JOHN HOR

GEOFFREY DE MANDEVILLE

A STUDY OF THE ANARCHY

Elibron Classics
www.elibron.com

Elibron Classics series.

© 2005 Adamant Media Corporation.

ISBN 1-4021-8299-6 (paperback)
ISBN 1-4021-5248-5 (hardcover)

This Elibron Classics Replica Edition is an unabridged facsimile of the edition published in 1892 by Longmans, Green, and Co., London.

Elibron and Elibron Classics are trademarks of Adamant Media Corporation. All rights reserved.

This book is an accurate reproduction of the original. Any marks, names, colophons, imprints, logos or other symbols or identifiers that appear on or in this book, except for those of Adamant Media Corporation and BookSurge, LLC, are used only for historical reference and accuracy and are not meant to designate origin or imply any sponsorship by or license from any third party.

GEOFFREY DE MANDEVILLE

A STUDY OF THE ANARCHY

BY

J. H. ROUND, M.A.

AUTHOR OF "THE EARLY LIFE OF ANNE BOLEYN: A CRITICAL ESSAY"

"Anno incarnationis Dominicæ millesimo centesimo quadragesimo primo inextricabilem labyrinthum rerum et negotiorum quæ acciderunt in Anglia aggredior evolvere." — *William of Malmesbury*

LONDON
LONGMANS, GREEN, & CO.
AND NEW YORK: 15 EAST 16th STREET
1892

All rights reserved

PREFACE

"THE reign of Stephen," in the words of our greatest living historian, "is one of the most important in our whole history, as exemplifying the working of causes and principles which had no other opportunity of exhibiting their real tendencies." To illustrate in detail the working of those principles to which the Bishop of Oxford thus refers, is the chief object I have set before myself in these pages. For this purpose I have chosen, to form the basis of my narrative, the career of Geoffrey de Mandeville, as the most perfect and typical presentment of the feudal and anarchic spirit that stamps the reign of Stephen. By fixing our glance upon one man, and by tracing his policy and its fruits, it is possible to gain a clearer perception of the true tendencies at work, and to obtain a firmer grasp of the essential principles involved. But, while availing myself of Geoffrey's career to give unity to my theme, I have not scrupled to introduce, from all available sources, any materials bearing on the period known as the Anarchy, or illustrating the points raised by the charters with which I deal.

The headings of my chapters express a fact upon which I cannot too strongly insist, namely, that the charters granted to Geoffrey are the very backbone of my work. By those charters it must stand or fall: for on their relation and their evidence the whole narrative is built. If the evidence of these documents is accepted, and the relation I have assigned to them established, it will, I trust, encourage the study of charters and their evidence, "as enabling the student both to amplify and to check such scanty knowledge as we now possess of the times to which they relate."[1] It will also result in the contribution of some new facts to English history, and break, as it were, by the wayside, a few stones towards the road on which future historians will travel.

Among the subjects on which I shall endeavour to throw some fresh light are problems of constitutional and institutional interest, such as the title to the English Crown, the origin and character of earldoms (especially the earldom of Arundel), the development of the fiscal system, and the early administration of London. I would also invite attention to such points as the appeal of the Empress to Rome in 1136, her intended coronation at Westminster in 1141, the unknown Oxford intrigue of 1142, the new theory on Norman castles suggested by Geoffrey's charters, and the genealogical discoveries in the Appendix on Gervase de Cornhill. The prominent part that the Earl of Gloucester played in the events of which I write may justify the inclusion of an essay on the creation of his historic earldom, which has, in the main, already appeared in another quarter.

In the words of Mr. Eyton, "the dispersion of error is the first step in the discovery of truth."[2] Cordially adopting this maxim, I have endeavoured throughout to correct

[1] Preface to my *Ancient Charters* (Pipe-Roll Society).
[2] *Staffordshire Survey*, p. 277.

errors and dispose of existing misconceptions. To "dare to be accurate" is, as Mr. Freeman so often reminds us, neither popular nor pleasant. It is easier to prophesy smooth things, and to accept without question the errors of others, in the spirit of mutual admiration. But I would repeat that "boast as we may of the achievements of our new scientific school, we are still, as I have urged, behind the Germans, so far, at least, as accuracy is concerned." If my criticism be deemed harsh, I may plead with Newman that, in controversy, "I have ever felt from experience that no one would believe me to be in earnest if I spoke calmly." The public is slow to believe that writers who have gained its ear are themselves often in error and, by the weight of their authority, lead others astray. At the same time, I would earnestly insist that if, in the light of new evidence, I have found myself compelled to differ from the conclusions even of Dr. Stubbs, it in no way impeaches the accuracy of that unrivalled scholar, the profundity of whose learning and the soundness of whose judgment can only be appreciated by those who have followed him in the same field.

The ill-health which has so long postponed the completion and appearance of this work is responsible for some shortcomings of which no one is more conscious than myself. It has been necessary to correct the proof-sheets at a distance from works of reference, and indeed from England, while the length of time that has elapsed since the bulk of the work was composed is such that two or three new books bearing upon the same period have appeared in the mean while. Of these I would specially mention Mr. Howlett's contributions to the Rolls Series, and Miss Norgate's well-known *England under the Angevin Kings.* Mr. Howlett's knowledge of the period, and especially of its MS. authorities, is of a quite exceptional character, while Miss Norgate's useful and painstaking work, which enjoys the advantage of a style that one cannot hope to rival, is a most welcome addition to our historical literature. To Dr. Stubbs, also, we are indebted for a new edition of William of Malmesbury. As I had employed for that chronicler and for the *Gesta Stephani* the English Historical Society's editions, my references are made to them, except where they are specially assigned to those editions by Dr. Stubbs and Mr. Howlett which have since appeared.

A few points of detail should, perhaps, be mentioned. The text of transcripts has been scrupulously preserved, even where it seemed corrupt; and all my extensions as to which any possible question could arise are enclosed in square brackets. The so-called "new style" has been adhered to throughout: that is to say, the dates given are those of the true historical year, irrespective of the wholly artificial reckoning from March 25. The form "fitz," denounced by purists, has been retained as a necessary convention, the admirable *Calendar of Patent Rolls,* now in course of publication, having demonstrated the impossibility of devising a satisfactory substitute. As to the spelling of Christian names, no attempt has been made to produce that pedantic uniformity which, in the twelfth century, was unknown. It is hoped that the index may be found serviceable and complete. The allusions to "the lost volume of the Great Coucher" (of the duchy of Lancaster) are based on references to that compilation by seventeenth-century transcribers, which cannot be identified in the volumes now preserved. It is to be feared that the volume most in request among antiquaries may, in those days, have been "lent out" (cf. p. 183), with the usual result. I am anxious to call attention to its existence in the hope of its ultimate recovery.

There remains the pleasant task of tendering my thanks to Mr. Hubert Hall, of H.M.'s Public Record Office, and Mr. F. Bickley, of the MS. Department, British Museum, for their invariable courtesy and assistance in the course of my researches. To Mr. Douglass Round I am indebted for several useful suggestions, and for much valuable help in passing these pages through the press.

J. H. ROUND.

Pau,
Christmas, 1891.

CONTENTS

CHAPTER I.
THE ACCESSION OF STEPHEN 1

CHAPTER II.
THE FIRST CHARTER OF THE KING 37

CHAPTER III.
TRIUMPH OF THE EMPRESS 55

CHAPTER IV.
THE FIRST CHARTER OF THE EMPRESS 81

CHAPTER V.
THE LOST CHARTER OF THE QUEEN 114

CHAPTER VI.
THE ROUT OF WINCHESTER 123

CHAPTER VII.
THE SECOND CHARTER OF THE KING 136

CHAPTER VIII.
THE SECOND CHARTER OF THE EMPRESS 163

CHAPTER IX.
FALL AND DEATH OF GEOFFREY 201

CHAPTER X.
THE EARLDOM OF ESSEX 227

APPENDICES.

		PAGE
A.	STEPHEN'S TREATY WITH THE LONDONERS	247
B.	THE APPEAL TO ROME IN 1136	250
C.	THE EASTER COURT OF 1136	262
D.	THE "FISCAL" EARLS	267
E.	THE ARRIVAL OF THE EMPRESS	278
F.	THE DEFECTION OF MILES OF GLOUCESTER	284
G.	CHARTER OF THE EMPRESS TO ROGER DE VALOINES	286
H.	THE "TERTIUS DENARIUS"	287
I.	"VICECOMITES" AND "CUSTODES"	297
J.	THE GREAT SEAL OF THE EMPRESS	299
K.	GERVASE DE CORNHILL	304
L.	CHARTER OF THE EMPRESS TO WILLIAM DE BEAUCHAMP	313
M.	THE EARLDOM OF ARUNDEL	316
N.	ROBERT DE VERE	326
O.	"TOWER" AND "CASTLE"	328
P.	THE EARLY ADMINISTRATION OF LONDON	347
Q.	OSBERTUS OCTODENARII	374
R.	THE FOREST OF ESSEX	376
S.	THE TREATY OF ALLIANCE BETWEEN THE EARLS OF HEREFORD AND GLOUCESTER	379
T.	"AFFIDATIO IN MANU"	384
U.	THE FAMILIES OF MANDEVILLE AND DE VERE	388
V.	WILLIAM OF ARQUES	397
X.	ROGER "DE RAMIS"	399
Y.	THE FIRST AND SECOND VISITS OF HENRY II. TO ENGLAND	405
Z.	BISHOP NIGEL AT ROME	411
AA.	"TENSERIE"	414
BB.	THE EMPRESS'S CHARTER TO GEOFFREY RIDEL	417

EXCURSUS.

THE CREATION OF THE EARLDOM OF GLOUCESTER	420
ADDENDA	437
INDEX	441

CHAPTER I.

THE ACCESSION OF STEPHEN.

BEFORE approaching that struggle between King Stephen and his rival, the Empress Maud, with which this work is mainly concerned, it is desirable to examine the peculiar conditions of Stephen's accession to the crown, determining, as they did, his position as king, and supplying, we shall find, the master-key to the anomalous character of his reign.

The actual facts of the case are happily beyond question. From the moment of his uncle's death, as Dr. Stubbs truly observes, "the succession was treated as an open question."[1] Stephen, quick to see his chance, made a bold stroke for the crown. The wind was in his favour, and, with a handful of comrades, he landed on the shores of Kent.[2] His first reception was not encouraging: Dover refused him admission, and Canterbury closed her gates.[3] On this Dr. Stubbs thus comments:—

"At Dover and at Canterbury he was received with sullen silence. The men of Kent had no love for the stranger who came, as his predecessor Eustace had done, to trouble the land."[4]

[1] *Early Plantagenets*, p. 13; *Const. Hist.* (1874), i. 319.
[2] *Gesta Stephani*, p. 3.
[3] "A Dourensibus repulsus, et a Cantuariuis exclusus" (*Gervase*, i. 94). As illustrating the use of such adjectives for the garrison, rather than the townsfolk, compare Florence of Worcester's "Hrofenses Cautuariensibus ... cædes inferunt" (ii. 23), where the "Hrofenses" are Odo's garrison. So too "Bristoenses" in the *Gesta* (ed. Howlett, pp. 38, 40, 41), though rendered by the editor "the people of Bristol," are clearly the troops of the Earl of Gloucester.
[4] *Early Plantagenets*. p. 14. Compare *Const. Hist.*, i. 319: "The men of

2   THE ACCESSION OF STEPHEN.

But "the men of Kent" were faithful to Stephen, when all others forsook him, and, remembering this, one would hardly expect to find in them his chief opponents. Nor, indeed, were they. Our great historian, when he wrote thus, must, I venture to think, have overlooked the passage in Ordericus (v. 110), from which we learn, incidentally, that Canterbury and Dover were among those fortresses which the Earl of Gloucester held by his father's gift.[1] It is, therefore, not surprising that Stephen should have met with this reception at the hands of the lieutenants of his arch-rival. It might, indeed, be thought that the prescient king had of set purpose placed these keys of the road to London in the hands of one whom he could trust to uphold his cherished scheme.[2]

Stephen, undiscouraged by these incidents, pushed on rapidly to London. The news of his approach had gone before him, and the citizens flocked to meet him. By them, as is well known, he was promptly chosen to be king, on the plea that a king was needed to fill the vacant throne, and that the right to elect one was specially vested in themselves.[3] The point, however, that I would here

Kent, remembering the mischief that had constantly come to them from Boulogne, refused to receive him." Miss Norgate adopts the same explanation (*England under the Angevin Kings*, i. 277).

[1] There is a curious incidental allusion to the earl's Kentish possessions in William of Malmesbury, who states (p. 759) that he was allowed, while a prisoner at Rochester (October, 1141), to receive his rents from his Kentish tenants ("ab hominibus suis de Cantia"). Stephen, then, it would seem, did not forfeit them.

[2] In the rebellion of 1138 Walchelin Maminot, the earl's castellan, held Dover against Stephen, and was besieged by the Queen and by the men of Boulogne. Curiously enough, Mr. Freeman made a similar slip, now corrected, to that here discussed, when he wrote that "whatever might be the feelings of the rest of the shire, the men of Dover had no mind to see Count Eustace again within their walls" (*Norm. Conq.*, iv. 116), though they were, on the contrary, quite as anxious as the rest of the shire to do so.

[3] "Id quoque sui esse juris, suique specialiter privilegii ut si rex ipsorum quoquo modo obiret, alius suo provisu in regno substituendus e vestigio succederet" (*Gesta*, p. 3). This audacious claim of the citizens to such right

ELECTION OF STEPHEN.

insist on, for it seems to have been scarcely noticed, is that this election appears to have been essentially conditional, and to have been preceded by an agreement with the citizens.[1] The bearing of this will be shown below.

There is another noteworthy point which would seem to have escaped observation. It is distinctly implied by William of Malmesbury that the primate, seizing his opportunity, on Stephen's appearance in London, had extorted from him, as a preliminary to his recognition, as Maurice had done from Henry at his coronation, and as Henry of Winchester was, later, to do in the case of the Empress, an oath to restore the Church her "liberty," a phrase of which the meaning is well known. Stephen, he adds, on reaching Winchester, was released from this oath by his brother, who himself "went bail" (made himself responsible) for Stephen's satisfactory behaviour to the Church.[2] It is, surely, to this incident that Henry so pointedly alludes in his speech at the election of the Empress.[3] It can only, I think, be explained on the

as vested in themselves is much stronger than Mr. Freeman's paraphrase when he speaks of "the citizens of London and Winchester [why Winchester?], who freely exercised their ancient right of *sharing in* the election of the king who should reign over them" (*Norm. Conq.*, v. 251; cf. p. 856).

[1] "Firmatâ prius utrimque pactione, peractoque, ut vulgus asserebat, mutuo juramento, ut eum cives quoad viveret opibus sustentarent, viribus tutarentur; ipse autem, ad regnum pacificandum, ad omnium eorundem suffragium, toto sese conatu accingeret" (*Gesta*, p. 4). See Appendix A.

[2] "Spe scilicet captus amplissima quod Stephanus avi sui Willelmi in regni moderamine mores servaret, precipueque in ecclesiastici vigoris disciplinâ. Quapropter districto sacramento quod a Stephano Willelmus Cantuarensis archiepiscopus exegit de libertate reddenda ecclesiæ et conservanda, episcopus Wintoniensis se mediatorem et vadem apposuit. Cujus sacramenti tenorem, postea scripto inditum, loco suo non prætermittam" (p. 704). See Addenda.

[3] "Enimvero, quamvis ego vadem me apposuerim inter eum et Deum quod sanctam ecclesiam honoraret et exaltaret, et bonas leges manuteneret, malas vero abrogaret; piget meminisse, pudet narrare, qualem se in regno exhibuerit," etc. (*ibid.*, p. 746).

4 THE ACCESSION OF STEPHEN.

hypothesis that Stephen chafed beneath the oath he had taken, and begged his brother to set him free. If so, the attempt was vain, for he had, we shall find, to bind himself anew on the occasion of his Oxford charter.[1] At Winchester the citizens, headed by their bishop, came forth from the city to greet him, but this reception must not be confused (as it is by Mr. Freeman) with his election by the citizens of London.[2] His brother, needless to say, met him with an eager welcome, and the main object of his visit was attained when William de Pont de l'Arche, who had shrunk, till his arrival, from embracing his cause, now, in concert with the head of the administration, Roger, Bishop of Salisbury, placed at his disposal the royal castle, with the treasury and all that it contained.[3]

Thus strengthened, he returned to London for coronation at the hands of the primate. Dr. Stubbs observes that "he returned to London for *formal election* and coronation."[4] His authority for that statement is Gervase (i. 94), who certainly asserts it distinctly.[5] But it will be found that he, who was not a contemporary, is the only authority for this second election, and, moreover, that he ignores the first, as well as the visit to Winchester, thus mixing up the two episodes, between which that visit intervened. Of course this opens the wider question as to

[1] The phrase "districto sacramento" is very difficult to construe. I have here taken it to imply a release of Stephen from his oath, but the meaning of the passage, which is obscure as it stands, may be merely that Henry became surety for Stephen's performance of the oath as in an agreement or treaty between two contracting parties (*vide infra passim*).
[2] *Ante*, p. 3.
[3] *Gesta*, 5, 6; *Will. Malms.*, 703. Note that William Rufus, Henry I., and Stephen all of them visited and secured Winchester even before their coronation.
[4] *Const. Hist.*, i. 319.
[5] "A cunctis fere in regem electus est, et sic a Willelmo Cantuarensi archiepiscopo coronatus."

whether the actual election, in such cases, took place at the coronation itself or on a previous occasion. This may, perhaps, be a matter of opinion; but in the preceding instance, that of Henry I., the election was admittedly that which took place at Winchester, and was previous to and unconnected with the actual coronation itself.[1] From this point of view, the presentation of the king to the people at his coronation would assume the aspect of a ratification of the election previously conducted. The point is here chiefly of importance as affecting the validity of Stephen's election. If his only election was that which the citizens of London conducted, it was, to say the least, "informally transacted."[2] Nor was the attendance of magnates at the ceremony such as to improve its character. It was, as Dr. Stubbs truly says, "but a poor substitute for the great councils which had attended the summons of William and Henry."[3] The chroniclers are here unsatisfactory. Henry of Huntingdon is rhetorical and vague; John of Hexham leaves us little wiser;[4] the Continuator of Florence indeed states that Stephen, when crowned, kept his Christmas court "cum totius Angliæ primoribus" (p. 95), but even the author of the *Gesta* implies that the primate's scruples were largely due to the paucity of magnates present.[5] William of Malmesbury alone is precise,[6] possibly because an adversary of Stephen could

---

[1] "The form of election was hastily gone through by the barons on the spot" (*Const. Hist.*, i. 303).
[2] *Select Charters*, p. 108.   [3] *Early Plantagenets*, p. 14.
[4] "Consentientibus in ejus promotionem Willelmo Cantuarensi archiepiscopo et clericorum et laicorum universitate" (*Sym. Dun.*, ii. 286, 287).
[5] "Sic profecto, sic congruit, ut ad eum in regno confirmandum omnes pariter convolent, parique consensu quid statuendum, quidve respuendum sit, ab omnibus provideatur" (pp. 6, 7). Eventually he represents the primate as acting "Cum episcopis frequentique, qui intererat, clericatu" (p. 8).
[6] "Tribus episcopis præsentibus, archiepiscopo, Wintoniensi, Salesbiriensi, nullis abbatibus, paucissimis optimatibus" (p. 704). See Addenda.

alone afford to be so, and his testimony, we shall find, is singularly confirmed by independent charter evidence (p. 11). It was at this stage that an attempt was made to dispel the scruples caused by Stephen's breach of his oath to the late king. The hint, in the *Gesta*, that Henry, on his deathbed, had repented of his act in extorting that oath,[1] is amplified by Gervase into a story that he had released his barons from its bond,[2] while Ralph "de Diceto" represents the assertion as nothing less than that the late king had actually disinherited the Empress, and made Stephen his heir in her stead.[3] It should be noticed that these last two writers, in their statement that this story was proved by Hugh Bigod on oath, are confirmed by the independent evidence of the *Historia Pontificalis*.[4]

The importance of securing, as quickly as possible, the performance of the ceremony of coronation is well brought out by the author of the *Gesta* in the arguments of Stephen's friends when combating the primate's scruples. They urged that it would *ipso facto* put an end to all question as to the validity of his election.[5] The advantage, in short, of "snatching" a coronation was that, in the language of modern diplomacy, of securing a *fait accompli*. Election was a matter of opinion; coronation a matter of fact. Or, to employ another expres-

[1] "Supremo eum agitante mortis articulo, cum et plurimi astarent et veram suorum erratuum confessionem audirent, de jurejurando violenter baronibus suis injuncto apertissime pænituit."
[2] "Quidam ex potentissimis Angliæ, jurans et dicens se præsentem affuisse ubi rex Henricus idem juramentum in bona fide sponte relaxasset."
[3] "Hugo Bigod senescallus regis coram archiepiscopo Cantuariæ sacramento probavit quod, dum Rex Henricus ageret in extremis, ortis quibus inimicitiis inter ipsum et imperatricem, ipsam exhæredavit, et Stephanum Boloniæ comitem hæredem instituit."
[4] "Et hæc juramento comitis (*sic*) Hugonis et duorum militum probata esse dicebant in facie ecclesie Anglicane" (ed. Pertz, p. 543).
[5] "Cum regis (*sic*) fautores obnixe persuaderent quatinus eum ad regnandum inungeret, quodque imperfectum videbatur, administrationis suæ officio suppleret" (p. 6).

sion, it was the "outward and visible sign" that a king had begun his reign. Its important bearing is well seen in the case of the Conqueror himself. Dr. Stubbs observes, with his usual judgment, that "the ceremony was understood as bestowing the divine ratification on the election that had preceded it."[1] Now, the fact that the performance of this essential ceremony was, of course, wholly in the hands of the Church, in whose power, therefore, it always was to perform or to withhold it at its pleasure, appears to me to have naturally led to the growing assumption that we now meet with, the claim, based on a confusion of the ceremony with the actual election itself, that it was for the Church to elect the king. This claim, which in the case of Stephen (1136) seems to have been only inchoate,[2] appears at the time of his capture (1141) in a fully developed form,[3] the circumstances of the time having enabled the Church to increase its power in the State with perhaps unexampled rapidity.

May it not have been this development, together with his own experience, that led Stephen to press for the coronation of his son Eustace in his lifetime (1152)? In this attempted innovation he was, indeed, defeated by the Church, but the lesson was not lost. Henry I., unlike his contemporaries, had never taken this precaution, and Henry II., warned by his example, succeeded in obtaining the coronation of his heir (1170) in the teeth of Becket's endeavours to forbid the act, and so to uphold the veto of the Church.

Prevailed upon, at length, to perform the ceremony, the primate seized the opportunity of extorting from the

[1] *Const. Hist.*, i. 146. [2] See his Oxford Charter.
[3] See the legate's speech at Winchester: "Ventilata est hesterno die causa secreto coram majori parte cleri Angliæ, *ad cujus jus potissimum spectat principem eligere, simulque ordinare*" (*Will. Malms.*, p. 746).

eager king (besides a charter of liberties) a renewal of his former oath to protect the rights of the Church. The oath which Henry had sworn at his coronation, and which Maud had to swear at her election, Stephen had to swear, it seems, at both, though not till the Oxford charter was it committed, in his case, to writing.[1]

We now approach an episode unknown to all our historians.[2]

The Empress, on her side, had not been idle; she had despatched an envoy to the papal court, in the person of the Bishop of Angers, to appeal her rival of (1) defrauding her of her right, and (2) breach of his solemn oath. Had this been known to Mr. Freeman, he would, it is safe to assert, have been fascinated by the really singular coincidence between the circumstances of 1136 and of 1066. In each case, of the rivals for the throne, the one based his pretensions on (1) kinship, fortified by (2) an oath to secure his succession, which had been taken by his opponent himself; while the other rested his claims on election duly followed by coronation. In each case the election was fairly open to question; in Harold's, because (*pace* Mr. Freeman) he was *not* a legitimate candidate; in Stephen's, because, though a qualified candidate, his election had been most informal. In each case the ousted claimant appealed to the papal court, and, in each case, on the same grounds, viz. (1) the kinship, (2) the broken oath. In each case the successful party was opposed by a particular cardinal, a fact which we learn, in each case, from later and incidental mention. And in each case that

---

[1] Henry had sworn "in ipso suæ consecrationis die" (Eadmer), Stephen "in ipsa consecrationis tuæ die" (Innocent's letter). Henry of Huntingdon refers to the "pacta" which Stephen "Deo et populo et sanctæ ecclesiæ concesserat in die coronationis suæ." William of Malmesbury speaks of the oath as "postea [*i.e.* at Oxford] scripto inditum." See Addenda.

[2] See Appendix B: "The Appeal to Rome in 1136."

cardinal became, afterwards, pope. But here the parallel ends. Stephen accepted, where Harold had (so far as we know) rejected, the jurisdiction of the Court of Rome. We may assign this difference to the closer connection between Rome and England in Stephen's day, or we may see in it proof that Stephen was the more politic of the two. For his action was justified by its success. There has been, on this point, no small misconception. Harold has been praised for possessing, and Stephen blamed for lacking, a sense of his kingly dignity. But *læsio fidei* was essentially a matter for courts Christian, and thus for the highest of them all, at Rome. Again, inheritance, so far as inheritance affected the question, was brought in many ways within the purview of the courts Christian, as, for instance, in the case of the alleged illegitimacy of Maud. Moreover, in 1136, the pope, though circumstances played into his hands, advanced no such pretension as his successor in the days of John. His attitude was not that of an overlord to a dependent fief: he made no claim to dispose of the realm of England. Sitting as judge in a spiritual court, he listened to the charges brought by Maud against Stephen in his personal capacity, and, without formally acquitting him, declined to pronounce him guilty.

Though the king was pleased to describe the papal letter which followed as a "confirmation" of his right to the throne, it was, strictly, nothing of the kind. It was simply, in the language of modern diplomacy, his "recognition" by the pope as king. If Ferdinand, elected Prince of Bulgaria, were to be recognized as such by a foreign power, that action would neither alter his status relatively to any other power, nor would it imply the least claim to dispose of the Bulgarian crown. Or, again, to take a mediæval illustration, the recognition as pope by an

English king of one of two rival claimants for the papacy would neither affect any other king, nor constitute a claim to dispose of the papal tiara. Stephen, however, was naturally eager to make the most of the papal action, especially when he found in his oath to the Empress the most formidable obstacle to his acceptance. The sanction of the Church would silence the reproach that he was occupying the throne as a perjured man. Hence the clause in his Oxford charter. To the advantage which this letter gave him Stephen shrewdly clung, and when Geoffrey summoned him, in later years, " to an investigation of his claims before the papal court," he promptly retorted that Rome had already heard the case.[1] He turned, in fact, the tables on his appellant by calling on Geoffrey to justify his occupation of the Duchy and of the Western counties in the teeth of the papal confirmation of his own right to the throne.

We now pass from Westminster to Reading, whither, after Christmas, Stephen proceeded, to attend his uncle's funeral.[2] The corpse, says the Continuator, was attended "non modica stipatus nobilium catervâ." The meeting of Stephen with these nobles is an episode of considerable importance. "It is probable," says Dr. Stubbs, "that it furnished an opportunity of obtaining some vague promises from Stephen."[3] But the learned writer here alludes to the subsequent promises at Oxford. What I am concerned with is the meeting at Reading. I proceed, therefore, to quote *in extenso* a charter which must have passed on this occasion, and which, this being so, is of great value and interest.[4]

[1] See Appendix B.
[2] *Hen. Hunt.*, 258; *Cont. Flor. Wig.*, 95; *Will. Malms.*, 705.
[3] *Const. Hist.*, i. 321.
[4] Lansdowne MS. 229, fol. 109, and Lansdowne MS. 259, fol. 66, both being excerpts from the lost volume of the Great Coucher of the Duchy.

STEPHEN AT READING.

Carta Stephani regis Angliæ facta Miloni Gloec' de honore Gloecestr' et Brekon'.

S. rex Angl. Archiepīs Epīs Abbatibus. Com̃. Baroñ. vic. præpositis, Ministris et omnibus fidelibus suis Francis et Anglicis totius Angliæ et Walliæ Sał. sciatis me reddidisse et concessisse Miloni Gloecestriæ et hæredibus suis post eum in feod et hæreditate totum honorem suum de Gloec', et de Brechenion, et omnes terras suas et tenaturas suas in vicecomitatibus et aliis rebus, sicut eas tenuit die quâ rex Henricus fuit viuus et mortuus. Quare volo et præcipio quod bene et honorifice et libere teneat in bosco et plano et pratis et pasturis et aquis et mariscis, in molendinis et piscariis, cum Thol et Theam et infangenetheof, et cum omnibus aliis libertatibus et consuetudinibus quibus unqũ melius et liberius tenuit tempore regis Henrici. Et sciatis q̃m ego ut dñs et Rex, convencionavi ei sicut Baroni et Justiciario meo quod eum in placitum non ponero quamdiu vixero de aliquâ tenatura q̃ tenuisset die quâ Rex Henricus fuit vivus et mortuus, neq' hæredem suum. T. Arch. Cantuar. et Epō Wintoñ. et Epō Sar'. et H. Big̃ et Rob filio Ricardi et Ing̃ de Sai. et W. de Pont et P. filio Joh. Apud Rading̃.

Sub magno sigillo suo.

The reflections suggested by this charter are many and most instructive. Firstly, we have here the most emphatic corroboration of the evidence of William of Malmesbury. The four first witnesses comprise the three bishops who, according to him, conducted Stephen's coronation, together with the notorious Hugh Bigod, to whose timely assurance that coronation was so largely due. The four others are Robert fitz Richard, whom we shall find present at the Easter court, attesting a charter as a royal chamberlain;

Enguerrand de Sai, the lord of Clun, who had probably come with Payne fitz John; William de Pont de l'Arche, whom we met at Winchester; and Payne fitz John. The impression conveyed by this charter is certainly that Stephen had as yet been joined by few of the magnates, and had still to be content with the handful by whom his coronation had been attended.

An important addition is, however, represented by the grantee, Miles of Gloucester, and the witness Payne fitz John. The former was a man of great power, both of himself and from his connection with the Earl of Gloucester, in the west of England and in Wales. The latter is represented by the author of the *Gesta* as acting with him at this juncture.[1] It should, however, be noted, as important in its bearing on the chronology of this able writer, that he places the adhesion of these two barons (p. 15) considerably after that of the Earl of Gloucester (p. 8), whereas the case was precisely the contrary, the earl not submitting to Stephen till some time later on. Both these magnates appear in attendance at Stephen's Easter court (*vide infra*), and again as witnesses to his Oxford charter. The part, however, in the coming struggle which Miles of Gloucester was destined to play, was such that it is most important to learn the circumstances and the date of his adhesion to the king. His companion, Payne fitz John, was slain, fighting the Welsh, in the spring of the following year.[2]

[1] Speaking of the late king's trusted friends, who hung back from coming to court, he writes: "Illi autem, intentâ sibi a rege comminatione, cum salvo eundi et redeundi conductu curiam petiere; omnibusque ad votum impetratis, peracto cum jurejurando liberali hominio, illius sese servitio ex toto mancipârunt. Affuit inter reliquos Paganus filius Johannis, sed et Milo, de quo superius fecimus mentionem, ille Herefordensis et Salopesbiriæ, iste Glocestrensis provinciæ dominatum gerens: qui in tempore regis Henrici potentiæ suæ culmen extenderant ut a Sabrinâ flumine usque ad mare per omnes fines Angliæ et Waloniæ omnes placitis involverent, angariis onerarent" (pp. 15, 16).

[2] *Cont. Flor. Wig.*

CHARTERS TO MILES OF GLOUCESTER. 13

It is a singular fact that, in addition to the charter I have here given, another charter was granted to Miles of Gloucester by the king, which, being similarly tested at Reading, probably passed on this occasion. The subject of the grant is the same, but the terms are more precise, the constableship of Gloucester Castle, with the hereditary estates of his house, being specially mentioned.[1] Though both these charters were entered in the Great Coucher (in the volume now missing), the latter alone is referred to by Dugdale, from whose transcript it has been printed by Madox.[2] Though the names of the witnesses are there omitted, those of the six leading witnesses are supplied by an abstract which is elsewhere found. Three of these are among those who attest the other charter— Robert fitz Richard, Hugh Bigod, and Enguerrand de Sai; but the other three names are new, being Robert de Ferrers, afterwards Earl of Derby, Baldwin de Clare, the spokesman of Stephen's host at Lincoln (see p. 148), and (Walter) fitz Richard, who afterwards appears in attendance at the Easter court.[3] These three barons should

---

[1] "S. rex Angliæ Archiepis etc. Sciatis me reddidisse et concessisse Miloni Gloec et heredibus suis post eum in feodo et hereditate totum honorem patris sui et custodiam turris et castelli Gloecestrie ad tenendum tali forma (*sic*) qualem reddebat tempore regis Henrici sicut patrimonium suum. Et totum honorem suum de Brechenion et omnia Ministeria sua et terras suas quas tenuit tempore regis Henrici sicut eas melius et honorificentius tenuit die qua rex Henricus fuit vivus et mortuus, et ego ei in convencionem habeo sicut Rex et dominus Baroni meo. Quare precipio quod bene et in honore et in pace et libere teneat cum omnibus libertatibus suis. Testes, W. filius Ricardi, Robertus de Ferrariis, Robertus filius Ricardi, Hugo Bigot, Ingelramus de Sai, Balduinus filius Gisleberti. Apud Radinges" (Lansdowne MS. 229, fols. 123, 124.

[2] *History of the Exchequer*, p. 135.

[3] I am inclined to believe that in Robert fitz Richard we have that Robert fitz Richard (de Clare) who died in 1137 (Robert de Torigny), being then described as paternal uncle to Richard fitz Gilbert (de Clare), usually but erroneously described as first Earl of Hertford. If so, he was also uncle to Baldwin (fitz Gilbert) de Clare of this charter, and brother to W(alter) fitz Richard (de Clare), another witness. We shall come across another of Stephen's

therefore be added to the list of those who were at Reading with the king.[1]

Possibly, however, the most instructive feature to be found in each charter is the striking illustration it affords of the method by which Stephen procured the adhesion of the turbulent and ambitious magnates. It is not so much a grant from a king to a subject as a *convencio* between equal powers. But especially would I invite attention to the words "ut dominus et Rex."[2] I see in them at once the symbol and the outcome of "the Norman idea of royalty." In his learned and masterly analysis of this subject, a passage which cannot be too closely studied, Dr. Stubbs shows us, with felicitous clearness, the twin factors of Norman kinghood, its royal and its feudal aspects.[3] Surely in the expression "dominus et Rex" (*alias* "Rex et dominus") we have in actual words the exponent of this double character.[4] And, more than this, we have here the needful and striking parallel which will illustrate and illumine the action of the Empress, so strangely overlooked or misunderstood, when she ordered herself, at Winchester, to be proclaimed "DOMINA ET REGINA."

charters to which the house of Clare contributes several witnesses. There is evidence to suggest that Robert fitz Richard (de Clare) was lord, in some way, of Maldon in Essex, and was succeeded there by (his nephew) Walter fitz Gilbert (de Clare), who went on crusade (probably in 1147).

[1] There is preserved among the royal charters belonging to the Duchy of Lancaster, the fragment of one grant of which the contents correspond exactly, it would seem, with those of the above charter, though the witnesses' names are different. This raises a problem which cannot at present be solved.

[2] In the fellow-charter the phrase runs: "sicut Rex et dominus Baroni meo."

[3] "The Norman idea of royalty was very comprehensive; it practically combined all the powers of the national sovereignty, as they had been exercised by Edgar and Canute, with those of the feudal theory of monarchy, which was exemplified at the time in France and the Empire. . . . The king is accordingly both the chosen head of the nation and the lord paramount of the whole of the land" (*Const. Hist.*, i. 338).

[4] Compare the words of address in several of the *Cartæ Baronum* (1166); "servitium ut domino;" "vobis sicut domino meo;" "sicut domino carissimo;" "ut domino suo ligio."

Henry of Huntingdon asserts distinctly that from Reading Stephen passed to Oxford, and that he there renewed the pledges he had made on his coronation-day.[1] That, on leaving Reading, he moved to Oxford, though the fact is mentioned by no other chronicler, would seem to be placed beyond question by Henry's repeated assertion.[2] But the difficulty is that Henry specifies what these pledges were, and that the version he gives cannot be reconciled either with the king's " coronation charter " or with what is known as his " second charter," granted at Oxford later in the year. Dr. Stubbs, with the caution of a true scholar, though he thinks it "probable," in his great work, that Stephen, upon this occasion, made " some vague promises," yet adds, of those recorded by Henry—

" Whether these promises were embodied in a charter is uncertain: if they were, the charter is lost ; it is, however, more probable that the story is a popular version of the document which was actually issued by the king, at Oxford, later in the year 1136." [3]

In his later work he seems inclined to place more credence in Henry's story.

" After the funeral, at Oxford or somewhere in the neighbourhood, he arranged terms with them; terms by which he endeavoured, amplifying the words of his charter, to catch the good will of each class of his subjects. . . . The promises were, perhaps, not insincere at the time ; anyhow, they had the desired effect, and united the nation for the moment."[4]

It will be seen that the point is a most perplexing one, and can scarcely at present be settled with certainty. But there is one point beyond dispute, namely, that the so-called " second charter " was issued later in the year,

---

[1] " Inde perrexit rex Stephanus apud Oxeneford ubi recordatus et confirmavit pacta quæ Deo et populo et sanctæ ecclesiæ concesserat in die coronationis suæ " (p. 258).
[2] " Cum venisset in fine Natalis ad Oxenefordiam " (*ibid.*).
[3] *Const. Hist.*, i. 321.
[4] *Early Plantagenets*, pp. 15, 16.

after the king's return from the north. Mr. Freeman, therefore, has not merely failed to grasp the question at issue, but has also strangely contradicted himself when he confidently assigns this "second charter" to the king's first visit to Oxford, and refers us, in doing so, to another page, in which it is as unhesitatingly assigned to his other and later visit after his return from the north.[1] If I call attention to this error, it is because I venture to think it one to which this writer is too often liable, and against which, therefore, his readers should be placed upon their guard.[2]

It was at Oxford, in January,[3] that Stephen heard of David's advance into England. With creditable rapidity he assembled an army and hastened to the north to meet him. He encountered him at Durham on the 5th of February (the day after Ash Wednesday), and effected a peaceable agreement. He then retraced his steps, after a stay of about a fortnight,[4] and returned to keep his Easter (March 22) at Westminster. I wish to invite special attention to this Easter court, because it was in many ways of great importance, although historians have almost ignored its existence. Combining the evidence of charters with that which the chroniclers afford, we can learn not a little about it, and see how notable an event it must have seemed at the time it was held. We should observe, in the first place, that this was no mere "curia de more":

[1] "The news of this [Scottish] inroad reached Stephen at Oxford, where he had just put forth his second charter" (*Norm.Conq.*, v. 258). "The second charter ... was put forth at Oxford before the first year of his reign was out. Stephen had just come back victorious from driving back a Scottish invasion (see p. 258)" (*ibid.*, p. 246).

[2] See Mr. Vincent's learned criticism on Mr. Freeman's *History of Wells Cathedral:* "I detect throughout these pages an infirmity, a confirmed habit of inaccuracy. The author of this book, I should infer from numberless passages, cannot revise what he writes" (*Genealogist*, (N.S.) ii. 179).

[3] "In fine Natalis" (*Hen. Hunt.*, 258). [4] *Sym. Dun.*, ii. 287.

it was emphatically a great or national council. The author of the *Gesta* describes it thus :—

"Omnibus igitur summatibus regni, fide et jurejurando cum rege constrictis, edicto per Angliam promulgato, summos ecclesiarum ductores cum primis populi ad concilium Londonias conscivit. Illis quoque quasi in unam sentinam illuc confluentibus ecclesiarumque columnis sedendi ordine dispositis, vulgo etiam confuse et permixtim,[1] ut solet, ubique se ingerente, plura regno et ecclesiæ profutura fuerunt et utiliter ostensa et salubriter pertractata."[2]

We have clearly in this great council, held on the first court day (Easter) after the king's coronation, a revival of the splendours of former reigns, so sorely dimmed beneath the rule of his bereaved and parsimonious uncle.[3]

Henry of Huntingdon has a glowing description of this Easter court,[4] which reminds one of William of Malmesbury's pictures of the Conqueror in his glory.[5] When, therefore, Dr. Stubbs tells us that this custom of the Conqueror "was restored by Henry II." (*Const. Hist.*, i. 370), he ignores this brilliant revival at the outset of Stephen's reign. Stephen, coming into possession of his predecessor's hoarded treasure, was as eager to plunge into costly pomp as was Henry VIII. on the death of his mean

---

[1] The curious words, "vulgo . . . ingerente," may be commended to those who uphold the doctrine of democratic survivals in these assemblies. They would doubtless jump at them as proof that the "vulgus" took part in the proceedings. The evidence, however, is, in any case, of indisputable interest.

[2] Ed. Howlett, p. 17.

[3] "Quem morem convivandi primus successor obstinate tenuit, secundus omisit" (*Will. Malms.*).

[4] "Rediens autem inde rex in Quadragesimâ tenuit curiam suam apud Lundoniam in solemnitate Paschali, quâ nunquam fuerat splendidior in Angliâ multitudine, magnitudine, auro, argento, gemmis, vestibus, omnimodaque dapsilitate" (p. 259).

[5] "[Consuetudo] erat ut ter in anno cuncti optimates ad curiam convenirent de necessariis regni tractaturi, simulque visuri regis insigne quomodo iret gemmato fastigiatus diademate" (*Vita S. Wulstani*). "Convivia in præcipuis festivitatibus sumptuosa et magnifica inibat; . . . omnes eo cujuscunque professionis magnates regium edictum accersiebat, ut exterarum gentium legati speciem multitudinis apparatumque deliciarum mirarentur" (*Gesta regum*).

and grasping sire. There were also more solid reasons for this dazzling assembly. It was desirable for the king to show himself to his new subjects in his capital, surrounded not only by the evidence of wealth, but by that of his national acceptance. The presence at his court of the magnates from all parts of the realm was a fact which would speak for itself, and to secure which he had clearly resolved that no pains should be spared.[1]

If the small group who attended his coronation had indeed been "but a poor substitute for the great councils which had attended the summons of William and Henry," he was resolved that this should be forgotten in the splendour of his Easter court.

This view is strikingly confirmed by the lists of witnesses to two charters which must have passed on this occasion. The one is a grant to the see of Winchester of the manor of Sutton, in Hampshire, in exchange for Morden, in Surrey. The other is a grant of the bishopric of Bath to Robert of Lewes. The former is dated "Apud Westmonasterium in presentia et audientia subscriptorum anno incarnationis dominicæ, 1136," etc.; the latter, "Apud Westmonasterium in generalis concilii celebratione et Paschalis festi solemnitate." At first sight, I confess, both charters have a rather spurious appearance. Their stilted style awakes suspicion, which is not lessened by the dating clauses or the extraordinary number of witnesses. Coming, however, from independent sources, and dealing with two unconnected subjects, they mutually confirm one another. We have, moreover, still extant the charter by which Henry II. confirmed the former of the two, and as this is among the duchy of Lancaster records, we have every reason to believe that

[1] See in *Gesta* (ed. Howlett, pp. 15, 16) his persistent efforts to conciliate the ministers of Henry I., and especially the Marchers of the west.

the original charter itself was, as both its transcribers assert, among them also. Again, as to the lists of witnesses. Abnormally long though these may seem, we must remember that in the charters of Henry I., especially towards the close of his reign, there was a tendency to increase the number of witnesses. Moreover, in the Oxford charter, by which these were immediately followed, we have a long list of witnesses (thirty-seven), and, which is noteworthy, it is similarly arranged on a principle of classification, the court officers being grouped together. I have, therefore, given in an appendix, for the purpose of comparison, all three lists.[1] If we analyze those appended to the two London charters, we find their authenticity confirmed by the fact that, while the Earl of Gloucester, who was abroad at the time, is conspicuously absent from the list, Henry, son of the King of Scots, duly appears among the attesting earls, and we are specially told by John of Hexham that he was present at this Easter court.[2] Miles of Gloucester and Brian fitz Count also figure together among the witnesses—a fact, from their position, of some importance.[3] It is, too, of interest for our purpose, to note that among them is Geoffrey de Mandeville. The extraordinary number of witnesses to these charters (no less than fifty-five in one case, excluding the king and queen, and thirty-six in the other) is not only of great value as giving us the *personnel* of this brilliant court, but is also, when compared with the Ox-

[1] See Appendix C.
[2] "In Paschali vero festivitate rex Stephanus eundem Henricum in honorem in reverentia præferens, ad dextoram suam sedere fecit" (*Sym. Dun.*, ii. 287).
[3] Dr. Stubbs appears, unless I am mistaken, to imply that they first appear at court as witnesses to the (later) Oxford charter. He writes, of that charter: "Her [the Empress's] most faithful adherents, Miles of Hereford" [*recte* Gloucester] "and Brian of Wallingford, were also among the witnesses; probably the retreat of the King of Scots had made her cause for the time hopeless" (*Const. Hist.*, i. 321, *note*).

ford charter, suggestive perhaps of a desire, by the king, to place on record the names of those whom he had induced to attend his courts and so to recognize his claims. Mr. Pym Yeatman more than once, in his strange *History of the House of Arundel*, quotes the charter to Winchester as from a transcript " among the valuable collection of MSS. belonging to the Earl of Egmont " (p. 49). It may, therefore, be of benefit to students to remind them that it is printed in Hearne's *Liber Niger* (ii. 808, 809). Mr. Yeatman, moreover, observes of this charter—

" It contains the names of no less than thirty-four noblemen of the highest rank (excluding only the Earl of Gloucester), but not a single ecclesiastical witness attests the grant, which is perhaps not remarkable, since it was a dangerous precedent to deal in such a matter with Church property, perhaps a new precedent created by Stephen" (p. 286).

To other students it will appear " perhaps not remarkable " that the charter is witnessed by the unusual number of no less than three archbishops and thirteen bishops.[1]

Now, although this was a national council, the state and position of the Church was the chief subject of discussion. The author of the *Gesta*, who appears to have been well informed on the subject, shows us the prelates appealing to Stephen to relieve the Church from the intolerable oppression which she had suffered, under the form of law, at the hands of Henry I. Stephen, bland, for the time, to all, and more especially to the powerful Church, listened graciously to their prayers, and promised all they asked.[2] In the grimly jocose language of the day, the keys of the Church, which had been held by Simon (Magus), were henceforth to be restored to Peter. To this

[1] See Appendix C.
[2] "His autem rex patienter auditis quæcumque postulârant gratuite eis indulgens ecclesiæ libertatem fixam et inviolabilem esse, illius statuta rata et inconcussa, ejus ministros cujuscunque professionis essent vel ordinis, omni reverentiâ honorandos esse præcepit" (*Gesta*).

STEPHEN AND THE CHURCH.

I trace a distinct allusion in the curious phrase which meets us in the Bath charter. Stephen grants the bishopric of Bath "*canonica prius electione præcedente.*" This recognition of the Church's right, with the public record of the fact, confirms the account of his attitude on this occasion to the Church. The whole charter contrasts strangely with that by which, fifteen years before, his predecessor had granted the bishopric of Hereford, and its reference to the counsel and consent of the magnates betrays the weakness of his position.

This council took place, as I have said, at London and during Easter. But there is some confusion on the subject. Mr. Howlett, in his excellent edition of the *Gesta*, assigns it, in footnotes (pp. 17, 18), to "early in April." But his argument that, as that must have been (as it was) the date of the (Oxford) charter, it was consequently that of the (London) council, confuses two distinct events. In this he does but follow the *Gesta*, which similarly runs into one the two consecutive events. Richard of Hexham also, followed by John of Hexham,[1] combines in one the council at London with the charter issued at Oxford, besides placing them both, wrongly, far too late in the year.

Here are the passages in point taken from both writers:—

RICHARD OF HEXHAM.	JOHN OF HEXHAM.
Eodem quoque anno Innocentius Romanæ sedis Apostolicus, Stephano regi Angliæ litteras suas transmisit, quibus eum Apostolica auctoritate in regno Angliæ confirmavit. . . . Igitur Stephanus his et aliis modis in regno Angliæ confirmatus, episcopos et proceres sui regni regali edicto in unum convenire præcepit; cum quibus hoc generale concilium celebravit.	Eodem anno Innocentius papa litteris ab Apostolica sede directis eundem regem Stephanum in negotiis regni confirmavit. Harum tenore litterarum rex instructus, generali convocato concilio bonas et antiquas leges, et justos consuetudines præcepit conservari, injustitias vero cassari.

[1] John's list of bishops attesting the (London) council is taken from Richard's list of bishops attesting the (Oxford) charter.

The point to keep clearly in mind is that the Earl of Gloucester was not present at the Easter court in London, and that, landing subsequently, he was present when the charter of liberties was granted at Oxford. So short an interval of time elapsed that there cannot have been two councils. There was, I believe, one council which adjourned from London to Oxford, and which did so on purpose to meet the virtual head of the opposition, the powerful Earl of Gloucester. It must have been the waiting for his arrival at court which postponed the issue of the charter, and it is not wonderful that, under these circumstances, the chroniclers should have made of the whole but one transaction.

The earl, on his arrival, did homage, with the very important and significant reservation that his loyalty would be strictly conditional on Stephen's behaviour to himself.[1]

His example in this respect was followed by the bishops, for we read in the chrönicler, immediately afterwards:

"Eodem anno, non multo post adventum comitis, juraverunt episcopi fidelitatem regi quamdiu ille libertatem ecclesiæ et vigorem disciplinæ conservaret."[2]

By this writer the incident in question is recorded in connection with the Oxford charter. In this he must be correct, if it was subsequent to the earl's homage, for this latter itself, we see, must have been subsequent to Easter.

Probably the council at London was the preliminary to that treaty (*convencio*) between the king and the bishops, at which William of Malmesbury so plainly hints,

[1] "Eodem anno post Pascha Robertus comes Glocestræ, cujus prudentiam rex Stephanus maxime verebatur, venit in Angliam. . . . Itaque homagium regi fecit sub conditione quadam, scilicet quamdiu ille dignitatem suam integre custodiret et sibi pacta servaret" (*Will. Malms.*, 705, 707).
Ibid., 707.

and of which the Oxford charter is virtually the exponent record. For this, I take it, is the point to be steadily kept in view, namely, that the terms of such a charter as this are the resultant of two opposing forces—the one, the desire to extort from the king the utmost possible concession; the other, his desire to extort homage at the lowest price he could. Taken in connection with the presence at Oxford of his arch-opponent, the Earl of Gloucester, this view, I would venture to urge, may lead us to the conclusion that this extended version of his meagre "coronation charter" represents his final and definite acceptance, by the magnates of England, as their king.

It may be noticed, incidentally, as illustrative of the chronicle-value of charters, that not a single chronicler records this eventful assembly at Oxford. Our knowledge of it is derived wholly and solely from the testing-clause of the charter itself—"Apud Oxeneford, anno ab incarnatione Domini MCXXXVI." Attention should also, perhaps, be drawn to this repeated visit to Oxford, and to the selection of that spot for this assembly. For this its central position may, doubtless, partly account, especially if the Earl of Gloucester was loth to come further east. But it also, we must remember, represented for Stephen, as it were, a post of observation, commanding, in Bristol and Gloucester, the two strongholds of the opposition. So, conversely, it represented to the Empress an advanced post resting on their base.

Lastly, I think it perfectly possible to fix pretty closely the date of this assembly and charter. Easter falling on the 22nd of March, neither the king nor the Earl of Gloucester would have reached Oxford till the end of March or, perhaps, the beginning of April. But as early as Rogation-tide (April 26–29) it was rumoured that the king was dead, and Hugh Bigod, who, as a royal *dapifer*, had been among the witnesses to this Oxford charter, burst into revolt at once.[1] Then followed the suppression of the rebellion, and the king's breach of the charter.[2] It would seem, therefore, to be beyond question that this assembly took place early in April (1136).

I have gone thus closely into these details in order to bring out as clearly as possible the process, culminating in the Oxford charter, by which the succession of Stephen was gradually and, above all, conditionally secured.

Stephen, as a king, was an admitted failure. I cannot, however, but view with suspicion the causes assigned to his failure by often unfriendly chroniclers. That their criticisms had some foundation it would not be possible to deny. But in the first place, had he enjoyed better fortune, we should have heard less of his incapacity, and in the second, these writers, not enjoying the same standpoint as ourselves, were, I think, somewhat inclined to mistake effects for causes. Stephen, for instance, has been severely blamed, mainly on the authority of Henry of Huntingdon,[3] for not punishing more severely the rebels who held Exeter against him in 1136. Surely, in doing so, his critics must forget the parallel cases of both his predecessors. William Rufus at the siege of Rochester (1088), Henry I. at the siege of Bridgnorth (1102), should both be remembered when dealing with Stephen at the siege of Exeter. In both these cases, the people had clamoured for condign punishment on the traitors; in both, the king, who had conquered by their help, was held back by the jealousy of his barons, from punishing their fellows as they deserved. We learn from the author of the *Gesta* that the same was the case at Exeter. The

---

[1] *Hen. Hunt.*, p. 259.   [2] *Ibid.*, p. 260.
[3] "Vindictam non exercuit in proditores suos, pessimo consilio usus; si enim eam tunc exercuisset, postea contra eum tot castella retenta non fuissent" (*Hen. Hunt.*, p. 259).

king's barons again intervened to save those who had rebelled from ruin, and at the same time to prevent the king from securing too signal a triumph. This brings us to the true source of his weakness throughout his reign. That weakness was due to two causes, each supplementing the other. These were—(1) the essentially unsatisfactory character of his position, as resting, virtually, on a compact that he should be king so long only as he gave satisfaction to those who had placed him on the throne; (2) the existence of a rival claim, hanging over him from the first, like the sword of Damocles, and affording a lever by which the malcontents could compel him to adhere to the original understanding, or even to submit to further demands.

Let us glance at them both in succession.

Stephen himself describes his title in the opening clause of his Oxford charter:—

"Ego Stephanus Dei gratia assensu cleri et populi in regem Anglorum electus, et a Willelmo Cantuariensi archiepiscopo et sanctæ Romanæ ecclesiæ legato consecratus, et ab Innocentio sanctæ Romanæ sedis pontifice confirmatus." [1]

On this clause Dr. Stubbs observes:—

"His rehearsal of his title is curious and important; it is worth while to compare it with that of Henry I., but it need not necessarily be interpreted as showing a consciousness of weakness." [2]

Referring to the charter of Henry I., we find the clause phrased thus:—

"HENRICUS FILIUS WILLELMI REGIS post obitum fratris sui Willelmi, Dei gratia rex Anglorum." [3]

Surely the point to strike us here is that the clause in Stephen's charter contains just that which is omitted in Henry's, and omits just that which is contained in Henry's. Henry puts forward his relationship to his father and his

[1] *Select Charters*, 114 (cf. *Will. Malms.*). [2] *Ibid.* [3] *Ibid.*, 96.

brother as the sole explanation of his position as king. Stephen omits all mention of his relationship. Conversely, the election, etc., set forth by Stephen, finds no place in the charter of Henry. What can be more significant than this contrast? Again, the formula in Stephen's charter should be compared not only with that of Henry, but with that of his daughter the Empress. As the father had styled himself "Henricus filius Willelmi Regis," so his daughter invariably styled herself "Matildis . . . Henrici regis [or regis Henrici] filia;" and so her son, in his time, is styled (1142), as we shall find in a charter quoted in this work, "Henricus filius filiæ regis Henrici." To the importance of this fact I shall recur below. Meanwhile, the point to bear in mind is, that Stephen's style contains no allusion to his parentage, though, strangely enough, in a charter which must have passed in the first year of his reign, he does adopt the curious style of "Ego Stephanus Willelmi Anglorum primi Regis nepos," etc.,[1] in which he hints, contrary to his practice, at a quasi-hereditary right.

Returning, however, to his Oxford charter, in which he did not venture to allude to such claim, we find him appealing (a) to his election, which, as we have seen, was informal enough; (b) to his anointing by the primate; (c) to his "confirmation" by the pope. It is impossible to read such a formula as this in any other light than that of an attempt to "make up a title" under difficulties. I do not know that it has ever been suggested, though the

[1] *Confirmation Roll*, 1 Hen. VIII., Part 5, No. 13 (quoted by Mr. J. A. C. Vincent in *Genealogist* (N. S.), ii. 271). This should be compared with the argument of his friends when urging the primate to crown him, that he had not only been elected to the throne (by the Londoners), but also "ad hoc justo germanæ propinquitatis jure idoneus accessit" (*Gesta*, p. 8), and with the admission, shortly after, in the pope's letter, that among his claims he "de præfati regis [Henrici] prosapia prope posito gradu originem traxisse."

hypothesis would seem highly probable, that the stress laid by Stephen upon the ecclesiastical sanction to his succession may have been largely due, as I have said (p. 10), to the obstacle presented by the oath that had been sworn to the Empress. Of breaking that oath the Church, he held, had pronounced him not guilty.

Yet it is not so much on this significant style, as on the drift of the charter itself, that I depend for support of my thesis that Stephen was virtually king on sufferance, or, to anticipate a phrase of later times, "Quamdiu se bene gesserit." We have seen how in the four typical cases, (1) of the Londoners, (2) of Miles of Gloucester, (3) of Earl Robert, (4) of the bishops, Stephen had only secured their allegiance by submitting to that "original contract" which the political philosophers of a later age evolved from their inner consciousness. It was because his Oxford charter set the seal to this "contract" that Stephen, even then, chafed beneath its yoke, as evidenced by the striking saving clause—

"Hæc omnia concedo et confirmo salva regia et justa dignitate meâ."[1]

And, as we know, at the first opportunity, he hastened to break its bonds.[2]

The position of his opponents throughout his reign would seem to have rested on two assumptions. The first, that a breach, on his part, of the "contract" justified *ipso facto* revolt on theirs;[3] the second, that their allegi-

---

[1] *Select Charters*, 115. But cf. *Will. Malms.*

[2] As further illustrating the compromise of which this charter was the resultant, note that Stephen retains and combines the formula "Dei gratiâ" with the recital of election, and that he further represents the election as merely a popular "*assent*" to his succession.

[3] Compare the clause in the *Confirmatio Cartarum* of 1265, establishing the right of insurrection: "Liceat omnibus de regno nostro contra nos insurgere."

ance to the king was a purely feudal relation, and, as such, could be thrown off at any moment by performing the famous *diffidatio*.[1] This essential feature of continental feudalism had been rigidly excluded by the Conqueror. He had taken advantage, as is well known, of his position as an English king, to extort an allegiance from his Norman followers more absolute than he could have claimed as their feudal lord. It was to Stephen's peculiar position that was due the introduction for a time of this pernicious principle into England. We have seen it hinted at in that charter of Stephen in which he treats with Miles of Gloucester not merely as his king (*rex*), but also as his feudal lord (*dominus*). We shall find it acted on three years later (1139), when this same Miles, with his own *dominus*, the Earl of Gloucester, jointly "defy" Stephen before declaring for the Empress.[2]

Passing now to the other point, the existence of a rival claim, we approach a subject of great interest, the theory of the succession to the English Crown at what may be termed the crisis of transition from the principle of

[1] See *inter alia*, Hallam's *Middle Ages*, i. 168, 169.

[2] "Fama per Angliam volitabat, quod comes Gloecestræ Robertus, qui erat in Normannia, in proximo partes sororis foret adjuturus, *rege tantummodo ante diffidato*. Nec fides rerum famæ levitatem destituit: celeriter enim post Pentecosten missis a Normanniâ suis regi *more majorum amicitiam et fidem interdixit, homagio etiam abdicato;* rationem præferens quam id juste faceret, quia et rex illicite ad regnum aspiraverat, et omnem fidem sibi juratam neglexerat, ne dicam mentitus fuerat" (*Will. Malms.*, 712). So, too, the Continuator of Florence: "Interim facta conjuratione adversus regem per prædictum Brycstowensem comitem et conestabularium Milonem, *abnegata fidelitate quam illi juraverant*, . . . Milo constabularius, *regiæ majestati redditis fidei sacramentis*, ad dominum suum, comitem Gloucestrensem, cum grandi manu militum se contulit" (pp. 110, 117). Compare with these passages the extraordinary complaint made against Stephen's conduct in attacking Lincoln without sending a formal "defiance" to his opponents, and the singular treaty, in this reign, between the Earls of Chester and of Leicester, in which the latter was bound not to attack the former, as his lord, without sending him the formal "diffidatio" a clear fortnight beforehand.

election (within the royal house) to that of hereditary right according to feudal rules.

For the right view on this subject, we turn, as ever, to Dr. Stubbs, who, with his usual sound judgment, writes thus of the Norman period:—

> "The crown then continued to be elective. . . . But whilst the elective principle was maintained in its fulness where it was necessary or possible to maintain it, it is quite certain that the right of inheritance, and inheritance as primogeniture, was recognized as co-ordinate. . . . The measures taken by Henry I. for securing the crown to his own children, whilst they prove the acceptance of the hereditary principle, prove also the importance of strengthening it by the recognition of the elective theory.[1]

Mr. Freeman, though writing with a strong bias in favour of the elective theory, is fully justified in his main argument, namely, that Stephen "was no usurper in the sense in which the word is vulgarly used."[2] He urges, apparently with perfect truth, that Stephen's offence, in the eyes of his contemporaries, lay in his breaking his solemn oath, and not in his supplanting a rightful heir. And he aptly suggests that the wretchedness of his reign may have hastened the growth of that new belief in the divine right of the heir to the throne, which first appears under Henry II., and in the pages of William of Newburgh.[3]

So far as Stephen is concerned the case is clear enough. But we have also to consider the Empress. On what did she base her claim? I think that, as implied in Dr. Stubbs' words, she based it on a double, not a single,

---

[1] *Const. Hist.*, i. 338, 340.   [2] *Norm. Conq.*, v. 251.
[3] "In a later stage, when the son of his rival was firm on the throne, the doctrine of female succession took root under a king who by the spindle-side sprang from both William and Cerdic, but who by the spear-side had nothing to do with either. Then it was that men began to find out that Stephen had been guilty not only of breaking his oath, but also of defrauding the heir to the crown of her lawful right" (*ibid.*, p. 252).

ground. She claimed the kingdom as King Henry's daughter ("regis Henrici filia"), but she claimed it further because the succession had been assured to her by oath ("sibi juratum") as such.[1] It is important to observe that the oath in question can in no way be regarded in the light of an election. To understand it aright, we must go back to the precisely similar oath which had been previously sworn to her brother. As early as 1116, the king, in evident anxiety to secure the succession to his heir, had called upon a gathering of the magnates "of all England," on the historic spot of Salisbury, to swear allegiance to his son (March 19).[2] It was with reference to this event that Eadmer described him at his death (November, 1120) as "Willelmum jam olim regni hæredem designatum" (p. 290). Before leaving Normandy in November, 1120, the king similarly secured the succession of the duchy to his son by compelling its barons to swear that they would be faithful to the youth.[3] On the destruction of his plans by his son's death, he hastened to marry again in the hope of securing, once more, a male heir. Despairing of this after some years, he took advantage of the Emperor's death to insist on his daughter's return, and brought her with him to England in the autumn of 1126. He was not long in taking steps to secure her recognition as his heir (subject however, as the Continuator and Symeon are both careful to point

[1] "Henrici regis filia, ... vehementer exhilarata utpote regnum sibi juratum ... jam adepta" (*Cont. Flor. Wig.*, 130). But the above duplex character of her claim is best brought out in her formal request that the legate should receive her "tanquam regis Henrici filiam et cui omnis Anglia et Normannia jurata esset."

[2] "Conventio optimatum et baronum totius Angliæ apud Salesbyriam xiv. kalend. Aprilis facta est, qui in præsentiâ regis Henrici homagium filio suo Willelmo fecerunt, et fidelitatem ei juraverunt" (*Flor. Wig.*, ii. 69).

[3] "Normanniæ principes, jubente rege, filio suo Willelmo jam tunc xviii. annorum, hominium faciunt, et fidelitatis securitatem sacramentis affirmant" (*Sym. Dun.*, ii. 258).

THE OATH TO THE EMPRESS. 31

out, to no son being born to him), by the same oath being sworn to her as, in 1116, had been sworn to his son. It was taken, not (as is always stated) in 1126, but on the 1st of January, 1127.[1] Of what took place upon that occasion, there is, happily, full evidence.[2] We have independent reports of the transaction from William of Malmesbury, Symeon of Durham, the Continuator of Florence, and Gervase of Canterbury.[3] From this last we learn (the fact is, therefore, doubtful) that the oath secured the succession, not only to the Empress, but to her heirs.[4] The Continuator's version is chiefly important as bringing out the action of the king in assigning the succession to his daughter, the oath being merely an undertaking to secure the arrangement he had made.[5] Symeon introduces the striking expression that

[1] Oddly enough, the correct date must be sought from Symeon of Durham, though, at first sight, he is the most inaccurate, as he places the event under 1128 (a date accepted, in the margin, by his editor) instead of 1126, the year given by the other chroniclers. But from him we learn that the Christmas court (i.e. Christmas 1126) was adjourned from Windsor to London, for the new year, "ubi Circumcisione Domini" (January 1) the actual oath was taken. William of Malmesbury dates it, loosely, at Christmas (1126), but the Continuator of Florence, more accurately, "finitis diebus festivioribus" (p. 84), which confirms Symeon's statement.

[2] It is scarcely realized so clearly as it should be that the oath taken on this occasion was that to which reference was always made. Dr. Stubbs (*Const. Hist.*, i. 341) recognizes "a similar oath in 1131" (on the authority of William of Malmesbury), and another in 1133 (on the authority of Roger of Hoveden). But the former is only incidentally mentioned, and is neither alluded to elsewhere, nor referred to subsequently by William himself; and the latter, which is similarly devoid of any contemporary confirmation, is represented as securing the succession, not to Matilda, but to her son. It is strange that so recent and important an oath as this, if it was really taken, should have been ignored in the controversy under Stephen, and the earlier oath, described above, alone appealed to.

[3] Henry of Huntingdon merely alludes to it, retrospectively, at Stephen's accession, as the "sacramentum fidelitatis Anglici regni filiæ regis Henrici" (p. 256).

[4] "Fecit principes et potentes adjurare eidem filiæ suæ et heredibus suis legitimis regnum Angliæ" (i. 93). This is, perhaps, somewhat confirmed by the words which the author of the *Gesta* places in the primate's mouth (p. 7).

[5] "In filiam suam, sororem scilicet Willelmi, . . . regni jura transferebat"

the Empress was to succeed "hæreditario jure,"[1] but William of Malmesbury, in the speech which he places in the king's mouth, far outstrips this in his assertion of hereditary right :—

"præfatus quanto incommodo patriæ fortuna Willelmum filium suum sibi surripuisset, *cui jure regnum competeret :* nunc superesse filiam, *cui soli legitima debeatur successio, ab avo, avunculo, et patre regibus ;* a materno genere multis retro seculis."[2]

Bearing in mind the time at which William wrote these words, it will be seen that the Empress and her partisans must have largely, to say the least, based their claim on her right to the throne as her father's heir, and that she and they appealed to the oath as the admission and recognition of that right, rather than as partaking in any way whatever of the character of a free election.[3] Thus her claim was neatly traversed by Stephen's advocates, at Rome, in 1136, when they urged that she was not her father's heir, and that, consequently, the oath which had been sworn to her as such (" sicut hæredi ") was void.

It is, as I have said, in the above light that I view her

(p. 85). The oath to secure her this succession was taken "ad jussum regis" (p. 84). Compare with this expression that of Gervase above, and that (*quantum valeat*) of Roger Hoveden, viz. "*constituit* eum regem;" also the "jubente rege" of Symeon in 1120. It was accordingly urged, at Stephen's accession, that the oath had been compulsory, and was therefore invalid.

[1] " Juraverunt ut filiæ suæ imperatrici fide servata regnum Angliæ *hæreditario jure* post eum servarent " (p. 281). Compare William of Newburgh, on Henry's accession : " Hæreditarium regnum suscepit." These expressions are the more noteworthy because of the contrast they afford to the Conqueror's dying words, " Neminem Anglici constituo heredem . . . non enim tantum decus hereditario jure possedi " (*Ord. Vit.*).

[2] *Will. Malms.*, 691.

[3] That the oath of January 1, 1127, preceding the marriage of the Empress, was, as I have urged, the ruling one seems to be further implied by the passage in William of Malmesbury : " Ego Rogerum Salesbiriensem episcopum sæpe dicentem audivi, 'Solutum se sacramento quod imperatrici fecerat: eo enim pacto se jurasse, ne rex præter consilium suum et cæterorum procerum filiam cuiquam nuptam daret extra regnum,' " etc., etc. (p. 693).

unvarying use of the style "regis Henrici filia," and that this was the true character of her claim will be seen from the terms of a charter I shall quote, which has hitherto, it would seem, remained unknown, and in which she recites that, on arriving in England, she was promptly welcomed by Miles of Gloucester "sicut illam quam justam hæredem regni Angliæ recognovit."

The sex of the Empress was the drawback to her claim. Had her brother lived, there can be little question that he would, as a matter of course, have succeeded his father at his death. Or again, had Henry II. been old enough to succeed his grandfather, he would, we may be sure, have done so. But as to the Empress, even admitting the justice of her claim, it was by no means clear in whom it was vested. It might either be vested (a) in herself, in accordance with our modern notions; or (b) in her husband, in accordance with feudal ones;[1] or (c) in her son, as, in the event, it was. It may be said that this point was still undecided as late as 1142, when Geoffrey was invited to come to England, and decided to send his son instead, to represent the hereditary claim. The force of circumstances, however, as we shall find, had compelled the Empress, in the hour of her triumph (1141), to take her

[1] As for instance when Henry II. obtained Aquitaine with his wife. There is, as it happens, a passage in Symeon of Durham, which may have been somewhat overlooked, where it is distinctly stated that in the autumn of the year (1127), Henry conceded, as a condition of the Angevin match, that, in default of his having a son, Geoffrey of Anjou should succeed him ("remque ad effectum perduxit eo tenore ut regi, de legitima conjuge hæredem non habenti, mortuo *gener illius* in regnum succederet"). That Geoffrey's claim was recognized at the time is clear from the striking passage quoted by Mr. Freeman from his panegyrist ("sceptro . . . non injuste aspirante"), and even more so from the explicit statement: "Volente igitur Gaufrido comite cum uxore suâ, quæ hæres erat [here again is an allusion to her hereditary right], in regnum succedere, primores terræ, juramenti sui male recordantes, *regem eum* suscipere noluerunt, dicentes 'Alienigena non regnabit super nos'" (*Select Charters*, p. 110).

own course, and to claim the throne for herself as queen, though even this would not decide the point, as, had she succeeded, her husband, we may be sure, would have claimed the title of king.

Broadly speaking, to sum up the evidence here collected, it tends to the belief that the obsolescence of the right of election to the English crown presents considerable analogy to that of canonical election in the case of English bishoprics. In both cases a free election degenerated into a mere assent to a choice already made. We see the process of change already in full operation when Henry I. endeavours to extort beforehand from the magnates their assent to his daughter's succession, and when they subsequently complain of this attempt to dictate to them on the subject. We catch sight of it again when his daughter bases her claim to the crown, not on any free election, but on her rights as her father's heir, confirmed by the above assent. We see it, lastly, when Stephen, though owing his crown to election, claims to rule by Divine right ("Dei gratia"[1]), and attempts to reduce that election to nothing more than a national "assent" to his succession. Obviously, the whole question turned on whether the election was to be held first, or was to be a mere ratification of a choice already made. Thus, at the very time when Stephen was formulating his title, he was admitting, in the case of the bishopric of Bath, that the canonical election had *preceded* his own nomination of the bishop.[2] Yet it is easy to see how, as the Crown grew in strength, the elections, in both cases alike, would become, more and more, virtually matters of form, while a weak sovereign or a disputed succession

[1] Compare the style of "Alphonso XIII., by the grace of God constitutional King of Spain."
[2] "Canonica prius electione præcedente."

would afford an opportunity for this historical survival, in the case at least of the throne, to recover for a moment its pristine strength.

Before quitting the point, I would venture briefly to resume my grounds for urging that, in comparing Stephen with his successor, the difference between their circumstances has been insufficiently allowed for. At Stephen's accession, thirty years of legal and financial oppression had rendered unpopular the power of the Crown, and had led to an impatience of official restraint which opened the path to a feudal reaction: at the accession of Henry, on the contrary, the evils of an enfeebled administration and of feudalism run mad had made all men eager for the advent of a strong king, and had prepared them to welcome the introduction of his centralizing administrative reforms. He anticipated the position of the house of Tudor at the close of the Wars of the Roses, and combined with it the advantages which Charles II. derived from the Puritan tyranny. Again, Stephen was hampered from the first by his weak position as a king on sufferance, whereas Henry came to his work unhampered by compact or concession. Lastly, Stephen was confronted throughout by a rival claimant, who formed a splendid rallying-point for all the discontent in his realm: but Henry reigned for as long as Stephen without a rival to trouble him; and when he found at length a rival in his own son, a claim far weaker than that which had threatened his predecessor seemed likely for a time to break his power as effectually as the followers of the Empress had broken that of Stephen. He may only, indeed, have owed his escape to that efficient administration which years of strength and safety had given him the time to construct.

It in no way follows from these considerations that Henry was not superior to Stephen; but it does, surely, suggest itself that Stephen's disadvantages were great, and that had he enjoyed better fortune, we might have heard less of his defects. It will be at least established by the evidence adduced in this work that some of the charges which are brought against him can no longer be maintained.

CHAPTER II.

THE FIRST CHARTER OF THE KING.

GEOFFREY DE MANDEVILLE was the grandson and heir of a follower of the conqueror of the same name. From Mandeville, a village, according to Mr. Stapleton, near Trevières in the Bessin,[1] the family took its name, which, being Latinized as "De Magnavilla," is often found as "De Magnaville." The elder Geoffrey appears in Domesday as a considerable tenant-in-chief, his estates lying in no less than eleven different counties.[2] On the authority of the *Monasticon* he is said by Dugdale to have been made constable of the Tower. Dugdale, however, has here misquoted his own authority, for the chronicle printed by him states, not that Geoffrey, but that his son and heir (William) received this office.[3] Its statement is confirmed

[1] *Rotuli Scaccarii Normanniæ,* II. clxxxviii. Such was also the opinion of M. Leopold Delisle. The French editors, however, of Ordericus write: "On ne sait auquel des nombreux Magneville, Mandeville, Manneville de Normandie rapporter le berceau de cette illustre maison" (iv. 108).

[2] There is a curious story in the Waltham Chronicle (*De Inventione,* cap. xiii.) that the Conqueror placed Geoffrey in the shoes of Esegar the staller. The passage runs thus: "Cui [Tovi] successit filius ejus Adelstanus pater Esegari qui stalra inventus est in Angliæ conquisitione a Normannis, cujus hereditatem postea dedit conquisitor terræ, rex Willelmus, Galfrido de Mandevile proavi presentis comitis Willelmi. Successit quidem Adelstanus patri suo Tovi, non in totam quidem possessionem quam possederat pater, sed in eam tantum quæ pertinebat ad stallariam, quam nunc habet comes Willelmus." The special interest of this story lies in the official connection of Esegar [or Ansgar] the staller with London and Middlesex, combined with the fact that Geoffrey occupied the same position. See p. 354, and Addenda.

[3] "Post cujus [*i.e.* Galfridi] mortem reliquit filium suum hæredem, cui firmitas turris Londoniarum custodienda committitur. Nobili cum Rege

by Ordericus Vitalis, who distinctly mentions that the Tower was in charge of William de Mandeville when Randulf Flambard was there imprisoned in 1101.[1] This may help to explain an otherwise puzzling fact, namely, that a Geoffrey de Mandeville, who was presumably his father, appears as a witness to charters of a date subsequent to this.[2]

Geoffrey de Mandeville founded the Benedictine priory of Hurley,[3] and we know the names of his two wives, Athelais and Leceline. By the former he had a son and heir, William, mentioned above, who in turn was the father of Geoffrey, the central figure of this work.[4]

The above descent is not based upon the evidence of the *Monasticon* alone, but is incidentally recited in those

magnificé plura gessit patri non immerito in rebus agendis coæqualis" (*Monasticon*). Dugdale's error, as we might expect, is followed by later writers, Mr. Clark treating Geoffrey as the first "hereditary constable," and his son, whom with characteristic inaccuracy he transforms from "William" into "Walter," as the second (*Mediæval Military Architecture*, ii. 253, 254). The French editors of Ordericus (iv. 108) strangely imagined that William was brother, not son, of Geoffrey de Mandeville.

[1] "In arce Lundoniensi Guillelmo de Magnavilla custodiendus in vinculis traditus est" (iv. 108).

[2] See for instance *Abingdon Cartulary*, ii. 73, 85, 116, where he attests charters of circ. 1110-1112.

[3] *Monasticon*, iii. 433. He founds the priory "pro anima Athelaisæ primæ uxoris meæ, matris filiorum meorum jam defunctæ;" and "Lecelina domina uxor mea" is a witness to the charter.

[4] It is necessary to check by authentic charters and other trustworthy evidence the chronicles printed in the *Monasticon* under Walden Abbey. One of these was taken from a long and interesting MS., formerly in the possession of the Royal Society, but now among the Arundel MSS. in the British Museum. This, which is only partially printed, and which ought to be published in its entirety, has the commencement wanting, and is, unfortunately, very inaccurate for the early period of which I treat. It is this narrative which makes the wild misstatements as to the circumstances of the foundation, which grossly misdates Geoffrey's death, etc., etc. All its statements are accepted by Dugdale. The other chronicle, which he printed from Cott. MS., Titus, D. 20, is far more accurate, gives Geoffrey's death correctly, and rightly assigns him as wife the *sister* (not the daughter) of the Earl of Oxford, thus correcting Dugdale's error. It is the latter chronicle which Dugdale has misquoted with reference to the charge of the Tower.

THE FAMILY OF MANDEVILLE.

royal charters on which my story is so largely based. It is therefore beyond dispute. But though there is no pedigree of the period clearer or better established, it has formed the subject of an amazing blunder, so gross as to be scarcely credible. Madox had shown, in his *History of the Exchequer* (ii. 400), that Geoffrey " Fitz Piers " (Earl of Essex from 1199 to 1213) was Sheriff of Essex and Herts in 1192-94 (4 & 5 Ric. I.). Now Geoffrey, the son of Geoffrey "Fitz Piers," assuming the surname of "De Mandeville," became his successor in the earldom of Essex, which he held from 1213 to 1216. The noble and learned authors of the *Lords' Reports on the Dignity of a Peer* began by confusing this Geoffrey with his namesake the earl of 1141, and bodily transferring to the latter the whole parentage of the former. Thus they evolved the startling discovery that the father of our Geoffrey, the earl of 1141, "was Geoffrey Fitz Peter [*i.e.* the earl of 1199-1213], and probably was son of Peter, the sheriff at the time of the Survey."[1] But not content even with this, they transferred the shrievalty of Geoffrey "Fitz Piers" from 1192-94 (*vide supra*)[2] to a date earlier than the grant to Geoffrey de Mandeville (his supposed son) in 1141. Now, during that shrievalty the Earls "of Clare" enjoyed the *tertius denarius* of the county of Hertford. Thus their lordships were enabled to produce the further discovery that the Earls "of Clare" enjoyed it before the date of this grant (1141), that is to say, "either before or early in the reign of King Stephen."[3] The authority of these Reports has

[1] Who was really Peter de Valognes.

[2] "Madox . . . has shown . . . that Geoffrey Fitzpeter, Earl of Essex, obtained from the Crown Grants of the shrievalty of the Counties of Essex and Hertford when the Earls, commonly called Earls of Clare, were Earls of Hertford, and had the Third Penny of the Pleas of that County " (iii. 69, ed. 1829).

[3] "The County of Hertford appears to have been, at the time of the Survey, in the King's hands, and Peter was then Sheriff; and the Sheriffwick

been so widely recognized that we cannot wonder at Courthope stating in his *Historic Peerage of England* (p. 248) that "Richard de Clare . . . was Earl of Hertford, and possessed of the third penny of that county, before or early in the reign of King Stephen." Courthope has in turn misled Dr. Stubbs,[1] and Mr. Doyle has now followed suit, stating that Richard de Clare was "created Earl of Hertford (about) 1136."[2] It is therefore something to have traced this error to its original source in the *Lords' Reports*.

The first mention, it would seem, of the subject of this study is to be found in the Pipe-Roll of 1130, where we read—

"Gaufridus de Mandeville reddit compotum de Dccclxvj*li*. et xiij*s*. et iiij*d*. pro terra patris sui. In thesauro cxxxiii*li*. et vi*s*. et viii*d*.
" Et debet Dcc et xxxiij*li*. et vj*s*. et viij*d*." (p. 55).

As he had thus, at Michaelmas, 1130, paid only two-thirteenths of the amount due from him for succession, that is the (arbitrary) "relief" to the Crown, we may infer that his father was but lately dead. He does not again meet us till he appears at Stephen's court early in 1136.[3] From the date of that appearance we pass to his creation as an earl by the first of those royal charters with which we are so largely concerned.[4]

of Hertfordshire was afterwards granted in Fee, by the Empress Maud, to Geoffrey de Mandeville, Earl of Essex, at a rent as his father and grandfather had held it. The father of Geoffrey was Geoffrey Fitz Peter, and probably was son of Peter, the Sheriff at the time of the Survey. The first trace which the Committee has discovered of the title of the Earls of Clare to the Third Penny of the County is in the reign of Henry the Second, subsequent to the grants under which the Earls of Essex claimed the Shrievalty in fee, at a fee-farm rent. But the grant of the Third Penny must have been of an earlier date, as the grant to the Earl of Essex was subject to that charge. The family of Clare must therefore have had the Third Penny either before or early in the Reign of King Stephen" (iii. 125).

[1] *Const. Hist.*, i. 362. [2] *Official Baronage*, ii. 175.
[3] See Appendix C. [4] See Frontispiece.

INTEREST OF THE CHARTER.

The date of this charter is a point of no small interest, not merely because we have in it the only surviving charter of creation of those issued by Stephen, but also because there is reason to believe that it is the oldest extant charter of creation known to English antiquaries. That distinction has indeed been claimed for the second charter in my series, namely, that which Geoffrey obtained from the Empress Maud. It is of the latter that Camden wrote, "This is the most ancient creation-charter that I ever saw."[1] Selden duly followed suit, and Dugdale echoed Selden's words.[2] Courthope merely observes that it "is presumed to be one of the very earliest charters of express creation of the title of earl;"[3] and Mr. Birch pronounces it "one of the earliest, if not the earliest, example of a deed creating a peerage."[4] In despite, however, of these opinions I am prepared to prove that the charter with which we are now dealing is entitled to the first place, though that of the Empress comes next.

We cannot begin an investigation of the subject better than by seeking the opinion of Mr. Eyton, who was a specialist in the matter of charters and their dates, and who had evidently investigated the point. His note on this charter is as follows:—

"Stephen's earlier deeds of 1136 exhibit Geoffrey de Magnaville as a baron only. There are three such, two of which certainly, and the third probably, passed at Westminster. He was custos of the Tower of London, an office which probably necessitated a constant residence. There are three patents of creation extant by which he became Earl of Essex. Those which I suppose to precede this were by the Empress. The first of them passed in the short period during which Maud was in London, i.e. between June 24 and July 25, 1141. The second within a month after, at Oxford. In the latter she alludes to grants of lands previously made by Stephen to the said Geoffrey, but to no patent of

[1] *Degrees of England.*
[2] "Note that this is the most ancient creation-charter which hath ever been known." Vide Selden, *Titles of Honour,* p. 647.
[3] *Historic Peerage,* p. 178.   [4] *Journ. Brit. Arch. Ass.,* xxxi. 386.

earldom except her own. Selden calls Maud's London patent the oldest on record. It is not perhaps that, but it is older than this, though Dugdale thought not. Having decided that Stephen's patent succeeded Maud's, it follows that it (viz. this charter) passed after Nov. 1, 1141, when Stephen regained his liberty and Geoffrey probably forsook the empress. The king was at London on Dec. 7. In 1142 we are told (Lysons, *Camb.*, 9) that this Geoffrey and Earl Gilbert were sent by Stephen against the Isle of Ely. He is called earl. We shall also have him attesting a charter of Queen Matilda (Stephen's wife).

"In 1143 he was seized in Stephen's court at St. Alban's.

"In 1144 he is in high rebellion against Stephen, and an ally of Nigel, Bishop of Ely. He is killed in Aug., 1144.

"On the whole then it would appear that the Empress first made him an earl as a means of securing London, the stronghold of Stephen's party, but that, on Stephen's release, the earl changed sides and Stephen opposed Maud's policy by a counter-patent (we have usually found counter-charters, however, to be Maud's). We have also a high probability that this charter passed in Dec., 1141, or soon after; for Stephen does not appear at London in 1142, when Geoffrey is earl and in Stephen's employ." [1]

Here I must first clear the ground by explaining as to the "three patents of creation" mentioned in this passage, that there were only *two* charters (not "patents") of creation—that of the king, which survives in the original, and that of the Empress, which is known to us from a transcript. As to the latter, it certainly "passed in the short period during which Maud was in London," but that period, so far from being "between June 24 and July 25, 1141," consisted only of a few days ending with "June 24, 1141." The main point, however, at issue is the priority of the creation-charters. It will be seen that Mr. Eyton jumped at his conclusion, and then proceeded: "Having decided," etc. This is the more surprising because that conclusion was at variance with what he admits to have been his own principle, namely, that he had "usually found counter-charters to be Maud's."[2] In

[1] *Addl. MSS.*, 31,943, fol. 97.
[2] Comp. fol. 96: "My position is that where this system of counter-

this case his conclusion was wrong, and his original principle was right. I think that Mr. Eyton's error was due to his ignorance of the second charter granted by the king to Geoffrey.[1] As he was well acquainted with the royal charters in the duchy of Lancaster collection it is not easy to understand how he came to overlook this very long one, which is, as it were, the keystone to the arch I am about to construct.

It is my object to make Geoffrey's charters prove their own sequence. When once arranged in their right order, it will be clear from their contents that this order is the only one possible. We must not attempt to decide their dates till we have determined their order. But when that order has been firmly established, we can approach the question of dates with comparative ease and confidence.

To determine from internal evidence the sequence of these charters, we must arrange them in an ascending scale. That is to say, each charter should represent an advance on its immediate predecessor. Tried by this test, our four main charters will assume, beyond dispute, this relative order.

(1) First charter of the king.
(2) First charter of the Empress.
(3) Second charter of the king.
(4) Second charter of the Empress.

The order of the three last is further established by the fact that the grants in the second are specifically confirmed by the third, while the third is expressly referred to in the fourth. The only one, therefore, about which there could possibly be a question is the first, and the fact that the second charter represents a great advance upon it

charters between Stephen and the Empress *is proved*, the former generally is the first in point of date."
[1] See p. 41 *ad pedem*.

is in this case the evidence. But there is, further, the fact that the place I have assigned it is the only one in the series that it can possibly occupy. Nor could Mr. Eyton have failed to arrive at this conclusion had he included within his sphere of view the second charter of the king.

It is clear that Mr. Eyton was here working from the statements of Dugdale alone. For the three charters he deals with are those which Dugdale gives. The order assigned to these charters by Dugdale and Mr. Eyton respectively can be thus briefly shown :—

Right order	1	2	3	4
Eyton's order		2	4	1
Dugdale's order	1	4	2	

How gravely Mr. Eyton erred in his conclusions will be obvious from this table. But it is necessary to go further still, and to say that of the seven charters affecting Geoffrey de Mandeville, three would seem to have been unknown to him, while of the rest, he assigned three, one might almost say all four, to a demonstrably erroneous date. It may be urged that this is harsh criticism, and the more so as its subject was never published, and exists only in the form of notes. There is much to be said for this view, but the fact remains that rash use is certain to be made of these notes, unless students are placed on their guard. That this should be so is due not only to Mr. Eyton's great and just reputation as a laborious student in this field, but also to the exaggerated estimate of the value and correctness of these notes which was set, somewhat prominently, before the public.[1]

Advancing from the question of position to that of actual date, we will glance at the opinion of another expert, Mr. Walter de Gray Birch. We learn from him, as to the date of this first creation-charter, that—

[1] *Notes and Queries*, 6th Series, v. 83.

DATE OF THE CHARTER. 45

"The dates of the witnesses appear to range between A.D. 1139 and
A.D. 1144. . . . The actual date of the circumstances mentioned in this
document is a matter of question. . . . He [Geoffrey] was slain on the
14th of September, A.D. 1144, and therefore this document must be
prior to that date."[1]

We see now that it is by no means easy to date this
charter with exactness. It will be best, in pursuance of
my usual practice, to begin by clearing the ground.

If we could place any trust in the copious chronicle of
Walden Abbey, which is printed (in part) in the *Monasticon*
from the Arundel manuscript, our task would be easy
enough. For we are there told that Stephen had already
created Geoffrey an earl when, in 1136, he founded Walden
Abbey.[2] And, in his foundation charter, he certainly
styles himself an earl.[3] But, alas for this precious narrative,
it brings together at the ceremony three bishops,
Robert of London, Nigel of Ely, and William of Norwich,
of whom Robert of London was not appointed till 1141,
while William of Norwich did not obtain that see till
1146!

Dismissing, therefore, this evidence, we turn to the
fact that no creation of an earldom by Stephen is mentioned
before 1138. But we have something far more
important than this in the occurrence at the head of the
witnesses to this creation-charter, of the name of William
of Ypres, the only name, indeed, among the witnesses that
strikes one as a note of time. Mr. Eyton wrote: "A
deed which I have dated 1140 . . . is his first known
attestation."[4] I have found no evidence contrary to this
conclusion. It would seem probable that when the arrest
of the bishops "gave," in Dr. Stubbs' words, "the signal

---

[1] *On the Great Seal of King Stephen*, pp. 19, 20.
[2] "Apud regem Stephanum, ac totius regni majores tanti erat ut nomine
comitis et re jampridem dignus haberetur" (*Mon. Angl.*, vol. iv. p. 141).
[3] "Gaufridus de Magnavillâ comes Essexe" (*ibid.*).
[4] *Addl. MSS.* 31,943, fol. 85 *dors.*

46 THE FIRST CHARTER OF THE KING.

for the civil war," Stephen's preparations for the approaching struggle would include the summons to his side of this experienced leader, who had hitherto been fighting in Normandy for his cause. Indeed, we know that it was so, for he was at once despatched against the castle of Devizes.[1]

Happily, however, there remains a writ, which should incidentally, we shall find, prove the key to the problem. This, which is printed among the foot-notes in Madox's *Baronia Anglica* (p. 231), from the muniments of Westminster Abbey, is addressed " Gaufrido de Magnavilla " simply, and is, therefore, previous to his elevation to the earldom. Now, as this writ refers to the death of Roger, Bishop of Salisbury, it must be later than the 11th of December, 1139.[2] Consequently Geoffrey's charter must be subsequent to that date. It must also be previous to the battle of Lincoln (February, 1141), because, as I observed at the outset, it must be previous to the charter of the Empress. We therefore virtually narrow its limit to the year 1140, for Stephen had set out for Lincoln before the close of the year.[3] Let us try and reduce it further still. What was the date of the above writ? Stephen, on the death of Bishop Roger, hastened to visit Salisbury.[4] He went there from Oxford to spend Christmas (1139), and then returned to Reading (*Cont. Flor. Wig.*). Going and returning he

---

[1] *Ordericus Vitalis*, vol. v. p. 120.   [2] See p. 282, n. 4.

[3] " Protractaque est obsidio [Lincolnie] a diebus Natalis Domini [1140] usque ad Ypapanti Domini " (*Will. Newburgh*, i. 39).

[4] To this visit may be assigned three charters (*Sarum Charters and Documents*, pp. 9–11) of interest for their witnesses. Two of them are attested by Philip the chancellor, who is immediately followed by Roger de Fécamp. The latter had similarly followed the preceding chancellor, Roger, in one of Stephen's charters of 1136 (see p. 263), which establishes his official position. Among the other witnesses were Bishop Robert of Hereford, Count Waleran of Meulan, Robert de Ver, William Martel, Robert d'Oilli with Fulk his brother, Turgis d'Avranches, Walter de Salisbury, Ingelram de Say, and William de Pont de l'Arche.

would have passed through Andover, the place at which this writ is tested. Thus it could have been, and probably was, issued at this period (December, 1139). Obviously, if it was issued in the course of 1140, this would reduce still further the possible limit within which Geoffrey's charter can have passed. Difficult though it is to trace the incessant movements of the king throughout this troubled year, he certainly visited Winchester, and (probably thence) Malmesbury. Still we have not, I believe, proof of his presence at Andover.[1] And there are other grounds, I shall now show, for thinking that the earldom was conferred before March, 1140.

William of Newburgh, speaking of the arrest of Geoffrey de Mandeville, assures us that Stephen bore an old grudge against him, which he had hitherto been forced to conceal. Its cause was a gross outrage by Geoffrey, who, on the arrival of Constance of France, the bride of Eustace the heir-apparent, had forcibly detained her in the Tower.[2] We fix the date of this event as February or March, 1140,

---

[1] The "P. cancellarius," by whom the writ is tested, was a chancellor of whom, according to Foss, virtually nothing is known. He was, however, Philip (de Harcourt), on whom the king conferred at Winchester, in 1140, the vacant see of Salisbury ("Rex Wintoniam veniens consilio baronum suorum cancellario suo Philippo Searebyriensem præsulatum . . . dedit" (*Cont. Flor. Wig.*). But the chapter refused to accept him as bishop, and eventually he was provided for by the see of Bayeux. He is likely, with or without the king, to have gone straight to Salisbury after his appointment at Winchester, in which case he would not have been present at Andover, even if Stephen himself was.

[2] "Acceptam ab eo injuriam rex caute dissimulabat, et tempus opportunum quo se ulcisceretur, observabat. Injuria vero quam regi nequam illo intulerat talis erat. Rex ante annos aliquot episcopi, ut dictum est, Salesbiriensis thesauros adeptus, summa non modica regi Francorum Lodovico transmissa, sororem ejus Constantiam Eustachio filio suo desponderat ; . . . eratque hæc cum socru sua regina Lundoniis. Cumque regina ad alium forte vellet cum eadem nuru sua locum migrare, memoratus Gaufridus arci tunc præsidens, restitit ; nuruque de manibus socrus, pro viribus obnitentis, abstracta atque retenta, illam cum ignominia abire permisit. Postea vero reposcenti, et justum motum pro tempore dissimulanti, regi socero insignem prædam ægre resignavit " (ii. 45).

from the words of the Continuator of Florence,[1] and that date agrees well with Henry of Huntingdon's statement, that Stephen had bought his son's bride with the treasure he obtained by the death of the great Bishop of Salisbury (December 11, 1139).[2]

It would seem, of course, highly improbable that this audacious insult to the royal family would have been followed by the grant of an earldom. We might consequently infer that, in all likelihood, Geoffrey had already obtained his earldom.

We have, however, to examine the movements of Stephen at the time. The king returned, as we saw, to Reading, after spending his Christmas at Salisbury. He was then summoned to the Fen country by the revolt of the Bishop of Ely, and he set out thither, says Henry of Huntingdon, "post Natale" (p. 267). He *may* have taken Westminster on his way, but there is no evidence that he did. He had, however, returned to London by the middle of March, to take part in a Mid-Lent council.[3] His movements now become more difficult to trace than ever, but it may have been after this that he marched on Hereford and Worcester.[4] Our next glimpse of him is at Whitsuntide (May 26), when he kept the festival in sorry state at the Tower.[5] It has been suggested that it was for security

[1] (1140) "Facta est desponsatio illorum mense Februario in transmarinis partibus, matre regina Anglorum præsente" (ii. 725).

[2] "Accipiens thesauros episcopi comparavit inde Constantiam sororem Lodovici regis Francorum ad opus Eustachii filii sui" (p. 265). It is amusing to learn from his champion (the author of the *Gesta Stephani*) that the king spent this treasure on good and pious works. This matrimonial alliance is deserving of careful attention, for the fact that Stephen was prepared to buy it with treasure which he sorely needed proves its importance in his eyes as a prop to his now threatened throne.

[3] *Annals of Waverley* (*Ann. Mon.*, ii. 228), where it is stated that, at this council, Stephen gave the see of Salisbury to his chancellor, Philip. According, however, to the Continuator of Florence, he did this not at London, but at Winchester (see p. 47, *supra*).

[4] See the Continuator of Florence.   [5] *Will. Malms.*

that he sought the shelter of its walls. But this explanation is disposed of by the fact that the citizens of London were his best friends and proved, the year after, the virtual salvation of his cause. It would seem more likely that he was anxious to reassert his impaired authority and to destroy the effect of Geoffrey's outrage, which might otherwise have been ruinous to his *prestige*.[1]

It was, as I read it, at the close of Whitsuntide, that is, about the beginning of June, that the king set forth for East Anglia, and, attacking Hugh Bigod, took his castle of Bungay.[2]

In August the king again set forth to attack Hugh Bigod;[3] and either to this, or to his preceding East Anglian campaign, we may safely assign his charter, granted at Norwich, to the Abbey of Reading.[4] Now, the first witness to this charter is Geoffrey de Mandeville himself, who is not styled an earl. We learn, then, that, at least as late as June, 1140, Geoffrey had not received his earldom. This would limit the date of his creation to June—December, 1140, or virtually, at the outside, a period of six months.

Such, then, is the ultimate conclusion to which our inquiry leads us. And if it be asked why Stephen should confer an earldom on Geoffrey at this particular time, the reply is at hand in the condition of affairs, which had now become sufficiently critical for Geoffrey to begin the game he had made up his mind to play. For Stephen

---

[1] See p. 81 as to the alleged riot in London and death of Aubrey de Vere, three weeks before.

[2] "Ad Pentecostem ivit rex cum exercitu suo super Hugonem Bigod in Sudfolc" *Ann. Wav.* (*Ann. Mon.*, ii. 228).

[3] "Item in Augusto perrexit super eum et concordati sunt, sed non diu duravit" (*ibid.*).

[4] Printed in *Archæological Journal*, xx. 291. Its second witness is Richard de Luci, whom I have not elsewhere found attesting before Christmas, 1141.

could not with prudence refuse his demand for an earldom.[1]

The first corollary of this conclusion is that "the second type" of Stephen's great seal (which is that appended to this charter) must have been already in use in the year 1140, that is to say, before his fall in 1141.

Mr. Birch, who, I need hardly say, is the recognized authority on the subject, has devoted one of his learned essays on the Great Seals of the Kings of England to those of Stephen.[2] He has appended to it photographs of the two types in use under this sovereign, and has given the text of nineteen original sealed charters, which he has divided into two classes according to the types of their seals. The conclusion at which he arrived as the result of this classification was that the existence of "two distinctly variant types" is proved (all traces of a third, if it ever existed, being now lost), one of which represents the earlier, and the other the later, portion of the reign.[3] To the former belong nine, and to the latter ten of the charters which he quotes in his paper. The only point on which a question can arise is the date at which the earlier was replaced by the later type. Mr. Birch is of opinion that—

"the consideration of the second seal tends to indicate the alteration of the type subsequent to his liberation from the hands of the Empress,

---

[1] If, as would seem, Hugh Bigod appears first as an earl at the battle of Lincoln, when he fought on Stephen's side, it may well be that the "concordia" between them in August, 1140, similarly comprised the concession by the king of comital rank. On the other hand, there is a noteworthy charter (*Harl. Cart.*, 43, c. 13) of Stephen, which seems to belong to the winter of 1140-1, to which Hugh Bigod is witness, not as an earl, so that his creation may have taken place very shortly before Stephen's fall. As this charter, according to Mr. Birch, has the second type of Stephen's seal, it strengthens the view advanced in the text.

[2] *Transactions of the Royal Society of Literature*, vol. xi., New Series.

[3] Mr. Birch points out the interesting fact that while the earlier type has an affinity to that of the great seal of Henry I., the later approximates to that adopted under Henry II.

and it is most natural to suppose that this alteration is owing to the destruction or loss of his seal consequent to his own capture and incarceration" (p. 15).

There can be no doubt that this is the most natural suggestion; but if, as I contend, the very first two of the charters adduced by Mr. Birch as specimens of the later type are previous to "his capture and incarceration," it follows that his later great seal must have been adopted before that event. One of these charters is that which forms the subject of this chapter; the other is preserved among the records of the duchy of Lancaster.[1] At the date when the latter was granted, the king was in possession of the temporalities of the see of Lincoln, which he had seized on the arrest of the bishops in June, 1139. As Alexander had regained possession of his see by the time of the battle of Lincoln, this charter must have passed before Stephen's capture, and most probably passed a year or more before. We have then to account for the adoption by Stephen of a new great seal, certainly before 1141, and possibly as early as 1139. Is it not possible that this event may be connected with the arrest of the chancellor and his mighty kinsmen in June, 1139, and that the seal may have been made away with in his and their interest, as on the flight of James II., in order to increase the confusion consequent on that arrest?[2]

And now we come to Geoffrey's charter itself[3]:—

"S. Rex Ang[lorum] Archiepiscopis Episcopis Abbatibus Comitibus Justiciis Baronibus Vicecomitibus et Omnibus Ministris et fidelibus suis francis et Anglis totius Angliæ salutem. Sciatis me fecisse Comitem de

---

[1] *Royal Charters*, No. 15. See my *Ancient Charters*, p. 39.
[2] Dr. Stubbs observes that the consequence of the arrest was that "the whole administration of the country ceased to work" (*Const. Hist.*, i. 326).
[3] Cotton Charter, vii. 4. See Frontispiece.

52 THE FIRST CHARTER OF THE KING.

Gaufr[ido] de Magnauillâ de Comitatu Essex[e] hereditarie. Quare uolo et concedo et firmiter precipio quod ipse et heredes sui post eum hereditario jure teneant de me et de heredibus meis bene et in pace et libere et quiete et honorifice sicut alii Comites mei de terrâ meâ melius vel liberius vel honorificentius tenent Comitatus suos unde Comites sunt cum omnibus dignitatibus et libertatibus et consuetudinibus cum quibus alii Comites mei prefati dignius vel liberius tenent.

" T[estibus] Will[elm]o de Iprâ et Henr[ico] de Essexâ [1] et Joh[ann]e fil[io] Rob[erti] fil[ii] Walt[eri] [2] et Rob[erto] de Nouo burgo [3] et Mainfen[ino] Briton [4] et Turg[esio] de Abrinc[is] [5] et Will[elm]o de S[an]c[t]o Claro [6] et Wil-

[1] This is the well-known Henry de Essex (see Appendix U), son of Robert (Rot. Pip., 31 Hen. I.), and grandson of Swegen of Essex (Domesday). He witnessed several of Stephen's charters, probably later in the reign, but was also a witness to the Empress's charters to the Earls of Oxford and of Essex (vide post).

[2] A John, son of Robert fitz Walter (sheriff of East Anglia, temp. Hen. I.), occurs in Ramsey Cartulary, i. 149.

[3] Robert de Neufbourg, said to have been a younger son of Henry, Earl of Warwick, occurs in connection with Warwickshire in 1130 (Rot. Pip., 31 Hen. I.). Mr. Yeatman characteristically advances " the idea that Robert de Arundel and Robert de Novoburgo were identical." He was afterwards Justiciary of Normandy (Ord. Vit.), having sided with Geoffrey of Anjou (Rot. Scacc. Norm.). He is mentioned in the Pipe-Rolls of 2 and 4 Henry II. According to Dugdale, he died (on the authority of the Chronicon Normanniæ), in August, 1158, a date followed by Mr. Yeatman. Mr. Eyton, however (Court and Itinerary, p. 47), on the same authority (with a reference also to Gervase, which I cannot verify) makes him die in August, 1159. The true date seems to have been August 30, 1159, when he died at Bec (Robert de Torigni).

[4] The Maenfininus Brito (Mr. Birch reads "Mamseu"), who, in the Pipe-Roll of 1130 (p. 100), was late sheriff of Bucks. and Beds. Probably father of Hamo filius Meinfelini, the Bucks. baron of 1166 (Cartæ). See also p. 201, n. 2.

[5] Turgis d'Avranches appears in the Pipe-Roll of 31 Hen. I. as having married the widow of Hugh " de Albertivillâ." We shall find him witnessing Stephen's second charter to the earl (Christmas, 1141).

[6] William de St. Clare occurs in Dorset and Huntingdonshire in 1130 (Rot. Pip., 31 Hen. I.). He was, I presume, of the same family as Hamon de St. Clare, custos of Colchester in 1130 (ibid.), who was among the witnesses to Stephen's Charter of Liberties (Oxford) in 1136.

GEOFFREY CREATED EARL OF ESSEX. 53

l[elm]o de Dammart[in]¹ et Ric[ardo] fil[io] Ursi² et Will[elm]o de Auco³ et Ric[ardo] fil[io] Osb[erti]⁴ et Radulfo de Wiret⁵ (*sic*) et Eglin[o]⁶ et Will[elm]o fil[io] Alur[edi]⁷ et Will[elmo] filio Ernald[i].⁸ Apud Westmonasterium."

Taking this, as I believe it to be, as our earliest charter of creation extant or even known, the chief point to attract our notice is its intensely hereditary character. Geoffrey receives the earldom "hereditarie," for himself "et heredes sui post eum hereditario jure." The terms in which the grant is made are of tantalizing vagueness; and, compared with the charters by which it was followed, this is remarkable for its brevity, and for the total omission of those accompanying concessions which the statements of our historians would lead us to expect without fail.⁹

---

¹ Odo de Dammartin states in his *Carta* (1166) that he held one fee (in Norfolk) of the king, of which he had enf.offed, *temp.* Hen. I., his brother, William de Dammartin.

² Richard fitz Urse is of special interest as the father (see *Liber Niger*) of Reginald fitz Urse, one of Becket's murderers. He occurs repeatedly in the Pipe-Roll of 31 Hen. I. After this charter he reappears at the battle of Lincoln (Feb. 2, 1141):—"Capitur etiam Ricardus filius Ursi, qui in ictibus dandis recipiendisque clarus et gloriosus comparuit" (*Hen. Hunt.*, p. 274). For his marriage to Sybil, daughter of Baldwin de Bollers by Sybil de Falaise (*neptis* of Henry I.), see Eyton's *Shropshire*, xi. 127, and *Genealogist*, N.S., iii. 195. One would welcome information on his connection, if any, with the terrible sheriff, Urse d'Abetot, and his impetuous son; but I know of none.

³ William de Eu appears as a tenant of four knights' fees *de veteri feoffamento* under Mandeville in the *Liber Niger*.

⁴ Richard fitz Osbert similarly figures (*Liber Niger*) as a tenant of four knights' fees *de veteri feoffamento*. He also held a knight's fee of the Bishop of Ely in Cambridgeshire. An Osbert fitz Richard, probably his son, attests a charter of Geoffrey's son, Earl William, to Walden Abbey.

⁵ A Ralph de *Worcester* occurs in the *Carta* and elsewhere under Henry II.

⁶ "Eglino," an unusual name, probably represents "Egelino de Furnes," who attests a charter of Stephen at Eye (*Formularium Anglicanum*, p. 154).

⁷ William fitz Alfred held one fee of Mandeville *de novo feoffamento*. He also attests the earl's foundation charter of Walden Abbey (*Mon. Ang.*, iv. 149). A William fitz Alfred occurs, also, in the Pipe-Roll of 31 Hen. I.

⁸ William fitz Ernald similarly held one knight's fee *de novo feoffamento*. He also attests the above foundation charter just after William fitz Alfred.

⁹ See Appendix D, on "Fiscal Earls."

We must now pass from the grant of this charter to the great day of Lincoln (February 2, 1141), where the fortunes of England and her king were changed "in the twinkling of an eye" by the wild charge of "the Disinherited," as they rode for death or victory.[1]

[1] "Acies exhæredatorum, quæ præibat, percussit aciem regalem . . . tanto impetu, quod statim, quasi in ictu oculi, dissipata est.

CHAPTER III.

TRIUMPH OF THE EMPRESS.

AT the time of this sudden and decisive triumph, the Empress had been in England some sixteen months. With the Earl of Gloucester, she had landed at Arundel,[1] on September 30, 1139,[2] and while her brother, escorted by a few knights, made his way to his stronghold at Bristol, had herself, attended by her Angevin suite, sought shelter with her step-mother, the late queen, in the famous castle of Arundel. Stephen had promptly appeared before its walls, but, either deeming the fortress impregnable or being misled by treacherous counsel,[3] had not only raised his blockade of the castle, but had allowed the Empress to set out for Bristol, and had given her for escort his brother the legate, and his trusted supporter the Count of Meulan.[4] From the legate her brother had received her at a spot appointed beforehand, and had then returned with her to Bristol. Here she was promptly visited by the constable, Miles of Gloucester, who at once acknowledged her claims as "the rightful heir" of England.[5] Escorted by him, she removed to Gloucester, of which he was hereditary cas-

[1] *Will. Malms.*, p. 724; *Gesta Stephani*, p. 56.
[2] *Will. Malms.*, p. 724. See Appendix E.
[3] Such are the alternatives presented by Henry of Huntingdon (p. 266). The treacherous counsel alluded to was that of his brother the legate (*Gesta Stephani*, p. 57). According to John of Hexham (*Sym. Dun.* ii. 302), Stephen acted "ex indiscretâ animi simplictate."
[4] *Will. Malms.*, p. 725.
[5] See Appendix F: "The Defection of Miles of Gloucester."

tellan, and received the submission of that city, and of all the country round about.[1] The statements of the chroniclers can here be checked, and are happily confirmed and amplified by a charter of the Empress, apparently unknown, but of great historical interest. The following abstract is given in a transcript taken from the lost volume of the Great Coucher of the duchy [2]:—

"Carta Matilde Imperatricis in quâ dicit, quod [3] quando in Angliam venit post mortem H. patris sui [4] Milo de Gloecestrâ quam citius potuit venit ad se [5] apud Bristolliam et recepit me ut dominam et sicut illam quam justum hæredem regni Angliæ recognovit, et inde me secum ad Gloecestram adduxit et ibi homagium suum mihi fecit ligie contra omnes homines. Et volo vos scire quod tunc quando homagium suum apud Gloecestram recepit, dedi ei pro servicio suo in feodo et hereditate sibi et heredibus suis castellum de Sancto Briavel(li) et totam forestam de Dene," [6] etc., etc.

It was at Gloucester that she received the news of her brother's victory at Lincoln (February 2, 1141), and it was there that he joined her, with his royal captive, on Quinquagesima Sunday (February 9).[7] It was at once decided that the king should be despatched to Bristol Castle,[8] and that he should be there kept a prisoner for life.[9]

In the utter paralysis of government consequent on the king's capture, there was not a day to be lost on the part of the Empress and her friends. The Empress herself was

[1] *Will. Malms.*, p. 725; *Cont. Flor.*, p. 118. Here the Continuator's chronology is irreconcilable with that of our other authorities. He states that the Empress removed to Gloucester on October 15, after a stay of two months at Bristol. This is, of course, consistent, it should be noticed, with the date (August 1) assigned by him for her landing.

[2] The text is taken from the transcript in Lansdowne MS. 229, fol. 123, collated with Dugdale's transcript in his MSS. at the Bodleian Library (L. 21). It will be seen that Dugdale transcribed *verbatim*, while the other transcript begins in *narratio obliqua*.

[3] "Sciatis quod" (D.). [4] "Mei" (D.). [5] "Me" (D.).

[6] These were specially excepted from the grants of royal demesne made by Henry II. to his son, the second earl.

[7] *Cont. Flor.*, p. 129; *Will. Malms.*, p. 742; *Gesta*, p. 72.

[8] *Ibid.*; *John Hex.*, p. 308; *Hen. Hunt.*, p. 275. [9] *Gesta*, p. 72.

PROGRESS OF THE EMPRESS.

intoxicated with joy, and eager for the fruits of victory.[1] Within a fortnight of the battle, she set out from Gloucester, on what may be termed her first progress.[2] Her destination was, of course, Winchester, the spot to which her eyes would at once be turned. She halted, however, for a while at Cirencester,[3] to allow time for completing the negotiations with the legate.[4] It was finally agreed that, advancing to Winchester, she should meet him in an open space, without the walls, for a conference. This spot a charter of the Empress enables us apparently to identify with Wherwell.[5] Hither, on Sunday, the 2nd of March, a wet and gloomy day,[6] the clergy and people, headed by the legate, with the monks and nuns of the religious houses, and such magnates of the realm as were present, streamed forth from the city to meet her.[7]

The compact ("pactum") which followed was strictly on the lines of that by means of which Stephen had secured the throne. The Empress, on her part, swore that if the legate would accept her as "domina," he should henceforth have his way in all ecclesiastical matters. And her leading followers swore that this oath should be kept. Thereupon the legate agreed to receive her as " Lady of

---

[1] "Ob illiusmodi eventum vehementer exhilirata, utpote regnum sibi juratum, sicut sibi videbatur, jam adepta" (*Cont. Flor.*, p. 130).

[2] *Cont. Flor.*, 130.

[3] "Simul et ejusdem civitatis sumens dominium" (*ibid.*).

[4] "Ut ipsam tanquam regis Henrici filiam et cui omnis Angliæ et Normannia jurata esset, incunctanter in ecclesiam et regnum reciperet" (*Will. Malms.*, p. 743). Compare the writer's description of the oath (1127) that the magnates "imperatricem *incunctanter* et sine ullâ retractione dominam susciperent" (p. 690).

[5] *Journ. B. A. A.*, xxxi. 389. Mr. Howlett asserts that the evidence of William of Malmesbury as to the date (2nd and 3rd of March) "is refuted" by this charter, which places them a fortnight earlier (Introduction to *Gesta Stephani*, p. xxii.). But I do not think the evidence of the charter is sufficiently strong to overthrow the accepted date.

[6] "Pluvioso et nebuloso die" (*Will. Malms.*, p. 743).

[7] *Cont. Flor.*, p. 130 ; *Will. Malms.*, p. 743.

England," and promised her the allegiance of himself and of his followers so long as she should keep her oath. The whole agreement is most important, and, as such, should be carefully studied.[1]

On the morrow (March 3) the Empress entered Winchester, and was received in state in the cathedral, the legate supporting her on the right, and Bernard of St. David's on the left.[2]

Now, it is most important to have a clear understanding of what really took place upon this occasion.

The main points to keep before us are—(1) that there are two distinct episodes, that of the 2nd and 3rd of March, and that of the 7th and 8th of April, five weeks intervening between them, during which the Empress left Winchester to make her second progress; (2) that the first episode was that of her *reception* at Winchester, the second (also at Winchester) that of her *election*.

It is, perhaps, not surprising that our historians are here in woeful confusion. Dr. Stubbs alone is, as usual, right. Writing from the standpoint of a constitutional historian, he is only concerned with the election of the

[1] "Juravit et affidavit imperatrix episcopo, quod omnia majora negotia in Anglia, præcipueque donationes episcopatuum et abbatiarum, ejus nutum spectarent, si eam ipse in sancta ecclesia in dominam reciperet, et perpetuam ei fidelitatem teneret. Idem juraverunt cum ea, et affidaverunt pro ea, Robertus frater ejus comes de Gloecestrâ, et Brianus filius comitis marchio de Walingeford et Milo de Gloecestrâ, postea comes de Hereford, et nonnulli alii. Nec dubitavit episcopus imperatricem in dominam Angliæ recipere et ei cum quibusdam suis affidare, quod, quamdiu ipsa pactum non infringeret, ipse quoque fidem ei custodiret" (*Will. Malms.*, 743, 744). The parallel afforded by the customs of Bigorre, as recorded (it is alleged) in 1097, is so striking as to deserve being quoted here. Speaking of the reception of a new lord, they provide that "antequam habitatorum terræ fidejussores accipiat, fide sua securos eos faciat ne extra consuetudines patrias vel eas in quibus eos invenerit aliquod educat; hoc autem sacramento et fide quatuor nobilium terræ faciat confirmari."

[2] "Crastino, quod fuit quinto nonas Martii, honorifica facta processione recepta est in ecclesia episcopatus Wintoniæ," etc., etc. (*ibid.*).

Empress, and to this he assigns its correct date.¹ In his useful and excellent *English History*, Mr. Bright, on the contrary, ignores the interval, and places the second episode " a few days after " the first.² Professor Pearson, whose work is that which is generally used for this period, omits altogether the earlier episode.³ Mr. Birch, on the other hand, in his historical introduction to his valuable *fasciculus* of the charters of the Empress, ignores altogether the later episode, though he goes into this question with special care. Indeed, he does more than this; for he transfers the election itself from the later to the earlier occasion, and assigns to the episode of March 2 and 3 the events of April 7 and 8. This cardinal error vitiates his elaborate argument,⁴ and, indeed, makes confusion worse confounded. Mr. Freeman, though, of course, in a less degree, seems inclined to err in the same direction, when he assigns to the earlier of the two episodes that importance which belongs to the later.⁵

Rightly to apprehend the bearing of this episode, we must glance back at the preceding reigns. Dr. Stubbs, writing of Stephen's accession, observes that "the example which Henry had set in his seizure and retention of the crown was followed in every point by his successor."⁶ But on at least one main point the precedent was older than this. The Conqueror, in 1066, and his heir, in 1087, had both deemed it their first necessity to obtain posses-

---

¹ *Const. Hist.*, i. 326 (*note*); *Early Plantagenets*, 22.
² *English History for the Use of Public Schools*, i. 83. The mistake may have arisen from a confusion with the departure of the Empress from Winchester a few days (" paucis post diebus ") after her reception.
³ *History of England during the Early and Middle Ages*, i. 478.
⁴ *Journ. Brit. Arch. Ass.*, xxxi. 377–380.
⁵ *Norm. Conq.*, v. 303. At the same time it is right to add that this is not a question of accuracy, but merely of treatment. In the marginal notes the two episodes are respectively assigned to their correct dates.
⁶ *Const. Hist.*, i. 318.

sion of Winchester. Winchester first, and then London, was a rule that thus enjoyed the sanction of four successive precedents. To secure Winchester with all that it contained, and with all the *prestige* that its possession would confer, was now, therefore, the object of the Empress. This object she attained by the *pactum* of the 2nd of March, and with it, as we have seen, the conditional allegiance of the princely bishop of the see.

Now, Henry of Blois was a great man. As papal legate, as Bishop of Winchester, and as brother to the captive king, he possessed an influence, in his triple capacity, which, at this eventful crisis, was probably unrivalled in the land. But there was one thing that he could not do—he could not presume, of his own authority, to depose or to nominate an English sovereign. Indeed the very fact of the subsequent election (April 8) and of his claim, audacious as it was, that that election should be the work of the clergy, proves that he had no thought of the even more audacious presumption to nominate the sovereign himself. This, then, is fatal to Mr. Birch's contention that the Empress was, on this occasion (March 3), elected "domina Angliæ." Indeed, as I have said, it is based on a confusion of the two episodes. The legate, as Mr. Birch truly says, " consented to recognize (*sic*) the Empress as *Domina Angliæ*, or Lady, that is, Supreme Governor of England," but, obviously, he could only do so on behalf of himself and of his followers. We ought, therefore, to compare his action with that of Miles of Gloucester in 1139, when, as we have seen, in the words of the Empress—

"*Recepit* me ut dominam et sicut illam quam justum hæredem regni Angliæ *recognovit* . . . et ibi homagium suum mihi fecit ligie contra omnes homines."[1]

[1] Compare also, even further back, the action, in Normandy, of Gingan Algasil in December, 1135, who, on the appearance of the Empress, "[eam]

RECEPTION OF THE EMPRESS. 61

Notice here the identity of expression—the "reception" of the Empress and the "recognition" of her claims. I have termed the earlier episode the "reception," and the later the "election" of the Empress. In these terms is precisely expressed the distinction between the two events. Take for instances the very passages appealed to by Mr. Birch himself :—

"The exact words employed by William of Malmesbury are 'Nec dubitavit Episcopus Imperatricem in Dominam Angliæ recipere' (*sic*). In another place the same Henry de Blois declares of her, 'In Angliæ Normanniæque Dominam eligimus' (*sic*). This regular election of Mathildis to the dignity and office of *Domina Angliæ* took place on Sunday, March 2, A.D. 1141" (p. 378).

Now we know, from William of Malmesbury himself, that "the regular election in question" took place on the 8th of April, and that the second of the passages quoted above refers to this later episode,[1] while the other refers to the earlier.[2] I have drawn attention to the two words (*recipere* and *eligimus*) which he respectively applies to the "reception" and the "election." The description of this "reception" by William of Malmesbury[3] completely tallies with that which is given by the Empress herself in a charter.[4] It should further be compared with the account by the author of the *Gesta Stephani*, of the similar reception accorded to Stephen in 1135.[5]

But though the legate could open to the Empress the cathedral and the cathedral city, he had no power over

ut naturalem dominam suscepit, eique . . . oppida quibus ut vicecomes, jubente rege præerat, subegit" (*Ord. Vit.*, v. 56).

[1] *Will. Malms.*, p. 747.   [2] *Ibid.*, p. 748.

[3] "Honorifica facta processione *recepta est* in ecclesia" (p. 744).

[4] "Idem prelatus et cives Wintonie honorifice in ecclesia et urbe Wintonie me *receperunt*" (*Journ. Brit. Arch. Ass.*, xxxi. 378)

[5] "Præsul Wintonie . . . cum dignioribus Wintonie civibus obvius ei advenit, habitoque in communi brevi colloquio, in civitatem, secundam duntaxat regni sedem, honorifice induxit" (p. 5). Note that in each case the "colloquium" preceded the entry.

the royal castle. This we saw in the case of Stephen, when his efforts to secure the constable's adherence were fruitless till the king himself arrived. Probably the constable, at this crisis, was the same William de Pont de l'Arche, but, whoever he was, he surrendered to the Empress the castle and all that it contained. In one respect, indeed, she was doomed to be bitterly disappointed, for the royal treasury, which her adventurous rival had found filled to overflowing, was by this time all but empty. One treasure, however, she secured; the object of her desires, the royal crown, was placed in her triumphant hands.[1]

To the one historian who has dealt with this incident it has proved a stumbling-block indeed. Mr. Freeman thus boldly attacks the problem :—

"William of Malmesbury (*Hist. Nov.*, iii. 42) seems distinctly to exclude a coronation; he merely says, 'Honorifica factâ processione, recepta est in ecclesia episcopatus Wintoniæ.' We must, therefore, see only rhetoric when the Continuator says, ' Datur ejus dominio corona Angliæ,' and when the author of the *Gesta* (75) speaks of 'regisque castello, et regni coronâ, quam semper ardentissime affectârat, . . . in deliberationem suam contraditis,' and adds that Henry 'dominam et *reginam* acclamare præcepit.' The Waverley Annalist, 1141, ventures to say, 'Corona regni est ei tradita.'"[2]

"Only rhetoric." Ah, how easily could history be written, if one could thus dispose of inconvenient evidence! So far from being "rhetoric," it is precisely because these statements are so strictly matter-of-fact that the writer failed to grasp their meaning. Had he known, or remembered, that the royal crown was preserved in the royal treasury, the passage by which he is so sorely puzzled would have proved simplicity itself.[3]

[1] "Regisque castello, et regni coronâ, quam semper ardentissimé affectârat thesaurisque quos licet perpaucos rex ibi reliquerat, in deliberationem suam contraditis" (*Gesta*, 75).
[2] *Norm. Conquest*, v. 304 (*note*).
[3] As an instance of the crown being kept at Winchester, take the entry in

THE TREASURY SECURED.

Here again, light is thrown on these events and on the action of the Empress by the precedent in the case of her father (1100), who, on the death of his brother, hastened to Winchester Castle ("ubi regalis thesaurus continebatur"), which was formally handed over to him with all that it contained ("arx cum regalibus gazis filio regis Henrico reddita est ").[1]

We have yet to consider the passage from the *Gesta*, to which Mr. Birch so confidently appeals, and which is dismissed by Mr. Freeman as "rhetoric." The passage runs:—

"In publica se civitatis et fori audientia dominam et reginam acclamare præcepit."[2]

By a strange coincidence it has been misconstrued by both writers independently. Mr. Freeman, as we saw, takes "præcepit" as referring to Henry himself, and so does Mr. Birch.[3] Though the sentence as a whole may be obscure, yet the passage quoted is quite clear. The words are "præcepit *se*," not "præcepit illam." Thus the proclamation, if made, was the doing of the Empress and not of the legate. Had the legate been indeed responsible, his conduct would have been utterly inconsistent. But as it is, the difficulty vanishes.[4]

To the double style, "domina et regina," I have made

the Pipe-Roll of 4 Hen. II.: "In conducendis coronis Regis ad Wirecestre de Wintoniâ," the crowns being taken out to be worn at Worcester, Easter, 1158. Oddly enough, Mr. Freeman himself alludes, in its place, to a similar taking out of the crown, from the treasury at Winchester, to be worn at York, Christmas, 1069. The words of Ordericus, as quoted by him, are: "Guillelmus ex civitate Guentâ jubet adferri coronam, aliaque ornamenta regalia et vasa" (cf. *Dialogus*, I. 14).

[1] *Ordericus Vitalis*. [2] *Gesta*, 75; *Journ. Brit. Arch. Ass.*, xxxi. 378.

[3] "He (*sic*) ordered that she should be proclaimed lady and queen."

[4] The *Gesta* itself is, on this point, conclusive, for it distinctly states that the Empress "solito severius, solito et arrogantius procedere et loqui, et cuncta cœpit peragere, adeo ut in ipso mox domini sui capite reginam se totius Angliæ fecerit, *et gloriata fuerit appellari*."

reference above. My object now is to examine this assumption of the style "regina" by the Empress. It might perhaps be urged that the author of the *Gesta* cannot here be implicitly relied on. His narrative, however, is vigorous and consistent; it is in perfect harmony with the character of the Empress; and so far as the assumption of this style is concerned, it is strikingly confirmed by that Oxford charter, to which we are now coming. After her election (April 8), the Empress might claim, as queen elect, the royal title, but if that were excusable, which is granting much, its assumption before her election could admit of no defence. Yet, headstrong and impetuous, and thirsting for the throne, she would doubtless urge that her rival's fall rendered her at once *de facto* queen. But this was as yet by no means certain. Stephen's brother, as we know, was talked of, and the great nobles held aloof. The Continuator, indeed, asserts that at Winchester (March) were "præsules pene totius Angliæ, barones multi, principes plurimi" (p. 130), but William, whose authority is here supreme, does not, though writing as a partisan of the Empress, make any allusion to their presence.[1] Moreover, the primate was still in doubt, and of the five bishops who were present with the legate, three (St. David's, Hereford, and Bath) came from districts under the influence of the Empress, while the other two (Lincoln and Ely) were still smarting beneath Stephen's action of two years before (1139).

The special interest, therefore, of this bold proclamation at Winchester lies in the touch it gives us of that feminine impatience of the Empress, which led her to grasp so eagerly the crown of England in her hands, and now to anticipate, in this hasty manner, her election and formal coronation.[2]

[1] *Will. Malms.*, 744.
[2] To this visit (if the only occasion on which she was at Winchester in

Within a few days of her reception at Winchester, she retraced her steps as far as Wilton, where it was arranged that she should meet the primate, with whom were certain bishops and some lay folk.[1] Theobald, however, professed himself unable to render her homage until he had received from the king his gracious permission to do so.[2] For this purpose he went on to Bristol, while the Empress made her way to Oxford, and there spent Easter (March 30th).[3] We must probably assign to this occasion her admission to Oxford by Robert d'Oilli.[4] The Continuator, indeed, assigns it to May, and in this he is followed by modern historians. Mr. Freeman, for instance, on his authority, places the incident at that stage,[5] and so does Mr. Franck Bright.[6]

But the movements of the Empress, at this stage, are

the spring) must belong the Empress's charter to Thurstan de Montfort. As it is not comprised in Mr. Birch's collection, I subjoin it *in extenso* (from Dugdale's MSS.):—

"M. Imperatrix H. Regis filia Rogero Comiti de Warwick et omnibus fidelibus suis Francis et Anglis de Warewicscire salutem. Sciatis me concessisse Thurstino de Monteforti quod habeat mercatum die dominica ad castellum suum de Bellodeserto. Volo igitur et firmiter præcipio quatenus omnes euntes, et stantes, et redeuntes de Mercato prædicto habeant firmam pacem. T. Milone de Glocestria. Apud Wintoniam."

As Milo attests not as an earl, this charter cannot belong to the subsequent visit to Winchester in the summer. The author of the *Gesta* mentions the Earl of Warwick among those who joined the Empress at once "sponte nulloque cogente."

[1] *Cont. Flor. Wig.*, p. 130.
[2] This he did on the ground that the recognition of Stephen as king by the pope, in 1136, was binding on all ecclesiastics (*Historia Pontificalis*). Vide infra, p. 69, n. 1.
[3] *Will. Malms.*, p. 744. Oddly enough, Miss Norgate gives this very reference for her statement that in a few days the Archbishop of Canterbury followed the legate's example, and swore fealty to the Empress at Wilton.
[4] "Convenitur ibi ab eadem de principibus unus, vocabulo Robertus de Oileio, de reddendo Oxenfordensi castello; quo consentiente, venit illa, totiusque civitatis et circumjacentis egionis suscepit dominium atque hominium" (*Cont. Flor. Wig.*, p. 131).
[5] "She then made her way to London by a roundabout path. She was received at Oxford by the younger Robert of Oily," etc. (*Norm. Conq.*, v. 306).
[6] *English History*, I. 83.

really difficult to determine. Between her presence at Oxford (March 30)[1] and her presence at Reading (May 5-7),[2] we know nothing for certain. One would imagine that she must have attended her own election at Winchester (April 7, 8), but the chroniclers are silent on the subject, though they, surely, would have mentioned her presence. On the whole, it seems most probable that the Continuator must be in error, when he places the adhesion of Robert d'Oilli so late as May (at Reading) and takes the Empress subsequently to Oxford, as if for the first time.

It was, doubtless, through her "brother" Robert "fitz Edith" that his step-father, Robert d'Oilli, was thus won over to her cause. It should be noted that his defection from the captive king is pointedly mentioned by the author of the *Gesta*, even before that of the Bishop of Winchester, thus further confirming the chronology advanced above.[3] At Oxford she received the submission of all the adjacent country,[4] and also executed an important charter. This charter Mr. Birch has printed, having apparently collated for the purpose no less than five copies.[5] Its special interest is derived from the fact that not only is it the earliest charter she is known to have issued after Stephen's fall (with the probable exception of that to Thurstan de Montfort), but it is also the only one of her charters in which we find the royal phrases "ecclesiarum *regni mei*" and "pertinentibus *coronæ meæ*." Mr.

---

[1] *Will. Malms.* [2] *Cont. Flor. Wig.*
[3] "Aliis quoque sponte, nulloque cogente, ad comitissæ imperium conversis (ut Robertus de Oli, civitatis Oxenefordiæ sub rege præceptor, et comes ille de Warwic, viri molles, et deliciis magis quam animi fortitudine affluentes)" (p. 74).
[4] *Cont. Flor. Wig. (ut supra).*
[5] *Journ. B. A. A.*, xxxi. 388, 389. It will also be found in the *Monasticon* (iii. 87).

Birch writes of its testing clause ("Apud Oxeneford Anno ab Incarnatione Domini mc. quatragesimo "):

> The date of this charter is very interesting, because it is the only example of an actual date calculated by expression of the years of the Incarnation, which occurs among the entire series which I have been able to collect. . . . Now, as the historical year in these times commenced on the 25th of March, there is no doubt but that this charter was granted to the Abbey of Hulme at some time between the 3rd and the 25th of March, A.D. 1140–41.[1]

Mr. Eyton has also independently discussed it (though his remarks are still in MS.), and detects, with his usual minute care, a difficulty, in one of the three witnesses, to which Mr. Birch does not allude.

> "St. Benet of Hulme.
> "The date given (1140) seems to combine with another circumstance to lead to error. Matilda's style is 'Matild' Imp. H. regis filia,' not, as usual, 'Anglorum domina.' One might therefore conclude that the deed passed before the battle of Lincoln, and so in 1140. However, this conclusion would be wrong, for though Mat* does not style herself Queen, she asserts in the deed Royal rights and speaks of matters pertaining 'coronæ meæ.' But we do not know that Maud was ever in Oxford before Stephen's captivity, nor can we think it. Again, it is certain that Rob* de Sigillo did not become Bishop of London till after Easter, 1141, for at Easter, 1142, he expressly dates his own deed 'anno primo pontif' mei.' He was almost certainly appointed when Maud was in London in July, 1141, for he attests Milo's patent of earldom on July 25."[2]

The omission of the style "Anglorum domina" is, however, strictly correct, and not, as Mr. Eyton thought, singular. For it was not till her election on the 8th of April that she became entitled to use this style. As for her assumption of the royal phrases, it is here simply *ultra vires*. Then, as to the attesting bishop ("R. episcopo Londoniensi"), his presence is natural, as he was a monk of Reading, and his position would seem to be paralleled

---

[1] *Journ. B. A. A.*, xxxi. p. 379. [2] *Addl. MSS.*, 31,943, fol. 118.

by that of his predecessor Maurice, who appears as bishop in the Survey, though, probably, only elect. As her father "gave the bishopric of Winchester" the moment he was elected, and before he was crowned,[1] so the Empress "gave," it would seem, the see of London to Robert "of the Seal," even before her formal election—an act, it should be noted, thoroughly in keeping with her impetuous assumption of the regal style. Besides the bishop and the Earl of Gloucester, there is a third witness to this charter —"Reginaldo filio Regis." No one, it seems, has noticed the fact that here alone, among the charters of the Empress, Reginald attests not as an earl, which confirms the early date claimed for this charter. A charter which I assign to the following May is attested by him: "Reginaldo *comite* filio regis." This would seem to place his creation between the dates of these charters, *i.e. circ.* April (1141).[2] To sum up, the evidence of this charter is in complete agreement with that of William of Malmesbury, when he states that the Empress spent Easter (March 30) at Oxford; and we further learn from it that she must have arrived there at least as early as the 24th of March.

The fact that Mr. Freeman, in common with others, has overlooked this early visit of the Empress in March, is no doubt the cause of his having been misled, as I have shown, by the Continuator's statement.

[1] *Ang. Sax. Chron.*, A.D. 1100.
[2] Relying on the explicit statement of the chronicler (*Will. Malms.*, p. 732), that the Earl of Gloucester "fratrem etiam suum Reinaldum in tanta difficultate temporis comitem Cornubiæ creavit," historians and antiquaries have assigned this creation to 1140 (see Stubbs' *Const. Hist.*, i. 362, *n.*; Courthope's *Historic Peerage*; Doyle's *Official Baronage*). In the version of Reginald's success given by the author of the *Gesta*, there is no mention of this creation, but that may, of course, be rejected as merely negative evidence. The above charter, however, certainly raises the question whether he had indeed been created earl at the time when he thus attested it. The point may be deemed of some importance as involving the question whether the Empress did really create an earl before the triumph of her cause.

ELECTION OF THE EMPRESS.

The Assembly at Winchester took place, as has been said, on the 7th and 8th of April. William of Malmesbury was present on the occasion, and states that it was attended by the primate "and all the bishops of England."[1] This latter phrase may, however, be questioned, in the light of subsequent charter evidence.

The proceedings of this council have been well described, and are so familiar that I need not repeat them. On the 7th was the private conclave; on the 8th, the public assembly. I am tempted just to mention the curiously modern incident of the legate (who presided) commencing the proceedings by reading out the letters of apology from those who had been summoned but were unable to be present.[2] On the 8th the legate announced to the Assembly the result of the previous day's conclave :—

"filiam pacifici regis . . . in Angliæ Normanniæque dominam eligimus, et ei fidem et manutenementum promittimus."[3]

On the 9th, the deputation summoned from London arrived and was informed of the decision; on the 10th the assembly was dissolved.

---

[1] "Concilium archiepiscopi Cantuariæ Thedbaldi, et omnium episcoporum Angliæ" (p. 744). Strange to say, Professor Pearson (I. 478) states that "Theobald remained faithful" to Stephen, though he had now formally joined the Empress. On the other hand, "Stephen's queen and William of Ypres" are represented by him as present, though they were far away, preparing for resistance. An important allusion to the primate's conduct at this time is found (under 1148) in the *Historia Pontificalis* (Pertz's *Monumenta Historica*, vol. xx.), where we read "propter obedienciam sedis apostolicæ proscriptus fuerat, quando urgente mandato domni Henrici Wintoniensis episcopi tunc legationem fungentis in Anglia post alios episcopos omnes receperat Imperatricem . . . licet inimicissimos habuerit regem et consiliarios suos."

[2] "Si qui defuerunt, legatis et literis causas cur non venissent dederunt. . . . Egregie quippe memini, ipsâ die, post recitata scripta excusatoria quibus absentiam suam quidem tutati sunt," etc. (*Will. Malms.*, pp. 744, 745). Is it possible that we have, in "legati," a hint at attendance by proxy?

[3] *Ibid.*, p. 746.

The point I shall here select for discussion is the meaning of the term "domina Angliæ," and the effect of this election on the position of the Empress.

First, as to the term "domina Angliæ." Its territorial character must not be overlooked. In the charters of the Empress, her style "Ang' domina" becomes occasionally, though very rarely, "Anglor' domina," proving that its right extension is "Anglorum Domina," which differs, as we have seen, from the chroniclers' phrase. The importance of the distinction is this. "Rex" is royal and national; "dominus" is feudal and territorial. We should expect, then, the first to be followed by the nation ("Anglorum"), the second by the territory ("Angliæ"). But, in addition to its normal feudal character, the term may here bear a special meaning.

It would seem that the clue to its meaning in this special sense was first discovered by the late Sir William (then Mr.) Hardy ("an ingenious and diligent young man," as he was at the time described) in 1836. He pointed out that "Dominus Anglie" was the style adopted by Richard I. "between the demise of his predecessor and his own coronation."[1] Mr. Albert Way, in a valuable paper on the charters belonging to Reading Abbey, which appeared some twenty-seven years later,[2] called attention to the styles "Anglorum *Regina*" and "Anglorum *Domina*," as used by the Empress.[3] As to the former, he referred to the charter of the Empress at Reading, granting lands to Reading Abbey.[4] As to the latter ("Domina Anglorum"), he quoted Mr. Hardy's paper on the charter

---

[1] *Archæologia*, xxvii. 110. See the charter in question in the Pipe-Roll Society's "Ancient Charters," Part I., p. 92.

[2] *Arch. Journ.* (1863), xx. 281–296.

[3] *Ibid.*, p. 283. Mr. Way adopts the extension "Anglo*rum*" throughout.

[4] "The only instances in which we have documentary evidence that she styled herself Queen of England occur in two charters of this period" (*ibid.*).

of Richard I., and urged that "the fact that Matilda was never crowned Queen of England may suffice to account for her being thus styled" (p. 283). He further quoted from William of Malmesbury the two passages in which that chronicler applies this style to the Empress,[1] and he carefully avoided assigning them both to the episode of the 2nd of March. Lastly, he quoted the third passage, that in the *Gesta Stephani*.

Mr. Birch subsequently read a paper "On the Great Seals of King Stephen" before the Royal Society of Literature (December 17, 1873), in which he referred to Mr. Way's paper, as the source of one of the charters of which he gave the text, and in which he embodied Mr. Way's observations on the styles "Regina" and "Domina."[2] But instead, unfortunately, of merely following in Mr. Way's footsteps, he added the startling error that Stephen was a prisoner, and Matilda consequently in power, till 1143. He wrote thus:—

"Did the king ever cease to exercise his regal functions? Were these functions performed by any other constitutional sovereign meanwhile? The events of the year 1141 need not to be very lengthily discussed to demonstrate that for a brief period there was a break in Stephen's sovereignty, and a corresponding assumption of royal power by another ruler unhindered and unimpeached by the lack of any formality necessary for its full enjoyment. . . . William of Malmesbury, writing with all the opportunity of an eye-witness, and moving in the royal court at the very period, relates at full length in his *Historia Novella* (ed. Hardy, for Historical Society, vol. ii. p. 774[3]), the particulars of the conference held at Winchester subsequent to the capture of Stephen after the battle of Lincoln, in the early part of the year, 4 Non. Feb. A.D. 1141. . . This election of Matilda as Domina of England in place of Stephen took place on Sunday, March 2, 1141. . . . Until the liberation of the king from his incarceration at Bristol, as a sequel to the battle at Winchester in A.D. 1143, so disastrous to the hopes of the Empress, she held her

---

[1] *Vide supra*, pp. 61, 69.   [2] Pp. xi.-xiv. (see foot-notes).
[3] The volume closes at p. 769.

TRIUMPH OF THE EMPRESS.

position as queen at London. The narrative of the events of this period, as given by William of Malmesbury in the work already quoted, so clearly points to her enjoyment of all temporal power needed to constitute a sovereign, that we must admit her name among the regnant queens of England" (pp. 12-14).

Two years later (June 9, 1875), Mr. Birch read a paper before the British Archæological Association,[1] in which, in the same words, he advanced the same thesis.

The following year (June 28, 1876), in an instructive paper read before the Royal Society of Literature,[2] Mr. Birch wrote thus :—

"As an example of new lights which the study of early English seals has thus cast upon our history (elucidations, as it were, of facts which have escaped the keen research of every one of our illustrious band of historians and chroniclers for upwards of seven hundred years), an examination into the history of the seal of Mathildis or Maud, the daughter and heiress of King Henry I. (generally known as the Empress Maud, or *Mathildis Imperatrix*, from the fact of her marriage with the Emperor Henry V. of Germany), has resulted in my being fortunately enabled to demonstrate that royal lady's undisputed right to a place in all tables or schemes of sovereigns of England; nevertheless it is, I believe, a very remarkable fact that her position with regard to the throne of England should have been so long, so universally, and so persistently ignored, by all those whose fancy has led them to accept facts at second hand, or from perfunctory inquiries into the sources of our national history rather than from careful step-by-step pursuit of truth through historical tracks which, like indistinct paths in the primæval forest, often lead the wanderer into situations which at the outset could not have been foreseen. In a paper on this subject which I prepared last year, and which is now published in the *Journal of the British Archæological Association*, I have fully explained my views of the propriety of inserting the name of Mathildis or Maud as Queen of England into the History Tables under the date of 1141-1143 ; and as this position has never as yet been impugned, we may take it that it is right in the main; and I have shown that until the liberation of King Stephen from his

[1] "A Fasciculus of the Charters of Mathildis, Empress of the Germans, and an Account of her Great Seal" (*Journ. Brit. Arch. Ass.*, xxxi. 376-398).
[2] "On the Seals of King Henry the Second and of his Son, the so-called Henry the Third" (*Transactions*, vol. xi. part 2, New Series).

imprisonment at Bristol, as a sequel to the battle at Winchester in 1143 (so disastrous to the prospects of Mathildis), she held her position as queen, most probably at London. . . .

"Now, I have introduced this apparent digression in this place to point to the importance of the study of historical seals, for my claim to the restoration of this queen's name is not due so much to my own researches as it is to the unaccountable oversight of others."[1]

I fear that, notwithstanding Mr. Birch's criticism on all who have gone before him, a careful analysis of the subject will reveal that the only addition he has made to our previous knowledge on this subject, as set forth in Mr. Way's papers, consists in two original and quite incomprehensible errors : one of them, the assigning of Maud's election to the episode of the 2nd and 3rd of March, instead of to that of the 7th and 8th of April (1141); the other, the assigning of Stephen's liberation to 1143 instead of 1141. When we correct these two errors, springing (may we say, in Mr. Birch's words?) "from perfunctory inquiries into the sources of our national history rather than from careful step-by-step pursuit of the truth," we return to the *status quo ante*, as set forth in Mr. Way's paper, and find that "the unaccountable oversight," by all writers before Mr. Birch, of the fact that the Empress "held her position as queen," for more than two years, "most probably at London," is due to the fact that her said rule lasted only a few months, or rather, indeed, a few weeks, while in London itself it was numbered by days.

But though it has been necessary to speak plainly on Mr. Birch's unfortunate discovery, one can probably agree with his acceptance of the view set forth by Mr. Hardy, and espoused by Mr. Way, that the style "domina" represents that "dominus" which was used as "a temporary title for the newly made monarch during the interval which was elapsing between the death of the

[1] Pp. 2, 3.

74 TRIUMPH OF THE EMPRESS.

predecessor and the coronation day of the living king."[1]
To Mr. Hardy's instance of Richard's style, "Dominus Angl[iæ]," August, 1189, we may add, I presume, that of John, "Dominus Angliæ," April 17th and 29th, (1199).[2] Now, if this usage be clearly established, it is certainly a complete explanation of a style of which historians have virtually failed to grasp the relevance.

But a really curious parallel, which no one has pointed out, is that afforded in the reign immediately preceding this, by the case of the king's second wife. Great importance is rightly attached to "the election of the Empress as 'domina Angliæ'" (as Dr. Stubbs describes it [3]), and to the words which William of Malmesbury places in the legate's mouth; [4] and yet, though the fact is utterly ignored, the very same formula of election is used in the case of Queen "Adeliza," twenty years before (1121)!

The expression there used by the Continuator is this: "Puella prædicta, *in regni dominam electa*, . . . regi desponsatur" (ii. 75). That is to say that before her marriage (January 29) and formal coronation as queen (January 30) she was elected, it would seem, "Domina Angliæ." The phrase "in regni dominam electa" precisely describes the *status* of the Empress after her election at Winchester, and before that formal coronation at Westminster which, as I maintain, was fully intended to follow. We might even go further still, and hold that the description of Adeliza as "futuram regni dominam," [5] when the envoys were despatched to fetch her, implies that she had been so elected at that great Epiphany council, in which the king "decrevit sibi in uxorem Atheleidem." [6] But I

---
[1] *Journ. B. A. A.*, xxxi. 383.
[2] Wells *Liber Albus*, fol. 10 (*Hist. MSS. Report* on Wells MSS.).
[3] *Const. Hist.*, i. 326, 341, 342.
[4] "In Angliæ Normanniæque dominam eligimus."
[5] *Cont. Flor. Wig.*, ii. 75. See Addenda.   [6] *Ibid.*

do not wish to press the parallel too far. In any case, precisely as with the Empress afterwards, she was clearly "domina Angliæ" before she was crowned queen. And, if "electa" means elected, the fact that these two passages, referring to the two elections (1121 and 1141), come from two independent chronicles proves that the terms employed are no idiosyncracy, but refer to a recognized practice of the highest constitutional interest.

Of course the fact that the same expression is applied to the election of Queen "Adeliza" as to that of the Empress herself, detracts from the importance of the latter event, regarded as an election to the throne.

At the same time, I hold that we should remember, as in the case of Stephen, the feudal bearing of "dominus." For herein lies its difference from "Rex." The "dominatus" of the Empress over England is attained step by step.[1] At Cirencester, at Winchester, at Oxford, she becomes "domina" in turn.[2] Not so with the royal title. She could be "lady" of a city or of a man: she could be "queen" of nothing less than England.

I must, however, with deep regret, differ widely from Mr. Birch in his conclusions on the styles adopted by the Empress. These he classes under three heads.[3] The second ("Mathildis Imperatrix Henrici regis filia et Anglorum regina") is found in only two charters, which I agree with him in assigning "to periods closely consecutive," not indeed to the episode of March 2 and 3, but to that of April 7 and 8. Of his remaining twenty-seven charters, thirteen belong to his first class and fourteen to his third, a proportion which makes it hard to understand

---

[1] "Pleraque tunc pars Angliæ dominatum ejus suscipiebat" (*Will. Malms.*, p. 749).
[2] "Ejusdem civitatis sumens dominium . . . totiusque civitatis suscepit dominium," etc. (*Cont. Flor. Wig.*).
[3] *Journ. B. A. A.*, xxxi. 382, 383.

why he should speak of the latter as "by far the most frequent."

Of the first class ("Mathildis Imperatrix Henrici Regis filia") Mr. Birch writes :—

"It is most probable that these documents are to be assigned to a period either before the death of her father, King Henry I., or at most to the initial years of Stephen, before any serious attempt had been made to obtain the possession of the kingdom."

Now, it is absolutely certain that not a single one of them can be assigned to the period suggested, that not one of them is previous to that 2nd of March (1141) which Mr. Birch selects as his turning-point, still less to "the death of her father" (1135). Nay, on Mr. Birch's own showing, the first and most important of these documents should be dated "between the 3rd of March and the 24th of July, A.D. 1141" (p. 380), and two others (Nos. 21, 28) "must be ascribed to a date between 1149 and 1151" (p. 397 n.). Nor is even this all, for as in two others the son of the Empress is spoken of as "King Henry," they must be as late as the reign of Henry II.

So, also, with the third class ("Mathildis Imperatrix Henrici regis filia et Anglorum domina"), of which we are told that it—

"was in the first instance adopted—I mean used—in those charters which contain the word and were promulgated between A.D. 1135 and A.D. 1141, by reason of the ceremony of coronation not yet having been performed ; and with regard to those charters which are placed subsequent to A.D. 1141, either because the ceremony was still unperformed, although she had the possession of the crown, or because of some stipulation with her opponents in power" (p. 383).

Here, again, it is absolutely certain that not a single one of these charters was "promulgated between A.D. 1135 and A.D. 1141." We have, therefore, no evidence that the Empress, in her charters, adopted this style until the election of April 7 and 8 (1141) enabled her justly to do

STYLE OF THE EMPRESS. 77

so. But the fact is that Mr. Birch's theory is not only based, as we have seen, on demonstrably erroneous hypotheses, but must be altogether abandoned as opposed to every fact of the case. For the two styles which he thus distinguishes were used at the same time, and even in the same document. For instance, in the very first of Mr. Birch's documents, that great charter to Geoffrey de Mandeville, to which we shall come in the next chapter, issued at the height of Matilda's power, and on the eve, as we shall see, of her intended coronation, "Anglorum domina" is omitted from her style, and the document is therefore, by Mr. Birch, assigned to the first of his classes. Yet I shall show that in a portion of the charter which has perished, and which is therefore unknown to Mr. Birch, her style is immediately repeated with the addition "Anglorum Domina." It is clear, then, on Mr. Birch's own showing, that this document should be assigned both to his first and to his third classes, and, consequently, that the distinction he attempts to draw has no foundation in fact.

Mr. Birch's thesis would, if sound, be a discovery of such importance that I need not apologize for establishing, by demonstration, that it is opposed to the whole of the evidence which he himself so carefully collected. And when we read of Stephen's "incarceration at Bristol, which was not terminated until the battle of Winchester in A.D. 1143, when the hopes of the Empress were shattered" (p. 378), it is again necessary to point out that her flight from Winchester took place not in 1143, but in September, 1141. Mr. Birch's conclusion is thus expressed :—

"We may, therefore, take it as fairly shown that until the liberation of the king from his imprisonment at Bristol (as a sequel to the battle at Winchester in A.D. 1143, so disastrous to the queen's hopes) she held her position, as queen, most probably at London," etc. (p. 380).

Here, as before, it is needful to remember that the date is all wrong, and that the triumph of the Empress, so far from lasting two years or more, lasted but for a few months of the year 1141, in the course of which she was not at London for more than a few days.

And now let us turn to my remaining point, " the effect of this election on the position of the Empress."

To understand this, we must glance back at the precedents of the four preceding reigns. The Empress, as I have shown, had followed these precedents in making first for Winchester : she had still to follow them in securing her coronation and anointing at Westminster. It is passing strange that all historians should have lost sight of this circumstance. For the case of her own father, in whose shoes she claimed to stand, was the aptest precedent of all. As he had been elected at Winchester, and then crowned at Westminster, so would she, following in his footsteps. The growing importance of London had been recognized in successive coronations from the Conquest, and now that it was rapidly supplanting Winchester as the destined capital of the realm, it would be more essential than ever that the coronation should there take place, and secure not merely the *prestige* of tradition, but the assent of the citizens of London.[1]

It has not, however, so far as I know, occurred to any writer that it was the full intention of the Empress and her followers that she should be crowned and anointed queen, and that, like those who had gone before her, she should be so crowned at Westminster. It is because they

[1] It is very singular that Mr. Freeman failed to perceive this parallel, since he himself writes of Henry (1100). "The Gemót of election was held at Winchester while the precedents of three reigns made it seem matter of necessity that the unction and coronation should be done at Westminster" (*Will. Rufus*, ii. 348). Such an admission as this is sufficient to prove my case.

THE INTENDED CORONATION. 79

failed to grasp this that Dr. Stubbs and Mr. Freeman are both at fault. The former writes :—

"Matilda became the Lady of the English; she was not crowned, because perhaps the solemn consecration which she had received as empress sufficed, or perhaps Stephen's royalty was so far forth indefeasible." [1]

"No attempt was made to crown the Empress; the legate simply proposes that she should be elected Lady of England and Normandy. It is just possible that the consecration which she had once received as empress might be regarded as superseding the necessity of a new ceremony of the kind, but it is far more likely that, so long as Stephen was alive and not formally degraded, the right conferred on him by coronation was regarded as so far indefeasible that no one else could be allowed to share it." [2]

Dr. Stubbs appears here to imply that we should have expected her coronation to follow her election. And in this he is clearly right. Mr. Freeman, however, oddly enough, seems to have looked for it *before* her election. This is the more strange in a champion of the elective principle. He writes thus of her reception at Winchester, five weeks before her election :—

"If Matilda was to reign, her reign needed to begin by something which might pass for an election and coronation. But her followers, Bishop Henry at their head, seem to have shrunk from the actual crowning and anointing ceremonies, which—unless Sexburh had, ages before, received the royal consecration—had never, either in England or in Gaul, been applied to a female ruler. Matilda was solemnly received in the cathedral church of Winchester; she was led by two bishops, the legate himself and Bernard of St. David's, as though to receive the crown and unction, but no crowning and no unction is spoken of." [3]

[1] *Early Plantagenets*, 22. [2] *Const. Hist.*, i. 339.
[3] *Norm. Conq.*, v. 308, 304. The foot-note to this statement ("William of Malmesbury seems distinctly to exclude a coronation," etc., etc.) has been already given (*ante*, p. 62). Mr. Birch confusing, as we have seen, the reception of the Empress with her election, naturally looks, like Mr. Freeman, to the former as the time when she ought to have been crowned: "The crown of England's sovereigns was handed over to her, a kind of *seizin* representing that the kingdom of England was under the power of her hands (although it does not appear that any further ceremony connected with the rite of

At the same time, he recurs to the subject, after describing the election, thus :—

"Whether any consecration was designed to follow, whether at such consecration she would have been promoted to the specially royal title, we are not told."[1]

But all this uncertainty is at once dispelled when we learn what was really intended. Taken in conjunction with the essential fact that "domina" possessed the special sense of the interim royal title, the intention of the Empress to be crowned at Westminster, and so to become queen in name as well as queen in deed, gives us the key to the whole problem. It explains, moreover, the full meaning of John of Hexham's words, when he writes that "David rex videns multa competere in imperatricis neptis suæ promotionem post Ascensionem Domini (May 8) ad eam in Suth-Anglia profectus est . . . plurimosque ex principibus sibi acquiescentes habuit ut ipsa promoveretur ad totius regni fastigium." We shall see how this intention was only foiled by the sudden uprising of the citizens; and in the names of the witnesses to Geoffrey's charter we shall behold those, "tam episcopi quam cinguli militaris viri, qui *ad dominam inthronizandam* posé Londonias et arroganter convenerant."[2]

coronation was then performed)" (*Journ. B. A. A.*, xxxi. p. 378). This assumes that the crown was "handed over to her" at a "ceremony" in the cathedral, whereas, as I explained, my own view is that she obtained it with the royal castle.

[1] *Norm. Conq.*, v. p. 305.

[2] *Gesta*, 79. In the word "inthronizandam," I contend, is to be found the confirmation of my theory, based on comparison and induction, of an intended coronation at Westminster. So far as I know, attention has never been drawn to it before.

CHAPTER IV.

THE FIRST CHARTER OF THE EMPRESS.

THOUGH the election of the Empress, says William of Malmesbury, took place immediately after Easter, it was nearly midsummer before the Londoners would receive her.[1] Hence her otherwise strange delay in proceeding to the scene of her coronation. An incidental allusion leads us to believe that this *interregnum* was marked by tumult and bloodshed in London. We learn that Aubrey de Vere was killed on the 9th of May, in the course of a riot in the city.[2] This event has been assigned by every writer that I have consulted to the May of the previous year (1140), and this is the date assigned in the editor's marginal note.[3] The context, however, clearly shows that it belongs to 1141. Aubrey was a man of some consequence. He had been actively employed by Henry I. in the capacity of justice and of sheriff, and was also a royal chamberlain. His death, therefore, was a notable event, and one is tempted to associate with it the fact that he was father-in-law to Geoffrey. It is not impossible that, on that occasion, they may have been acting in concert, and resisting a popular movement of the citizens, whether directed against the Empress or against Geoffrey himself.

[1] "Itaque multæ fuit molis Londoniensium animos permulcere posse, ut, cum hæc statim post Pascha (ut dixi) fuerint actitata, vix paucis ante Nativitatem beati Johannis diebus imperatricem reciperent" (p. 748).
[2] "Galfridus de Mandevilla firmavit Turrim Londoniensem. Idibus Maii Albericus de Ver Londoniis occiditur" (M. Paris, *Chron. Major.*, ii. 174).
[3] *Ibid.*

82   THE FIRST CHARTER OF THE EMPRESS.

The comparison of the Empress's advance on London with that of her grandfather, in similar circumstances, is of course obvious. The details, however, of the latter are obscure, and Mr. Parker, we must remember, has gravely impugned the account of it given in the *Norman Conquest*.[1]

Of the ten weeks which appear to have elapsed between the election of the Empress and her reception in London, we know little or nothing. Early in May she came to Reading,[2] the Continuator's statement to that effect being confirmed by a charter which, to all appearance, passed on this occasion.[3] It is attested by her three constant companions, the Earl of Gloucester, Brian fitz Count, and Miles of Gloucester (acting as her constable), together with John (fitz Gilbert) the marshal, and her brothers Reginald (now an earl)[4] and Robert (fitz Edith).[5] But a special significance is to be found in the names of the five attesting bishops (Winchester, Lincoln, Ely, St. David's, and Hereford). They are, it will be found, the same five who attest the charter to Geoffrey de Mandeville (midsummer), and they are also the five who (with the Bishop of Bath) had attended, in March, the Empress at Winchester. This creates a strong presumption that, in despite of chroniclers' vague assertions, the number of bishops who joined the Empress was, even if not limited to these, at least extremely small.[6]

[1] *The Early History of Oxford*, cap. x.
[2] "Ad Radingum infra Rogationes veniens, suscipitur cum honoribus, hinc inde principibus cum populis ad ejus imperium convolantibus" (*Cont. Flor. Wig.*, 130).
[3] *Add. Chart.* (Brit. Mus.), 19,576; *Arch. Journ.*, xx. 289; *Journ. B. A. A.*, xxxi. 389.
[4] "Reginaldo *comite* filio regis." He had attested, as we have seen, an Oxford charter (*circ.* March 24) as Reginald "filius regis" simply. This would seem to fix his creation to *circ.* April, 1141 (see p. 68).
[5] "Roberto fratre ejus."
[6] We obtain incidentally, in another quarter, unique evidence on this very point. There is printed in the *Cartulary of Ramsey* (Rolls Series),

This is one of the two charters in which the Empress employs the style "Regina." It is probable that the other also should be assigned to this period.[1] These two exceptional cases would thus belong to the interim period during which she was queen elect, though technically only "domina." Here again the fact that, during this period, she adopted, alternatively, both styles ("regina" and "domina"), as well as that which Mr. Birch assigns to his first period, proves how impossible it is to classify these styles by date.

If we reject the statement that from Reading she returned to Oxford,[2] the only other stage in her progress that is named is that of her reception at St. Albans.[3] In this case also the evidence of a charter confirms that of

vol. ii. p. 254, a precept from Nigel, Bishop of Ely, to William, Prior of Ely, and others, notifying the agreement he has made with Walter, Abbot of Ramsey:—"Sciatis me et Walterum Abbatem de Rameseia consilio et assensu dominæ nostræ Imperatricis et Episcopi Wynton' Apost' sedis legati aliorumque coepiscoporum meorum scilicet Linc', Norwycensis, Cestrensis, Hereford', Sancti Davidis, et Roberti Comitis Gloecestrie, et Hugonis Comitis et Brienni et Milonis ad voluntatem meam concordatos esse. Quapropter mando et præcipio sicut me diligitis," etc., etc. This precept, in the printed cartulary, is dated "1133-1144." These are absurdly wide limits, and a little research would, surely, have shown that it must belong to the period in which the Empress was triumphant, and during which the legate was with her. This fixes it to March—June, 1141. Independent of the great interest attaching to this document as representing a "concordia" in the court of the Empress during her brief triumph, it affords in my opinion proof of the *personnel* of her court at the time. Five of the seven bishops mentioned were, as observed in the text, in regular attendance at her court, and we may therefore, on the strength of this document, add those of "Chester" and Norwich, as visiting it, at least, on this occasion. So with the laity. Three of the four magnates named (of whom Miles had not yet received the earldom of Hereford) were her constant companions, so that we may safely rely on this evidence for the presence at her court on this occasion of Hugh, Earl of Norfolk.

[1] *Journ. B. A. A.*, xxxi. 389. Note that in this case Seffrid, Bishop of Chichester, appears as a witness, doubtless because he had been Abbot of Glastonbury, to which abbey the charter was granted.

[2] See above, p. 66.

[3] "Proficiscitur inde cum exultatione magna et gaudio, et in monasterio Sancti Albani cum processionali suscipitur honore, et jubilo" (*Cont. Flor. Wig.*, 131).

the chronicler.[1] At St. Albans she received a deputation from London, and the terms on which the city agreed to receive her must have been here finally arranged.[2] She then proceeded in state to Westminster,[3] no doubt by the Edgware Road, the old Roman highway, and was probably met by the citizens and their rulers, according to the custom, at Knightsbridge.[4]

Meanwhile, she had been joined in her progress by her uncle, the King of Scots, who had left his realm about the middle of May for the purpose of attending her coronation.[5]

The Empress, according to William of Malmesbury, reached London only a few days before the 24th of June.[6] This is the sole authority we have for the date of her visit, except the statement by Trivet that she arrived on the 21st (or 26th) of April.[7] This latter date we may certainly reject. If we combine the statement that her flight took

[1] "Apud sanctum Albanum" (Duchy of Lancaster: Royal Charters, No. 16; *Journ. B. A. A.*, xxxi. 388).

[2] "Adeunt eam ibi cives multi ex Londoniâ, tractatur ibi sermo multimodus de reddenda civitate" (*Cont. Flor. Wig.*, 131).

[3] "Imperatrix, ut prædiximus, habito tractatu cum Londoniensibus, comitantibus secum præsulibus multis et principibus, secura properavit ad urbem, et apud Westmonasterium cum processionali suscipitur honorificentiâ" (*ibid.*).

[4] *i.e.* Hyde Park Corner, as it now is. See, for this custom, the *Chronicles of the Mayors of London*, which record how, a century later (1257), upon the king approaching Westminster, "exierunt Maior et cives, *sicut mos est* ad salutandum ipsum usque ad Kniwtebrigge" (p. 31). The Continuator (p. 132) alludes to some such reception by the citizens ("cum honore susceperunt").

[5] "Videns itaque David rex multa competere in imperatricis neptis suæ promotionem, post Ascensionem Domini ad eam in Suthangliam profectus est: . . . Venit itaque rex ad neptem suam, plurimosque ex principibus sibi acquiescentes habuit ut ipsa promoveretur ad totius regni fastigium" (*Sym. Dun.*, ii. 309). As he did not join her till after her election, I have taken this latter phrase as referring to her coronation (see p. 80). Cf. p. 5, *n*. 5.

[6] "Vix paucis ante Nativitatem beati Johannis diebus."

[7] "Cives . . . Imperatricem . . . favorabiliter susciperunt undecimo [*al.* Sexto] Kal. Maii."

place on Midsummer Day [1] with that of the Continuator that her visit lasted for "some days," [2] they harmonize fairly enough with that of William of Malmesbury. If it was, indeed, after a few days that her visit was so rudely cut short, we are able to understand why she left without the intended coronation taking place.

From another and quite independent authority, we obtain the same day (June 24th) as the date of her flight from London, together with a welcome and important glimpse of her doings. The would-be Bishop of Durham, William Cumin, had come south with the King of Scots (whose chancellor he was), accompanied by certain barons of the bishopric and a deputation from the cathedral chapter. Nominally, this deputation was to claim from the Empress and the legate a confirmation of the chapter's canonical right of free election; but, in fact, it was composed of William's adherents, who purposed to secure from the Empress and the legate letters to the chapter in his favour. The legate not having arrived at court when they reached the Empress, she deferred her reply till he should join her. In the result, however, the two differed; for, while the legate, warned from Durham, refused to support William, the Empress, doubtless influenced by her uncle, had actually agreed, as sovereign, to give him the ring and staff, and would undoubtedly have done so, but for the Londoners' revolt.[3] It must be remembered

[1] See the *Liber de Antiquis Legibus:* "Tandem a Londonensibus expulsa est in die Sancti Johannis Bapt." So also Trivet.

[2] "Ibique aliquantis diebus . . . resedit" (p. 131).

[3] "[Legatus] rem exanimans, præscriptam factionem invenit, fautoribusque ipsius dignâ animadversione interdixit ne Willelmum in Episcopum nisi canonicâ electione susciperent. Ipsi quoque Willelmo interdixit omnem ecclesiasticam communionem, si Episcopatum susciperet nisi Canonice promotus. Actum id in die S. Johannis Baptistæ. Pactus erat Willelmus ab Imperatrice baculum et annulum recipere; et data hæc ei essent, nisi, facta a Londoniensibus dissentione, cum omnibus suis discederet *ipso die* a Londonia Imperatrix." — Continuatio Historiæ Turgoti (*Anglia Sacra*, i. 711).

86 THE FIRST CHARTER OF THE EMPRESS.

that, for her own sake, the Empress would welcome every opportunity of exercising sovereign rights, as in her prompt bestowal of the see of London upon Robert. And though she lost her chance of actually investing William, she had granted, before her flight, letters commending him for election.[1]

Thus we obtain the date of the charter which is the subject of this chapter. In this case alone was Mr. Eyton right in the dates he assigned to these documents. Nor, indeed, is it possible to be mistaken. For this charter can only have passed on the occasion of this, the only visit that the Empress paid to Westminster. Yet, even here, Mr. Eyton's date is not absolutely correct. For he holds that it "passed in the short period during which Maud was in London, *i.e.* between June 24 and July 25, 1141";[2] whereas "June 24" is the probable date of her departure, and not of her arrival, which was certainly previous to that day.

There is but one other document (besides a comparatively insignificant precept[3]) which can be positively

This passage further proves (though, indeed, there is no reason to doubt it) that the legate remained in London till the actual flight of the Empress. It also illustrates their discordance.

[1] "Literas Imperatricis directas ad Capitulum, quarum summa hæc erat: Quod vellet Ecclesiam nostram de Pastore consultam esse, et nominatim de illo quem Robertus Archidiaconus nominaret, et quod de illo vellet, et de alio omnino nollet. Quæsitum est ergo quis hic esset. Responsum est quod Willelmus" (*ibid.*). This has, of course, an important bearing on the question of episcopal election. Strong though the terms of her letter appear to have been, the Empress here waives the right, on which her father and her son insisted, of having the election conducted in her presence and in her own chapel, and anticipated the later practice introduced by the charter of John.

[2] *Add. MSS.*, 31,943, fol. 97. So too fol. 115: "After June 24, 1141, when the Empress was received in London; before July 25, when Milo was created Earl of Hereford."

[3] Mandate to Sheriff of Essex in favour of William fitz Otto (*Journ. B. A. A.*, xxxi. 387). It is possible that the charter to Christ Church, London (*ibid.*, p. 388), may also belong to this occasion; but, even if so, it is of no importance.

IMPORTANCE OF THE CHARTER. 87

assigned to this visit.[1] This consideration alone would invest our charter with interest, but when we add to this its great length, its list of witnesses, and its intrinsic importance, it may be claimed as one of the most instructive documents of this obscure and eventful period.

Of the original, now among the Cottonian Charters (xvi. 27), Mr. Birch, who is exceptionally qualified to pronounce upon these subjects, has given us as complete a transcript as it is now possible to obtain.[2] To this he has appended the following remarks :—

"This most important charter, one of the earliest, if not the earliest example of the text of a deed creating a peerage, does not appear to have been ever published. I cannot find the text in any printed book or MS. Fortunately Sir William Dugdale inspected this charter before it had been injured in the disastrous Cottonian fire, which destroyed so many invaluable evidences of British history. In his account of the Mandevilles, Earls of Essex (*Baronage*, vol. i. p. 202), he says that 'this is the most antient creation-charter, which hath ever been known, *vide* Selden's *Titles of Honour*, p. 647,' and he gives an English rendering of the greater portion of the Latin text, which has enabled me to conjecture several emendations and restorations in the above transcript."

Mr. Birch having thus, like preceding antiquaries, borne witness to the interest attaching to "this most important charter," it is with special satisfaction that I find myself enabled to print a transcript of the entire document, supplying, there is every reason to believe, a complete and accurate text. Nor will it only enable us to restore the portions of the charter now wanting,[3] for it further convicts the great Dugdale of no less serious an error than the omission of two most important witnesses and the garbling of the name of a third.[4]

[1] A charter to Roger de Valoines. See Appendix G.
[2] *Journ. B. A. A.*, pp. 384-386.
[3] The portions which are wanting in the charter and which are supplied from my transcript will be found enclosed in brackets.
[4] Robert, Earl of Gloucester, and William the chancellor are omitted

The accuracy of my authorities can be tested by collation with those portions of the original that are still perfect. This test is quite satisfactory, as is also that of comparing one of the passages they supply with Camden's transcript of that same passage, taken from the original charter. Camden's extract, of the existence of which Mr. Birch was evidently not aware, was printed by him in his *Ordines Anglicani*,[1] from which it is quoted by Selden in his well-known *Titles of Honour*.[2] It is further quoted, as from Camden and Selden, at the head of the Patents of Creation appended to the *Lords' Reports on the Dignity of a Peer*,[3] as also in the Third Report itself (where the marginal reference, however, is wrong).[4] It is specially interesting from Camden's comment: "This is the most ancient creation-charter that I ever saw" (which is clearly the origin of the statement as to its unique antiquity), and from the fact of that great antiquary speaking of it as "now in my hands."

The two transcripts I have employed for the text (D. and A.) are copies respectively found in the Dugdale MSS. (L. fol. 81) and the Ashmole MSS. (841, fol. 3). I have reason to believe that this charter was among those duly recorded in the missing volume of the Great Coucher.

CHARTER OF THE EMPRESS TO GEOFFREY DE MANDEVILLE

(Midsummer, 1141).

"Archiepis-
copis, etc."
(D.).

M. Imperatrix regis Henrici filia Archiepiscopis Episcopis Abbatibus (Comitibus Baronibus Justiciariis Vice-

altogether, and Ralph *Lovell* becomes Ralph *de London*. Dugdale has, of course, misled Mr. Birch.

[1] Appended (as the "Degrees of England") to Gibson's well-known edition of the *Britannia* (1772), vol. i. p. 125.
[2] Second edition, p. 647.
[3] Appendix V., p. 1 (ed. 1829).   [4] Page 164.

TEXT OF THE CHARTER. 89

comitibus et ministris et omnibus baronibus et fidelibus) suis Francis et Anglis totius Angliæ et Normanniæ salutem. (Sciatis omnes tam præsentes quam futuri quod Ego Matildis regis Henrici filia et Anglor[um] domina) do et concedo Gaufrido de Magnavillâ (pro servitio suo et heredibus suis post eum hereditabiliter ut sit comes de Essex[iâ] et habeat tertium denarium Vicecomitatus de placitis sicut comes habere debet in comitatu suo [1] in omnibus rebus, et præter hoc reddo illi in feodo et hereditate de me et heredibus meis totam terram quam) tenuit [2] (Gaufridus de Magnavilla avus suus et Serlo de Matom in Angliâ et Normanniâ ita libere et [3]) bene et quiete sicut aliquis antecessorum suorum illam unquam melius (et liberius tenuit, vel ipsemet) postea (aliquo in tempore, sibi dico) et heredibus suis (post eum), et concedo illi et heredibus suis Custodiam turris Londonie (cum parvo Castello quod) fuit Ravengeri in feodo et hereditate de me (et heredibus) meis cum terris et liberationibus et omnibus Consuetudinibus quæ ad (eandem terram [3]) pertinerent, et ut inforciet illa secundum voluntatem suam. (Et similiter [4]) do ei et concedo et heredibus suis C libratas terræ de me et de (heredibus) meis in dominio, videlicet Niweport [5] pro tanto quantum reddere solebat die qua rex H[enricus] pater meus fuit vivus et mortuus, et ad rem(ovend') mercatum de Niweport in Castellum suum de Waldena cum omnibus Consuetudinibus que prius mercato illi melius

---

[1] " Ego Matildis filia regis Henrici et Anglorum domina do et concedo Gaufredo de Magnavilla pro servicio suo et heredibus suis post eum hereditabiliter ut sit Comes de Essexia, et habeat tertium denarium Vicecomitatus de placitis sicut Comes habere debet in comitatu suo " (Camden).

[2] Mr. Birch reads " tenuit bene," omitting the intervening words.

[3] Mr. Birch for "eandem terram" (*rectius* "turrem") conjectures "illam."

[4] Mr. Birch conjectures " Preterea."

[5] Newport (the name hints at a market-town) was ancient demesne of the Crown. It lay about three miles south-west of (Saffron) Walden.

90 *THE FIRST CHARTER OF THE EMPRESS.*

"passagio" (A.).
"Newport" (A.).

pertinuerunt in (Thelon[eo] et passag[io] [1]) et aliis consuetudinibus, (et) ut vie de Niweport quæ sunt juxta littus aquæ [2] dirigantur ex consuetudine ad Waledenam (sup[er] foris)facturam meam et Mercatum de Waldenâ sit ad diem dominicam et ad diem Jovis et ut feria [3] habeatur apud Waledenam et incipiat in (Vigiliâ Pentecost [4]) et duret per totam hebdomadam pentecostes Et Meldonam [5] ad perficiendum predictas C libratas terræ pro tanto quantum inde reddi solebat die quâ (Rex Henricus fuit) vivus et mortuus cum omnibus Appendiciis et rebus que adjacebant in terrâ et mari ad Burgum illud predicto die mortis Regis Henrici, et (Deopedenam [6]) similiter pro tanto quantum inde reddi solebat die quâ rex Henricus fuit vivus et mortuus cum omnibus Appendiciis suis et Boscum de chatelegâ [7] cum (hominibus pro) [8] xx solidis, et terram de Banhunta [9] pro xl solidis, et si quid defuerit ad C libratas perficiendas perficiam ei in loco competenti in Essexa (aut in Hert)-fordescirâ aut in Cantebriggscirâ tali tenore quod si

"dictam" (A.).
"Vigilia Pentecost" (A.); "vigil' pentecostes" (D.).

"quanto" (A.);
"quantum" (D.).

"et si" in D.; "et" omitted in A.
"perfici end'" (D.).
"Heortfordescira" (D.);
"Hertfordscira" (A.).

[1] There was still a toll bridge there in the last century. For table of tolls and exemptions, see Morant's *Essex*.

[2] Apparently, the high road on the left bank, and the way on the right bank, of the Cam.

[3] Neither this market nor this fair are, it would seem, to be traced afterwards.

[4] Mr. Birch conjectures "vigiliam."

[5] This was presumably a grant of the borough of Maldon (*i.e.* the royal rights in that borough), though Peverel's fee in Maldon was an escheat at the time. The proof of this is not only that it is here described as a "borough" (*burgus*), but also that its annual value was to be deducted from the sheriff's ferm, which could only be the case if it formed part of the *corpus comitatus*, *i.e.* was Crown demesne. In Domesday, Peverel's fee in Maldon was valued at £12, and the royal manor at £16 ("ad pondus"), though it had been £24. It was probably the latter which Henry II. granted to his brother William as representing ("pro") £22 ("numero") (see Pipe-Rolls).

[6] Depden, three miles south of Walden. It had formed part, at the Survey, of the fief of Randulf Peverel.

[7] Catlidge, according to Morant.

[8] Mr. Birch conjectures "tenentibus ibidem pro."

[9] Bonhunt, now part of Wickham Bonhunt, adjoining Newport. It had been held by Saissclinus at the Survey. In 1485 it was held of the honour of Lancaster.

TEXT OF THE CHARTER.

(reddi)dero Comiti Theobaldo totam terram quam (tenebat)[1] in An(gliâ dabo Gaufrido Comiti Essex[ie] escambium suum ad valentiam in his prædictis tribus Comitatibus antequam de) predictis terris dissais(iatur ; si etiam reddidero totum honorem et totam terram) heredibus Willelmi peur[elli] de Lond[oniâ][2] dabo similiter ei escambium ad valens antequam dissaisiatur de illâ quæ fuit peurelli et illud (escambium erit) de terrâ que remanebit illi hereditabiliter Et preter hoc do et concedo ei et heredibus suis de me et heredibus meis tenendum feodum (et servicium) xx militum et infra servicium istorum xx militum do ei feodum et servicium terre quam Hasculf[us] de tania[3] tenuit in Angliâ die quâ fuit (vivus et) mortuus, quam tenet Graeleng[us][4] et mater sua pro tanto servicii quantum de feodo illo debent et totum superplus istorum xx militum[5] ei perficiam in (prenomina)tis[6] tribus comitatibus. Et servicium istorum xx militum faciet mihi separatim preter aliud servicium alterius feodi sui. Et preterea concedo (illi ut)[6] castella sua que habet stent et ei remaneant (ad) inforcia(nd[um])[6] ad voluntatem suam Et ut ille et omnes homines sui teneant terras (et tenaturas) suas omnes de

"Gaufrido" (D.); "Galfrido" (A.).
"valens" (D.); "valentiam" (A.).
"his tribus" (A.).
"et etiam" (A.)

"inforciand'" (A.).
"inforciancum" (D.).

"terras et tent'" (A.).

---

[1] Mr. Birch conjectures "ipse habuit."

[2] This, apparently, refers to Depden, as forming part of Peverel's fief, which had been an escheat, in the king's hands, as early as 1130 (*Rot. Pip.*, 31 Hen. L).

[3] Hasculf de Tany was ancestor of the Essex family of Tany, of Stapleford-Tany, Theydon Bois, Elmstead, Great Stambridge, Latton, etc. He appears repeatedly in the Pipe-Roll of 31 Hen. I. (pp. 53, 56, 58, 60, 99, 152), when he was in litigation with William de Bovill and Rhiwallon d'Avranches.

[4] "Graelengus" is proved to be identical with "Graelandus de Thania," the Essex tenant-in-capite of 1166, by Stephen's second charter (Christmas, 1141), which gives his holding as 7½ fees, the very amount at which he returns it in his *Carta* (see p. 142). But his contemporary, Graeland "fitz Gilbert" de Tany, on the Pipe-Rolls of Henry II., was probably so styled for distinction, being a son of Gilbert de Tany who figures on the Essex Pipe-Roll of 1158.

[5] Compare the phrase "superplus militum" in *Rot. Pip.* 31 H. I. (p. 47).

[6] "Predictis;" "ei quod omnia;" "et sint inforciata" (Mr. Birch).

92 THE FIRST CHARTER OF THE EMPRESS.

quocunque teneant sicut tenuerunt die quâ ipse homo meus effectus est salvo servitio dominorum Et ut ipse et homines sui (sint quieti) de omnibus debitis que debuerunt regi Henrico aut regi Stephano et ut ipse et omnes homines sui per totam Angliam sint quieti de Wastis fores(tariis et) "Gaufridi" (D.); Gal- assartis que facta sunt in feodo ipsius Gaufredi usque ad fridi" (A.). (diem quo) homo meus devenit Et ut a die illo in antea omnia illa ess(arta sint amodo excultibilia et arrabilia sine "anno inci- forisfacto et ut habeat mercatum die Jovis apud Bisseiam [1] piat" (A.) "preteria" et feriam similiter ibidem quoque anno; et incipiat vigiliâ (A.); "prœ- terea" (D.). Sancti Jacobi et duret tres dies. Et [preterea] do et "Essex" concedo ei et heredibus suis in feodo et hereditate ad (A.); "de Essexâ" tenendum de me et heredibus meis vicecomitatum Es- (D.). sex[ie] reddendo inde rectam firmam que inde reddi solebat "firmæ" die quâ rex Henricus pater meus fuit vivus et mortuus, (D.); "firma" ita quod auferat de summâ firmâ vice)comitatus quantum (A.). "Newport" pertinuerit [2] (ad) Meldonam et Niweport que ei (donavi et) (A.). "donu'" quantum (pertinuerit [3] ad tertium) denarium de placitis (A.); "do- navi" (D.). Vicecomitatus unde eum feci Comitem, et ut teneat omnia "Dominica" (D.) excidamenta mea que mihi exciderint (in com)itatu Essexe reddendo inde firmam rectam quamdiu erunt in Dominio "Essexiâ" meo Et ut sit capitalis Justicia in Essexâ hereditabiliter (A.). "meo" (A.). mea (et hered[um]) meorum de placitis et forisfactis que pertinuerint ad Coronam meam, ita quod non mittam aliam Justiciam super eum in Comitatu illo nisi [4] (ita sit quod ali)quando mittam aliquem de paribus suis qui audiat cum illo quod placita mea juste tractentur Et ut ipse et omnes homines sui sint (quieti versus) me et versus heredes meos "malevo- de omni forisfacto et omni malivolentiâ preteritâ ante diem lentia" (A.). "anno et die quo meus homo devenit Et ei firmiter concedo et (here- quo" (A.); "ante diem" (D.).

---

[1] Bushey in Hertfordshire. Part of Mandeville's Domesday fief.
[2] Mr. Birch reads "pertinuerunt."
[3] "Pertinuit"—Mr. Birch's conjecture.
[4] "Quod aliquando"—Mr. Birch's conjecture.

TEXT OF THE CHARTER. 93

dibus suis) quod bene et in pace et libere et sine placito habeat et[1] teneat hereditabiliter, sicut hæc carta confirmat, omnia tenementa sua (que ei concessi, in terris) et tenaturis et in feodis et firmis et Castellis et libertatibus et in omnibus Conventionibus inter nos factis (sicut aliquis Comes) terre[2] mee melius et quietius et liberius tenet ad modum Comitis in omnibus rebus ita quod ipse vel aliquis hominum suorum non (ponantur[3] in ullo modo) in placitum de aliquo forisfacto quod fecissent antequam homo meus factus esset, nec pro aliquo forisfacto quod facturus sit in (antea ponatur in) placit[um] de feodo vel Castello vel terrâ vel tenurâ quam ei concesserim quamdiu se defendere potuerit de scelere sive (traditione) ad corpus meum pertinente per se aut per unum militem si quis coram venerit qui eum appellare inde voluerit.

"tenaturis" (D.); "tenu. tis" (A.).
"consuetudinibus" (A.).
"ponantur ullo" (D.). "placitum" (D.); "placita" (A.).
"de traditione" (A., D.).

(T[estibus] H[enrico] Ep[iscop]o Winton[ensi]) et A[lexandro] Ep[iscop]o Lincoln[ensi] et R[oberto] Ep[iscop]o Heref[ordensi] et N[igello] Ep[iscop]o Ely[ensi] (et B[ernardo] Ep[iscop]o de S[ancto] David et W[illelmo] Cancellario et Com[ite] R[oberto] de Glocestr[iâ] et Com[ite] B[aldewino[4]]) et Com[ite] W[illelmo] de Moion et B[riano] fil[io] Com[itis] (et M[ilone] Glocestr[ie] et R[oberto] Arundell[5] et R[oberto] Malet[6] et Rad[ulfo]

---

[1] Mr. Birch reads "placito hac teneat."
[2] Mr. Birch reads "tre mee."
[3] Mr. Birch conjectures "ponantur in (placitum)."
[4] Mr. Birch conjectures "Baldewino Comite Devonie."
[5] On Robert Arundell, see Yeatman's *History of the House of Arundel*, p. 49 (where too early a date is suggested for this charter), and p. 105 (where it is implied that he was a tenant of the Earl of Gloucester). He occurs repeatedly in the Pipe-Roll of 31 Hen. I., and again in the Westminster charters (1136) of Stephen. (See Appendix C.)
[6] Robert Malet also was a west-country baron. He figures in connection with Warminster in the Pipe-Roll of 31 Hen. I., and is among the witnesses to the Westminster charters (1136), being there styled "Dapifer" (see Appendix C.). The *carta* of the Abbot of Glastonbury (1166) proves that he was the predecessor of William Malet, *dapifer* to Henry II.

(*vide infra.*) Lovell[1] et Rad[ulfo] Painell[2]) et W[alkelino] Maminot[3] et Rob[erto] fil[io] R[egis][4] et Rob[erto] fil[io] Martin[5]

[1] Another west-country baron. He was one of the rebels of 1138, when he held Castle Carey against the king (*Hen. Hunt.*, p. 261; *Ord. Vit.*, v. 310; *Gesta*, p. 43). According to Mr. Yeatman, he was son of "William Gouel de Percival, called Lovel," Lord of Ivry (*History of the House of Arundel*, p. 136). He is however wrongly termed by him "Robert (*sic*) Lovel" on p. 268. He witnessed an early charter of the Empress to Glastonbury (*Journ. B. A. A.*, xxxi. 390).

[2] Ralph Paynell had instigated the Earl of Gloucester's raid on Nottingham the previous September (*Cont. Flor. Wig.*, 128), and was one of the rebels in 1138, when he held Dudley against the king (*ibid.*, 110). He was presumably identical with the "Rad[ulfus] Paen[ellus]" of 1130 (*Rot. Pip.*, 31 Hen. I.). He witnessed the charter to Roger de Valoines (see p. 286), and three other charters of the Empress (*Journ. B. A. A.*, xxxi. 391, 395, 398), including the creation of the earldom of Hereford (25 July, 1141).

[3] Walchelin Maminot had been among the witnesses to the above Westminster charters of (Easter) 1136, but had held Dover against the king in 1138 (*Ord. Vit.*, v. 310), when Ordericus (v. 111, 112) speaks of him as a son-in-law of Robert de Ferrers (Earl of Derby). He witnessed the charter to Roger de Valoines (see p. 286), and five other charters of the Empress (*Journ. B. A. A.*, xxxi. 388, 391, 394 *bis*, 398), including the creation of the earldom of Hereford (25 July 1141), and he appears in the Pipe-Rolls and other records under Henry II. from 1155 to 1170.

[4] Robert, natural son of Henry I. by Edith (afterwards married to Robert d'Oilli of Oxford), and uterine brother, as Mr. Eyton observes (*Addl. MSS.*, 31,943, fol. 115), "to Henry d'Oilli of Hook-Norton." He appears in connection with Devonshire in the Pipe-Roll of 31 Hen. I., and is probably identical with Robert "brother" of Earl Reginald of Cornwall (*vide ante*. p. 82). He is mentioned as present (as "Robert fitz Edith") at the siege of Winchester, a few weeks later (*Sym. Dun.*, ii. 310), and he was among the witnesses to the Empress's charters (Oxford, 1142) to the earls of Oxford and of Essex, and to her charter (Devizes) to Geoffrey de Mandeville the younger (*vide post*). He subsequently witnessed Henry II.'s charter (? 1156) to Henry de Oxenford (*Cart. Ant.*, D., No. 42). See also *Liber Niger*. Working from misleading copies, Mr. Eyton wrongly identifies this Robert "filius Regis," as a witness to three charters of the Empress, with a Robert fitz Reginald (de Dunstanville) (*History of Shropshire*, ii. 271).

[5] Robert fitz Martin occurs in the Pipe-Roll of 31 Hen. I. in connection with Dorset. Dugdale and Mr. Eyton (*Addl. MSS.*, 31,943, fol. 90) affiliate him as son of a Martin of Tours, who had established himself in Wales. He witnessed two other charters of the Empress (*Journ. B. A. A.*, xxxi. 391, 395), both of them at Oxford. A son of his (filius Roberti filii Martini) held five knights' fees of Glastonbury Abbey in 1166.

(et Rob[ert]o fil[io] Heldebrand[i])[1] Apud Westmonaster[ium]).[2]

One cannot but be greatly struck by the names of the witnesses to this charter. The legate and his four brother prelates, who had been with the Empress in Winchester, at her reception on March 3, are here with her again at Westminster. So are her three inseparable companions; but where are the magnates of England? Two west-country earls, one of them of her own making,[3] and a few west-

[1] Robert fitz Hildebrand witnessed the Empress's second charter to Geoffrey with that to the Earl of Oxford (*vide post*). See for his adultery, treason, and shocking death (? 1143), *Gesta Stephani*, pp. 95, 96, where he is described as "virum plebeium quidem, sed militari virtute approbatum." He is also spoken of as "vir infimi generis, sed summæ semper militiæ machinator" (*ibid.*, p. 93). He is affiliated by the editors of Ordericus (Société de l'Histoire de France) as "Robert fils de Herbrand de Sauqueville" (iii. 45, iv. 420), where also we learn that he had refused to embark upon the White Ship. He was perhaps a brother of Richard fitz Hildebrand, who held five fees from the Abbot of Sherborne and five from the Bishop of Salisbury in 1166.

[2] As the closing names vary somewhat in the two transcripts, I give both versions:—

DUGDALE MS.	ASHMOLE MS.
"Rad Lond' et Rad' painel et W. Maminot et Rob' fil. R. et Rob' fil. Martin et Rob' fil Heldebrand' apud Westmonasterium."	"Rad lovell et Rad Painell et W. Maminot et Roberto filio R. et Roberto filio Martin Roberto filio *Haidebrandi apud Oxford*."

The three last words are added in a different hand, and "Oxford" appears to have been substituted for "Westmr" by yet another hand.

[3] William de Moiun (Mohun) had attested *eo nomine* the charter to Glastonbury (*Journ. B. A. A.*, xxxi. 389; *Adam de Domerham*) which probably passed soon after the election of the Empress (April 8) at Winchester (see p. 83). He now attests, among the earls, as "*Comite Willelmo de Moion*." This fixes his creation as April—June, 1141. Courthope gives no date for the creation, and no authority but his foundation-charter to Bruton, in which he styles himself "Comes Somersetensis." Dr. Stubbs, following him, gives (under "dates and authorities for the empress's earldoms") no date and no further authority (*Const. Hist.*, i. 362). Mr. Maxwell Lyte, in his learned and valuable monograph on *Dunster and its Lords* (1882), quotes the *Gesta Stephani* for the fact "that at the siege of Winchester, in 1140, the empress bestowed on William de Mohun the title of Earl of Dorset" (p. 6). But Winchester was besieged in (August—September) 1141, not in

country barons virtually complete the list. I do not say that these were, of necessity, the sole constituents of her court; but there is certainly the strongest possible presumption that had she been joined in person by any number of bishops or nobles, we should not have found so important a charter witnessed merely by the members of the *entourage* that she had brought up with her from the west. We have, for instance, but to compare this list with that of the witnesses to Stephen's charter six months later.[1] Or, indeed, we may compare it, to some disadvantage, with that of the Empress herself a month later at Oxford.[2] Where were the primate and the Bishop of London? Where was the King of Scots? These questions are difficult to answer. It may, however, be suggested that the general disgust at her intolerable arrogance,[3] and her harshness to the king,[4] kept the magnates from attending her court.[5] Her inability to repel the queen's forces, and

1140, and though the writer does speak of "Willelmus de Mohun, quem comitem ibi statuit Dorsetiæ" (p. 81), this charter proves that he postdates the creation, as he also does that of Hereford, which he assigns to the same siege (cf. pp. 125, n., 194). Mr. Doyle, with his usual painstaking care, places the creation (on the same authority) "before September, 1141" (which happens, it will be seen, to be quite correct), and assigns his use of the above style ("comes Somersetensis") to 1142. See also, on this point, p. 277 *infra*.

[1] See p. 143.

[2] The grant of the earldom of Hereford to Miles of Gloucester.

[3] "Erecta est autem in superbiam intolerabilem . . . et omnium fere corda a se alienavit" (*Hen. Hunt.*, 275).

[4] "Interpellavit dominam Anglorum regina pro domino suo rege capto et custodiæ ac vinculis mancipato. Interpellata quoque est pro eadem causa et a majoribus seu primoribus Angliæ; . . . at illa non exaudivit eos" (*Cont. Flor. Wig.*, 132).

[5] All this, however, is subject to the assumption that this charter passed at Westminster. That assumption rests on Dugdale's transcript and his statement to that effect in his *Baronage*. There is nothing in the charter (except, of course, the above difficulty) inconsistent with this statement, which is strongly supported by the Valoines charter; but, unfortunately, the transcript I have quoted from gives *Oxford* as the place of testing. But, then, the word (*vide supra*) appears to have been added in a later hand, and may have been inserted from confusion with the Empress's *second* charter to Geoffrey, which did pass at Oxford. Still, there is no actual reason why

CONTRAST WITH STEPHEN'S CHARTER. 97

her instant flight before the Londoners, are alike suggestive of the fact that her followers were comparatively few.

There are several points of constitutional importance upon which this instructive charter sheds some welcome light.

In the first place we should compare it with Stephen's charter (p. 51), to which, in Mr. Eyton's words, it forms the "counter-patent."[1] In the former the words of creation are: "Sciatis me fecisse comitem de Gaufredo," etc. In the charter of the Empress they run thus: "Sciatis ... quod ... do et concedo Gaufredo de Magnavilla ... ut sit Comes," etc. This contrast is in itself conclusive as to the earldom having been first *created* by Stephen and then *recognized* by the Empress. This being so, it is the more strange that Mr. Eyton should have arrived at the contrary conclusion, especially as he noticed the stronger form in the charter creating the earldom of Hereford (" Sciatis me fecisse Milonem de Glocestriâ Comitem"), a form corresponding with that in Stephen's charter to Geoffrey. The earldom of Hereford being *created* by the Empress, as that of Essex had been by Stephen, we find the same formula duly employed by both. The distinction thus established is one of considerable importance.

The special grant of the "tertius denarius" is a point of such extreme interest in its bearing on earls and earldoms that it requires to be separately discussed in a note devoted to the subject.[2]

But without dwelling at greater length upon the peerage aspect of this charter, let us see how it illustrates the

this charter may not have passed at Oxford, though its subject makes Westminster, perhaps, the more likely place of the two. Personally, I feel no doubt whatever that Westminster was the place.

[1] See p. 42.
[2] See Appendix H : "The Tertius Denarius."

98 THE FIRST CHARTER OF THE EMPRESS.

ambitious policy pursued in this struggle by the feudal nobles. Dr. Stubbs writes :—

"It is possible that the frequent tergiversations which mark the struggle may have been caused by the desire of obtaining confirmation of the rank [of earl] from both the competitors for the crown."[1]

But it is my contention that Geoffrey and his fellows were playing a deeper game. We find each successive change of side on the part of this unscrupulous magnate marked by a distinct advance in his demands and in the price he obtained. Broadly speaking, he was master of the situation, and he put himself and his fortress up to auction. Thus he obtained from the impassioned rivals a rapid advance at each bid. Compare, for instance, this charter with that he had obtained from Stephen, or, again, compare it with those which are to follow.

The very length of this charter, as compared with Stephen's, is significant enough in itself. But its details are far more so. Stephen's grant had not explicitly included the *tertius denarius ;* the Empress grants him the *tertius denarius* "sicut comes habere debet in comitatu suo."[2] But what may be termed the characteristic features are to be found in such clauses as those dealing with the license to fortify, and with the grants of lands.[3] These latter, indeed, teem with information, not only for the local, but for the general historian, as in the case of Theobald's forfeiture. But their special information is rather in the light they throw on the nature of these grants, and on the sources from which the Empress, like her rival, strove to gratify the greed of these insatiable nobles.

Foremost among these were those "extravagant grants

---

[1] *Const. Hist.*, i. 362.

[2] This, however, raises the question of comital rights, on which see pp. 143, 169, 269, and Appendix H.

[3] Cf. William of Malmesbury : "Hi prædia, hi castella, postremo quæcunque semel collibuisset, petere non verebantur."

of Crown lands" spoken of by Dr. Stubbs and by Gneist.[1]
Now, in this charter, and in those which follow, we are
enabled to trace the actual working of this fatal policy in
practice. The Empress begins, in this charter, by granting Geoffrey, for this is its effect, £100 a year in land
("C libratas terræ"). Stephen, we shall find, a few
months later, regains him to his side by increasing the
bid to £300 a year ("CCC libratas terræ"). But how is the
amount made up? It is charged on the Crown lands in
his own county of Essex. But observe, for this is an
important point, that it is not charged as a lump sum on
the entire *corpus comitatus* (or, to speak more exactly, on
the annual *firma* of that *corpus*), but on certain specified
estates. Here we have a welcome allusion to the practice
of the early Exchequer. The charter authorizes Geoffrey,
as sheriff, to deduct from the annual ferm of the county,
for which he was responsible at the Exchequer (being that
recorded on the *Rotulus exactorius*), that portion of it
represented by the annual rents (*redditus*) of Maldon and
Newport, which, as estates of Crown demesne, had till
then been included in the *corpus*.[2] From the earliest
Pipe-Rolls now remaining we know that the estates so
alienated were usually entered by the sheriff under the
head of "*Terræ Datæ*," with the amount due from each,
for which amounts, of course, he claimed allowance in his
account. I think we have here at least a suggestion that
even at the height of the anarchy and of the struggle,
the Exchequer, with all the details of its practice, was
recognized as in full existence. I have never been able

[1] See also Mr. S. R. Bird's valuable essay on the Crown Lands in vol. xiii. of the *Antiquary*. He refers (p. 160) to the "extensive alienations of these lands during the turbulent reign of Stephen, in order to enable that monarch to endow the new earldoms."

[2] "Quod auferat de summâ firma vicecomitatus quantum pertinuerit ad Meldonam et Niweport que ei donavi."

to reconcile myself to the accepted view, as set forth by Dr. Stubbs, of the "stoppage of the administrative machinery"[1] under Stephen. He holds that on the arrest of the bishops (June, 1139) "the whole administration of the country ceased to work," and that Stephen was "never able to restore the administrative machinery."[2] Crippled and disorganized though it doubtless was, the Exchequer, I contend, must have preserved its existence, because its existence was an absolute necessity. Without an exchequer, the income of the Crown would, obviously, have instantly disappeared. Moreover, the case of William of Ypres, and others to which reference will be made below, will go far to establish the important fact that the Exchequer system remained in force, and that accounts of some kind must have been kept.

The next point to which I would call attention is the expression "pro tanto quantum inde reddi solebat die quâ Rex Henricus fuit vivus et mortuus," which is applied to Maldon and Newport. The Pipe-Rolls, it should be remembered, only took cognizance of the total ferm of the shire. The constituents of that ferm were a matter for the sheriff. At first sight, therefore, these expressions might seem to cause some difficulty. Their explanation, however, is this. Just as I have shown in *Domesday Studies*[3] that the ferm of a town, as in the case of Huntingdon, was in truth the aggregate of several distinct and separate ferms, so the ferm of a county must have comprised the separate and distinct ferms of each of the royal estates. That ferm would be a customary, that is, fixed, *redditus* (or, as the charter expresses it, "quantum inde reddi solebat"). A particularly striking case in point is afforded by Hatfield Regis (*alias* Hatfield Broadoak). When Stephen increased the alienation of Crown demesne

[1] *Select Charters.*   [2] *Const. Hist.*, i. 326, 327.
[3] *Domesday Studies*, vol. i. (Longmans), 1887.

to Geoffrey, he granted him Hatfield *inter alia* "pro quater xx libris," that is, as representing £80 a year. This same estate, after the fall of Geoffrey, was alienated anew to Richard de Luci, and in the early Pipe-Rolls of Henry II. we read, under "Terræ Datæ" in Essex, "Ricardo de Luci quater xx libræ numero in Hadfeld." That is to say, in his annual account, the sheriff claimed to be allowed £80 off the amount of his ferm, in respect of the alienated estate. Now, the Domesday valuation of this manor is fortunately very precise : "Tunc Manerium valuit xxxvi libras. Modo lx. Sed vicecomes recipit inde lxxx libras et c solidos de gersuma" (ii. 2 b). The Domesday *redditus* of the manor, therefore, had remained absolutely unchanged. In such cases of alienation of demesne, it was, obviously, the object of the grantee that the manor should be valued as low as possible, while that of the sheriff was precisely the reverse. It was on this account doubtless, to prevent dispute, that these charters carefully named the sum at which the manor was to be valued, either in figures, as in the case of Bonhunt,[1] or, as in that of Maldon and Newport, in the formula "quantum inde reddi solebat" at the death of Henry I., this formula probably implying that the earlier ferm had been forced up in the days of the Lion of Justice.

The conclusion I would draw from the above argument is that the sheriff was not at liberty to exact arbitrary sums from the demesne lands of the Crown. A fixed annual render (*redditus*) was due to him from each, though this, like the *firma* of the sheriff himself, was liable to revision from time to time.[2]

[1] It is in this case alone, in the Empress's charter, that we can compare the value with that in Domesday. The charter grants it "pro xl solidis." In Domesday we read "Tunc et post valuit xl solidos. Modo lv" (ii. 98).

[2] See an illustration of this principle, some years later, in the *Chronicle of Ramsey* (p. 287): "Sciatis me concessisse Abbati de Rameseia ut ad

But it would be difficult to overestimate the importance of evidence which forms a connecting link between Domesday and the period of the Pipe-Rolls, especially if it throws some fresh light on the vexed question of Domesday values. Moreover, we have here an obvious suggestion as to the purpose of the Conqueror in ascertaining values, at least so far as concerned the demesne lands of the Crown, for he was thus enabled to check the sheriffs, by obtaining a basis for calculating the amount of the *firma comitatus*. With this point we shall have to deal when we come to Geoffrey's connection with the shrievalty of Essex and Herts.

Attention may also be called to the formula of "excambion" (as the Scottish lawyers term it) here employed, for it would seem to be earlier than any of those quoted in Madox's *Formularium*. But the suggested exchange is specially interesting in the case of Count Theobald, because it gives us an historical fact not elsewhere mentioned, namely, that the Empress, on obtaining the mastery, forfeited his lands at once. Her doing so, we should observe, is in strict accordance with the chroniclers' assertions as to her wholesale forfeitures and her special hostility to Stephen's house. And we can go further still. We can ascertain not only that Count Theobald was forfeited, as we have seen, by the Empress, but also that the land she forfeited had been given him by Stephen himself. In a document which I have previously referred to, we read that Stephen had given him the "manor" of Maldon,[1] being that manor of Crown demesne which the Empress here bestows upon Geoffrey.

firmam habeat hundredum de Hyrstintan reddendo inde quoque anno quatuor marcas argenti, quicunque sit vicecomes ita ne vicecomes plus ab eo requirat."

[1] "Die quâ dedi Manerium illud [de Meldonâ] Comiti Theobaldo."— Westminster Abbey Charters (Madox's *Baronia*, p. 232, note).

Another important though difficult subject upon which this charter bears is that of knight-service. Indeed, considering its early date—a quarter of a century earlier than the returns contained in the *Liber Niger*—it may, in conjunction with Stephen's charter of some six months later, be pronounced to be among our most valuable evidences for what Dr. Stubbs describes as "a subject on which the greatest obscurity prevails."[1]

Let us first notice that the Empress grants "feodum et servicium xx militum," while Stephen grants "lx milites feudatos . . . scilicet servicium" of so and so "pro [lx] militibus." Thus, then, the "milites feudatos" of Stephen equates the "feodum et servicium . . . militum" of the Empress. And, further, it repeats the remarkable expression employed by Florence of Worcester when he tells us that the Conqueror instructed the Domesday Commissioners to ascertain "quot milites feudatos" his tenants-in-chief possessed, that is to say, how many knights they had enfeoffed. But the Empress in her charter complicates her grant by adding the special clause: "Et servicium istorum xx militum faciet mihi separatim preter aliud servicium alterius feodi sui." Had it not been for this clause, one might have inferred that the object of the grant was to transfer to Earl Geoffrey the "servicium" of these twenty knights' fees due, of right, to the Crown, so that he might enjoy all such profits as the Crown would have derived from that "servicium," and, at the same time, have employed these knights as substitutes for those which he was bound to furnish, from his own fief, to the Crown. But the above clause is fatal to such a view. Again, both in the charters

---

[1] *Const. Hist.*, i. 260. See my articles on the "Introduction of Knight Service into England" in *English Historical Review*, July and October, 1891, January, 1892. See also Addenda (p. 439).

of the Empress and of her rival, these special grants of knights and their "servicium" are kept entirely distinct from those of Crown demesne or escheated land, which, moreover, are expressed in terms of the "librata terræ." On the whole I lean strongly to the belief that, although the working of the arrangement may be obscure, the object of Geoffrey was to add to the number of the knights who followed his standard, and thus to increase his power as a noble and the weight that he could throw into the scale. And the special clause referred to above would imply that the Crown was to have a claim on him for twenty knights more than those whom he was bound to furnish from his own fief.

Lastly, we may note the identity of the formula employed for the grant of lands and for that of knights' service. In each case the grant is made "pro tanto,"[1] and in each case the Empress undertakes to make good ("perficere") the balance to him within the limit of the three counties of Essex, Cambridgeshire, and Herts.[2]

With the subject of castles I propose to deal later on. But there is one point on which the evidence of this charter is perhaps more important than on any other, and that is in the retrospective light which it throws on the system of reform introduced by the first Henry.

Incidentally, we have here witness to that system, of which the Pipe-Roll of 1130 is the solitary but vivid

---

[1] The lands were granted "pro tanto quantum inde reddi solebat," and the knights' service (of Graaland de Tany) " pro tanto servicii quantum de feodo illo debent," which amount is given in Stephen's charter as 7½ knights' service (as also in the *Liber Niger*).

[2] "Et si quid defuerit ad C libratas perficiendas, perficiam ei in loco competenti in Essexiâ aut in Hertfordescirâ aut in Cantebriggscirâ . . . . et totum superplus istorum xx. militum ei perficiam in prenominatis tribus comitatibus."

exponent, and under which the very name of "plea" became a terror to all men. Every man was liable, on the slightest pretext, to be brought within the meshes of the law, with the object, as it seemed, and at least with the result, of swelling the royal hoard (cf. pp. 11, 12, *n.* 1). Even to secure one's simplest rights money had always to be paid. Thus, here, Geoffrey stipulates that he and his men are to hold their possessions " sine placito," and " ita quod . . . non ponantur in ullo modo in placito de aliquo forisfacto," etc., etc. So again, in his later charter, we find him insisting that he and they shall hold all their possessions " sine placito et sine pecuniæ donatione," and that " Rectum eis teneatur de eorum calumpniis sine pecuniæ donatione." The exactions he dreaded meet us at every turn on the Pipe-Roll of 1130.

But, on the other hand, the charter, broadly speaking, illustrates, by the retrograde concessions it extorts, the cardinal factor in the long struggle between the feudal nobles and their lord the king, namely, their jealousy of that royal jurisdiction by which the Crown strove, and eventually with success, to break their semi-independent power, and to bring the whole realm into uniform subjection to the law.

After the clauses conferring on Geoffrey the *hereditary* shrievalty of Essex, a matter which I shall discuss further on, there immediately follows this passage, the most significant, as I deem it, in the whole charter :—

" Et ut sit Capitalis Justicia in Essexiâ hereditabiliter mea et heredum meorum de placitis et forisfactis que pertinuerint ad coronam meam, ita quod non mittam aliam justiciam super eum in comitatu illo nisi ita sit quod aliquando mittam aliquem de paribus suis qui audiat cum illo quod placita mea juste tractentur."

The first point to be dealt with here is the phrase " *Capitalis* Justicia in Essexiâ." Here we have the term "capitalis" applied to the *justicia* of a single county. On this I would lay some stress, for it has been generally supposed that this style was reserved for the Great Justiciary, the *alter ego* of the king himself.[1]

In his learned observations on the "obscurities" of the style "*justitia* or *justitiarius*," Dr. Stubbs writes that "the *capitalis justitia* seems to be the only one of the body to whom a determinate position as the king's representative is assigned in formal documents" (i. 389). It was probably the object of Geoffrey, when he secured this particular style, to obtain for himself all the powers vested in "the king's representative," and so to provide against his supersession by a justiciar claiming in that capacity.

Let us now examine the witness of the charter to the differentiation of the sheriff (*vicecomes*) and the justice (*justitia*), for that is the development which its terms involve.

Dr. Stubbs points out that, under the Norman kings, "the authority of the sheriff, when he was relieved from the company of the ealdorman, . . . would have no check except the direct control of the king" (i. 272); and Gneist similarly observed that "After the withdrawal of the eorl, the Anglo-Saxon shir-gerefa became the regular governor of the county, who was henceforth no longer dependent upon the eorl, but upon the personal orders of

[1] Dr. Stubbs writes: "From the reign of Henry I. we have distinct traces of a judicial system, a supreme court of justice, called the Curia Regis, presided over by the king or justiciary, and containing other judges also called justiciars, the chief being occasionally distinguished by the title of 'summus,' 'magnus,' or 'capitalis'" (*Const. Hist.*, i. 377). But, in another place, he points out, of the Great Justiciar, Roger of Salisbury, that "several other ministers receive the same name [*justitiarius*] even during the time at which he was actually in office; even the title of *capitalis justitiarius* is given to officers of the *Curia Regis* who were acting in subordination to him" (i. 350). Of this he gives instances in point (i. 389). On the whole it is safest, perhaps, to hold, as Dr. Stubbs suggested, that the style "capitalis" was not reserved to the Great Justiciar alone till the reign of Henry II. (i. 350).

the king, and upon the organs of the Norman central administration" (i. 140). And for a period of transition between the two systems, the Anglo-Saxon and the late Norman, the sheriff not only presided, in his court, as its sole lay head, but also in a dual capacity. Dr. Stubbs, it is true, with his wonted caution, does but suggest it as "probable that whilst the sheriff in his character of sheriff was competent to direct the customary business of the court, it was in that of *justitia* that he transacted special business under the king's writ."[1] But Gneist treats of him, under a separate heading, in his capacity of "royal justiciary" (i. 142). It is from this dual position that there developed, by specialization of function, two distinct officers, the sheriff (*vicecomes*) and the justice (*justicia*). This is the development which, as yet, has been somewhat imperfectly apprehended.

The centralizing policy of Henry I., operating through the *Curia Regis*, has, I need hardly observe, been admirably explained by Dr. Stubbs. He has shown how two methods were employed to attain the end in view: the one, to call up certain pleas from the local courts to the *curia*; the other, to send down the officers of the *curia* to sit in the local courts.[2] In the latter case, the royal officer ("justicia") appeared as the representative of the central power of which the *Curia Regis* was the exponent. Thus, there were, again, for the county court two lay presidents, but they were now the sheriff, as local authority, and the justice, who represented the central. Such an arrangement was, of course, a step in advance for the Crown, which had thus secured for itself, through its justice, a footing in the local courts.[3] But with this arrangement

---

[1] *Const. Hist.*, i. 389, *note*.
[2] See Appendix I.
[3] I cannot quite understand Gneist's view that "A better spirit is infused

neither side was able to rest satisfied. Broadly speaking, if I may be allowed the expression, the Crown sought to centralize the sheriff, and to exclude the local element; the feudatories would fain have localized the justice, and so have excluded the central. Thus, before the close of Henry's reign, he had actually employed on a large scale the officers of his *curia* as sheriffs of counties, and "by these means," as Dr. Stubbs observes, "the king and justiciar kept in their hands the reins of the entire judicial administration" (i. 392).[1] The same policy was faithfully followed by his grandson, a generation later, on the occasion of the inquest of sheriffs (1170), when, says Dr. Stubbs, "the sheriffs removed from their offices were most of them local magnates, whose chances of oppression and whose inclination towards a feudal administration of justice were too great. In their place Henry instituted officers of the Exchequer, less closely connected with the counties by property, and more amenable to royal influence, as well as more skilled administrators—another step towards the concentration of the provincial jurisdiction under the *Curia Regis*."[2]

into this portion of the legal administration by the severance of the farm-interest (*firma*) from the judicial functions, which was effected by the appointment of royal *justitiarii* in the place of the *vicecomes*. The reservation of the royal right of interference now develops into a periodical delegation of matters to criminal judges" (i. 180). It is probable that this eminent jurist has a right conception of the change, and that, if it is obscured, it is only by his mode of expression. But, when arguing from the laws of Cnut and of Henry, as to pleas "in firma," he might, if one may venture to say so, have added the higher evidence of Domesday. There are several passages in the Great Survey bearing upon this subject, of which the most noteworthy is, I think, this, which is found in the passage on Shrewsbury:—" Siquis pacem regis manu propria datam scienter infringebat utlagus fiebat. Qui vero pacem regis a vicecomite datam infringebat, C solidos emendabat, et tantundem dabat qui Forestel vel Heinfare faciebat. *Has iii forisfacturas* habebat in dominio rex E. in omni Angliâ extra firmas" (i. 152).

[1] See Appendix I : "Vicecomites" and "Custodes."
[2] *Select Charters*, 141.

This passage enables us to see how essentially contrary to the policy of the Crown were the provisions of Geoffrey's charter. It not only feudalized the local shrievalty by placing it in the hands of a feudal magnate, and, further still, making it hereditary, but it seized upon the centralizing office of justice, and made it as purely local, nay, as feudal as the other.

But let us return to the point from which we started, namely, the witness of Geoffrey's charter to the differentiation of the sheriff and the justice. It proves that the sheriff could no longer discharge the functions of "a royal justiciary," without a separate appointment to that distinct office. When we thus learn how Geoffrey became both sheriff and justice of Essex, we can approach in the light of that appointment the writ addressed " Ricardo de Luci Justic' et Vicecomiti de Essexa," on which Madox relies for Richard's tenure of the post of chief justiciary.[1] It may be that Richard's appointment corresponded with that of Geoffrey. But whatever uncertainty there may be on this point, there can be none on the parallel between Geoffrey's charter and that which Henry I. granted to the citizens of London. Indeed, in all municipal charters of the fullest and best type, we find the functions of the sheriff and the justice dealt with in the same successive order. The striking thought to be drawn from this is that the feudatories and the towns, though their interests were opposed *inter se*, presented to the Crown the same attitude and sought from it the same exemptions. In proof of this I here adduce three typical charters, arranged in chronological order. The first is an extract from that important charter which London obtained from Henry I., the second is taken from Geoffrey's charter, and the third

---

[1] Foss's *Judges*, i. 145.

from that of Richard I. to Colchester, which I quote because it contains the same word "justicia," and also because it is, probably, little, if at all, known.

CHARTER OF HENRY I. TO LONDON.	CHARTER OF THE EMPRESS TO GEOFFREY.	CHARTER OF RICHARD I. TO COLCHESTER.
"Ipsi cives ponent *vicecomitem* qualem voluerint de se ipsis, *et justitiarium* qualem voluerint de se ipsis ad custodiendum placita coronæ meæ et eadem placitanda; et nullus alius erit Justitiarius super ipsos homines Londoniarum."	"Concedo ei et heredibus suis . . . *vicecomitatum* Essexie. Et ut sit Capitalis *Justicia* . . . de placitis et forisfactis que pertinuerint ad coronam meam, ita quod non mittam aliam Justiciam super eum in comitatu illo," etc.	"Ipsi ponant de se ipsis *Ballivos* quoscunque voluerint et *Justiciam* ad servanda placita Coronæ nostræ et ad placitanda eadem placita infra Burgum suum et quod nullus alius sit inde Justicia nisi quem elegerint."

Here we have the two offices similarly distinct throughout. We have also the *ballivi*, representing to the town what the *vicecomes* represents to the shire, a point which it is necessary to bear in mind. The "bailiff," so far as the town was concerned, stood in the sheriff's shoes. So also did the "coroner" (or "coroners") in those of the justice. Indeed, at Colchester, two "coroners" represented the "justice" of the charter. I cannot find that Dr. Stubbs calls attention to the fact of this twin privilege, the fact that exemption from the sheriff and from the justice went, in these charters, hand in hand.

Lastly, we should observe that though, in these charters, the clause relating to the sheriff precedes that which relates to the justice, yet, conversely, in the enumeration of those to whom a charter is directed, "justices" are invariably, I believe, given the precedence of "sheriffs." This, which would seem to have passed unnoticed, may have an important bearing. Ordericus, in a famous passage (xi. 2) describing Henry's ministers, tells us how the king

"favorabiliter illi obsequentes de ignobili stirpe illustravit, de pulvere, ut ita dicam, extulit, dataque multiplici facultate *super* consules et illustres oppidanos exaltavit. . . . Illos . . . rex, cum de infimo genere essent, nobilitavit, regali auctoritate de imo erexit, in fastigio potestatum constituit, ipsis etiam spectabilibus regni principibus formidabiles effecit."

Observe how vivid a light such a passage as this throws upon the clause in Geoffrey's charter:—

"Non mittam aliam Justiciam *super* eum in Comitatu illo, nisi ita sit quod aliquando mittam aliquem de paribus suis qui audiat cum illo quod placita mea juste tractentur."

The whole clause breathes the very spirit of feudalism. It betrays the hatred of Geoffrey and his class for those upstarts, as they deemed them, the royal justices, who, clad in all the authority of the Crown, intruded themselves into their local courts and checked them in the exercise of their power. Henceforth, in the courts of the favoured earl, the representative of the Crown was to make his appearance not regularly, but only now and then ("aliquando"); moreover, when he came, he was to figure in court not as the superior ("super eum"), but as the colleague ("cum illo") of the earl; and, lastly, he was not to belong to the upstart ministerial class: he was to be one of his own class—of his "peers" ("de paribus suis").

As an illustrative parallel to this clause, I am tempted to quote a remarkable charter, unnoticed, it would seem, not only by our historians, but even by Mr. Eyton himself. The Assize of Clarendon, a quarter of a century (1166) after the date of our charter to Geoffrey, contained clauses specially aimed against such exemption as he sought. Referring to these clauses, Dr. Stubbs writes:—

"No franchise is to exclude the justices. . . . In the article which directs the admission of the justices into every franchise may be

112 THE FIRST CHARTER OF THE EMPRESS.

detected one sign of the anti-feudal policy which the king had all his life to maintain."[1]

But the clauses in question, though their sweeping character fully justifies this description,[2] contrast strangely with the humble, almost apologetic, charter in which Henry II., immediately afterwards, announces that he is only sending his "justicia" into the patrimony of St. Cuthbert "by permission" of the bishop, and as a quite exceptional measure, not to be taken again. It throws, perhaps, some new light on the character and methods of the king, when we find him thus stooping, in form, to gain his point in fact.

"Henricus Rex Angl' et Dux Normann' et Aquitan' et Comes Andegav', justiciariis Vicecomitibus et omnibus ministris suis de Eborac'sir et de Nordhummerlanda salutem. Sciatis quod consilio Baronum meorum,[3] et Episcopi Dunelmensis licencia, mitto hac vice in terram sancti Cuthberti justiciam meam, quæ[4] videat ut fiat justicia secundum assisam meam de latronibus et murdratoribus et roboratoribus;[5] non quia velim ut trahatur in consuetudinem tempore meo vel heredum meorum, sed ad tempus hoc facio, pro prædicta necessitate; quia volo quod terra beati Cuthberti suas habeat libertates et antiquas consuetudines, sicut unquam melius habuit. T. Gavfrido Archiepiscopo [sic] Cant. Ric. Arch. Pictav. Comite Gaufrido, Ricardo de Luci. Apud Wodestoc."[6]

[1] *Const. Hist.*, i. 470.
[2] "Nulli sint in civitate vel burgo vel castello, vel extra, nec in honore etiam de Walingeford, qui vetent vicecomites [sic] intrare in terram suam vel socam suam." Strictly speaking, this refers to sheriffs, but *à fortiori* it would apply to the king's "justicia."
[3] The Assize of Clarendon describes itself as passed "de consilio omnium baronum suorum."
[4] Notice the "justicia . . . quæ videat," as answering to the "aliquis . . . qui audiat" in Geoffrey's charter.
[5] These are the words of the Assize itself, which deals throughout with "robatores," "murdratores," and "latrones."
[6] This charter is limited, by the names of the witnesses, to 1163-1166.

The first charter of the Empress has now been sufficiently discussed. It was, of course, his possession of the Tower that enabled Geoffrey to extort such terms, the command of that fortress being essential to the Empress, to overawe the disaffected citizens.

It can only, therefore, refer to the Assize of Clarendon, which conclusion is confirmed by its language. It must consequently have been granted immediately after it, before the king left England in March. Observe that the two last witnesses are the very justices who were entrusted with the execution of the Assize, and that "Earl Geoffrey," by the irony of fate, was no other than the son and successor of Geoffrey de Mandeville himself.

CHAPTER V.

THE LOST CHARTER OF THE QUEEN.

It was at the very hour when the Empress seemed to have attained the height of her triumph that her hopes were dashed to the ground.[1] The disaster, as is well known, was due to her own behaviour. As Dr. Stubbs has well observed, " She, too, was on the crest of the wave and had her little day . . . she had not learned wisdom or conciliation, and threw away opportunities as recklessly as her rival."[2] Indeed, even William of Malmesbury hints that the fault was hers.[3]

The Queen, having pleaded in vain for her husband, resolved to appeal to arms. Advancing on Southwark at the head of the forces which she had raised from Kent, and probably from Boulogne, she ravaged the lands of the citizens with fire and sword before their eyes.[4] The

---

[1] " Ecce, dum ipsa putaretur omni Anglia statim posse potiri, mutata omnia " (*Will. Malms.*, p. 749).

[2] *Early Plantagenets*, p. 22 ; *Const. Hist.*, i. 330.

[3] " Satisque constat quod si ejus (*i.e.* comitis) moderationi et sapientiæ a suis esset creditum, non tam sinistrum postea sensissent aleæ casum " (p. 749).

[4] " Regina quod prece non valuit, armis impetrare confidens, splendidissimum militantium decus ante Londonias, ex alterâ fluvii regione, transmisit, utque raptu, et incendio, violentiâ, et gladio, in comitissæ suorumque prospectu, ardentissime circa civitatem desævirent præcepit " (*Gesta Stephani*, p. 78). These expressions appear to imply that she not only wasted the southern bank, but sent over (*transmisit*) her troops to plunder round the walls of the city itself (*circa civitatem*). Mr. Pearson strangely assigns this action not to the Queen, but to the Empress : " Matilda brought up troops, and cut off the trade of the citizens, and wasted their lands, to punish their disaffection " (p. 478).

citizens, who had received the Empress but grudgingly, and were already alarmed by her haughty conduct, were now reduced to desperation. They decided on rising against their new mistress, and joining the Queen in her struggle for the restoration of the king.[1] There is a stirring picture in the *Gesta* of the sudden sounding of the *tocsin*, and of the citizens pouring forth from the gates amidst the clanging of the bells. The Empress was taken so completely by surprise that she seems to have been at table at the time, and she and her followers, mounting in haste, had scarcely galloped clear of the suburbs when the mob streamed into her quarters and rifled them of all that they contained. So great, we are told, was the panic of the fugitives that they scattered in all directions, regardless of the Empress and her fate. Although the *Gesta* is a hostile source, the evidence of its author is here confirmed by that of the Continuator of Florence.[2] William of Malmesbury, however, writing as a partisan, will not allow that the Empress and her brother were thus ignominiously expelled, but asserts that they withdrew in military array.[3]

The Empress herself fled to Oxford, and, afraid to remain even there, pushed on to Gloucester. The king, it is true, was still her prisoner, but her followers were almost all dispersed ; and the legate, who had secured her triumph, was alienated already from her cause. Expelled

[1] The *Annals of Plympton* (ed. Liebermann, p. 20) imply that the city was divided on the subject:—"In mense Junio facta est sedicio in civitate Londoniensi a civibus; sed tamen pars sanior vices imperatricis agebat, pars vero quedam eam obpugnabat."

[2] "Facta conjuratione adversus eam quam cum honore susceperunt, cum dedecore apprehendere statuerunt. At illa a quodam civium præmunita, ignominiosam cum suis fugam arripuit omni sua suorumque supellectili post tergum relicta."

[3] "Sensim sine tumultu quadam militari disciplina urbe cesserunt." This is clearly intended to rebut the story of their hurried flight (see also p. 132, *infra*).

from the capital, and resisted in arms by no small portion of the kingdom, her *prestige* had received a fatal blow, and the moment for her coronation had passed away, never to return.[1]

Here we may pause to glance for a moment at a charter of singular interest for its mention of the citizens of London and their faithful devotion to the king.

" Hugo dei gratia Rothomagensis archiepiscopus senatoribus inclitis civibus honoratis et omnibus commune London concordie gratiam, salutem eternam. Deo et vobis agimus gratias pro vestra fidelitate stabili et certa domino nostro regi Stephano jugiter impensa. Inde per regiones notæ vestra nobilitas virtus et potestas."[2]

It is tempting to see in this charter—unknown, it would seem, to the historians of London—a mention of the famous "communa," the "tumor plebis, timor regni," of 1191. But the term, here, is more probably employed, as in the "communa liberorum hominum " of the Assize of Arms (1181), and the "communa totius terre " of the Great Charter (1215). At the same time, there are two expressions which occur at this very epoch, and which might support the former view. One is *conjuratio*, which, as we have seen, the Continuator applies to the action of the Londoners in 1141,[3] and which Richard of Devizes similarly applies to the commune of 1191.[4] The other is *communio*, which William of Malmesbury applies to their government in the previous April, and which the keen eye of Dr. Stubbs noted as "a description of municipal unity which suggests that the communal idea was already in existence as a basis of civil organization."[5] But he failed, it would seem, to observe the passage

[1] See Appendix J: "The Great Seal of the Empress."
[2] *Harl. MS.* 1708, fo. 113.   [3] "Conjuratione facta."
[4] "In indulta sibi conjuratione . . . quanta quippe mala ex conjuratione proveniunt" (ed. Howlett, p. 416).
[5] *Const. Hist.*, i. 407.

GEOFFREY SEIZES THE BISHOP. 117

which follows, and which speaks of "omnes barones, qui in eorum communionem jamdudum recepti fuerant." For in this allusion we recognize a distinctive practice of the "sworn commune," from that of Le Mans (1073),[1] to that of London (1191), "in quam universi regni magnates et ipsi etiam ipsius provinciæ episcopi jurare coguntur."[2]

Meanwhile, what of Geoffrey de Mandeville? A tale is told of him by Dugdale, and accepted without question by Mr. Clark,[3] which, so far as I can find, must be traced to the following passage in Trivet:—

"Igitur in die Nativitatis Præcursoris Domini [June 24], *obsessâ turri*, fugatur imperatrix de Londoniâ. Turrim autem Galfridus de Magnavillâ potenter defendit, et egressu facto, Robertum civitatis episcopum, partis adversæ fautorem, cepit apud manerium de Fulham."[4]

It is quite certain that this tale is untrustworthy as it stands. We have seen above that Trivet's date for the arrival of the Empress at London is similarly, beyond doubt, erroneous.[5] That the citizens, when they suddenly rose against the Empress, may also have blockaded Geoffrey in his tower, not only as her ally, but as their own natural enemy, is possible, nay, even probable. But that he ventured forth, through their ranks, to Fulham, when thus blockaded, is improbable, and that he captured the bishop as an enemy of the Empress is impossible, for the Empress herself had just installed him,[6] and we find him

---

[1] "Facta conspiratione quam *communionem* vocabant sese omnes pariter sacramentis adstringunt, et . . . ejusdem regionis proceres quamvis invitos, sacramentis suæ conspirationis obligari compelluut."

[2] *Richard of Devizes* (ed. Howlett, p. 416).

[3] *Mediæval Military Architecture*, ii. 254.

[4] Trivet's *Annals* (Eng. Hist. Soc., p. 13).   [5] See p. 84.

[6] "Primo quidem [apud Westmonasterium] quod decuit, sanctæ Dei Ecclesiæ, juxta bonorum consilium, consulere procuravit. Dedit itaque Lundoniensis ecclesiæ præsulatum cuidam Radingensi monacho viro venerabili præsente et jubente reverendo abbate suo Edwardo" (*Cont. Flor. Wig.*, 131).

118 *THE LOST CHARTER OF THE QUEEN.*

at her court a month later.[1] At the same time Trivet, we must assume, cannot have invented all this. His story must preserve a confused version of the facts as told in some chronicle now lost, or, at least, unknown.[2] On this assumption it may, perhaps, be suggested that Geoffrey was indeed blockaded in the Tower, but that when he accepted the Queen's offers, and thus made, as we shall see, common cause with the citizens, he signalized his defection from the cause of the Empress by seizing her adherent the bishop,[3] and holding him a prisoner till, as Holinshed implies, he purchased his freedom, and so became free to join the Empress at Oxford.[4]

And now let us come to the subject of this chapter, the lost charter of the Queen.

That this charter was granted is an historical fact hitherto absolutely unknown. No chronicler mentions the fact, nor is there a trace of any such document, or even of a transcript of its contents. And yet the existence of this charter, like that of the planet Neptune, can be established, in the words of Sir John Herschel, "with a certainty hardly inferior to ocular demonstration." The discovery, indeed, of that planet was effected (*magnis componere parva*) by strangely similar means. For as the perturbations of Uranus pointed to the existence of

---

[1] See p. 123.

[2] We have, indeed, a glimpse of this incident in the *Liber de Antiquis Legibus* (fol. 35), where we read: "Anno predicto, statim in illa estate, obsessa est Turris Londoniarum a Londoniensibus, quam Willielmus (*sic*) de Magnavilla tenebat et firmaverat."

[3] The city, it must be remembered, lay between him and Fulham, so that, obviously, he is more likely to have made this raid when the city was no longer in arms against him.

[4] We have a hint that the bishop was disliked by the citizens in the *Historia Pontificalis* (p. 532), where we learn (in 1148) that they had disobeyed the papal authority: "Quando episcopus bone memorie Robertus expulsus est, cui hanc exhibuere devocionem ut omni diligentia procurarent ne patri exulanti in aliquo prodessent."

GEOFFREY JOINS THE QUEEN.

Neptune, so the "perturbations" of Geoffrey de Mandeville point to the existence of this charter.

We know that the departure of the Empress was followed by the arrival of the Queen, with the result that Geoffrey was again in a position to demand his own terms. Had he continued to hold the Tower in the name of the Empress, he would have made it a thorn in the side of the citizens now that they had declared for her rival. We hear, moreover, at this crisis, of offers by the Queen to all those whom bribes or concessions could allure to her side.[1] We have, therefore, the strongest presumption that Geoffrey would be among the first to whom offers were made. But it is not on presumption that we depend. Stephen, we shall find, six months later, refers distinctly to this lost charter ("Carta Reginæ"),[2] and the Empress in turn, in the following year, refers to the charters of the king *and of the queen* ("quas Rex Stephanus *et Matildis regina* ei dederunt . . . sicut habet inde cartas illo*rum*").[3] Thus its existence is beyond question. And that it passed about this time may be inferred, not only from the circumstances of the case, but also from the most significant fact that, a few weeks later, at the siege of Winchester, we find Geoffrey supporting the Queen in active concert with the citizens.[4]

What were the terms of the charter by which he was

---

[1] "Regina autem a Londoniensibus suscepta, sexusque fragilitatis, feminæque mollitiei oblita, viriliter sese et virtuose continere; invictos ubique coadjutores prece sibi et pretio allicere, regis conjuratos ubi ubi per Angliam fuerant dispersi ad dominum suum secum reposcendum constanter sollicitare" (*Gesta Stephani*, 80). "Regina omnibus supplicavit, omnes pro ereptione mariti sui precibus, promissis, et obsequiis sollicitavit" (*Sym. Dun.*, ii. 310).

[2] See p. 143.   [3] See p. 167.

[4] "Gaufrido de Mandevillâ (*qui jam iterum auxilio eorum cesserat*, antea enim post captionem regis imperatrici fidelitatem juraverat) et Londoniensibus maxime annitentibus, nihilque omnino quod possent prætermittentibus quo imperatricem contristarent" (*Will. Malms.*, p. 752).

thus regained to his allegiance we cannot now tell. To judge, however, from that of Stephen, which was mainly a confirmation of its terms, it probably represented a distinct advance on the concessions he had wrung from the Empress.

It is an interesting fact, and one which probably is known to few, if any, that there is still preserved in the Public Record Office a solitary charter of the Queen, granted, I cannot but think, at this very crisis. As it is not long, I shall here quote it as a unique and instructive record.

"M. Regina Angl[ie] Omnibus fidelibus suis francis et Anglis salutem. Sciatis quod dedi Gervasio Justiciario de Lond[oniâ] x marcatas terræ in villâ de Gamelingeia pro servicio suo . . . donec ei persolvam debitum quod ei debeo, ut infra illum terminum habeat proficua que exibunt de villa predictâ . . . testibus Com[ite] Sim[one] et Ric[ardo] de Bolon[iâ] et Sim[one] de Gerardmot[a] et Warn[erio] de Lisor[iis]. apud Lond[oniam].[1]

The first of the witnesses, Earl Simon (of Northampton), is known to have been one of the three earls who adhered to the Queen during the king's captivity.[2] Richard of Boulogne was possibly a brother of her *nepos*, " Pharamus " of Boulogne, who is also known to have been with her.[3] Combining the fact of the charter being the Queen's with that of its subject-matter and that of its place of testing, we obtain the strongest possible presumption that it passed at this crisis, a presumption confirmed, as we have seen, by the name of the leading witness. The endeavour to fix the date of this charter is well worth the making. For it is not merely of interest

[1] *Royal Charters* (Duchy of Lancaster), No. 22. N.B.—The above is merely an extract from the charter.
[2] Waleran of Meulan, William of Warrenne, and Simon of Northampton (*Ord. Vit.*, v. 130).
[3] See p. 147.

as a record unique of its kind. If it is, indeed, of the date suggested, it is, to all appearance, the sole survivor of all those charters, such as that to Geoffrey, by which the Queen, in her hour of need, must have purchased support for the royal cause. We see her, like the queen of Henry III., like the queen of Charles I., straining every nerve to succour her husband, and to raise men and means. And as Henrietta Maria pledged her jewels as security for the loans she raised, so Matilda is here shown as pledging a portion of her ancestral "honour" to raise the sinews of war.[1]

But this charter, if the date I have assigned to it be right, does more for us than this. It gives us, for an instant, a precious glimpse of that of which we know so little, and would fain know so much—I mean the government of London. We learn from it that London had then a "justiciary," and further that his name was Gervase. Nor is even this all. The Gamlingay entry in the *Testa de Nevill* and *Liber Niger* enables us to advance a step further and to establish the identity of this Gervase with no other than Gervase of Cornhill.[2] The importance of this identification will be shown in a special appendix.[3]

Among those whom the Queen strove hard to gain was her husband's brother, the legate.[4] He had headed, as we have seen, the witnesses to Geoffrey's charter, but he was

---

[1] Gamlingay, in Cambridgeshire, had come to the Queen as belonging to "the honour of Boulogne."

[2] "Gamenegheia valet xxx li. Inde tenent . . heredes Gervas[ii] de Cornhill x li." (*Liber Niger*, 395; *Testa*, pp. 274, 275). This entry also proves that the loan (1141 ?) to the Queen was not repaid, and the property, therefore, not redeemed.

[3] See Appendix K : "Gervase de Cornhill."

[4] "Nunc quidem Wintoniensem episcopum, totius Angliæ legatum, ut fraternis compatiens vinculis ad eum liberandum intenderet, ut sibi maritum, plebi regem, regno patronum, toto secum nisu adquireret, viriliter supplicare" (*Gesta*, 80).

deeply injured at the failure of his appeal, on behalf of his family, to the Empress, and was even thought to have secretly encouraged the rising of the citizens of London.[1] He now kept aloof from the court of the Empress, and, having held an interview with the Queen at Guildford, resolved to devote himself, heart and soul, to setting his brother free.[2]

[1] *Gesta*, 79.
[2] *Will. Malms.*, p. 750; *Cont. Flor. Wig.*, 132; *Gesta*, 80; *Annals of Winchester.*

CHAPTER VI.

THE ROUT OF WINCHESTER.

THE Empress, it will be remembered, in the panic of her escape, on the sudden revolt of the citizens, had fled to the strongholds of her cause in the west, and sought refuge in Gloucester. Most of her followers were scattered abroad, but the faithful Miles of Gloucester was found, as ever, by her side. As soon as she recovered from her first alarm, she retraced her steps to Oxford, acting upon his advice, and made that fortress her head-quarters, to which her adherents might rally.[1]

To her stay at Oxford on this occasion we may assign a charter to Haughmond Abbey, tested *inter alios* by the King of Scots.[2] But of far more importance is the well-known charter by which she granted the earldom of Hereford to her devoted follower, Miles of Gloucester.[3] With singular unanimity, the rival chroniclers testify to the faithful service of which this grant was the reward.[4]

---

[1] "Porro fugiens domina per Oxenefordiam venit ad Glavorniam, ubi cum Milone ex-constabulario consilio inito statim cum eodem ad Oxenefordensem revertitur urbem, ibi præstolatura seu recuperatura suum dispersum militarem numerum" (*Cont. Flor. Wig.*, 132).

[2] The other witnesses were Robert, Bishop of London, Alexander, Bishop of Lincoln, William the chancellor, R[ichard] de Belmeis, archdeacon, G[ilbert?], archdeacon, Reginald, Earl of Cornwall, William Fitz Alan and Walter his brother, Alan de Dunstanville (*Harl. MS.*, 2188, fol. 123). The two bishops and the King of Scots also witnessed the charter to Miles.

[3] *Fœdera*, N.E., i. 14.

[4] "Et quia ejusdem Milonis præcipue fruebatur consilio et fovebatur auxilio, utpote quæ eatenus nec unius diei victum nec mensæ ipsius apparatum aliunde quam ex ipsius munificentiâ sive providentiâ acceperat sicut ex ipsius Milonis ore audivimus, ut eum suo arctius vinciret ministerio, comitatum ei Here-

It is an important fact that this charter contains a record of its date, which makes it a fixed point of great value for our story. This circumstance is the more welcome from the long list of witnesses, which enables us to give with absolute certainty the *personnel* of Matilda's court on the day this charter passed (July 25, 1141), evidence confirmed by another charter omitted from the fasciculus of Mr. Birch.[1] From a comparison of the dates we can assign these documents to the very close of her stay at Oxford, by which time her scattered followers had again rallied to her standard. It is also noteworthy that the date is in harmony with the narrative of the Continuator of Florence. This has a bearing on the chronology of that writer, to which we have now in the main to trust.

William of Malmesbury, who on the doings of his patron is likely to be well informed, tells us that the rumours of the legate's defection led the Earl of Gloucester to visit Winchester in the hope of regaining him to his sister's cause. Disappointed in this, he rejoined her at Oxford.[2] It must have been on his return that he witnessed the charter to Miles of Gloucester.

The Empress, on hearing her brother's report, decided to march on Winchester with the forces she had now assembled.[3] The names of her leading followers can be recovered from the various accounts of the siege.[4]

---

fordensem tunc ibi posita pro magnæ remunerationis contulit præmio" (*Cont. Flor. Wig.*, 133). Comp. *Gesta*, 81 : " Milo Glaornensis, quem ibi cum gratiâ et favore omnium comitem præfecit Herefordiæ."

[1] See Appendix L : " Charter of the Empress to William de Beauchamp."

[2] " Ad hos motus, si possit, componendos comes Gloecestrensis non adeo denso comitatu Wintoniam contendit; sed, re infecta, ad Oxeneford rediit, ubi soror stativâ mansione jamdudum se continuerat " (p. 751). The "jamdudum" should be noticed, as a hint towards the chronology.

[3] " Ipsa itaque, et ex his quæ continue audiebat et a fratre tunc cognovit nihil legatum molle ad suas partes cogitare intelligeus, Wintoniam cum quanto potuit apparatu venit " (*ibid.*).

[4] They were her uncle, the King of Scots ; * her three brothers, the Earls

THE EMPRESS MARCHES ON WINCHESTER. 125

The Continuator states that she reached Winchester shortly before the 1st of August.[1] He also speaks of the siege having lasted seven weeks on the 13th of September.[2] If he means by this, as he implies, the siege by the queen's forces, he is clearly wrong; but if he was thinking of the arrival of the Empress, this would place that event not later than the 27th of July. We know from the date of the Oxford charter that it cannot well have been earlier. The *Hyde Cartulary* (Stowe MSS.) is more exact, and, indeed, gives us the day of her arrival, Thursday, July 31 ("pridie kal. Augusti"). According to the *Annals of Waverley*, the Empress besieged the bishop the next day.[3]

Of the struggle which now took place we have several independent accounts. Of these the fullest are those given by the Continuator, who here writes with a bitter feeling against the legate, and by the author of the *Gesta*, whose sympathies were, of course, on the other side. John of Hexham, William of Malmesbury, and Henry of Huntingdon have accounts which should be carefully consulted, and some information is also to be gleaned from the *Hyde Cartulary* (Stowe MSS.).

It is John of Hexham alone who mentions that the bishop himself had commenced operations by besieging the royal castle, which was held by a garrison of the

of Gloucester,* and of Cornwall,* and Robert fitz Edith; the Earls of Warwick and Devon ("Exeter"), with their newly created fellows, the Earls of Dorset (or Somerset) and Hereford; Humphrey de Bohun,* John the Marshal,* Brien fitz Count,* Geoffrey Boterel (his relative), William fitz Alan, "William" of Salisbury, Roger d'Oilli, Roger "de Nunant," etc. The primate * was also of the company. N.B.—Those marked with an asterisk attested the above charter to Miles de Gloucester.

[1] "Inde [*i.e.* from Oxford] jam militum virtute roborata et numero, appropinquante festivitate Sancti Petri, quæ dicitur ad Vincula" [August 1] (*Cont. Flor. Wig.*, 133).

[2] "Septem igitur septimanis in obsidione transactis" (*ibid.*).

[3] "Die kalendarum Augusti" (*Ann. Mon.*, ii. 229).

Empress.[1] It was in this castle, says the Continuator, that she took up her quarters on her arrival.[2] She at once summoned the legate to her presence, but he, dreading that she would seize his person, returned a temporizing answer, and eventually rode forth from the city (it would seem, by the east gate) just as the Empress entered it in state.[3]

Though the Continuator asserts that the Empress, on her arrival, found the city opposed to her, William of Malmesbury, whose sympathies were the same, asserts, on the contrary, that the citizens were for her.[4] Possibly, the former may only have meant that she had found the gates of the city closed against her by the legate. In any case, she now established herself, together with her followers, within the walls, and laid siege to the episcopal palace, which was defended by the legate's garrison.[5]

[1] "Imperatrix, collectis viribus suis, cum rege Scotiæ et Rodberto comite ascendit in Wintoniam, audiens milites suos inclusos in regia munitione expugnari a militibus legati qui erant in mœnibus illius" (*Sym. Dun.*, ii. 310).

[2] "Ignorante fratre suo, comite Bricstowensi (*i.e.* Earl Robert), Wintoniensem venit ad urbem, sed eam a se jam alienatam inveniens, in castello suscepit hospitium" (p. 133). It seems impossible to understand what can be meant by the expression "ignorante fratre suo." So too *Will. Malms.*: "intra castellum regium sine cunctatione recepta."

[3] *Will. Malms.*, p. 751; *Gesta*, p. 80; *Cont. Flor. Wig.*, 133. The *Gesta* alone represents the Empress as hoping to surprise the legate, which is scarcely probable.

[4] "Wintonienses porro vel tacito ei favebant judicio, memores fidei quam ei pacti fuerant cum inviti propemodum ab episcopo ad hoc adacti essent" (p. 752).

[5] There is some confusion as to what the Empress actually besieged. The *Gesta* says it was "(1) castellum episcopi, quod venustissimo constructum schemate in civitatis medio locarat, sed et (2) domum illius, quam ad instar castelli fortiter et inexpugnabiliter firmarat." We learn from the *Annals of Winchester* (p. 51) that, in 1138, the bishop "fecit ædificare domum quasi palatium cum turri fortissima in Wintonia," which would seem to be Wolvesey, with its keep, at the south-east angle of the city. Again, Giraldus has a story (vii. 46) that the bishop built himself a residence from the materials of the Conqueror's palace: "Domos regios apud Wintoniam ecclesie ipsius atrio nimis enormiter imminentes, . . . funditus in brevi

THE BISHOP BURNS WINCHESTER.

The usual consequence followed. From the summit of the keep its reckless defenders rained down fire upon the town, and a monastery, a nunnery, more than forty (?) churches, and the greater part of the houses within the walls are said to have been reduced to ashes.[1]

Meanwhile, the legate had summoned to his aid the Queen and all the royal party. His summons was

raptim et subito ... dejecit, et ... ex dirutis ædificiis et abstractis domos episcopales egregias sibi in eadem urbe construxit." On the other hand, the *Hyde Cartulary* assigns the destruction of the palace to the siege (*vide infra.*).

[1] "Interea ex turre pontificis jaculatum incendium in domos burgensium (qui, ut dixi, proniores erant imperatricis felicitati) comprehendit et combussit abbatiam totam sanctimonialium intra urbem, simulque cænobium quod dicitur ad Hidam extra" (*Will. Malms.*, p. 752). "Qui intus recludebantur ignibus foras emissis majorem civitatis partem sed et duas abbatias in favillas penitus redegerunt" (*Gesta*, p. 83). "Siquidem secundo die mensis Augusti ignis civitati immissis, monasterium sanctimonialium cum suis ædificiis, ecclesias plus XL cum majori seu meliori parte civitatis, postremo cænobium monachorum Deo et Sancto Grimbaldo famulantium, cum suis ædibus redegit in cineres" (*Cont. Flor. Wig.*, p. 133). It is from this last writer that we get the date (August 2), which we should never have gathered from William of Malmesbury (who mentions this fire in conjunction with the burning of Wherwell Abbey, at the close of the siege) or from the *Gesta*. M. Paris (*Chron. Maj.*, ii. 174) assigns the fire, like William of Malmesbury, to the end of the siege, but his version, "Destructa est Wintonia XVIII kal. Oct., et captus est R. Comes Glovernie die exaltationis Sancte Crucis," is self-stultifying, the two dates being one and the same. The Continuator's date is confirmed by the independent evidence of the *Hyde Cartulary* (among the Stowe MSS.), which states that on Saturday, the 2nd of August ("Sabbato IIII. non. Augusti"), the city was burned by the bishop's forces, "et eodem die dicta civitas Wyntonie capta est et spoliata." From this source we further obtain the interesting fact that the Conqueror's palace in the city ("totum palatium cum aula sua") perished on this occasion. Allusion is made to this fact in the same cartulary's account of a council held by Henry of Winchester in the cathedral, in November, 1150, where the parish of St. Laurence is assigned the site "super quam aulam suam et palacium edificari fecit (Rex Willelmus)," which palace "in adventu Roberti Comitis Gloecestrie combustum fuit." The Continuator (*more suo*) assigns the fire to the cruelty of the bishop; but it was the ordinary practice in such cases. As from the tower of Le Mans in 1099 (*Ord. Vit.*), as from the tower of Hereford Cathedral but a few years before this (*Gesta Stephani*), so now at Winchester the firebrands flew : and so again at Lewes, in far later days (1264), where on the evening of the great battle there blazed forth from the defeated Royalists, sheltered on the castle height, a mad shower of fire.

promptly obeyed;[1] even the Earl of Chester, "who," says Dr. Stubbs, "was uniformly opposed to Stephen, but who no doubt fought for himself far more than for the Empress,"[2] joined, on this occasion, the royal forces, perhaps to maintain the balance of power. But his assistance, naturally enough, was viewed with such deep suspicion that he soon went over to the Empress,[3] to whom, however, his tardy help was of little or no value.[4] From London the Queen received a well-armed contingent, nearly a thousand strong;[5] but Henry of Huntingdon appears to imply that their arrival, although it turned the scale, did not take place till late in the siege.[6]

The position of the opposing forces became a very strange one. The Empress and her followers, from the castle, besieged the bishop's palace, and were in turn themselves besieged by the Queen and her host without.[7] It was the aim of the latter to cut off the Empress from her base of operations in the west. With this object they burnt Andover,[8] and harassed so successfully the enemy's convoys, that famine was imminent in the city.[9] The

---

[1] "Statimque propter omnes misit quos regi fauturos sciebat. Venerunt ergo fere omnes comites Angliæ; erant enim juvenes et leves, et qui mallent equitationum discursus quam pacem" (*Will. Malms.*, p. 751). Cf. *Hen. Hunt.*, p. 275, and *Gesta*, pp. 81, 82.

[2] *Early Plantagenets*, p. 25. Compare *Const. Hist.*, i. 329 : "The Earl of Chester, although, whenever he prevailed on himself to act, he took part against Stephen, fought rather on his own account than on Matilda's."

[3] *Sym. Dun.*, ii. 310.

[4] "Reinulfus enim comes Cestrie tarde et inutiliter advenit" (*Will. Malms.*, p. 751.

[5] "Invictâ Londoniensium catervâ, qui, fere mille, cum galeis et loricis ornatissime instructi convenerant" (*Gesta*, p. 82).

[6] "Venit tandem exercitus Lundoniensis, et aucti numerose qui contra imperatricem contendebant, fugere eam compulerunt" (p. 275).

[7] *Gesta*, p. 82. The *Annals of Winchester* (p. 52) strangely reverse the respective positions of the two: "Imperatrix cum suis castellum tenuit regium et orientalem (*sic*) partem Wintonie et burgenses eum ea; legatus cum suis castrum suum cum parte occidentali" (*sic*).

[8] *Will. Malms.*, p. 752.   [9] *Ibid.*; *Gesta*, p. 83.

THE QUEEN BESIEGES THE EMPRESS. 129

Empress, moreover, was clearly outnumbered by the forces of the Queen and legate. It is agreed on all hands that the actual crisis was connected with an affair at Wherwell, but John of Hexham and the author of the *Gesta* are not entirely in accord as to the details. According to the latter, who can hardly be mistaken in a statement so precise, the besieged, now in dire straits, despatched a small force along the old Icknield Way, to fortify Wherwell and its nunnery, commanding the passage of the Test, in order to secure their line of communication.[1] John of Hexham, on the contrary, describing, it would seem, the same incident, represents it as merely the despatch of an escort, under John the Marshal and Robert fitz Edith, to meet an expected convoy.[2] In any case, it is clear that William of Ypres, probably the Queen's best soldier, burst upon the convoy close to Wherwell, and slew or captured all but those who sought refuge within the nunnery walls.[3] Nor are the two accounts gravely inconsistent.

On the other hand, the Continuator of Florence appears at first sight to imply that the Marshal and his followers took refuge at Wherwell in the course of the general flight,[4] and this version is in harmony with the *Histoire*

[1] "Provisum est igitur, et communi consilio provisé, ut sibi videbatur, statutum, quatinus penes abbatiam Werwellensem, quæ a Ventâ civitate VI. milliariis distabat, trecentis (*sic*) ibi destinatis militibus, castellum construerent, ut scilicet inde et regales facilius arcerentur, et ciborum subsidia competentius in urbe dirigerentur" (p. 83).

[2] "Emissi sunt autem ducenti (*sic*) milites, cum Rodberto filio Edæ et Henrici regis notho et Johanne Marascaldo, ut conducerent in urbem eos qui comportabant victualia in ministerium imperatricis et eorum qui obsessi fuerant" (*Sym. Dun.*, ii. 310).

[3] "Quos persecuti Willelmus Dipre et pars exercitus usque ad Warewella (ubi est congregatio sanctimonialium) et milites et omnem apparatum, qui erat copiosus, abduxerunt" (*ibid*). "Subito et insperaté, cum intolerabili multitudine Werwellam advenerunt, fortiterque in eos undique irruentes captis et interemptis plurimis, cedere tandem reliquos et in templum se recipere compulerunt" (*Gesta*, p. 83).

[4] *Vide infra.* Since the above was written Mr. Howlett, in his edition of

de Guillaume le Maréchal.[1] But putting aside William of Malmesbury, whose testimony is ambiguous on the point, I consider the balance to be clearly in favour of the *Gesta* and John of Hexham, whose detailed accounts must be wholly rejected if we embrace the other version, whereas the Continuator's words can be harmonized, and indeed better understood, if we take "ad monasterium Warewellense fugientem" as referring to John taking refuge in the nunnery (as described in the other versions) when surprised with his convoy. Moreover, the evidence (*vide infra*) as to the Empress leaving Winchester by the west instead of the north gate, appears to me to clinch the matter. As to the Marshal poem, on such a point its evidence is of little weight. Composed at a later period, and based on family tradition, its incidents, as M. Meyer has shown, are thrown together in wrong order, and its obvious errors not a few. I may add that the Marshal's position is unduly exalted in the poem, and that Brian fitz Count (though it is true that he accompanied the Empress in her flight) would never have taken his orders from John the Marshal.[2] Its narrative cannot be explained away, but it is the one that we are most justified in selecting for rejection.

the *Gesta* (p. 82, *note*), has noted the contradiction in the narrative, but seems to lean to the latter version as being supported by the Marshal poem.

[1] As has been duly pointed out by its accomplished editor, M. Paul Meyer (*Romania*, vol. xi.), who will shortly, it may be hoped, publish the entire poem.

[2] "Li Mareschals de son afaire
Ne sout que dire ne que feire,
N'i vit rescose ne confort.
A Brien de Walingofort
Commanda a mener la dame,
E dist, sor le peril de s'alme
Q'en nul lieu ne s'aresteiisent,
Por nul besoing que il eiisent,
N'en bone veie ne en male,
De si qu'a Lothegaresale ;
E cil tost e hastivemeut
En fist tot son commandement" (Lines 225-236).

THE STRUGGLE AT WHERWELL.

To expel the fugitives from their place of safety, William and his troopers fired the nunnery. A furious struggle followed in the church, amidst the shrieks of the nuns and the roar of the flames; the sanctuary itself streamed with blood; but John the Marshal stood his ground, and refused to surrender to his foes.[1] "Silence, or I will slay thee with mine own hands," the undaunted man is said to have exclaimed, as his last remaining comrade implored him to save their lives.[2]

[1] "Cumque vice castelli ad se defendendos templo uterentur, alii, facibus undique injectis, semiustulatos eos e templo prodire, et ad votum suum se sibi subdere coegerunt. Erat quidem horrendum," etc. (*Gesta*, p. 83). "Johannem etiam, fautorem eorum, ad monasterium Warewellense fugientem milites episcopi persequentes, cum exinde nullo modo expellere valuissent, in ipsâ die festivitatis Exaltationis Sanctæ Crucis [Sept. 14], immisso igne ipsam ecclesiam Sanctæ Crucis cum sanctimonialium rebus et domibus cremaverunt, . . . prædictum tamen Johannem nec capere nec expellere potuerunt" (*Cont. Flor. Wig.*, p. 135). So also *Will. Malms.* (p. 752): "Combusta est etiam abbatia sanctimonialium de Warewellâ a quodam Willelmo de Iprâ homine nefando, qui nec Deo nec hominibus reverentiam observaret, quod in eâ quidam imperatricis fautores se contutati essent."

[2] "Li Mareschas el guié s'estut,
A son poer les contrestut.
Tute l'ost sur lui descarcha
Qui si durement le charcha
Que n'i pont naint plus durer;
Trop lui fui fort a endurer,
Einz s'enbati en un mostier ;
N'ont o lui k'un sol chevaler.
Quant li real les aperçurent
Qu'el mostier enbatu se furent :
' Or ça, li feus !' funt il, ' or sa,
Li traitres ne li garra.'
Quant li feus el moster se prist,
En la vis de la tor se mist.
Li chevaliers li dist : 'Beau sire,
Or ardrum ci a grant martire :
Ce sera pecchiez e damages.
Rendom nos, si ferom que sages.'
Cil respundi mult cruelment :
N'en parler ja, gel te defent ;
Ke, s'en diseies plus ne mains,
Ge t'occirreie de mes mains.'
Por le grant feu qui fu entor
Dejeta li pluns de la tor,

On receiving intelligence of this disaster, the besieged were seized with panic, and resolved on immediate retreat.[1] William of Malmesbury, as before, is anxious to deny the panic,[2] and the Continuator accuses the legate of treachery.[3] The account, however, in the *Gesta* appears thoroughly trustworthy. According to this, the Empress and her forces sallied forth from the gates in good order, but were quickly surrounded and put to flight. All order was soon at an end. Bishops, nobles, barons, troopers, fled in headlong rout. With her faithful squire by her side the Empress rode for her life.[4] The Earl of Gloucester, with

> Si que sor le vis li chaï,
> Dunt leidement li meschaï,
> K'un de ses elz i out perdu
> Dunt molt se tint a esperdu,
> Mais, merci Dieu, n'i murust pas.
> E li real en es le pas
> Por mort e por ars le quiderent;
> A Vincestre s'en returnerent,
> Mais n'i fu ne mors ne esteinz " (Lines 237-269).

[1] " Ubi lacrymabilem præfati infortunii audissent eventum de obsidione diutius ingereudâ ex toto desperati, fugæ quammaturé inire præsidium sibi consuluere " (*Gesta*, pp. 83, 84). "Qui jam non in concertatione sed in fuga spem salutis gerentes egressi sunt, ne forte victores cum Willelmo d'Ipre ad socios regressi, sumptâ fiduciâ ex quotidianis successibus, aliquid subitum in eos excogitarent" (*Sym. Dun.*, ii. 310).

[2] "[Comes] cedendum tempori ratus, compositis ordinibus discessionem paravit" (p. 753).

[3] P. 134. His strong bias against the legate makes this somewhat confused charge unworthy of credit.

[4] " La fist tantost metre a la voie
Tot dreit a Lotegaresale.
. . . . .
Ne[l] purrent suffrir ne atendre
Cil qui o l'empereriz erent:
Al meis ku'il purent s'en alerent,
Poingnant si que regne n'i tindrent
[J]esque soz Varesvalle vindrent;
Mès forment les desavancha
L'empereriz qui chevacha
Cumme femme fait en seant:
Ne sembla pas buen ne seant
Al Marechal, anceis li dist :

the rear-guard, covered his sister's retreat, but in so doing was himself made prisoner, while holding, at Stockbridge, the passage of the Test.[1]

The mention of Stockbridge proves that the besieged must have fled by the Salisbury road, their line of retreat by Andover being now barred at Wherwell. After crossing the Test, the fugitive Empress must have turned northwards, and made her way, by country lanes, over Longstock hills, to Ludgershall. So great was the dread of her victorious foes, now in full pursuit, that though she had ridden more than twenty miles, and was overwhelmed with anxiety and fatigue, she was unable to rest even here, and, remounting, rode for Devizes, across the Wiltshire downs.[2] It was not, we should notice, thought safe for her to make straight for Gloucester, through Marlborough and Cirencester; so she again set her face due west, as if making for Bristol. Thus fleeing from fortress to fortress, she came to her castle at Devizes. So great, however, was now her terror that even in this celebrated stronghold[3] she would

> 'Dame, si m'ait Jesucrist,
> L'em ne puet pas en seant poindre;
> Les jambes vos covient desjoindre
> E metre par en son l'arçun.'
> El le fiat, volsist ele ou non,
> Quer lor enemis le[s] grevoient
> Qui de trop près les herd[i]oient" (Lines 198, 199, 208–224)

The quaint detail here given is confirmed, as M. Meyer notes, by the Continuator's phrase (vide infra, note 2).

[1] "In loco qui Stolibricge dicitur a Flammensibus cum comite Warrennensi captus" (Cont. Flor. Wig., p. 135). Cf. p. 134, and Will. Malms. (j p 753, 758, 759), Gesta (p. 84), Sym. Dun. (ii. 311), Hen. Hunt (p. 275) As in Matilda's flight from London, so in her flight from Winchester, the author of the Gesta appears to advantage with his descriptive and spirited account.

[2] "Hæc audiens domina, vehementer exterrita atque turbata, ad castellum quo tendebat de Ludkereshala tristris ac dolens advenit, sed ibi locum tutum quiescendi, propter metum episcopi, non invenit. Unde, hortantibus suis, equo iterum usu masculino supposita, atque ad Divisas perducta" (Cont. Flor. Wig., p. 134).

[3] "Castellum quod vocatur Divise, quo non erat aliud splendidius intra fines Europæ" (Hen. Hunt., p. 265). "Castellum .. multis et vix numerabi-

not, she feared, be safe. She had already ridden some forty miles, mainly over bad country, and what with grief, terror, and fatigue, the erst haughty Empress was now " more dead than alive " (*pene exanimis*). It was out of the question that she should mount again ; a litter was hurriedly slung between two horses, and, strapped to this, the unfortunate Lady was conveyed in sorry guise (*sat ignominiose*) to her faithful city of Gloucester.[1]

On a misunderstanding, as I deem it, of the passage (and especially of the word *feretrum*), writers have successively, for three centuries, represented the Continuator as stating that the Empress, "to elude the vigilance of her pursuers," was "laid out as a corpse!" Lingard, indeed, while following suit, gravely doubts if the fact be true, as it is recorded by the Continuator alone ; but Professor Pearson improves upon the story, and holds that the versatile " Lady " was in turn " a trooper " and a corpse.[2]

libus sumptibus, non (ut ipse præsul dictabat) ad ornamentum, sed (ut se rei veritas habet) ad ecclesiæ detrimentum, ædificatum " (*Will. Malms.*, pp. 717, 718). It had been raised by the Bishop of Salisbury, and it passed, at his fall, into Stephen's hands. It is then described by the author of the *Gesta* (p. 66) as " castellum regis, quod Divisa dicebatur, ornanter et inexpugnabiliter muratum." It was subsequently surprised by Robert fitz Hubert, who held it for his own hand till his capture, when the Earl of Gloucester tried hard to extort its surrender from him. In this, however, he failed. Robert was hanged, and, soon after, his garrison sold it to Stephen, by whom it was entrusted to Hervey of Brittany, whom he seems to have made Earl of Wilts. But on Stephen's capture, the peasantry rose, and extorted its surrender from Hervey. Thenceforth, it was a stronghold of the Empress (see for this the Continuator and the *Gesta*).

[1] " Cum nec ibi secure se tutari posse, ob insequentes, formidaret, jam pene exanimis feretro invecta, et funibus quasi cadaver ligata, equis deferentibus, sat ignominiose ad civitatem deportatur Glaornensem " (*Cont. Flor. Wig.*, 134). The author of the *Gesta* (p. 85) mentions her flight to Devizes (" Brieno tantum cum paucis comite, ad Divisas confugit"), and incidentally observes (p. 87) that she was " ex Wintoniensi dispersione quassa nimis, et usque ad defectum pené defatigata " (*i.e.* " tired to death ; " cf. *supra*). John of Hexham merely says : " Et imperatrix quidem non sine magno conflictu et plurima difficultate erepta est" (*Sym. Dun.*, ii. 310).

[2] Camden, in his *Britannia*, gives the story, but Knighton (De eventibus

RELEASE OF THE KING.

On the 1st of November the king was released, and a few days later the Earl of Gloucester, for whom he had been exchanged, reached Bristol.[1] Shortly after, it would seem, there were assembled together at Bristol, the Earl, the Empress, and their loyal adherents, Miles, now Earl of Hereford, Brian fitz Count, and Robert fitz Martin.[2]

Angliæ, lib. ii., in *Scriptores* X.) seems to be the chief offender. Dugdale follows with the assertion that "she was necessitated . . . for her more security to be put into a coffin, as a dead corps, to escape their hands" (i. 537 *b*). According to Milner (*History of Winchester*, p. 162), "she was enclosed like a corpse in a sheet of lead, and was thus suffered to pass in a horse-litter as if carried out for interment, through the army of her besiegers, a truce having been granted for this purpose." Even Edwards, in his introduction to the *Liber de Hyda* (p. xlviii.), speaks of "the raising of the siege; a raising precipitated, if we accept the accounts of Knighton and some other chroniclers who accord with him, by the strange escape of the Empress Maud from Winchester Castle concealed in a leaden coffin." *Sic crescit eundo.*

[1] *Will. Malms.*, p. 754.

[2] See donation of Miles (*Monasticon*, vi. 137), stated to have been made in their presence, and in the year 1141, in which he speaks of himself as "apud Bristolium positus, jamque consulatus honorem adeptus." Brian had escorted the Empress in her flight, but Miles, intercepted by the enemy, had barely escaped with his life ("de solâ vita lætus ad Gluornam cum dedecore fugiendo pervenit lassus, solus, et pene nudus."—*Cont. Flor. Wig.*, p. 135).

CHAPTER VII.

THE SECOND CHARTER OF THE KING.

THE liberation of the king from his captivity was hailed with joy by his adherents, and not least, we may be sure, in his loyal city of London. The greatness of the event is seen, perhaps, in the fact that it is even mentioned in a private London deed of the time, executed "Anno MCXLI., Id est in exitu regis Stephani de captione Roberti filii regis Henrici."[1]

In spite of his faults we may fairly assume that the king's imprisonment had aroused a popular reaction in his favour, as it did in the case of Charles I., five centuries later. The experiences also of the summer had been greatly in his favour. For, however unfit he may have been to fill the throne himself, he was able now to point to the fact that his rival had been tried and found wanting.

He would now be eager to efface the stain inflicted on his regal dignity, to show in the sight of all men that he was again their king, and then to execute vengeance on those whose captive he had been. The first step to be taken was to assemble a council of the realm that should undo the work of the April council at Winchester, and formally recognize in him the rightful possessor of the throne. This council met on the 7th of December at Westminster, the king himself being present.[2] The ingenious legate was now as ready to prove that his

---

[1] *Ninth Report Hist. MSS.*, App. i. p. 62 b.
[2] "Regem ipsum in concilium introisse" (*Will. Malms.*, 755).

brother, and not the Empress, should rightly fill the throne, as, we saw, he was in April to prove the exact reverse. The two grounds on which he based his renunciation were, first, that the Empress had failed to fulfil her pledges to the Church;[1] second, that her failure implied the condemnation of God.[2]

A solemn coronation might naturally follow, to set, as it were, the seal to the work of this assembly. Perhaps the nearest parallel to this second coronation is to be found in that of Richard I., in 1194, after his captivity and humiliation.[3] I think we have evidence that Stephen himself looked on this as a second coronation, and as no mere "crown-wearing," in a precept in favour of the monks of Abingdon, in which he alludes incidentally to the day of his *first* coronation.[4] This clearly implies a second coronation since; and as the precept is attested by Richard de Luci, it is presumably subsequent to that second coronation, to which we now come.

It cannot be wondered that this event has been unnoticed by historians, for it is only recorded in a single copy of the works of a single chronicler. We are indebted to Dr. Stubbs and his scholarly edition of the writings of Gervase of Canterbury for our knowledge of the fact that in one, and that comparatively imperfect, of the three manuscripts on which his text is based, we read of a coronation of Stephen, at Canterbury, "placed under

---

[1] "Ipsam quæcunque pepigerat ad ecclesiarum jus pertinentia obstinate fregisse" (*ibid.*).

[2] "Deum, pro sua clementia, secus quam ipsa sperasset vertisse negotia" (*ibid.*).

[3] Dr. Stubbs well observes of this coronation of Richard: "His second coronation was understood to have an important significance. He had by his captivity in Germany ... impaired or compromised his dignity as a crowned king. The Winchester coronation was not intended to be a reconsecration, but a solemn assertion that the royal dignity had undergone no diminution" (*Const. Hist.*, i. 504).

[4] "Die qua primum coronatus fui" (*Cartulary of Abingdon*, ii. 181).

1142." We learn from him that in this MS. "it is probably inserted in a wrong place," as indeed is evident from the fact that at Christmas, 1142, Stephen was at Oxford. Here is the passage in question:—

> "Deinde rex Stephanus una cum regina et nobilitate procerum ad Natale Domini gratiosus adveniens, in ipsa solempnitate in ecclesiâ Christi a venerabili Theobaldo ejusdem ecclesiæ archiepiscopo coronatus est; ipsa etiam regina cum eo ibidem coronam auream gestabat in capite" (*Gervase*, i. 123).

It should perhaps be noticed that, while the Queen is merely said to have worn her crown, Stephen is distinctly stated to have been crowned. I cannot but think that this must imply a distinction between them, and supports the view that this coronation was due to the captivity of the king.

My contention is that the date of this event was Christmas, 1141, and that the choice, for its scene, of the Kentish capital was a graceful compliment to that county which, in the darkest hour of the king's fortunes, had remained faithful to his cause, and to the support of which his restoration had been so largely due.[1]

I further hold that the second charter granted to Geoffrey de Mandeville was executed on this occasion, and that in its witnesses we have the list of that "nobilitas procerum" by which, according to Gervase, this coronation was attended.

This charter, when rightly dated, is indeed the keystone of my story. For without it we could not form that series on which the sequence of events is based. It is admittedly subsequent to the king's liberation, for it refers to the battle of Lincoln. It must also be previous to Geoffrey's death in 1144. These are the obvious limits given in the official calendar.[2] But it must further be previous to

---

[1] "Cantia quam solam casus non flexerat regius" (*Will. Newburgh*, i. 41).
[2] *Thirty-first Report of Deputy Keeper*, p. 3 (based on the late Sir

Geoffrey's fall in 1143. Lastly, it must be previous to the Oxford, or second, charter of the Empress, in which we shall find it is referred to. As that charter cannot be later than the summer of 1142, our limit is again narrowed. Now the charter is tested at Canterbury. Stephen cannot, it seems, have been there in the course of 1142. This accordingly leaves us, as the only possible date, the close of 1141; and this is the very date of the king's coronation at Canterbury. When we add to this train of reasoning the fact that the number of earls by whom the charter is witnessed clearly points to some great state ceremonial, we cannot feel the slightest doubt that the charter must, as I observed, have passed on this occasion. With this conclusion its character will be found in complete accordance, for it plainly represents the price for which the traitor earl consented to change sides again, and to place at the disposal of his outraged king that Tower of London, its citadel and its dread, the possession of which once more enabled him to dictate his own terms.

Those terms were that, in the first place, he should forfeit nothing for his treason in having joined the cause of the Empress, and should be confirmed in his possession of all that he held before the king's capture. But his demands far exceeded the mere *status quo ante*. Just as he had sold his support to the Empress when she gave him an advance on Stephen's terms, so the Queen must have brought him back by offering terms, at the crisis of the struggle, in excess even of those which he had just wrung from the Empress. He would now insist that these great concessions should be confirmed by the king himself. Such is the explanation of the strange character of this Canterbury charter.

William Hardy's register of these charters). Mr. Birch, in his learned paper on the seals of King Stephen, also assigns these limits to the charter.

Charter of the King to Geoffrey de Mandeville
(Christmas, 1141).

S. rex Angl[orum] Archiepiscopis Episcopis Abbatibus Comitibus Justic[iariis] Vicecomitibus Baronibus et Omnibus Ministris et fidelibus suis francis et Anglis totius Anglie salutem. Sciatis me reddidisse et firmiter concesisse Gaufr[ido] Comiti de Essexâ omnia sua tenementa que tenuit, de quocunque illa tenuerit, die quâ impeditus fui apud Linc[olniam] et captus. Et præter hoc dedi ei et concessi ccc libratas terræ scilicet Meldonam [1] et Neweport et Depedenam et Banhunte et Ingam et Phingriam [2] et Chateleam cum omnibus suis Appendiciis pro c libris. Et Writelam [3] pro vi.xx libris. Et Hadfeld [4] pro quater.xx libris cum omnibus appendiciis illorum Maneriorum. Et præter hec dedi ei et concessi in feodo et hereditate de me et de meis hæredibus sibi et suis heredibus c libratas terræ de terris excaatis, scilicet totam terram Roberti de Baentona [5] quam tenuit in Essexâ, videlicet

[1] "Meldona." This manor, and those which follow are the same, with the addition of 'Inga' and 'Phingria,' as had been granted Geoffrey by the Empress to make up his £100 a year. Thus these two manors represent the "si quid defuerit ad c libratas perficiendas" of the Empress's charters. Maldon itself had, we saw (p. 102), been held by Stephen's brother Theobald, forfeited by the Empress on her triumph, and granted by her to Geoffrey. Theobald's possession is further proved by a writ among the archives of Westminster (printed in Madox's *Baronia Anglica*, p. 232), in which Stephen distinctly states (1139) that he had given it him. Thus, in giving it to Geoffrey, he had to despoil his own brother.

[2] The "Phenge" and "Inga" of Domesday (ii. 71 *b*, 72 *a*), which were part of the fief of Randulf Peverel ("of London").

[3] Writtle was ancient demesne of the Crown (Pipe-Roll, 31 Hen. I.). Its *redditus*, at the Survey, was "c libras ad pondus et c solidos de gersumâ."

[4] Hatfield Broadoak, *alias* Hatfield Regis. This also was ancient demesne, its *redditus*, at the Survey, being "lxxx libras et c solidos de gersumâ." Here the Domesday *redditus* remained unchanged, an important point to notice.

[5] Robert de Baentonâ was lord of Bampton, co. Devon. He occurs in the

TEXT OF THE CHARTER. 141

Reneham[1] et Hoilandam,[2] Et Amb[er]denam[3] et Wodeham[4] et Eistan',[5] quam Picardus de Danfront[6] tenuit. Et Ichilintonam[7] cum omnibus eorum appendiciis pro c libris. Et præterea dedi ei et firmiter concessi in feodo et hereditate c libratas terræ ad opus Ernulfi de Mannavilla de ipso Comite Gaufredo tenendas, scilicet Anastiam,[8] et Braching,[9] et Hamam[10] cum omnibus eorum appendiciis. Et c solidatas terræ in Hadfeld ad præfatas c libratas terræ perficiend[um]. Et præterea dedi ei et concessi custodiam turris Lond[oniæ] cum Castello quod ei subest habend[um] et tenendum sibi et suis hæredibus de me et de meis heredibus cum omnibus rebus et libertatibus et consuetudinibus prefate turri pertinentibus. Et Justicias et Vicecomitat' de Lond[oniâ] et de Middlesexâ in feodo et hereditate

Pipe-Roll of 31 Hen. I. (p. 153, 154). He is identical with the Robert "de Bathentona" whose rebellion against Stephen is narrated at some length in the *Gesta*. His lands were forfeited for that rebellion, and consequently appear here as an escheat (see my note on him in *English Historical Review*, October, 1890).

[1] Rainham, on the Thames, in South Essex. It had formed part of the Domesday (*D. B.*, ii. 91) barony of Walter de Douai, to whose Domesday fief Robert de Baentonâ had succeeded.

[2] Great Holland, in Essex, adjacent to Clacton-on-Sea. It had similarly formed part of the Domesday barony of Walter de Douai.

[3] Amberden, in Depden, with which it had been held by Randulf Peverel at the Survey.

[4] Woodham Mortimer, Essex. This also had been part of the fief of Randulf Peverel.

[5] Easton, Essex. Geoffrey de Mandeville had held land, at the Survey in (Little) Easton.

[6] Picard de Domfront occurs in the Pipe-Roll of 31 Hen. I. as a landowner in Wilts and Essex (pp. 22, 53).

[7] Ickleton, Cambridgeshire, on the borders of Essex, the "Ichilintone" of Domesday (in which it figures), was *Terra Regis*. In the *Liber Niger* (special inquisition), however (p. 394), it appears as part of the honour of Boulogne.

[8] Anstey, Herts, the "Anestige" of Domesday, part of the honour of Boulogne.

[9] Braughing, Herts, the "Brachinges" of Domesday. Also part of the honour of Boulogne.

[10] Possibly that portion of Ham (East and West Ham), Essex, which formed part of the fief of Randulf Peverel.

142 THE SECOND CHARTER OF THE KING.

eadem firma qua Gaufridus de Mannavilla avus suus eas tenuit, scilicet pro ccc libris. Et Justitias et Vicecomitat' de Essexâ et de Heortfordiscirâ eâdem firmâ quâ avus ejus eas tenuit, ita tamen quod dominica que de prædictis Comitatibus data sunt ipsi Comiti Gaufredo aut alicui alii a firmâ præfatâ subtrahantur et illi et hæredibus suis ad scaccarium combutabuntur. Et præterea firmiter ei concessi ut possit firmare quoddam castellum ubicunque voluerit in terrâ suâ et quod stare possit. Et præterea dedi eidem Comiti Gaufr[edo] et firmiter concessi in feodo et hereditate sibi et hæredibus suis de me et de meis heredibus lx milites feudatos, de quibus Ernulfus de Mannavillâ tenebit x in feodo et hereditate de patre suo, scilicet servicium Graalondi de Tania [1] pro vii militibus et dimidio Et servicium Willelmi filii Roberti pro vii militibus Et servicium Brient[ii] filii Radulfi [2] pro v militibus Et servicium Roberti filii Geroldi pro xi militibus Et servicium Radulfi filii Geroldi pro i milite Et servicium Willelmi de Tresgoz [3] pro vi militibus Et servicium Mauricii de Chic[he] pro v militibus et servicium Radulfi Maled[octi] pro ii militibus Et servicium Goisb[erti] de Ing[â] pro i milite Et servicium Willelmi filii Heru[ei] pro iii militibus Et servicium Willelmi de Auco pro j milite et dimidio Et servicium Willelmi de Bosevillâ [4] pro ii militibus

---

[1] On Graaland de Tany, see p. 91.

[2] Brien fitz Ralf may have been a son of the Ralf fitz Brien who appears in Domesday as an under-tenant of Randulf Peverel. According to the inquisition on the honour of Peverel assigned to 13th John, "Brien filius Radulfi" held five fees of the honour, the very number here given.

[3] William de Tresgoz appears in the Pipe-Roll of 31 Hen. I. as a landowner in Essex (where the family held Tolleshunt Tregoz of the honour of Peverel) and elsewhere. He was then fermor of the honour of Peverel. In the above inquisition "William de Tregoz" holds six fees of the honour.

[4] William "de Boevilla" (*sic*) appears in the same roll as a landowner in Essex (pp. 53, 60), and William "de Bosevill" (*sic*) is found in (Hearne's) *Liber Niger* (p. 229) as a tenant of the Earl of Essex (1½ fees de vet. fef.).

TEXT OF THE CHARTER. 143

Et servicium Mathei Peur[elli][1] pro iiij militibus Et servicium Ade de Sum[er]i de feodo de Elmedonâ[2] pro iij militibus Et servicium Rann[ulfi] Briton[is][3] pro i milite. Et præterea quicquid Carta Regine testatur ei dedi et concessi. Omnia autem hec prædicta tenementa, scilicet in terris et dominiis et serviciis militum et in Custodia turris Lon[doniæ] et Castelli quod turri subest et in Justiciis et Vicecomitatibus et omnibus prædictis rebus et consuetudinibus et libertatibus, dedi ei et firmiter concessi Comiti Gaufredo in feodo et hereditate de me et de meis heredibus sibi et heredibus suis pro servicio suo. Quare volo et firmiter præcipio quod ipse et heredes sui post eum habeant et teneant omnia illa tenementa et concessiones adeo libere et quiete et honorifice sicut aliquis omnium Comitum totius Angliæ aliquod suum tenementum tenet vel tenuit liberius et honorificentius et quietius et plenius.

T[estibus] M. Regina et H[enrico] Ep[iscop]o Wint[onensi] et W[illelmo] Com[ite] Warenn[a] et Com[ite] Gisl[eberto] de Pembroc et Com[ite] Gisl[eberto] de heortford et W[illelmo] Com[ite] de Albarm[arlâ] et Com[ite] Sim[one] et Comite Will[elmo] de Sudsexâ et Com[ite] Alan[o] et Com[ite] Rob[erto] de Ferrers et Will[elmo]

But what is here granted is the manor of Springfield Hall, which William de Boseville held of the honour of Peverel "of London," by the service of two knights. Mathew Peverel, the Tresgoz family, and the Mauduits were all tenants of the same honour.

[1] Mathew Peverel similarly appears in the Pipe-Roll of 31 Hen. I. as holding land in Essex and Norfolk. In the above inquisition William Peverel holds five fees of the honour.

[2] Elmdon (Essex) had been held of Eustace of Boulogne at the Survey by Roger de Someri, ancestor of the family of that name seated there. Stephen was of course entitled to their *servicium* in right of his wife. Adam de Sumeri held seven fees of the Earl of Essex in 1166.

[3] Possibly the *Ralph* Brito who appears in the Pipe-Rolls of Hen. II. as holding *terræ datæ* "in Chatelegâ," and who also figures as "Ralph le Bret," under Essex, in the *Liber Niger* (p. 242), and as Radulfus Brito, a tenant of Robert de Helion (*ibid.*, p. 240).

de Ip[rà] et Will[elmo] Mart[el] et Bald[wino] fil[io] Gisl[eberti] et Rob[erto] de V[er] et Pharam[o] et Ric[ardo] de Luci et Turg[isio] de Abrincis et Ada de Belum. Apud Cantuar[iam].[1]

It will at once be seen that this charter is one of extraordinary interest.

The first point to strike one, on examining the list of witnesses, is the presence of no less than eight earls and of no more than one bishop. To these, indeed, we may add perhaps, though by no means of necessity, the Earl of Essex himself. Though the evidence is, of course, merely negative, it is probable, to judge from similar cases, that had other bishops been present, they would appear among the witnesses to the charter. The absence of their names, therefore, is somewhat difficult to explain, unless (if present) they were at enmity with Geoffrey.

Another point deserving of notice is that this great gathering of earls enables us to draw some important conclusions as to the origin and development of their titles. We may, for instance, safely infer that when a Christian name was borne by one earl alone, he used for his style that name with the addition of "Comes" either as a prefix or as a suffix. Thus we have in this instance "Comes Alanus" and "Comes Simon." But when two or more earls bore the same Christian name, they had to be distinguished by some addition. Thus we have "Comes Gislebertus de Pembroc" and "Comes Gislebertus de Heortford," or "Comes Robertus de Ferrers," as distinguished from Earl Robert "of Gloucester." The addition of "de Essexa" to Earl Geoffrey himself, which is found in this and other charters (see pp. 158, 183), can only, it would seem, be intended to distinguish him from Count

[1] Duchy of Lancaster, *Royal Charters*, No. 18.

Geoffrey of Anjou. But here the striking case is that of "Willelmo Comite Warenna," "Willelmo Comite de Albarmarlâ," and "Comite Willelmo de Sudsexâ." These examples show us how perfectly immaterial was the source from which the description was taken. "Warenna" is used as if a surname; "Albarmarla" is "Aumâle," a local name; and "Sudsexa" needs no comment. The same noble who here attests as Earl of "Albarmarla" elsewhere attests as Earl "of York," while the Earl "of Sussex" is elsewhere a witness as Earl "of Chichester" or "of Arundel." In short, the "Comes" really belongs to the Christian name alone. The descriptive suffix is distinct and immaterial. But the important inference which I draw from the conclusion arrived at above is that where we find such descriptive suffix employed, we may gather that there was in existence at the time some other earl or count with the same Christian name.[1]

Among the earls, we look at once, but we look in vain, for the name of Waleran of Meulan. But his half-brother, William de Warenne, one, like himself, of the faithful three,[2] duly figures at the head of the list. He is followed by their brother-in-law, the Earl of Pembroke, whose nephew and namesake, the Earl of Hertford, and brother, Baldwin fitz Gilbert, are also found among the witnesses. With them is another of the faithful three, Earl Simon of Northampton. There too is Earl Alan of Richmond, and

[1] This same principle is well illustrated by two *cartæ* which follow one another in the pages of the *Liber Niger*. They are those of "Willelmus filius Johannis *de Herpetreu*" and "Willelmus filius Johannis *de Westena*." Here the suffix (which in such cases is rather a crux to genealogists) clearly distinguishes the two Williams, and is not the appellation of their respective fathers (as it sometimes is). This leads us to such styles as "Beauchamp de Somerset" and "Beauchamp de Warwick," "Willoughby d'Eresby" and "Willoughby de Beke." Many similar instances are to be found in writs of summons, and, applying the above principle, we see that, in all cases, the suffix must originally have been added for the sake of distinction only.

[2] See p. 120.

the fortunate William of Albini, now Earl William of Sussex. Robert of Ferrers and William of Aumâle, both of them heroes of the Battle of the Standard, complete the list of earls.[1]

It would alone be sufficient to make this charter of importance that it affords the earliest record evidence of the existence of two famous earldoms, that of Hertford or Clare, and that of Arundel or Sussex.[2] Indeed I know of no earlier mention in any contemporary chronicler. We further learn from it that William of Ypres was not an earl at the time, as has been persistently stated. Nor have I ever found a record in which he is so styled. Lastly, we have here a noteworthy appearance of one afterwards famous as Richard de Luci the Loyal, who was destined to play so great a part as a faithful and trusted minister for nearly forty years to come.[3] His appearance as an attesting witness at least as early as this (Christmas, 1141) is a fact more especially deserving of notice because it must affect the date of many other charters. Mr. Eyton thought that "his earliest attestation yet proved is 1146,"[4] and hence found his name a difficulty, at times, as a witness. William Martel was another official in constant attendance on Stephen. He is described in the *Gesta* (p. 92) as "vir illustris, fide quoque et amicitiâ potissimum regi connexus." At the affair of Wilton, with its disgraceful surprise and rout of the royal forces, he was made prisoner and forced to give Sherborne Castle as the

---

[1] Of the absentees, the Earl of Chester and his half-brother the Earl of Lincoln will be found accounted for below, as will also the Earl of Warwick; the Earl of Leicester was absent, like his brother the Count of Meulan, but he generally, as here, held aloof; the Earls of Gloucester, Cornwall, Devon, and Hereford were, of course, with the Empress. Thus, with the nine mentioned in the charter, we account for some eighteen earls.

[2] See Appendix M, on the latter earldom.

[3] See p. 49, n. 4.

[4] *Add. MSS.*, 31,943, fol. 85 dors.

price of his liberty (*ibid.*). By his wife "Albreda" he was father of a son and heir, Geoffrey.[1]

Of the remaining witnesses, Pharamus (fitz William) de Boulogne was *nepos* of the queen. In 1130 he was indebted £20 to the Exchequer "pro placitis terre sue [Surrey] et ut habeat terram suam quam Noverca sua tenet" (*Rot. Pip.*, 31 Hen. I., p. 50). In the present year (1141) he had been in joint charge of the king's *familia* during his captivity:—"Rexit autem familiam regis Stephani Willelmus d'Ipre, homo Flandrensis et Pharamus nepos reginæ Matildis, et iste Bononienisis" (*Sym. Dun.*, ii. 310). His ravages—"per destructionem Faramusi"—are referred to in the Pipe-Roll of 1156 (p. 15), but he retained favour under Henry II., receiving £60 annually from the royal dues in Wendover and Eton. In May, 1157, he attested, at Colchester, the charter of Henry II. to Feversham Abbey (Stephen's foundation). He held six fees of the honour of Boulogne. His grandfather, Geoffrey, is described as a *nepos* of Eustace of Boulogne. With his daughter and heiress Sibyl, his lands passed to the family of Fiennes.

Robert de V(er) would be naturally taken for the younger brother of Aubrey the chamberlain, slain in 1141.[2] This might seem so obvious that to question it may appear strange. Yet there is reason to believe that his identity was wholly different. I take him to be Robert (fitz *Bernard*) de Vere, who is presumably the "Robert de Vere" who figures as an Essex landowner in the Pipe-Roll of 1130, for he is certainly the "Robert de Vere" who is entered in that same roll as acquiring lands

[1] *Colchester Cartulary* (Stowe MSS.). See also p. 406.

[2] As by Mr. Eyton (*Addl. MSS.*, 31,943, fol. 96). The said Robert appears in the latter part of this reign as "Robertus filius Alberici de Ver" (*Report on MSS. of Wells Cathedral*, p. 133), and sent in his *carta* in 1166 as "Robertus filius Alberici Camerarii," not as Robert de Vere.

148 THE SECOND CHARTER OF THE KING.

in Kent, with his wife, for whom he had paid the Crown £210, at that time a large sum. She was an heiress, (sister of Robert and) daughter of Hugh de Montfort, a considerable landowner in Kent and in the Eastern Counties. With her he founded, on her Kentish estate, the Cluniac priory of Monks Horton, and in the charters relating to that priory he is spoken of as a royal constable. As such he attested the Charter of Liberties issued by Stephen at Oxford in 1136. I am therefore of opinion that he is the witness who attests this Canterbury charter, the Oxford charter of about a year later,[1] and some others in the course of this reign.[2] He had also witnessed some charters towards the close of the preceding reign, and would seem to be the Robert de Ver who was among those who took charge of the body of Henry I. at his death.[3]

Baldwin fitz Gilbert occurs repeatedly in the Pipe-Roll of 31 Hen. I. He was a younger son of Gilbert de Clare, a brother of Gilbert, afterwards Earl of Pembroke, and uncle of Gilbert, Earl of Hertford. He appears, as early as January, 1136, in attendance on Stephen, at Reading, where he witnessed one of the charters to Miles of Gloucester. He was then sent by the king into Wales to avenge the death of his brother Richard (de Clare); but, on reaching Brecknock, turned back in fear (*Gesta*, p. 12). At the battle of Lincoln (February 2, 1141), he acted as spokesman on the king's behalf, and was captured by the forces of the Empress, after he had been covered with wounds.[4]

[1] *Abingdon Cartulary*, ii. 179.
[2] See Appendix N, on " Robert de Vere."
[3] See *Ord. Vit.*, v. 52 (where the French editors affiliate him wrongly).
[4] " Tunc, quia rex Stephanus festivâ carebat voce, Baldewino filio Gilleberti, magnæ nobilitatis viro et militi fortissimo, sermo exhortatorius ad universum cœtum injunctus est. . . . Capitur etiam Baldewinus qui orationem

STEPHEN OUTBIDS THE EMPRESS. 149

Turgis of Avranches (the namesake of its bishop) we have met with as a witness to Stephen's former charter to Geoffrey. He seems to have been placed, on Geoffrey's fall (1143), in charge of his castle of Walden, and, apparently, of the whole property. Though Stephen had raised him, it was said, from the ranks and loaded him with favours, he ended by offering him resistance, but was surprised by him, in the forest, when hunting, and forced to surrender (*Gesta*, p. 110).

Passing now from the witnesses to the subject-matter of the charter, we have first the clause replacing Geoffrey in the same position as he was before the battle of Lincoln, in despite of his treason to the king's cause. The next clause illustrates the system of advancing bids. Whereas the Empress had granted Geoffrey £100 a year, charged on certain manors of royal demesne in Essex, Stephen now increased that grant to £300 a year, by adding the manors of Writtle (£120) and Hatfield (£80). He further granted him another £100 a year payable from lands which had escheated to the Crown. And lastly, he granted to his son Ernulf £100 a year, likewise charged on land.

The next clause grants him, precisely as in the charter of the Empress, the constableship of the Tower of London and of its appendant "castle,"[1] with the exception that the Empress uses the term "concedo" where Stephen has "dedi et concessi." The latter expression is somewhat strange in view of the fact that Geoffrey had been in full possession of the Tower before the struggle had begun, and, indeed, by hereditary right.

We then return to what I have termed the system of

---

fecerat persuasoriam, multis confossus vulneribus, multis contritus ictibus, ubi egregie resistendo gloriam promeruit sempiternam" (*Hen. Hunt.*, pp. 271, 274).

[1] See Appendix O: "Tower and Castle."

advancing bids. For where the Empress had granted Geoffrey the office of justice and sheriff of Essex alone, Stephen makes him justice and sheriff, not merely of Essex, but of Herts and of London and Middlesex to boot. Nor is even this all ; for, whereas the Empress had allowed him to hold Essex to farm for the same annual sum which it had paid at her father's death,[1] Stephen now leases it to him at the annual rent which his grandfather had paid.[2] The fact that in the second charter of the Empress she adopts, we shall find, the original rental,[3] instead of, as before, that which was paid at the time of her father's death, proves that, in this Canterbury charter, Stephen had outbid her, and further proves that Henry I. had increased, after his wont, the sum at which the sheriff held Essex of the Crown. This, indeed, is clear from the Pipe-Roll of 1130, which records a *firma* far in excess of the £300 which, according to these charters, Geoffrey's grandfather had paid.[4] It may be noted that while Stephen's charter gives in actual figures the "ferm" which had been paid by Geoffrey's grandfather, and which Geoffrey himself was now to pay for London and Middlesex, it merely provides, in the case of Essex and Hertfordshire, that he was to pay what his grandfather had paid, without mentioning what that sum was. Happily, we obtain the information in the subsequent charter of the Empress, and we are tempted to infer

---

[1] "Reddendo mihi rectam firmam que inde reddi solebat die quâ rex Henricus pater meus fuit vivus et mortuus." Perhaps this indefinite phrase was due to the fact that Essex and Herts had a *joint* firma at the time (see *Rot. Pip.*, 31 Hen. I.).

[2] "Eadem firma qua avus ejus . . . tenuit."

[3] "Pro CCC libris sicut idem Gaufredus avus ejus tenuit."

[4] The *firma* of Essex with *Herts*, in 1130, was £420 3s. "ad pensum," *plus* £26 17s. "numero," *plus* £86 19s. 9d. "blancas," whereas Geoffrey secured the two for £360. The difference between this sum and the joint *firma* of 1130 curiously approximates that at London (see Appendix, p. 366, *n.*).

THE "FIRMA" OF LONDON AND MIDDLESEX.

from the silence of this earlier charter on the point, that while the ancient *firma* of London and Middlesex was a sum familiar to men, that of Essex and Herts could only be ascertained by research, pending which the Crown declined to commit itself to the sum.

It is scarcely necessary that I should insist on the extraordinary value of this statement and formal admission by the Crown that London and Middlesex had been held to farm by the elder Geoffrey de Mandeville—that is, towards the close of the eleventh century, or, at latest, in the beginning of the twelfth—and that the amount of the *firma* was £300 a year. One cannot understand how such a fact, of which the historical student cannot fail to grasp the importance, can have been overlooked so long, when it has virtually figured in Dugdale's *Baronage* for more than two centuries. The only writer, so far as I know, who has ventured on an estimate of the annual render from London at the time of Domesday arrives at the conclusion that "we can hardly be wrong in putting the returns at . . . about £850 a year."[1] We have seen that, on the contrary, the rental, even later than Domesday, was £300 a year, and this not for London only, but for London and Middlesex together.[2]

Nothing, indeed, could show more plainly the necessity for such a work as I have here undertaken, and the new light which the evidence of these charters throws upon the history of the time, than a comparison of the results here obtained with the statements in Mr. Loftie's work,[3] published under the editorship of Professor Freeman, which, though far less inaccurate than his earlier and larger work, contains such passages as this:—

[1] Pearson's *History of England during the Early and Middle Ages*, i. 664 ("County Rentals in Domesday").

[2] See Appendix P: "The Early Administration of London."

[3] *Historic Towns: London* (1887).

"Matilda had one chance of conciliating the citizens, and she threw it away. The immemorial liberties which had been enjoyed for generations, and confirmed by William and Henry, were taken from the city, which for the first and last time in its history was put 'in demesne.' The Earl of Essex, Geoffrey de Mandeville, whose father is said by Stow to have been portreeve, was given Middlesex 'in farm' with the Tower for his castle, and no person could hold pleas either in city or county without his permission. The feelings of the Londoners were fully roused. Though Stephen was actually a prisoner, and Matilda's fortunes never seemed brighter, her cause was lost. . . . The citizens soon saw that her putting them in demesne was no mistake committed in a hasty moment in times of confusion, but was part of a settled policy. This decided the waverers and doubled the party of Stephen. . . . Stephen was exchanged for the Earl of Gloucester, the Tower was surrendered, the dominion was removed, and London had its liberty once more; but after such an experience it is not wonderful that the citizens held loyally to Stephen during the short remainder of his life" (pp. 36, 37).[1]

A more complete travesty of history it would not be possible to conceive. "The immemorial liberties" were no older than the charter wrung from Henry a few years before, and so far from the city being "put 'in demesne'" (whatever may be meant by this expression),[2] "for the first and last time in its history," the Empress, had she done what is here charged to her, would have merely placed Geoffrey in the shoes of his grandfather and namesake.[3] But the strange thing is that she did nothing of the kind, and that the facts, in Mr. Loftie's narrative, are

[1] The two omitted portions amount to but a few lines. There is, however, an error in each. The first implies that the charter to Geoffrey was granted before the Empress reached, or was even invited to, London. The second contains the erroneous statement that the Empress, on her flight from London, "withdrew towards Winchester," and that her brother was captured by the Londoners in pursuit, whereas he was not captured till after the siege of Winchester, later in the year, and under different circumstances.

[2] It looks much as if Mr. Loftie had here again attempted to separate London from Middlesex, and to treat the former as granted "in demesne," and the latter "in farm." Such a conception is quite erroneous.

[3] It was his grandfather and not (as Mr. Loftie writes) his "father" who "is said by Stow to have been portreeve."

turned topsy-turvey. It was not by Matilda in June, but by Stephen in December, that London and Middlesex were placed in Geoffrey's power. The Empress did not do that which she is stated to have done; and Stephen did do what he is said to have undone. The result of his return to power, so far as London was concerned, was that the Tower was *not* surrendered, but, on the contrary, confirmed to Geoffrey, and that so far from "the dominion" (an unintelligible expression) being "removed," or London regaining its liberty, it was now deprived of its liberty by being placed, as even the Empress had refrained from placing it, beneath the yoke of Geoffrey. Thus it was certainly not due to his conduct on this occasion "that the citizens of London held loyally to Stephen during the short remainder of his life." Nor, it may be added, is it possible to understand what is meant by that "short remainder," for these events happened early in Stephen's reign, not a third of which had elapsed at the time.

But the important point is this. Here was Stephen anxious on the one hand to reward the Londoners for their allegiance, and, on the other, to punish Geoffrey for his repeated offences against himself, and yet compelled by the force of circumstances actually to reward Geoffrey at the cost of the Londoners themselves. We need no more striking illustration of the commanding position and overwhelming power which the ambitious earl had now obtained by taking advantage of the rival claims, and skilfully holding the balance between the two parties, as was done by a later king-maker in the strife of Lancaster and York.

Passing over for the present the remarkable expressions which illustrate my theory of the differentiation of the offices of justice and sheriff, I would invite attention to Geoffrey's claim to be placed in the shoes of his grand-

THE SECOND CHARTER OF THE KING.

father, as an instance of the tendency, in this reign, of the magnates to advance quasi-hereditary claims, often involving, as it were, the undoing of the work of Henry I. William de Beauchamp was anxious to be placed in the shoes of Robert le Despenser; the Beaumont Earl of Leicester in those of William Fitz Osbern; the Earl of Oxford in those of William of Avranches; and Geoffrey himself, we shall find, in those of "Eudo Dapifer."

A point of great importance awaits us in the reference which, in this charter, is made to the Exchequer. I expressed a doubt, when dealing with the first charter of the Empress,[1] as to the supposed total extinction of the working of the Exchequer under Stephen. The author of the *Dialogus*, though anxious to emphasize its re-establishment under Henry II., goes no further than to speak of its system being "*pene* prorsus abolitam" in the terrible time of the Anarchy (I. viii.). Now here, in 1141, at the very height, one might say, of the Anarchy, we not only find the Exchequer spoken of as in full existence, but, which is most important to observe, we have the precise Exchequer *formulæ* which we find under Henry II. The "Terræ datæ," or alienated Crown demesnes, are represented here by the "dominia que de predictis comitatibus data sunt," and the provision that they should be subtracted from the fixed ferm ("a firma subtrahantur") is a formula found in use subsequently, as is, even more, the phrase "ad scaccarium computabuntur."[2]

The next clause deals with castles, that great feature of the time. Here again the accepted view as to Stephen's laxity on the subject is greatly modified by this evidence that even Geoffrey de Mandeville, great as was his power,

[1] See p. 99.
[2] "Et computabitur tibi ad scaccarium" is the regular form found in the precepts of Henry II. (*Dialogus*, ii. 8).

deemed it needful to secure the royal permission before erecting a castle, and that this permission was limited to a single fortress.[1]

In the next clause we return to the system of counter-bids. As the king had trebled the grants of Crown demesne made to Geoffrey by the Empress, and trebled also the counties which had been placed in his charge by her, so now he trebled the number of enfeoffed knights ("milites feudatos"). The Empress had granted twenty; Stephen grants sixty. Of these sixty, ten were to be held of Geoffrey by his son Ernulf. Here, as before,[2] the question arises: what was the nature of the benefits thus conferred on the grantee? They were, I think, of two kinds. In the first place, Geoffrey became entitled to what may be termed the feudal profits, such as reliefs, accruing from these sixty fees. In the second, he secured sixty knights to serve beneath his banner in war. This, in a normal state of affairs, would have been of no consequence, as he would only have led them to serve the Crown. But in the then abnormal condition of affairs, and utter weakness of the crown, such a grant would be equivalent to strengthening *pro tanto* the power of the earl as arbiter between the two rivals for the throne.

Independently, however, of its bearing at the time, this grant has a special interest, as placing at our disposal a list of sixty knights' fees, a quarter of a century older than the "cartæ" of the *Liber Niger*.[3]

[1] See also, for Stephen's attitude towards the "adulterine" castles, the *Gesta Stephani* (p. 66): "Plurima adulterina castella, alia solâ adventus sui famâ vacuata, alia viribus virtuose adhibitis conquisita subvertit: omnesque circumjacentes provincias, quas castella inhabitantes intolerabili infestatione degravabant, purgavit tunc omnino, et quietissima reddidit" (1140).

[2] See p. 103.

[3] Note here the figures 60, 20, 10, as confirming the theory advanced by me in the *English Historical Review* (October, 1891) as to knight-service being grouped in multiples of ten (the *constabularia*).

At the close of all these specified grants comes a general confirmation of the lost charter of the Queen ("Carta Regine").

Our ignorance of the actual contents of that charter renders it difficult to speak positively as to whether Geoffrey obtained from Stephen all the concessions he had wrung from the Empress, or had to content himself, on some points, with less, while on most he secured infinitely more. Thus, in the matter of "the third penny," which was specially granted him by the Empress, we find this charter of Stephen as silent as had been the former.[1] And the omission of a clause authorizing the earl to deduct it from the ferm of the county virtually implies that he did not receive it. He gained, however, infinitely more by the great reduction in the total ferm. The grant by the Empress of a market at Bushey, and her permission that the market at Newport should be transferred to his castle at Walden, are not repeated in this charter; nor does the king, as his rival had done, grant the earl permission to fortify the Tower at his will, or to retain and strengthen the castles he already possessed. On the other hand, he allowed him, by a fresh concession, to raise an additional stronghold. It may also be mentioned, to complete the comparison, that the curious reference to appeal of treason is not found in the king's charter.

We will now turn from this charter to the movements by which it was followed.

At the close of the invaluable passage from Gervase alluded to above, we read:—

"Rex Stephanus a Cantuariâ recedens vires suas reparare studuit, quo severius et acrius imperatricem et omnes ipsius complices debellaret."[2]

His first step in this direction was to make a progress

---

[1] See Appendix H.   [2] *Gervase of Canterbury*, i. 123.

through his realm, or at least through that portion over which he reigned supreme. William of Malmesbury writes of his movements after Christmas :—

"Utræque partes imperatricis et regis se cum quietis modestiâ egerunt a Natale usque ad Quadragesimam; magis sua custodire quam aliena incursare studentes: rex in superiores regiones abscessit nescio quæ compositurus" (p. 763).

This scrupulous reluctance of the writer to relate events of which he had no personal knowledge is evidently meant to confirm his assurance, just above, that he had the greatest horror of so misleading posterity.[1] The thread of the narrative, however, which he drops is taken up by John of Hexham, who tells us that "after Easter" (April 19) the king and queen arrived at York, put a stop to a projected tournament between the two great Yorkshire earls, and endeavoured to complete the preparations for the king's revenge upon his foes.[2]

Before proceeding, I would call attention to two charters which must, it seems, have passed between the king's visit to Canterbury (Christmas, 1141), and his

---

[1] "Semper quippe horrori habui aliquid ad posteros transmittendum stylo committere, quod nescirem solidâ veritate subsistere. Ea porro, quæ de præsenti anno dicenda, hoc habebunt principium."

[2] "Post Pascha Stephanus, prosequente eum reginâ suâ Mathilde, venit Eboracum militaresque nundinas a Willelmo comite Eboraci et Alano comite de Richemunt adversus alterutrum conductas solvit; habuitque in votis pristinas suas injurias ultum ire, et regnum ad antiquam dignitatem et integritatem reformare" (*Sym. Dun.*, ii. 312). Notice that John of Hexham always speaks of Alan as Earl "of Richmond" and William as Earl "of York." He is probably the first writer to speak of an Earl "of Richmond," and this early appearance of the title was clearly unknown to the Lords' committee when they drew up their elaborate account of its origin and descent (*Third Report on the Dignity of a Peer*). If, as I believe, no county could, at this period, have two earls, it follows that either Alan "Comes" did not hold an English earldom, and was merely described as of Richmond because that was his seat; or, that "Richmondshire" was, at that time, treated as a county of itself. One or other of these alternatives must, I think, be adopted. But see also p. 290, n. 2.

appearance with the queen in Yorkshire (Easter, 1142). I do so, firstly, because their witnesses ought to be compared with those by whom the Canterbury charter was attested; secondly, because one of them is a further instance of how, as in the case of the Canterbury charter, chronicles and charters may be made to confirm and explain each other.

The first of these charters is the confirmation by Stephen of the foundation, by his constable Robert de Vere, of Monks Horton Priory, Kent.[1] If we eliminate from its eleven witnesses those whose attendance was due to the special contents of the charter, namely, the Count of Eu and two Kentish barons,[2] there remain eight names, every one of which appears in the Canterbury charter, one as grantee and seven as witnesses. Here is the list:

"Testibus Comite Gaufrido de Essex et Willelmo Comite de Warrenne . . . Et Comite Gilleberto de Penbroc et Willelmo de Iprâ et Willelmo Mart[el] et Turgisio de Abrincis et Ricardo de Luci et Adam de Belu[n] . . . apud Gipeswic."

Here then we have what might be described as King Stephen's Restoration Court, or at least the greater portion of its leading members; and this charter is therefore evidence that Stephen must have visited the Eastern Counties early in 1142. It is also evidence that Earl Geoffrey was with him on that occasion, and thus throws a gleam of light on the earl's movements at the time.

The other charter is known to us only from a transcript in the Great Coucher (vol. ii. fol. 445), and is

[1] *Harl. MS.*, 2044, fol. 55 *b*; *Addl. MSS.*, 5516, No. 9, p. 7 (printed in *Archæologia Cantiana*, x. 272, but not in Dugdale's *Monasticon*).

[2] Robert de Crevecœur and William de Eynsford. The Count of Eu was a benefactor to the priory.

strangely assigned in the official calendar to 1135-37.¹ The grantee is William, Earl of Lincoln, and the list of witnesses is as follows :—

"T. Com. Rann. et Com. Gisl. de Pembroc * et Com. Gisl. de hertf.* et Com. Sim.* et Com. R. de Warwic' et Com. R. de Ferr.* et W. mart.* et Bald. fil. Gisl.* et W. fil. Gisl. et Ric. de Camvill et Ric. fil. Ursi * et E[ustachio] fil. John' et Rad. de Haia et h' Wac' et W. de Coleuill apud Stanf'."

Of these fifteen witnesses at least five are local men, and of the remaining ten no fewer than seven (here distinguished by an asterisk) had attested the Canterbury charter. But further evidence of the close connection, in date, between these two charters is found in yet another quarter. This is the *English Chronicle*. We there read that after the release of Stephen from his captivity, "the king and Earl Randolf agreed at Stamford and swore oaths and plighted troth, that neither of them should prove traitor to the other." For this is the earliest occasion to which that passage can refer. Stephen would pass through Stamford on his northward progress to York, and here, clearly, at his entrance into Lincolnshire, he was met by the two local magnates, William, Earl of Lincoln, and Randolf, Earl of Chester. Their revolt at Lincoln, at the close of 1140, had led directly to his fall, but it was absolutely needful for the schemes he had in view that he should now secure their support, and overlook their past treason. He therefore came to terms with the two brother earls, and, further, bestowed on the Earl of Lincoln the manor of Kirton in Lindsey ("Chircheton"), and confirmed him in possession of his castle of Gainsborough and his bridge over Trent, "libere et quiete tenendum omnibus liberis consuetudinibus cum quibus

¹ *Thirty-first Report of Deputy Keeper*, p. 2.

aliquis comes Anglie tenet castella sua,"—a formula well deserving attention as bearing on the two peculiar features of this unhappy time, its earls and its castles.

Lastly, we should observe the family relationship between the grantee and the witnesses of this charter. The first witness was his half-brother, Earl Randolf of Chester, who was uncle of Earl Gilbert of Hertford, who was nephew of Earl Gilbert of Pembroke, who was brother of W(alter) fitz Gilbert and Baldwin fitz Gilbert, of whom the latter's daughter married H(ugh) Wac (Wake). Of the other witnesses, Ralph de Haye was of the family which then, and Richard de Camville of that which afterwards, held the constableship of Lincoln Castle. Earl R(oger) of Warwick (a supporter of the Empress) should be noticed as an addition to the Canterbury list of earls, and the descriptive style "de Warwicâ" may perhaps be explained as inserted here to distinguish him from Earl R(obert) "de Ferrers."

Gervase of Canterbury and John of Hexham alike lay stress on the fact that the king, eager for revenge, was bent on renewing the strife. William of Malmesbury echoes the statement, but tells us that the king was struck down just as he was about, we gather, to march south. As it was at Northampton that this took place he must have been following the very same road as he had done at this same time of year in 1138.[1] Nor can we doubt that his objective was Oxford, now again the head-quarters of his foe.[2] So alarming was his illness that his death was rumoured,

[1] He held a council at Northampton on his way south in Easter week, 1138.
[2] William of Malmesbury writes: "In ipsis Paschalibus feriis regem quædam (ut aiunt) dura meditantem gravis incommodum morbi apud Northamptunam detinuit, adeo ut in tota propemodum Angliâ sicut mortuus conclamaretur" (p. 763). There is a discrepancy of date between this statement and that of John of Hexham, who states that Stephen did not reach York till "post Pascha." William's chronology seems the more probable.

GEOFFREY SENT AGAINST ELY.

and the forces he had gathered were dismissed to their homes.[1]

But, meanwhile, where was Earl Geoffrey? We have seen that early in the year he was present with Stephen at Ipswich.[2] If we turn to the *Ely History*, printed in Wharton's *Anglia Sacra*, we shall find evidence that he was, shortly after, despatched with Earl Gilbert of Pembroke, who had been with him at Ipswich, to Ely.[3] When Stephen had successfully attacked Ely two years before (1140), the bishop had fled, with three companions, to the Empress at Gloucester. His scattered followers had now reassembled, and it was to expel them from their stronghold in the isle that Stephen despatched the two earls. Geoffrey soon put them to flight, doubtless at Aldreth, and setting his prisoners on horseback, with their feet tied together, led them in triumph to Ely.[4] To the monks, who came forth to meet him with their crosses and reliquaries, he threatened plunder and death, and their possessions were at once seized into the king's hands. But, meanwhile, their bishop's envoy to the pope, "a man skilled in the use of Latin, French, and English," had returned from Rome with letters to the primates of England and Normandy, insisting that Nigel should be restored to his see. The monks, also, had approached Stephen and obtained from him a reversal of Geoffrey's violent action. Nigel, therefore, returned to Ely, to the

[1] "Præventus vero infirmitate copias militum quas contraxerat remisit ad propria" (*Sym. Dun.*, ii. 312).

[2] *Supra*, p. 158.

[3] "Dirigitur enim in Ely a rege Stephano cum militari manu in armis strenuus Comes Gaufridus de Mannavillâ, associante ei Comite Gileberto, ut homines episcopi, qui tunc latenter affugerent, inde abigeret, aut gladiis truncaret" (*Anglia Sacra*, i. 621). Earl Gilbert was uncle to Earl Geoffrey's wife.

[4] "Qui festinus adveniens, hostilem turbam fugavit; milites vero teneri jussit; et equis impositos pedes eorum sub equis ligatos spectante populo usque in Ely perduxit" (*ibid.*).

joy, we are told, of his monks and people; and the two earls delivered into his hands the isle and Aldreth, its key.[1]

The point to insist upon, for our own purpose, is that the Earls Geoffrey and Gilbert were both concerned in this business, and that their names will again be found in conjunction in the records of that intrigue with the Empress which is the subject of the next chapter.

[1] See Appendix Z: "Bishop Nigel at Rome."

CHAPTER VIII.

THE SECOND CHARTER OF THE EMPRESS.

WE left, it may be remembered, the Empress and her supporters assembled at Bristol, apparently towards the close of the year 1141. Their movements are now somewhat obscure, and the hopes of the Empress had been so rudely shattered, that for a time her party were stunned by the blow. We gather, however, from William of Malmesbury that Oxford became her head-quarters,[1] and it was at Oxford that she granted the charter which forms the subject of this chapter.

From internal evidence it is absolutely certain that this charter is subsequent to that dealt with in the last chapter. That is to say, it must be dated subsequent to Christmas, 1141. But it is also certain, from the fact that the Earl of Gloucester is a witness, that it must have passed previous to his departure from England at the end of June, 1142.[2]

It may, at first sight, excite surprise that, after having extorted such concessions from Stephen, Geoffrey should so quickly turn to his rival, more especially when Stephen appeared triumphant, and the chances of his rival desperate. But, on the one hand, in accordance with his

---

[1] He states that the Earl of Gloucester, on his release, "circa germanam sedulo apud Oxeneford mansitabat; quo loco, ut præfatus sum, illa sedem sibi constituens, curiam fecerat" (p. 754).

[2] He set sail "aliquanto post festum sancti Johannis" (*Will. Malms.*, p. 765).

persistent policy, he hoped, by the offer of a fresh treason, to secure from the Empress an even higher bid than that which he had wrung from Stephen; and, on the other, the very weakness of the Empress, he must have seen, would place her more completely at his mercy. In short, he now virtually aspired to the *rôle* of "the king-maker" himself.[1]

Even he, however, strong though he was, could scarcely have attempted to stem the tide, while the flood of reaction was at its height. He watched, no doubt, for the first signs of an ebb in Stephen's triumph. It was not long before this ebb came in the form of that illness by which the king, as we saw, was struck down about the end of April, on his way south, at Northampton.[2] The dismissal of the host he had so eagerly collected was followed by a rumour of his death.[3] No one, it would seem, has ever noticed the strange parallel between this illness and that of 1136. In each case it was about the end of April that the king was thus seized, and in each case his seizure gave rise to a widespread rumour of his death.[4] On the previous occasion that rumour had been followed by an outburst of treason and revolt,[5] and it is surely, to say the

[1] See the dazzling description of his power given by the author of the *Gesta*, who speaks of him as one "qui omnes regni primates et divitiarum potentiâ et dignitatis excedebat opulentiâ; turrim quoque Londoniarum in manu, sed castella inexpugnabilis fortitudinis circa civitatem constructa habebat, omnemque regni partem, quæ se regi subdiderat, ut ubique per regnum regis vices adimplens, et, in rebus agendis, rege avidius exaudiretur, et in præceptis injungendis, plus ei quam regi obtemperaretur" (p. 101). William of Newburgh, in the same spirit, speaks of him as "regi terribilis" (i. 44).

[2] See p. 160.

[3] "In totâ propemodum Angliâ sicut mortuus conclamaretur" (*ibid.*).

[4] William of Malmesbury (*ut supra*) is the authority for 1142, and Henry of Huntingdon for 1136: "Ad Rogationes vero divulgatum est regem mortuum esse" (p. 259).

[5] "Jam ergo cœpit rabies prædicta Normannorum, perjurio et proditione pullulare" (*ibid.*).

DATE AND AUTHORITIES. 165

least, not improbable that it now gave the sign for which Geoffrey was watching, and led to the extraordinary charter with which we have here to deal.

The movements of the Empress have also to be considered in their bearing on the date of the charter. We learn from William of Malmesbury that she held two councils at Devizes, one about the 1st of April (Mid-Lent), and one at Whitsuntide (7–14 June). The latter council was held on the return of the envoys who had been despatched, after the former one, to request Geoffrey of Anjou to come to his wife's assistance. Geoffrey had replied that the Earl of Gloucester must first come over to him, and the earl accordingly sailed from Wareham about the end of June. It is most probable that he went there straight from Devizes, in which case he was not at Oxford after the beginning of June. In this case, that is the latest date at which the charter can have passed.

Although the original of this charter cannot, like its predecessor of the previous year, be traced down to this very day, we have the independent authorities of Dugdale and of another transcriber for the fact that it was duly recorded in the Great Coucher of the duchy.[1] If the missing volume, or volumes, of that work should come to light, I cannot entertain the slightest doubt that this charter will be found there entered. Collateral evidence in its favour is forthcoming from another quarter, for the record with which, as I shall show, it is so closely connected that the two form parts of one whole, has its existence proved by cumulative independent evidence.

I have taken for my text, in this instance, the fine

---

[1] It would seem to have been entered immediately after that charter to Miles of Gloucester which I have printed on p. 11, and which precedes it in the transcripts.

166 *THE SECOND CHARTER OF THE EMPRESS.*

transcript from the Great Coucher in *Lansd. MS.* 229 (fol. 109), with which I have collated Dugdale's transcript, among his MSS. at Oxford (L. 19), " ex magno registro in officio Ducatus Lancastrie." I have also collated another transcript which is among the Dodsworth MSS. (xxx. 113), and which was made in 1649. It is, unfortunately, incomplete. Yet another transcriber began to copy the charter, but stopped almost at once.[1] I have given in the notes the variants (which are slight) in the Dodsworth and Dugdale transcripts.

" Carta M. Imperatricis facta Com̄ Gaufredo Essexiæ de pluribus terris et libertatibus.

M. Imperatrix. H. regis filia et Anglorum Domina. Archiepiscopis.[2] Episcopis. Abbatibus. Comitibus. Baronibus. Justiciariis. Vicecomitibus. Ministris. et omnibus fidelibus suis Francis et Anglis totius Angliæ et Normanniæ Salutem. Sciatis me reddidisse et concessisse Comiti Gaufr[edo] Essexe omnia tenementa sua, sicut Gaufredus avus suus,[3] aut Willelmus pater suus,[4] aut ipsemet postea unquam melius vel liberius tenuerit[5] aliquo tempore in feodo et hæreditate sibi et hæredibus suis, ad tenendum de me et de hæredibus meis. Videlicet in terris et turribus, in Castellis et Bailliis. Et nominatim Turrim Lund[oniæ] cum Castello quod subtus[6] est, ad firmandum et efforciandum ad voluntatem suam. Et Vicecomitatum Lund[oniæ][7] et Middelsex per CCC lib[ras] sicut Gaufredus auus eius tenuit. Et vicecomitatum Essex per CCC lib[ras] sicut idem Gaufredus auus eius tenuit.[8] Et vicecomitatum

---

[1] *Lansdowne MS.* 259, fol. 66.
[2] " Archiepiscopis, etc." (Dug.).
[3] " suus " omitted (Dug.).
[4] " ejus " (Dug.).
[5] " tenuerunt " (Dug., Dods.).
[6] " subjectum " (Dods.).
[7] " Lundoniæ et Middlesexiæ " (Dug.).
[8] " Et . . . tenuit " (Essex shrievalty) omitted by Dugdale (and, consequently, in his *Baronage* also).

de Heortfordscirâ per LX libras sicut avus eius tenuit. Et præter hoc do et concedo eidem Gaufredo quod habeat hæreditabiliter Justiciã Lund[oniæ] et Middelsex et Essex et de Hertfordscirâ, ita quod nulla alia justicia placitet in hiis supradictis vicecomitatibus nisi per eis[1] [*sic*]. Et concedo illi,[2] ut habeat illas C libratas terræ quas dedi illi, et servicium illorum XX militum sicut illud ei dedi et per aliam cartam meam confirmavi. Et illas CC libratas terræ quas Rex Stephanus et Matildis regina ei dederunt. Et illas C libratas terræ de terris Eschaetis quas idem Rex et Regina ei dederunt, et servicium militum quod ei dederunt, sicut habet inde cartas illorum. Et do ei totam terram quæ fuit[3] Eudonis Dapiferi in Normanniâ et Dapiferatum ipsius. Et hæc reddo ei ut Rectum suum ut habeat et teneat hæreditabiliter, ita ne ponatur inde in placitum versus aliquem. Et si dominus meus Comes Andegaviæ et ego voluerimus, Comes Gaufredus accipiet pro dominiis et terris quas habet Eschaetis et pro servicio militum[4] quod habet totam terram quæ fuit Eudonis Dapiferi in Anglia sicut tenuit ea die qua fuit et vivus et[5] mortuus, quia hoc est Rectum suum, Præter illas[6] libratas terræ quas ego dedi ei Et præter seruicium XX militum quod ei dedi, Et præter terram Ernulfi de Mannavill sicut eam tenet de Comite Gaufredo ex servicio X militum Et si potero perquirere erga Episcopum Lund[oniæ] et erga ecclesiam Sancti Pauli Castellum de Storteford per Escambium ad Gratum suum tunc do et concedo illud ei et hæredibus suis in feodo et hereditate tenendum de me et hæredibus meis. Quod si facere non potero, tunc ei convenciono quod faciam illud prosternere

---

[1] Dodsworth transcript closes here. [2] "illi" omitted by Dugdale.
[3] "quæ fuit" omitted by Dugdale.
[4] "per servicium militare" (wrongly, Dug.).
[5] "et" omitted by Dugdale. [6] "centum libratas" (Dug.).

et ex toto cadere. Et concedo quod **Ernulf[us]** de **Manna-vill** teneat illas C libratas terræ quas ei dedi, et servicium X militum de Comite Gaufredo patre suo. Et præter hoc do et concedo eidem Ernulfo C libratas terræ de terris Eschaetis Et servicium X militum ad tenendum de domino meo Comite Andegau[ie] et de me in capite hæreditarie sibi et hæredibus suis de nobis et de hæredibus nostris videlicet Cristeshalam[1] et Benedis[2] pro quanto valent. Et superplus perficiam ei per considerationem Comitis Gaufredi. Et convenciono eidem Gaufredo Comiti Essex quod dominus meus Comes Andegauie vel ego vel filii nostri nullam pacem aut concordiam cum Burgensibus Lund[oniæ] faciemus, nisi concessu et assensu prædicti Comitis Gaufredi quia inimici eius sunt mortales. Concedo etiam eidem Gaufredo quod novum castellum quod firmavit super Lviam[3] stet et remaneat ad efforciandum ad voluntatem suam. Concedo etiam ei quod firmet unum Castellum ubicunque voluerit in terrâ suâ sicut ei per aliam cartam meam concessi, et quod stet et remaneat. Concedo etiam eidem Gaufredo quod ipse et omnes homines sui habeant et lucrentur omnia essarta sua libera et quieta de omnibus placitis facta usque ad diem qua servicio domini mei Comitis Andegavie ac meo adhesit. Hæc autem omnia supradicta tenementa in omnibus rebus concedo ei tenenda hæreditarie sibi et hæredibus suis de me et hæredibus meis. Quare volo et firmiter præcipio quod ipse Gaufredus comes et hæredes sui teneant hæc omnia supradicta tenementa ita bene et in pace et libere et quiete et honorifice et

---

[1] Chreshall, *alias* Christhall, Essex. Part of the honour of Boulogne. Was held by Count Eustace, at the Survey, in demesne. Stephen granted it to his own son William, who gave it to Richard de Luci.

[2] Bendish Hall, in Radwinter, Essex. Part of the honour of Boulogne. It was given by Stephen's son William to Faversham Abbey, Kent.

[3] This word is illegible. It baffled the transcriber in *Lansd. MS.* 259. Dugdale has "wiam." The right reading is "luiam," the river Lea being meant, as is proved by the Pipe-Roll of 14 Hen. II.

plenarie sicut unquam aliquis Comitum meorum totius
Angliæ melius vel liberius tenuit vel tenet Et præter hoc
dedi Willelmo filio Otuet [1] fratri ejusdem Comitis Gaufredi
C libratas terræ de terris Escaetis tenendis de me et de
hæredibus meis in feudo et hæreditate pro seruicio suo,
et pro amore fratris sui Comitis Gaufredi. Concedo etiam
quod Willelmus de Sai [2] habeat omnes terras et tenementa
quæ fuerunt patris sui, et ipse et hæredes sui, et quod
Willelmus Cap'.[3] habeat terram patris sui sine placito
et ipse et hæredes sui. Concedo etiam eidem Comiti Gaufredo quod Willelmus filius Walteri [4] et hæredes sui
habeant custodiam Castelli de Windesh' et omnia sua

[1] William fitz Otwel, Earl Geoffrey's "brother," is referred to by Earl
William (Geoffrey's son) as his uncle ("avunculus") in a charter confirming
his grant of lands (thirty-three acres) in "Abi et Toresbi" to Greenfield
Nunnery, Lincolnshire (*Harl. Cart.*, 53, C, 50). He is also a witness, as
"patruus meus," to a charter of Earl Geoffrey the younger (*Sloane Cart.*,
xxxii. 64), early in the reign of Henry II. He was clearly a "uterine"
brother of Earl Geoffrey the elder, so that his father must have married
William de Mandeville's widow—a fact unknown to genealogists.

[2] William de Sai had married Beatrice, sister (and, in her issue, heiress)
of the earl, by whom he was ancestor of the second line of Mandeville, Earl
of Essex. In the following year he joined the earl in his furious revolt
against the king.

[3] This was William "Capra" (*Chèvre*), whose family gave its name to
the manor of "Chevers" in Mountnessing, county Essex. He was probably
another brother-in-law of the earl, for I have seen a charter of Alice
(*Adelid[is]*) Capra, in which she speaks of Geoffrey's son, Earl William, as
her nephew ("nepos"). There is also a charter of a Geoffrey Capra and
Mazelina (*sic*) his wife, which suggests that the name of Geoffrey may have
come to the family from the earl. Thoby Priory, Essex, was founded (1141-
1151) by Michael Capra, Roesia his wife, and William, their son. The
founder speaks of Roger fitz Richard ("ex cujus munificentiâ mihi idem
fundus pervenit"), who was the second husband (as I have elsewhere
explained) of "Alice of Essex," *née* de Vere, the sister of Earl Geoffrey's
wife. A Michael Capra and a William Capra, holding respectively four and
four and a half knights' fees, were feudal tenants of Walter fitz Robert (the
lord of Dunmow) in 1166.

[4] William, son of Walter (Fitz Other) de Windsor, castellan of Windsor.
In the Pipe-Roll of 31 Hen. I., he appears as in charge of Windsor
Forest, for which he renders his account. It is probably to this charter
rather than to any separate grant that Dugdale refers in his account of the
family.

170 THE SECOND CHARTER OF THE EMPRESS.

tenementa sicut ipse Willelmus et antecessores sui eam habuerunt de Rege H. patre meo et antecessoribus ipsius. Et quod Matheus de Rumilli[1] habeat terram patris sui quam Gaufridus de Turevill[2] tenet. Et Willelmus de Auco[3] habeat Lauendonam sicut Rectum suum hæreditarie. Concedo etiam eidem Comiti Gaufredo quod omnes homines sui teneant terras et tenementa sua de quocunque teneant sine placito et sine pecuniæ donatione et ut Rectum eis teneatur de eorum Calumpnijs sine pecuniæ donatione Et quod Osb[ertus] Octod[enarii][4] habeat illas XX libratas terræ quas ei dedi et confirmaui per cartam meam.

"Hanc[5] autem convencionem et donationem tenendam affidavi manu mea propria in manu ipsius Comitis Gaufredi. Et hujus fiduciæ sunt obsides per fidem et Testes Robertus Comes Gloec': et Milo Com' Heref':[6] et Brianus filius Comitis: et Rob' fil' Reg':[7] et Rob' de Curc' Dap:[8]

---

[1] This is an unusual name. As William de Say is mentioned just before, it may be noted that his son (Earl Geoffrey's nephew) promised (in 1150-1160) to grant to Ramsey Abbey "marcatam redditus ex quo adipisci poterit quadraginta marcatas de hereditate sua, scilicet de terra Roberti de *Rumele*" (*Chron. Ram.*, p. 305). Mathew de Romeli, according to Dugdale, was the son of Robert de Romeli, lord of Skipton, by Cecily his wife. A Mathew de Romeli, with Alan his son, occur in a plea of 1236-7 (*Bracton's Note-Book*, ed. Maitland, iii. 189).

[2] Geoffrey de Tourville appears in 1130 as holding land in four counties (*Rot. Pip.*, 31 Hen. I.).

[3] William de Ou (Auco) or Eu is returned in the *carta* of the Earl of Essex (1166) as holding four fees of him.

[4] See Appendix Q, on "Osbertus Octodenarii."

[5] Dodsworth's transcript begins again here, and is continued down to "Belloc[ampo]."

[6] "Comes Herefordiæ" (Dug.).

[7] So also Dodsworth; but Dugdale wrongly extends: "Robertus filius Reginaldi." See p. 94, *n.* 4.

[8] Robert de Courci of Stoke (Courcy), Somerset. He figures in the Pipe-Roll of 31 Hen. I. As "Robert de Curci" he witnessed the Empress's charter creating the earldom of Hereford (July 25, 1141), and as "Robert de Curci Dapifer" her confirmation of the Earl of Devon's gift (*Mon. Aug.*, v. 106; *Journ. B. A. A.*, xxxi. 391), both of them passing at Oxford, the latter (probably) in 1142, subsequent to the above charter. He was slain at Counsylth, 1157.

et Joh'es filius Gisleberti:[1] et Milo de Belloc':[2] et Rad' Paganell:[3] et Rob' de Oilli Conest':[4] et Rob' fil' Heldebrand'.[5]

"Et[6] convencionavi eidem Comiti Gaufredo pro posse meâ quod Comes Andegavie dominus meus assecurabit ei manu sua propria illud idem[7] tenendum et Henricus filius meus similiter. Et quod rex Franciæ erit inde[8] obses si facere potero. Et si non potero, faciam quod ipse Rex capiet in manu illud tenendum. Et de hoc debent esse

[1] John Fitz Gilbert, marshal to the Empress, and brother, as the succeeding charter proves, to William, her chancellor. With his father, Gilbert the Marshal (*Mariscallus*), he was unsuccessfully impleaded, under Henry I., by Robert de Venoiz and William de Hastings, for the office of marshal (*Rot. Cart.*, 1 John), and in 1130, as John the Marshal (*Mariscallus*), he appears as charged, with his relief, in Wiltshire, for his father's lands and office (*Rot. Pip.*, 31 Hen. I.). He is mentioned among the "barons" on the side of the Empress at the siege of Winchester (*Gesta Stephani*), and he was, with Robert de Curcy, witness to her (Oxford) charter, which I assign in the last note to later in this year, as he also had been to her charter creating the earldom of Hereford (July 25, 1141). Subsequently, he witnessed the charter to the son of the Earl of Essex (*vide post*). He played some part in the next reign from his official connection with the Becket quarrel. See also p. 131.

[2] Miles de Beauchamp, son of Robert de Beauchamp, and nephew to Simon de Beauchamp, hereditary castellan of Bedford. In 1130 he appears in connection with Beds. and Bucks. (*Rot. Pip.*, 31 Hen. I.). With his brother (*Salop Cartulary*) Payn de Beauchamp (who afterwards married Rohaise, the widow of this Geoffrey de Mandeville), he had held Bedford Castle against the king for five weeks from Christmas, 1137, as heir-male to his uncle, whose daughter and heir, with the Bedford barony, Stephen had conferred on Hugh *Pauper*, brother of his favourite, the Count of Meulan (*Ord. Vit.; Gesta Steph.*). Dugdale's account is singularly inaccurate. Simon, the uncle, must have been living in the spring of 1136, for he then witnessed, as a royal *dapifer*, Stephen's great (Oxford) charter.

[3] See p. 94, n. 2.

[4] Robert de Oilli the second, castellan of Oxford, and constable. Founder of Osney Priory. He appears in the Pipe-Roll of 31 Hen. I., and had witnessed, as a royal *constabularius*, Stephen's great (Oxford) charter of 1136, but had embraced the cause of the Empress in 1141 (see p. 66). He witnessed five others of the Empress's charters, all of which passed at Oxford (*Journ. B. A. A.*, xxxi. 391, 392, 396, 397).

[5] See p. 95, note [1].

[6] Dodsworth's transcript recommences and is continued to the end.

[7] "Ibidem" (Dods., wrongly).

[8] "Ijdem" (Dods., wrongly).

obsides per fidem: Juhel de Moduana,[1] et Robertus de Sabloill et Wido de Sabloill[2] et Pagan' de Clarevall'[3] et Gaufredus de Clarevall' et Andreas de Aluia:[4] et Pipinus de Turon': et Absalon Rumarch'[5] et Reginaldus comes Cornubiæ et Balduinus Comes Devon': et Gislebertus Comes de Penbr': et Comes Hugo de Norff': et Comes Albericus: et Henricus de Essex: et Petrus de Valon':[6] et alii Barones mei quos habere voluerit et ego habere potero, erunt inde obsides similiter. Et quod x'rianitas Angliæ quæ est in potestate meâ capiet in manu istam supradictam conventionem tenendam eidem Comiti[7] Gaufredo et hæredibus suis de me et de hæredibus meis. Apud Oxineford.[8]

"Sub magno sigillo dictæ Matildis Imperatricis."

Let us now, in accordance with the guiding principle on which I have throughout insisted, compare this charter *seriatim* with those by which it was preceded, with a view to ascertaining what further concessions the unscrupulous

[1] "Meduana" (Dug., rightly).

"Johelus de Meduanâ" (Juhel of Mayenne) figures in the Pipe-Roll of 31 Hen. I. as holding land in Devonshire. At the commencement of Stephen's reign, Geoffrey of Anjou had entrusted him with three of the castles he had captured in Normandy, on condition of receiving his support (*R. of Torigni*).

[2] Guy de Sablé had accompanied the Empress to England in the autumn of 1139 (*Ord. Vit.*, v. 121).

[3] Clairvaux was a castle in Anjou. Payn de Clairvaux (*de Claris vallibus*) had, in 1130, and for some time previously, been fermor of Hastings, in Sussex (*Rot. Pip.*, 31 Hen. I. p. 42). Later on, in Stephen's reign, he appears at Caen, witnessing a charter of Geoffrey, Duke of Normandy (Bayeux *Liber Niger*).

[4] "Alvia" (Dug.).   [5] Or "Rumard." Dugdale has "Rumard."

[6] "Valoniis" (Dug.).

Peter de Valoines. The occurrence of this great Hertfordshire baron is of special interest, because we have seen the Empress granting a charter to his father, Roger, in 1141. It is probable, therefore, that Roger had died in the interval. Peter himself died before 1166, when his younger brother, Robert, had succeeded him. His widow, Gundred (de Warrenne), was then living.

[7] "Comiti . . . meis." Dodsworth has only "Com etc."

[8] "cum sigillo" (Dods.).

INCREASED DEMANDS OF GEOFFREY.

earl had won by this last change of front. We shall find that, as we might expect, it marks a distinct advance.

The earlier clauses do little more than specifically confirm the privileges and possessions that he had inherited from his father or had already wrung from the eager rivals for the Crown. This was by no means needless so far as the Empress was concerned, for his desertion of her cause since her previous charter involved, as an act of treason, his forfeiture at her hands. These are followed by a new grant, namely, "totam terram quæ fuit Eudonis Dapiferi in Normannia et Dapiferatum ipsius," with a conditional proposal that Geoffrey should also, in exchange for the grants he had already received, obtain that portion of the Dapifer's fief which lay in England. The large estate which this successful minister had accumulated in the service of the Conqueror and his sons had escheated to the Crown at his death, and is entered accordingly in the Pipe-Roll of 31 Hen. I. This has an important bearing on the noteworthy admission in the charter that Geoffrey is to receive the Dapifer's fief not as a gift, but as his right ("rectum suum"). This expression is referred to by Mr. Eyton in his MSS., as placing beyond doubt the received statement that Geoffrey was maternally a grandson of the Dapifer, whose daughter and heiress Margaret had married his father William. But this statement is taken from Dugdale, who derived it solely from the *Historia Fundationis* of St. John's Abbey, Colchester, a notoriously inaccurate and untrustworthy document printed in the *Monasticon*. The fact that this fief escheated to the Crown, instead of passing to the Mandevilles with the Dapifer's alleged daughter, is directly opposed to a story which has no foundation of its own.[1]

[1] The clause certainly favours the belief that a relationship existed, but it was probably collateral, instead of lineal.

The next clause to be noticed is that which refers to Bishop's Stortford. It implies a peculiar antipathy to this castle on the part of Earl Geoffrey, an antipathy explained by the fact of its position, lying as it did on the main road from London to (Saffron) Walden, and thus cutting communications between his two strongholds. We have a curious allusion to this episcopal castle a few years before (1137), when Abbot Anselm of St. Edmund's, who claimed to have been elected to the see, seized and held it.[1]

The next additional grant made in this charter is that of " C libratas terræ de terris eschaetis et servicium X militum " to the earl's son Ernulf. This is followed by what is certainly the most striking clause in the whole charter, that which binds the Empress and her husband "to make no peace and come to no terms with the burgesses (*sic*) of London, without the permission and assent of the said Earl Geoffrey, because they are his mortal foes." Comment on the character of such a pledge on the part of one who claimed the crown, or on the light it throws on Geoffrey's doings, is surely needless.

The clauses relating to Geoffrey's castles are deserving of special attention on account of the important part which the castle played in this great struggle. The erection of unlicensed ("adulterine") castles and their rapid multiplication throughout the land is one of the most notorious features of the strife, and one for which Stephen's weakness has been always held responsible. It is evident, however, from these charters that the Crown struggled hard against the abdication of its right to control the building of castles, and that even when reduced to sore straits, both Stephen and the Empress made this

---

[1] "Possessiones omnes ad ecclesiam pertinentes, castellum quoque de Storteford in sua dominatione recepit" (*Rad. de Diceto*, i. 250).

privilege the subject of special and limited grant. By this charter the earl secures the license of the Empress for a new castle which he had erected on the Lea. He may have built it to secure for himself the passage of the river, it being for him a vital necessity to maintain communication between the Tower of London and his ancestral stronghold in Essex. But the remainder of the passage involves a doubt. The Empress professes to repeat the permission in her former charter that he may construct one permanent castle, in addition to those he has already, anywhere within his fief. Yet a careful comparison of this permission with that contained in her former charter, and that which was granted by Stephen, in his charter between the two, proves that she was really confirming what he, not she, had granted.

MAUD (1141).	STEPHEN.	MAUD (1142).
"Et præterea concedo illi ut castella sua que habet stent ei et remaneant ad inforciandum ad voluntatem suam."	"Et præterea firmiter ei concessi ut possit firmare quoddam castellum ubicunque voluerit in terra sua, et quod stare possit."	"Concedo etiam ei quod firmet unum castellum ubicunque voluerit in terra sua, *sicut ei per aliam cartam meam concessi*, et quod stet et remaneat."

As we can trace, in every other instance, the relation of the various charters without difficulty or question, it would seem that we have here to do with an error, whether or not intentional.

We then come to the clauses in favour of Geoffrey's relatives and friends. This is a novel feature which we cannot afford to overlook. It is directly connected with the question of that important De Vere charter to which we shall shortly come.

Lastly, there is the remarkable arrangement for securing the validity of the charter. Let us look at this closely.[1] We should first notice that the Empress describes it, not as a charter, but as a "convencio et donatio." Now this "convencio" is a striking term, for it virtually denotes a treaty between two contracting powers. This conception of treaty relations between the Crown and its subjects is one of the marked peculiarities of this singular reign. It is clearly foreshadowed in those noteworthy charters which the powerful Miles of Gloucester secured from Stephen at his accession, and it meets us again in the negotiations between the youthful Henry of Anjou, posing as the heir to the crown, and the great nobles, towards the close of this same reign. It is in strict accordance with this idea that we here find the Empress naming those who were to be her sureties for her observance of this "convencio," precisely as was done in the case of a treaty between sovereign powers.[2] The

[1] This negotiation between the Empress and Geoffrey should be compared with that between her and the legate in the spring of the preceding year. Each illustrates the other. In the latter case the expression used is, "Juravit et *affidavit* imperatrix episcopo quod," etc. In the former, the empress is made to say, "Hanc autem convencionem et donacionem tenendam *affidavi*," etc. But the striking point of resemblance is that in each case her leading followers are made to take part in the pledge of performance. At Winchester, we read in William of Malmesbury, "Idem juraverunt cum ea, et affidaverunt pro eâ, Robertus frater ejus comes de Gloecestrâ, et Brianus filius comitis marchio de Walingeford, et Milo de Gloecestriâ, postea comes de Hereford, et nonnulli alii" (see p. 58). At Oxford, we read in these charters, "Et hujus fiduciæ sunt obsides per fidem et Testes, Robertus comes Gloecestrie, et Milo comes Herefordie, et Brianus filius comitis et," etc. So close a parallel further confirms the genuineness of these charters.

Another remarkable document illustrative of this negotiation is the alliance ("Confederatio amoris") between the Earls of Hereford and Gloucester (see Appendix S). Each earl there "affidavit et juravit" to the other, and each named certain of his followers as his "obsides per fidem"—the very phrase here used. See also p. 385, n. 3.

[2] That these securities were modelled on the practice of contracting sovereign powers is seen on comparing them with the treaty between Henry I. and the Count of Flanders (see Appendix S). But most to the point is the treaty between King Stephen and Duke Henry, where the clause for securing the "conventiones" runs:—"Archiepiscopi vero et episcopi ab utraque parte in manu ceperunt quod si quis nostrum a predictis conventioni-

exact part which the King of France was to play in this transaction is not as clear as could be wished, but the expression "capere in manu" is of course equivalent to his becoming her "manucaptor," and "tenere" is here used in the sense of "to hold good."[1] The closing words in which "the Lady of England" declared that all the Church of Christ then beneath her sway shall undertake to be responsible for her keeping faith, present a striking picture: but yet more vivid, in its dramatic intensity, is that of the undaunted Empress, the would-be Queen of the English, standing in her water-girdled citadel, surrounded by her faithful followers, and playing, as it were, her last card, as she placed her hand, in token of her faith, in the grip of the Iron Earl.[2]

It was only, indeed, the collapse, to all appearance, of her fortunes, that could have tempted Geoffrey to demand, or have induced the Empress to concede, terms so preposterously high. The fact that she was hoping, at this moment, to allure her husband to her side, that he might join her in a crowning effort, explains her eagerness to secure allies, at the cost of whatever sacrifice, and also, in consequence, the anxiety of those allies to bind her to her promises hard and fast. It further throws light on the constant reference throughout this charter to Geoffrey of Anjou and his son.

Turning to the names of her proposed sureties, we find

bus recederet, tam diu eum ecclesiastica justicia coercebunt, quousque errata corrigat et ad predictam pactionem observandam redeat. Mater etiam Ducis et ejus uxor et fratres ipsius Ducis et omnes sui quos ad hoc applicare poterit, hæc assecurabunt."

[1] We may perhaps compare the oath taken by the French king some years before, to secure the charter ("Keure") granted to St. Omer by William, Count of Flanders (April 14, 1127):—"Hanc igitur Communionem tenendam, has supradictas consuetudines et conventiones esse observandas fide promiserunt et sacramento confirmaverunt Ludovicus rex Francorum, Guillelmus Comes Flandriæ," etc., etc.

[2] See Appendix T, on "Affidatio in manu."

among them five earls, of whom the Earls of Norfolk and of Pembroke invite special notice. The former had played a shifty part from the very beginning of the reign. He appears to have really fought for his own hand alone, and we find him, the year after this, joining the Earl of Essex in his wild outburst of revolt. With Pembroke the case was different. He had been among the nobles who, the Christmas before, had assembled at Stephen's court, and had attested the charter there granted to the Earl of Essex. He may, in the interval, have quarrelled with Stephen and joined the party of the Empress; but I think the occurrence of his name may be referred, with more probability, to another cause, that of his family ties. It is, indeed, to family ties that we must now turn our attention.

The Earl of Essex had included, as we have seen, in his demands on this occasion, provisions in favour of certain of his relatives, including apparently his sisters' husbands. But these by no means exhausted the concessions he had resolved to exact. He had come prepared to offer the Empress the support, not only of himself, but of a powerful kinsman and ally. This was his wife's brother, Aubrey de Vere.

It will be better to relegate to an appendix the relationship of these two families, without a clear understanding of which it is impossible to grasp Geoffrey's scheme, or to interpret aright these charters in their relation to one another, and in their bearing as parts of a connected whole. Unfortunately, the errors of past genealogists have rendered it a task of some difficulty to ascertain the correct pedigree.[1]

When the fact has been established on a sure footing that Aubrey stood in the relation of wife's brother to Geoffrey, we may turn to the charter upon which my narrative is here founded.

[1] See Appendix U: "The Families of Mandeville and De Vere."

This is a charter of the Empress to Aubrey at Oxford. Mr. Eyton had, of course, devoted his attention to this, as to the other charters, in his special studies on the subject, but his fatal mistake in assigning both this and the above charter to Geoffrey to the year 1141 deprives his conclusions of all value. We may note, however, that he argued from the mention, in the charter granted to Geoffrey, of "Earl Aubrey," that it must, in any case, be subsequent to the charter by which Aubrey was created an earl. He, therefore, dated the latter as "*circ.* July, 1141," and the former "*circ.* August, 1141" (or "between July 25 and Aug. 15, 1141").[1] This reasoning could at once be disposed of by pointing out that the Empress accepted her new ally and supporter as "Earl Aubrey" already. Of this, however, more below. But the true answer is to be found in the fact, which Mr. Eyton failed to perceive, that these two charters were not only granted simultaneously, but formed the two complements of one connected whole. In the light of this discovery the whole episode is clear.

It is now time to give the charter with the grounds for believing in its existence and authenticity. We have two independent transcripts to work from. One of them was taken from the Vere register by Vincent in 1622, and printed by him in his curious *Discoverie of Brook's Errors*. The other was taken, apparently, in 1621, and was used by Dugdale for his *Baronage*. Vincent's original transcript is preserved at the College of Arms, and this I have used for the text. But we have, fortunately, strong external testimony to the existence of the actual document. There is printed in Rymer's *Fœdera* (xiii. 251) a confirmation by Henry VIII. (May 6, 1509) of this very charter, in which he is careful to state that it was duly exhibited before

[1] *Add. MSS.*, 31,943, fols 96 b, 99, 116 b

him.[1] Thus, from an unexpected source we obtain the evidence we want. It must further be remembered that our knowledge of these twin charters comes from two different and unconnected quarters, one being recorded in the duchy coucher (see p. 165), while the other was found among the muniments of the heir of the original grantee (see p. 183). If, then, these two independent documents confirm and explain one another, there is every reason to believe that their contents are wholly authentic.

Charter of the Empress to Aubrey de Vere (1142).

M. Imp'atrix H. Regis filia et Anglorum Domina Archiepiscopis Episcopis Abbatibus Comitibus Baronibus Justiciariis Vicecomitibus ministris et omnibus fidelibus suis Francis et Anglis totius Angliæ salutem. Sciatis me reddidisse et concessisse Comiti Alberico omnes terras et tenementa sua, sicut pater eius Albericus de Veer tenuit, die quâ fuit vivus et mortuus, videlicet, in terris, in feodis, in firmis, in ministeriis, in vadiis, in empcionibus, et hæreditatibus. Et nominatim Camerariam Angliæ sicut Albericus de Veer pater eius vel Robertus Malet vel aliquis Antecessorum suorum eam melius vel liberius tenuit cum omnibus consuetudinibus et libertatibus quæ ad ea pertinent sicut alia Carta mea quam inde habuit testatur. Et do et concedo ei totam terram Willelmi de Albrincis sine placito pro seruicio suo, simul cum hæreditate et iure quod clamat ex parte uxoris sue sicut umquam Willelmus de Archis[2] ea melius tenuit. Et turrim et Castellum de Colecestr' sine placito finaliter et sine escampa[3] quam citius ei deliberare potero. Et omnes tenuras suas de

[1] It is headed "Pro Comite Oxoniæ Carta Matildæ Imperatricis confirmata," and it confirms the grants made by her "prout per cartam illam (*i.e.* Matildæ) plenius liquet."
[2] See Appendix V, on "William of Arques."   [3] *i.e.* escambio.

TEXT OF THE CHARTER TO AUBREY.

quocunque eas teneat in omnibus rebus sicut Carta sua alia quam inde habuit testatur. Et preter hoc do ei et concedo quod sit Comes de Cantebruggescr' et habeat inde tertium denarium sicut Comes debet habere, ita dico si Rex Scotiæ non habet illum Comitatum. Et si Rex habuerit perquiram illum ei ad posse meum per escambium. Et si non potero tunc do ei et concedo quod sit Comes de quolibet quatuor Comitatuum subscriptorum, videlicet Oxenefordscira, Berkscira, Wiltescira, et Dorsetscira per consilium et consideracionem Comitis Gloecestrie fratris mei et Comitis Gaufridi et Comitis Gisleberti et teneat Comitatum suum cum omnibus illis rebus que ad comitatum suum pertineat ita bene et in pace et libere et quiete et honorifice et plenarie sicut unquam aliquis Comes melius vel liberius tenuit vel tenet comitatum suum. Concedo etiam ei in feodo et hæreditate seruicium Willelmi de Helion,[1] videlicet decem militum ut ipse Willelmus teneat de Comite Alberico et ipse Comes faciat inde michi seruicium et michi et hæredibus meis. Concedo etiam ei et hæredibus suis de cremento Diham[2] que fuit Rogeri de Ramis[3] rectum nepotum ipsius comitis Alberici, videlicet filiorum Rogeri de Ramis.[4] Et similiter concedo ei et heredibus suis Turroč[5] que fuit Willelmi Peuerelli de Nottingh', et terram Salamonis Presbiteri[6] de Tilleberiâ.[7]

[1] Of Helions in Bumsted Helion, Essex, the other portion of the parish, viz. Bumsted Hall, being, at and from the Survey, a portion of the De Vere fief. These his ten fees duly figure in the *Liber Niger*.

[2] Dedham, Essex.

[3] They were named, I presume, from the castle of Rames, adjoining the forest of Lillebonne.

[4] This would seem to imply that Roger de Ramis had married a sister of Aubrey de Vere. See Appendix X: "Roger de Ramis."

[5] Grey's Thurrock, in South Essex, being that portion of it which had been held by William Peverel at the Survey.

[6] Query, the "Salamon clericus de Sudwic" (Northants) of the Pipe-Roll of 31 Hen. I. (p. 85)?

[7] This was not Tilbury on the Thames, but Tilbury (Essex) near Clare,

THE SECOND CHARTER OF THE EMPRESS.

Concedo etiam eidem Alberico Comiti quod ipse et omnes homines sui habeant et lucrentur omnia essarta sua libera et quieta de omnibus placitis que fecerant usque ad diem quâ seruicio domini mei Comitis Andegavie et meo adhæserunt.[1] Hec omnia supradicta tenementa concedo ei tenenda hæreditarie in omnibus rebus sibi et hæredibus suis de me et de hæredibus meis. Quare volo et firmiter præcipio quod ipse Albericus Comes et heredes sui teneant omnia tenementa sua ita bene et in pace et libere et quiete et honorifice et plenarie sicut unquam aliquis Comitum meorum melius vel liberius tenuit vel tenet et preter hoc do et concedo Galfrido de Ver totam terram que fuit Galfridi Talebot[2] in dominiis in militibus si eam ei Warantizare potero. Et si non potero, escambium ei inde dabo ad valentiam per consideracionem Comitis Galfridi Essex et Comitis Gisleberti et Comitis Alberici fratris sui. Et preter hoc concedo Roberto de Ver unam baroniam ad valentiam honoris Galfridi de Ver infra annum quo potestatiua fuero regni Angliæ. Vel aliam terram ad valentiam illius terræ. Et preter hoc do et concedo eidem Comiti Alberico Cancellariam ad opus Willelmi de Ver fratris sui ex quo deliberata fuerit de Willelmo Cancellario fratre Johannis filii Gisleberti qui eam modo habet. Hanc autem convencionem et donacionem tenendam affidaui manu mea propria in manu Galfridi Comitis Essex. Et hujus fiduciæ sunt obsides per fidem et Testes: Robertus Comes Gloec', et Milo Comes Heref', et Brianus

---

as is proved by *Liber Niger* (p. 393), where this land of Salamon proves to be part of the honour of Boulogne, held as a fifth of a knight's fee.

[1] See Appendix R: "The Forest of Essex."

[2] Geoffrey Talbot appears in the Pipe-Roll of 31 Henry I. as paying two hundred marks of silver for his father's land in Kent (p. 67). As "Agnes Vxor Gaufredi Talebot" is charged, at the same time, "pro dote et maritagio suo" (*ibid.*), it would seem that our Geoffrey had a father of the same name. We learn from the *Liber Niger* (i. 58) that at the death of Henry I. (1135) he held twenty knights' fees in Kent.

TEXT OF THE CHARTER TO AUBREY. 183

filius Comitis, et Robertus filius Regis[1] et Robertus de Curci Dap', et Johannes filius Gisleb', et Milo de Belloc', et Radulfus Paganel, et Robertus filius Heldebrandi et Robertus de Oileio Conestabularius. Et Convencionaui eidem Comiti Alberico quod pro posse meo Comes Andegavie dominus meus assecurabit ei manu suâ propriâ illud idem tenendum et Henricus filius meus similiter. Et quod Rex ffrancie erit mihi obses si facere potero Et si non potero, faciam quod rex capiet in manu illud idem tenendum. Et de hoc debent esse obsides per fidem Juhel de Meduana et Rob[ertus] de Sabloill et Wido de Sabloill et Paganus de Clarievall' et Gaufridus de Clarievall et Andreas de Alvia et Pepinus de Turcin, et Absalon de Ruinard[2] et Reginaldus Comes Cornubiæ et Baldwinus Comes Deuoniæ et Comes Gislebertus de Pembroc et Comes Hugo de Norfolc et Comes de Essex Gaufridus et Patricius[3] (sic) de Valoniis, et alii barones mei quos habere voluerit et ego habere potero erunt inde obsides similiter et quod Christianitas Angliæ quæ in potestate meâ est capiat in manu supradictam convencionem tenendam eidem Comiti Alberico et hæredibus suis de me et hæredibus meis Apud Oxin.[4]

The first point to which I would call attention is the identity of expression in the two charters, proving, as I urged above, their close and essential connection. It may be as well to place the passages to which I refer side by side.

CHARTER TO GEOFFREY.   CHARTER TO AUBREY.

Hanc autem conventionem et   Hanc autem conventionem et
donationem tenendam affidavi   donationem tenendam affilavi
manu mea propria in manu   manu mea propria in manu

[1] "Rogeri" in MS.   [2] Or "Rumard."   [3] *Rectius* Petr[us]
[4] "Ex libro quodam pervetusto in pergamena manuscripto in custodia Henrici Vere nunc Comitis Oxoniæ, et mihi per Capitan: Skipwith, mutuato 21 April, 1622."

184 THE SECOND CHARTER OF THE EMPRESS.

<table>
<tr><td>ipsius Comitis Gaufredi. Et hujus fiduciæ sunt obsides per fidem et Testes, Robertus etc.

Et conventionavi eidem Comiti Gaufrido pro posse meâ quod Comes Andegavie dominus meus assecurabit ei manu suâ propriâ illud idem tenendum et Henricus filius meus similiter, etc., etc.</td><td>Galfredi Comitis Essex. Et hujus fiduciæ sunt obsides per fidem et Testes, Robertus, etc.

Et conventionavi eidem Comiti Alberico quod pro posse meo Comes Andegavie dominus meus assecurabit ei manu suâ propriâ illud idem tenendum et Henricus filius meus similiter, etc., etc.</td></tr>
</table>

Putting together these passages with the fact that the witnesses also are the same in both charters, we see plainly that these two documents, while differing from all others of the kind, correspond precisely with each other. Above all, we note that it was to Geoffrey, not to Aubrey, that the Empress pledged her faith for the fulfilment of Aubrey's charter. This shows, as I observed, that Aubrey obtained this charter as Geoffrey's relative and ally, just as Geoffrey's less important kinsmen were provided for in his own charter.

Here we may pause for a moment, before examining this record in detail, to glance at another which forms its corollary and complement.

It will have been noticed that in both these charters the Empress undertook to obtain their confirmation by her husband and her son. We know not whether the charter to Geoffrey was so confirmed, but presumably it was. For, happily, in the case of its sister-charter, the confirmation by the youthful Henry was preserved. And there is every reason to believe that when this was confirmed the other would be confirmed also.

The confirmation by the future King Henry II. of his mother's charter to Aubrey de Vere may be assigned to July—November, 1142. His uncle Robert crossed to Normandy shortly after witnessing the original charter, and returned to England, accompanied by his nephew, about the end of December.[1] We may assume that no time was lost in obtaining the confirmation by the youthful heir, and though the names of the witnesses and the place of testing are, unluckily, omitted in the transcript, the fact that a Hugh "de Juga" acted as Geoffrey's proxy for the occasion supports the hypothesis that the confirmation took place over sea. That we have a confirmation by Henry, but not by his father, is doubtless due to Geoffrey of Anjou refusing, on this occasion, to come to his wife's assistance, and virtually, by sending his son in his stead, abdicating in his favour whatever pretensions he had to the English throne.

As Henry's charter is printed at the foot of his mother's by Vincent, I shall content myself with quoting its distinctive features, for the subject matter is the same except for some verbal differences.[2] There is some confusion as to the authority for its text. Vincent transcribed it, like that of the Empress, from the Hedingham Castle Register. Dugdale, in his *Baronage*, mixes it up with the charter granted by Henry when king, so that his marginal reference would seem to apply to the latter. In his MSS., however, he gives as his authority "Autographum in custodia Johis. Tindall unius magror. Curie cancellarie temp. Reg. Eliz." If the original charter itself was in existence so late as this there is just a hope that it may yet be found in some unexplored collection. From time to time such "finds" are made,[3] and few discoveries would be more welcome than that of

---

[1] See Appendix Y.

[2] As "turrim de Colcestr' et castellum" for "turrim et castellum de Colcestr'." The only difference of any importance is that Dugdale reads "Albenejo" in this charter, where he has "Albrincis" in that of the Empress.

[3] I may perhaps be permitted to refer to my own discovery, in a stable loft, of a document bearing the seal of the King-maker, and bearing his rare autograph, which antiquaries had lost sight of since the days of Camden.

the earliest charter of one of the greatest sovereigns who have ever ruled these realms, the first Plantagenet king.[1]

Charter of Henry of Anjou to Aubrey de Vere.

July—November, 1142.

"Henricus filius filiæ Regis Henrici, rectus heres Angl. et Normann. etc. Sciatis quod sicut Domina mea, viz. mater mea imperatrix reddidit et concessit, ita reddo et concedo. . . . Hanc autem convencionem tenendam affidavi manu mea propria in manu Hugonis de Juga,[2] sicut mater mea Imperatrix affidavit in manu Comitis Gaufr. Testibus," etc.

Henry "fitz Empress" was at this time only nine and a half years old. The claim he is here made to advance as "rightful heir" of England and Normandy sounds the key-note of the coming struggle. Not only till he had obtained the crown, but also after he had obtained it, he steadily dwelt on his "right" to the throne, of which Stephen had wrongfully deprived him.

We should also note that he claims to be "heir" of England and Normandy, but not of Anjou. I take this to imply that he posed as no mere heir-expectant, but as one who ought, by right, to be in actual possession of his realm. He could not, in the lifetime of his father, assume this attitude to Anjou. Hence its omission. As for his mother, he seems, from the first, to have claimed her inheritance, as he eventually obtained it, not for her, but for himself.

[1] Mr. Eyton must have strangely overlooked this charter, for he begins his series of Henry's charters in 1149.

[2] "Inga" in Dugdale's transcript, and rightly so, for we find this same Hugh, as "Hugo de Ging'," a witness to a charter on behalf of Earl Aubrey, about this time (*infra*, p. 190). There were several places in Essex named "Ging" *alias* "Ing."

Let us now return to the charter of the Empress.

It will be best to discuss its successive clauses *seriatim*. The opening portion, from "Sciatis me reddidisse" to "sicut alia Carta mea quam inde habuit testatur," is merely a confirmation of her previous charter, granted, as we learn from this, for the purpose of securing him in the possession of his father's fief and office of royal chamberlain. His father, who is said to have been slain in May, 1141, had been granted the chamberlainship by Henry I. in 1133, the charter being printed by Madox from Dugdale's transcript. This confirmation repeats its terms.

The next portion extends from the words "Et do et concedo" to "sicut Carta sua alia quam inde habet testatur." About this there is some obscurity. The word is "do," not "*red*do," and the expression "Carta sua" replaces "Carta mea." The clause clearly refers to grants made to Aubrey himself since his father's death, but whether by the king or by the Empress is not so clear as could be wished. The point need not be discussed at length, but the former seems the more probable.

Fortunately, there is no such doubt about the clauses of creation. Here the question of the formula becomes all-important. The case stands thus. There are only two instances in the course of this reign in which we can be quite certain that we are dealing with creations *de novo*. The one is that by which the king "made" Geoffrey Earl of Essex; the other, that by which the Empress "made" Miles Earl of Hereford. We know that neither grantee had been created an earl before; and we find that the sovereign, in each instance, speaks of having "made" ("fecisse") him an earl.[1] So, again, in the only instance of a "counter-patent" of creation, of which we can be quite

[1] Compare the famous Lewes charter of William de Warenne, Earl of Surrey, said (if genuine) to be the earliest allusion to a peerage creation. There the earl speaks of William Rufus, "qui me Surreæ comitem *fecit*."

188 THE SECOND CHARTER OF THE EMPRESS.

certain, namely, that by which the Empress recognized Geoffrey as Earl of Essex after he had received that title from Stephen, the formula used is: "Do et concedo ut sit Comes." The two are essentially distinct. Now, applying this principle to the present charter, we find the latter of the two *formulæ* employed on this occasion. The words are: "Do ei et concedo ut sit Comes." We infer, therefore, if my view be right, that Aubrey was already in enjoyment of comital rank when he received this charter. It might be, and indeed has been, supposed that he was so by virtue of a creation by Stephen. I have noted an instance in which he attests a charter of Stephen (at the siege of Wallingford) as a "comes,"[1] and it is not likely that Stephen would allow him this title in virtue of a creation by the Empress. On the other hand, in this charter the Empress treats him as already a *comes*, which she does not do in the case of Geoffrey, who had been created a *comes* by Stephen.[2] The difference between the two cases is accounted for by the fact that Aubrey was *comes* not by a creation of Stephen, but in right of his wi'e Beatrice, heiress of the *Comté* of Guisnes. This has been clearly explained by Mr. Stapleton in his paper on "The Barony of William of Arques,"[3] although he is mistaken in his dates. He wrongly thought, like others, that Aubrey's father, the chamberlain, was killed in May, 1140, instead of May, 1141, and, like Mr. Eyton, he wrongly assigned this charter of the empress to 1141, instead of 1142.[4] His able identification of "Albericus *Aper*" with

[1] *Abingdon Cartulary*, ii. 179.
[2] It should, however, be observed that in this same charter she refers to Earl Gilbert (of Pembroke) and Earl Hugh (of Norfolk) by their comital style, though, so far as we know, they were earls of Stephen's creation alone. But such a reference as this is very different from the style formally given in a charter of creation.
[3] *Archæologia*, vol. xxxi.
[4] "Its date is subsequent to the 25th of July, 1141, when the Empress

AUBREY WAS COUNT OF GUISNES.

Aubrey de Vere may be supplemented by a reference to the fact that "the blue *boar*" was the badge of the family through a pun on the Latin *verres*.

Aubrey was already the husband of Beatrice, the heiress of Guisnes, at the death of her grandfather Count Manasses (? 1139). He thereupon went to Flanders and became (says Lambart d'Ardes) Count of Guisnes. Returning to England, he sought and obtained from Stephen his wife's English inheritance and executed, as Mr. Stapleton observes, in his father's lifetime (*i.e.* before May, 1141), the charter printed in Morant's *Essex* (ii. 506). Aubrey was divorced from Beatrice a few years later, when she married (between 1144 and 1146, thinks Mr. Stapleton) Baldwin d'Ardres, the claimant of Guisnes. Thus did Aubrey come to be for a time "Count of Guisnes," as recorded, according to Weever, on his tomb at Colne Priory.

Mr. Stapleton was unable to produce any English record or chronicle in which Aubrey is given the style of "Count of Guisnes." It is, therefore, with much satisfaction that I print, from the original charter, the following record, conclusively establishing that he actually had that style:—

COTT. CHART. xxi. 6.

"Ordingus dei gratia Abbas ecclesie sancti eadmundi Omnibus hominibus suis et amicis et fidelibus francis et anglis salutem. Sciatis me concessisse Alberico comiti Gisnensi per concessum totius conuentus totum feudum et seruitium Rogeri de Ver auunculi sui sicut tenet de honore sancti eadmundi uidelicet per seruitium unius militis et dimidii et totum feudum et seruitium Alani filii Frodonis

created Milo de Gloucester Earl of Hereford at Oxford, who has this title in the charter, and, from its having been given at Oxford, there can be little doubt that it was contemporaneous with that creation, and certainly prior to the siege of Winchester in the month of August following" (*ibid.*, pp. 231, 232).

sicut tenet de honore sancti eadmundi uidelicet per seruitium iii militum, et insuper singulis annis centum solidos ad pascha de camera mea. Hec omnia illi concedo in feudo et hereditate, ipsi et heredibus suis de ecclesia sancti eadmundi et de meis successoribus. Quare uolo et firmiter precipio quod idem Albericus comes Gisnensis et heredes sui jure hereditario teneant de ecclesia sancti eadmundi bene et honorifice heo supradicta omnia per seruitium quod supradiximus. Huius donationis sunt testes ex parte mea Willelmus prior Radulfus sacrista Gotscelinus et Eudo monachi Mauricius dapifer Gilebertus blundus Adam de cocef' Radulfus de lodn' Willelmus filius Ailb'. Helias de melef' Gauffridus frater eius. Ex parte comitis, Gauffridus de ver Robertus filius humfridi Robertus filius Ailr' Garinus filius Geroldi Hugo de ging' Albericus de capella Radulfus filius Adam Guarinus frater eius Radulfus de gisnes Gauffridus filius Humfridi Gauffridus Arsic Rodbertus de cocef' Radulfus carboneal et Hugo filius eius et plures alii."[1]

But, to return to Maud's charter, the point which I am anxious to emphasize is that of the formula she employs, namely, "do et concedo," as against the "sciatis me fecisse" of an original creation. I trace this distinction in later years, when her son, who had already, as we have seen, confirmed this charter to Aubrey, again confirmed it when king (1156), employing for that purpose the same formula: "Sciatis me dedisse et concessisse comiti Alberico." Conversely, in the case of Hugh Bigod,

[1] Of these witnesses "ex parte comitis," Geoffrey de Ver held half a knight's fee of him, Robert fitz Humfrey held one, Robert fitz "Ailric" one, Ralph fitz Adam a quarter, Ralph de Guisnes one, Geoffrey Arsic two, Robert de Cocefeld three, Ralph Carbonel one and a half. Hugh de Ging' was the "Hugo de Inga" who acted as proxy (*vide supra*) at Henry's confirmation of his mother's charter. This charter has an independent value for its bearing on knights' fees. See also Addenda.

he employs the formula: "Sciatis me fecisse Hugonem Bigot comitem de Norfolca " (1155), this being an earldom of Stephen's creation, and, so far as we know, of his alone. This is a view which should be accepted with caution, but which has, if correct, an important bearing.

The very remarkable shifting clause as to the county of which the grantee should be earl requires separate notice. The axiom from which I start is this: When a feudatory was created an earl, he took if he could for his "comitatus" the county in which was situated the chief seat of his power, his "Caput Baroniæ." If this county had an earl already he then took the nearest county that remained available. Thus Norfolk fell to Bigod, Essex to Mandeville, Sussex to Albini, Derby to Ferrers, and so on. De Clare, the seat of whose power was in Suffolk, though closely adjoining Essex, took Herts, probably for the reason that Mandeville had already obtained Essex, while Bigod's province, being in truth the old earldom of the East Angles—" Comes de Estangle," as Henry of Huntingdon terms him,—took in Suffolk. So now, Aubrey de Vere probably selected Cambridgeshire as the nearest available county to his stronghold at Castle Hedingham.[1]

But the Empress, we see, promised it only on the strange condition that her uncle was not already in possession. I say "the strange condition," for one would surely have thought that she knew whether he was or not. Moreover, the dignity was then held not by her uncle, but by his son, and is described as the earldom of Huntingdon, never as the earldom of Cambridge. The first of these difficulties is explained by the fact that the

[1] At the same time, we must remember that he held a considerable fief in Cambridgeshire (see Domesday), which, if he could not have Essex, might lead him to select that county.

King of Scots had, early in the reign, made over the earldom to his son Henry, to avoid becoming himself the "man" of the King of England. The second requires special notice.

We are taken back, by this provision, to the days before the Conquest. Mr. Freeman, in his erudite essay on *The Great Earldoms under Eadward*, has traced the shifting relations of the counties of Northamptonshire, Huntingdonshire, Cambridgeshire, and Northumberland. The point, however, which concerns us here is that, "under William," Earl Waltheof, "besides his great Northumbrian government, was certainly Earl of Northamptonshire (*Ord. Vit.*, 522 C.), and of Huntingdonshire (*Will. Gem*, viii. 37)."[1] His daughter Matilda married twice, and between the heirs of these two marriages the contest for her father's inheritance was obstinate and long. Restricting ourselves to his southern province, with which alone we have here to deal, its western half, the county of Northampton, had at this time passed to Simon of St. Liz as the heir of the first marriage, while Huntingdon had conferred an earldom on Henry, the heir of her marriage with the Scottish king. The house of St. Liz, however, claimed the whole inheritance, and as the Earl of Huntingdon, of course, sided with his cousin, the Empress, Earl Simon of Northampton was the steadfast supporter, even in their darkest hours, of Stephen and his queen. Now, the question that arises is this: Was not Earl Henry's province Huntingdonshire *with* Cambridgeshire? Mr. Freeman writes of Huntingdonshire, that "in 1051 we find it, together with Cambridgeshire, a shire still so closely connected with it as to have a common sheriff, detached altogether from Mercia," etc.[2] It is true that when the

[1] *Norm. Conq.*, ii. 559.   [2] *Ibid.*

AUBREY BECOMES EARL OF OXFORD.

former county became "an outlying portion of the earldom of Northumberland," it does not, he observes, "appear that Cambridgeshire followed it in this last migration;"[1] but when we compare this earlier connection with that in the Pipe-Roll of 1130,[2] and with the fact that under another David of Scotland, this earldom, some seventy years later, appears as that of Huntingdon and Cambridge,[3] we shall find in this charter a connecting link, which favours the view that the two counties had, for comital purposes, formed one throughout. We have a notable parallel in the adjacent counties of Norfolk and Suffolk, which still formed one, the East Anglian earldom. Dorset and Somerset, too, which were under one sheriff, may have been also intended to form one earldom, for the Lord of Dunster is found both as Earl of "Dorset" and of "Somerset." I suspect also that the Ferrers earldom was, in truth, that of the joint shrievalty of Derbyshire and Notts, and that this is why the latter county was never made a separate earldom till the days of Richard II.

The doubt of the Empress must therefore be attributed to her anxiety not to invade the comital rights of her cousin, in case he should deem that her creation of an earldom of Cambridgeshire would constitute such invasion. It is evident, we shall find, that he did so. The accepted view is, it would appear, that Aubrey, by virtue of this charter, became Earl "of Cambridge."[4] Mr. Doyle, indeed, in his great work, goes so far as to state that he was "cr. Earl of CAMBRIDGE by the Empress

[1] *Norm. Conq.*, ii. 559.

[2] Where they form one shrievalty with one *firma*, though the county of Surrey as well is inexplicably combined with them.

[3] And the "tertius denarius" of Cambridgeshire was actually held by its earl (1205).

[4] Stubbs, *Const. Hist.*, i. 362, *note.*

Maud (after March 2) 1141; . . . cr. Earl of Oxford (*in exchange*) 1155."[1] But in Cole's (unpublished) transcript of the Colne Cartulary (fols. 34, 37), we have a charter of this Aubrey, "Pro animâ patris mei Alberici de Vere," which must have passed between 1141 and 1147, for it is attested by Robert, Bishop of London, appointed 1141, and Hugh, Abbot of Colchester, who died in 1147. In this charter his style is "Albericus Comes Oxeneford." Here, then, we have evidence that, in this reign, he was already Earl " of Oxford," not Earl of Cambridge.

Before quitting the subject of Aubrey's creation, we may note the bearing of the shifting clause on the creation of the earldom of Wiltshire. It implies that Patrick of Salisbury had not yet received his earldom. This conclusion is confirmed by a charter of the Empress tested at Devizes, which he witnesses merely as "Patricio de Sarum conestabulo."[2] The choice of Dorset is somewhat singular, as it suggests an intrusion on the Mohun earldom. But this rather shadowy dignity appears, during its brief existence, as an earldom of Somerset rather than of Dorset.

The specific grant of the " tertius denarius," as in the creation charters of the earldoms of Essex and of Hereford, should also be noticed.

The "Earl Gilbert" who is repeatedly mentioned in the course of this charter is Earl Gilbert "of Pembroke," maternal uncle to Aubrey. It is this relationship that, perhaps, accounts for the part he here plays.

Of the remaining features of interest in the record, attention may be directed to the phrase concerning the knights' fees of William de Helion: " Ut ipse Willelmus

[1] *Official Baronage*, i. 291.
[2] *Mon. Ang.*, v. 440; *Journ. B. A. A.*, xxxi. 392. This conclusion reveals a further error in the *Histoire de Guillaume le Maréchal*, which gives a very incomprehensible account of this Patrick's action.

teneat de Comite Alberico, et ipse Comes faciat inde michi servitium;" also to the implied forfeiture of William Peverel of Nottingham, he having been made prisoner at Lincoln, fighting on Stephen's side. Lastly, the promise to the earl of the chancellorship for his brother William becomes full of interest when we know that this was the Canon of St. Osyth,[1] and that he was to be thus rewarded as being the clerical member of his house. It enables us further to identify in William, the existing chancellor, the brother of John (fitz Gilbert) the marshal.

We have now examined these two charters, parts, I would again insist, of one connected negotiation. What was its object? Nothing less, in my opinion, than a combined revolt in the Eastern Counties which should take Stephen in the rear, as soon as the arrival from Normandy of Geoffrey of Anjou and his son should give the signal for a renewal of the struggle, and a fresh advance upon London by the forces of the west country. Earl Geoffrey himself was now at the height of his power. If he were supported by Aubrey de Vere, and by Henry of Essex with Peter de Valoines (who are specially named in Geoffrey's charter), he would be virtually master of Essex. And if the restless Earl of the East Angles (p. 178 *supra*) would also join him, as eventually he did, while Bishop Nigel held Ely, Stephen would indeed be placed between two fires. I cannot but think that it is to the rumour of some such scheme as this that Stephen's panegyrist refers, when he tells us, the following year, that Geoffrey "had arranged to betray the realm into the hands of the Countess of Anjou, and that his intention to do so had been matter of common knowledge."[2]

I would urge that in the charters I have given above

[1] See Appendix U.
[2] "Regnum, ut in ore jam vulgi celebre fuerat, comitissæ Andegavensi

we find the key to this allusion, and that they, in their turn, are explained, and at the same time confirmed, by the existence of this concerted plot. We have now to trace the failure of the scheme, and to learn how it was that all came to nought.

Stephen's illness, to which, it may be remembered, I had attributed in part the inception of the scheme, only lasted till the middle of June. By the time that Robert of Gloucester had set forth to cross the Channel, Stephen was restored to health, and ready and eager for action.[1] Swift to seize on such an opportunity as he had never before obtained, he burst into the heart of the enemy's country and marched straight on Wareham. He found its defenders off their guard; the town was sacked and burnt, and the castle was quickly his.[2] The precautions of the Earl of Gloucester had thus been taken in vain, and the port he had secured for his return was now garrisoned by the king.

The effect of this brilliant stroke was to paralyze the party of the Empress. Her brother, who had left her with great reluctance, dreading the fickleness of the nobles, had made her assembled supporters swear that they would defend her in his absence, and had further taken with him hostages for their faithful behaviour.[3] He had also so strengthened her defences at Oxford that the city seemed

conferre disposuerat" (*Gesta Stephani*, p. 101). This very remarkable incidental allusion should be compared with that in which Henry of Huntingdon justifies the earl's arrest by Stephen: "Nisi enim hoc egisset, perfidio consulis illius regno privatus fuisset" (p. 276).

[1] "Duravit improspera valetudo usque post Pentecostem (June 7); tum enim sensim refusus salutis vigor eum in pedes erexit" (*Will. Malms.*, p. 763).

[2] "Rex ... comitis absentiam aucupatus, subito ad Waram veniens, et non bene munitum propugnatoribus offendens, succensa et depredata villa, statim etiam castello potitus est" (*ibid.*, p. 766).

[3] "Obsides poposcit sigillatim ab his qui optimates videbantur, secum in Normannia ducendos, vadesque futuros tam comiti Andegavensi quam impera-

almost impregnable.[1] Lastly, a series of outlying posts secured the communications of its defenders with the districts friendly to their cause.[2]

But Stephen, in the words of his panegyrist, had "awaked as one out of sleep." Summoning to his standard his friends and supporters, he marched on Gloucestershire itself, and appeared unexpectedly at Cirencester on the line of the enemy's communications. Its castle, taken by surprise, was burnt and razed to the ground. Then, completing the isolation of the Empress, by storming, as he advanced, other of her posts,[3] he arrived before the walls of Oxford on the 26th of September.[4] The forces of the Empress at once deployed on the left bank of the river. The action which followed was a curious anticipation of the struggle at Boyne Water (1690). The king, informed of the existence of a ford, boldly plunged into the water, and, half fording, half swimming, was one of the first to reach the shore. Instantly charging the enemy's line, he forced the portion opposed to him back towards the walls of the city, and when the bulk of his forces had followed him across, the whole line was put to flight, his victorious troops entering the gates pell-mell with the routed fugitives. The torch was as familiar as the sword to the soldier of the Norman age, and Oxford was quickly buried in a sheet of smoke and fire.[5] The castle, then of great strength, alone held out. From the

---

trici quod omnes, junctis umbonibus ab ea, dum ipse abesset, injurias propulsarent, viribus suis apud Oxeneford manentes" (*Will. Malms.*, p. 764). The phrase "junctis umbonibus" revives memories of the shield-wall. See also Appendix S.

[1] "Civitatem . . . ita comes Gloecestrie fossatis munierat, ut inexpugnabilis præter per incendium videretur" (*ibid.*, p. 766).
[2] *Gesta*, pp. 87, 88.   [3] *Gesta*, p. 88.
[4] "Tribus diebus ante festum Sancti Michaelis" (*Will. Malms.*, p. 766).
[5] See the brilliant description of this action in the *Gesta Stephani*, pp. 88, 89.

summit of its mound the Empress must have witnessed the rout of her followers; within its walls she was now destined to stand a weary siege.

It is probable that Stephen's success at Oxford was in part owing to the desertion of the Empress by those who had sworn to defend her. For we read that they were led by shame to talk of advancing to her relief.[1] The project, however, came to nothing, and Earl Robert, hearing of the critical state of affairs, became eager to return to the assistance of his sister and her beleaguered followers.

Geoffrey of Anjou had, on various pretences, detained the earl in Normandy, instead of accepting his invitation and returning with him to England. But Robert's patience was now exhausted, and, bringing with him, instead of Geoffrey, the youthful Henry "fitz Empress," he sailed for England with a fleet of more than fifty ships. Such was the first visit to this land of the future Henry II., being then nine years and a half, not (as stated by Dr. Stubbs) eight years old.[2]

The earl made it a point of honour to recapture Wareham as his first step. He also hoped to create a diversion which might draw off the king from Oxford.[3] This was not bad strategy, for Stephen was deemed to be stronger behind the walls of Oxford than he would be in the open country. The position of affairs resembled, in fact, that at Winchester, the year before. But the two sides had changed places. As the Empress, in Winchester, had besieged Wolvesey, so now, in Oxford, Stephen did the

---

[1] "Mox igitur optimates quidem omnes imperatricis, confusi quia a domina sua præter statutum abfuerant, confertis cuneis ad Walengeford convenerunt," etc. (*Will. Malms.*, p. 766).

[2] Dr. Stubbs has erroneously placed his landing in 1141 instead of in the autumn of 1142. See Appendix Y, on "The First and Second Visits of Henry II. to England."

[3] *Will. Malms.*, pp. 767, 768.

same. It would, therefore, have been necessary to besiege him in turn as the Empress was besieged the year before. Well aware of the advantage he enjoyed, Stephen refused to be decoyed away, and allowed the castle of Wareham to fall into Robert's hands. The other posts in the neighbourhood were also secured by the earl, who then advanced to Cirencester, where he had summoned his friends to meet him. Thus strengthened, he was already marching to the relief of Oxford, when he received the news of his sister's perilous escape and flight. A close siege of three months had brought her to the extremity of want, and Stephen was pressing the attack with all the artillery of the time. A few days before Christmas, in a long and hard frost, when the snow was thick upon the ground, she was let down by ropes from the grim Norman tower, which commanded the approach to the castle on the side of the river. Clad in white from head to foot, and escorted by only three knights, she succeeded under cover of the darkness of night, and by the connivance of one of the besiegers' sentries, in passing through their lines undetected and crossing the frozen river. After journeying on foot for six miles, she reached the spot where horses were in waiting, and rode for Wallingford Castle, her still unconquered stronghold.[1]

On receiving the news of this event Robert changed his course, and proceeded to join his sister. In her joy at the return of her brother and the safe arrival of her

[1] See, for the story of her romantic escape, the *Gesta Stephani* (pp. 89, 90), *William of Malmesbury* (pp. 768, 769), *John of Hexham* (*Sym. Dun.*, ii. 317), *William of Newburgh* (i. 43), and the *Anglo-Saxon Chronicle* (p. 384). This last is of special value for its mention of her escape from the tower of the castle. It states that Stephen "besæt hire in the tur," and that she was on the night of her escape let down by ropes from the tower ("me læt hire dun on niht of the tur mid rapes"). It is difficult to see how this can mean anything else than that she was lowered to the ground from the existing tower, instead of leaving by a gate.

son, the Empress forgot all her troubles. She was also in safety now, herself, behind the walls of Wallingford, the support of that town and its fidelity to her cause being gratefully acknowledged by her son on his eventual accession to the throne.[1]

But her husband had declined to come to her help; her city of Oxford was lost; her *prestige* had suffered a final blow; the great combination scheme was at an end.

[1] See his charter to Wallingford (printed in Hearne's *Liber Niger* [1771], pp. 817, 818), in which he grants privileges "pro servitio et labore magno quem pro me sustinuerunt in acquisitione hereditarii juris mei in Anglia."

CHAPTER IX.

FALL AND DEATH OF GEOFFREY.

THE movements of Geoffrey during the latter half of 1142 are shrouded in utter darkness. After the surrender of the isle of Ely, we lose sight of him altogether, save in the glimpse afforded us by the Oxford intrigue. It is, however, quite possible that we should assign to the period of the siege of Oxford Castle (September—December, 1142) a charter to Abingdon Abbey which passed at Oxford.[1] For if we deduct from its eight witnesses the two local barons (Walter de Bocland and Hugh de Bolbec), five of the remaining six are found in the Canterbury charter.[2] In that case, Geoffrey, who figures at their head, must have been at Oxford, in Stephen's quarters, at some time in the course of the siege. He would obviously not declare for the Empress till the time was ripe for the scheme,

[1] *Chronicle of Abingdon*, ii. 178, 179. Assigned to "probably about the Christmas of 1135" (p. 542).
[2] See p. 143. They are Earl Geoffrey, Robert de Ver, William of Ypres, Adam "de Belnaio," and Richard de Luci. The sixth, "Mainfeninus Brito," we have seen attesting Stephen's first charter to Geoffrey in 1140 (p. 52). Another charter, perhaps, may also be assigned to this period, namely, that of Stephen (at Oxford) to St. Frideswide's, of which the original is now preserved in the Bodleian Library. For this, as for the preceding charter, the date suggested is 1135 (*Calendar of Charters and Rolls*), but the names of William of Ypres and Richard de Luci prove that this date is too early. These names, with that of Robert de Ver, are common to both charters, and if Richard de Luci's earliest attestation is in the summer of 1140, it is quite possible that this charter should be assigned to the siege of 1142.

and, in the meanwhile, it might disarm suspicion, and secure his safety in the case of the capture or defeat of the Empress, if he continued outwardly in full allegiance to the king.

It was not till the following year that the crisis at length came. Stephen, at Mid-Lent, had attended a council at London, at which decrees were passed against the general disregard of the rights and privileges of the Church. Her ministers were henceforth to be free from outrage, and her sanctuaries from violation, under penalty of an excommunication which only the pope himself could remove.[1]

At some period in the course of the year (1143) after this council—possibly about the end of September—the king held a court at St. Albans, to which, it would seem, there came the leading nobles of the realm.[2] Among them was the Earl of Essex, still at the height of his power. Of what passed on this occasion we have, from independent quarters, several brief accounts.[3] Of the main fact there is no question. Stephen, acting on that sudden impulse which roused him at times to unwonted vigour, struck at last, and struck home. The mighty earl was seized and bound, and according to the regular practice throughout this internecine warfare, the surrender of the castles on which his strength was based was made the price of his liberty. As with the arrest of the bishops at Oxford in 1139, so was it now with the arrest of the great earl at St. Albans, and so it was again to be at Northampton, with

---

[1] *Rog. Wend.*, ii. 233 ; *Mat. Paris* (*Hist. Angl.*), i. 270 ; *Hen. Hunt.*, p. 276.

[2] No clue to this date, important though it is for our story, is afforded by any of the ordinary chroniclers. The London Chronicle, however, preserved in the *Liber de Antiquis Legibus* (fol. 35), carefully dates it "post festum Sancti Michaelis."

[3] *Mon. Ang.*, iv. 142 ; *Mat. Paris* (*Hist. Angl.*), i. 270, 271 ; *William of Newburgh*, cap. xi. ; *Gesta Stephani*, pp. 103, 104 ; *Hen. Hunt.*, p. 276.

the arrest of the Earl of Chester some three years later. What it was that decided Stephen to seize this moment for thus reasserting his authority, it is not so easy to say. William of Newburgh, who is fullest on the subject, gives us the story, which is found nowhere else, of the earl's outrage on the king more than three years before,[1] and tells us that Stephen had been ever since awaiting an opportunity for revenge.[2] He adds that the height of power to which the earl had attained had filled the king with dread, and hints, I think, obscurely at that great conspiracy of which the earl, as we have seen, was the pivot and the moving spirit.[3] Henry of Huntingdon plainly asserts that his seizure was a necessity for the king, who would otherwise have lost his crown through the King-maker's treacherous schemes.[4] We may, indeed, safely believe that the time had now come when Stephen felt that it must be decided whether he or Geoffrey were master.[5] But, as with the arrest of the bishops at Oxford four years before, so, at this similar crisis, his own feelings and his own jealousy of a power beneath which he chafed were assiduously fostered and encouraged by a faction among the nobles themselves. This is well brought out in the Chronicle of Walden Abbey,[6] and still more so in the *Gesta*. It is there distinctly asserted that this faction worked upon the king, by reminding him of Geoffrey's

---

[1] See p. 47.
[2] "Acceptam ab eo injuriam rex caute dissimulabat, et tempus opportunum quo se ulcisceretur, observabat."
[3] "Subtili astutia ingentia moliens."
[4] "Nisi enim hoc egisset, perfidia consulis illius regno privatus fuisset."
[5] Compare the words of the *Gesta*: "Ubique per regnum regis vices adimplens et in rebus agendis rege avidius exaudiretur et in præceptis injungendis plus ei quam regi obtemperaretur."
[6] "Tandem vero a quibusdam regni majoribus, stimulante invidia, iniqua loquentibus, quasi regis proditor ac patriæ dilator erga regem mendaciter clanculo accusatus est. . . . Vir autem iste magnanimus subdola malignantium fraude, ut jam dictum est, delusus" (*Mon. Ang.*, iv. 142).

unparalleled power, and of his intention to declare for the Empress, urging him to arrest the earl as a traitor, to seize his castles and crush his power, and so to secure safety for himself and peace for his troubled realm.[1] It is added that, Stephen hesitating to take the decisive step, the jealousy of the barons blazed forth suddenly into open strife, taunts and threats being hurled at one another by the earl and his infuriated opponents.[2] On the king endeavouring to allay the tumult, the earl was charged to his face with plotting treason. Called upon to rebut the charge, he did not attempt to do so, but laughed with cynical scorn. The king, outraged beyond endurance, at once ordered his arrest, and his foes rushed upon him.[3]

The actual seizure of the earl appears to have been attended by circumstances of which we are only informed from a somewhat unexpected quarter. Mathew Paris, from his connection with St. Albans, has been able to preserve in his *Historia Anglorum* the local tradition of the event. From this we learn, firstly, that there was a struggle; secondly, that there was a flagrant violation of the right of sanctuary. The struggle, indeed, was so sharp that the Earl of Arundel, whom we know to have been an old opponent of Geoffrey (see p. 323), was rolled

[1] "Tum quia Galfridus, ut videbatur, omnia regni jura sibi callide usurparat, tum quia regnum ut in ore jam vulgi celebre fuerat, comitissæ Andegavensi conferre disposuerat, ad hoc regem secreta persuasione impulerunt, quatinus Galfridum de proditionis infamia notatum caperet, et redditis quæcunque possederat castellis, et rex post hinc securus, et regnum ipsius haberetur pacatius" (*Gesta*).

[2] "Rege multo tempore differente, ne regia majestas turpi proditionis opprobrio infameretur, subito inter Galfridum et barones, injuriis et minis utrinque protensis, orta seditio" (*ibid.*).

[3] "Cumque rex habitam inter eos dissensionem, sedatis partibus, niteretur dirimere, affuerunt quidam, qui Galfridum de proditionis factione in se et suos machinatâ, libera fronte accusabant. Cumque se de objecto crimine minime purgaret, sed turpissimam infamiam verbis jocosis alludendo infringeret, rex et qui præsentes erant Barones Galfridum et suos repente ceperunt" (*ibid.*).

over, horse and all, and nearly drowned in "Holywell."
The fact that this tussle took place in the open would
seem to imply that the whole of this highly dramatic
episode took place out of doors.[1] As to the other of these
two points, it is clear that there was something discredit-
able to Stephen, according to the opinion of the time, in
his sudden seizure of the earl. William of Newburgh
observes that he acted "non quidem honeste et secundum
jus gentium, sed pro merito ejus et metu; scilicet, quod
expediret quam quod deceret plus attendens." Henry of
Huntingdon similarly writes that such a step was "magis
secundum retributionem nequitiæ consulis quam secundum
jus gentium, magis ex necessitate quam ex honestate."[2]
The Chronicle of Walden, also, complains of the circumstances of his arrest;[3] and even the panegyrist of Stephen

[1] This story, being told by Mathew Paris alone, and evidently as a matter of tradition, must be accepted with considerable caution. He makes the singular and careless mistake of speaking of Earl Geoffrey as William (*sic*) de Mandeville, though he properly terms him, the following year, "Gaufridus consul de Mandeville." On the other hand, it is possible to apply a test which yields not unsatisfactory results. Mathew tells us that the Earl of Arundel was unhorsed "a Walkelino de Oxeai [*alias* Oxehaie] milite strenuissimo." Now there was, contemporary with Mathew himself, a certain Richard "de Oxeya," who held by knight-service of St. Albans Abbey, and who, in 1245, was jointly responsible with "Petronilla de Crokesle" for the service of one knight (*Chron. Majora*, vi. 437). Turning to a list of the abbey's knights, which is dated by the editor in the Rolls Series as "1258," but which is quite certainly some hundred years earlier, we find this same knight's fee held jointly by Richard "de Crokesle" and a certain "Walchelinus." Here then we may perhaps recognize that very "Walchelinus de Oxeai" who figures in Mathew's story, a story which Richard "de Oxeya" may have told him as a family tradition. Indeed, there is evidence to prove that this identification is correct.

[2] The coincidence of language between these two passages, beginning respectively "eodem tempore" and "eodem anno," ought to be noticed, for it has been overlooked by Mr. Howlett in his valuable edition of William of Newburgh for the Rolls Series, though he notes those on p. 34 before it, and on p. 48 after it, in his instructive remarks on the indebtedness of William of Newburgh to others (p. xxvi.).

[3] "Vir iste nobilis, cæteris in pace recedentibus, solus, rege jubente, fraudulenter comprehensus, et, ne abiret, custodibus designatis, detentus est" (*Mon. Ang.*, iv. 142).

is anxious to clear his fame by imputing to the barons the suggestion of what he admits to be a questionable act, and claiming for the king the credit of reluctance to adopt their advice.[1]

But there was a more serious charge brought against the king than that of dishonourable behaviour to the earl. He was accused of violating by his conduct the rights of sanctuary of St. Albans, though he had sworn, we are told, not to do so, and had taken part so shortly before in that council of London at which such violations were denounced. The abbot's knights, indeed, went so far as to resist by force of arms this outrage on the Church's rights.[2] It is clearly to the contest thus caused, rather than (as implied by Mathew) to the actual arrest of Geoffrey, that we must assign the struggle in which the Earl of Arundel was unhorsed by Walchelin de Oxeai, for Walchelin was one of the abbey's knights, and was, therefore, fighting in her cause.[3]

Though the friends of the earl interceded on his

---

[1] "Ne regia majestas turpi proditionis opprobio infamaretur."

[2] "Milites autem beati Albani, qui tunc, ad ecclesiæ ejus custodiam et villæ fossatis circumdatæ, ipsum vicum, qui juxta cænobium est, inhabitabant, ipsi regi in faciem viriliter restiterunt, donec ecclesiæ, quam quidam ex regiis ædituis violaverant, satisfecisset ipse rex, et ejus temerarii invasores. . . . Et hoc fecit rex contra jusjurandum, quod fecerat apud Sanctum Albanum, et contra statuta concilii nuper, eo consentiente, celebrati" (Mathew Paris, *Historia Anglorum*, i. 271).

[3] An incidental allusion to this conflict between the followers of the king and the abbey's knights is to be found, I think, in a curious passage in the *Gesta Abbatum S. Albani* (i. 94). We there read of Abbot Geoffrey (1119-1146): "Tabulam quoque unam ex auro et argento et gemmis electis artificiose constructam ad longitudinem et latitudinem altaris Sancti Albani, quam deinde, ingruente maxima necessitate, idem Abbas in igne conflavit et in massam confregit. Quam dedit Comiti de Warrena et Willelmo de Ypra et Comiti de Arundel et Willelmo Martel, temporibus Regis Stephani, *Villam Sancti Albani volentibus concremare*." The conjunction of William of Ypres with Abbot Geoffrey dates this incident within the limits 1139-1146, and there is no episode to which it can be so fitly assigned as this of 1143, especially as the Earl of Arundel figures in both versions.

behalf,[1] the king had no alternative but to complete what he had begun. After what he had done there could be no hope of reconciliation with the earl. Geoffrey was offered the usual choice; either he must surrender his castles, or he must go to the gallows. Taken to London, he was clearly made, according to the practice in these cases, to order his own garrison to surrender to the king. Thus he saw the fortress which he had himself done so much to strengthen, the source of his power and of his pride, pass for ever from his grasp. He had also to surrender, before regaining his freedom, his ancestral Essex strongholds of Pleshy and Saffron Walden.[2]

The earl's impotent rage when he found himself thus overreached is dwelt on by all the chroniclers.[3] The king's move, moreover, had now forced his hand, and the revolt so carefully planned could no longer be delayed, but broke out prematurely at a time when the Empress was not in a position to offer effective co-operation.

We must now return to the doings of Nigel, Bishop of

---

[1] "Et licet multi amicorum suorum, talia ei injuste illata ægre ferentium, pro eo regem interpellarent" (*Mon. Ang.*, iv. 142).

[2] "Rex igitur Galfridum, custodiis arctissime adhibitis, Londonias adducens, ni turrim et quæ miro labore et artificio erexerat castella in manus ejus committeret, suspendio cruciari paravit; cum salubri amicorum persuasus consilio, ut imminens inhonestæ mortis periculum, castellis redditis, devitaret, regis voluntati tandem satisfecit" (*Gesta*, p. 104). "Igitur, ut rex liberaret eum reddidit ei turrim Lundoniæ et castellum de Waledene et illud de Plaisseiz" (*Hen. Hunt.*, p. 276). "Eique arcem Lundoniensem cum duobus reliquis quæ possidebat castellis extorsit [rex]" (*W. Newburgh*, i. 45). The castle of (Saffron) Walden, with the surrounding district, was placed by Stephen in charge of Turgis d'Avranches, whom we have met with before, and who refused, some two years later, to admit the king to it (*Gesta*, ed Howlett, p. 101). Mr. Howlett appears to have confused it with another castle which Stephen took "in the Lent of 1139," for Walden was Geoffrey's hereditary seat and had always been in his hands.

[3] "Regnique totius communem ad jacturam, tali modo liberatus de medio illorum evasit" (*Gesta*, p. 104). "Quo facto, velut equus validus et infrænis, morsibus, calcibus quoslibet obvios dilaniare non cessavit" (*Mon. Ang.*, iv. 142).

Ely. That prelate had for a year (1142-43) been peacefully occupied in his see. But at the council of 1143 his past conduct had been gravely impugned. Alarmed at the turn affairs were taking, he decided to consult the Empress.[1] He must, I think, have gone by sea, for we find him, on his way at Wareham, the port for reaching her in Wiltshire. Here he was surprised and plundered by a party of the king's men.[2] He succeeded, however, in reaching the Empress, and then returned to Ely. He had now resolved to appeal to the pope in person, a resolve quickened, it may be, by the fact that the legate, who was one of his chief opponents, had gone thither in November (1143). With great difficulty, and after long debate, he prevailed on the monks to let him carry off, from among the remaining treasures of the church, a large amount of those precious objects without the assistance of which, especially in a doubtful cause, it would have been but lost labour to appeal to the heir of the Apostles. As it was Pope Lucius before whom he successfully cleared his character, and as Lucius was not elected till the March of the following year (1144), I have placed his departure for Rome subsequent to that of the legate. He may, of course, have arrived there sooner and applied to Cœlestine without success, but as that pontiff favoured the Empress, this is not probable. Indeed, the wording of the narrative is distinctly opposed to the idea.[3] In any case, my object is to show that the period of his absence abroad har-

[1] "Episcopus vero Elyensis pro tam imminenti sibi negotio auxilium Dominæ Imperatricis et suorum colloquium requirendum putavit" (*Anglia Sacra*, i. 622).

[2] This might lead us to suppose that the incident belonged to the latter half of 1142, when Wareham was in the king's hands. The date (1143), however, cannot be in question.

[3] *Historia Eliensis*, p. 623. Theobald, from his Angevin sympathies, supported Nigel's cause.

monizes well with the London Chronicle, which places Geoffrey's revolt about the end of the year. For the bishop had been gone some time when the earl obtained possession of Ely.[1]

Hugh Bigod, the Earl of Norfolk, whose allegiance had ever sat lightly upon him, appears to have eventually become his ally,[2] but for the time we hear only of his brother-in-law, William de Say, as actively embracing his cause.[3] He must, however, have relied on at least the friendly neutrality of his relatives, the Clares and the De Veres, in Cambridgeshire, Suffolk, and Essex, as well as on the loyalty of his own vassals. It is possible, from scattered sources, to trace his plan of action, and to reconstruct the outline of what we may term the fenland campaign.

Fordham, in Cambridgeshire, on the Suffolk border, appears to have been his base of operations. Here supplies could reach him from Suffolk and North Essex. He was thence enabled to advance to Ely, the bishop being at this time absent at Rome, and his forces being hard pressed by those which Stephen had despatched against them. The earl gladly accepted their appeal to himself for assistance, and was placed by them in possession of the isle, including its key, Aldreth Castle.[4] He soon made a further advance, and, pushing on in the same direction, burst upon Ramsey Abbey on a December[5] morning at

---

[1] See Appendix Z: "Bishop Nigel at Rome."
[2] "Hugone quoque, cognomente Bigot, viro illustri et in illis partibus potenti, sibi confœderato" (*Gesta*, p. 106).
[3] *Mon. Ang.*, iv. 142.
[4] "Homines regis erga locum fratrum Ely insidias unanimiter paraverunt, adversum quos cum custodes insulæ non sufficerent rebellare, Galfridum comitem, tunc adversarium [Stephani regis,] incendiis patriam et seditione perturbantem, suscipiunt; cui etiam castrum de Ely, atque Alrehede, ob firmamentum tuitionis, submiserunt" (*Historia Eliensis*, p. 623).
[5] Here again we are indebted for the date to the London Chronicle (*Liber*

P

daybreak, seized the monks in their beds, drove them forth clad as they were, and turned the abbey into a fortified post.[1]

He was probably led to this step by the confusion then reigning among the brethren. A certain scheming monk, Daniel by name, had induced the abbot to resign in his favour. The resignation was indignantly repudiated by the monks and the tenants of the abbey, but Stephen, bribed by Daniel, had visited Ramsey in person, and installed him by force as abbot only eighteen days before the earl's attack.[2] It is, therefore, quite possible that, as stated in the Walden Chronicle, Daniel may have been privy to this gross outrage. In any case the earl's conduct excited universal indignation.[3] He stabled his horses in the cloisters; he plundered the church of its most sacred treasures; he distributed its manors among his lawless followers, and he then sent them forth to ravage far and wide. In short, in the words of the pious chronicler, he made of the church of God a very den of thieves.[4]

de Ant. Leg., fol. 35), which states that Geoffrey "in adventu Domini fecit castellum Ecclesiam de Rameseya." Geoffrey's doings may well have been of special interest to the Londoners.

[1] "Ira humanum excedente modum, ita efferatus est, ut procurantibus Willelmo de Saye et Daniele quodam falsi nominis ac tonsuræ monacho, navigio cum suis subvectus Rameseiam peteret, ecclesiam Deo ac beato patri Benedicto dicatam summo mane ausu temerario primitus invadendo subintraret, monachosque omnes post divinum nocturnale officium sopori deditos comprehenderet, et vix habitu simplici indutos expellendo statim perturbaret, nullaque interveniente mora, ecclesiam illam satis pulcherrimam, non ut Dei castrum sed sicut castellum, superius ac inferius, intus ac extra, fortiter munivit" (*Mon. Ang.*, iv. 142).

"Hic totus in rabiem invectus Ramesiam, nobile monasterium invadens, fugata monachorum caterva, custodiam posuit" (*Leland's Collectanea*, i. 600).

[2] *Chronicon Abbatiæ Ramesiensis*, pp. 327-329.

[3] "Monachis expulsis, raptores immisit, et ecclesiam Dei speluncam fecit latronum" (*Hen. Hunt.*, p. 277).

[4] "Vasa autem altaris aurea et argentea Deo sacrata, capas etiam cantorum lapidibus preciosis ac opere mirifico contextas, casulis cum albis, et

STRATEGY OF THE REBELS.

But for the time these same enormities enabled the daring earl at once to increase the number of his followers and to acquire a strategical position unrivalled for his purpose. The soldiers of fortune and mercenary troopers who now swarmed throughout the land flocked in crowds to his standard, and he was soon at the head of a sufficient force to undertake offensive operations.[1] From his advanced post at Ramsey Abbey, he was within striking distance of several important points, while himself comparatively safe from attack. His front and right flank were covered by the meres and fens; his left was to some extent protected by the Ouse and its tributaries, and was further strengthened by a fortified work, erected by his son Ernulf at one of the abbey's manors, Wood Walton.[2] In his rear lay the isle of Ely, with its castles in the hands of his men, and its communications with the Eastern Counties secured by his garrison at Fordham.[3] His positions at Ely and Ramsey were themselves connected by a garrison, on the borders of the two counties, at Benwick.[4]

cæteris ecclesiastici decoris ornamentis rapuit, et quibuslibet eruere volentibus vili satis precio distraxit unde militibus et satellitibus suis debita largitus est stipendia" (*Mon. Ang.*, iv. 142). "Cœnobiumque sancti Benedicti de Rameseiâ non solum, captis monachorum spoliis, altaribus quoque et sanctorum reliquiis nudatis, expilavit, sed etiam expulsis incompassive monachis de monasterio, militibusque impositis castellum sibi adaptavit" (*Gesta*, p. 105). "Cum manu forti monasterium ipsum occupavit, monachos dispersit, thesaurum et omnia ecclesiæ ornamenta sacrilega manu surripuit et ex ipso monasterio stabulum fecit equorum, villas adjacentes commilitonibus pro stipendiis distribuit" (*Chron. Ram.*, p. 329).

[1] "Galfridus igitur, ubique in regno fide sibi et hominio conjuratis in unum secum cuneum convocatis, gregariæ quoque militiæ sed et prædonum, qui undecumque devote concurrerant, robustissima manu in suum protinus conspirata collegium, ignibus et gladio ubique locorum desævire" (*Gesta*, p. 105). "Crebris eruptionibus atque excursionibus vicinas infestavit provincias" (*W. Newburgh*, i. 45).

[2] "Castellum quoddam fecerat apud Waltone" (*Chron. Ram.*, p. 332).

[3] "Inde recessum habuit per Ely quiete : Fordham quoque contra hostes sibi cum valida manu firmare usurpavit" (*Historia Eliensis*, p. 623).

[4] "Similiter apud Benewik in transitu aquarum" (*ibid.*).

Thus situated, the earl was enabled to indulge his thirst for vengeance, if not on Stephen himself, at least on his unfortunate subjects. From his fastness in the fenland he raided forth; his course was marked by wild havoc, and he returned laden with plunder.[1] Cambridge, as being the king's town, underwent at his hands the same fate that Nottingham had suffered in 1140, or Worcester in 1139, at the hands of the Earl of Gloucester.[2] Bursting suddenly on the town, he surprised, seized, and sacked it. As at Worcester, the townsmen had stored in the churches such property as they could; but the earl was hardened to sacrilege: the doors were soon crashing beneath the axes of his eager troopers, and when they had pillaged to their hearts' content, the town was committed to the flames.[3] The whole country round was the scene of similar deeds.[4] The humblest village church was not safe from his attack,[5] but the religious houses, from their own wealth, and from the accumulated treasures which, for safety, were then stored within their walls, offered the most alluring prize. It is only from the snatch of a popular rhyme that we learn incidentally the fact that St. Ives was treated even as the abbey of which it was a daughter-

---

[1] "Omnia adversus regiæ partis consentaneos abripere et consumere, nudare et destruere" (*Gesta*, p. 105). "Maneria, villas, ceteraque proprietatem regiam contingentia primitus invasit, igni combussit, prædasque cum rapinis non minimis inde sublatas commilitonibus suis larga manu distribuit" (*Monasticon*, iv. 142).

[2] *Cont. Flor. Wig.*, ii. 119, 128. Compare the Peterborough Chronicle: "Ræuedan hi & brendon alle the tunes" (*Ang. Sax. Chron.*, i. 382).

[3] *Gesta.*

[4] "Talique ferocitate in omnem circumquaque provinciam, in omnibus etiam, quascunque obviam habebat, ecclesiis immiseranter desæviit; possessiones cœnobiorum, distractis rebus, depopulatis omnibus in solitudinem redegit; sanctuaria eorum, vel quæcumque in ærariis concredita reponebantur sine metu vel pietate ferox abripuit" (*ibid.*).

[5] "Locis sacris vel ipsis de ecclesiis nullam deferendo exhibuit reverentiam" (*Monasticon*, iv. 142).

house. In a MS. of the *Historia Anglorum* there is preserved by Mathew Paris the tradition that the earl and his lawless followers mockingly sang of their wild doings—

"I ne mai a live
For Benoit ne for Ive."[1]

It may not have been observed that this jingle refers to St. Benedict of Ramsey and its daughter-house of St. Ives.[2]

Emboldened by success, he extended his ravages, till his deeds could no longer be ignored.[3] Stephen, at length fairly roused, marched in strength against him, determined to suppress the revolt. But the earl, skilfully avoiding an encounter in the open field, took refuge in the depths of the fenland and baffled the efforts of the king. Finding it useless to prolong the chase, Stephen fell back on his usual policy of establishing fortified posts to hem the rebels in. In these he placed garrisons, and so departed.[4]

Geoffrey was now at his worst. Checked in extending his sphere of plunder, he ravaged, with redoubled energy, the isle itself. His tools, disguised as beggars, wandered from door to door, to discover those who were still able to relieve them from their scanty stores. The hapless

[1] "Facti enim amentes cantitabat unusquisque Anglice," etc. The "Anglice" reads oddly. Strange that the sufferings of the people should be bewailed and made merry over in the same tongue!

[2] Stephen himself behaved no better, to judge from the story in the *Chronicle of Abingdon* (ii. 292), where it is alleged that the king, being informed of a large sum of money stored in the treasury of the abbey, sent his satellite, William d'Ypres, who, gaining admission on the plea of prayer, broke open the chest with an axe, and carried off the treasure.

[3] "Militum suorum numerositate immanior factus, per totam circumcirca discurrendo provinciam nulli cuicunque pecuniam possidenti parcere vovit" (*Mon. Ang.*, iv. 142).

"Crebris eruptionibus et excursionibus vicinas infestavit provincias. Deinde sumpta ex successu fiducia longius progrediens, regem Stephanum acerrimis fatigavit terruitque incursibus" (*Will. Newb.*, i. 45).

[4] *Gesta*.

victims of this stratagem were seized at dead of night, dragged before the earl as a great prize, and exposed in turn to every torture that a devilish ingenuity could devise till the ransom demanded by their captors had been extorted to the uttermost farthing.[1] I cannot but think that the terrible picture of the cruelties which have made this period memorable for ever in our history was painted by the Peterborough chronicler from life, and that these very doings in his own neighbourhood inspired his imperishable words.

Nor was it only the earl that the brethren of Ely had to fear. Stephen, infuriated at the loss of the isle, laid the blame at their bishop's door, and seized all those of their possessions which were not within the earl's grasp. The monks, thus placed "between the devil and the deep sea," were indeed at their wits' end.[2] A very interesting reference to this condition of things is found in a communication from the pope to Archbishop Theobald, stating

[1] "Exploratores vero illius, habitu mutato, more egenorum ostiatim oberrantes, villanis et cæteris hujusmodi hominibus pecunia a Deo data abundantibus insidiabantur, quibus taliter compertis intempestæ noctis silentio, tempore tamen primitus considerato, Sathanæ satellites a comite transmittebantur qui viros innocuos alto sopore quandoque detentos raperent raptos vero quasi pro magno munere ei presentarent. Qui mox immani supplicio, per intervalla tamen, vexabantur et tamdiu per tormenta varia vicissim sibi succedentia torquebantur, donec pecuniæ eis impositæ ultimum solverent quadrantem" (*Monasticon*, iv. 142). An incidental allusion to this system of robbery by ransom is found in an inquisition (*temp.* John) on the royal manor of Writtle, Essex (*Testa de Nevill*, p. 270 b). It is there recorded that Godebold of Writtle, who held land at Boreham, was captured by Geoffrey and forced to mortgage his land to raise the means for his ransom: "Godebold de Writel' qui eam tenuit captus a comite Galfrido, patre Willelmi de Mandevilla, tempore regis Stephani, pro redemptione sua versus predictum comitem acquietanda posuit in vadimonium," etc.

[2] "Propterea Rex Stephanus, irâ graviter accensus, omnia hæc reputavit ab Episcopo Nigello machinari; et jussit e vestigio possessiones Ecclesiæ a suis undequaque distrahi in vindictam odiorum ejus. Succisâ igitur Monachis rerum facultate suarum, nimis ægre compelluntur in Ecclesiâ, maxime ciborum inedia. Unde non habentes victuum, gementes et anxii reliquas thesaurorum," etc. (*Historia Eliensis*, p. 623).

that Bishop Nigel of Ely has written to complain that
he found on his return from Rome that Earl Geoffrey, in
his absence, had seized and fortified the isle, and ravaged
the possessions of his church within it, while Stephen had
done the same for those which lay without it. As it
would seem that this document has not been printed, I
here append the passage:—

"Venerabilis frater noster N. elyensis episcopus per literas suas
nobis significavit quod dum apostolicorum limina et nostram presentiam visitasset, Gaufridus comes de mandeuilla elyensem insulam ubi
sedes episcopalis est violenter occupavit et quasdam sibi munitiones
in ea parauit. Occupatis autem ab ipso comite interioribus, Stephanus rex omnes ejusdem ecclesie possessiones exteriores occupavit et
pro voluntate sua illicite distribuit."[1]

This letter would seem to have been written subsequent
to Nigel's return. The bishop, however, had heard while
at Rome of these violent proceedings,[2] and had prevailed
on Lucius to write to Theobald and his fellow-bishops,
complaining—

"Quod a quibusdam parrochianis vestris bona et possessiones
elyensis ecclesie, precipue dum ipse ab episcopatu expulsus esset,
direpta sunt et occupata et contra justitiam teneantur. Quidam
etiam sub nomine *tenseriarum* villas et homines suos spoliant et
injustis operationibus et exaccionibus opprimunt."[3]

But the bishop was not the only sufferer who turned
to Rome for help. When Stephen installed the ambitious
Daniel as Abbot of Ramsey in person, Walter, the late
abbot, had sought "the threshold of the Apostles."
Daniel, whether implicated or not in Geoffrey's sacrilegious deeds, found himself virtually deposed when the

[1] *Cotton. MS.*, Tib. A. vi. fol. 117.
[2] "Hæc omnia episcopo, quamvis Romæ longius commoranti, satis
innotuerunt, et gratiâ Domini Papæ sublimiter donatus, his munimentis
tandem roboratus contra deprimentum ingenia, ad domum gaudens rediit"
(*Historia Eliensis*, p. 623).
[3] *Cotton. MS.*, Tib. A. vi. fol. 116 b. See Appendix AA: "Tenserie."

abbey became a fortress of the earl. Alarmed also for the possible consequence of Walter's appeal to Rome, he resolved to follow his example and betake himself to the pope, trusting to the treasure that he was able to bring.[1] The guileless simplicity of Walter, however, carried the day; he found favour in the eyes of the curia and returned to claim his abbey.[2] But though he had been absent only three months, the scene was changed indeed. That which he had left "the House of God," he found, as we have seen, "a den of thieves." But the "dove" who had pleaded before the papal court could show himself, at need, a lion. Filled, we are told, with the Holy Spirit, he entered, undaunted, the earl's camp, seized a flaming torch, and set fire not only to the tents of his troopers, but also to the outer gate of the abbey, which they had made the barbican of their stronghold. But neither this novel adaptation of the orthodox "tongues of fire," nor yet the more appropriate anathemas which he scattered as freely as the flames, could convert the mailed sinners from the error of their unhallowed ways. Indeed, it was almost a miracle that he escaped actual violence, for the enraged soldiery threatened him with death and brandished their weapons in his face.[3]

[1] *Chronicle of Ramsey*, p. 329.
[2] "Quum autem negotium feliciter ibi consummasset, reversus in Angliam infra tres menses per judices delegatos abbatiam suam, Rege super hoc multum murmurante, recuperavit" (*ibid.*, p. 330).
[3] "Quum vero sæpedictus abbas in possessionem abbatiæ suæ corporaliter mitti debuisset, invenit sceleratam familiam prædicti comitis sibi fortiter resistentem. Sed ipse, Spiritu Dei plenus, inter sagittas et gladios ipsorum sæpius in caput ejus vibratos, accessit intrepidus, ignem arripuit, et tentoria ipsorum portamque exteriorem quam incastellaverant viriliter incendit et combussit. Sed nec propter incendium nec propter anathema quod in eos fuerat sententiatum locum amatum deserere vel abbati cedere voluerunt. Creditur a multis miraculose factum esse quod nullus ex insanis prædonibus illis manus in eum misit dum eorum tecta combureret quamvis lanceis et sagittis, multum irati, dum hæc faceret, mortem ei cominus intentarent" (*ibid.*).

DESECRATION OF RAMSEY ABBEY.   217

In the excited state of the minds of those by whom such sights were witnessed, portents would be looked for, and found, as signs of the wrath of Heaven. Before long it was noised abroad that the very walls of the abbey were sweating blood, as a mark of Divine reprobation on the deeds of its impious garrison.[1] Far and wide the story spread; and men told with bated breath how they had themselves seen and touched the abbey's bleeding walls. Among those attracted by the wondrous sight was Henry, Archdeacon of Huntingdon, who has recorded for all time that he beheld it with his own eyes.[2] And as they spoke to one another of the miracle, in which they saw the finger of God, the starving peasants whispered their hopes that the hour of their deliverance was at hand.

The time, indeed, had come. As the now homeless abbot wandered over the abbey's lands, sick at heart, in weariness and want, the sights that met his despairing eyes were enough to make him long for death.[3] Barely a plough remained on all his broad demesnes; all provisions had been carried off; no man tilled the land. Every lord had now his castle, and every castle was a robber's nest.[4] In vain he boldly appealed to Earl

[1] "Aliud etiam illis diebus fertur contigisse miraculum, quod lapides murorum ecclesiæ Ramesensis, claustri etiam et officinarum quas prædones inhabitaverant, in magna quantitate guttas sanguinis emiserunt, unde per totam Angliam rumor abiit admirabilis, et magnæ super hoc habitæ sunt inter omnes ad invicem collationes. Erat enim quasi notorium, et omnibus intueri volentibus visu et tactu manifestum" (*ibid.*).

[2] "Dum autem ecclesia illa pro castello teneretur, ebullivit sanguis a parietibus ecclesie et claustri adjacentis, indignationem divinam manifestans, exterminationem sceleratorum denuntians; quod multi quidem, et ipse ego, oculis meis inspexi" (*Hen. Hunt.*, p. 277).

[3] "Miserabilis abbas iste post tot labores et ærumnas quietem habere et domum suam recuperasse sperabat a qua dolens et exspes recessit, laboribus expensis ita fatigatus ut jam tæderet eum vivere. Non enim habebat unde modicæ familiæ suæ equitaturas et sumptus necessarios posset providere" (*Chron. Ram.*, p. 331).

[4] "In omnibus terris dominicis totius abbatiæ unam tantum carucam reperit et dimidiam, reperit victualium nihil; debitum urgebat; terræ jace-

218   FALL AND DEATH OF GEOFFREY.

Geoffrey himself, warning him to his face that he and his would remain cut off from the communion of Christians till the abbey was restored to its owners. The earl listened with impatience, and gave him a vague promise; but he kept his hold of the abbey.[1] The heart of the spoiler was hardened like that of Pharaoh of old, and not even miracles could move him to part with his precious stronghold.[2]

But if Ramsey had thus suffered, what had been the fate of Ely? A bad harvest, combined with months of systematic plunder, had brought about a famine in the land. For the space of twenty or even thirty miles, neither ox nor plough was to be seen; barely could the smallest bushel of grain be bought for two hundred pence. The people, by hundreds and thousands, were perishing

bant incultæ.... Oportuit præfatum abbatem xxiiii castell[?anis] vel amplius singulis mensibus pro rusticis suis redemptiones seu tenserias præstare, qui tam per Danielem quam per ipsos malefactores multum exhausti fuerant, et extenuati" (*Chron. Ram.*, 333, 334). This description, though it is applied to the state of things which awaited the abbot on Earl Geoffrey's death, is obviously in point here. It is of importance for its allusion to the plough, which illustrates the language of Domesday (the plough-teams being always the first to suffer, and the most serious loss: compare Bishop Denewulf's tenth-century charter in *Liber de Hyda*), but still more for its mention of the *tenseriæ*. Here we have the very same word, used at the very same time, at Peterborough, Ramsey, and Ely. The correction, therefore, of the English Chronicle is utterly unjustifiable (see Appendix AA). Moreover, a comparison of this passage with the letter of Pope Lucius (*ante*, p. 215) shows that at Ramsey, as at Ely, the evil effect of this state of things continued in these *tenseriæ* even after the bishop and the abbot had respectively regained possession.

[1] "Suorum tandem consilio fretus, comitem Gaufridum adiit, monasterii sui detentorem, patenter et audacter ei ostendens tam ipsum quam totam familiam ipsius, tam ex ipso facto quam apostolica auctoritate interveniente, a Christianâ communione esse privatos, domum suam sibi postulans restitui si vellet absolvi. Quod comes vix patienter audiens, plures ei terminos de reddenda possessione sua constituit, sed promissum nunquam adimplevit ita ut cum potius deludere videretur quam ablatam possessionem sibi velle restituere; unde miser abbas miserabiliter afflictus mortis debitum jam vellet exsolvisse" (*Chron. Ram.*, p. 331).

[2] "Sed prophani milites in sua malitia pertinaces nec sic domum Dei quam polluerant reddere voluerant; induratum enim erat cor eorum" (*ibid.*, p. 330).

HORRORS OF THE ANARCHY. 219

for want of bread, and their corpses lay unburied in the fields, a prey to beasts and to fowls of the air. Not for ages past, as it seemed to the monks, had there been such tribulation upon earth.[1] Nor were the peasants the only sufferers. Might was then right, for all classes, throughout the land;[2] the smaller gentry were themselves seized, and held, by their captors, to ransom. As they heard of distant villages in flames, as they gazed on strings of captives dragged from their ravaged homes, the words of the psalmist were adapted in the mouths of the terrified monks: " They bind the godly with chains, and the nobles with links of iron."[3] In the mad orgie of wickedness neither women nor the aged were spared. Ransom was wrung from the quivering victims by a thousand refinements of torture. In the groans of the sufferers, in the shrieks of the tortured, men beheld the fulfilment of the words of St. John the Apostle, "In those days shall men . . . desire to die, and death shall flee from them."[4]

Again we are tempted to ask if we have not in these very scenes the actual original from which was drawn the

[1] "Oppresserat enim fames omnem regionem; et ægra seges victum omnem negaverat; per viginti milliaria seu triginta non bos non aratrum est inventus qui particulam terræ excoleret; vix parvissimus tunc modius emi poterat ducentis denariis. Tantaque hominum clades de inopiâ panis sequuta est, ut per vicos et plateas centeni et milleni ad instar uteris inflati exanimes jacerent: feris et volatilibus cadavera inhumata relinquebantur. Nam multo retro tempore talis tribulatio non fuit in cunctis terrarum regnis " (*Historia Eliensis*, p. 623).

[2] "Efferbuit enim per totam Angliam Stephani regis hostilis tribulatio, totaque insula vi potius quam ratione regebatur " (*Chron. Ram.*, p. 334).

[3] " Potentes, per circuitum late vastando, milites ex rapinâ conducunt; villas comburunt: captivos de longe ducentes miserabiliter tractabant; pios alligabant in compedibus et nobiles in manicis ferreis" (*Historia Eliensis*, p. 623).

[4] " Furit itaque rabies vesana. Invicta lætatur malitia: non sexui non parcunt ætati. Mille mortis species inferunt, ut ab afflictis pecuniam excutiant: fit clamor dirus plangentium: inhorruit luctus ubique mærentium; et constat fuisse completum quod nunciatur in Apocalypsi Joannis: 'quærent homines mori et fugiet mors ab eis'" (*ibid.*).

picture in the English Chronicle, a picture which might thus be literally true of the chronicler's own district, while not necessarily applicable, as the latest research suggests, to the whole of Stephen's realm.

It was now that men "said openly that Christ slept, and His saints." The English chronicler seems to imply, and Henry of Huntingdon distinctly asserts, that the wicked, emboldened by impunity, said so in scornful derision; but William of Newburgh assigns the cry to the sufferings of a despairing people. It is probable enough that both were right, that the people and their oppressors had reversed the parts of Elijah and the priests of Baal. For a time there seemed to rise in vain the cry so quaintly Englished in the paraphrase of John Hopkins :—

> "Why doost withdraw thy hand aback,
> And hide it in thy lappe?
> O pluck it out, and be not slack
> To give thy foes a rappe!"

But when night is darkest, dawn is nearest,[1] and the end of the oppressor was at hand. It was told in after days how even Nature herself had shown, by a visible sign, her horror of his impious deeds. While marching to the siege of Burwell on a hot summer's day, he halted at the edge of a wood, and lay down for rest in the shade. And lo! the very grass withered away beneath the touch of his unhallowed form![2]

The fortified post which the king's men had now established at Burwell was a standing threat to Fordham, the key of his line of communications. He was therefore

---

[1] "Sed verum est quod vulgariter dicitur: 'Ubi dolor maximus ibi proxima consolatio'" (*Chron. Ram.*, p. 331).

[2] "Herba viridissima emarcuit, ut eo surgente quasi præmortua videretur, nec toto fere anno viridatis suæ vires recuperavit. Unde datur intelligi quam detestandum sit consortium excommunicatorum" (*Gervase*, i. p. 128).

compelled to attack it. And there he was destined to die the death of Richard Cœur de Lion. As he reconnoitred the position to select his point of attack, or as, according to others, he was fighting at the head of the troops, he carelessly removed his headpiece and loosened his coat of mail. A humble bowman saw his chance: an arrow whizzed from the fortress, and struck the unguarded head.[1]

There is a conflict of testimony as to the date of the event. Henry of Huntingdon places it in August, while M. Paris (*Chron. Maj.*, ii. 177) makes him die on the 14th of September, and the Walden Chronicle on the 16th. Possibly he was wounded in August and lingered on into September, but, in any case, Henry's date is the most trustworthy.

The monks of Ramsey gloried in the fact that their oppressor had received his fatal wound as he stood on ground which their abbey owned, as a manifest proof that his fate was incurred by the wrong he had done to their

[1] "Accessit paulo post cum exercitu suo ad quoddam castellum expugnandum quod apud Burewelle de novo fuerat constructum, et quum elevata casside illud circuiret ut infirmiorem ejus partem eligeret ad expugnandum, . . . quidam vilissimus sagittarius ex hiis qui intra castellum erant capiti ipsius comitis lethale vulnus impressit" (*Chron. Ram.*, 331, 332).

"Hic, cum . . . in obsidione supradicti castelli de Burwelle in scuto et lancea contra adversarios viriliter decertasset, ob nimium calorem cassidem deposuit, et loricæ ventilabrum solvit, sicque nudato capite intrepidus militavit. Æstus quippe erat. Quem cum vidisset quispiam de castello, et adversarium agnosceret, telo gracili quod ganea dicitur eum jam cominus positum petiit, que testam capitis ipsius male nudati perforavit" (*Gervase*, i. 128).

"Dum nimis audax, nimisque prudentiæ suæ innitens regiæ virtutis castella frequentius circumstreperet, ab ipsis tandem regalibus circumventus prosternitur" (*Gesta*, p. 106).

"Post hujusmodi tandem excessibus aliisque multis his similibus publicam anathematis non immerito incurrit sententiam, in qua apud quoddam oppidulum in Burwella lethaliter in capite vulneratus est" (*Mon. Ang.*, iv. 142).

"Inter acies suorum confertas, a quodam pedite vilissimo solus sagitta percussus est. Et ipse, vulnus ridens, post dies tamen ex ipso vulnere excommunicatus occubuit" (*Hen. Hunt.*, 276).

222   FALL AND DEATH OF GEOFFREY.

patron saint.[1] At Waltham Abbey, with equal pride, it was recorded that he who had refused to atone for the wrong he had done to its holy cross received his wound in the self-same hour in which its aid was invoked against the oppressor of its shrine.[2] But all were agreed that such a death was a direct answer to the prayer of the oppressed, a signal act of Divine vengeance on one who had sinned against God and man.[3]

For the wound was fatal. The earl, like Richard in after days, made light of it at first.[4] Retiring, it would seem, through Fordham, along the Thetford road, he reached Mildenhall in Suffolk, and there he remained, to die. The monks of his own foundation believed, and perhaps with truth, that when face to face with death, he displayed heartfelt penitence, prayed earnestly that his sins might be forgiven, and made such atonement to God and man as his last moments could afford. But there was none to give him the absolution he craved; indeed, after the action which the Church had taken the year

---

[1] "In quodam prædio consisteret quod . . . ad Ramesense monasterium pertinebat, et pertinet usque in hodiernum diem . . . Quod iccirco in fundo beati Benedicti factum fuisse creditur ut omnes intelligere possent quod Deus ultionum dominus hoc fecerat in odium et vindictam injuriarum quas monasterio beati Benedicti sacrilegus comes intulerat" (*Chron. Ram.*, p. 331).

[2] "Cum nollet satisfacere, placuit fratribus ibidem Deo servientibus in transgressionis huius vindictam Crucem deponere si forte dives ille compunctus hoc facto vellet resipiscere. Tradunt autem qui hiis inquirendis diligentiam adhibuerunt eadem depositionis hora Comitem illum ante castrum de Burewelle ad quod expugnandum diligenter operam dabat letale vulnus suscepisse et eo infra xl dies viam universe Carnis ingressum fuisse" (*Harl. MS.*, 3776). See also Appendix M.

[3] "Verum tantarum tamque immanium persecutionum, tam crudelium quoque, quas in omnes ingerebat, calamitatum justissimus tandem respector Deus dignum malitiæ suæ finem imposuit" (*Gesta*, p. 106).

"Quia igitur improbi dixerunt Deum dormitare, excitatus est Deus, et in hoc signo, et in significato" (*Hen. Hunt.*, p. 277).

[4] "Letiferum sui capitis vulnus deridens nec sic a suo cessavit furore" (*Gervase*, i. 128, 129).

before, it is doubtful if any one but the pope could absolve so great a sinner.[1]

In the mean time the Abbot of Ramsey heard the startling news, and saw that his chance had come. The earl might be willing to save his soul at the cost of restoring the abbey. To Mildenhall he flew in all haste, but only to find that the earl had already lost consciousness. There awaited him, however, the fruit of his oppressor's tardy repentance in the form of instructions from the earl to his son to surrender Ramsey Abbey. Armed with these, the abbot departed as speedily as he had come.[2]

The tragic end of the great earl must have filled the thoughts of men with a strange awe and horror. That one who had rivalled, but a year ago, the king himself in power, should meet an inglorious death at the hands of a wretched churl, that he who had defied the thunders of the Church should fall as if by a bolt from heaven, were facts which, in the highly wrought state of the minds of men at the time, were indeed signs and wonders.[3] But even more tragic than his death was the fate which awaited his corpse. Unshriven, he had passed away laden with the curses of the Church. His soul was lost for ever; and his body no man might bury.[4] As the earl was drawing his

[1] "Pœnitens itaque valde et Deo cum magna cordis contritione pro peccatis suis supplicans, quantum taliter moriens poterat, Deo et hominibus satisfecit, licet a præsentibus absolvi non poterat" (*Mon. Ang.*, iv. 142). Cf. p. 202, *supra*.

[2] "Quum igitur apud Mildehale mortis angustia premeretur, hoc audiens præfatus abbas ad eum citissime convolavit. Quo cum venisset, nec erat in ipso comite vox neque sensus, familiares tamen ipsius, domino suo multum condolentes, eum benigne receperunt et cum literis ipsius comitis eum ad filium suum scilicet Ernaldum de Magna Villa . . . statim miserunt ut sine mora cœnobium suum sibi restitueret" (*Chron. Ram.*, p. 332).

[3] "Gaufridus de Magna Villa regem validissime vexavit et in omnibus gloriosus effulsit. Mense autem Augusti miraculum justitia sua dignum Dei splendor exhibuit" (*Hen. Hunt.*, p. 277).

[4] "Et sicut, dum viveret, ecclesiam confudit, terram turbavit, sic, ad eum confundendum tota Angliæ conspiravit ecclesia; quia et anathematis

last breath there came upon the scene some Knights Templar, who flung over him the garb of their order so that he might at least die with the red cross upon his breast.[1] Then, proud in the privileges of their order, they carried the remains to London, to their "Old Temple" in Holborn. There the earl's corpse was enclosed in a leaden coffin, which was hung, say some, on a gnarled fruit tree, that it might not contaminate the earth, or was hurled, according to others, into a pit without the churchyard.[2] So it remained, for nearly twenty years, exposed to the gibes of the Londoners, the earl's "deadly foes." But with the characteristic faithfulness of a monastic house to its founder, the monks of Walden clung to the hope that the ban of the Church might yet be removed, and the bones of the great earl be suffered to rest among them. According to their chronicle, Prior William, who had obtained his post from Geoffrey's hands, rested not till he had wrung his absolution from Pope Alexander III.[3] (1159-1181). But the *Ramsey Chronicle*, which appears to be a virtually contemporary record, assigns the eventual

gladio percussus et inabsolutus abscessit, et terræ sacrilegum dari non licuit" (*Gesta*, p. 106).

[1] "Illo autem, in discrimine mortis, ultimum trahente spiritum, quidam supervenere Templarii qui religionis suæ habitum cruce rubea signatum ei imposuerunt" (*Mon. Ang., ut supra*). But the red cross is said not to have been assumed by the order till the time of Pope Eugene (1145). See *Monasticon Ang.*, ii. 815, 816.

[2] "Ac deinde jam mortuum secum tollentes, et in pomerio suo, veteris scilicet Templi apud London' canali inclusum plumbeo in arbore torva suspenderunt" (*Mon. Ang.*, iv. 142).

"Corpus vero defuncti comitis in trunco quodam signatum, et propter anathema quo fuerat innodatus Londoniis apud Vetus Templum extra cimiterium in antro quodam projectum est" (*Chron. Ram.*, p. 332). This would seem to be the earliest mention of the Old Temple. *Pomerium* in Low Latin is, of course, an orchard, and not, as Mr. Freeman so strangely imagines (at Nottingham, in Domesday), a town wall.

[3] "Post aliquod vero tempus industria et expensis Willelmi quem jam pridem in Waldena constituerat priorem, a papa Alexandro, more taliter decedentium meruit absolvi, inter Christianos recipi, et pro eo divina celebrari" (*Mon. Ang.*, iv. 142).

removal of the ban to Geoffrey's son and namesake, and to the atonement which he made to Ramsey Abbey on his father's behalf.[1] The latter story is most precise, but both may well be true. For, although the Ramsey chronicler would more especially insist on the fact that St. Benedict had to be appeased before the earl could be absolved, the absolution itself would be given not by the abbot, but by the pope. The grant to Ramsey would be merely a condition of the absolution itself being granted. The nature of the grant is known to us not only from the chronicle, but also from the primate's charter confirming this final settlement.[2] As this confirmation is dated at Windsor, April 6, 1163, we thus, roughly, obtain the date of the earl's Christian burial.[3]

[1] "Ibique jacuit toto tempore Regis Stephani magnaque parte Regis Henrici Secundi, donec Gaufridus filius ejus, Comes Essexie, vir industrius et justitiarius Domini Regis jam factus Dominum Willelmum abbatem cæpit humiliter interpellare pro patre suo defuncto offerens satisfactionem, et quum ab eo benignum super hoc responsum accepisset, statuta die convenerunt ambo sub præsentia domini Cantuarensis, scilicet beati Thomæ martyris, super hoc tractaturi. . . . Quo facto, pater ipsius comitis Christianæ traditus est sepulturæ."

The earl's grant runs as follows :—

"Gaufridus de Magna Villa Comes Essexie, omnibus amicis suis et hominibus et universis sanctæ Ecclesiæ filiis salutem.

"Satis notum est quanta damna pater meus, Comes Gaufridus, tempore guerrarum monasterio de Rameseia irrogaverit.

"Et quia tanta noxia publico dinoscitur indigere remedio, ego tam præ eo quam pro suis satisfacere volens, consilio sanctæ Ecclesiæ cum Willelmo Abbate monachisque suprascripti cœnobii in hanc formam composui. . . . Et quia constat sepedictum patrem meum in irrogatione damnorum memoratæ ecclesiæ bona thesauri in cappis, et textis, et hujusmodi plurimum delapidasse, ad eorundem reparationem ad ecclesiæ ornatum dignum duxi redditum istum assignari" (*Cart. Ram.*, i. 197). Compare p. 276, n. 3, and p. 415.

[2] *Chron. Ram.*, pp. 306, 333. The king was probably at Windsor at the time, and the date is a useful one for Becket's movements.

[3] A curious archæological question is raised by this date. According to the received belief, the Templars did not remove to the New Temple till 1185, but, according to this evidence, they already had their churchyard there consecrated in 1163, and had therefore, we may presume, begun their church. The church of the New Temple was consecrated by Heraclius on his visit in 1185, but may have been finished sooner.

The Prior of Walden had gained his end, and he now hastened to the Temple to claim his patron's remains. But his hopes were cruelly frustrated at the very moment of success. Just as the body of the then earl (1163) was destined to be coveted at his death (1166) by two rival houses, so now the remains of his father were a prize which the indignant Templars would never thus surrender. Warned of the prior's coming, they instantly seized the coffin, and buried it at once in their new graveyard, where, around the nameless resting-place of the great champion of anarchy, there was destined to rise, in later days, the home of English law.[1]

[1] "Cumque Prior ille corpus defunctum deponere et secum Waldenam deferre satageret, Templarii illi caute premeditati statim illud tollentes, et in cimiterio novi templi ignobili satis tradiderunt sepulturæ" (*Mon. Ang.*, iv. 142). It was generally believed that his effigy was among those remaining at the Temple, but this supposition is erroneous, as has been shown by Mr. J. G. Nichols in an elaborate article on "The Effigy attributed to Geoffrey de Magnaville, and the Other Effigies in the Temple Church" (*Herald and Genealogist* [1866], iii. 97, *et seq.*).

CHAPTER X.

THE EARLDOM OF ESSEX.

THE death of Geoffrey was a fatal blow to the power of the fenland rebels. According, indeed, to one authority, his brother-in-law, William de Say, met his death on the same occasion,[1] but it was the decease of the great earl which filled the king's supporters with exultant joy and hope.[2] For a time Ernulf, his son and heir, clung to the abbey fortress, but at length, sorely against his will, he gave up possession to the monks.[3] Before the year was out, he was himself made prisoner and straightway banished from the realm.[4] Nor was the vengeance of Heaven even yet complete. The chief officer of the wicked earl was thrown from his horse and killed,[5] and

[1] "Willelmi de Say et Galfridi de Mandeville, qui apud Borewelle interfecti fuerunt" (*Chron. Ram.*, App. p. 347).

[2] "Isto itaque tali modo ad extrema deducto, nox quædam et horror omnes regis adversarios implevit, quique ex dissensione a Galfrido exorta regis annisum maxime infirmari putabant, nunc, eo interfecto, liberiorem et ad se perturbandum, ut res se habebat, expediorem fore æstimabant" (*Gesta*, p. 104). "Sicque Dei judicio patriæ vastatore sublato, virtus bellatorum qui secum manum ad perniciem miserorum firmaverunt plurimum labefacta est, cognoscentes Dominum Christum fideli suo Regi de hostibus dare triumphum, et adversantes ei potenter elidere, ad hoc expavit cor inimicorum illius" (*Historia Eliensis*, p. 628).

[3] "Quod post dilationes, non sine difficultate, tandem invitus fecit; locum enim illum et vicinas ejus partes multum dilexerat. Prophani milites recedunt cum iniquo satellite" (*Chron. Ram.*, p. 332).

[4] "Eodem quoque anno, Ernulfus filius comitis, qui post mortem patris ecclesiam incastellatam retinebat, captus est et in exilium fugatus" (*Gervase*, i. 129. Cf. *Hen. Hunt.*).

[5] "Cujus princeps militum ab equo corruens effuso cerebro spiritum exhalavit" (*ibid.*).

the captain of his foot, who had made himself conspicuous in the violating and burning of churches, met, as he fled beyond the sea, with the fate of Jonah, and worse.[1]

Chroniclers and genealogists have found it easiest to ignore the subsequent fate of Ernulf (or Ernald) de Mandeville.[2] He has even been conveniently disposed of by the statement that he died childless.[3] It may therefore fairly be described as a genealogical surprise to establish the fact, beyond a shadow of doubt, not only that he left issue, but that his descendants flourished for generations, heirs in the direct male line of this once mighty house. Ernulf himself first reappears, early in the following reign, as a witness to a royal charter confirming Ernald *de Bosco's* foundation at Betlesdene.[4] He also occurs as a principal witness in a family charter, about the same time.[5] This document,[6] which is addressed by Earl Geoffrey "baronibus suis," is a confirmation of a grant of lands in Sawbridgeworth, by

---

[1] "Magister autem peditum suorum, qui plus cæteris solitus erat ecclesias concremare et frangere, dum mare transiret cum uxore sua, ut multi perhibuerant, navis immobilis facta est. Quod monstrum nautis stupentibus et sorte data rei causam inquirentibus, sors cecidit super eum. Quod cum ille totis viribus, nec mirum, contradiceret, secundo et tertio sors jacta in eum devenit: formidantibus igitur nautis positus est in cymbam parvulam ipse et uxor ejus et eorum pecunia nequiter adquisita, ut cum illis esset in perditione; quo facto, navis ut prius maria libera sulcavit, cymba vero in voragine subsistens circumducta et absorpta est" (*Hen. Hunt.*).

[2] There is abundant evidence that the two names are used indifferently.

[3] Burke's *Extinct Peerage*. So also Dr. Stubbs.

[4] *Harl. Cart.*, 84. C. 4. The charter being attested by Thomas the Chancellor must be previous to August, 1158, as it passed at Westminster. It has a rather unusual set of witnesses.

[5] This charter may fairly be dated 1157-1158, on the following grounds. It speaks of Warine fitz Gerold as the king's chamberlain, and as living. But he died in the summer of 1158. It is, however, subsequent to Henry's accession, because it was not till after that event that Fitz Gerold was enfeoffed in Sawbridgeworth (*Liber Niger*), and also subsequent to 1155, because Geoffrey occurs as earl. But as Maurice (de Tiretei) was not sheriff, within these limits, till Michaelmas, 1157, we obtain the date 1157-1158.

[6] *Sloane Cart.*, xxxii. 64.

his tenant Warine fitz Gerold "Camerarius Regis" and his brother Henry, to Robert Blund of London, who is to hold them "de predictis baronibus meis." The witnesses are: "Roesia Com[itissa] matre mea, Eust[achia] Com[itissa], Ernulfo de Mannavilla fratre meo, Willelmo filio Otuwel patruo meo, Mauricio vicecomite, Willelmo de Moch' capellano meo, Otuwel de bouile, Ricardo filio Osberti, Radulfo de Bernires, Willelmo et Ranulfo fil' Ernaldi, Gaufrido de Gerp[en]villa, Hugone de Augo, Waltero de Mannavilla, Willelmo filio Alfredi, Gaufredo filio Walteri, Willelmo de Plaisiz, Gaufrido pincerna." He is, doubtless, also the "Ernald de Mandevill" who holds a knight's fee, in Yorkshire, of Ranulf fitz Walter in 1166.[1] But in the earliest Pipe-Rolls of Henry II. he is already found as a grantee of *terræ datæ* in Wilts., to the amount of £11 10s. 0d. (blanch) "in Wurda." This grant was not among those repudiated by Henry II., and Geoffrey de Mandeville, Ernulf's heir, was still in receipt of the same sum in 1189[2] and 1201–2.[3] Later on, in a list of knights' fees in Wilts., which must belong, from the mention of Earl William de Longespée, to 1196—1226, and is probably *circ.* 1212, we read: "Galfridus de Mandevill tenet in Wurth duas partes unius militis de Rege."[4] That Ernulf should have received a grant in Wilts., a county with which his family was not connected, is probably accounted for by the fact that he

---

[1] *Liber Niger* (ed. 1774), p. 326. The return of the Barony of Helion (p. 242), in which an Ernulf de Mandeville appears as holding half a knight's fee in Bumsted (Helion), is of later date.

[2] *Rot. Pip.*, 1 Ric. I. The "Ernald de Magneville" who was among the Crusaders that reached Acre in June, 1191, may have been a younger son of the disinherited Ernald, if the latter was then dead. An Ernulf de Mandeville is found among the witnesses to a star of Abraham fitz Muriel (1214), granting a house in Westcheap to Geoffrey "de Mandeville," Earl of Essex and Gloucester.

[3] *Rot. Pip.*, 3 John.   [4] *Testa*, p. 142 b.

obtained it in the time of the Empress, who, as in the case of Humfrey de Bohun, found the revenues of Wilts. convenient as a means of rewarding her partisans.[1] But we now come to a series of charters of the highest importance for this discovery. These were preserved among the muniments of Henry Beaufoe of Edmondescote, county Warwick, Esq., when they were seen by Dugdale, who does not, however, in his *Baronage*, allude to their evidence. By the first of these Earl Geoffrey (died 1166) grants to his brother Ernulf one knight's fee in Kingham, county Oxon. :—

"Sciatis me dedisse et firmiter concessisse Ernulfo de Mandavilla fratri meo terram de Caingeham, ... pro servitio unius militis in excambitione terre Radulfi de Nuer. ... Et si Caingeham illi garantizare non potero dabo illi excambium ad valorem de Caingeham antequam inde sit dissaisitus. ... T. Com[ite] Albrico auunculo meo, Henry (*sic*) fil[io] Ger[oldi], Galfr[ido] Arsic, Rad[ulf]o de Berner[iis], Waltero de Mandavilla, Will[elm]o de Aino, Galfrido de Jarpeuill, Will[elmo] de Plais', Jurdan[o] de Taid' Hug[one] de Auc[o], Willelm[o] fil[io] Alured[i] Rad[ulfo] Magn[?avilla], Audoenus (*sic*) Pincerna, Rad[ulfo] frater (*sic*) eius, Aluredus (*sic*) Predevilain."[2]

Ralph "de Nuers," is entered in 1166 as a former holder of four fees from Earl Geoffrey (II.).[3] Of the witnesses to the charter,[4] Henry fitz Gerold (probably the chamberlain) held four fees (*de novo*) of the earl in 1166, Ralph de Berners four (*de veteri*), Walter de Mandeville four (*de veteri*), Geoffrey de Jarpe[n]ville one (*de novo*), Hugh de Ou and William fitz Alfred one each (*de novo*), "Audoenus Pincerna" and Ralph his brother the fifth of a fee (*de novo*) jointly. The relative precedence, according to hold-

---

[1] See, for the exceptionally heavy alienations in this country (some £440 a year), the Pipe-Roll of 2 Henry II., p. 57.
[2] *Dugdale MS.*, 15 (H) fol. 129.
[3] "Feod[um] Rad[ulfi] de Nuers iiii. milites" (*Liber Niger*).
[4] Compare them with the preceding charter of Earl Geoffrey.

ERNULF DE MANDEVILLE AND HIS HEIRS. 231

ing, is not unworthy of notice. The second charter is from Earl William, confirming his brother's gift:—

"Willelmus de Mandavilla comes Essexie Omnibus hominibus, etc. Sciatis me concessisse Ernulfo de Mandauilla fratri meo donationem quam Comes Galfridus illi fecit de villa de Kahingeham. . . . T. Comite Albrico, Simone de Bellocampo, Gaufrido de Say, Wil-l[elm]o de Bouilla, Radu[lfo] de Berneres, Seawal' de Osonuɔlla, Ric[ard]o de Rochellâ, Osberto fil[io] Ric[ard]i, Dauid de Gerponuilla, Wiscardo Leidet, Waltero de Bareuilla, Albot Fulcino, Hugone clerico," etc.[1]

Here Earl "Alberic" was uncle both to the grantor and the grantee; Simon de Beauchamp was their uterine brother; Geoffrey de Say their first cousin. William de Boville would be related to Otuel de Boville, the chief tenant of Mandeville in 1166.[2] "Sewalus de Osevill" then (1166) held four fees (*de veteri*) of the earl. Richard "de Rochellâ" held three-quarters of a fee (*de novo*). Osbert fitz Richard was probably a son of Richard fitz Osbert, who held four fees (*de veteri*) in 1166. Wiscard Ledet was a tenant *in capite* in Oxfordshire (*Testa*, p. 103).[3]

The third charter transfers the fee from the grantee himself to his son:—

"Notum sit . . . quod ego Arnulfus de Mandeuilla concessi et dedi Radulfo de Mandeuilla filio meo pro suo servicio et homagio villam de

---

[1] *Dugdale MS., ut supra.*
[2] William's succession to Otwel suggests that they were somehow related to William fitz Otuel (p. 169).
[3] With this charter of Earl William may be compared another (*Cart. Cott.*, x. 1), in which he confirms to Westminster Abbey the church of Sawbridgeworth. The witnesses are " Willielmo de Ver, Asculfo Capellano, Ricardo de Vercorol, Willelmo de Lisoris, David de Jarpouilla, Symone fratre eius, Osberto filio Ricardi, Osberto de sancto Claro, Willelmo de Norhala, Johanne de Rochella, Eustachio Camerario, Rogero et Simone clericis Abbatis West'." The second and third witnesses are also found attesting the earl's charter to the nuns of Greenfield (see p. 169). Compare further "A charter of William, Earl of Essex" (*Eng. Hist. Review*, April, 1891). "Asculfus (or Hasculfus) Capellanus" was the hero of the adventure, on the earl's death, thus related by Dugdale: "A chaplain of the earl's, called Hasculf, took out his best saddle-horse in the night, and rode to Chicksand, where the Countess Rohese then resided," etc., etc.

Chaingeham . . . et hospitium meum Oxenfordie ad prædictam villam pertinens¹ . . . T. Henrico Danuers," etc.²

From another quarter we are enabled to continue the chain of evidence. We have first a charter to Osney :—

"Ego Gaufridus de Mandeuile . . . confirmavi mercatam terre quam Aaliz mater mea eis diuisit in Hugato, sic[?ut] Ernulfus de Mandeuile pater meus eis assignavit."³

Then we have a charter which thus carries us a step further :—

"Ego Galfridus de Mandeuilla filius Galfridi de Mandeuillâ concessi Domino Galfrido patri meo, filio Arnulfi de Mandeuillâ," etc., etc.⁴

Among the witnesses to this last charter are Robert de Mandeville, and Ralph his brother, and Hugh de Mandeville. Lastly, we have a charter of Ralph de Mandeville, to which the first witness is "Galfridus de Mandauilla frater meus."⁵

We have now established this pedigree :—

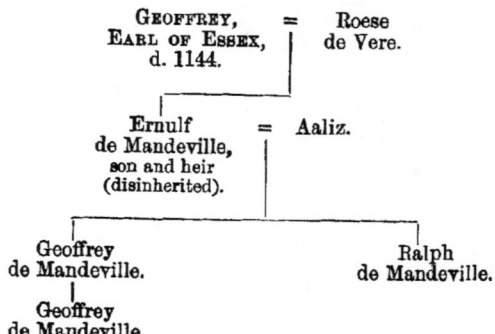

A further charter (*Harl. Cart.*, 54, I. 44) can now be fitted into this pedigree. It is a notification by Adam de

¹ This is a good instance of the custom, so constantly met with in Domesday, by which a house in a county town was attached to a manor.
² *Dugdale MS.*, *ut supra*.   ³ *Dodsworth MS.*, vii. fol. 299.
⁴ *Ibid.*   ⁵ *Ibid.*, xxx. fol. 104.

ERNULF DE MANDEVILLE DISINHERITED. 233

Port, to the Bishop of Lincoln, etc., of his grant of the church of "Hattele." The witnesses are : "Hernaldo de Mandeville et domina Alicia uxore sua, domina Matilside uxore dicti Adæ de Port, Henrico de Port, fratre ejusdem, Galfrido de Mandeville," etc.[1] Here we have a clue to the parentage of Ernulf's wife.

Passing to the reign of Henry III., we find Kingham then still in possession of the family.[2] In Wiltshire they are found yet later, Worth being still held by them in 1292–93 (21 Edw. I).[3]

The importance of the existence of Ernulf and his heirs is seen when we come to deal with the fate of the earldom of Essex. That Ernulf was "exiled" even for a time becomes a remarkable fact, when we remember that he might have found shelter from the king among the followers of the Empress in the west. But he and his father had offended a power greater than the king. The Empress could not shield him from the vengeance of the outraged Church. It is, I think, in his doings at Ramsey, and in the penalties he had thus incurred, that we must seek the reason of his being, as we shall find, so strangely passed over, in favour of his younger brother Geoffrey, who had not partaken of his guilt.

To another charter, hitherto unknown, we owe our knowledge of the fact that Geoffrey was recognized as his father's heir, by the Empress, on his death. Instructive as its contents would doubtless be, it is known to us only from the following note, made by one who had inspected its transcript in the lost volume of the Great Coucher :—

"Carta M. Imperatricis per quam dat Gaufredo de Mannevill filio

---

[1] "Alano de Matem" is among them (cf. p. 89).

[2] "Willelmus de Mandevill tenet in Kaingham feodum unius militis de feod[o] Comitis Hereford[ie]" (*Testa*, pp. 102 *a*, 106 *a*).

[3] *Lansdowne MS.*, 865, fol. 118 *dors.*; *Harl. MS.*, 154, fol. 45.

Gaufredi Comitis Essexie totam hereditatem suam et omnes tenuras quas concessit patri suo. Testes R. Com. Gloec., Rag. Com. Cornub., Rog. Com. Hereford, R. Regis filio, Umfridus de Bohun Dap., Johannes filius Gisleberti, W. de Poutlarch' Camerario. Apud Divisas.[1]

The names of Robert, Earl of Gloucester, and Roger, Earl of Hereford, limit the date of this charter to 1144-1147, and the father of the grantee died, as we have seen, in August, 1144. It should be noted that nothing is said here of the earldom of Essex, and that only an absolutely new creation could confer the dignity on Geoffrey, as he was not his father's heir.

Here, however, yet another charter, also at present unknown, comes to our assistance with its unique evidence that Geoffrey must have held his father's title before 1147.[2] He then disappears from view for the time.

We must now skip some twelve years, and pass to that most important charter in which the earldom was conferred anew on Geoffrey by Henry II. Only those who have made a special study of these subjects can realize the value of this charter, a record hitherto unknown. The attitude of Henry II. to the creations of Stephen and Matilda, the extent to which he recognized them, and the method in which he did so, are subjects on which the historian is peculiarly anxious for information, but on which our existing evidence is singularly and lamentably slight. Of the four charters quoted in the *Reports on the Dignity of a Peer*, only two can be said to have a real bearing on the question, and of these one is of uncertain date, while the meaning of the other is doubtful. But the charter I am about to deal with is remarkably clear in

---

[1] *Lansdowne MS.*, 229, fol. 123 b. This note is followed by one of the charter by which the Empress confirmed Humfrey de Bohun in his post of *Dapifer*, and of which the original is still extant among the Duchy of Lancaster Royal Charters (Pipe-Roll Society : *Ancient Charters*, p. 45).

[2] See Appendix BB.

its meaning, and possesses the advantage that its contents enable us to date it with precision.

The original charter was formerly preserved in the Cottonian collection, but was doubtless among those which perished in the disastrous fire.[1] The copy of it made by Dugdale, and now among his MSS. at Oxford, is unfortunately imperfect, but the discovery of an independent copy among the Rawlinson MSS. has enabled me not only to fill the gaps in Dugdale's copy (which I have here placed within brackets), but also to establish by collation the accuracy of the text.

CHARTER OF HENRY II. TO GEOFFREY DE MANDEVILLE THE YOUNGER (Jan. 1156).

H. Rex Angl[orum] (et) Dux Normannie et Aquitanie et Comes Andegavie Archiepiscopis Episcopis Abbatibus Comitibus Justiciariis Baronibus Vicecomitibus ministris et omnibus fidelibus suis Francis et Anglis Anglie et Normannie salutem. Sciatis me fecisse Gaufridum de Magna Villa Comitem de Essexa et dedisse et hereditarie concessisse sibi et heredibus suis ad tenendum de me et heredibus meis Tertium Denarium de placitis meis ejusdem Comitatus. Et volo et concedo et firmiter precipio quod ipse Comes et heredes sui[2] post eum [habeant] et teneant comitatum suum ita bene et in pace et libere et quiete et plene et honorifice sicut aliquis Comes in Angliâ vel Normanniâ melius, liberius, quietius, plenius, et honorificentius tenet Comitatum suum. Præterea reddidi ei et concessi totam terram Gaufridi de MagnaVilla proavi sui, et avi sui, et patris sui, et omnia tenementa illorum, tam in dominiis quam in feodis militum, tam in Anglia quam in

---

[1] It was, I believe, duly entered in the lost volume of the Great Coucher.
[2] "Sui" omitted in Rawlinson MS.

Normannia, que de me tenet in capite, et de quocunque teneat et de cujuscunque feodo sint, et nominatim Waledenam et Sabrichteswordam[1] et Walteham. Et vadium quod Rex Henricus avus meus habuit super predicta tria maneria sua imperpetuum ei clamavi quietum sibi et heredibus suis de me et de meis heredibus. Quare volo (et firmiter precipio) quod ipse et heredes sui habeant et teneant (de me et de meis heredibus) comitatum suum predictum ita libere (et quiete et plene) sicut aliquis Comes in Anglia (vel Normannia) melius, (liberius quietius et plenius comitatum suum) tenet. Et habeant et teneant ipse et heredes sui omnia predicta tenementa antecessorum suorum predictorum et nominatim predicta tria maneria ita bene (et in pace et libere et quiete et honorifice et plene, in bosco et plano et pratis et pascuis in Aquis et molendinis in viis et semitis in forestis et warrennis in rivariis et piscariis infra Burgum et extra et in omnibus locis et nominatim infra Civitatem London[ie], cum Soco et Saca et Toll et Team et Infangtheof et cum omnibus Libertatibus et liberis consuetudinibus et quietanciis suis) sicut Gaufridus de MagnaVilla proavus suus et avus suus et pater suus unquam melius, (liberius, quietius, et honorificentius et plenius) tenuerunt, tempore Regis Willelmi et Regis Henrici avi mei. Testibus T[heobaldo] Archiepiscopo Cantuar' (Rog[er]o Archiep[iscop]o Eborac' Ric[ardo] Ep[iscop]o London', Rob[erto] Ep[iscop]o Lincoln', Nigello Ep[iscop]o Eliensi, Tom[a] Canc[ellario], Rag[inaldo] Com[ite] Cornub', R[oberto] Com[ite] Legrec', Rog[ero] Com[ite] de Clara, H[enrico] de Essex Conesta[bulo], Ric[ardo] de Hum[ez] Conest[abulo], Ric[ardo] de Lucy, War[ino] fil[io] Ger[oldi] Cam[er]ario, Man[assero] Bisset dap[ifero], Rob[er]to de Dunest[anvilla] et Jos[celino] de Baillolio) Apud Cantuariam.

[1] "Dabrichteswordam" (Rawlinson).

DATE OF GEOFFREY'S RESTORATION. 237

The first point to be considered is that of the date. It is obvious at once from the names of the primate and the chancellor that the charter must be previous to the king's departure from England in 1158. But the only occasion within this limit on which the charter can have passed is that of the king's visit to Canterbury on his way to Dover and the Continent in January, 1156 (115⅔). On no other occasion within this limit did he land at or depart from Dover. Now, it is quite certain that the charter to Earl Aubrey (de Vere), which is tested "Apud Dover in transitu Regis," passed at the time of this departure from Dover (January 10, 1156).[1] We find, then, that as in 1142 the charters to Earl Geoffrey and Earl Aubrey were part of one transaction and passed on the same occasion, so now, the charters to Earl Geoffrey the second and Earl Aubrey, his uncle, passed almost on the same day. The long list of witnesses to the former, for which we are indebted to the Rawlinson MS., enables us to compare it closely with those of the four other charters which passed, according to Mr. Eyton, about the same time.[2] The proportions of their witnesses found among the witnesses to this charter are respectively: seven out of ten in the first; nine out of eighteen in the second; the whole ten in the third; and seven out of fourteen in the fourth. As the king had spent his Christmas at Westminster, we can thus fix the date almost to a day, viz. *circ.* January 2, 1156. And this harmonizes well enough with the evidence of the Pipe-Rolls, which show that Earl Geoffrey was in receipt of the *tertius denarius* in 1157, as from Michaelmas, 1155.

On looking at the terms of this instrument, we are

[1] *R. Diceto*, p. 531.

[2] (1) To the church of St. Jean d'Angely (Canterbury); (2) to Christchurch, Canterbury (Dover); (3) to St. Mary's Abbey, Leicester (Dover); (4) to Earl Aubrey (Dover) (*Court and Itinerary of Henry II.*, pp. 15, 16).

struck at once by the fact that it is a charter of actual creation. This is in perfect accordance with the view advanced above, namely, that the charter granted at Devizes to this Geoffrey, as his father's son, has no bearing on the earldom of Essex, "and that only an absolutely new creation could confer the earldom on Geoffrey, as he was not his father's heir." It is thus that the existence of his brother Ernulf became a factor in the problem of no small consequence.[1]

Being thus an undoubted new creation, its terms should be examined most carefully. It will then be found that the precedent they follow is not the charter of the Empress (1141), but the original charter of the king (1140).

STEPHEN (1140).	MAUD (1141).	HENRY (1156).
Sciatis me fecisse Comitem de Gaufrido de Magnauillâ de Comitatu Essexe hereditarie.	Sciatis omnes . . . quod ego . . . do et concedo Gaufrido de Magnavilla . . . ut sit Comes de Essexâ.	Sciatis me fecisse Gaufridum de Magnauillâ Comitem de Essexâ.

The explanation is, of course, that the first and third are new creations, while the second is virtually but a confirmation of the previous creation by Stephen. So again, comparing this creation with that of Hugh Bigod, the only instance in point—

(1155.)	(1156.)
Sciatis me fecisse Hugonem Bigot Comitem de Norfolca,	Sciatis me fecisse Gaufridum de Mandavillâ Comitem de Essexa,

[1] It is true that the charter to Geoffrey Ridel (Appendix BB) proves that Geoffrey de Mandeville the younger enjoyed, at the court of the Empress, the title of Earl of Essex. But the same charter proves that Henry did not hold himself bound by his mother's charters or deeds.

THE EARLDOM WAS CREATED ANEW. 239

scilicet de tercio denario de Nordwic et de Norfolca.

et dedisse et hereditarie concessisse sibi et heredibus suis. . . . Tertium denarium de placitis meis ejusdem Comitatus.

Here the absolute identity of the actual formula of creation accentuates the difference between the clauses relating to the "Tertius Denarius." It will therefore be desirable to compare the clauses as they stand in the Mandeville and the Vere charters (January, 1156) :—

MANDEVILLE.

Sciatis me . . . dedisse et hereditarie concessisse sibi et heredibus suis ad tenendum de me et heredibus meis tertium denarium de placitis meis ejusdem Comitatus.

VERE

Sciatis me dedisse et concessisse Comiti Alberico in feodo et hereditate tertium denarium de placitis Oxenfordscyre ut sit inde Comes.

It is said with truth in the Lords' Reports that "inde" is an ambiguous word, as it might refer either to the county or to the "third penny" itself. And, indeed, the above extract from the charter to Hugh Bigod would lend support to the latter view. But the case of Earl Aubrey was, we must remember, peculiar. As we saw in the charter of the empress (1142), she recognized him as already a "comes" in virtue of his rank as Count of Guisnes (p. 188). It is my belief that in the present charter he is styled "comes" by Henry on precisely the same ground. For if Henry had recognized him as Earl of Oxford in virtue of his mother's charter (1142), he must also have recognized his right to "the third penny" of the shire which was granted by that same charter.[1] But he clearly did not recognize that right, for he here makes a fresh grant. Therefore he did not recognize the validity

[1] "Do et concedo quod sit Comes de . . . et habeat inde tertium denarium sicut comes debet habere."

of his mother's charter. Consequently, he styled Aubrey "comes" in virtue only of the comital rank he enjoyed as Count of Guisnes. And as he could not *make* a "comes" of a man who was a "comes" already (p. 187), he merely grants him "the third penny of the pleas" of Oxfordshire, "that he may be earl of that county" ("ut sit inde Comes"). Hence the anomalous form in which the charter is drawn.[1]

Different, again, yet no less instructive, is the case of the Earl of Sussex. There the grant runs—

"Sciatis me dedisse Willelmo Comiti Arundel castellum de Arundel cum toto honore Arundel . . . et tercium denarium de placitis de Suthsex unde comes est."

This charter has been looked upon as relating to the earldom itself, whereas it is clearly nothing but a grant of the castle and honour of Arundel and of the "Tertius Denarius" of Sussex, "of which county he is earl."[2] When these two phrases are compared—"ut sit inde Comes" and "unde Comes est"—their meaning is, surely, clear. William was *already* Earl of Sussex (*alias* Arundel *alias* Chichester), but his right to the "Tertius Denarius" of the county was not recognized by the king. The fact that this right required to be granted *nominatim* confirms my view that it was not conveyed by Stephen's charter to Geoffrey.[3]

The distinction between the "dedi et concessi" of the "Tertius Denarius" clause and the "reddidi" and "concessi" of those by which the king confirms to Geoffrey his ancestral estates is one always to be noted. The

[1] It is one of the mysteries of the Pipe-Rolls that no such payment to the earl is to be traced on them, though the grant is quite unmistakable in its terms. See Appendix H.

[2] The "unde" of this charter answers to the "inde" in the charters to Earl Aubrey.

[3] See Appendix H.

PECULIARITIES OF THE NEW CHARTER. 241

terms of what one may call this general confirmation are remarkably comprehensive, going back as they do to the days of King William and of the grantee's great-grandfather; and the profusion of legal verbiage in which they are enwrapped is worthy of later times. The charter also illustrates the adaptation in Latin of the old Anglo-Saxon *formulæ*, themselves the relics of those quaint jingles which must bear witness to oral transmission in an archaic state of society.[1]

The release of the lien (upon three manors) which Henry I. had held is a very curious feature. One of these manors, Sawbridgeworth in Herts., is surveyed in Domesday at great length. Its value had then sunk from £60 to £50; but early in the reign of Henry II., Earl Geoffrey gave it in fee to Warine fitz Gerold, the chamberlain, "per (*sic*) LXXIIII libratas terræ, singulas xx libratas pro servitio unius militis."[2]

Under this charter Earl Geoffrey held the dignity till

---

[1] See, for instance, survivals of them in the charters of Henry I. to Christchurch, Canterbury, and of Henry II. to Oxford. The former runs, "on strande and on stream, on wudan and on feldan" (Campbell Charter, xxix. 5); the latter, "by water and by stronde, by Gode (*sic*) and by londe" (Hearne's *Liber Niger*, Appendix).

The formula "cum omnibus ad hoc rebus rite pertinentibus, sive *litorum*, sive camporum, agrorum, saltuumve" (Kemble, *Cod. Dipl.*, No. 425; Earle, *Land Charters*, p. 186), suggested to Prof. Maitland (*Select Pleas in Manorial Courts*) a connection with the "leet" through the "litus" of early Teutonic law, but Mr. W. H. Stevenson, correcting him, observed (*Academy*, June 29, 1889) that *litorum* referred to the seashore at Reculver (with which this grant deals). Both these distinguished scholars are mistaken, for the words only render the general formula: "by lande and by strande (' litorum '), by wede and by felde." So for instance—

> "bi water and bi lande
> mid inlade and mid utlade
> wit inne burghe and wit outen
> bi lande and by strande
> bi wode and by felde" (*Ramsey Cart.*, ii. 80, 81).

Thus we have "in bosco et plano . . . infra burgum et extra" (*supra*, p. 236). See also pp. 286, 314, 381. [2] *Liber Niger* (1774), i. 239.

his death, at which time we find him lord of more than a hundred and fifty knights' fees. The earldom then (1166) passed to his younger brother William, and did so, as far as we know, without a fresh creation. For the limitation, it is important to observe, in this as in other early creations, is not restricted to heirs *of the body*—a much later addition. As this point is of considerable importance it may be as well here to compare the essential words of inheritance in the three successive charters :—

STEPHEN (1140).	MAUD. (1141).	HENRY II. (1156).
Sciatis me fecisse Comitem de Gaufrido de Magnavillâ de Comitatu Essexe *hereditarie*. Quare volo ... quod ipse *et heredes sui post eum hereditario jure* teneant de me et de heredibus meis ... sicut alii Comites mei de terrâ meâ, etc.	Sciatis ... quod ego do et concedo Gaufrido de Magnavillâ ... *et heredibus suis post eum hereditabiliter* ut sit Comes de Essexâ.	Sciatis me fecisse Gaufridum de Magna Villa Comitem de Essexa. ... Et volo ... quod ipse Comes *et heredes sui post eum* habeant et teneant Comitatum suum ... sicut aliquis Comes in Angliâ, etc.

It is noteworthy that the earliest of these three—the earliest of all our creation-charters—has the most intensely hereditary ring, a fact at variance with the favourite doctrine that the hereditary principle was a late innovation, and ousted but slowly the official position. It is further to be observed that the term "Comitatus," of which the denotation in Scottish charters has been so long and fiercely debated, has here the abstract signification which it possesses in our own day, namely, that of the dignity of an earl.

When we think of their father's stormy career, it is not a little strange to find these two successive Earls of

Essex high in favour with the order-loving king, throughout whose reign, for more than thirty years (1156–1189), we find them honoured and trusted in his councils, in his courts, and in his host. Of Earl William Miss Norgate writes: "The son was as loyal as his father was faithless; he seems, indeed, to have been a close personal friend of the king, and to have well deserved his friendship."[1] His fidelity was rewarded by the hand of the heiress of the house of Aumâle, so that, already an earl in England, he thus became, also, a count beyond the sea.

Yet well might men believe that the awful curse of Heaven rested on this great and able house. At the very moment when Earl William seemed to have attained the pinnacle of power, when he had reached the point which his father had reached some half a century before, then, as in his father's case, the prize was snatched from his grasp. King Richard, rightly prizing the earl's loyalty and worth, announced his intention, at the Council of Pipewell (September, 1189), of leaving him, with the Bishop of Durham as his assessor, in charge of the kingdom, as Justiciar, during his own absence in the East. Such an office would have made the earl the foremost layman in the realm. But before the time had come for entering on his exalted duties, indeed within a few weeks of his appointment, he was dead (November 14, 1189).

Like his brother Geoffrey before him, the earl died childless; the vast estates of the house of Mandeville passed to the descendants of his aunt; to his earldom there was no heir.[2] Such was the end that awaited the

---

[1] *Angevin Kings*, ii. 144.

[2] The inheritance was in dispute for some time between his aunt's younger son and the two daughters and co-heirs of her elder son deceased. As the latter were eventually successful in their claim, there was no one heir to whom the earldom could pass, as of right, under the charter of 1156 (accepting it as representing a limitation to heirs whatsoever). I have,

ambition of Geoffrey de Mandeville. The earldom for which he had schemed and striven, the strongholds on which his power was based, the broad lands which owned his sway—all were lost to his house. And as if by the very irony of fate, Ernulf, his disinherited son, alone continued the race, that there might not be wanting in his hapless heirs an ever-standing monument to the greatness at once of the guilt and of the fall of the man whose story I have told.

however, elsewhere suggested (Pipe-Roll Society : *Ancient Charters*, p. 99) that the *salvo* to the elder of the two daughters of her *antenatio* may have been connected with a claim to the dignity by her husband, in her right.

APPENDICES.

APPENDIX A.

STEPHEN'S TREATY WITH THE LONDONERS.

(See p. 3.)

THERE are few more suggestive passages in the chronicles of Stephen's reign than that which describes, in the *Gesta*, his "pactio" with the citizens of London. This, because of the striking resemblance between the "pactio . . . mutuo juramento" there described and the similar practice in those foreign towns which enjoyed the rights of a "communa." Thus at Bazas, in Aquitaine, " quum dominus rex venit apud Vasatum, omnes cives Vasatenses jurant ei fidelitatem et obedientiam . . . similiter et rex et senescallus jurant dictis civibus Vasatensibus quod sit bonus dominus eis et teneat consuetudines, et custodiat eos de omni injuria de se et aliis pro posse suo." At Issigeac, in the Perigord, it was (as was usual) the lord who had to swear first before the citizens would do so : " en aital manieira que'l seinher reis . . . cant requerra et queste sagrament . . . ; deu jurar a lor premeirament qu'il los defendra de si et d'autrui de tot domnage, et las bonas custumas que il ont et que il auront lor gardet et lor amelhoret, à bona fe, . . . et que las males lor oste et lor tolha de tot. Et en après, li prohome deven li far lo sagrament sobredich, que'l garderon son corps et sas gentz qui par lui esseron et sas dreituras de tort et de forsa," etc., etc. At Bourg-sur-Mer, in Gascony, the clause runs : " Dum dominus rex venit primo in Vasconia, juratur ab eo, dum est sistens et coram senescallo suo (vel a senescallo suo, dum ipse non est præsens, qui pro tempore veniet) quod villam et jus custodiet et defendet et de se et de alio ab omni injuria, et quod servabit foros et consuetudines suas. Nos juramus ei et senescallo fidelitatem." So too at Bayonne, when the Great Seneschal of Aquitaine, as representing the king,

first arrived, he was called upon to swear by all the saints that he would be a good and loyal lord; that he would protect the citizens from all wrong and violence, either from himself or from others; that he would preserve all their rights, customs, and privileges, as granted them by the Kings of England and Dukes of Guyenne, to the utmost of his power, so long as he held the office, saving his fealty to the king.[1] When he had done so, the mayor and jurats swore in their turn to him:—
"By those saints, will we be good, faithful, loyal, and obedient to you; your life and limbs we will guard; good and loyal counsel will we give you to the best of our power, and your secrets will we keep."[2] These examples, which could be widely paralleled, not only in municipalities, but also in the rural commonwealths of the Pyrenean valleys, illustrate the principle and uniform character of this "mutuum juramentum."

We are tempted then to ask whether it was not by some such transaction as this that Stephen secured the adhesion of the citizens. We shall find the Empress securing the city in 1141, after a formal "tractatus" at St. Albans with its authorized representatives, and we know that the Conqueror himself made some terms with the citizens before he entered London. Comparing these facts with the reception at Winchester of Stephen and the Empress in turn, it may fairly be questioned whether we should accept the startling assertion in the *Gesta* as literally correct. It would seem at least highly probable that what the Londoners really claimed in 1135 was not the right to elect a king of all England, but to choose their own lord independently of the rest of the kingdom, and to do so by a *separate negotiation* between himself and them. They were not, in any case, prepared to receive the king as their

[1] "Lo senescaut de Guiayne deu jurar en sa nabere vengude au mayre juratz et eent partz et a laut poble et comunautat de Baione . . . en questo forme : Per aques sentz Job serey bon seinhor et leyau, de tort et de force vos guoarderey de mi medichs et dautruy ; a mon leyau poder vostres fors vostres costumes et vostres priviledges sa en rer per los reys Dangleterre et dux de Guiayne autreyatz vos sauberey, tant quoant serey en lodit offici, sauban le fideutat de nostre seinhor lo Rey."

[2] "Et losditz maire et juratz deben jurar en le mancyre seguent disent assi : Per aques sentz nos vos seram bons, fideus, leyaus, et hobediens; vite et menbres vos guarderam; bon cosseilh et leyau vos deram, a nostre leyau poder ; et segretz vos thieram."

lord unless he would first guarantee them the possession of all their liberties. This semi-independent attitude, which was virtually that assumed by Exeter when it attempted to treat with the Conqueror, was distinctly foreign to the English polity so far as our knowledge goes. There are faint hints, however, in Domesday that such towns as London, York, Winchester, and Exeter may have possessed a greater independence than it has hitherto been the custom to believe.

APPENDIX B.

THE APPEAL TO ROME IN 1136.

(See p. 8.)

ONE of the most interesting and curious discoveries that I have made in the course of my researches has been the true story of the appeal to Rome as arbiter between Stephen and Maud. Considering the exceptional importance of this episode, in many ways, it has received strangely little attention, with the result that it has been imperfectly understood and almost incredibly misdated.

Mr. Freeman, working, in the *Norman Conquest*, from the *Historia Pontificalis*,[1] writes of this episode as taking place on and in consequence of Stephen's attempt to secure the coronation of Eustace in 1152.[2] Miss Norgate has gone into the matter far more fully than Mr. Freeman, but at first assigned the debate described in the *Historia Pontificalis* to "1151."[3]

In so doing, she was guided merely by the *Historia* passage itself, which she did not connect, as did Mr. Freeman, with the episode of the proposed coronation in 1152. But on inves-

---

[1] Pertz's *Monumenta Historica*, vol. xx.

[2] "The application to Rome and the debate which followed it there are to be found in the *Historia Pontificalis*, 41 (Pertz, xx. 543). Bishop (*sic*) Henry 'promisit se daturum operam et diligentiam ut apostolicus Eustachium filium regis coronaret. Quod utique fieri non licebat, nisi Romani pontificis veniâ impetratâ.' I have already (see above, p. 251) had to refer to some of the points urged in this debate" (*Norm. Conq.*, v. 325, note). On turning to "p. 251," we similarly find the debate spoken of as belonging to "later years," and at p. 354 also, while at p. 857 we read: "At a later time, in the argument before Pope Innocent (*sic*), when Stephen is trying to get the pontiff's consent to the coronation of his son Eustace (p. 325)," etc., etc. How an argument could be held before Innocent, many years after his death, Mr. Freeman does not explain.

[3] *England under the Angevin Kings*, i. 278, *note*.

tigating the matter more closely, she was clearly led to reject the date she had first given :—

"From the way in which the trial is brought into the *Historia Pontificalis*, it would at first sight seem to have taken place in 1151. But the presence of Bishop Ulger of Angers and Roger of Chester, both of whom died in 1149, and the account of the proceedings written by Gilbert Foliot to Brian fitz Count, clearly prove the true date to be 1148." [1]

As to the time of the bishop's death, Roger died, not in 1149, but in April, 1148, and at Antioch, so that the chronology is no less fatal to Miss Norgate's date than to Mr. Freeman's own. But the additional evidence she obtains from Gilbert Foliot's letter requires a special examination.

The sequence of events at which she arrives is this :—

(1) Theobald goes, in defiance of Stephen, to the council convened at Rheims by Eugenius III. for Mid-Lent Sunday, (March) 1148 (N.S.).

(2) Stephen forfeits Theobald, and is threatened in consequence by the Pope.

(3) Geoffrey of Anjou, thereupon, challenges Stephen "to an investigation of his claims before the papal court." Stephen, in reply, calls on Geoffrey to surrender Normandy "before he would agree to any further proceeding in the matter."

(4) Geoffrey surrenders Normandy—but to his son Henry, and Stephen "appears to have consented, as if in desperation, to the proposed trial at Rome."

(5) "The trial" takes place, as recorded in the *Historia Pontificalis*, and is attended, *inter alios*, by Gilbert Foliot, Abbot of Gloucester, who had obtained "the succession to the vacant see" of Hereford at the Council of Rheims, and had added, in consequence, to his style the words "et Herefordiensis ecclesiæ mandato Domini Papæ vicarius."

(6) Gilbert Foliot writes the letter to Brian fitz Count, reviewing the treatise which Brian had just composed in support of the claims of the Empress, and alluding to the above "trial" at Rome which he (Gilbert) had attended.

(7) Gilbert Foliot is consecrated Bishop of Hereford by Theobald, at St. Omer, in September (1148).[2]

Of these events, the cession of Normandy by Geoffrey to his

[1] *England under the Angevin Kings*, i. 370, *note*.
[2] *Ibid.*, i. 370, 371, 495, 496.

son Henry belongs, as Mr. Howlett has pointed out, not to 1148, but to 1150 or 1151.[1] This, however, scarcely affects Miss Norgate's sequence of events. It is when we turn to Foliot's letter that our suspicions begin to be aroused. Although Dr. Giles has placed it at the end of those letters which belong to the period of his rule as abbot (1139–1148), we must be struck by the fact that if (as Miss Norgate holds) it was written just before his consecration as Bishop of Hereford, the style would have been "elect of Hereford," or, at least, "Vicar of the Diocese (*ut supra*)," instead of "Abbot of Gloucester" only. Moreover, as Henry was *ex hypothesi* now Duke of Normandy, the "trial" would have been, surely, of his own claims, not of those of his mother, who had virtually retired in his favour. Lastly, we must see that the date assigned by her to this "trial" at Rome (1148) is a mere hypothesis unsupported by any direct evidence.

But, indeed, we have only to read the letter and the *Historia Pontificalis* to see that they must have been perused with almost incredible carelessness. For Gilbert Foliot distinctly mentions (*a*) that he is writing in the time of Pope Celestine,[2] (*b*) that the "trial" took place under Pope Innocent.[3] Now, Celestine died in March, 1144, and his predecessor Innocent had died in September, 1143. The letter, therefore, must have been written within these six months, and the "trial" at Rome must have taken place before September 24, 1143. This being clear, we naturally ask :—How came Innocent thus to hear the case argued, when he had admittedly "confirmed" Stephen at the very beginning of his reign? Having decided the question at the outset, how could he ignore that decision, and begin, as it were, *de novo?* Moreover, Stephen's champion is described by the *Historia* writer as Arnulf, Archdeacon of Séez, afterwards Bishop of Lisieux. Now, Miss Norgate, with her usual care, fixes the date of his elevation to the see as 1141.[4] A council, therefore, which he attended as archdeacon must, on her own showing, be not later than this.[5] Lastly, now that we know the council

[1] *Academy*, November 12, 1887.
[2] "Sed jam nunc Deo propitio et favente parti huic domino papa Celestino."
[3] "Audisti dominum papam Innocentium convocasse ecclesiam et Romæ conventum celebrem habuisse."
[4] *England under the Angevin Kings*, i. 500.
[5] Perhaps she did not recognize his name (see below).

to be previous to 1141, do not the words of the writer—"Magno illi conventui cum domino et patre nostro domino abbate Cluniacensi interfui et ego Cluniacensium minimus "—suggest that it was, further, previous to his becoming Abbot of Gloucester in 1139? Turning again to the passage in the *Historia Pontificalis* (41), we find that, in the light of the above evidence, its meaning is beyond dispute. So, indeed, it should be of itself, but for a most incomprehensible blunder by which two passages of the *narrative* are printed in Pertz as part of the arguments advanced in the debate. The fact is that the writer of the *Historia*, when he comes to the proposal to crown Eustace, is anxious to show us how the matter stood by tracing the attitude of the Papacy to Stephen since the beginning of his reign. He, therefore, takes us right back to the year of the king's accession, and tells us how, and to what extent, his claim came to be confirmed.

This discovery at once explains Gilbert Foliot's expression. For, the trial at Rome taking place, as I shall show, early in 1136, he attended it, not as Abbot of Gloucester, but merely as " minimus Cluniacensium," in attendance on his famous abbot, Peter the Venerable (1122–1158). It may have been as prior ("claustral" prior?) of the abbey that he thus attended him, for we know from himself that he had held that office.

Everything now fits into place. We find that, following in her grandfather's footsteps, Maud at once appealed to Rome against Stephen's usurpation, charging him, precisely as William, in his day, had charged Harold, (1) with defrauding her of her rightful inheritance, (2) with breach of his oath. Stephen, when he had overcome the scruples of William of Corbeuil, and had secured coronation at his hands, hastened to take his next step by despatching to Rome three envoys to plead his cause before the pope. These envoys were Roger, Bishop of Chester, Arnulf, Archdeacon of Séez (the spokesman of the party), and " Lovel," a clerk of Archbishop William.[1] This last was, of course, intended to represent his master in the matter, and to justify his action in crowning Stephen by explaining the

[1] " Ex adverso steterunt a rege missi Rogerus Cestrensis episcopus Lupellus clericus Guillelmi bone memorie Cantuarensis archiepiscopi, et qui eis in causa patrocinabatur Ernulfus archidiaconus Sagiensis" (*Hist. Pontif.*, 41).

grounds on which his scruples had been overruled. The envoys were abundantly supplied with the requisite motive power—or, shall we say, the oil for lubricating the wheels of the Curia?—from the hoarded treasure of the dead king, which was now in his successor's hands. The pope resolved that so important a cause required no ordinary tribunal: he convoked for the purpose a great council, and among those by whom it was attended was Peter, Abbot of Cluny, with Gilbert Foliot in his train.[1]

The name of Cluny leads me to break the thread for a moment for the purpose of insisting on the important fact that the sympathies of the house, under its then abbot, must have been with the Angevin cause. This is certain from the documents printed by Sir George Duckett,[2] especially from the Mandatory Epistle of this same Abbot Peter relating to the Empress.[3] We have here, I think, the probable explanation of the energy with which that cause was espoused by Gilbert Foliot.

To return to the council. The case for the prosecution, as we might term it, was opened by the Bishop of Angers, who charged Stephen both with perjury, that is, with breaking the oath he had sworn to Henry I., and with usurpation in seizing the throne to the detriment of the rightful heir.[4] Stephen's

[1] "Audisti dominum papam Innocentium convocasse ecclesiam et Romæ conventum celebrem habuisse. Magno illi conventui cum domino et patre nostro domino abbato Cluniacensi interfui et ego Cluniacensium minimus. Ibi causa hæc in medium deducta est, et aliquandiu ventilata" (Foliot's letter, lxxix., ed. Giles, i. 100).

[2] *Charters and Records of the Ancient Abbey of Cluni* (1888).

[3] "Felicis memoriæ rex Anglorum et Dux Normannorum, Henricus, Willelmi primo ducis dein regis filius, speciali eam [Cluniacensem ecclesiam] amore coluit et veneratus est. Donis autem multiplicibus et magnis omnes jam dictos exsuperans, etiam majorem ecclesiam . . . miro et singulari opere inter universas pene tocius orbis ecclesias consummavit. Ea de causa, specialis apud universos Cluniacensis ordinis fratres ejus memoria habetur et in perpetuum per Dei gratiam habebitur. Cui in paterna hereditate succedens Matildis, ejus filia, Henrici magni Romanorum imperatoris conjux . . . paternæ imaginis et prudentiæ formam velut sigillo impressam representavit, et præter alia digna relatu, Cluniacensem ecclesiam more patris sincere dilexit" (*ibid.*, ii. 104).

[4] "Stabat ab Imperatrice dominus Andegavensis episcopus, qui . . . duo inducebat precipue, jus scilicet hereditarium et factum imperatrici juramentum" (Foliot's letter, *ut supra*). "Querimoniam imperatricis ad papam

supporters, with Arnulf at their head, met these charges by a defence, the two reports of which are not in absolute harmony. It is quite certain that to the charge of usurpation they retorted that the Empress was the offspring of an unlawful alliance, and had, therefore, suffered no wrong.[1] But how they disposed of the oath is not so clear. According to Gilbert Foliot, whose account we may safely follow, they advanced the subtle and ingenious plea that fidelity had only been sworn to the Empress as heir ("sicut heredi") to the throne, and since (they urged) she was not such heir (for the reason given above), the oath was *ipso facto* void, and the charge fell to the ground.[2] The other writer asserts that the defence was based, first, on the plea that the oath had been forcibly extorted, and, second, on the cunning pretence that the king had reserved to himself the right of appointing another heir, and had exercised that right on his deathbed, to the extent of disinheriting the Empress and nominating Stephen in her stead.[3]

A careful study of the two versions has led me to believe that both writers were, probably, right in their facts. Gilbert Foliot would be the last man to invent an argument in favour of Stephen, nor would the other writer have any inducement to

Innocentium Ulgerius Andegavorum venerandus antistes detulit, arguens regem periurii et illicité presumptionis regni" (*Hist. Pontif.*, 41).

[1] "Hic [Ernulfus] adversus episcopum allegavit publice, quod imperatrix patris erat indigna successione, eo quod de incestis nupciis procreata et filia fuerat monialis, quam Rex Henricus de monasterio Romeseiensi extraxerat eique velum abstulerat" (*Hist. Pontif.*). "Imperatricem, de qua loquitur, non de legitimo matrimonio ortam denuntiamus. Deviavit a legitimo tramite Henricus rex, et quam non licebat sibi junxit matrimonio, unde istius sunt natalitia propagata: quare illam patri in heredem non debere succedere et sacra denuntiant" (Foliot's letter).

[2] "Sublato enim jure principali, necessario tollitur et secundarium. In hac igitur causâ principale est, quod dominus Andegavensis de hereditate inducit et ab hoc totum illud dependet, quod de juramento subjungitur. Imperatrici namque sicut heredi juramentum factum fuisse pronunciat. Totum igitur quod de juramento inducitur, exinaniri necesse est, si de ipso hereditario jure non constiterit" (*ibid.*).

[3] "Juramentum confessus est [Ernulfus], sed adjecit violentur extortum, et sub conditione scilicet imperatrici successionem patris se pro viribus servaturum, nisi patrem voluntatem mutare contingeret et heredem alium instituere; poterat enim esse ut ei de uxore filius nasceretur. Postremo subjecit quod rex Henricus mutaverat voluntatem et in extremis agens filium sororis suæ Stephanum designavit heredem" (*Hist. Pontif.*).

do so, writing (as he did) long after that king's death. Moreover, the pleas that (1) the oath had been extorted, (2) Henry I. had released his barons from its obligation, are precisely those which the author of the *Gesta* and William of Malmesbury [1] respectively mention as being advanced on Stephen's behalf. Lastly, we have yet another plea advanced by Bishop Roger of Salisbury, namely, that, so far as he was himself concerned, he looked on the re-marriage of the Empress, without the consent of the Great Council, as absolving him from his oath. Now, all this points to one conclusion. The thorn in the side of Stephen and of his friends was, clearly, this unlucky oath. Their various attempts to excuse its breach betray their consciousness of the fact. More especially was this the case before a spiritual court. Hence their ingenious endeavour, described by Gilbert Foliot, to keep the oath in the background as the lesser of the two points. Hence, too, their accumulated pleas. First, they urge that the oath was void because the Empress was not the heir; then, that it was void, because extorted; lastly, that it was void because the dying king had released them from their obligation. Such an argument as this speaks for itself.

The only point on which the two witnesses do, at first sight, differ, is the attitude taken by the Bishop of Angers with regard to the plea that the Empress was not of legitimate birth. Did he contravene this plea? The *Historia* asserts that when Stephen's advocates had stated the case for the defence, the bishop rose and traversed their pleadings, rejecting them one by one. But Gilbert, writing to Brian fitz Count, admits that the attack on the birth of the Empress (the only argument which he discusses) had not been replied to.[2] Now, the version found in the *Historia*, though composed much later, is a more detailed account, and bears the stamp of truth. Yet Gilbert's admission to his friend and ally betrays an uneasy consciousness that the charge had not been disposed of. For he asks him to suggest an effectual reply, and proceeds to suggest one himself.[3] He

[1] So also Gervase of Canterbury.

[2] "Hoc in communi audientiâ multum vociferatione declamatum est, et nihil omnino ab altera parte responsum."

[3] "Rogo, mihi in parte ista respondeas. Interim dicam ipse quod sentio. Majores natu, personas religiosas et sanctas, sæpius de re ista conveni. Audio illius matrimonii copulam sancto Anselmo archiepiscopo minis-

relies on St. Anselm's consent to her parents' marriage. We have here possibly the clue we seek. For the Bishop of Angers, in his speech, as given by the writer of the *Historia*, had not alluded to St. Anselm's consent.[1] Perhaps he was taken by surprise, and had not expected the plea.

Stephen's advocates seem, from a hint of Gilbert Foliot,[2] to have simply "stampeded the convention" (*conventus*), and the wrath of the Angevin champion rose to a white heat.[3] The pope commanded that the wrangling should cease, and announced that he would neither pass sentence nor allow the trial to be adjourned. This was equivalent to a verdict that the king was not guilty, and was duly followed by a letter to Stephen confirming him in his possession of the kingdom and the duchy.[4]

Seeing that he had lost his case, the aged Bishop of Angers relieved his feelings by a bitter jest at the cost of the heir of St. Peter.[5]

But we are more immediately concerned with that letter by which the pope (the writer tells us) confirmed Stephen in possession. For this connecting link is no other than the letter which meets us in the pages of Richard of Hexham.[6]

Its relevant portion runs thus:—

"Nos cognoscentes vota tantorum virorum in personam tuam, præunte

---

trante celebratam .... Manus autem sibi præcidi permisisset [Anselmus], quam eas ad opus illicitum extendisset."

[1] His reply was: "Ipsa [Romana ecclesia] enim confirmavit matrimonium quod accusas, filiamque ex eo susceptam domnus Pascalis Romanus pontifex inunxit in imperatricem. Quod utique non fecisset de filia monialis. Nec eum veritas latere poterat, quia non fuit obscurum matrimonium aut contractum in tenebris."

[2] "Multorum vociferatione declamatum est."

[3] "In Archidiaconum excandescens" (*Hist. Pontif.*).

[4] "Non tulit ulterius contentiones eorum domnus Innocentius nec sententiam ferre voluit aut causam in aliud differre tempus, sed contra consilium quorundam cardinalium et maxime Guidonis presbiteri sancti Marci, receptis muneribus regis Stephani, ei familiaribus litteris regnum Angliæ confirmavit et ducatum Normanniæ." This is the passage so inexplicably printed in Pertz as part of the bishop's speech, which immediately precedes it.

[5] "Ulgerius vero cum cognitioni cause supersederi videret, verbo comico utebatur dicens: 'De causa sua querentibus intus despondebitur:' et adjiciebat: 'Petrus enim peregre profectus est, nummulariis relicta domo'" (*Hist. Pontif.*).   [6] Ed. Howlett, p. 147.

divina gratia, convenisse, pro spe etiam certa,[1] et [quia] beato Petro in ipsa consecrationis tuæ die obedientiam et reverentiam promisisse, et quia de præfati regis prosapia prope posito gradu originem traxisse dinosceris, quod de te factum est gratum habentes, te in specialem beati Petri et sanctæ Romanæ ecclesie filium affectione paterna recipimus, et in eadem honoris et familiaritatis prærogativa, qua predecessor tuus egregiæ recordationis Henricus a nobis coronabatur, te propensius volumus retinere."

The chronicler, observing that Stephen was "his et aliis modis in regno Angliæ confirmatus," passes straight from this letter to the King's Oxford charter, in which he describes himself as "ab Innocentio sanctæ Romanæ sedis pontifice confirmatus." Of this "confirmation," as we find it styled by the author of the *Historia*, by Richard of Hexham, by John of Hexham, and lastly, by Stephen himself, I speak more fully in the text. For the present the point to be grasped is that (1) the "conventus" at Rome was previous to (2) this letter of the pope, which was previous itself to (3) Stephen's charter, which is assigned to the spring (after Easter) of 1136. Thus we arrive at the fact that the council and debate at Rome belong to the early months of 1136.

To complete while we are about it the explanation of the *Historia* narrative, we will now take the second passage which has been erroneously printed in Pertz—

"Postea, cum prefatus Guido cardinalis promoveretur in papam Celestinum, favore imperatricis scripsit domno Theobaldo Cantuarensi archiepiscopo inhibens ne qua fieret innovatio in regno Anglie circa coronam, quia res erat litigiosa cujus translatio jure reprobata est. Successores eius papæ Lucius et Eugenius eandem prohibitionem innovaverunt."

This passage is absurdly given as part of Bishop Ulger's sneer.

The above cardinal is Guy, cardinal priest of St. Mark, referred to in the previous misplaced passage as opposing the confirmation of Stephen. Observe here that three writers allude quite independently to his sympathy with the Angevin cause. These are—(1) the writer (*ut supra*) of the *Historia Pontificalis*; (2) Gilbert Foliot, who speaks of him, when pope, as "favente parti huic domino papa Celestino," and (3) John of Hexham, who describes him as " Alumpnus Andegavensium."
A coincidence of testimony, so striking as this, strengthens the

---

[1] Compare the description of Henry of Winchester, shortly before this, as "spe scilicet captus amplissima" that Stephen would do his duty by the Church.

THE SUBSEQUENT PAPAL POLICY. 259

authority of all three, including that of the writer of the *Historia Pontificalis*.

The step taken by Pope Celestine was based on the alleged doubt in which his predecessor had left the question. It was, he held, still "res litigiosa," and, therefore, without reversing the action of Innocent in the matter, he felt free to forbid any further step in advance. His instructions to that effect, to the primate, were duly renewed by his successors, and covered, when the time arrived, the case of the coronation of Eustace as being an "innovatio in regno Anglie circa coronam." Stephen had, indeed, been confirmed as king, and this could not be undone. But that confirmation did not extend to the son of the "perjured" king.[1]

With the character and meaning of the "confirmation" obtained by Stephen from the pope, I have dealt in the body of this work. There are, however, a few minor points which had better be disposed of here. Of these the first is Miss Norgate's contention that when, in 1148, Stephen met Geoffrey's challenge to submit his claims to Rome, " by a counter challenge calling upon Geoffrey to give up his equally ill-gotten duchy before he would agree to any further proceeding in the matter."

"Geoffrey took him at his word, but in a way which he was far from desiring. He did give up the duchy of Normandy, by making it over to his own son, Henry Fitz-Empress."[2]

A reference to the passage in the *Historia*[3] on which Miss Norgate relies, will show at once that Geoffrey, on receiving the counter-challenge, abandoned all thought of carrying the matter further.[4] It also incidentally proves that Geoffrey had

[1] "Ne filium regis, qui contra jusjurandum regnum obtinuisse videbatur in regem sublimaret" (*Gervase*).

[2] Vol. i. p. 369.

[3] Pertz, xx. p. 531. Bishop Miles is sent to England, "ad petitionem Gaufridi comitis Andegavorum, ut regem super perjurio et regni occupatione conveniret et ducatu Normanniæ, quem invaserat."

[4] Mr. Howlett has duly pointed out that Geoffrey did not, as Miss Norgate imagines, hand over Normandy to his son in consequence of this challenge; but I would point out further that Stephen demanded not merely the surrender of Normandy, but also that of the *English* districts then under Angevin sway ("Hoc retulit responsum: quod rex *utrumque* honorem et jure suo *et ecclesie Romane auctoritate* adeptus erat, *nec refugerat stare judicio apostolicæ sedis*, quando eum comes violenter ducatu spoliavit et parte regni *Quibus* non restitutis non debebat subire judicium " (p. 531).

refused admission to his dominions to either pope or legate. This is a fact of interest.

This was not the only occasion on which Stephen's "recognition" by the pope stood him in good stead. At the crisis of 1141, the sensitive conscience of Archbishop Theobald had prevented his transferring his allegiance to the Empress, badly though Stephen had treated him, till he received permission from the Lord's anointed to follow in the footsteps of his brother prelates.[1]

The loyal primate explained the position when Gilbert Foliot had enraged the Angevins by doing homage to Stephen for the see of Hereford. Wholly Angevin though they were in their sympathies, the prelates maintained that they were bound as Churchmen to follow the pope's ruling, and that the Papacy had "received" Stephen as king.[2]

Another point deserving notice is the choice of Arnulf, afterwards the well-known Bishop of Lisieux, as Stephen's chief envoy in 1136. For Miss Norgate, oddly enough, misses this point in her sketch of this distinguished man's career.[3] She has nothing to say of his doings between his *Tractatus de Schismate*, "about 1130," and his appointment to the see of Lisieux in 1141, from which date "for the next forty years there was hardly a diplomatic transaction of any kind, ecclesiastical or secular, in England or in Gaul, in which he was not at some moment or in some way or other concerned."[4] This, therefore, constitutes a welcome addition to his career, and, moreover, gives us the reason of Geoffrey's aversion to him, when duke, and of the "heavy price" with which his favour had to be bought by Arnulf.[5]

[1] "Confiscata sunt [1148] bona ejus et secundo proscriptus pro obediencia Romane ecclesie. Nam et alia vice propter obedienciam sedis Apostolicæ proscriptus fuerat, quando, urgente mandato domini Henrici Wintoniensis episcopi tunc legatione fungentis in Anglia post alios episcopos omnes receperat imperatricem . . . licet inimicissimos habuerit regem et consiliarios suos" (*Hist. Pontif.*).

[2] [Stephen] "quem tota Anglicana ecclesia sequebatur ex constitutione ecclesie Romane. Licet proceres divisi diversos principes sequerentur, unum tamen habebat ecclesia . . . quod episcopo non licuerat ecclesiam scindere ei subtrahendo fidelitatem quem ecclesia Romana recipiebat ut principem" (*Ibid.*, pp. 532, 533).

[3] *England under the Angevin Kings*, i. 500–502.   [4] *Ibid.*

[5] The stinging taunts of the Bishop of Angers on Arnulf's humble origin,

THE FACTS ARE NOW ESTABLISHED. 261

The last point concerns the "most interesting and valuable" letter from Gilbert Foliot to Brian fitz Count. A careful perusal of this composition has led me to believe, from internal evidence, that it refers not (as Miss Norgate puts it) to a "book" by Brian fitz Count, or "a defence of his Lady's rights in the shape of a little treatise,"[2] but to a justification of his own conduct in reply to hostile criticism. And I venture to think that so far from this composition being "unhappily lost,"[3] it may be, and probably is, no other than that lengthy epistle from Brian to the Bishop of Winchester, of which a copy was entered in Richard de Bury's *Liber Epistolaris*. And there, happily, it is still preserved.[4] This can only be decided when the contents of that epistle are made accessible to the public, as they should have been before now.

To resume. I have now established these facts. The "trial" at Rome took place, not, as Mr. Freeman assumes, in 1152, nor, as Miss Norgate argues, in 1148, but early in 1136. The letter of Gilbert Foliot, in which he refers to it, was written, not in 1148, but late in 1143 or early in 1144. The whole of Miss Norgate's sequence of events (i. 369, 370) breaks down entirely. The great debate before the pope at Rome was not the result of Stephen's attempt to get Eustace crowned, nor of Geoffrey's challenge to Stephen by the mouth of Bishop Miles, but of the charge brought against Stephen at the very outset of his reign. The true story of this debate and of Stephen's "confirmation," by the pope, as king is here set forth for the first time, and throws on the whole chain of events a light entirely new.

as given in the *Hist. Pontif.*, are of great importance in their bearing on Henry I.'s policy of raising men to power "from the dust." They should be compared with the well-known sneer of Ordericus (see p. 111).

[1] *England under the Angevin Kings*, i. p. 496, *note*.
[2] *Ibid.*, p. 369.   [3] *Ibid.*, p. 496, *note*.
[4] I called attention to this letter in a communication to the *Athenæum*, pointing out that in Mr. Horwood's report on the *Liber Epistolaris* in an Historical MSS. Commission Report on Lord Harlech's MSS. (1874), mention was made, among its contents, of a letter from the Bishop of Winchester to Brian fitz Count, and of Brian's reply, which is merely described as "a long reply to the above" (it extends over three folios), and of which a *précis* should certainly have been given.

APPENDIX C.

THE EASTER COURT OF 1136.

(See p. 19.)

I HERE give in parallel columns the witnesses to (I.) Stephen's grant to Winchester; (II.) his grant of the bishopric of Bath; (III.) his great charter of liberties subsequently issued at Oxford.

I.	II.	III.
King Stephen.	William, Archbishop of Canterbury.	William, Archbishop of Canterbury.
Queen Matilda.	Thurstan, Archbishop of York.	Hugh, Archbishop of Rouen.
William, Earl Warenne.	Hugh, Archbishop of Rouen.	Henry, Bishop of Winchester.
Ranulf, Earl of Chester.	Henry, Bishop of Winchester.	Roger, Bishop of Salisbury.
Henry, son of the King of Scotland [Scotie].	Roger, Bishop of Salisbury.	Alexander, Bishop of Lincoln.
Roger, Earl of Warwick.	Alexander, Bishop of Lincoln.	Nigel, Bishop of Ely.
Waleran, Count of Meulan.	Nigel, Bishop of Ely.	Ebrard, Bishop of Norwich.
William de Albemarla.	Seffrid, Bishop of Chichester.	Simon, Bishop of Worcester.
Simon de Silvanecta.	Robert, Bishop of Hereford.	Bernard, Bishop of St. David's.
Aubrey de Vere, Camerarius.	John, Bishop of Rochester.	Audoen, Bishop of Evreux.
William de Albini, Pincerna.	Bernard, Bishop of St. David's.	Richard, Bishop of Avranches.
Robert de Ver, Conestabularius.	Simon, Bishop of Worcester.	Robert, Bishop of Hereford.
Miles de Gloucester, Conestabularius.	Ebrard, Bishop of Norwich.	John, Bishop of Rochester.
Brian fitz Count, Conestabularius.	Audoen, Bishop of Evreux.	Athelwulf, Bishop of Carlisle.
Robert fitz Richard, Dapifer.	John, Bishop of Séez.	Roger the Chancellor.
Robert Malet, Dapifer.	"Algarus," Bishop of Coutances.	Henry, the nephew of the king.
[William] Martel, Dapifer.		
Simon de Beauchamp, Dapifer.		
William, Archbishop of Canterbury.		

WITNESSES TO STEPHEN'S CHARTERS.

I.

Thurstan, Archbishop of York.
Hugh, Archbishop of Rouen.
Roger, Bishop of Salisbury.
Nigel, Bishop of Ely.
Seffrid, Bishop of Chichester.
Ebrard, Bishop of Norwich.
Simon, Bishop of Worcester.
Robert, Bishop of Bath.
Bernard, Bishop of St. David's.
Robert, Bishop of Hereford.
John, Bishop of Rochester.
Audoen, Bishop of Evreux.
John, Bishop of Séez.
Richard, Bishop of Avranches.
"Algarus," Bishop of Coutances.
Roger the Chancellor.
Roger de Fecamp, Capellanus.
Henry, nephew of King Stephen.
Reginald, son of King Henry.
Robert de Ferrers. ⎫
William Peverel de Nottingham. ⎪
Ilbert de Lacy. ⎬ Barones.
Walter Espec. ⎪
Payn fitz John. ⎭

II.

Richard, Bishop of Avranches.
Athelwulf, Bishop of Carlisle.
Roger the Chancellor.
Henry, the nephew of the king.
Henry, son of the King of Scotland.
William, Earl Warenne.
Waleran, Count of Meulan.
Roger, Earl of Warwick.
Robert de Ver, Conestabularius.
Miles de Gloucester, Conestabularius.
Aubrey de Vere, Camerarius.
William de Pont de l'arche, Camerarius.
Robert fitz Richard, Camerarius.
William de Albini, Pincerna.
Robert de Ferrars.
Robert Arundel.
Geoffrey de Mandeville.
Ilbert de Lacy.
William Peverel.
Geoffrey Talbot.

III.

Robert, Earl of Gloucester.
William, Earl Warenne.
Ranulf, Earl of Chester.
Roger, Earl of Warwick.
Robert de Ver. ⎫
Miles de Gloucester. ⎬ Conestabuli.
Brian fitz Count. ⎪
Robert de Oilli. ⎭
William Martel. ⎫
Hugh Bigot. ⎪
Humphrey de Bohun. ⎬ Dapiferi.
Simon de Beauchamp. ⎭
William de Albini. ⎫
Eudo Martel. ⎬ Pincernae.
Robert de Ferrers. ⎭
William Peverel de Nottingham.
Simon de Saintliz.
William de Albamarla.
Payn fitz John.
Hamo de St. Clare.
Ilbert de Lacy.[1]

---

[1] This list is taken from that in Stubbs' *Select Charters*, which is derived, through the *Statutes of the Realm*, from a copy at Exeter Cathedral. There is another version in Richard of Hexham (ed. Howlett, pp. 149, 150), in which Payn fitz John is omitted and *Hugh* de St. Clare entered in error for *Hamon*. But the reading "Silvanecta" (for "Saint liz") is confirmed by Charter No. I., as well as by a charter in *Cott. MSS.*, Nero, C. iii. (fol. 177). Both versions of this list are questionable as to the second "pincerna," the statutes reading "Eudonc Mart'," while Richard gives "Martel de Alb'."

264 THE EASTER COURT OF 1136.

I.	II.	III.
Eustace fitz John.		
Walter de Salisbury.		
Robert Arundel.		
Geoffrey de Mandeville.		
Hamo de St. Clare.	Barones.	
Roger de Valoines.		
Henry de Port.		
Walter fitz Richard.		
Walter de Gant.		
Walter de Bolebec.		
Walcholin Maminot.		
William de Percy.[1]		

There were thus assembled at the Easter court of 1136 the two primates of England and twelve of their suffragans, and the primate of Normandy, with four of his—nineteen prelates in all. Next to these, in order of precedence, were Henry, the king's nephew,[2] Henry, son of the King of Scots, and Reginald, afterwards Earl of Cornwall, whose presence, as a son of the late king, was of importance in the absence of the Earl of Gloucester. The names in all three lists repay careful study. Among them we find all those of the leading supporters of the Empress in the future, while in Robert de Ferrers, William de Aumale, and Geoffrey de Mandeville, we recognize three of those who were to receive earldoms from Stephen. The style and place of William de Aumale deserves special notice, because they prove that he did not, as is supposed, enjoy comital rank at the time.[3] This fact, further on, will have an important bearing. So, too, Simon de St. Liz ("de Silva Necta") was clearly not an earl at the time of these charters. It is believed indeed that he was Earl of Northampton, while

[1] This list is here printed as it is given by Hearne, but the order of the names, of course, is wholly erroneous, the prelates being placed low down instead of at the head. The right order would be prelates, chancellor (and chaplain), the "royalties," the earls, the household officers, and the "barones." But it would not be safe to rearrange the names in the absence of the original charter, in which they probably stood in parallel columns.

[2] Henry de Soilli (or Sully), son of Stephen's brother William. I find him attesting a charter of Stephen abroad, subsequently, as "H. de Soilli, nepote regis." He was a monk, and failing to obtain the bishopric of Salisbury or the archbishopric of York, in 1140, was consoled with the Abbey of Fécamp.

[3] For if he had even been then a count over sea, he would have ranked, like the Count of Meulan, among English earls.

Henry of Scotland was Earl of Huntingdon. But it is clear that when Henry received from Stephen, as he had just done, Waltheof's earldom, that grant must have comprised Northampton as well as Huntingdon; and I have seen other evidence pointing to the same conclusion. In after years, when Simon was as loyal as the Scotch court was hostile to Stephen, he may well have received the earldom of Northampton from the king he served so well. But for the present, Henry of Scotland was in high favour with Stephen, so high that the jealousy of the Earl of Chester, stirred by the alienation of Carlisle, blazed forth at this very court.[1] Their mention of Ranulf's presence, as of Henry's, confirms the authenticity of our charters.

The document with which they should be compared is the charter granted to the church of Salisbury by Henry I. at his Northampton council in 1131 (September 8).[2] Its witnesses are the Archbishops of Canterbury and York, ten bishops (Gilbert of London, Henry of Winchester, Alexander of Lincoln, John of Rochester, Seffrid of Chichester, William of Exeter, Robert of Hereford, Symon of Worcester, Roger of "Chester," and Ebrard of Norwich), seven abbots (Anscher of Reading, Ingulf of Abingdon, Walter of Gloucester, Geoffrey of St. Albans, Herbert of Westminster, Warner of Battle, and Hugh of St. Augustine's), Geoffrey the chancellor,[3] with Robert "de Sigillo,"[4] and Nigel the Bishop of Salisbury's nephew,[5] five earls (Robert of Gloucester, William of Warenne, Randulf of Chester, Robert of Leicester, and Roger of Warwick), nineteen barons (Brian fitz Count, Miles de Gloucester, Hugh Bigod, Humfrey de Bohun, Payne fitz John, Geoffrey de Clinton, William de Pont de l'Arche, Richard Basset, Aubrey de Ver, Richard fitz Gilbert, Roger fitz Richard, Walter fitz

---

[1] "Fuit quoque Henricus filius regis Scottiae ad curiam Stephani regis Angliae in proxima Pascha, quam apud Londoniam festive tenuit, cum maximo honore susceptus, atque ad mensam ad dexteram ipsius regis sedit. Unde et Willelmus archiepiscopus[?] antiquaronsia[?] se a rege abstraxit, et quidam proceres Angliae erga regem indignati coram ipso Henrico calumpniam intulerant" (*Ric. Hexham*). Among these "proceres" was the Earl of Chester.
[2] *Sarum Charters and Documents* (Rolls Series), pp. 6, 7.
[3] Afterwards Bishop of Durham.
[4] Afterwards Bishop of London.
[5] Afterwards the celebrated Bishop of Ely.

Richard, Walter de Gant, Robert de Ferrers, William Peverel of Nottingham, Baldwin de Redvers, Walter de Salisbury, William de Moion, Robert de Arundel), forty-six in all. In many ways a very noteworthy list, and not least in its likeness to the future House of Lords, with its strong clerical element. It is impossible to comment on all the magnates here assembled at Henry's court, many of whom we meet with again, but attention may be called to the significant fact that nine of the earldoms created under Stephen were bestowed on houses represented among the nineteen barons named above.[1]

[1] See Appendix D: "The 'Fiscal' Earls."

APPENDIX D.

THE "FISCAL" EARLS.

(See p. 53.)

"STEPHEN's earldoms are a matter of great constitutional importance." Such are the words of the supreme authority on the constitutional history of the time. I propose, therefore, to deal with this subject in detail and at some length, and to test the statements of the chroniclers—too readily, as I think, accepted—by the actual facts of the case, so far as they can now be recovered.

The two main propositions advanced by our historians on this subject are: (1) that Stephen created many new earls, who were deposed by Henry II. on his accession;[1] (2) that these new earls, having no means of their own, had to be provided for "by pensions on the Exchequer."[2] That these propositions are fairly warranted by the statements of one or two chroniclers may be at once frankly conceded; that they are true in fact, we shall now find, may be denied without hesitation.

Let us first examine Dr. Stubbs's view as set forth in his own words:—

"Not satisfied with putting this weapon into the hands of his enemies, he provoked their pride and jealousy by conferring the title of earl upon some of those whom he trusted most implicitly, irrespective of the means which they might have of supporting their new dignity. Their poverty was

"Stephen also would have a court of great earls, but in trying to make himself friends he raised up persistent enemies. He raised new men to new earldoms, but as he had no spare domains to bestow, he endowed them with pensions charged on the Exchequer . . . the new and unsub-

---

[1] So also Gneist: "Under Stephen, new comites appear to be created in great numbers, and with extended powers; but these pseudo-earls were deposed under Henry II." (*Const. Hist.*, i. 140, *note*).

[2] Stubbs, *Const. Hist.*, i. 362. Hence the name of "fiscal earls," invented, I believe, by Dr. Stubbs. See also Addenda.

relieved by pensions drawn from the Exchequer. . . . Stephen, almost before the struggle for the crown had begun, attempted to strengthen his party by a creation of new earls. To these the third penny of the county was given, and their connection with the district from which the title was taken was generally confined to this comparatively small endowment, the rest of their provision being furnished by pensions on the Exchequer" (*Const. Hist.*, i. 324, 362).

stantial earldoms provoked the real earls to further hostility; and the newly created lords demanded of the king new privileges as the reward and security for their continued services" (*Early Plants.*, p. 19).[1]

Now, these "pensions on the Exchequer" must, I fear, be dismissed at once as having an existence only in a misapprehension of the writer. Indeed, if the Exchequer machinery had broken down, as he holds, it is difficult to see of what value these pensions would be. But in any case, it is absolutely certain that such grants as were made were alienations of lands and rents, and not "pensions" at all.[2] The passages bearing on these grants are as follows. Robert de Torigny (*alias* "De Monte") states that Stephen "omnia pene ad fiscum pertinentia minus caute distribuerat," and that Henry, on his accession, "coepit revocare in jus proprium urbes, castella, villas, quæ ad coronam regni pertinebant."[3] William of Newburgh writes:—

"Considerans autem Rex [Henricus] quod regii redditus breves essent, qui avito tempore uberes fuerant, eo quod regia dominica per mollitiem regis Stephani ad alia multosque dominos majori ex parte migrassent, præcepit

---

[1] See also *Select Charters*, p. 20.

[2] The error arises from a not unnatural, but mistaken, rendering of the Latin. The term "fiscus" was used at the time in the sense of Crown demesne. Thus Stephen claimed the treasures of Roger of Salisbury " quia eas tempore regis Henrici, avunculi et antecessoris sui, *ex fisci regii redditibus* Rogerius episcopus collegisset" (*Will. Malms.*). So, too, in the same reign, the Earl of Chester is suspected of treason, "quia *regalium fiscorum redditus* et castella, quæ violentur possederat reddere negligebat" (*Gesta*). This latter passage has been misunderstood, Miss Norgate, for instance, rendering it: "to pay his dues to the royal treasury." It means that the earl refused to surrender the Crown castles and estates which he had seized. Again, speaking of the accession of Henry of Essex's fief to the Crown demesne, William of Newburgh writes: "amplissimo autem patrimonio ejus *fiscum* auxit."

[3] Anno 1155. Under the year 1171 he records a searching investigation by Henry into the alienated demesnes in Normandy.

ea cum omni integritate a quibuscunque detentioribus resignari, et in jus statumque pristinum revocari."

In the vigorous words of William of Malmesbury :—

"Multi siquidem . . . a rege, hi prædia, hi castella, postremo quæcumque semel collibuisset, petere non verebantur; . . . Denique multos etiam comites, qui ante non fuerant, instituit, applicitis possessionibus et redditibus quæ proprio jure regi competebant."

It is on this last passage that Dr. Stubbs specially relies; but a careful comparison of this with the two preceding extracts will show that in none of them are " pensions " spoken of. The grants, as indeed charters prove, always consisted of actual estates.

The next point is that these alienations were, for the most part, made in favour not of "fiscal earls," but, on the contrary, in favour of those who were not created earls.[1] There is reason to believe, from such evidence as we have, that, in this matter, the Empress was a worse offender than the king, while their immaculate successor, as his Pipe-Rolls show, was perhaps the worst of the three. It is, at any rate, a remarkable fact that the only known charter by which Stephen creates an earldom —being that to Geoffrey de Mandeville (1140)—does not grant a pennyworth of land, while the largest grantee of lands known to us, namely, William d'Ypres, was never created an earl.[2] Then, again, as to " the third penny." It is not even mentioned in the above creation-charter, and there is no evidence that " the third penny of the county was given " to all Stephen's earls; indeed, as I have elsewhere shown, it was probably limited to a few (see Appendix H).

The fact is that the whole view is based on the radically false assumption of the "poverty" of Stephen's earls. The idea that his earls were taken from the ranks is a most extraordinary delusion. They belonged, in the main, to that class

[1] The erroneous view is also found in a valuable essay on "The Crown Lands," by Mr. S. R. Bird, who writes: " It is true that extensive alienations of those lands [the demesne lands of the Crown] took place during the turbulent reign of Stephen, in order to enable that monarch to endow the new earldoms " (*Antiquary*, xiii. 160).

[2] The king's "second charter" to Geoffrey de Mandeville is not in point, for it was unconnected with his creation as earl, and was necessitated by the grants of the Empress.

of magnates from whom, both before and after his time, the earls were usually drawn. Dr. Stubbs's own words are in themselves destructive of his view:—

"Stephen made Hugh Bigod Earl of Norfolk, Aubrey de Vere Earl of Oxford, Geoffrey de Mandeville Earl of Essex, Richard de Clare Earl of Hertford, William of Aumâle Earl of Yorkshire, Gilbert de Clare Earl of Pembroke, Robert de Ferrers Earl of Derby, and Hugh de Beaumont Earl of Bedford."[1]

Were such nobles as these "new men"? Had *their* "poverty" to be "relieved"? Why, their very names are enough; they are those of the noblest and wealthiest houses in the baronage of Stephen's realm. Even the last, Hugh de Beaumont, though not the head of his house, had two elder brothers earls at the time, nor was it proposed to create him an earl till, by possession of the Beauchamp fief, he should be qualified to take his place among the great landowners of the day.

Having thus, I hope, completely disposed of this strange delusion, and shown that Stephen selected his earls from the same class as other kings, I now approach the alleged deposition of the earls created by the Empress and himself, on the accession of Henry II.

I would venture, on the strength of special research, to make several alterations in the lists given by Dr. Stubbs.[2]

The earldoms he assigns to Stephen are these:—

NORFOLK. Hugh Bigod (before 1153).
OXFORD. Aubrey de Vere (*questionable*).
ESSEX. Geoffrey de Mandeville (before 1143).
HERTFORD. Richard de Clare (uncertain).
YORKSHIRE. William of Aumâle (1138).
PEMBROKE. Gilbert de Clare (1138).
DERBY. Robert de Ferrers (1138).
BEDFORD. Hugh de Beaumont.
KENT. William of Ypres (*questionable*).

From these we must at once deduct the two admitted to be "questionable:" William of Ypres, because I am enabled to state

[1] *Const. Hist.*, i. 362.
[2] "As Stephen's earldoms are a matter of great constitutional importance, it is as well to give the dates and authorities" (*Ibid.*, i. 362).

CREATIONS BY STEPHEN AND MAUD. 271

absolutely, from my own knowledge of charters, that he never received an English earldom,[1] and Aubrey de Vere, because there is no evidence whatever that Stephen created him an earl. On the other hand, we must add the earldoms of Arundel (or Chichester or Sussex) and of Lincoln.[2] When thus corrected, the list will run:—

DERBY. Robert de Ferrers (1138).
YORKSHIRE. William of Aumâle (1138).
PEMBROKE. Gilbert de Clare (1138).
ESSEX. Geoffrey de Mandeville (1140).
LINCOLN. William de Roumare (? 1139–1140).
NORFOLK. Hugh Bigod (before February, 1141).
ARUNDEL. William de Albini (before Christmas, 1141).
HERTFORD. Gilbert de Clare[3] (before Christmas, 1141).
BEDFORD. Hugh de Beaumont (? 1138).

A glance at this list will show how familiar are these titles to our ears, and how powerful were the houses on which they were bestowed. With the exception of the last, which had a transitory existence, the names of these great earldoms became household words.

Turning now to the earldoms of the Empress, and confining ourselves to new creations, we obtain the following list:—

CORNWALL. Reginald fitz Roy (? 1141).
DEVON. Baldwin de Redvers (before June, 1141).
DORSET (or SOMERSET). William de Mohun (before June, 1141).
HEREFORD. Miles of Gloucester (July, 1141).
OXFORD. Aubrey de Vere (1142).
WILTSHIRE ("SALISBURY"). Patrick of Salisbury (in or before 1149).[4]

---

[1] There is a curious allusion to him in John of Salisbury's letters (ed. Giles, i. 174, 175) as "famosissimus ille tyrannus et ecclesiæ nostræ gravissimus persecutor, Willelmus de Ypra" (cf. pp. 129, 206 n., 213 n., 275 n.).

[2] A shadowy earldom of Cambridge, known to us only from an Inspeximus temp. Edward III., and a doubtful earldom of Worcestershire bestowed on the Count of Meulan, need not be considered here.

[3] Son of Richard de Clare, who, in Dr. Stubbs's list and elsewhere, is erroneously supposed to have been the first earl.

[4] The earliest mention of Patrick, as an earl, that I have yet found is in the Devizes charter of Henry (1149).

This varies from Dr. Stubbs's list in omitting ESSEX (Geoffrey de Mandeville) as only a confirmation, and adding DEVON (Baldwin de Redvers), an earldom which is always, but erroneously, stated to have been conferred upon Baldwin's father *temp.* Henry I.[1] Of these creations, Hereford is the one of which the facts are best ascertained, while Dorset or Somerset is that of which least is known.[2]

The merest glance at these two lists is sufficient to show that the titles conferred by the rival competitors for the crown were chosen from those portions of the realm in which their strength respectively lay. Nor do they seem to have encroached upon the sphere of one another by assigning to the same county rival earls. This is an important fact to note, and it leads us to this further observation, that, contrary to the view advanced by Dr. Stubbs, the earls created in this reign took their title, wherever possible, from the counties in which lay their chief territorial strength. Of the earldoms existing at the death of Henry (Chester, Leicester, Warwick, Gloucester, Surrey, [Northampton?], Huntingdon, and Buckingham[3]), Surrey was the one glaring exception to this important rule. Under Stephen and Matilda, in these two lists, we have fifteen new earls, of whom almost all take their titles in accordance with this same rule. Hugh Bigod, Robert de Ferrers, William of Aumâle, Geoffrey de Mandeville, William de Albini, William de Roumare, William de Mohun, Baldwin de Redvers, Patrick of Salisbury, are all instances in point. The only exceptions suggest the conclusion that where a newly created earl could not take for his title the county in which his chief possessions lay, he chose the nearest county remaining vacant at the time. Thus the head of the house of Clare must have taken Hertford

---

[1] In an interesting charter (transcribed in *Lansdowne MS.*, 229, fol. 116 b) of this Earl Baldwin as "Comes Exonie," granted at Carisbrooke, he speaks, "Ricardi de Redvers patris mei."

[2] I have shown (p. 95 n.) that William de Mohun was already an earl in June, 1141, though the *Gesta* assigns his creation to the siege of Winchester, later in the year.

[3] Buckingham is a most difficult and obscure title, and is only inserted here *carendi causa*. Northampton, also, and Huntingdon are most troublesome titles, owing to the double set of earls with their conflicting claims, and the doubt as to their correct title.

for his title, because Essex had already been given to Geoffrey, while Suffolk was included in the earldom of Hugh, as "Earl of the East Angles." So, too, Miles of Gloucester must have selected Hereford, because Gloucester was already the title of his lord. Aubrey de Vere, coming, as he did, among the later of these creations, could not obtain Essex, in which lay his chief seat, but sought for Cambridge, in which county he held an extensive fief. But here, too, he had been forestalled. He had, therefore, to go further afield, receiving his choice of the counties of Oxford, Berks, Wilts, or Dorset. And of these he chose the nearest, Oxford to wit. Here then we have, I think, a definite principle at work, which has never, so far as I know, been enunciated before.

It may have been observed that I assume throughout that each earl is the earl of a county. It would not be possible here to discuss this point in detail, so I will merely give it as my own conviction that while comital rank was at this period so far a personal dignity that men spoke of Earl Hugh, Earl Gilbert, or Earl Geoffrey, yet that an earl without a county was a conception that had not yet entered into the minds of men.[1] In this, of course, we have a relic of the earl's *official* character. To me, therefore, the struggles of antiquaries to solve puzzles of their own creation as to the correct names of earldoms are but waste of paper and ink, and occasionally, even, of brain-power. "Earl William" might be spoken of by that style only, or he might be further distinguished by adding "of Arundel," "of Chichester," or "of Sussex." But his earldom was not affected or altered by any such distinctive addition to his style. A firm grasp of the broad principle which I have set forth above should avoid any possibility of trouble or doubt on the question.

But, keeping close to the "fiscal earls," let us now see whether, as alleged, they were deposed by Henry II., and, if so, to what extent.

According to Dr. Stubbs, "amongst the terms of pacifica-

[1] This view is not affected by the fact that two or even more counties (as in the case of Waltheof's earldom) might be, officially, linked together, for where this arrangement had lingered on, the group might (or might not) be treated as one county, as regarded the earl. Warwick and Leicester are an instance one way; Norfolk and Suffolk the other.

tion which were intended to bind both Stephen and Henry ... the new earldoms [were] to be extinguished."[1] Consequently, on his accession as king, "Henry was bound to annul the titular creations of Stephen, and it was by no means certain within what limits the promise would be construed."[2] But I cannot find in any account of the said terms of pacification any allusion whatever to the supposed "fiscal earls." Nor indeed does Dr. Stubbs himself, in his careful analysis of these terms,[3] include anything of the kind. The statement is therefore, I presume, a retrospective induction.

The fact from which must have been inferred the existence of the above promise is that "cashiering of the supposititious earls" which rests, so far as I can see, on the statement of a single chronicler.[4] Yet that statement, for what it is worth, is sufficiently precise to warrant Dr. Stubbs in saying that "to abolish the 'fiscal' earldoms" was among the first of Henry's reforms.[5] The actual words of our great historian should, in justice, be here quoted:—

"Another measure which must have been taken at the coronation [December 19, 1154], when all the recognized earls did their homage and paid their ceremonial services, seems to have been the degrading or cashiering of the supposititious earls created by Stephen and Matilda. Some of these may have obtained recognition by getting new grants; but those who lost endowment and dignity at once, like William of Ypres, the leader of the Flemish mercenaries, could make no terms. They sank to the rank from which they had been so incautiously raised" (*Early Plantagenets*, pp. 41, 42).

"We have no record of actual displacement; some, at least, of the fiscal earls retained their dignity: the earldoms of Bedford, Somerset, York, and perhaps a few others, drop out of the list; those of Essex and Wilts remain. Some had already made their peace with the king; some, like Aubrey de Vere, obtained a new charter for their dignity: this part of the social reconstruction was despatched without much complaint or difficulty" (*Const. Hist.*, i. 451).

Before examining these statements, I must deal with the assertion that William of Ypres was a fiscal earl who "lost

[1] *Select Charters*, pp. 20, 21. Cf. *Early Plants.*, p. 37: "All property alienated from the Crown was to be resumed, especially the pensions on the Exchequer with which Stephen endowed his newly created earls."
[2] *Const. Hist.*, i. 451.　　　　[3] *Ibid.*, i. 333, 334.
[4] Robert de Monte.　　　　[5] *Select Charters*, p. 21.

endowment and dignity at once." That he ever obtained an English earldom I have already ventured to deny ; that he lost his "endowment" at Henry's accession I shall now proceed to disprove. It is a further illustration of the danger attendant on a blind following of the chroniclers that the expulsion of the Flemings, and the fall of their leader, are events which are always confidently assigned to the earliest days of Henry's reign.[1] For though Stephen died in October, 1154, it can be absolutely proved by record evidence that William of Ypres continued to enjoy his rich "endowment" down to Easter, 1157.[2] Stephen had, indeed, provided well for his great and faithful follower, quartering him on the county of Kent, where he held ancient demesne of the Crown to the annual value of £261 "blanch," *plus* £178 8*s.* 7*d.* "numero" of Crown escheats formerly belonging to the Bishop of Bayeux. Such a provision was enormous for the time at which it was made.

Returning now to the "cashiering" of the earls, it will be noticed that Dr. Stubbs has great difficulty in producing instances in point, and can find nothing answering to any general measure of the kind. But I am prepared to take firm ground, and boldly to deny that a single man, who enjoyed comital rank at the death of Stephen, can be shown to have lost that rank under Henry II.

Rash though it may seem thus to impugn the conclusions of Dr. Stubbs *in toto*, the facts are inexorably clear. Indeed, the weakness of his position is manifest when he seeks evidence for its support from a passage in the *Polycraticus* :—

"The following passage of the *Polycraticus* probably refers to the transient character of the new dignities, although some of the persons mentioned in it were not of Stephen's promoting: "Ubi sunt, ut de domesticis loquar, Ganfridus, Milo, Ranulfus, Alanus, Simon, Gillibertus, non tam comites regni quam hostes publici? Ubi Willelmus Sarisberiensis?" (*Const. Hist.*, i. 451 note).

---

[1] The chroniclers are positive on the point. At the opening of 1155, writes Gervase (i. 161), "Guillelmus de Ypre et omnes fere Flandrenses qui in Angliam confluxerant, indignationem et magnanimitatem novi regis metuentes, ab Anglia recesserunt." So, too, Fitz Stephen asserts that "infra tres primos menses coronationis regis Willelmus de Ypra violentus incubator Cantiæ cum lachrymis emigravit."

[2] Pipe-Rolls, 2 and 3 Hen. II. (published 1844).

For this passage has nothing to do with "the transient character of the new dignities": it alludes to a totally different subject, the *death* of certain magnates, and is written in the spirit of Henry of Huntingdon's *De Contemptu Mundi*.[1] The magnates referred to are Geoffrey, Earl of Essex (d. 1144); Miles, Earl of Hereford (d. 1143); Randulf, Earl of Chester (d. 1153); Count Alan of Richmond (d. 1146?); Simon, Earl of Northampton (d. 1153); and Gilbert, Earl of Pembroke (d. 1148).[2] Their names alone are sufficient to show that the passage has been misunderstood, for no one could suggest that the Earl of Chester or Earl Simon, Waltheof's heir, enjoyed "new dignities," or that their earldoms proved of a "transient character."[3]

Of the three cases of actual displacement tentatively selected by Dr. Stubbs, Bedford may be at once rejected; for Hugh de Beaumont had lost the dignity (so far as he ever possessed it[4]), together with the fief itself, in 1141.[5] York requires separate treatment : William of Aumâle sometimes, but rarely, styled himself, under Stephen, Earl of York; he did not, however, under Henry II., lose his comital rank,[6] and that is sufficient for my

---

[1] Compare also the moralizing of Ordericus on the death of William fitz Osbern (1071): "Ubi est Guillelmus Osberni filius, Herfordensis comes et Regis vicarius," etc.

[2] This is the date given for his death in the *Tintern Chronicle* (*Monasticon*, O. E., i. 725).

[3] "William of Salisbury" was a deceased magnate, but is mentioned by himself in the above passage because he was not an earl. As he is overlooked by genealogists, it may be well to explain who he was. He fought for the Empress at the siege of Winchester, where he was taken prisoner by the Earl of Hertford (*Will. Malms.*, ed. Stubbs, ii. 587). He was also the "Willelmus ... civitatis Saresbiriæ præceptor ... et municeps" (*Gesta*, ed. Howlett, p. 96), who took part in the attack on Wilton nunnery in 1143, and "lento tandem cruciatu tortus interiit." This brings us to a document in the register of St. Osmund (i. 237), in which "Walterus, Edwardi vicecomitis filius, et Sibilla uxor mea et heres noster Comes Patricius" make a grant to the church of Salisbury "nominatim pro anima Willelmi filii nostri fratris comitis Patricii in restauramentum dampnorum quæ prænominatus filius noster Willelmus Sarum ecclesie fecerit." The paternity of William is thus established.

[4] I have never found him attesting any charter as an earl, though this does not, of course, prove that he never did so.

[5] *Gesta* (ed. Howlett), pp. 32, 73.

[6] Aumâle ("Albemarle") is notoriously a difficult title, as one of those

purpose. The earldom of Dorset (or Somerset) is again a special case. Its existence is based—(1) on "Earl William de Mohun" appearing as a witness in June, 1141; (2) on the statement in the *Gesta* that he was made Earl of Dorset in 1141; (3) on his founding Bruton Priory, as "William de Mohun, Earl of Somerset," in 1142. The terms of the charter to Earl Aubrey may imply a doubt as to the *status* of this earldom, even in 1142, but, in any case, it does not subsequently occur, so far as is at present known, and there is nothing to connect the disappearance of the title with the accession of Henry II.[1]

Such slight evidence as we have on the dealings of Henry with the earls is opposed to the view that anything was done, as suggested, "at the coronation" (December 19, 1154). It was not, we have seen, till January, 1156, that charters were granted dealing with the earldoms of Essex and of Oxford. And it can only have been when some time had elapsed since the coronation that Hugh Bigod obtained a charter creating him anew Earl of Norfolk.[2]

To sum up the result of this inquiry, we have now seen that no such beings as "fiscal" earls ever existed. No chronicler mentions the name, and their existence is based on nothing but a false assumption. Stephen did not "incautiously" confer on men in a state of "poverty" the dignity of earl; he did not make provision for them by Exchequer pensions; no promise was made, in the terms between Henry and himself, to degrade or cashier any such earls; and no proof exists that any were so cashiered when Henry came to the throne. Indeed, we may go further and say that Stephen's earldoms all continued, and that their alleged abolition, as a general measure, has been here absolutely disproved.

of which the bearer enjoyed comital rank, though whether as a Norman count or as an English earl, it is, at first, difficult to decide. Eventually, of course, the dignity became an English earldom.

[1] Nor was it an earldom of Stephen's creation.

[2] It was granted at Northampton. Its date is of importance as proving that the charter to the Earl of Arundel, being attested by Hugh as earl, must be of later date. Mr. Eyton, however, oddly enough, reverses the order of the two (*Itinerary of Henry II.*, pp. 2, 3). He was thus misled by an error in the witnesses to the Earl of Arundel's charter, which Foss had acutely detected and explained long before.

APPENDIX E.

THE ARRIVAL OF THE EMPRESS.

(See p. 55.)

THE true date of this event is involved in considerable obscurity. The two most detailed versions are those of William of Malmesbury and of the Continuator of Florence of Worcester. The former states precisely that the Ecclesiastical Council lasted from August 29 to September 1 (1139), and that the Empress landed, at Arundel, on September 30; the latter gives no date for the council, but asserts that the Empress landed, at Portsmouth, before August 1—that is, two months earlier. These grave discrepancies have been carefully discussed by Mr. Howlett,[1] though he fails to note that the Continuator is thoroughly consistent in his narrative, for he subsequently makes the Empress remove from Bristol, after spending "more than two months" there, to Gloucester in the middle of October. He is, however, almost certainly wrong in placing the landing at Portsmouth,[2] and no less mistaken in placing it so early in the year. The "in autumno" of Ordericus clearly favours William rather than the Continuator.

Mr. Howlett, in his detailed investigation of this "exceedingly complex chronological difficulty," endeavours to exalt the value of the *Gesta* by laying peculiar stress on its mention of Baldwin de Redvers' landing, as suggestive of a fresh conjecture. Urging that "Baldwin's was in very truth the main army of invasion," he advances the

"theory that the expedition came in two sections, for the *Gesta Stephani* say that Baldwin de Redvers arrived 'forti militum catervâ,' as no doubt

---

[1] Introduction to *Gesta Stephani*, pp. xxi.-xxv.
[2] The *Gesta* and Robert "De Monte" concur with William that it was at Arundel.

he did, for it was only his presence in force that could render the coming of Maud and her brother with twenty or thirty retainers anything else than an act of madness."

Here we see the danger of catching at a phrase. For if the *Gesta* says that Baldwin landed "forti militum catervâ" (p. 53), it also asserts that the Empress came "cum robustâ militum manu" (p. 55)—a phrase which Mr. Howlett ignores—while it speaks of her son, in later years, arriving "cum florida militum catervâ," when, according to Mr. Howlett, "his following was small" (p. xvii.), and when, indeed, the *Gesta* itself (p. 129) explains that this "florida militum catervâ" was in truth "militum globum exiguum." But this is not all. Mr. Howlett speaks, we have seen, of "twenty or thirty retainers," and asserts that "Malmesbury and Robert of Torigny agree that he [Earl Robert] had but a handful of men—twenty, or even twelve as the former has it" (p. xxiv.). It is difficult to see how he came to do so, for William of Malmesbury distinctly states that he brought with him, not twelve, but a hundred and forty knights,[1] and, in his recapitulation of the earl's conduct, repeats the same number. Now, if the *Gesta* admits that the little band of knights who accompanied, in later years, the young Henry to England, was swollen by rumour to many thousands,[2] surely it is easy to understand how the hundred and forty knights, who accompanied the earl to England, were swollen by rumour (when it reached the Continuator of Florence of Worcester) to a "grandis exercitus,"—without resorting to Mr. Howlett's far-fetched explanation that the Continuator confused the two landings and imagined that the Empress had arrived with Baldwin, who "landed at Wareham . . . about August 1." But if he was so ill informed, what is the value of his evidence? And indeed, his statement that she landed "at Portsmouth" (not, be it observed, at Wareham, nor with Baldwin) places him out of court, for it is accepted by no one. Mr. Howlett offers the desperate explanation, which he terms "no strained conjecture," that "Earl

---

[1] " Centum et quadraginta milites tunc secum adduxit."

[2] " Ut fama adventus ejus se latius, sicut solet, diffunderet, multa scilicet millia secum adduxisse . . . postquam certum fuit . . . militum eum globum exiguum, non autem exercitum adduxisse" (p. 130).

Robert went on by sea to Portsmouth," a guess for which there is no basis or, indeed, probability, and which, even if admitted, would be no explanation; for the Continuator takes the Empress and her brother to Portsmouth first and to Arundel afterwards.

The real point to strike one in the matter is that the Empress should have landed in Sussex when her friends were awaiting her in the west—for Mr. Howlett fails to realize that she trusted to them and not to an "army" of her own.[1] The most probable explanation, doubtless, is that she hoped to evade Stephen, while he was carefully guarding the roads leading from the south-western coast to Gloucester and Bristol. Robert of Torigny distinctly implies that Stephen had effectually closed the other ports ("Appulerunt itaque apud Harundel, quia tunc alium portum non habebant").

In any case Mr. Howlett's endeavour to harmonize the two conflicting dates—the end of July and the end of September—by suggesting as a compromise the end of August, cannot be pronounced a success.[2]

It may afford, perhaps, some fresh light if we trace the king's movements after the arrival of the Empress.

Though the narratives of the chroniclers for the period between the landing of the Empress and the close of 1139 are at first sight difficult to reconcile, and, in any case, hard to understand, it is possible to unravel the sequence of events by a careful collation of their respective versions, aided by study of the topography and of other relative considerations.

[1] William of Malmesbury, who was well informed, lays stress on this, describing the earl as "fretus pietate Dei et fide legitimi sacramenti; ceterum multo minore armorum apparatu quam quis alius tam periculosum bellum aggredi temptaret . . . in sancti spiritus et dominæ sanctæ Mariæ patrocinio totus pendulus erat."

[2] Mr. Freeman (*Norm. Conq.*, v. 291) takes the place of landing (Portsmouth) from the one account, and the date (September 30) from the other, without saying so. I notice this because it is characteristic. Thus Mr. James Parker (*Early History of Oxford*, p. 191) observes of Mr. Freeman's account of the Conqueror's advance on London: "Though by leaving out here and there the discrepancies, the residue may be worked up into a consecutive and consistent series of events, such a process amounts to making history, not writing it. Amidst a mass of contradictory evidence it is impossible to arrive at any sure conclusion. . . . It is, however, comparatively easy to piece together such details as will fit out of the various stories; and more easy still to discover reasons for the results which such mosaic work produces."

On the landing of the Empress, the Earl of Gloucester, leaving her at Arundel, proceeded to Bristol (*Will. Malms.*, p. 725). Stephen, who, says Florence's Continuator (p. 117), was then besieging Marlborough, endeavoured to intercept him (*Gesta*, p. 56), but, failing in this, returned to besiege the Empress at Arundel (*ibid.*; *Cont. Flor. Wig.*, p. 117; *Gervase*, i. 110). Desisting, however, from this siege, he allowed her to set out for Bristol.[1] Meanwhile, her brother, on his way to Bristol, had held a meeting with Brian fitz Count (*Will. Malms.*, p. 725), and had evidently arranged with him a concerted plan of action (it must be remembered that they intended immediate revolt, for they had promised the Empress possession of her realm within a few months[2]). Brian had, accordingly, returned to Wallingford, and declared at once for the Empress (*Gesta*, p. 58). Stephen now marched against him, but either by the advice of his followers (*ibid.*) or from impatience at the tedium of the siege,[3] again abandoned his undertaking, and leaving a detachment to blockade Brian (*Cont. Flor. Wig.*, p. 118), marched west, himself, to strike at the centre of the revolt. He first attacked and captured Cerney (near Cirencester), a small fortress of Miles of Gloucester (*Gesta*, p. 59; *Will. Malms.*, p. 726), and was then called south to Malmesbury by the news that Robert fitz Hubert had surprised it (on the 7th of October) and expelled his garrison (*Will. Malms.*, p. 726; *Cont. Flor. Wig.*, p. 119; *Gesta*, p. 59). Recovering the castle, within a fortnight of its capture (*Will. Malms.*, p. 726), after besieging it eight days (*Cont. Flor. Wig.*, p. 125), he was then decoyed still further south by the news that Humphrey de Bohun, at the instigation of Miles, had garrisoned Trowbridge against him. Here, however, he was not so fortunate (*Will. Malms.*, p. 726; *Gesta*, p. 59). In the meanwhile Miles of Gloucester, with the instinct of a born warrior, had seized the opportunity thus afforded him, and, striking out boldly from his stronghold at Gloucester, marched to the relief of Brian fitz Count. Bursting by night on the blockading force, he scattered them in all directions, and returned in triumph to Gloucester (*Gesta*, p. 60). It was probably the tidings of this disaster (though the fact is

---

[1] See p. 55. [2] *Cont. Flor. Wig.*, p. 115.
[3] "Obsidionis diutinæ pertæsus" (*ibid.*, p. 118).

not so stated) that induced Stephen to abandon his unsuccessful siege of Trowbridge, and retrace his steps to the Thames valley (*ibid.*, pp. 61, 62). This must have been early in November.[1]

Seizing his chance, the active Miles again sallied forth from Gloucester, but this time toward the north, and, on the 7th of November, sacked and burnt Worcester (*Cont. Flor. Wig.*, pp. 118-120). About the same time he made himself master of Hereford and its county for the Empress (*Will. Malms.*, p. 727; *Gesta*, p. 61). Stephen was probably in the Thames valley when he received news of this fresh disaster, which led him once more to march west. Advancing from Oxford, he entered Worcester, and beheld the traces of the enemy's attack (*Cont. Flor. Wig.*, p. 121). After a stay there of a few days, he heard that the enemy had seized Hereford and were besieging his garrison in the castle (*ibid.*).[2] He therefore advanced to Leominster by way of Little Hereford,[3] but Advent Sunday (December 3) having brought about a cessation of hostilities, he retraced his steps to Worcester (*ibid.*). Thence, after another brief stay, he marched back to Oxford, probably making for Wallingford and London. Evidently, however, on reaching Oxford, he received news of the death of Roger, Bishop of Salisbury.[4] It

[1] It is an instance of the extraordinary confusion, at this point, in the chroniclers that the author of the *Gesta* makes him go from Trowbridge to London, and thence to Ely, omitting all the intervening events, which will be found set forth above.

[2] "Fama volante regiæ majestati nunciatur inimicos suos, juratæ quidem pacis violatores Herefordiam invasisse, monasterium S. Æthelberti regis et martyris, velut in castellinum munimen penetrasse." It seems absolutely certain, especially if we add the testimony of the other MSS., that this passage refers to the attack on the royal garrison in the castle so graphically described by the author of the *Gesta*, but (apparently) placed by him among the events of the summer of the following year. As, however, his narrative breaks off just at this point, his sequence of events is left uncertain, and in any case the chronology of the local chronicler, who here writes as an eyewitness, must be preferred to his.

[3] This passage (p. 121) should be compared with that on pp. 123, 124 ("Rex et comes . . . Oxenefordiam"), which looks extremely like a repetition of it (as the passage on pp. 110, 111 is an anticipation of that on pp. 116, 117).

[4] Assigned to December 11 by William of Malmesbury (p. 727), and to December 4 by the Continuator (p. 113). The above facts are rather in favour of the former of the two dates.

THE CHRONOLOGICAL DIFFICULTY. 283

was probably this which led him to keep his Christmas at Salisbury. Thither, therefore, he proceeded from Oxford, returning at the close of the year to Reading (*ibid.*).

The question, then, it will be seen, is this. Assuming, as we must do, that William of Malmesbury is right in the date he assigns to Stephen's visit to Malmesbury and recovery of Malmesbury Castle, is it consistent with the date he assigns to the landing of the Empress and her brother? That is to say, is it possible that the events which, we have seen, must have occurred between the above landing and Stephen's visit to Malmesbury can have been all comprised within the space of a fortnight? This is a matter of opinion on which I do not pronounce.

APPENDIX F.

THE DEFECTION OF MILES OF GLOUCESTER.

(See p. 55.)

MISS NORGATE assigns this event to the early summer of the year 1138,[1] on the authority of Gervase of Canterbury (i. 104). The statement of that writer is clear enough, but it is also clear that he made it on the authority of the Continuator of Florence. Now, the Continuator muddled in inextricable confusion the events of 1138 and 1139. In this he was duly followed by Gervase, who gives us, under 1138, first the arrest of the bishops at Oxford (June, 1139), then the *diffidatio* of the Earl of Gloucester, next the revolt of 1138 and the defection of Miles, next the invitation to the Empress (1139), followed by the Battle of the Standard (1138), and lastly the death of the Bishop of Salisbury (December, 1139). This can be clearly traced to the Continuator,[2] and conclusive evidence, if required, is afforded by the fact that Gervase, like the Continuator, travels again over the same ground under 1139. Thus the defection of Miles is told twice over, as will be seen from these parallel extracts :—

CONT. FLOR. WIG. (1138.)	GERV. CANT. (1138.)
"Interim facta conjuratione adversus regem per predictum Bryostowensem comitem et conestabularium Milonem, abnegata fidelitate quam illi juraverant, missis nuntiis ad Andegavensem civitatem accersunt ex-imperatricem," etc., etc.	"Qui [Comes Glaornensis] . . . fidei et sacramentis quibus regi tenebatur renuntiavit. . . . Milo quoque princeps militiæ regis avertit se a rege, . . . Interea conjuratio in regem facta per comitem Glaornensem et Milonem summum regis constabularium invaluit, nam missis nuntiis . . . asciverunt ex-imperatricem," etc., etc.

---

[1] *England under the Angevin Kings*, i. 295.
[2] Ed. Eng. Hist. Soc., ii. 107–113.

CONFUSION OF THE CHRONICLERS. 285

(1139.)
"Milo constabularius, regiæ majestati redditis fidei sacramentis, ad dominum suum, comitem Gloucestrensem, cum grandi manu militum se contulit, illi spondens in fide auxilium contra regem exhibiturum.'

(1139.)
"Milo regis constabularius multique procerum cum multa militum manu ab obsequio regis recesserunt, et pristinis fidei sacramentis innovatis ad partem imperatricis tuendam conversi sunt."

It is obvious from these extracts that the Continuator tells the tale of the constable's *diffidatio* and defection twice over; it is further obvious, from his own evidence, that the second of the two dates (1139) is the right one, for he tells us that so late as February, 1139, Stephen gave Gloucester Abbey to Gilbert Foliot "petente constabulario suo Milone."[1] When we find that this event is assigned by the author of the *Gesta* to 1139, that the constableship of Miles was not transferred to William de Beauchamp till the latter part of 1139, and that Miles is not mentioned among the rebels in 1138 (though his importance would preclude his omission), nor is any attack on Gloucester assigned to Stephen in that year, we may safely decide that the defection of Miles did not take place till the arrival of the Empress in 1139.

Since writing the above I have noted the presence of Miles of Gloucester among the followers of Stephen at the siege of Shrewsbury (August, 1138).[2] This is absolutely conclusive, proving as it does that Miles was still on the king's side in the revolt of 1138.

---

[1] ii. 114. Miss Norgate, having accepted the date of 1138 for the defection of Miles, finds it difficult to explain this passage. She writes (i. 494): "Stephen's consent to his appointment can hardly have been prompted by favour to Miles, who had openly defied the king a year ago."

[2] Charter dated in third year of Stephen, "Apud Salopesbiriam in obsidione" (Nero, C. iii. fol. 177).

APPENDIX G.

CHARTER OF THE EMPRESS TO ROGER DE VALOINES.

(See p. 87.)

As this charter is not included in Mr. Birch's *Fasciculus*, and is therefore practically unknown, I here give it *in extenso* from the *Cartæ Antiquæ* (K. 24). It will be observed that, of its six witnesses, five attest the Westminster charter to Geoffrey de Mandeville. The sixth is Humfrey de Bohun, a frequent witness to charters of the Empress. This charter is preceded in the *Cartæ Antiquæ* by enrolments of two charters to the grantee's predecessors from William Rufus and Henry I. respectively. The "service" of Albany de Hairon, a Herts tenant-in-capite, is an addition made by the Empress to these grants of her predecessors. The *cartæ* of 1166 prove that it was subsequently ignored.

"M. Imperatrix regis H. filia archiepiscopis episcopis abbatibus comitibus baronibus justiciariis vicecomitibus ministris et omnibus fidelibus suis Francis et Anglis tocius Anglie salutem. Sciatis me reddidisse et concessisse Rogero de Valoniis in feodo et hereditate sibi et heredibus suis Esendonam et Begefordiam et molendina Heortfordie et servitium Albani de Hairon et omnes alias terras et tenaturas patris sui sicut pater suus eas tenuit die qua fuit vivus et mortuus et preter hoc quicquid modo tenet de quocunque teneat. Quare volo et firmiter precipio quod bene et in pace et honorifice et libere et quiete teneat in bosco et plano in pratis et pascuis in turbariis in via et semita in exitibus in aquis et molendinis in vivariis et stagnis in foro et navium applicationibus infra burgum et extra cum socha et saka et thol et theam et infanenethef et cum omnibus libertatibus et consuetudinibus et quietantiis cum quibus pater suus melius et quietius et liberius tenuit tempore patris mei regis Henrici et ipse post patrem. T. R[oberto] Com[ite] Gloec[estrie] et M[ilone] Gloec[estrie] et Brientio fil[io] Com[itis] et Rad[ulfo] Painel et Walchel[ino] Maminot et Humfr[ido] de Buh[un] apud Westmonasterium."

APPENDIX H.

THE "TERTIUS DENARIUS."

(See p. 97.)

SPECIAL research has led me to discover that all our historians are in error in their accounts of this institution.

The key to the enquiry will be found in the fact that the term "tertius denarius" had two distinct denotations; that is to say, was used in two different senses. Dr. Stubbs and Mr. Freeman have both failed to grasp this essential fact. The two varieties of the "tertius denarius" were these:—

(1) The "tertius denarius placitorum comitatus." This is the recognized "third penny" of which historians speak. Observe that this was not, as it is sometimes loosely termed, and as, indeed, Gneist describes it, "the customary third of the revenues of the county,"[1] but, as Dr. Stubbs accurately terms it, "the third penny of the pleas."[2] So here the Empress grants to Geoffrey de Mandeville "tertium denarium vice-comitatus *de placitis*" (cf. p. 239). This distinction is all-important, for "the pleas" only represented a small portion of the total "revenues of the county" as compounded for in the sheriff's *firma*.

(2) The "tertius denarius redditus burgi." This "third penny," which has been strangely confused with the other, differs from it in these two respects. Firstly, it is that, not of the pleas ("placitorum"), but of the total revenues ("redditus"); secondly, it is that, not of the county ("comitatus"), but of a town alone ("burgi").

This distinction, which is absolutely certain from Domesday and from record evidence, is fortunately shown, with singular

---

[1] *Constitutional History*, i. 139. [2] *Ibid.*, i. 363.

clearness, in the charter of the Empress to Miles of Gloucester, creating him Earl of Hereford. In it she grants—

"Tertium denarium redditus burgi Hereford quicquid unquam reddat,[1] et tertium denarium placitorum totius comitatus Hereford."

Nor is it less clear in the charter (1155), by which Henry II. creates Hugh Bigod Earl of Norfolk "scilicet de tercio denario de Norwic et de Norfolca."

Now, let us trace how the "tertius denarius redditus burgi" has been erroneously taken for the "tertius denarius placitorum totius comitatus," the only recognized "third penny."

Dr. Stubbs writes: "The third penny of the county which had been a part of the profits of the English earls is occasionally referred to in Domesday."[2] The passage on which this statement is based is found earlier in the volume. Our great historian there writes:—

"Each shire was under an ealdorman, who sat with the sheriff and bishop in the folkmoot, and received a third part of the profits of jurisdiction. (The third penny of the county appears from Domesday [i. 1. 26, 203, 246, 252, 280, 298, 336] to have been paid to the earl in the time of Edward the Confessor.—Ellis, *Introduction to Domesday*, i. 167)."[3]

The argument that the ealdorman, or earl, of the days before the Conquest, received "a third part of the profits of jurisdiction" in the county, rests here, it will be seen, wholly on the evidence of Domesday. But in six of the eight passages on which Dr. Stubbs relies we are distinctly dealing, not with the county ("comitatus"), but with a single town ("burgus"). These are Dover, Lewes, Huntingdon, Stafford, Shrewsbury, and Lincoln. In these, therefore, the third penny could only be that of the *redditus burgi*, not of the *placita comitatus*.[4] Huntingdon is specially a case in point, for there the earl received a third of each of the items out of which the render

[1] This insured him his participation *pro rata* in any future increase ("crementum") of the render.
[2] *Const. Hist.*, i. 361.   [3] *Ibid.*, p. 113.
[4] We must, further, observe that, of these six, Lewes, of which we are not told if, or how, its *redditus* was divided before the Conquest, and Shrewsbury, of which we are told that the "third penny" of its redditus went, not to the earl, but to the sheriff ("Tempore Regis E . . . duas partes habebat rex et *vicecomes* tertiam") are not in point for the earl's share.

("redditus") of the town was composed. The only cases of those mentioned which could possibly concern the third penny "placitorum comitatus" are those of Yorkshire (298), Lincolnshire (336), and Nottinghamshire with Derbyshire (280). Even in these, however, "the third penny of the pleas" is only vaguely implied, the passages referring to a peculiar system which has, I believe, never obtained the attentive study it deserves. This system was confined to the Danish district, to which these counties all belonged.

The main point, however, which we have to keep in view is that "the third penny" of the *revenues* of the *town* has nothing to do with "the third penny" of the *pleas* of the *county*, and that the passages in Domesday concerning the former must not be quoted as evidence for the latter. I do not find that Ellis (*Introduction*, i. 167, 168) is responsible for so taking them, but Dr. Stubbs, as we have seen, clearly confused the two kinds of *tertius denarius*, and we find that Mr. Freeman does the same when he tells us that at Exeter "six pounds— that is, the earl's third penny—went to the Sheriff Baldwin."[1]

We are reminded by this last instance that not only the earl, but the sheriff, was concerned with "the third penny" of the *revenues* of the *town*. This—which (I would here again repeat) is not the earl's "third penny" to which historians allude—sometimes, as for instance at Shrewsbury and Exeter, fell to the sheriff's share. Dr. Stubbs mentions the case of Shrewsbury only, and takes it as evidence that "the sheriff as well as the ealdorman was entitled to a share of the profits of administration."[2]

This third penny "redditus burgi" is in Domesday absolutely erratic. In the Wiltshire and Somersetshire towns, it seems to have been held by the king himself, though at Cricklade both he and Westminster Abbey are credited with it (64 *b*, 67). At Leicester it was held by Hugh de Grantmesnil, but we are not told by what right (i. 230). At Stafford it had been held

[1] *Exeter*, p. 43 (cf. p. 55).
[2] This passage appears to imply that Dr. Stubbs, who sees in the "third penny" of the county the perquisite of the earl, would look on that of the borough as the perquisite of the sheriff. But the latter, as we have seen, was held, as a rule, by the earl, though occasionally by the sheriff.

by the English earl, and had fallen with his estates to the Crown. The Conqueror kept it, but, halving his own two-thirds share, made a fresh "third," which he granted to Robert de Stafford.[1] At Ipswich it had, with the "tertius denarius [*i.e.* placitorum] de duobus hundret," been annexed to an estate held by the local earl. The whole of this was granted by the Conqueror to his follower, Earl Alan.[2] At Worcester, by a curious arrangement, the total render had been divided, in unequal portions, between the king and the earl, while a third of the whole was received by the bishop. At Fordwich "the third penny" fell to Bishop Odo, and was bestowed by him, with the king's consent, on St. Augustine's, Canterbury, to which the other two-thirds had been given already by the Confessor. The case of Bristol has led Mr. Freeman into a characteristic error. We read in Domesday:—

"Burgenses dicunt quod episcopus G. habet xxxiii marcas argenti et unam marcam auri p[re]ter firmam regis" (i. 163).

Mr. Freeman, who is never weary of insisting on the value of Domesday, is clearly not so familiar as one could wish with its normal contractions, for he renders the closing words "*propter* firmam regis." On this he observes: "This looks like the earl's third penny; but Geoffrey certainly had no formal earldom in Gloucestershire."[3] When we substitute for the meaningless "propter" the right reading "preter" ("in addition to"), we see at once that the figures given no longer suggest a "third penny."

Leaving now the third penny of the revenues of the country town, let us turn our attention to that of the pleas of the whole county. Independent of the system in the Danelaw to which I have referred above, we have two references in Domesday to

[1] This has been strangely misunderstood by Mr. Eyton in his analysis of the Staffordshire survey. See my paper in *Domesday Studies*.
[2] *Domesday*, ii. 280, 294. We read of Alan's heir, Conan, in 1156, "Comiti Conano de tercio denario Comit' ix *li.* et x *sol*" (*Rot. Pip*, 2 Hen. II., p. 8). It is a singular circumstance that Robert de Torigny alludes to this under 1171, when, at the death of Conan, "tota Britannia, et *comitatus de Gippewis* [Ipswich], et honor Richemundie" passed to the king,—and still more singular that his latest editor, Mr. Howlett, identifies "Gippewis" with Guingamp (p. 391).
[3] *Will. Rufus*, i. 40.

ORIGIN OF THE EARL'S RIGHT. 291

this "third penny." Firstly, the "tercius denarius de totâ scirâ Dorsete" (i. 75); secondly (in the case of Warwickshire) "tercio denario placitorum siræ" (i. 278), yet neither of these is among the cases appealed to by Dr. Stubbs. Now, the curious point about them is that in neither instance was the right annexed to the dignity of earl, but to a certain manor, which manor was held by the earl. That is to say, he was entitled to this "third penny of the pleas" not *quâ* earl, but *quâ* lord of that estate. The distinction is vital. Whether "the third penny of the pleas" be that of the whole shire or only of a single hundred, it is always attached, under the Confessor, to the possession of some manor. We find the "tercius denarius" of one, of two, of three, of even six hundreds so annexed.[1] This peculiarity would seem to have been an essential feature of the system, and I need scarcely point out how opposed it is to the alleged tenure *ex officio* in days before the Conquest, or to that granted to the earl *quâ* earl under the Norman and Angevin kings. Let us seek to learn when the latter institution, the recognized "tertius denarius," became first annexed to the dignity of earl.

The prevailing view would seem to be that it was so annexed from the first; that its possession, in fact, was part of, or rather was connoted by, the dignity of an earl. Madox held that the oldest mode of conferring the dignity of earl, a mode "coeval to the Norman Conquest," was by charter; and he further held that "By the charter the king granted to the earl the *tertius denarius comitatus*."[2] Dr. Stubbs writes, of the investiture of earls in the Norman period:—

"The idea of official position is not lost sight of, although the third penny of the pleas and the sword of the shire alone attest its original character" (*Const. Hist.*, i. 363).

Mr. Freeman puts the case thus:—

"Earldoms are now in their transitional stage. They have become hereditary; but they carry with them the official perquisite of the ancient official earls, the third penny of the king's revenues in the shire."[3]

Here it may at once be pointed out that the mistake which I referred to at the outset is again made, "the third penny" being

[1] *Domesday*, i. 38 b, 101, 87 b, 186 b, 253; ii. 294 b.
[2] *Baronia Anglica*, pp. 137, 138.   [3] *Exeter*, p. 55.

described as that not of the pleas, but "of the revenues" of the county. Then there is the question whether this perquisite was indeed the right of "the ancient official earls." Lastly, we must ask whether the earldoms granted in this period did unquestionably "carry with them" this "official perquisite."

To answer this last question, we must turn to our record evidence. Now, the very first charter quoted by Madox himself, in support of his own view, is the creation by Stephen of the earldom of Essex in favour of Geoffrey de Mandeville. The formula there is quite vague. Geoffrey is to hold "bene et in pace et libere et quiete et honorifice sicut alii Comites mei de terrâ meâ melius vel honorificentius tenent Comitatus suos unde Comites sunt." Here there is nothing about the "third penny," and we must therefore ask whether its grant is included in the above formula; that is to say, whether an earl received his "third penny" as a mere matter of course. The contrary is, it would seem, implied by the special way in which the "third penny" is granted him in the charter of the Empress, together with the curious added phrase, "sicut comes habere debet in comitatu suo." This phrase may, of course, be held to imply that an earl had, as earl, a recognized right to the sum, but the fact that in the other charters of the Empress (those of the earldoms of Hereford and Oxford) the "tertius denarius" is made the subject of a special grant, and that in her son's charters it is the same, would suggest that, without such special grant, the right was not conveyed. This is the view taken by Gneist (who founds, in the main, on Madox):—

"It is only a *donatio sub modo*, the grant of a permanent income 'for the better support of the dignity of an earl;' it consists in a mere order or precept addressed to the sheriff, and is therefore a right of demand, but no feudal right, and is accompanied by no investiture."[1]

That the grant of "the third penny" (of the pleas of the county) was not an innovation introduced in this reign, is proved by the solitary surviving Pipe-Roll of Henry I., in which, however, there is but one mention of this "third penny," namely, in the case of the Earl of Gloucester. Indeed, with the exception of this entry, and of the special arrangement

[1] *Const. Hist.*, i. 139.

which existed before the Conquest in the Danish districts (*ut supra*), it may be said that the charters of the Empress, in 1141, represent the first occurrence of this "third penny."

Again, if we turn to the succeeding reign, we find, though the fact appears to have hitherto escaped notice, that, as far as the printed Pipe-Rolls take us—that is, for the first few years —less than half the existing earls were in receipt of the "third penny." Careful examination of the Rolls of 2–7 Hen. II. reveals this fact. The earls to whom was paid "the third penny of the pleas" were these: Essex, Hertford, Norfolk, Gloucester, Wiltshire (Salisbury), Devon, and Sussex. Those who are not entered in the Rolls, and who, therefore, it would seem, cannot have received it, are Warwick, Leicester, Huntingdon, Northampton, Derby (Ferrers), Oxford, Surrey, Chester,[1] Lincoln, and Cornwall. Thus seven received this sum, and ten did not. The inference, of course, from this discovery is that the possession of the dignity of an earl did not *per se* carry with it "the third penny of the pleas," the right to which could only be conferred by a special grant.[2] This, apparently conclusive, evidence illustrates and confirms the words of the *Dialogus* :—

"Comes autem est qui tertiam portionem eorum quæ de placitis proveniunt in quolibet comitatu percipit. Summa namque illa quæ nomine firmæ requiritur a vicecomite tota non exsurgit ex fundorum redditibus, sed ex magna parte de placitis provenit; et horum tertiam partem comes percipit, qui ideo sic dici dicitur, quia fisco socius est et comes in percipiendis."

D. "Nunquid ex singulis comitatibus comites ista percipiunt."

M. "Nequaquam: sed hii tantum ista percipiunt, quibus regum munificentia, obsequii præstiti vel eximiæ probitatis intuitu comites sibi creat et ratione dignitatis illius hæc conferenda decernit, quibusdam hæreditarie, quibusdam personaliter." [3]

This passage requires to be read as a whole, for the answer might easily be differently understood, as indeed it has been in the Lords' Reports,[4] where it is taken to apply to the earls as well as to "the third penny." The point is of no small

[1] The Palatinate of Chester is, of course, anomalous, and does not, strictly, tell either way.

[2] In the third and fifth years the Earl of Arundel is entered as receiving the third penny " per breve regis."

[3] *Dialogus de Scaccario*, ii. 17.

[4] *Reports on the Dignity of a Peer*, iii. 68.

importance, for the conclusion drawn is that "both [the dignity and the third penny] were either hereditary or personal, at the pleasure of the Crown." Careful reading, however, will show, I think, that, like the question, the reply deals with "the third penny" alone. The "hæc conferenda decernit" of the latter refers to the "ista" of the former.

Confirmed as they are by the evidence of the Pipe-Rolls, the words of the *Dialogus* clearly prove that the view I take is right, and that Professor Freeman is certainly wrong in stating that "earldoms," at this stage, "carry with them the third penny."[1] Mr. Hunt, who, here as elsewhere, seems to follow Dr. Stubbs, writes that :—

"The earl still received the third penny of all profits of jurisdiction in his county. With this exception, however, the policy of the Norman kings stripped the earls of their official character."[2]

This view must now be abandoned, and the total absence of any allusion, in Stephen's creation of the earldom of Essex, to "the third penny of the pleas," must be taken to imply that the charter in question did not convey a right to that sum. Thus the charter of the Empress to Geoffrey in 1141 remains the first record in which that perquisite is granted.

We should also note that the *Dialogus* passage establishes the fact that the only recognized "third penny" of the earl was "the third penny of the pleas," and that the third penny "redditus burgi," which, we saw, had been taken for it, is not alluded to at all.

Before leaving this subject it may be well to record the sums actually received under this heading :—

	£	s.	d.
Devon	18	6	8
Essex	40	10	10
Gloucestershire	20	0	0
Herts.	33	1	6

[1] Gueist is right in insisting on the fact that an earl was only entitled to the "tertius denarius" in virtue of a distinct grant, but he fails to grasp the important point that such grant was not made to every earl as a matter of course, but only as a special favour. He is also, as we have seen, quite mistaken as to the extent of the third penny (see p. 287).

[2] *Norman Britain*, p. 168.

				£	s.	d.
Norfolk	...	...	...	28	4	0
Sussex	...	...	...	13	6	8
Wilts.	...	...	...	22	16	7[1]

These figures are sufficient to disprove the view that the third penny actually formed an endowment for the dignity of an earl, but their chief interest is found in the light they throw on the farming of the "pleas," illustrating, as they do, the statement in the *Dialogus* that the sheriff's *firma* "ex magna parte de placitis provenit." For multiplying these sums by three we obtain the total for which the pleas were farmed in their respective shires. It will be observed that "the third penny" is stereotyped in amount, but an important passage bearing upon this point is quoted by Madox (*Baronia Anglica*, p. 139) from the Roll of 27 Hen. II. :—

"Idem Vicecomes redd. comp. de £xxviii de tercio denario Comitatus de Legercestria de vii annis præteritis, quos Comes Leg. accipere noluit, nisi haberet similiter de cremento, sicut prædecessores sui recipere consueverunt tempore Regis Henrici" (*sic*).

The meaning of this entry is that the earl demanded the "third penny," not only of the old composition for the "pleas," but also of the increased sum now paid for them. The passage, of course, is puzzling in its statement that the earl's predecessors had received "the third penny," for, so far as the printed Rolls take us, they never did so. A similar difficulty is caused, in the case of Oxfordshire, by the charter of Henry II. (see p. 239) granting to Aubrey de Vere its "third penny" "ut sit inde Comes;" for there is no trace in the printed Rolls of such payment being made, and in 7 John the then earl actually owes "cc marcas pro habendo tercio denario Comitatus Oxoniæ de placitis, et ut sit Comes Oxoniæ."[2]

Passing from these perplexing cases, on which we need fuller knowledge, we have a simple example in 12 Hen. III., when, on the death of the Earl of Essex (February 15, 1228), his

[1] These figures are taken from the Rolls of 2-7 Hen. II., a range sufficiently wide to establish their permanence. Occasionally, as in the case of Wilts and Sussex, the "tertius denarius" seems to be omitted for a year or two, but this does not affect the general result.

[2] Pipe-Roll of John, quoted by Madox (*Baronia Anglica*, p. 139).

annual third penny, as £40 10s. 10d., was allowed to count, for his heirs, towards the payment of his debts to the Crown.[1] A much later and most important instance is that of Devon, where Hugh de Courtenay, as the heir of the Earls of Devon, is found receiving their "third penny" in 8 Edw. III., though not an earl, a state of things which provoked a protest, a decision against him, and, eventually, his elevation to comital rank.

[1] Madox (*Baronia Anglica*, p. 139).

APPENDIX I.

"VICECOMITES" AND "CUSTODES."

(See pp. 107, 108.)

DR. STUBBS writes: "A measure dictated still more distinctly by this policy may be traced in the list of sheriffs for A.D. 1130. Richard Basset and Aubrey de Vere, a judge and a royal chamberlain, act as joint sheriffs in no less than eleven counties; Geoffrey de Clinton, Miles of Gloucester, William of Pont l'Arche, the treasurer, are also sheriffs as well as justices of the king's court" (i. 392). But this statement requires a certain qualification. For though they appear as sheriffs (*vicecomites*) on the Roll, and have been always so reckoned, we gather from one passage in the record that they were, strictly speaking, not *vicecomites*, but *custodes*. The difference is this. By the former a county was held *ad firmam;* by the latter it was held *in custodia*. In the Inquest of Sheriffs (1170) the distinction is clearly recognized. We there find the expressions used: "sive eos tenuerint ad firmam, sive in custodia." By the true sheriff (*vicecomes*) the county was, in fact, leased. He, as its farmer (*firmarius*), was responsible for its annual rent (*firma*). It was thus, virtually, a speculation of his own, and the profit, if any, was his. But by a process exactly analogous to that of a modern landlord taking an estate into his own hands, and farming it himself through a bailiff, the king could, under special circumstances, take a county into his own hands, and farm it himself through a bailiff (*custos*). Henry II., in his twentieth year, did this with London, putting in his own *custodes* in the place of the regular sheriffs, and, in later days, Henry III. and Edward I.

did the same. It was this, I contend, that Henry I. had done with the counties in question. The proof of it is found in this passage:—

"Ricardus basset et Albericus de Ver reddunt Compotum de M marcis argenti de superplus Comitatuum, quas habent *in custodia*" (p. 63).

Here we have the very same phrase as that in the Inquest of Sheriffs, while the enormous "superplus" of a thousand marcs must represent the excess of receipts over the amount required for the *firmæ*, which excess, the counties being "in custodia," fell to the share of the Crown. Thus we obtain the right explanation of the employment in this capacity of royal officers, and we further get a glimpse, which we would not lose, of one of those administrative changes which, as under Henry II., tell of a system of government as yet empirical and imperfect.

It is clear that this measure was no mere development, but a sudden and unforeseen step. For in the case of Essex, the scene of our story, William de Eynsford ("Æginesford"), a Kentish landowner, had leased the county for five years, from Michaelmas, 1128, the consideration he paid for his lease being a hundred marcs (£66 13s. 4d.). Early in the second year of his lease, that is between Michaelmas, 1129, and Easter, 1130, he must have been superseded by the royal *custodes*, on the king taking the county into his own hands. He, however, received "compensation for disturbance," four-fifths of his hundred marcs ("de Gersoma") being remitted to him in consideration of his losing four out of his five years' lease. All this we learn from the brief record in the Roll (p. 63).

Another point that should be here noticed is the use of the term "Gersoma." Retrospectively, its use in this Roll illustrates its use in Domesday. In those cases, where a *firmarius* was willing, as a speculation, to give for an estate more than its fixed rental (*firma*), he gave the excess "de Gersoma," either in the form of a lump sum, or in that of an annual payment.

APPENDIX J.

THE GREAT SEAL OF THE EMPRESS.

(See p. 116.)

THERE yet remains one point, in connection with this remarkable charter, perhaps the most striking, certainly the most novel, of all. This is that of the seal. According to the transcript in the Ashmole MSS., the legend "in circumferentia sigillo" was this : " Matildis Imperatrix Rom' et Regina Angliæ."

Now, that any such seal was designed for the Empress has never been suspected by any historian. We cannot, on a question of royal seals, appeal to a higher or more recognized authority than Mr. Walter de Gray Birch. He has written as follows on the subject :—

"The type of seal of the empress which is invariably fixed to every document among this collection that bears a seal is that used by her in Germany as 'Queen of the Romans.' . . . From this date [1106] to that of her death, which took place on the 16th of December, A.D. 1167, long after the solution of the troubles of the years 1140-1142 in England, she was accustomed to use this seal, and this only. It has never been suggested by any writer upon the historic seals of England that Mathildis employed any Great Seal as Queen of England, made after the conventional characteristics which obtain in the Great Seals of Stephen, her predecessor, or of her son, King Henry II. The troubled state of this country, the uncertain movements of the lady, the unsettled confidence of the people, and the consequent inability of attending to such a matter as the engraving of a Great Seal—a work, it must be borne in mind, involving some time and care—are, when taken together, more than sufficient causes to account for the continued usage of this type ; although we may fairly presume that it was intended to supersede this foreign seal with one more consentaneously in keeping with English tradition."[1]

The seal to which Mr. Birch refers bore the legend "Mathildis dei Gratia Romanorum regina."

[1] *Journ. Brit. Arch. Ass.*, **xxxi**. 381.

The question, of course, at once arises as to the amount of reliance that can be placed on the above transcriber's note. For my part, while fully admitting the right to reject such evidence, I cannot believe that any transcriber would for his own private gratification have forged such a legend, which he could not hope to foist upon the world, if it were indeed a forgery, since a reference to the original would at once expose him.[1] And it is quite certain that we cannot account for it by any misreading, however gross. A comparison of the two legends will put this out of the question:—

MATHILDIS DEI GRATIA ROMANORUM REGINA.
MATILDIS IMPERATRIX ROM' ET REGINA ANGLIÆ.

If we accept the fact, and believe the legend genuine, the first point to strike us is the substitution of "*Imperatrix*" for "*Regina* Romanorum."

It is passing strange that Maud should have retained, indeed that she should ever have possessed, a seal which gave her no higher style than that of "Queen of the Romans." It is true that at the time of her actual betrothal (1110), her husband was not, in strictness, "emperor," not having yet been crowned at Rome; yet the performance of that ceremony a few months later (April, 1111) made him fully "emperor." At the time therefore of their marriage and joint coronation (1114), they were, one would imagine, "emperor" and "empress;" and indeed we read in the *Lüneburg Chronicle*, "dar makede he se to *keiserinne*." At the same time, as has been well observed, "matters of phrase and title are never unimportant, least of all in an age ignorant and superstitiously antiquarian,"[2] and there must be some good reason for what appears to be a singular contradiction, though the point is overlooked by Mr. Birch. Two explanations suggest themselves. The one is that while Henry was fully and strictly "emperor," having been duly crowned at Rome, his wife, having only been crowned in Germany (1114), was not entitled to the style of "empress," but only to that of "Queen of the Romans." As against this, it would seem impossible that the wife of a crowned emperor can have been anything

---

[1] This transcript was taken before the fire in which the charter was so badly injured.
[2] Bryce's *Holy Roman Empire*.

but an empress. Moreover, from the pleadings of her advocate at Rome, in 1136 (see p. 257 n.), we learn incidentally that she had duly been "anointed to empress." The only other explanation is that her seal had been engraved in 1110—when the emperor was, as I have shown, only "Rex Romanorum"—and had not been altered since.

It is important to remember that a seal is evidence of formal style, and not of current phraseology. In spite of the efforts of Messrs. Bryce and Freeman to insist on accuracy in the matter, it is certain that at the time of which I write a most loose usage prevailed. Thus William of Malmesbury, although he specially records the solemn coronation of Henry V. as "Imperator Romanorum," at Rome in 1111, speaks of him as "Imperator Alemanniæ," or "Imperator Alemannorum," both before and after that event. This circumstance is the more notable, because I cannot find that style recognized in Mr. Bryce's work, where the terms "German Emperor" and "Emperor of Germany" are treated as recent corruptions.[1] Its common use in the twelfth century is shown by the scene, in the next reign, between Herbert of Bosham and the king (May 1, 1166), when the latter takes the former to task for speaking of Frederick as "King," not as "Emperor" *of the Germans*. Had Henry enjoyed the advantage of sitting under our own professors, he would have insisted on Frederick being styled Emperor *of the Romans;* but as he lived in the twelfth century, he employed, to the annoyance of modern pedants, the current language of his day.[2]

It was natural and fitting that, the legend on her seal being at variance with her style, the Empress should embrace the opportunity afforded, by the making of a wholly new seal, to bring the two into harmony.

The next point is the adoption of the form "Angliæ," not "Anglorum." This, at first sight, seemed suspicious. For though the abbreviation found in charters ("Angl'") might

[1] P. 317 (3rd edition).

[2] "*Rex*. Quare in nomine dignitatis derogas ei, non vocans eum imperatorem Alemannorum? *Herbertus*. Rex est Alemannorum; sed ubi scribit, scribit 'Imperator Romanorum, semper Augustus'" (*Becket Memorials*, iii. 100, 101).

stand for "Anglorum" or for "Angliæ," the legend on the seal of Stephen, as on that of Henry I., contains the form "Anglorum;" and Matilda styled herself in her charters "Anglorum" (not "Anglie) Domina." But the remarkable fact that both the queens of Henry I. bore on their seals the legend "Sigillum . . . Reginæ Ang*lie*" led me to the conclusion that, so far from impugning, this form actually confirmed the genuineness of the alleged legend.

It will doubtless be asked why this seal should have been affixed, so far as we know, to this charter alone. But it is precisely this that gives it so great an interest. For this is the only known instance of an original charter, still surviving, belonging to the brief but eventful period of the Empress's stay at Westminster on the eve of her intended coronation.[1] It may safely be presumed that a Great Seal was made in readiness for this event, and that its legend would necessarily include the style of "Queen of England." The Empress, in at least two of her charters, had already, though irregularly, assumed this style,[2] and was clearly eager to adopt it. As to her retention of her foreign style on her seal as an English sovereign, it might be suggested that she clung to the loftiest style of all[3] from that haughty pride which was to prove fatal to her claims; but it is more likely that she found it needful to distinguish thus her style from that of her rival's queen. For by a singular coincidence, they would both have had, in the ordinary course, upon their seals precisely the same legend, viz. "Mathildis dei gratia Regina Anglie."[4]

We may then, I think, thus account for the presence of this seal at Westminster, and for its use, with characteristic eagerness, by the Empress on this occasion. We may also no less

[1] The two other charters which belong (certainly) to this visit are known to us only from transcripts.

[2] "M. Imperatrix Henrici regis filia et Angl[ie] regina."

[3] We must remember the then supreme position and lofty pretensions of "the Emperor."

[4] Original charters of Stephen's queen are so extremely rare, that we know but little of her seal. Transcripts, however, of two fine charters of hers, formerly in the Cottonian collection, will be found in *Add. MS.* 22,641 (fols. 29, 31), and to one of them is appended a sketch of the seal, the first half of the legend being "Matildis Dei Gratia," and the second being lost.

MAUD WAS TO BE "QUEEN OF ENGLAND."

satisfactorily account for the fact that it was never used again. For this, indeed, the events that followed the fall of the Empress from her high estate, and the virtual collapse of her hopes, may be held sufficiently to account. But it is quite possible that in the headlong flight of the Empress and her followers from Westminster, the Great Seal may have fallen, with the rest of her abandoned treasure, into the hands of her triumphant foes.

APPENDIX K.

GERVASE DE CORNHILL.

(See p. 121.)

FEW discoveries, in the course of these researches, have afforded me more satisfaction and pleasure than that of the origin of Gervase de Cornhill, the founder of an eminent and wealthy house, and himself a great City magnate who played, we shall find, no small part in the affairs of an eventful time.

The peculiar interest of the story lies in the light it throws on the close amalgamation of the Normans and the English, even in the days of Henry I., thereby affording a perfect illustration of the well-known passage in the *Dialogus*:—

"Jam cohabitantibus Anglicis et Normannis, et alterutrum uxores ducentibus vel nubentibus, sic permixtæ sunt nationes, ut vix discerni possit hôdie, de liberis loquor, quis Anglicus, quis Normannus sit genere."[1]

It also affords us a welcome glimpse of the territorial aristocracy of the City, as yet its ruling class.

It has hitherto been supposed, as in Foss's work, that Gervase de Cornhill first appears in 1155–56 (2 Hen. II.), in which year he figures on the Pipe-Roll as one of the sheriffs of London. I propose to show that he first appears a quarter of a century before, and so to bridge over Stephen's reign, and to connect the Pipe-Roll of Henry I. with the earliest Pipe-Rolls of Henry II. The problem before us is this. We have to identify the "Gervasius filius Rogeri nepotis Huberti," who figures prominently on the Pipe-Roll of 1130 (31 Hen. I.), with "Gervase, Justiciary of London," who meets us twice under Stephen, with "Gervase" who was one of the sheriffs of London in 1155 and 1156, and with Gervase de Cornhill, whose name occurs at least twice under Stephen, and innumerable times under Henry II., both in a public and private capacity.

[1] *Dialogus*, i. 10.

GERVASE WAS JUSTICIAR OF LONDON. 305

Let us first identify Gervase de Cornhill with Gervase, the Justiciary of London. The latter personage occurs once in the legend on the seal affixed to "a 'star' with Hebrew words," which reads, "Sigillum Gervas' justitia' Londoniar';"[1] and once in a charter which confirms this legend, dealing, as it does, with a grant : " Gervasio Justic' de Lond'."[2] But the land (in Gamlingay) granted to " Gervase, Justiciary of London," is entered in a survey of the reign of John as held by "the heirs of Gervase *de Cornhill*" (see p. 121). Similarly, the land mortgaged in the former transaction to " Gervase, Justiciary of London," is afterwards found in possession of Henry, son and heir of Gervase *de Cornhill*. Thus is established the identity of the two.

The identity of the Gervase who thus flourished in the reigns of Stephen and Henry II. with the Gervase fitz Roger of 1130 must next occupy our attention. Here are the entries relating to the latter:—

"Radulfus filius Ebrardi debet cc marcas argenti pro placitis pecunie Rogeri nepotis Huberti."

"Andreas bucca uncta reddit compotum de lxiiij libris et vii solidis et viiij denariis pro xx libratis terre de terra Rogeri nepotis Huberti."

"Johannes filius Radulfi filii Ebrardi et Robertus frater suus reddunt Compotum de dcccc et ij marcis argenti iiij denarios minus de debitis Gervasii filii Rogeri pro totâ terrâ patris sui exceptis xx libratis terræ quas rex retinuit ad opus Andr' bucca uncta. . . . Et Idem debent iij marcas auri pro concessione terrarum quas Gervasius eis dedit."

"Ingenolda uxor Rogeri Nepotis Huberti debet ij marcas auri ut habeat maritagium et dotem et res suas."

"Gervasius filius Rogeri nepotis Huberti debet vj libras et xii solidos et vj denarios de debitis patris sui."

"Robertus filius Radufi et Johannes frater ejus reddunt Compotum de lij marcis auri ut rex concederet eis vadimonium et terras quas Gervasius eis concessit."[3]

These entries are explained by the charter subjoined, which shows how John and Robert came to have charge of the estate:—

" H. rex Angl[orum] Vic' Lund' et omnibus Baronibus et Vicecomitibus in quorum Bailiis Gervasius filius Rogeri terram habet salutem. Precipio

---

[1] Such is the reading given by Anstis, who saw this star among the duchy records. It is greatly to be hoped that it may still be found. Anstis describes the device as " a Lyon."

[2] Duchy of Lancaster : Royal Charters, No. 22.

[3] *Rot. Pip.*, 31 Hen. I., pp. 144, 145, 147-149. Compare the clause in Henry's charter guaranteeing to the citizens "terras suas et vadimonia." Here the possession has to be paid for.

quod Gervasius filius Rogeri sit saisitus et tenens de omnibus terris et rebus patris sui sicut pater ejus erat die quo movit ire ad Jerosolimam. . . . Et ipse et tota terra sua interim sint in custodia et saisina Johannis et Roberti filiorum Radulfi. . . . T. Comite Gloecestrie. Apud West'."[1]

John fitz Ralph (fitz Ebrard) was another London magnate, who was more or less connected with Gervase throughout his career. He is found with him at St. Albans, late in Stephen's reign, witnessing a charter of the king;[2] and the two men, as " Gervase and John," were joint sheriffs of London in 2 Hen. II. He is also the first witness to one of Gervase's charters after his brother Alan.[3]

We further find Gervase fitz Roger excused (in the Pipe-Roll of 1130) the payment of two shillings "de veteri Danegeldo" (? 1127-28) in Middlesex, and seven shillings "de preterito Danegeldo" (1128-29) because his land is "waste."[4] The inference to be drawn from all these passages is that Gervase had then (1130) recently succeeded his father, a man of unusual wealth and considerable property in land. We should therefore expect to find him, in his turn, a man of some importance, as was our own Gervase the Justiciar (*alias* Gervase de Cornhill), the only Gervase who meets us as a man of any consequence. Fortunately, however, we are not dependent on mere inference. The manor of Chalk was granted by the Crown to Roger "nepos Huberti;"[5] it was subsequently regranted to Gervase de Cornhill,[6] whom I identify with Gervase his son. Moreover, the adoption by Gervase of the surname " de Cornhill " can, as it happens, be accounted for. Among the records of the duchy of Lancaster is a grant by William, Archbishop of Canterbury (1123-1136), of land at " Eadintune" to Gervase and Agnes his wife, Agnes being described as daughter of " Godeleve."[7] By the aid of another document relating to the same property,[8] we identify this " Godeleve " as the wife of Edward de Cornhill. To the eye of a trained genealogist all is thus made clear.

---

[1] Duchy of Lancaster: Royal Charters, No. 8.

[2] "Gervasio de Corn . . ., Johanne filio Radulfi" (Madox's *Formularium*, 293).

[3] Duchy of Lancaster: *Cart. Misc.*, ii. 57.

[4] *Rot. Pip.*, 31 Hen. I., pp. 150, 151.

[5] Duchy of Lancaster: Royal Charters, No. 3.

[6] *Ibid.*, No. 26 (see Pipe-Roll Society: *Ancient Charters*, p. 66).

[7] Grants in boxes, A., No. 156.

[8] *Ibid.*, 154.

But we now find ourselves in the midst of a most interesting family connection. For these same records carry us back to the father of this "Godeleve," namely, Edward of Southwark.[1] It is true that here he figures merely as a "æ. desudwerc," but we have only to turn to another quarter, and there we find "Edwardo de Suthwerke et Willelmo filio ejus" among the leading witnesses to the invaluable document recording the surrender by the English Cnihtengild of their soke to the priory of Christchurch (1125).[2] I need scarcely lay stress on the interest and importance of everything bearing on that remarkable and as yet mysterious institution. We find ourselves now brought into actual contact with the gild. For in one of its members, as named in that document, "Edwardus Hupcornhill," we recognize no other than that "Edward of Cornhill" who was son-in-law to "Edward of Southwark."[3] Following up our man in yet another quarter, we find him witnessing a London deed (*temp.* William the Dean),[4] and another one of about the middle of the reign of Henry I.,[5] though wrongly assigned in the (Hist. MSS.) Report to "about 1127."[6] Lastly, turning to still another quarter, we find his name among those of the witnesses to an agreement between Ramsey Abbey and the priory of Christchurch soon after 1125.[7]

We are now in a position to construct this remarkable pedigree:—

---

[1] "Ego Radulfus Archiepiscopus [1114-1122] concedo Æadwardo de Cornhelle et uxori ejus Godelif et hæredibus suis terram de Eadintune . . . quam æ. desudwerc dedit cum filia sua æ. de Cornhelle" (*ibid.*, 154). We have here an instance of the caution with which official calendars should be used. In the official abstract of the above record (*Thirty-fifth Report of Dep. Keeper,* p. 15), the above words are rendered, "with his daughter æ. de Cornhelle," the dative being taken for an ablative, and the wife transformed into her husband! [2] *London and Middlesex Arch. Journ.,* v. 477.

[3] The curious form "Hupcornhill" should, of course, be noted. I have met with a similar form at Colchester, where the name "Opethewalle," which has been supposed to have been connected with the town-wall, occurs earlier (under Edward I.) as "Opethehelle," *i.e.* up the hill. The idiom still survives in such forms as "up town" and "up the street." It probably accounts for the strange name, "Hoppeoverhumber," *i.e.* a man who came from "up beyond the Humber" (cf. for aspirate "Huppelanda de Berchamstede").

[4] *Ninth Report Hist. MSS.,* i. 61 b. [5] *Ibid.,* p. 66 a.

[6] *Ibid.,* p. 31 b. It is certainly earlier than 1120, when Otuel fitz Count (the leading witness) was drowned, and probably earlier than the spring of 1116.

[7] Pipe-Roll Society: *Ancient Charters,* p. 26 (Eadwardus de Corhulle).

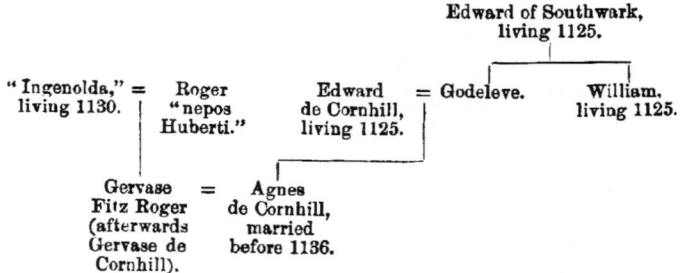

I say that this is a remarkable pedigree because, from the dates, Edward of Southwark must have been born within a very few years of the Conquest, and also because we can feel sure, in the case both of him and of his son-in-law, that we are dealing with men of the old stock, connected with the venerable gild of English "Cnihts." But it further shows us how the elder of the two bestowed on his English son the name of the Norman Conqueror, and how the Norman settlers intermarried with the English stock.

Let us now return to the father of Gervase, Roger "nepos Huberti." Here, again, there come to our help the records of the duchy of Lancaster. Among them are two royal charters, the first of which grants to Roger the manor of Chalk, in Kent,[1] while the second was consequent on his death,[2] and should be read in connection with the above extracts from the Pipe-Roll of 1130. This charter has a special interest from its mention of the fact that Roger had gone "ad Jerosolima." We may infer from this that he had died on pilgrimage.[3] As Gervase inherited from his father so large an estate, Roger must have been, in his day, a man of some consequence. It is, therefore, rather strange that his name does not occur in the report on the muniments of St. Paul's, nor in any other quarter to which I have been able to refer. Luckily, however, Stow has preserved for us the gist of a document which he had

---

[1] Royal Charters, No. 3. This charter must belong to the years 1116–1120.

[2] *Ibid.*, No. 8 (see p. 305).

[3] This has a curious bearing on the legend that Gilbert Becket, the primate's father, had journeyed to Palestine, as showing that this was actually done by a contemporary City magnate.

ROGER, THE FATHER OF GERVASE. 309

seen, when he tells us that on the grant of their soke, in 1125, by the Cnihtengild—

",The king sent also his sheriffs, to wit Aubrey de Vere and *Roger nephew to Hubert*, which (upon his behalf) should invest this church with the possessions thereof; which the said sheriffs accomplished, coming upon the ground, Andrew Buchevite [1] and the forenamed witnesses and others standing by." [2]

If we can trust to this passage, as I believe we certainly can, our Roger was a sheriff of London in 1125. This makes it highly probable that he was identical with the "Roger" named in a document addressed, a few years earlier:—

" Hugoni de Bocheland, *Rogero*, Leofstano, Ordgaro, et omnibus aliis baronibus Lundoniæ." [3]

I do not know of any other Roger who is likely to have been thus addressed.

We are given by Gervase de Cornhill a further clue as to his parentage in a charter of his, under Henry II., in which he mentions Ralph fitz Herlwin as his uncle ("avunculus"). Ralph fitz Herlwin was in 1130 joint-Sheriff of London.[4] This clue, therefore, is worth following up. Now, Ralph must either have been a brother of the father or of the mother of Gervase. It is highly improbable that Ralph "filius Herlwini" was a brother of Roger "nepos Huberti," each of the two being always mentioned by the same distinctive suffix. It may, therefore, be presumed that Ralph was brother to Roger's wife. Now, we happen to have two documents which greatly concern this Ralph and his son, and which belong to one transaction, although they figure widely apart in the report on the muniments of St. Paul's.[5] Nicholas, son of Ælfgar, parish priest of the church of St. Michael's, Cheap, a living which, like his father before him, he held at lease from St. Paul's, exercised his right to the next presentation in favour of a son of Ralph fitz Herlwin, who had married his niece Mary. From the evidence now in our possession, we may construct this pedigree:—

---

[1] This name should be Andrew Buccuinte (Bucca uncta).

[2] Strype's *Stow*, ii. 4.

[3] *Ramsey Cartulary*, i. 130. The date there assigned is 1114-1130, but Hugh de Bocland appears to have died several years before 1130.

[4] *Rot. Pip.*, 31 Hen. I., p. 149.

[5] *Ninth Report Hist. MSS.*, App. i. pp. 20 *a*, 64 *a*.

GERVASE DE CORNHILL.

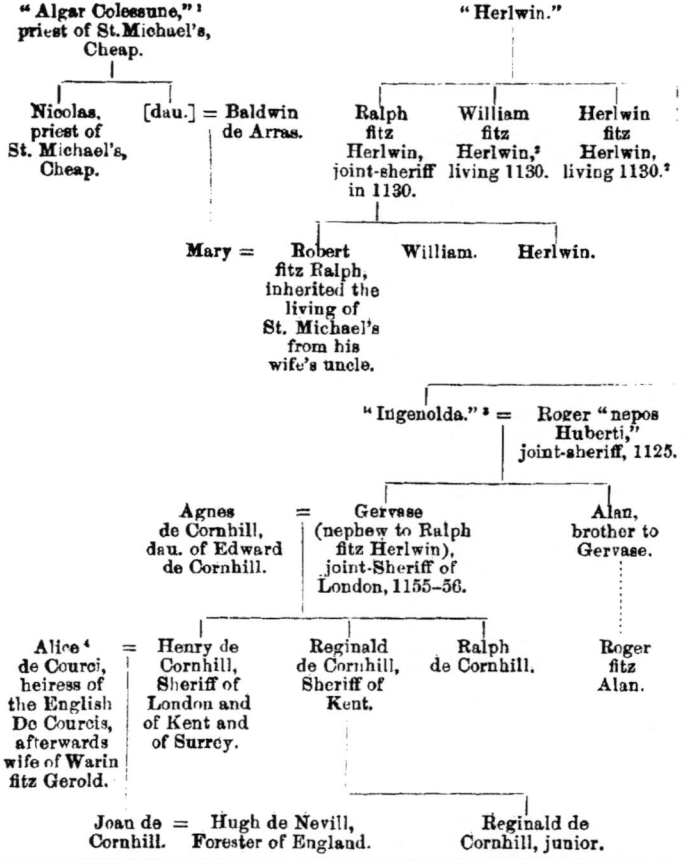

[1] The form of this surname should be noted as illustrating the practice of abbreviation. The name of Ælfgar's father must have been Colswegen, or some other compound of "Col—"

[2] See Pipe-Roll of 1130.

[3] This involves a double supposition: (*a*) that "Ingenolda," who is proved to have been the widow of Roger, was the mother of his son Gervase; (*b*) that Ralph fitz Herlwin was brother to the mother, not the father, of Gervase. These assumptions seem tolerably certain, but, at present, they can only be provisionally accepted.

[4] For this descent see Stapleton's preface to the *Liber de Antiquis Legibus* (Cam. Soc.).

HIS RELATIVES AND DESCENDANTS. 311

It will have been noticed that in this pedigree I assign to Gervase a brother Alan. I do so on the strength of a charter of Archbishop Theobald, late in the reign of Stephen, to Holy Trinity, witnessed *inter alios* by "Gervasio de Cornhill et Alano fratre ejus,"[1] also of a charter I have seen (Duchy of Lanc., *Cart. Misc.*, ii. 57), in which the first witness to a charter of Gervase is Alan, his brother. The "Roger fitz Alan" for whom I suggest an affiliation to this Alan occurs among the witnesses to a grant made by Ralph, and witnessed by Reginald de Cornhill.[2] This suggests such paternity, and his name, Roger, would then be derived from Roger, his paternal grandfather. We have here, at least, another clue which ought to be followed up, for Roger fitz Alan is repeatedly found among the leading witnesses to London documents of the close of the twelfth and beginning of the thirteenth centuries, his career culminating in his appointment as mayor on the death of the well-known "Henry fitz Ailwin" in 1212.[3]

The fact that Gervase and Alan were brothers tempts one to recognize in them the "Alanus juvenis et Gervasius fratres," who witness a grant to (their cousin) Robert fitz Ralph fitz Herlwin,[4] and the "Alanus juvenis" and "Gervasius frater Alani" of a similar document.[5] But, unluckily, we find this same Alan elsewhere styled "Alanus filius *Huberti* juvenis."[6] Possibly they were sons of that Hubert to whom his father was "nepos." But the question, for the present, must be left in doubt.

Both Gervase de Cornhill and Henry his son appear, it may be added, from the evidence of charters, to have lent money on mortgage, and to have acquired landed property by foreclosing. A curious allusion to the mercantile origin and the profitable money-lending transactions of Geoffrey is found in a sneer of Becket's biographer, when, as Sheriff of Kent, he opposed the primate's landing.[7] The contemporary allusion to

[1] From a MS. note of Dugdale (L. 41, dors.).
[2] *Ninth Report Hist. MSS.*, i. 52 b.
[3] This, it must be well understood, is thrown out merely as a suggestion.
[4] *Ninth Report Hist. MSS.*, i. 64 a.
[5] *Ibid.*, 66 b.
[6] *Ibid.*, 20 a.
[7] "Cujus jurisdictioni Cantia subjiciebatur, plus besses et centesimas usuras quam bonum et æquum attendens" (*Becket Memorials*, iii. 100).

such pursuits, in the *Dialogus*, breathes the same scornful spirit for the trader and all his works.[1] Gervase, I think, may have been that "Gervase" who, at the head of the citizens of London, met Henry II. in 1174 (*Fantosme*, l. 1941); he would seem to have lived on till 1183, and was probably, at his death, between seventy and seventy-five years old. Among his descendants were a Dean of St. Paul's (1243–1254) and a Bishop of Coventry and Lichfield (1215–1223).

[1] "Quod si forte miles aliquis vel liber alius a sui status dignitate, quod absit, degenerans, multiplicandis denariis per publica mercimonia, vel per turpissimum genus quæstus, hoc est per fœnus extiterit . . . Hiis similis qui multiplicant quocunque modo rem." Compare *Quadripartitus: ein Englisches Rechtsbuch von* 1114 (ed. Liebermann): "qui, vera morum generositate carentes et honesta prosapia, longo nummorum stemmate gloriantur, . . . qui vetitum pecunie fenus exercent, . . . miseram pecunie stipem, pauperum lacrimis et anxietatibus cruentatam, omni veritatis et justicie sanctioni mentes perdite prefecerunt et id solum sapientiam reputant quod eis obtatum pecunie fenus quibuscunque machinationibus insusurrat" (Dedicatio, § 16, § 33). Compare also with these Cicero (*De Officiis*, i. 42): "Jam de artificiis et quæstibus, qui liberales habendi, qui sordidi sint, hæc præaccepimus. Primum improbantur ii quæstus qui in odia hominum incurrunt, ut portitorum, ut feneratorum. . . . Sordidi etiam putandi qui mercantura mercatoribus quod statim vendant. Nihil enim proficiunt nisi admodum mentiantur."

APPENDIX L.

CHARTER OF THE EMPRESS TO WILLIAM DE BEAUCHAMP.

(See p. 124.)

As this important charter has never, I believe, been printed, I have taken the present opportunity of publishing it *in extenso*. The grantee must, at first, have staunchly supported Stephen, for he received in 1139, from the king, a grant of that constableship which Miles of Gloucester had forfeited on his defection.[1] It is evident, however, from the terms of this charter that he was jealous of Stephen's favourite, Gualeran, Count of Meulan, and of the power which the king had given him at Worcester. The grant of Tamworth also should be carefully noted, because that portion of the Despencer inheritance had fallen to the share of Marmion, which suggests that the Beauchamps and the Marmions were at strife, and that therefore, in this struggle, they embraced opposite sides. An intermarriage between Robert Marmion and Maud de Beauchamp was probably, as in other cases, a compromise of the quarrel.

"M. Imperatrix H. Regis filia et Anglor[um] domina Archiepiscopis Episcopis Abbatibus Comitibus Baronibus Justic[iariis] vicecomitibus ministris et omnibus fidelibus suis francis et Anglis tocius Angliæ salutem. Sciatis me dedisse et reddidisse Willelmo de Bellocampo hereditario jure Castellum de Wigorn[ia] cum mota sibi et heredibus suis ad tenendum de me in capite et heredibus meis. Dedi ei et reddidi vicecomitatum Wigorn[ie] et forestas cum omnibus appendiciis suis in feodo et hereditarie per eandem firmam quam pater eius Walterus de Bellocampo inde reddebat. Et de hoc devenit ipse

[1] See Appendix F

314 CHARTER TO WILLIAM DE BEAUCHAMP.

Willelmus meus ligius homo contra omnes mortales et nominatim contra Gualerann[um] Comitem de Mellent et ita quod nec ipse Comes Gualeran[us] nec aliquis alius de hiis predictis mecum finem faciet quin semper ipse Willelmus de me in capite teneat nisi ipse bona voluntate et gratuita concessione de predicto Comite tenere voluerit. Et præter hoc dedi ei et reddidi castellum et honorem de Tamword ad tenend[um] ita bene et in pace et quiete et plenarie et honorifice et libere sicut unquam melius et quietius et plenarius et honorificentius et liberius Robertus Dispensator frater Ursonis de Abbetot ipsum castellum et honorem tenuerit. Et eciam dedi ei et reddidi Manerium de Cokeford cum omnibus appendiciis suis ut rectum suum sine placito. Et cum hoc dedi ei et reddidi Westonam et Luffenham in Roteland cum omnibus appendiciis suis ut rectum suum similiter sine placito. Dedi eciam ei et concessi de cremento lx libratas terræ de perquisitione Angl' pro servicio suo. Et iterum dedi ei et reddidi conestabulatum quem Urso de Abetot tenuit et dispensam ita hereditarie sicut Walterus pater ejus eam de patre meo H. Rege tenuit. Et item dedi ei et concessi terras et hereditates suorum proximorum parentum qui contra me fuerint in Werra mea et mecum finem facere non poterunt nisi de sua parentela propinquiore michi in ipsa Werra servierit. Quare volo et firmiter precipio quod de me et de quocunque teneat bene et honorifice in pace et hereditarie et libere et quiete teneat ipse Willelmus et heres suus post eum in bosco in plano in pratis et pasturis in forestis et fugaciis in percursibus et exitibus in aquis et molendinis in vivariis et piscariis in stagnis et mariscis et salinis et viis et semitis in foris et in feriis infra burgum et extra in civitate et extra et in omnibus locis cum saca et soka et toll et team et Infangenthef et cum omnibus consuetudinibus et libertatibus et quietudinibus T[estibus] Ep'o Bern[ardo] de S'cto D., et Nigello Ep'o de Ely, et Rob[erto] Com[ite] Gloec[estrie] et Milon[e] Com[ite] He[re]ford et Brienc[io] fil[io] Com[itis] et Unfr[ido] de Bub[un] et Joh[ann]e fil[io] Gilleb[erti] et Walkel[ino] Maminot et Milon[e] de Belloc[ampo] et Gaufr[edo] de Walt[er]vyll[a] et Steph[ano] de Belloc[ampo] et Rob[er]to de Colevill et Isnardo park[?ario] Gaufr[edo] de Abbetot Gilleb[erto] Arch' Nich[olao] fil[io] Isnardi. Apud Oxineford."

NOTES ON THE CHARTER.

There can, I think, be little question that this charter passed at Oxford just after that by which Miles of Gloucester was created Earl of Hereford (July 25, 1141). It is certainly previous to the Earl of Gloucester's departure from England in the summer of 1142, and I do not know of any evidence for the presence of these bishops with the Empress at Oxford after the rout of Winchester. The names of the eight first witnesses to this charter are all found in Miles's charter (*Fœdera*, *N.E.*, i. 14). As to the others, Miles de Beauchamp had held his castle of Bedford against Stephen (Christmas, 1137), and, though compelled to surrender it, had regained it on the triumph of the Empress. Stephen de Beauchamp heads the list of William de Beauchamp's under-tenants in his *Carta* (1166), and the Abetots—Heming's "Ursini"—also held of him. "Isnardus" was a landowner in Worcestershire and witnessed a charter to Evesham Abbey in 1130.

The text of this charter—which is taken from the Beauchamp Cartulary (*Add. MSS.*, 28,024, fol. 126 *b*), a most precious volume, of which the existence is little known—is perhaps corrupt in places, but the document affords several points of considerable interest. Among them are the formula "dedi et reddidi" applied to the grantee's previous possessions, as contrasted with the "dedi et concessi" of the new grant (60 "librates" of land) and of the grant of his relatives' inheritance; the reference to the hereditary shrievalty of Worcester; the allusion to Tamworth Castle as the head of its "honour" (as at Arundel); and the phrase "de hoc devenit . . . meus ligius homo contra omnes mortales," to be compared with "pro hiis . . . devenit homo noster ligius contra omnes homines" in the charter (1144) to Humfrey de Bohun (Pipe-Roll Society: *Ancient Charters*, p. 46), and the "homagium suum fecit ligie contra omnes homines" in the charter to Miles of Gloucester (see p. 56). The statement that active opponents of the Empress were precluded from compounding for their offence, except by special intervention, occurs, I think, here alone. The facts that Urse de Abetot was a constable and Walter de Beauchamp an hereditary "Dispenser" are also noteworthy, the latter bearing on the question of the succession to Robert "Dispensator" (see my remarks in *Ancient Charters*, p. 2).

APPENDIX M.

THE EARLDOM OF ARUNDEL.

(See p. 146.)

It is difficult to overrate the importance of the Canterbury charter to Geoffrey in its bearing on the origin and nature of this far-famed earldom. For centuries, antiquaries and lawyers have wrangled over this dignity, the premier earldom of England, but its true character and history have remained an unsolved enigma.

The popular belief that the dignity is "an earldom by tenure" and is annexed to the possession of Arundel Castle, is based on the petitions of John fitz Alan in 11 Hen. IV. and of Thomas Howard in 3 Car. I. This view would be strenuously upheld, of course, by the possessors of the castle, but neither their own *ex parte* statements, nor even the tacit admission of them by the Crown, can override the facts of the case as established by the evidence of history. The problem is for us, it should be added, of merely historical interest, as the dignity is now, and has been since 1627, held under a special parliamentary entail created in that year.

Even the warmest advocates of the "earldom by tenure" theory would admit that such an anomaly was absolutely unique of its kind. The *onus* of proving the fact must therefore rest on them, and the presumption, to put it mildly, is completely against them, for I do not hesitate to say that to a student of the dignity of an earl the proposition they ask us to accept is more than impossible : it is ludicrous.

Tierney endeavoured, with some skill, to rebut the arguments of Lord Redesdale in the *Reports of the Lords' Committee*, but the advance of historical research leaves them both behind. The latest words on the subject have been spoken by Mr. Pym

Yeatman, the confidence of whose assertions and the size of whose work[1] might convey the erroneous impression that he had solved this ancient riddle. I shall therefore here examine his arguments in some detail, and, having disposed of his theories, shall then discuss the facts.

An enthusiastic champion of the "earldom by tenure" theory, Mr. Yeatman has further advanced a view which is quite peculiar to himself. So far as this view can be understood, it "dimidiates" the first earl (d. 1176), and converts him into two, viz. a father who died about 1156, and a son who died in 1176. This is first described as "certain" (p. 281),[2] then as "probable" (p. 288),[3] lastly, as "possible" (p. 285).[4] But when we look for the foundation of the theory, and for evidence that the first earl died in 1156, we only read, to our confusion, that the doings of the Becket earl are "possibly" to be attributed to "his [the first earl's] son, and we must come to that conclusion, if we believe the only evidence we possess in relation to the death of his father in 1156; at any rate, before it is rejected some reason should be shown for doing so." Yet the only scrap of "evidence" given us is the incidental remark (p. 283) that "the year 1156 is usually assigned as that of the death of the first Earl of Arundel." Now, this is directly contrary to fact. For Mr. Yeatman himself tells us that Dugdale's is "the generally received account" (p. 282), and Dugdale, like every one else, kills the first earl in 1176.[5] Again, it is "very certain," we learn, that the Earl of Arundel "died the 3rd (*sic*) of October, 1176" (p. 281), while "Diceto is the authority for the statement that William Albini, Earl of Arundel, died the 17th (*sic*) of October, 1176" (p. 285), the actual words of the chronicler being given as "iv. die Octobus"

---

[1] *The Early Genealogical History of the House of Arundel* (1882).

[2] "Very certain it is that William Earl of Arundel died the 3rd (*sic*) of October, 1176, and equally certain is it that this was the son of the first earl."

[3] Where the earl of the Becket quarrel is described as "probably his [the first earl's] son."

[4] "It is possible that the new earl [son of the earl who died 1176] was the grandson of the first Earl of Arundel."

[5] Weever similarly kills him in 1176, though he wrongly assigns the death of his father (the founder of Wymondham) to 3 Hen. II.

(*sic*). Now, all three dates, as a matter of fact, are wrong, though this is only introduced to show how the laborious researches of the author are marred by a carelessness which is fatal to his work.

Let us now turn to this argument :—

"The foundation charter of Bungay, in Suffolk, contains the first entry known to the author of the title of Earl of Sussex. It was founded in 1160 by Roger de Glanville. . . . This charter seems to confirm the statement that the first Earl of Arundel died about 1156. If not, he too was styled Earl of Sussex. It disposes as well of the theory that the first (*sic*) Earl of Arundel was so created [1] in 1176" (p. 284).

This argument is based on the fact that the house was "founded in 1160." The *Monasticon* editors indeed say that this was "about" the date, but, unluckily, a moment's examination of the list of witnesses to the charter shows that its date must be much later,[2] while Mr. Eyton unhesitatingly assigns it to 1188. All the above argument, therefore, falls to the ground.

Another point on which the author insists as of great importance is that the first earl was never Earl of *Sussex* :—

"The first Earl of Arundel was never called Earl of Sussex, nor did he bear that title. . . . His son was the first Earl of Sussex, and he would certainly have given his father the higher title if he ever bore it. Yet in confirming his charter to Wymondham, William, Earl of Sussex, confirms the grants of his . . . father, William, the venerable Earl of Arundel. . . . An earl could not call himself the earl of a county unless he had a grant of it, and of this, with respect to the husband of Queen Adeliza, there is no evidence" (p. 282).

"That his son was called Earl of Sussex, and that he was the first earl, is equally clear" (p. 282).

"The chartulary of the Abbey of Buckenham, which the first Earl of Arundel founded, preserves the distinction in the titles of himself and his son and successor already insisted upon. It was founded *tempe* Stephen, and the founder is styled William, Count of Chichester. William, Count of Sussex, confirms the charter" (p. 284).

But on the very next page he demolishes his own argument by quoting Hoveden to the effect that "Willielmus (*sic*) de Albineio filio Willielmi Comitis de *Arundel* [Rex] dedit comi-

[1] ? created Earl of Sussex.
[2] Bishop John of Norwich, for instance, was not elected till 1175.

THE EARLDOM WAS THAT OF SUSSEX. 319

tatum de *Southsex*." For here his own rule would require that if the late earl was, as he admits, Earl of *Sussex*, he would not be described as Earl of *Arundel*.[1]

But, in any case, the still existing charter to Geoffrey de Mandeville (1141), which the earl attests as "Earl of Sussex" (evidence which does not stand alone), is absolutely conclusive on the subject, and simply annihilates Mr. Yeatman's attempts to deny to the husband of Queen Adeliza the possession of that title.

With this there falls to the ground the argument based on that denial, viz. :—

"There is another argument which appears to have been lost sight of, which proves distinctly that there was (*sic*) at least five earls, and probably six, of the name of William de Albini. The record of the 12 Henry III. which was made *after* the last earl of that name was dead three years proves that there were four Earls of Sussex. . . . Now, the first Earl of Arundel was never called Earl of Sussex, nor did he bear that title," etc. (p. 282).

The above argument that the record in question proves the existence of *five*, not of four, earls thus falls to the ground. But this is by no means all. Mr. Yeatman first asserts (p. 281 *a*) that there were five Albini Earls of Arundel in all, "if indeed there were not six of them." Deducting the last earl, Hugh de Albini, this leaves us *four* or *five* Earl Williams in succession. Yet on the very next page he urges it (in the above passage) as "distinctly proved" that "there was (*sic*) at least *five* earls, and probably *six*, of the name of William de Albini." And, lastly, on p. 284, he announces that "there must have been *six*"!

We will now dismiss from our minds all that has been written on the point by Mr. Yeatman and other antiquaries, and turn to the facts of the case, which are few and beyond dispute. It is absolutely certain, from the evidence of contemporary chronicles and charters, that the first Albini earl,

[1] Mr. Yeatman attempts to get over this difficulty by suggesting that "Henry's charter to William, Earl of Arundel, styling himself [? him] incidentally Earl of Sussex, shows that these earls bore both titles [*i.e.* Arundel and Sussex], just as the first earl was called of Chichester as well as of Arundel" (p. 285). But this alternative use of Arundel and Sussex is precisely what the author denies above, in the case of the first earl, as impossible.

the husband of Queen Adeliza, was indifferently styled at the time (1) Earl of Sussex, (2) Earl of Chichester, (3) Earl of Arundel, (4) Earl William de Albini. The proofs of user of these styles are as follows. First, he attests as Earl of Sussex the Canterbury charter to the Earl of Essex (Christmas, 1141);[1] he also attests as Earl of Sussex Stephen's charter to Barking Abbey, which may have passed about the same time. As this charter is of importance for the argument, I append the full list of witnesses as extracted by me from the Patent Rolls:—

"Matild[a] Regina & Will[elm]o Comite de Sudsexa, & Will[elm]o Mart[el], & Adam de Belum, & Rog[ero] de Fraxin[eto] & Reinald[o] fil[io] Comitis, & Henr[ico] de Novo Mercato, & Ric[ard]o de Valderi, & Godefrid[o] de Petrivilla, & Warn[erio] de Lusoris, Apud Berching[es]."[2]

Secondly, it is as "Earl of Chichester" that he attests four charters,[3] one of which is dated 1147, and is confirmed by King Stephen as the grant "quod Comes Willelmus de *Arundel* fecit;" it is also as Earl of Chichester that he appears in the Buckenham foundation charter,[4] and that he confirms the grants to Boxgrove.[5] As to the two other styles no question arises.

Thus the case of the earldom of Arundel is one of special interest in its bearing on the adoption of comital titles. For it affords, according to the view I have advanced, an example of the use, in a single case, of all the four possible varieties of an earl's title. These four possible varieties are those in which the title is taken (1) from the county of which the bearer is earl, (2) from the capital town of that county, (3) from the earl's chief residence, (4) from his family name. Strictly speaking, when an earl was created, it was always (whatever may be pretended) as the earl of a particular county. The earl and his county were essentially correlative; nor was it then possible to conceive an earl unattached to a county. Titles, however, like surnames in that period of transition, had not yet crystallized into a hard and fast form, and it was

[1] *Supra*, p. 143.
[2] It is not safe from the concurrence of only three witnesses to assign this charter positively to the same period as the Canterbury one. The grant which it records is that of the hundred of Barstable, which Stephen offered "super altare beatæ Mariæ et beatæ Athelburgæ in ecclesia de Berching[es] per unum cultellum" (Pat. 2 Hen. VI., p. 3, m. 18).
[3] *Monasticon*, vi. 1169.   [4] *Ibid.*, vi. 419.   [5] *Ibid.*, vi. 645.

deemed unnecessary, when speaking of an earl, that his county should always be mentioned. Men spoke of "Earl Geoffrey," or of "Geoffrey, Earl of Essex," just as they spoke of "King Henry," or of "Henry, King of the English." If the simple "Earl Geoffrey" was not sufficiently distinctive, they added his surname, or his residence, or his county for the purpose of identification. The secondary importance of this addition is the key to Norman polyonomy. The founder, for instance, of the house of Clare was known as Richard "Fitz-Gilbert," or "de Tunbridge," or "de Bienfaite," or "de Clare." The result of this system, or rather want of system, was, as we might expect, in the case of earls, that no fixed principle guided the adoption of their styles. It was indeed a matter of haphazard which of their *cognomina* prevailed, and survived to form the style by which their descendants were known. Thus, the Earls of Herts and of Surrey, of Derby and of Bucks, were usually spoken of by their family names of Clare and of Warenne, of Ferrers and of Giffard; on the other hand the Earls of Norfolk and of Essex, of Devon and of Cornwall, were more usually styled by those of their counties. Where the name of the county was formed from that of its chief town, the latter, rather than the county itself, was adopted for the earl's style. Familiar instances are found in the earldoms of Chester, Gloucester, and Hereford, of Lincoln, of Leicester, and of Warwick. Rarest, perhaps, are those cases in which the earl took his style from his chief residence, as the Earls of Pembroke-(shire) from Striguil (Chepstow), and, perhaps, of Wiltshire from Salisbury, though here the case is a doubtful one, for "de Salisbury" was already the surname of the family when the earldom was conferred upon it. The Earl of Gloucester is spoken of by the Continuator of Florence of Worcester as "Earl of Bristol" (see p. 284), and the Earls of Derby occasionally as Earls "of Tutbury," but the most remarkable case, of course, is that of Arundel itself. It was doubtful for a time by which style this earldom would eventually be known, and "Sussex," under Henry II., seemed likely to prevail. The eventual adoption of Arundel was, no doubt, largely due to the importance of that "honour" and of the castle which formed its "head."

Having now established that the earldom of "Arundel"

was from the first the earldom of a county, and thus similar to every other, one is led to inquire on what ground there is claimed for it an absolutely unique and wholly anomalous origin. I reply: on none whatever. There is nothing to rebut the legitimate assumption that William de Albini was created an earl in the ordinary course of things. Here, again, the facts of the case, few and simple though they are, have been so overlaid by assumption and by theory that it is necessary to state them anew. All that has been hitherto really known is that Queen Adeliza married William de Albini between King Henry's death (December, 1135) and the landing of the Empress in the autumn of 1139, and that her husband subsequently appears as an earl. The assertion that he became an earl on his marriage, in virtue of his possession of Arundel Castle, is pure assumption and nothing else.[1] I have already dwelt on the value of the Canterbury charter to Geoffrey as evidence not only that William was Earl "of Sussex," but also that he was already an earl at Christmas, 1141. In that charter I claim to have discovered the earliest contemporary record mention of this famous earldom.[2] William, therefore, became an earl between Christmas, 1135, and Christmas, 1141. This much is certain.

The key to the problem, however, is found in another quarter. The curious and valuable *Chronicle of the Holy Cross of Waltham* (*Harl. MS.*, 3776) was the work of one who was acquainted—indeed, too well acquainted—with the persons and

[1] Robert of Torigny, a contemporary witness, speaks of him, in 1139, as "Willelmus de Albinneio, qui duxerat Aeliz quondam reginam, quæ habebat castellum et comitatum Harundel, quod rex Henricus dederat ei in dote." The possession of Arundel by Queen Adeliza may probably be accounted for by William of Malmesbury's statement that Henry I. had settled Shropshire on her,—" uxori suæ . . . comitatum Salopesberiæ dedit" (ed. Stubbs, ii. 529),—for this would represent the forfeited inheritance of the house of Montgomery, including Arundel and its rights over Sussex. A curious incidental allusion in the *Dialogus* (i. 7) to "Salop, *Sudsex*, Northumberland, et Cumberland" having only come to pay their *firmæ* to the Crown "per incidentes aliquos casus," suggests that, like his neighbour in Cheshire, Roger de Montgomery had palatine rights, including the *firmæ* of both his counties, Shropshire and Sussex, which escheated to the Crown on the forfeiture of his heir.

[2] See p. 146.

THE CASTLE DID NOT CONFER THE EARLDOM. 323

the doings of those two nobles, Geoffrey de Mandeville and William de Albini. His own neighbourhood became their battleground, and when William harried Geoffrey's manors, and Geoffrey, in revenge, fired Waltham, he was among the sufferers himself.[1] The pictures he draws of these rival magnates are, therefore, of peculiar interest, and his admiration for Geoffrey is so remarkable, in the face of the earl's wild deeds, that no apology is needed for quoting the description in full :—

"E contra Gaufridus iste præcellens multiformi gratia, præcipuus totius Anglie, militia quidem præclivis, morum venustate præclarus, in consiliis regis et regni moderamine cunctis præminens, agebat se inter ceteros quasi unus ex illis, nullius probitatis suæ garrulus, nullius probitatis sibi collatæ vel dignitatis nimius ostensator, rei suæ familiaris providus dispensator, omnium virtutum communium quæ tantum decerent virum affluentia exuberans, si Dei gratiam diligentius acceptam et ceteris prelatam, diligens executor menti suæ sedulus imprimeret; novit populus quod non mentior, quem si laudibus extulerim, meritis ejus assignari potius quam gratiæ nostræ id debere credimus, verumptamen gratiæ divinæ de cujus munere venit quicquid boni provenit homini" (cap. 29).

"Tempore igitur incendii supra memorati, dum observaret comes ille ecclesiam cum multis ne succenderetur, amicissimus ipse et devotus ecclesiæ, afflictus multo dolore quod periclitarentur res ecclesiæ (non tamen poterat manentibus illis injuriam sibi illatam vindicare)," etc. (cap. 31).

As eager to denounce the character of William as to palliate the excesses of Geoffrey, the chronicler thus sketches the husband of Queen Adeliza :—

"Seditionis tempore, cum se inæqualiter agerent homines in terra nostra, et de pari contenderet modicus cum magno, humilis cum summo, et fide penitus subacta, nullo respectu habito servi ad dominum, sic vacillaret regnum et regni status miserabili ductore premeretur fere usque ad exanimationem, e vicino contendebant inter se duo de præcipuis terræ baronibus, Gaufridus de Mandeville, et Comes de Harundel, quem post discessum Regis Henrici conjugio Reginæ Adelidis contigit honorari, unde et superbire et supra se extolli cœpit ultra modum, ut [non] posset sibi pati parem, et vilesceret in oculis suis quicquid præcipuum præter regem in se habebat noster mundus. Habebat tunc temporis Willelmus ille, pincerna, nondum

---

[1] "Intra se igitur tanti viri pacis et tranquillitatis metas excedentes et seditiose alter alterius predia vastantes contigit Gaufridum furore exagitatum, quia succenderat Willelmus domos suas et universam predam terræ suæ abigi fecerat villam Walthamensem succendere nec posse domibus canonicorum parcere quia reliquis domibus erant contigue, testimonium prohibemus qui et dampna cum ceteris sustinuimus" (*Harl. MS.*, 3776). Compare p. 222. supra.

comes, dotem reginæ Waltham, contiguam terris comitis Gaufridi de Mandeville, impatiens quidem omnium comprovincialium terras suo dominio non mancipari.[1]

In the words "nondum comes" we find the clue we seek. If the writer had merely abstained from giving William his title, the value of his evidence would be slight; but when he goes, as it were, out of his way to inform us that though William, in virtue of his marriage, was already in possession of the queen's dower, he was "not yet an earl," he tells us, in unmistakable language, the very thing that we want to know. It was probably in order to accentuate his pride that his critic reminds us that the future earl was as yet only a *pincerna*;[2] but, whatever the motive, the fact remains, on first-hand evidence, that William was "not yet an earl" at a time when he possessed his wife's dower, and consequently Arundel Castle. This fact, hitherto overlooked, is completely destructive of the time-honoured belief that he acquired the earldom on, and by, obtaining possession of the castle.

So far, all is clear. But the question is further complicated by William appearing in two distinct documents as earl, not of Arundel or Chichester, but of Lincoln! That he held this title is a fact so utterly unsuspected, and indeed so incredible, that Mr. Eyton, finding him so styled in a cartulary of Lewes

---

[1] There is a curious incidental allusion to the possession of Waltham by the Earl of Arundel (jure uxoris) in the *Testa de Nevill* (p. 270 b). In an inquisition of John's reign we have the entry: "Menigarus le Napier dicit quod Rex Henricus, avus [*lege* proavus] domini Regis feodavit antecessores suos per serjantiam de Naperie et dicit quod *quando comes de Arundel duxit Reginam Aliciam in uxorem* removit illud servicium et fecit inde reddere xx sol. per annum et predictus Menigarus tenet," etc. That is, that while Waltham was in Henry's hands, he had enfeoffed this man's predecessor by serjeanty, but that, this tenure becoming inept when the manor passed to a private owner, the earl substituted for it an annual money rent. Note here how Henry provided for his widow from escheats rather than Crown demesne, and observe the origin of the name "Napier," comparing *Testa*, p. 115: "Robertus Napparius habet feodum unius militis de hereditate uxoris suæ . . . dominus Rex perdonavit predicto Roberto et heredibus ejus per cartam suam predictum servicium militare per unam nappam de precio iii sol. vel per tres solidos reddendo pro precio illius nappæ." And p. 118: "Thomas Napar tenet terram suam . . . per serjantiam reddendo singulis annis unam nappam . . . et debet esse naparius domini Regis."

[2] This proves, incidentally, the fact that he had succeeded his father in this office at the time.

WILLIAM STYLED EARL OF LINCOLN.

Priory, dismissed the title, without hesitation, as an obvious error of the scribe.[1] But I have identified in the Public Record Office the actual charter from which the scribe worked, and the same style is there employed. Even so, error is possible; but the evidence does not stand alone. In a cartulary of Reading[2] we find William confirming, as Earl of Lincoln, a grant from the queen, his wife, and here again the original charter is there to prove that the cartulary is right.[3] The early history of the earldom of Lincoln is already difficult enough without this additional complication, of which I do not attempt to offer any solution.

But so far as the earldom of "Arundel" is concerned, I claim to have established its true character, and to have shown that there is nothing to distinguish it in its origin from the other earldoms of the day. The erratic notion of "earldom by tenure," held when the strangest views prevailed as to peerage dignities, was a fallacy of the *post hoc propter hoc* kind, based on the long connection of the castle with the earls. Nor has Mr. Freeman's strange fancy that the holder of this earldom is "the only one of his class left" any better foundation in fact.

[1] Speaking of the earl's confirmation of a grant by Alan de Dunstanville to Lewes Priory, of lands at Newtimber, he writes: "This confirmation purports to be that of William, Earl of *Lincoln*, but is addressed to his barons and men of the honour of Arundel. The mistake of the transcriber is obvious" (*History of Shropshire*, ii. 273).

[2] *Harl. MS.*, 1708, fol. 97.

[3] *Add. Cart.*, 19,586: "Ego Willelmus, Comes Lincolnie."

APPENDIX N.

ROBERT DE VERE.

(See p. 128.)

THIS personage, who, as charters show, was in constant attendance on Stephen, is usually, and very naturally, taken by genealogists, from Mr. Eyton downwards, for a younger brother of Aubrey de Vere (the chamberlain) and uncle of the first Earl of Oxford. He was, however, quite distinct, being a son of Bernard de Vere. He owed his position to a marriage with Adeline, daughter of Hugh de Montfort, as recorded on the Pipe-Roll of 1130. By this marriage he became possessed of the honour of Haughley ("Haganet"), and with it (it is important to observe) of the office of constable, in which capacity he figures among the witnesses to Stephen's Charter of Liberties (1136). In conjunction with his wife he founded, on her Kentish estate, the Cluniac priory of Monks Horton. They were succeeded, in their tenure of the honour, by the well-known Henry of Essex, who thus became constable in his turn. As supporting this view that the honour carried the constableship, attention may be drawn to its *compotus* as "Honor Constabularie" in 1189–90 (*Rot. Pip.*, 1 Ric. I., pp. 14, 15), just before that of the "Terra que fuit Henrici de Essex." It is therefore worth consideration whether Robert de Montfort, general to William Rufus—" strator Normannici exercitus hereditario jure "—may not have really held the post of constable.

The history of the Montfort fief in Kent is of interest from the Conquest downwards owing to its inclusion of Saltwood and other estates claimed by the Archbishops of Canterbury.[1]

---

[1] Saltwood was granted by the Conqueror to Hugh de Montfort, was recovered by Lanfranc in the great *placitum* on Pennenden Heath, was thereafter held by the Montforts from the archbishop as two knights' fees,

THE HEREDITARY CONSTABLESHIP. 327

Dugdale is terribly at sea in his account of the Montfort descent, wrongly affiliating the Warwickshire Thurstan (ancestor of the Lords Montfort) to the Kentish house, and confusing his generations wholesale (especially in the case of Adeline, wife of William de Breteuil).

The fact that Henry of Essex was appealed of treason and defeated in the trial by battle by a Robert de Montfort (1163), suggests that a grudge on the part of a descendant of the dispossessed line against himself as possessor of their fief may have been at the bottom of this somewhat mysterious affair.

was so held by Henry of Essex as their successor, was seized by the Crown upon his forfeiture, was persistently claimed by Becket, and was finally restored to the see by Richard I.

NOTE.—Since the above was in type, there has appeared (*Rot. Pip.*, 15 Hen. II., p. 111) a most valuable *compotus* of the 'Honor Constabularie' (with a misleading head-line) for 1169, proving that Gilbert de Gant had held it, at one time, under Stephen, and had alienated nearly a third of it.

APPENDIX O.

"TOWER AND CASTLE."

(See p. 149.)

The description of the Tower by the Empress, in her charter, as "turris Londonie cum parvo castello quod fuit Ravengeri," and its similar description in Stephen's charter as "turris Lond[oniæ] cum castello quod ei subest," though at first sight singular and obscure, are fraught, when explained, with interest and importance in their bearing on military architecture.

It will be found, on reference to the charter granted to Aubrey de Vere (p. 180), that the Empress gives him Colchester Castle as "turrim et castellum de Colcestr[a]," a grant confirmed by her son as that of "turrim de Colcestr[a] et castellum" (p. 185 n.), and, in later days, by Henry VIII., as "Castrum et turrim de Colcestr[a]."[1] Further, in the charter to William de Beauchamp (p. 313), we find Worcester Castle described as "castellum de Wigorn[ia] cum mota," Hereford Castle being similarly described in the charter granted at the same time to Miles de Gloucester as "motam Hereford cum toto castello." Before proceeding to the inferences to be drawn from these expressions, it may be as well to strengthen them by other parallel examples. Taking first the case of Colchester, we turn to a charter of Henry I., granted to his favourite, Eudo Dapifer, at the Christmas court of 1101,[2] in which Colchester Castle is similarly described:—

"Henricus Rex Angliæ Mauricio Lond. Episcopo et Hugoni de Bochelanda et omnibus baronibus suis Anglis et Francis de Essex salutem. Sciatis me dedisse benigne et ad amorem concessisse Eudoni Dapifero meo Civitatem de Colecestrâ et *turrim et castellum* et omnes ejusdem civitatis firmitates Cum omnibus quæ ad illam pertinent sicut pater meus et frater et ego eam melius

---

[1] *Fœdera* (O.E.), xiii. 251. See p. 179.
[2] The internal evidence determines its date.

habuimus et cum omnibus consuetudinibus illis quas pater meus et frater et ego in eâ unquam habuimus. Et hæc concessio facta fuit apud Westmonaster in primo natali post concordiam Roberti comitis fratris mei de me et de illo.

"T. Rob. Ep. Lincoln et W. Gifardo Wintoniensi electo et Rob. Com. de Mellent. et Henr. Com. fr. ejus et Roger Bigoto et Gisleberti fil. Richard et Rob. fil. Baldwin et Ric. fratr. ejus."[1]

Turning to Hereford, we find its description as "mota cum toto castello" recurring in the confirmation by Henry II. and the recital of that confirmation by John.[2] There is another example sufficiently important to deserve separate treatment. This is that of Gloucester.

We find that, in 1137, "Milo constabularius Glocestrie" granted to the canons of "Llanthony the Second"

"Tota oblatio custodum *turris et castelli* et Baronum ibi commorantium."[3]

Here again the correctness of the description is fortunately confirmed by subsequent evidence; for John recites (April 28, 1200) a charter of his father, Henry II. (which is assigned by Mr. Eyton to the spring of 1155), granting to Miles's son, Roger, Earl of Hereford,

"custodiam *turris Gloc'* cum toto castello," etc., etc. . . . "per eandem firmam quam reddere solebat comes Milo pater ejus tempore H. R. avi mei;"[4]

while Robert of Torigny speaks, independently, of "discordia quæ erat inter regem Anglorum Henricum et Rogerium, filium Milonis de Gloecestria, propter *turrim* Gloecestrie."[5] The

---

[1] "Collectanea quædam eorum quæ ad Historiam illustrandam conducunt selecta ex Registro MSS. sive breviario Monasterii sancti Johannis Baptistæ Colecestriæ collecto (*sic*) a Joh. Hadlege spectante Johanni Lucas armigero. Anno Domini, 1633" (*Harl. MS.*, 312, fol. 92). This charter (which, being in MS., was unknown, of course, to Prof. Freeman) has also an incidental value for its evidence on the Clare pedigree, Gilbert, Robert, and Richard, the witnesses, being all grandsons of Count Gilbert, the progenitor of the house. Among the documents in the *Monasticon* relating to Bec, we find mention of " Emmæ uxoris Baldewini filii Comitis Gilberti et filiorum ejus Roberti et Ricardi," which singularly confirms the accuracy of this charter and its list of witnesses. This is worth noting, because the charter is curious in form, and has been described as having "a suspicious ring." It is also found in (Morant's) transcript of the Colchester cartulary (*Stowe MSS.*).

[2] *Cart.*, 1 John, m. 6.   [3] *Mon. Ang.* (1661), ii. 66 b.

[4] *Cart.*, 1 John, m. 6 (printed in Appendix 5 to *Lords' Reports on Dignity of a Peer*, pp. 4, 5).

[5] Ed. Howlett, p. 184.

"tower" of Gloucester is also referred to in the Pipe-Roll of 1156,[1] and in the Cartulary of Gloucester Abbey.[2] The importance of its mention lies in the fact that it establishes the character of Gloucester Castle, and proves that what the leading authority has written on the subject is entirely erroneous. Mr. G. T. Clark, in his great work on our castles, refers thus to Gloucester:—

"The castle of Gloucester . . . was the base of all extended operations in South Wales. Here the kings of England often held their court, and here their troops were mustered. Brichtric had a castle at Gloucester, *but his mound has long been removed, and with it all traces of the Norman building.*"[3]

In another place he goes further still:—

"Gloucester, a royal castle, stood on the Severn bank, at one angle of the Roman city. *It had a mound and a shell-keep, now utterly levelled,* and the site partially built over. It was the muster-place and starting-point for expeditions against South Wales, and the not infrequent residence of the Norman sovereigns."[4]

It may seem rash, in the teeth of these assertions, to maintain that this mound and its shell-keep are alike imaginary, but the word "turris" proves the fact. For, as Mr. Clark himself observes with perfect truth,

"in the convention between Stephen and Henry of Anjou [1153] the distinction is drawn between '*Turris* Londinensis et *Mota* de Windesorâ,' London having a square keep or tower, and Windsor a shell-keep upon a mound."[5]

So the keep of Gloucester, being a "turris" and not a "mota," was clearly "a square tower" and not "a shell-keep upon a mound." The fact is that Mr. Clark's assertions would seem to be a guess based on the hypothesis, itself (as could be shown) untenable, that "Brichtric had a castle at Gloucester." Assuming from this the existence of a mound, he must further have assumed that the Normans had crowned it, as elsewhere, with a shell-keep. But the true character of this great fortress is now determined.

[1] "In operibus Turris de Gloec' vii *li.* vi *s.* ii *d.*" (Pipe-Roll, 2 Hen. II., p. 78).
[2] Henry I. gave land to the abbey (1109) "in escambium pro placia ubi nunc turris stat Gloecestrie" (i. 59).
[3] *Mediæval Military Architecture*, i. 108.   [4] *Ibid.*, i. 79.
[5] *Ibid.*, i. 29 (cf. "Mota de Hereford"—*Rot. Pip.*, 15 Hen. II., p. 140).

TWO FACTORS IN A FORTRESS. 331

Two examples of the double style shall now be adduced from castles outside England. In Normandy we have an entry, in 1180, referring to expenditure "in operationibus domorum *turris et castri*," etc., at Caen;[1] in Ireland the grant of Dublin Castle to Hugh de Laci (1172) is thus related in the so-called poem of Matthew Regan (ll. 2713-2716):—

> "Li riche rei ad dunc baillé
> Dyvelin en garde la cité
> *E la chastel e le dongun*
> A Huge de Laci le barun."

The phrase, it will be seen, corresponds exactly with those employed to describe the castles of Carlisle and Appleby, at the same period:—

> "Mès voist au rei Henri, si face sa clamur
> Que jo tieng Carduil, *le chastel e la tur.*"
> "Li reis out ubblié par itant sa dolur
> Quant avait Appelbi, *le chastel e la tur.*"[2]

Having thus established the use of the phrase, let us now pass to its origin.

I would urge that it possesses the peculiar value of a genuine transition form. It preserves for us, as such, the essential fact that there went to the making of the mediæval "castle" two distinct factors, two factors which coalesced so early that the original distinction between them was already being rapidly forgotten, and is only to be detected in the faint echoes of this "transition form."

The two factors to which I refer were the Roman *castrum* or *castellum* and the mediæval "motte" or "tour." The former survived in the *fortified enclosure*; the latter, in the *central keep*. The Latin word *castellum* (corresponding with the Welsh *caer*) continued to be regularly used as descriptive of a fortified enclosure, whether surrounded by walls or earthworks.[3] It is

[1] *Rotuli scaccarii Normanniæ* (ed. Stapleton), i. 56. The "turris" had been added by Henry I. (*vide infra*, p. 333). With the above entry may be compared the phrase in one of Richard's despatches (1198)—"castrum cepimus cum turre" (*R. Howden*, iv. 58); also the expression, "tunc etiam comes turrem et castellum funditus evertit," applied to Geoffrey's action at Montreuil (*circ.* 1152) by Robert de Torigny (ed. Howlett, p. 159).

[2] *Chronique de Jordan Fantosme* (ed. Howlett), ll. 1423, 1424, 1469, 1470.

[3] It is even applied by Giraldus Cambrensis to the turf entrenchment thrown up by Arnulf de Montgomery at Pembroke.

singular how much confusion has resulted from the overlooking of this simple fact and the retrospective application of the denotation of the later "castle." Thus Theodore, in the seventh century, styles the Bishop of Rochester, "Episcopus *Castelli* Cantuariorum, *quod dicitur Hrofesceaster* " (*Bæda*, iv. 5); and Mr. Clark gives several instances, from the eighth and ninth centuries, in which Rochester is alternatively styled a " civitas " and a " castellum." [1] So again, in the ninth century, where the chroniclers, in 876 A.D., describe how " bestæl se here into Werham," etc., Asser and Florence paraphrase the statement by saying that the host "*castellum quod dicitur Werham* intravit." Now, it is obvious that there could be no " castle " at Wareham in 876, and that even if there had been, an "army " could not have entered it. But when we bear in mind the true meaning of "castellum," at once all is clear. As Professor Freeman observes, "Wareham is a fortified town."[2] Its famous and ancient defences are thus described by Mr. Clark:—

"In figure the town is nearly square, the west face about 600 yards, the north face 650 yards . . . The outline of this rectangular figure is an earthwork, within which the town was built." [3]

Such then was the nature of the " castellum," within which the host took shelter.[4] Passing now to a different instance, we find the Greek κώμη (" a village ") represented by "castellum " in the Latin Gospels (Matt. xxi. 2), and this actually Englished as " castel " in the English Gospels of 1000 A.D.[5] Here again, confusion has resulted from a misunderstanding.

---

[1] *M. M. A.*, ii. 420.   [2] *English Towns and Districts*, p. 152.

[3] *Mediæval Military Architecture*, ii. 514.

[4] There is a strange use of "castellum," apparently in this sense, in William of Malmesbury's version (ii. 119) of Godwine's speech on the Dover riot (1051). The phrase is " magnates *illius castelli*," which Mr. Freeman unhesitatingly renders " the magistrates of that *town* " (*Norm. Conq.*, 2nd ed., ii. 135), a rendering which should be compared with his remarks on " castles " on the next page but one, and in Appendix S. Mr. Clark is of opinion that " whether ' castellum ' can [here] be taken for more than the fortified town is uncertain " (*M. M. A.*, ii. 8).

[5] Skeat's *Etymological Dictionary;* Oliphant's *Old and Middle English*, p. 37. It is not, therefore, strictly accurate to say of the expression "æune castel," in the chronicle for 1048, that it was "no English name," as Mr. Freeman asserts (*Norm. Conq.*, 2nd ed., ii. 137), or to imply that it then first appeared in the language.

As against the *castellum*, the fortified enclosure, we have a new and distinct type of fortress, the outcome of a different state of society, in the single "motte" or "tour." I shall not here enter into the controversy as to the relation between these two forms, my space being too limited. For the present, we need only consider the "motte" (*mota*) as a mound (*agger*) crowned by a stronghold (whether of timber or masonry), but *not*, as Mr. Clark has clearly shown, "crowned with the square donjon," as so strangely imagined by Mr. Freeman.[1] In the "tour" (*turris*) we have, of course, the familiar keep of masonry, rectangular in form, and independent of a mound.

The process, then, that we are about to trace is that by which the "motte" or "tour" coalesced with the *castellum*, and by which, from this combination, there was evolved the later "castle." For my theory amounts to this: in the mediæval fortress, the keep and the *castellum* were elements different in origin, and, for a time, looked upon as distinct. It was impossible that the compound fortress, the result of their combination, should long retain a compound name: there must be one name for the entire fortress, either "tour" (*turris*) or "chastel" (*castellum*). Which was to prevail?

This question may have been decided by either of two considerations. On the one hand, the relative importance of the two factors in the fortress may have determined the ultimate form of its style; on the other—and this, perhaps, is the more probable explanation—the older of the two factors may have given its name to the whole. For sometimes the keep was added to the "castle," and sometimes the "castle" to the keep. The former development is the more familiar, and three striking instances in point will occur below. For the present I will only quote a passage from Robert de Torigny, to whom we are specially indebted for evidence on military architecture:—

[1123] "Henricus rex . . . turrem nihilominus excelsam fecit in castello Cadomensi, et murum ipsius castelli, quem pater suus fecerat, in altum crevit. . . . Item castellum quod vocatur Archas, turre et mœnibus mirabiliter firmavit. . . . Turrem Vernonis similiter fecit."[2]

---

[1] *Norman Conquest* (2nd ed.), ii. 189.

[2] Ed. Howlett, p. 106. Robert also mentions (p. 126) the "towers" of Evreux, Alençon, and Coutances as among those constructed by Henry I.

More interesting for us is the other case, that in which the "castle" was added to the keep, because it is that of the respective strongholds in the capitals of Normandy and of England. The "Tower of Rouen" and the "Tower of London" —for such were their well-known names—were both older than their surrounding wards (*castra* or *castella*). William Rufus built a wall "circa turrim Londoniæ" (*Henry of Huntingdon*):[1] his brother and successor built a wall "circa turrim Rothomagi."[2] The former enclosed what is now known as "the Inner Ward" of the Tower,[3] the "parvum castellum" of Maud's charter.[4]

Of "the Tower of Rouen" I could say much. Perhaps its earliest undoubted mention is in or about 1078 (the exact date is doubtful), when Robert "Courthose," revolting from his father "Rotomagum expetiit, et *arcem regiam* furtim præoccupare sategit. Verum Rogerius de Iberico . . . qui turrim

---

[1] "About the Tower," as the chronicle expresses it.

[2] "Henricus Rex circa turrem Rothomagi . . . murum altum et latum cum propugnaculis ædificat, et ædificia ad mansionem regiam congrua infra eundem murum parat" (*Robert of Torigny*, ed. Howlett, p. 106).

[3] I can make nothing of Mr. Clark's chronology. In his description of the Tower he first tells us that "all save the keep [*i.e.* the White Tower] is later, and most of it considerably later than the eleventh century" (*M. M.A.*, ii. 205), and then that "the Tower of the close of the reign of Rufus" (i.e. *before the end of* "the eleventh century") . . . was probably composed of the White Tower with a palace ward upon its south-east side, and a wall, probably that we now see, and certainly along its general course, including what is now known as the inner ward" (*ibid.*, ii. 253). Again, as to the Wakefield Tower, which "deserves very close attention, its lower story being next to the keep in antiquity" (*ibid.*, ii. 220), Mr. Clark tells us that Gundulf (who died in 1108) was the founder "perhaps of the Wakefield Tower" (*ibid.*, ii. 252); nay, that "Devereux Tower ". . . may be as old as Wakefield, and therefore in substance *the work of Rufus*" (*ibid.*, ii. 253); and yet we learn of this same basement, that "the basement of Wakefield Tower is probably late Norman, perhaps of the reign of Stephen or Henry II., although this is no doubt early for masonry so finely jointed" (*ibid.*, ii. 224). In other words, a structure which was "the work of Rufus," *i.e.* of 1087-1100, can only be attributed, at the very earliest, to the days of "Stephen or Henry II.," *i.e.* to 1135-1189.

[4] The very same phrase is employed by Robert de Torigny in describing her husband's action at Torigny ten years later (1151): "dux obsederat castellum Torinneium, sed propter adventum Regis infecto negotio discesserat; combustis tamen domibus infra muros usque ad turrem et *parvum castellum circa eam*" (ed. Howlett, p. 161).

custodiebat . . . diligenter arcem præmunivit," Ordericus here, as often, using *turris* and *arx* interchangeably.¹ Passing over other notices of this stronghold, we come in 1090 to one of those tragic deeds by which its history was destined to be stained.² Mr. Freeman has told the tale of Conan's attempt and doom.³ The duke, who was occupying the Tower, left it at the height of the struggle,⁴ but on the triumph of his party, and the capture of Conan, the prisoner was claimed by Henry for his prey and was led by him to an upper story of the Tower.⁵ At this point I pause to discuss the actual scene of the tragedy. Mr. Freeman writes as follows:—

"Conan himself was led into the castle, and there Henry took him . . . The Ætheling led his victim up through the several stages of the loftiest tower of the castle," etc., etc.⁶

Here the writer misses the whole point of the topography. The scene of Conan's death was no mere "tower of the castle," but "*the* Tower," the Tower of Rouen—*Rotomagensis turris*, as William here terms it. He fails to realize that the Tower of Rouen held a similar position to the Tower of London. Thus, in 1098, when Helias of Le Mans was taken prisoner, we read that "Rotomagum usque productus, in arce ipsius civitatis in vincula conjectus est" (*Vetera Analecta*), which Wace renders:—

> "Li reis à Roem l'enveia
> E garder le recomenda
> En la tour le rova garder."

---

¹ *Ord. Vit.*, ii. 296.

² A curious touch in a legend of the time brings before us in a vivid manner the impression that this mighty tower had made upon the Norman mind. Hugh de Glos, an oppressor of the poor, appearing, after death, to a priest by night (1090), declared that the burden he was compelled to bear seemed "heavier to carry than the Tower of Rouen" ("Ecce candens ferrum molendini gesto in ore, quod sine dubio mihi videtur ad ferendum gravius Rotomagensi arce."—*Ord. Vit.*, iii. 373).

³ *W. Rufus*, i. 245-260.

⁴ "De arce prodiit" (*Ord. Vit.*, iii. 353). *Arx*, here as above, is used as a substitute for *turris*.

⁵ "Conanus autem a victoribus in arcem ductus est. Quem Henricus per solaria turris ducens" (*ibid.*, iii. 355). "In superiora Rotomagensis turris duxit" (*W. Malms.*).

⁶ *W. Rufus*, i. 256, 257.

Again, even in the next reign, a royal charter, assigned by Mr. Eyton to 1114–15, is tested, not at the "castle" of Rouen, but "in *turre* Rothomagensi."[1] And so, two reigns after that, a century later than Conan's death, we find the *custodes* of "the Tower of Rouen" entered in the Exchequer Rolls, where it is repeatedly styled "turris."

Thus at Rouen, as at London, the "Tower" not only preserved its name, but ultimately imposed it on the whole fortress. And precisely as the Tower of London is mentioned in 1141 by the transition style of "turris Londoniæ cum castello," so in 1146 we find Duke Geoffrey repairing "sartatecta turris Rothomagensis et castelli," after it fell into his hands.[2]

Here then we have at length the explanation of a difficulty often raised. Why is "the Tower of London" so styled?[3] And although, in England, the style may now be unique, men spoke in the days of which I write of the "Tower" of Bristol or of Rochester as of the Tower of Gloucester.[4] Abroad, the form was more persistent, and special attention may be drawn to the Tower of Le Mans ("Turris Cenomannica),"[5] because the expression "regia turris" which Ordericus applies to it is precisely that which Florence of Worcester applies, in 1114, to the Tower of London, to which it bore an affinity in its relation to the Roman Wall.[6]

All that I have said of the "turris" keep is applicable to the "mota" also, *mutatis mutandis*, for the *motte*, though its name was occasionally extended to the whole fortress, was essentially the actual keep, the crowned mound, as is well brought out in the passages quoted by Mr. Clark from French charters:—

"Le motte *et les fossez d'entour* . . . le motte de Maiex . . . le motte de mon manoir de Caieux *et les fossez d'entour.*"[7]

---

[1] *Ord. Vit.*, v. (Appendix) 199. See p. 422.

[2] *Robert of Torigny* (ed. Howlett), p. 153.

[3] My alternative explanation of the choice of style, namely, the importance of the keep itself relatively to the "castellum," must also be borne in mind.

[4] "[Rex] in *turri* de Bristou captivus ponitur . . . [Imperatrix] obsedit *turrim* Wintonensis episcopi . . . Robertus frater Imperatricis in cujus *turri* Rex captivus erat" (*Hen. Hunt.*, p. 275).

[5] "In turri Cenomannica" (*Annales Veteres*, 311).

[6] The Tower of Rouen, we have seen (p. 334), was styled "arx regia."

[7] A fine "motte" is visible from the line between Calais and Paris (on

Here the "fossez d'entour" represent the surrounding works, the "castellum" referred to in the charters of the Empress. But between "the right to hold a moot there," "the moat (*sic*) and castle" as Mr. Hallam rendered it, "the moat (*sic*) probably the *motte*" of Mr. Clark (ii. 112), and the clever evasion "mote" in the *Reports on the Dignity of a Peer* (*Third Report*, p. 163), the unfortunate "mota" of Hereford has had a singular fate.

And now for the results of those conclusions that I have here endeavoured to set forth. The three castles to which I shall apply them are those of Rochester, of Newcastle, and of Arques.

In an elaborate article on the keep of Rochester, Mr. Hartshorne showed that it was erected, not as was believed by Gundulf, but by Archbishop William of Corbeuil,[1] between 1126 and 1139. But he did not attempt to explain what was the "castle of stone" which Gundulf is recorded to have there constructed. As everything turns on the exact wording, I here give the relevant portions of the document in point:—

"Quomodo Willelmus Rex filius Willelmi Regis rogatu Lanfranci Archiepiscopi concessit et confirmavit Rofensi ecclesiæ S. Andreæ Apostoli ad victum Monachorum manerium nomine Hedenham; quare Gundulfus Episcopus *Castrum* Rofense *lapideum* totum de suo proprio Regi construxit.

"Gundulfus . . . illis contulit beneficium . . . *castrum* etenim, quod situm est in pulchriore parte Hrovecestræ. . . . Regi consuluerunt [duo amici] quatinus . . . Gundulfus, quia in opere cæmentarii plurimum sciens et efficax erat, *castrum* sibi Hrofense *lapideum* de suo construeret . . . Dixerunt [Archiepiscopus et Episcopus] . . . quotiescunque quidlibet ex infortunio aliquo casu in *castro* illo contingeret aut infractione muri aut fissura maceriei, id protinus . . . exigeretur. . . . Hoc pacto coram Rege inito fecit *castrum* Gundulfus Episcopus de suo ex integro totum, costamine, ut reor, lx librarum."[2]

Though *castrum* is the term used throughout, Mr. Parker in his essay on *The Buildings of Gundulph*, 1863, assumed that a *tower* must be meant, and wrote of "Gundulf's tower" in the Cathedral: "This is probably the tower which Gundulph

the right); another, as I think, stood on the Lea, between Bow Bridge and the "Old Ford," and is (or was) well seen from the Great Eastern line.

[1] *Archæological Journal*, xx. 205–223 (1863).
[2] *Anglia Sacra* (ed. Wharton), i. 337, 338.

is recorded to have built at the cost of £60."¹ So too, Mr. Clark wrote :—

"As to his architectural skill and his work at Rochester Castle, . . . the bishop [was] to employ his skill, and spend £60 in building a castle, *that is, a tower* of some sort. What Gundulf certainly built is the tower which still bears his name. . . . It may be that Gundulf's tower was removed to make way for the new keep, but in this case its materials would have been made use of, and some trace of them would be almost certain to be detected. But there is no such trace, so that probably the new keep did not supersede the other tower." ²

Mr. Freeman guardedly observes :—

"The noble tower raised in the next age by Archbishop Walter (*sic*) of Corbeuil . . . had perhaps not even a forerunner of its own class.

"Mr. Hartshorne showed distinctly that the present tower of Rochester was not built by Gundulf, but by William of Corbeuil. . . . But we have seen (see *N. C.*, vol. iv. p. 366) that Gundulf did build a stone castle at Rochester for William Rufus ('castrum Hrofense lapidum' [*sic*]), and we should most naturally look for it on the site of the later one. On the other hand, there is a tower seemingly of Gundulf's building and of a military rather than an ecclesiastical look, which is now almost swallowed up between the transepts of the cathedral. But it would be strange if a tower built for the king stood in the middle of the monastic precinct." ³

Thus the problem is left unsolved by all four writers. But the true interpretation of *castrum*, as established by me above, solves it at once. For just as William of Corbeuil is recorded to have built the "turris" or rectangular keep,⁴ so Gundulf is described as constructing the *castrum* or fortified enclosure.⁵ We must look, therefore, for his work in the wall that girt it round. And there we find it. Mr. Clark himself is witness to the fact :—

"Part of the curtain of the *enceinte* of Rochester Castle may also be Gundulph's work. The south wall looks very early, as does the east wall." ⁶

But Mr. Irvine had already, in 1874, pointed out, in a brief but valuable communication, that a distinctive peculiarity of

¹ *Gentleman's Magazine*, N.S., xv. 260.
² *Mediæval Military Architecture*, ii. 421, 422.   ³ *William Rufus*, i. 53, 54.
⁴ "Egregia turris" is the expression of Gervase (*Actus Pontificum*).
⁵ The "castrum lapideum" (compare the three "castra lapidea' erected for the blockade of Montreuil in 1149) is so styled to distinguish it from the "castrum ligneum," which occurs so often, and which Mr. Freeman so persistently renders "tower."
⁶ *Mediæval Military Architecture*, ii. 419.

THE KEEP OF NEWCASTLE. 339

Gundulf's work—the absence of plinth to his buttresses—is found "in the castle wall at Rochester (also his)."[1] Thus, it will be seen, the character of the work independently confirms my own conclusion.

Some confusion, it may be well to add, has been caused by such forms as "castellum Hrofi" and "castrum quod nominatur Hrofesceaster." In these early forms (as in some other cases), "castrum" denotes the whole of Rochester, girt by its Roman wall, and not (as Mr. Hartshorne assumed throughout) the castle enclosure. Mr. Clark leaves the point in doubt.[2]

Before leaving Rochester, I would point out that, unlike the rest of Gundulf's work, this *castrum* can be closely dated. The conjunction of Lanfranc and William Rufus, in the story of its building, limits it to September, 1087—March, 1089, while Odo's rebellion would probably postpone its construction till his surrender. It is most unfortunate, therefore, that Mr. Clark should write, "This transaction between the bishop and the king occurred about 1076,"[3] when neither Gundulf was bishop nor William king.

To the case of Newcastle and its keep, I invite special attention, because we have here the tacit admission of Mr. Clark himself that he has antedated, incredible though it may seem, by more than ninety years the erection of this famous keep. To prove this, it is only necessary to print his own conclusions side by side:—

(1080.)	(1172-74.)
"Of this masonry there is but little which can be referred to the reign of the Conqueror or William Rufus,—that is, to the eleventh century. Of that period are certainly (*sic*) . . . the keeps of Chester, . . . and Newcastle, though this last looks later than its recorded (*sic*) date. . . . Carlisle . . . received from Rufus a castle and a keep, now standing;	"Newcastle is an excellent example of a rectangular Norman keep. "Its condition is perfect, its date known (*sic*), and being late (1172-74) in its style, it is more ornate than is usual in its details, and is furnished with all the peculiarities of a late (*sic*) Norman work. "The present castle is an excellent

---

[1] *Journ. Brit. Arch. Ass.*, xxxi., 471, 472.
[2] Both writers, also, mistake a general exemption from the *trinoda necessitas* for a special allusion to Rochester keep.
[3] *Mediæval Military Architecture*, ii. 421.

and Newcastle, similarly provided in 1080, also retains its keep. . . . The castle of Newcastle . . . was built by Robert Curthose in 1080, and is a very perfect example of a rectangular Norman keep. Newcastle, built in 1080, has very many chambers" (*Mediæval Military Architecture*, 1884, i. 40, 49, 94, 128.

example of the later (*sic*) form of the rectangular Norman keep. . . . Newcastle has its fellow in the keep of Dover, known to have been the work of Henry the Second " (*Archæological Journal*, 1884).

The origin, of course, of the astounding error by which "the great master of military architecture" misdated this keep by nearly a century,[1] and took an essentially late work for one of the earliest in existence, was the same fatal delusion that *castrum* or *castellum* meant precisely what it did not mean, namely, a tower. "Castellum novum super flumen Tyne condidit" is the expression applied to Robert's work in 1080, and the absence of a "tower" explains the fact that Fantosme makes no mention of a "tur" when describing "Le Noef Chasteau sur Tyne," the existing keep not being available at the time of which he wrote.

We now come to our last case, that of the Château d'Arques.

"Arques," writes Mr. Clark, "is one of the earliest examples of a Norman castle."[2] It is, Mr. Freeman holds, "a fortress which is undoubtedly one of the earliest and most important in the history of Norman military architecture."[3] No apology, therefore, is needed for discussing the date of this celebrated structure, so long a subject of interest and of study both to English and to French archæologists.

As at Colchester and in other places, the very wildest theories have been generally advanced, and archæologists have only gradually sobered down till they have virtually agreed upon a date for this keep which is actually, I venture to think, less than a century wrong.

In his noble monograph upon the fortress, the basis of all subsequent accounts,[4] M. Deville enumerates, with contemptuous

[1] Mr. J. R. Boyle has shown that nearly £1000 was spent upon it between 1172 and 1177, when it was, therefore, in course of erection.
[2] *Mediæval Military Architecture*, i. 186.
[3] *Norman Conquest*, iii. 182.
[4] *Histoire du Château d'Arques*, by A. Deville, pp. x., 412 (Rouen).

amusement (pp. 49, 268–272), the rival theories that it was built (1) by the Romans; (2) by "Clotaire I." in 553—the date 1553 on one of the additions for the structure having actually been so read; (3) by "Charles Martel" in 745, 747, or 749 (on the strength of another reading of the same date, confirmed by a carving of his coat-of-arms)—these being the dates given by Houard and Toussaint-Duplessis. At the time when Deville himself wrote the study of castles was still in its infancy, and of the two sources of evidence now open to us, the internal (that of the structure itself) and the external (that of chronicles and records), the latter alone was ripe for use. Now, at Arques, precisely as at our own Rochester, the written evidence has hitherto appeared conflicting to archæologists, but only because the language employed has never yet been rightly understood. On the one hand we read in William of Jumièges, an excellent authority in the matter, that "Hic Willelmus [the Conqueror's uncle] castrum Archarum in cacumine ipsius montis condidit;" and in the *Chronicle of Fontenelle*, that this same William "Arcas castrum in pago Tellau primus statuit;" also, in William of Poitiers, that "id munimentum . . . ipse primus fundavit:" on the other, we read in Robert du Mont, a first-rate and contemporary authority, who may indeed be termed a specialist on the subject, that "Anno MCXXIII. castellum quod vocatur Archas turre et mœnibus mirabiliter firmavit [Rex Henricus]."[1]

M. de Caumont, that industrious pioneer, whose work appeared four years before that of M. Deville, boldly followed Robert du Mont, and confidently assigned the existing keep to 1123.[2] Guided, however, by M. Le Prévost (1824), he held that the original structure was raised by the Conqueror's uncle, and that Henry I. merely "fit reconstruire en entier le donjon et une partie des murs d'enceinte." M. Deville, on the contrary, in his eager zeal for the honour and glory of the castle, stoutly maintained that, keep and all, it was clearly Count William's work. He admitted that his Norman brother-antiquaries assigned it to Henry I., but urged that they had overlooked the evidence of the structure, and its resemblance to English keeps

[1] Ed. Howlett, p. 106.
[2] *Cours d'antiquités monumentales* (1835), v. 227, 228.

assigned (but, as we now know, wrongly) to the eleventh century, or earlier;[1] and that they had misunderstood the passage in Robert du Mont, which must have referred to mere alterations. In order thus to explain it away, he contends (and this contention Mr. Clark strangely accepts) that Robert says the same—which he does not—of "Gisors, Falaise, and other castles known"—which they are not[2]—"to be of earlier date" (*M. M. A.*, i. 194). Lastly, he appeals, though with an apology for doing so ("s'il nous était permis d'invoquer à l'appui de notre opinion"), to the far later "Chronique de Normandie" for actual evidence, elsewhere wanting, that the keep itself (*turris*) was built by William of Arques,[3] that is, in 1039–1043.[4]

"I went over the castle minutely," Professor Freeman writes, "in May, 1868, with M. Deville's book in hand, and can bear witness to the accuracy of his description, though I cannot always accept his inferences" (*N. C.*, iii. 124, *note*). He accordingly doubts M. Deville's date for the gateway and walls of the inner ward, but sees "no reason to doubt that the ruined keep is part of the original work" (*ibid.*). We must remember, however, that the Professor is at direct variance with Mr. Clark on the Norman rectangular keeps, for which he claims an earlier origin than the latter can concede.

Turning now to Mr. Clark himself, we learn from him that—

"it seems probable that the keep is the oldest part of the masonry, and the work of the Conqueror's uncle, Guillaume d'Arques, and it is supposed to be one of the earliest, if not the earliest, of the rectangular keeps known" (*M. M. A.*, i. 194).

He adds that the passage in Robert du Mont

"has been held to show that the whole structure was the work of Henry, who reigned from 1105 (*sic*) to 1135, and the extreme boldness of the buttresses and superincumbent constructions of the keep no doubt favour

---

[1] Colchester, in *Archæologia*, to which he refers, was attributed to Edward the Elder, and Rochester was, of course, as yet, believed to be the work of Gundulf.

[2] Compare Professor Freeman on Falaise: "More probably, I think, of the twelfth than of the eleventh [century]" (*Norm. Conq.*, ii. 175).

[3] *Château d'Arques*, pp. 307–312.   [4] *Ibid.*, pp. 48, 267.

THE KEEP WAS BUILT BY HENRY I.   343

this view; but, as M. Deville remarks in the same passage, similar reference is made to Gisors, Falaise, and other castles, known to be of earlier date" (*ibid.*).

To resume. The external or written evidence is as follows. On the one hand, we have the clear and positive statement of a contemporary writer, Robert du Mont, that Henry I. built this keep in 1123. On the other, we have no statement from any contemporary that it was built by William of Arques (in 1039–1043). He is merely credited with founding the *castellum*, and in none of the contemporary accounts of its blockade and capture by his nephew is there any mention of a *turris*. The distinction between a *castellum* and a *turris*, with their respective independence, has not, as I have shown, hitherto been realized, and it is quite in the spirit of older students that M. Deville confidently exclaims—

"Or, conçoit-on un château-fort sans murailles? Un château-fort sans donjon, dans le cours du XIe siècle, en Normandie, n'est guère plus rationnel" (p. 310).

As to the "murailles," Mr. Clark has taught us that palisades were not replaced by walls till a good deal later than has been usually supposed; and as to the "donjon," if, as I have established, so important a fortress as Rochester was without a keep in the eleventh, and indeed well into the twelfth century, other *castella* must have been similarly destitute—probably, for instance, Newcastle, as we have seen, and certainly Exeter, of which Mr. Clark writes: "There is no evidence of a keep, nor, at so great a height, was any needed" (*M. M. A.*, ii. 47). The same argument from strength of position would *à fortiori* apply to Arques, and there is, in short, no reason for doubting that the *castrum* of William of Arques need not have included a *turris*.[1]

On what, then, rests the assertion that the keep was the work of the Conqueror's uncle? Strange as it may seem, it rests solely on the so-called *Chronique de Normandie*, an anonymous production, not of the eleventh, but of the fourteenth century! "Si fist faire une tour moult forte audessus du chastel d'Arques," runs the passage, which is quoted by Mr.

[1] Compare the "castrum in cacumine ipsius montis condidit" at Arques with the "castellum novum super flumen Tyne condidit" at Newcastle.

Clark (i. 194), from Deville (pp. 311, 312), who, however, apologized for appealing to that authority. This "Chronique" is admitted to have been based on the poetical histories of Wace and Benoit de St. More, themselves written several generations later than the alleged erection of this keep. Of the former, Mr. Freeman holds that, except where repeating contemporary authorities, "his statements need to be very carefully weighed" (*N. C.*, ii. 162); and of the latter, that he is "of much smaller historical authority" (*ibid.*). To this I may add that, in my opinion, Wace, writing as he did in the reign of Henry II., at the close of the great tower-building epoch, spoke loosely of towers, when mentioning castles, as if they had been equally common in the reign of the Conqueror. A careful inspection of his poem will be found to verify this statement. "La tur d'Arques" was standing when he wrote: consequently he talks of "La tur d'Arques" when describing the Conqueror's blockade of the castle in 1053. There is no contemporary authority for its existence at that date.[1]

And now let us pass from documentary evidence to that of the structure itself. We may call Mr. Clark himself to witness that the presumption is against so early a date as 1039–1043. He tells us, of the rectangular keep in general, that—

"not above half a dozen examples can be shown with certainty to have been constructed in Normandy before the latter part of the eleventh century, and but very few, if any, before the English conquest" (i. 35).

Therefore, on Mr. Clark's own showing, we ought to ask for conclusive evidence before admitting that any rectangular keep is as old as 1039–1043. But what was the impression produced on him by an inspection of the structure itself? This is a most significant fact. While rejecting, apparently on what he be-

---

[1] Compare, on this point, the acute criticism of Dr. Bruce (repeated by Mr. Freeman) that "Wace (v. 12,628) speaks of the horse of William Fitz Osbern [in 1066] as 'all covered with iron,' whereas in the [Bayeux] Tapestry 'not a single horse is equipped in steel armour; and if we refer to the authors who lived at that period, we shall find that not one of them mentions any defensive covering for the horse.'" Compare also the expression of William of Malmesbury, who lived and wrote under the tower-building king, that the Norman barons took advantage of the Conqueror's minority "*turres agere*," these being the structures with the building of which the writer was most familiar.

lieved to be documentary evidence, the theory that the keep (*turris*) was the work of Henry I., he confessed that the features of the building "no doubt favour this view" (i. 194, *ut supra*).

But leaving, for the present, Mr. Clark's views, to which I shall return below, I take my stand without hesitation on certain features in this keep. It is not needful to visit Arques —I have myself never done so—to appreciate their true significance and their bearing on the question of the date. The first of these is the forebuilding. Mr. Clark tells us that Arques possesses "the usual square appendage or forebuilding common in these keeps" (*M. M. A.*, i. 198). But this unscientific treatment of the forebuilding, ignoring so completely its origin and development, cannot too strongly be resisted. Restricting ourselves to the case before us, we at once observe the peculiarity of an external staircase, not only leading up to a forebuilding, through which the keep is entered, but actually carried, through a massive buttress, round an angle of the keep.[1] Rochester being believed to be the work of Gundulf, in the days when M. Deville wrote, it was natural that he should have supposed "cette savante combinaison" to have been familiar to Gundulf (p. 299). But now that, on these points, we are better informed, let us ask where can Mr. Clark produce an instance of this elaborate and striking device as old even as the days of Gundulf, to say nothing of those of Count William (1039–1043)? Where we do find it is in such keeps as Dover, the work of Henry II., or Rochester, where the resemblance is even more remarkable. Now, Rochester, as we know, was actually built within a few years of the date given by Robert du Mont, and upheld by me, as that of the construction of Arques. Oddly enough, it is Mr. Clark himself who thus points out another resemblance:—

"In the basement of the forebuilding . . . was a vaulted chamber, opening into the basement of the keep, *as at Rochester*, either a store or prison" (*M. M. A.*, p. 188).

Lastly, both at Arques and at Rochester, we find on the first

[1] "A flight of steps, beginning upon the north face, passing by a doorway through its most westerly buttress, and which then, turning, is continued along the west face" (*M. M. A.*, i. 188). Cf. Deville (p. 298), and the plan of 1708 (*ibid.*, Pl. XII.).

floor, near the entrance, the very peculiar feature of a smaller doorway communicating with the rampart of the curtain.[1] This parallel, which is not alluded to by Mr. Clark, is the more remarkable, as such a device is foreign to the earlier rectangular keeps, and also implies that the keep must have been built certainly no earlier, and possibly later, than the curtain, which curtain, Mr. Clark, as we shall find, admits, cannot be so old as the days of Count William.

No one, in short, unbiassed by supposed documentary evidence, could study this keep, with its "petites galeries avec d'autres petites chambres ou prisons pratiquées dans l'épaisseur des murs"[2] (as at Rochester), with the elaborate defences of its entrance, and with those other special features which made even Mr. Clark uneasy, without rejecting as incredible the accepted view that it was built by Count William of Arques (1039–1043). And this being so, there is, admittedly, no alternative left but to assign it to Henry I. (1123), the date specifically given by Robert du Mont himself.

But, it may be urged, though there is nothing improbable in Mr. Freeman being wrong, is it conceivable that so unrivalled an expert as Mr. Clark himself can have mistaken a keep of 1123 for one of 1039–1043, when we remember the wonderful development of these structures in the course of those eighty years? To this objection, I fear, there is a singularly complete answer in the case of Newcastle, where, as we have seen, he was led by the same misconception into no less amazing an error.[3]

In short, the view I have brought forward as to the separate existence of "tower" and "castle" may be said, from these examples, to revolutionize the study of Norman military architecture.

[1] *M. M. A.*, i. 188, ii. 432.
[2] Report of 1708 (*Deville*, p. 294).
[3] It is only right to mention that, according to the *Academy*, "Mr. Clark has long been recognized as the first living authority on the subject of castellated architecture;" that, in the opinion of the *Athenæum*, all those "who in future touch the subject may safely rely on Mr. Clark;" that his is "a masterly history of mediæval military architecture" (*Saturday Review*); and that, according to *Notes and Queries*, "no other Englishman knows so much of our old military architecture as Mr. Clark."

APPENDIX P.

THE EARLY ADMINISTRATION OF LONDON.

(See p. 151.)

THE new light which is thrown by the charters granted to Geoffrey upon a subject so interesting and so obscure as the government and *status* of London during the Norman period requires, for its full appreciation, detailed and separate treatment. But, before advancing my own conclusions, it is absolutely needful to dispose of that singular accretion of error which has grown, by gradual degrees, around the recorded facts.[1]

The cardinal error has been the supposition that when the citizens of London, under Henry I., were given Middlesex *ad firmam*, the " Middlesex " in question was only Middlesex *exclusive of London.* The actual words of the charter are these:—

"Sciatis me concessisse civibus meis London[iarum], tenendum Middlesex ad firmam pro ccc libris ad compotum, ipsis et hæredibus suis de me et hæredibus meis ita quod ipsi cives ponent vicecomitem qualem voluerint de se ipsis; et justitiarium qualem voluerint de se ipsis, ad custodiendum placita coronæ meæ et eadem placitanda, et nullus alius erit justitiarius super ipsos homines London[iarum]."

Now, it is absolutely certain that the shrievalty (*vicecomitatus*) and the ferm (*firma*) mentioned in this passage are the shrievalty and the ferm not of Middlesex apart from London, nor of London apart from Middlesex, but of "London *and* Middlesex." For there is never, from the first, but one ferm.

[1] On the somewhat thorny question of the right extension of "Lond'" (London*ia* or Londoni*æ*) I would explain at the outset that both forms, the singular and the plural, are found, so that either extension is legitimate. I have seen no reason to change my belief (as set forth in the *Athenæum*, 1887) that "Londonia" is the Latinization of the English "Londone," and "Londoniæ" of the Norman "Londres."

It is here called the ferm of "Middlesex;" in the almost contemporary Pipe-Roll (31 Hen. I.) it is called the ferm of "London" (there being no ferm of Middlesex mentioned); and Geoffrey's charters clinch the matter. For while Stephen grants him "the shrievalties of London and Middlesex,"[1] the Empress, in her turn, grants him "the shrievalty of London and Middlesex."[2] Further, the Pipe-Rolls of Henry II. describe this same *firma* both as the ferm of "London," and as that of "London and Middlesex;" while in the Roll of 8 Ric. I. we find the phrase, "de veteri firma *Comitat'* Lond' et Middelsexa." Lastly, the charter of Henry III. grants to the citizens of London—

"Vicecomitatum Londoniæ et de Middelsexia, cum omnibus rebus et consuetudinibus quæ pertinent ad predictum Vicecomitatum, infra civitatem et extra per terras et aquas; ... Reddendo inde annuatim ... trescentas libras sterlingorum blancorum.[3]

And so, to this day, the shrievalty is that of "London and Middlesex."[4]

The royal writs and charters bear the same witness. When they are directed to the local authorities, it is to those of "London and Middlesex," or of "London," or of "Middlesex." The three are, for all purposes, used as equivalent terms. There was never, as I have said, but one ferm, and never but one shrievalty.[5]

[1] "Vicecomitatus de Londonia et de Middelsexa ... pro ccc libris."
[2] "Vicecomitatum Lundoniæ et Middelsex pro ccc libris."
[3] Madox's *Firma Burgi*, p. 242, *note*.
[4] These words were written before the late changes.
[5] A remarkable illustration of this loose usage is afforded by the case of the archdeaconry. Take the styles of Ralph "de Diceto." Dr. Stubbs writes of his archdeaconry: "That it was the archdeaconry of Middlesex is certain ... it is beyond doubt, and wherever Ralph is called Archdeacon of London, it is only loosely in reference to the fact that he was one of the four archdeacons of the diocese" (*Radulfi de Diceto Opera*, I. xxxv., xxxvi.). But, as to this explanation, the writer adduces no evidence in support of this view, that all "four archdeacons" might be described, loosely, as "of London." Indeed, he admits, further on (p. xl., *note*), "that the title of Essex or Colchester is generally given to the holders of these two archdeaconries, so that really the only two between which confusion was likely to arise were London and Middlesex." Now, in a very formal document, quoted by Dr. Stubbs himself (p. l., *note*), Ralph is emphatically styled "Archdeacon of London." It is clear, therefore, that, in the case of this archdeaconry, that style was fully recognized, and the explanation of this is

MIDDLESEX NEVER SEPARATE FROM LONDON.

Now, this completely disposes of the view that the "Middlesex" of Henry I.'s charter was Middlesex *apart from London*. This prevalent but erroneous assumption has proved the cause of much confusion and misunderstanding of the facts of the case. It has nowhere, perhaps, been assigned such prominence as in that account of London by Mr. Loftie which may derive authority in the eyes of some from the editorial *imprimatur* of Mr. Freeman.[1] We there read as follows:—

"It may be as well, before we proceed, to remember one thing. That London is not in Middlesex, that it never was in Middlesex, . . . is a fact of which we have to be constantly reminded" (p. 125).

From this interpretation of the "Middlesex" of the charter, it, of course, followed that the writer took the *firma* of £300 to be paid in respect of Middlesex *exclusive of London*.[2] We need not wonder, therefore, that to him the grant is difficult to understand. Here are his comments on its terms:—

"If we could estimate the reasons which led to this grant with any degree of certainty, we should understand better what the citizens expected to gain by it besides rights of jurisdiction. . . . The meaning and nature of the grant are subjects of which we should like to know more. But here we can obtain little help from books . . . and we may inquire in vain for a definition of the position and duties of the sheriff who acts for the citizens in their subject county. . . . There must have been advantages to accrue from the payment by London of £300 a year, a sum which, small as it seems to us, was a heavy tax in those days. We may be sure the willing citizens expected to obtain correspondingly valuable liberties" (pp. 121–123).

Then follow various conjectures, all of them necessarily wide of the mark. And as with the ferm, so with the sheriff. Mr. Loftie, taking the sheriff (*vicecomes*) in question to be a sheriff of Middlesex exclusive of London (which he hence terms a "subject county"), is of necessity baffled by the charter. For by it the citizens are empowered to appoint (*a*) a "vice-

to be found, I would suggest, in the use, exemplified in the text *ut supra*, of "London" and "Middlesex" as convertible terms.

[1] Mr. Freeman himself makes the same mistake, and insists on regarding Middlesex as a subject district round the City.

[2] Even Dr. Sharpe, the learned editor of the valuable *Calendar of Hustings Wills*, is similarly puzzled by a grant of twenty-five marks out of the king's ferm "de civitate London," to be paid annually by the sheriffs of London and Middlesex (i. 610), because he imagines that the *firma* was paid in respect of the sheriffwick of Middlesex alone.

comes," (*b*) a "justitiarius." As the "vicecomes," according to his view, had nothing to do with the City itself, Mr. Loftie has to account for "the omission of any reference to the portreeve in the charter," his assumption being that the City itself was at this time governed by a portreeve. Though his views are obscurely expressed, his solutions of the problem are as follows. In his larger work he dismisses the supposition that the "justitiarius" of the charter was the "chief magistrate" of the City, *i.e.* the portreeve, because the citizens must have been "already" entitled to elect that officer. Yet in his later work, with equal confidence, he tells us that by "justitiarius" the portreeve is "evidently intended." The fact is that he is really opposing two different suppositions; the one that Henry granted by his charter the right to elect a portreeve, the other that he did not grant it, but retained the appointment in his hands. Mr. Loftie first denies the former, and then, in his later work, asserts the former to deny the latter. But really his language is so confused that it is doubtful whether he realized himself the contradictory drift of his two arguments, both based on the same assumption, which " it is manifestly absurd," we learn, to dispute.[1] And the strange part of the

[1] "It has been supposed that the justiciar here mentioned means a mayor or chief magistrate, and that the grant includes that of the election of the supreme executive officer of the City. It may be so, but all probability is against this view. For by this time the citizens already appear to have selected their own portreeve, by whatever name he was called; and it is absurd to suppose that the king gave them power to appoint a sheriff of Middlesex, if they were not already allowed to appoint their own. The omission of any reference to the portreeve in the charter cannot, in fact, be otherwise accounted for" (*History of London*, i. 90).

"The next substantial benefit they derived from the charter was the leave to elect their own justiciar. They may place whom they will to hold pleas of the Crown. The portreeve is here evidently intended, for it is manifestly absurd to suppose, as some have done, that Henry allowed the citizens to elect a reeve for Middlesex, if they could not elect one for themselves; and if proof were wanting, we have it in the references to the trials before the portreeve which are found in very early documents. In one of these, which cannot be dated later than 1115, Gilbert Proudfoot, or Prutfot, described as vicecomes, is mentioned as having some time before given judgment against the dean and chapter as to a piece of land on the present site of the Bank of England" (*London*, p. 29).

THE CONCESSIONS OF HENRY I.

business is this, What is the "proof" that Mr. Loftie offers for the later of his two hypotheses? If the "trial" to which he refers had ever taken place at all, and, still more, if it had taken place before 1115, the fact would have an important bearing. But, in the first place, he has wrongly assigned to the record too early a date, and, in the second, it represents Gilbert Prutfot, not as a judge, but as a culprit. The expression used is, "Terra quam Gillebertus Prutfot nobis disfortiat."[1] Now "defortiare" (or "disfortiare") is rendered by Dr. Stubbs, in his *Select Charters* (p. 518), "to deforce, to dispossess by violence." We have here, therefore, an interesting, because early, example of the legal offence of "deforcement," defined by Johnson as "a withholding of lands and tenements by force from the right owner." But the point to which I would call attention is that, even if this writer were correct in his facts (which he is not), his "proof" that (a *vicecomes* and a *justitiarius* being mentioned in the charter) the *justitiarius* was "evidently" the portreeve consists in the fact that a *vicecomes* had "given judgment" in a trial, and being styled *vicecomes*, was the portreeve! That is to say, the *justitiarius* must have been the portreeve *because* the portreeve was styled (*not* "justitiarius," but, on the contrary,) *vicecomes*. Such is actually his argument.[2]

I have dwelt thus fully on these observations, because they illustrate the hopeless wandering which is the inevitable result of the adoption of the above fundamental error.

We have a curiously close parallel to this use of "London and Middlesex" in the expression "turris et castellum," on which I have elsewhere dwelt.[3] Just as the relative importance of the "Tower" of London to the encircling "castle" at its feet led to the term "turris" alone being used to describe the two,—while, conversely, in the provinces, "castellum" was the term adopted,—so did the relative greatness of London to the county that lay around its walls lead to the occasional use of "London" as a term descriptive of both together, a usage

[1] *Ninth Report Hist. MSS.*, i. 66 b.

[2] Reference to p. 110, *supra*, will show at once how vain is the effort to wrench "justitiarius" from its natural and well-known meaning.

[3] See Appendix O.

impossible in the provinces. Whether a "turris et castellum" were destined to become known as a "turris" or a "castellum," whether "Londonia et Middelsex" were described as "Londonia" merely, or as "Middlesex," in each case the entity is the same. For fiscal, and therefore for our purposes, "London and Middlesex," under whatever name, remain one and indivisible.

The special value of the charters granted to Geoffrey de Mandeville lies not so much in their complete confirmation of the view that the *firma* of "Middlesex" was that of "London *and* Middlesex" (for that would be evident without them), as in their proof of the fact, so strangely overlooked, that this connection was at least as old as the days of William the Conqueror, and in their treatment of Middlesex (including London) as an ordinary county like Essex or Herts, "farmed" in precisely the same way. The *firma* of Herts was £60, of Essex £300, and of Middlesex (because containing London) £300 also.

But now let us leave our record evidence and turn to geography and to common sense. What must have always been the salient feature which distinguished Middlesex internally from every other county? Obviously, that the shire was abnormally small, and its chief town abnormally large. Nor was it a mere matter of size, but, still more, of comparative wealth. This is illustrated by the taxation recorded in the Pipe-Roll of 1130. Unlike the *firma*, the taxes were raised, as elsewhere, from the town and the shire respectively, the town contributing an *auxilium*, and the shire, without the walls, a Danegeld. We thus learn that London paid a sum about half as large again as that raised from the rest of the shire.[1] The normal relation of the "shire" to the "port" was accordingly here reversed, and so would be also, in consequence, that of the shire-reeve to the portreeve. Where, as usual, the "port" formed but a small item in the *corpus comitatus*, it was possible to sever it from the rest of the county, to place it *extra firmam*, and to give it a reeve who should stand towards it in the same relation as the shire-reeve to the shire, and would therefore be termed the "port-

[1] Here and elsewhere I use "shire" on the strength of Middlesex having a "sheriff" (*i.e.* a shire-reeve).

reeve." But to have done this in the case of Middlesex would have been to reverse the nature of things, to place a mere "portreeve" in a position greater than that of the "shire-reeve" himself. This is why that change which, in the provinces, was the aim of every rising town, never took place in the case of London, though the greatest town of all. I say that it "never took place," for, as we have seen, the city of London was never severed from the rest of the shire. As far back as we can trace them, they are found one and indivisible.

What, then, was the alternative? Simply this. The "reeve," who, in the case of a normal county, took his title from the "shire" and not from the "port," took it, in the abnormal case of Middlesex, from the "port" and not from the "shire." In each case both "port" and "shire" were alike within his jurisdiction; in each case he took his style from the most important part of that jurisdiction. Such is the original solution I offer for this most interesting problem, and I claim that its acceptance will explain everything, will harmonize with all existing *data*, and will dispose of difficulties which, hitherto, it has been impossible to surmount.

My contention is, briefly, that the Norman *vicecomes* of "London," or "Middlesex," or "London and Middlesex" was simply the successor, in that office, of the Anglo-Saxon "portreeve." With the sphere of the *vicecomes* I have already dealt, and though we are not in a position similarly to prove the sphere of the Anglo-Saxon "portreeve," I might appeal to the belief of Mr. Loftie himself that "Ulf the Sheriff of Middlesex is identical with Ulf the Portreeve of London"[1] (though he adds, contrary to my contention, that "as yet their official connection was only that of neighbourhood "),[2] and that Ansgar, though one of the "portreeves" (p. 24), "was Sheriff of Middlesex for a time there can be no doubt" (p. 127).[3] But I would rather appeal to the vital fact that the shire-reeve and the portreeve are, so far I know, never mentioned together, and that writs are directed to a port-

[1] *London*, p. 126.
[2] This springs, of course, from what I have termed "the fundamental error."
[3] See p. 37, *ante*, and *Norm. Conq.*, iii. (1869) 424, 544, 729.

reeve or to a shire-reeve,[1] but never to both. Specially would I insist upon the indisputable circumstance that such writs as were addressed to the "portreeve" by the Anglo-Saxon kings, were addressed to the *vicecomes* by the Norman, and that the turning-point is seen under the Conqueror himself, whose Anglo-Saxon charter is addressed to the "bisceop" and the "portirefan," and whose Latin writs are, similarly, addressed to the *episcopus* and the *vicecomes*. More convincing evidence it would not be easy to find.

The acceptance of this view will at once dispose of the alleged "disappearance of the portreeve," with the difficulties it has always presented, and the conjectures to which it has given rise.[2] The style of the "portreeve" indeed disappears, but his office does not. In the person of the Norman *vicecomes*, it preserves an unbroken existence. Geoffrey de Mandeville steps, as sheriff, into the shoes of Ansgar the portreeve.[3]

The problem as to what became of the portreeve, a problem which has exercised so many minds, sprang from the delusion that in the Norman period the City must have had a portreeve for governor independent of the Sheriff of Middlesex. I term this an undoubted "delusion," because I have already made it clear that the City was part of the sheriff's jurisdiction and contributed its share to his *firma*. There was, therefore, no room for an independent portreeve; nor indeed does a "portreeve" of London, I believe, ever occur after the Conqueror's charter.

But we must here glance at the contrary view set forth by Mr. Loftie:—

"The succession of portreeves is uninterrupted. We have the names of some of them in the records of the Exchequer. Occasionally two or three,

---

[1] I would suggest that, as in the case of Ulf, the Reeve of "London and Middlesex" might be addressed as portreeve in writs affecting the City and as shire-reeve in those more particularly affecting the rest of Middlesex.

[2] Dr. Stubbs, in a footnote, hazards "the conjecture" that "the disappearance of the portreeve" may be connected with "a civic revolution, the history of which is now lost, but which might account for the earnest support given by the citizens to Stephen," etc. In another place (*Select Charters*, p. 300) he writes: "How long the Portreeve of London continued to exist is not known; perhaps until he was merged in the *mayor*." I have already dealt with Mr. Loftie's explanation of "the omission of any reference to the portreeve in the charter.

[3] See p. 37, *ante*, and Addenda.

once as many as five, came to answer for the City and pay the £300 which was the farm of Middlesex. In 1129, a few years only after the retirement of Orgar and his companions, we read of 'quatuor vicecomites' as attending for London. The following year we hear of a single 'camerarius.' The 'Hugh Buche' of Stowe may be identified with the Hugo de Bock of the St. Paul's documents, and his 'Richard de Par' with Richard the younger, the chamberlain. 'Par' is probably a misreading for Parvus contracted. In the reign of Stephen two members of the Buckerel family hold office, and we have Fulcred and Robert, who were related to each other. Another early portreeve was Wluardus, who attends at the Exchequer in 1138, and who continued to be an alderman thirty years later" (*Historic Towns: London*, p. 34).

Where are "the records of the Exchequer" from which we learn all this? The only Pipe-Roll of the period is that of 1130, in which "the farm of Middlesex" is not £300, but a much larger sum, a fact which, as we shall find, has a most important bearing. The "quatuor vicecomites" appear "as attending," not in 1129, but in 1130. The "camerarius" does not (and could not) appear "in the following year," but, on the contrary, belonged to a preceding one ("Willelmus *qui fuit* camerarius de *veteribus* debitis"); nor does he account for the *firma*. The *firma* was always accounted for by "vicecomites," and not (as implied on p. 108) by a chamberlain, or by a "prefect." The "Hugh Buche" is given in Mr. Loftie's former work (p. 98) as "Hugh de Buch." He is meant (as even Foss perceived) for the well-known Hugh de Bocland (the minister of Henry I.), who cannot be shown to have been a "portreeve." No "Hugo de Bock" occurs in the St. Paul's documents, which only mention "Hugo de Bochelanda" and "Hugo de Bock[elanda]," the latter imperfection being the source of the error. "Richard, the younger, chamberlain" only occurs in these documents a century later (1204–1215), and "the younger," I presume, there translates "juvenis," and not "parvus." It is, moreover, quite certain that Stowe's "de Par" was not "a misreading for 'parvus' contracted," but for "delpare," as may easily be ascertained. No member of the Bucherel family occurs in these documents as holding office "in the reign of Stephen," though some do in the next century. Fulcred was not a "portreeve," but a "chamberlain;" and Robert, Fulcred's brother, was neither one nor the other. But what are we to say to "Wluardus" the portreeve, "who attends at the Exchequer in 1138"?

Where are the "records of the Exchequer for 1138"? They are known to Mr. Loftie alone.[1] Moreover, his identification, here, of the *vicecomes* with the portreeve is in direct antagonism to the principle laid down just before (p. 29), that, on the contrary, it was the *justitiarius* who should "evidently" be identified with the portreeve (see p. 350, *supra*).

Perhaps the assumption of a portreeve's existence springs from forgetfulness or misapprehension of the condition of London at the time. Its corporate unity, we must always remember, had not yet been developed. As Dr. Stubbs so truly observes, London was only

"a bundle of communities, townships, parishes, and lordships, of which each has its own constitution."[2]

I cannot indeed agree with him in his view that the result of the charter of Henry I. was to replace this older system by a new "shire organization."[3] For my contention is that our great historian not only misdates the charter in question, but also misunderstands it (though not so seriously as others), and that it made no difference in the "organization" at all. But I would cordially endorse these his words :—

"No new incorporation is bestowed: the churches, the barons, the citizens retain their ancient customs; the churches their sokens, the barons their manors, the citizens their township organization, and possibly their guilds. The municipal unity which they possess is of the same sort as that of the county and hundred."[4]

And he further observes that the City "clearly was organized under a sheriff like any other shire." Thus the local government of the day was to be found in the petty courts of these various "communities," and not in any central corporation. The only centralizing element was the sheriff, and his office was not so much to "govern," as to satisfy the financial claims of the Crown in ferm, taxes, and profits of jurisdiction. There was,

[1] See *Athenæum*, February 5, 1887, p. 191; also my papers on "The First Mayor of London" in *Academy*, November 12, 1887, and *Antiquary*, March, 1887.

[2] *Const. Hist.*, i. 404.

[3] "The ... shire organization which seems to have displaced early in the century" [*i.e.* by Henry's charter] "the complicated system of guild and franchise" (*ibid.*, i. 630).

[4] *Ibid.*, i. 405.

LONDON NOT YET A CORPORATE UNIT. 357

of course, the general "folkmote" over which, with the bishop, he would preside, but the true corporate organisms were those of the several communities. The sheriff and the folkmote could no more mould these self-governing bodies into one coherent whole, than they could, or did, accomplish this in the case of an ordinary shire. Here we have a somewhat curious parallel between such a polity as is here described and that of the present metropolis outside the City. There, too, we have the local communities, with their quasi-independent vestries, etc., and the Metropolitan Board of Works is a substitute for their "folkmote" or "shiremote."[1] But, to revert to the days of Henry I., the Anglo-Saxon system of government, its strength varying in intension conversely with its sphere in extension, possessed the toughest vitality in its lowest and simplest forms. Thus the original territorial system might never have led to a corporate unity. But what the sheriff and the folkmote could not accomplish, the mayor and the *communa* could and did. The territorial arrangement was overthrown by the rising power of commerce. To quote once more from Dr. Stubbs's work:

"The establishment of the corporate character of the City under a mayor marks the victory of the communal principle over the more ancient shire organization.... It also marks the triumph of the mercantile over the aristocratic element."[2]

At the risk of being tedious I would now repeat the view I have advanced on the shrievalty, because the point is of such paramount importance that it cannot be expressed too clearly. The great illustrative value of Geoffrey's charters is this. They prove, in the first place, that Middlesex (inclusive of London) was treated financially on the same footing as Essex or Herts or any other shire; and in the second they give us that all-important information, the amount of the *firma* for each of these counties at the close of the eleventh century. All we have to do in the case of Middlesex is to keep steadily in view its *firma* of £300. Sometimes described as the *firma* of "London," sometimes "of Middlesex," and sometimes "of London and Middlesex," its identity never changes; it is always, and beyond the shadow of question, the *firma* of Middlesex

[1] This was written before the days of the London County Council.
[2] *Ibid.*, i. 630.

inclusive of London. The history of this ancient payment reveals a persistent endeavour of the Crown to increase its amount, an endeavour which was eventually foiled. Under the first Geoffrey de Mandeville (William I. and William II.), it was £300. Nearly doubled by Henry I., it was yet reduced to £300 by his charter to the citizens of London. In the succeeding reign, the second Geoffrey eventually secured it from both claimants at the same low figure (£300). Under Henry II., as the Pipe-Rolls show, it was again raised as under Henry I. John, we shall find, reduced it again to the original £300, and the reduction was confirmed by his successor on his assuming the reins of power. For we find a charter of Henry III. conceding to the citizens of London (February 11, 1227)—

"Vicecomitatum Londoniæ et de Middlesexiâ cum omnibus rebus et consuetudinibus quæ pertinent ad prædictum Vicecomitatum, infra Civitatem et extra per terras et aquas; Habendum et tenendum eis et heredibus suis de nobis et heredibus nostris; Reddendo inde annuatim nobis et heredibus nostris *trescentas libras* sterlingorum blancorum . . . Hanc vero concessionem et confirmationem fecimus Civibus Londoniæ propter emendationem ejusdem Civitatis, et *quia antiquitus consuevit esse ad firmam pro trecentis libris.*"

The adhesion of the City to Simon de Montfort resulted in the forfeiture of its rights, and when, in 1270, the citizens were restored to favour, on payment of heavy sums to the king and to his son, they received permission "to have two sheriffs of their own who should hold the shrievalty of the City and Middlesex as they used to have." But the *firma* was raised from £300 to £400 a year.[1] Finally, on the accession of

[1] *Liber de Antiquis Legibus*, p. 124: "Circa idem tempus, scilicet Pentecosten [1270], ad instantiam domini Edwardi concessit Dominus Rex civibus ad habendum de se ipsis duos Vicecomites, qui tenerent Vicecomitatum Civitatis et Midelsexiæ ad firmam sicut ante solebant: Ita, tamen, cum temporibus transactis solvissent inde tantummodo per annum ccc libras sterlingorum blancorum, quod de cetero solvent annuatim cccc libras sterlingorum computatorum. . . . Et tunc tradite sunt civibus omnes antique carte eorum de libertatibus suis que fuerunt in manu Domini Regis, et concessum est eis per Dominum Regem et per Dominum Edwardum ut eis plenarie utantur, excepto quod pro firma Civitatis et Comitatus solvent per annum cccc libras, sicut præscriptum est.

"Tunc temporis dederunt Cives Domino Regi centum marcas sterlingorum. . . . Dederunt etiam Domino Edwardo V^c. marcas ad expensas suas in itinere versus Terram Sanctam." This passage is quoted in full because, important though the transaction is, not a trace of it is to be found in *The*

THE "FIRMA" OF LONDON AND MIDDLESEX. 359

Edward III. (March 9, 132$\frac{5}{6}$), the *firma* was reduced to the original sum of £300 a year, at which figure, Mr. Loftie says, " it has remained ever since." [1]

This one *firma*, of which the history has here been traced, represents one *corpus comitatus*, namely, Middlesex inclusive of London.[2] From this conclusion there is no escape.

Hence the *firmarii* of this *corpus comitatus* were from the first the *firmarii* (that is, the sheriffs) of Middlesex inclusive of London. This, similarly, is beyond dispute. As with the *firma* so with the sheriffs. Whether described as "of London," or "of Middlesex," or "of London and Middlesex," they are, from the first, the sheriffs of Middlesex inclusive of London.

This conclusion throws a new light on the charter by which Henry I. granted to the citizens of London Middlesex (*i.e.* Middlesex inclusive of London) at farm. Broadly speaking, the transaction in question may be regarded in this aspect. Instead of leasing the *corpus comitatus* to any one individual for a year, or for a term of years, the king leased it to the citizens as a body, leased it, moreover, in perpetuity, and at the low original *firma* of £300 a year. The change effected was simply that which was involved in placing the citizens, as a body, in the shoes of the Sheriff "of London and Middlesex." [3]

The only distinction between this lease and one to a private individual lies in the corporate character of the lessee, and in the consequent provision for the election of a representative of that corporate body: "Ita quod ipsi cives ponent vicecomites qualem voluerint de seipsis."

It would seem that under the *régime* adopted by Henry I.,

Historical Charters and Constitutional Documents of the City of London (1884), the latest work on the subject. So, in 1284, when Edward I., who had " taken into his hands " the town of Nottingham for some years, restored the burgesses their liberties, it was at the price of their *firma* being raised from £52 to £60 a year.

[1] *History of London*, ii. 208, 209.

[2] A curious illustration of the fact that this *firma* arose out of the city and county alike is afforded by Henry III.'s charter (1253): "quod vii libre sterlingorum per annum allocarentur Vicecomitibus in firma eorum pro libertate ecclesiæ sancti Pauli."

[3] This is illustrated by the subsequent prohibition of the sheriffs themselves underletting the county at "farm " (*Liber Custumarum*, p. 91 ; *Liber Albus*, p. 46).

the financial exactions of which a glimpse is afforded us in the solitary Pipe-Roll of his reign, included the leasing of the counties, etc. (*i.e.* of the financial rights of the Crown in them), at the highest rate possible. This was effected either by adding to the annual *firma*, a sum " de cremento," or by exacting from the *firmarius*, over and above his *firma*, a payment "de gersoma" for his lease. Where the lease was offered for open competition it would be worth the while of the would-be *firmarius* to offer a large payment " de gersoma " for his lease, if the *firma* was a low one. But if the *firma* was a high one, he would not offer much for his bargain. In the case of Oxfordshire we find the sheriff paying no less than four hundred marks " de gersoma, pro comitatu habendo."[1] But in Berkshire the payment "de gersoma" would seem to have been considerably less.[2] Sometimes the county (or group of counties) was leased for a specified term of years. Thus " Maenfininus " had taken a lease of Bucks. and Beds. for four years,[3] for which, seemingly, he paid but a trifling sum "de gersoma," while William de Eynsford (Æinesford) paid a hundred marks for a five years' lease of Essex and Herts.[4] Now, the fact that William de Eynsford was not an Essex but a Kentish landowner obviously suggests that in taking this lease he was actuated by speculative motives. It is, indeed, an admitted fact that the Norman gentry, in their greed for gain, were by no means above indulging in speculations of the kind. But when we make the interesting discovery that William de Eynsford, in this same reign, had acted as Sheriff of London,[5] may we not infer that, there also, he had indulged in a similar speculation ? That the shrievalty of London (*i.e.* London and Middlesex) was purchased by payments " de gersoma " is a matter, itself, not of inference, but of fact. Fulcred fitz Walter is debited in the Pipe-Rolls with a sum of " cxx marcas argenti de Gersoma pro Vicecomitatu Londoniæ."[6]

The *firmarius* who had succeeded in obtaining a lease would

---

[1] *Rot. Pip.*, 31 Hen. I., p. 2. [2] *Ibid.*, p. 122. [3] *Ibid.*, p. 100.
[4] *Ibid.*, p. 52.
[5] "William de Einesford, vicecomes de Londoniâ," heads the list of witnesses to a London agreement assigned to 1114–1130 (*Ramsey Cartulary*, i. 139).
[6] *Rot. Pip.*, 31 Hen. I., p. 144.

have to recoup himself, of course, from his receipts the amount of the actual "firma" *plus* his payment "de gersoma," before he could derive for himself any profit whatever from the transaction. This implied that he had closely to shear the flock committed to his charge. If he was a mere speculator, unconnected with his sphere of operations, he would have no scruple in doing this, and would resort to every means of extortion. What those means were it is now difficult to tell, for, obscure as the financial system of the Norman period may be, it is clear that just as the *rotulus exactorius* recorded the amounts to which the king was entitled from the *firmarii* of the various counties, so these *firmarii*, in their turn, were entitled to sums of ostensibly fixed amount from the various constituents of their counties' "corpora." Domesday, however, while recording these sums, shows us, in many remarkable cases, a larger "redditus" being paid than that which was strictly due. The fact is that we are, and must be, to a great extent, in the dark as to the fixity of these ostensibly stereotyped payments. That the remarkable rise in the annual *firmæ* exacted from the towns which, Domesday shows us, had taken place since, and consequent on, the Conquest would seem to imply that these *firmæ*, under the loose *régime* of the old system, had been allowed to remain so long unaltered that they had become antiquated and unduly low. In any case the Conqueror raised them sharply, probably according to his estimate of the financial capacity of the town. And this step would, of course, involve a rise in the total of the *firma* exacted from the *corpus comitatus*. The precedent which his father had thus set was probably followed by Henry I., who appears to have exacted, systematically, the uttermost farthing. It was probably, however, to the oppressive use of the "placita" included in the "firma comitatus" that the sheriffs mainly trusted to increase their receipts.

But whatever may have been the means of extortion possessed by the sheriffs in the towns within their rule,[1] and exercised by them to recoup themselves for the increased demands of the Crown, we know that such means there must have been, or it would not have been worth the while of the towns to

[1] Probably the mysterious "scotale" was among them (cf. Stubbs, *Const. Hist.*, i. 628).

offer considerable sums for the privilege of paying their *firmæ* to the Crown directly, instead of through the sheriffs.[1]

I would now institute a comparison between the cases of Lincoln and of London. In both cases the city formed part of the *corpus comitatus*; in both, therefore, its *firma* was included in the total ferm of the shire. Lincoln was at this time one of the largest and wealthiest towns in the country. Its citizens evidently had reason to complain of the exactions of the sheriff of the shire. London, we infer, was in the same plight. Both cities were, accordingly, anxious to exclude the financial intervention of the sheriff between themselves and the Crown. How was this end to be attained? It was attained in two different ways varying with the circumstances of the two cases. London was considerably larger than Lincoln, and Middlesex infinitely smaller than Lincolnshire. Thus while the *firma* of Lincoln represented less than a fifth of the ferm of the shire,[2] that of London would, of course, constitute the bulk of the ferm of Middlesex. Lincoln, therefore, would only seek to sever itself financially from the shire; London, on the contrary, would endeavour to exclude, still more effectually, the sheriff, by itself boldly stepping into the sheriff's shoes. The action of the citizens of Lincoln is revealed to us by the Roll of 1130:—

"Burgenses Lincolie reddunt compotum de cc marcis argenti et iiij marcis auri ut teneant ciuitatem de Rege in capite" (p. 114).

The same Roll is witness to that of the citizens of London:—

"Homines Londonie reddunt compotum de c marcis argenti ut habeant Vic[ecomitem?] ad electionem suam" (p. 148).

I contend that these two passages ought to be read together. No one appears to have observed the fact that the sequel to the above Lincoln entry is to be found in the Pipe-Roll of 1157 (3 Hen. II.). We there find £140 deducted from the ferm of the shire in consideration of the severance of the city from the *corpus comitatus* ("Et in Civitate Lincol[nie] CXL libræ blancæ"). But we further find the citizens of Lincoln, in accounting for their *firma* to the Crown direct, accounting not for £140, but for

[1] Cf. Stubbs, *Const. Hist.*, i. 410.
[2] The ferm of Lincolnshire in 1130 was rather over £750 (£40 "numero" *plus* £716 16s. 3d. "blanch").

THE "FIRMA" LEASED TO THE LONDONERS. 363

£180. It must, consequently, have been worth their while to offer the Crown a sum equivalent to about a year's rental for the privilege of paying it £180 direct rather than £140 through the sheriff.[1] Such figures are eloquent as to the extortions from which they had suffered. The citizens of London, as I have said, set to work a different way. They simply sought to lease the shrievalty of the shire themselves. I can, on careful consideration, offer no other suggestion than that the hundred marcs for which they account in the Roll of 1130, represent the payment by which they secured a lease of the shrievalty for the year 1129–1130, the shrievalty being held in that year by the "quatuor vicecomites" of the Roll. I gather from the Roll that Fulcred fitz Walter had been sheriff for 1128–29, and his payment "de gersoma" is, I take it, represented in the case of the following year (1129–30) by these hundred marks, the "quatuor vicecomites" themselves having paid nothing "de gersoma." On this view, the citizens must have leased the shrievalty themselves and then put in four of their fellows, as representing them, to hold it. But, obviously, such a post was not one to be coveted. To exact sufficient from their fellow-citizens wherewith to meet the claims of the Crown would be a task neither popular nor pleasant. Indeed, the fact of the citizens installing four "vicecomites" may imply that they could not find any one man who would consent to fill a post as thankless as that of the hapless *decurio* in the provinces of the Roman Empire, or of the chamberlain, in a later age, in the country towns of England. Hence it may be that we find it thus placed in commission. Hence, also, the eagerness of these *vicecomites* to be quit of office, as shown by their payment, for that privilege, of two marcs of gold apiece.[2] It may, however, be frankly confessed that the nature of this payment is not so clear as could be wished. Judging from the very ancient practice with regard to municipal offices, one

[1] We have a precisely similar illustration, ninety years later, in the case of Carlisle. In 5 Hen. III. (1220-21) the citizens of Carlisle obtained permission to hold their city *ad firmam* for £60 a year payable to the Crown direct, in the place of £52 a year payable through the sheriff ("per vicecomitem") and his ferm of the shire (*Ninth Report Hist. MSS.*, App. i. pp. 197, 202).

[2] *Rot. Pip.*, 31 Hen. I., p. 149.

would have thought that such payments would probably have been made to their fellow-citizens who had thrust on them the office rather than to the Crown. Moreover, if their year of office was over, and the city's lease at an end, one would have thought they would be freed from office in the ordinary course of things. The only explanation, perhaps, that suggests itself is that they purchased from the Crown an exemption from serving again even though their fellow-citizens should again elect them to office.[1] But I leave the point in doubt.

The hypothesis, it will be seen, that I have here advanced is that the citizens leased the shrievalty (so far as we know, for the first time) for the year 1129–30. We have the names of those who held the shrievalty at various periods in the course of the reign, before this year, but there is no evidence that, throughout this period, it was ever leased to the citizens. The important question which now arises is this : How does this view affect the charter granted to the citizens by Henry I. ?

We have first to consider the date to which the charter should be assigned. Mr. Loftie characteristically observes that Rymer, "from the names appended to it or some other evidence, dates it in 1101."[2] As a matter of fact, Rymer assigns no year to it; nor, indeed, did Rymer himself even include it in his work. In the modern enlarged edition of that work the charter is printed, but without a date, nor was it till 1885 that in the Record Office *Syllabus*, begun by Sir T. D. Hardy, the date 1101 was assigned to it.[3] That date is possibly to be traced to Northouck's *History of London* (1773), in which the commencement of Henry's reign is suggested as a probable period (p. 27). This view is set forth also in a modern work upon the subject.[4] It is not often that we meet with a charter so difficult to date. The *formula* of address, as

---

[1] Compare Henry III.'s charter to John Gifard of Chillington, conceding that during his lifetime he should not be made a *sheriff*, coroner, or any other bailiff against his will (*Staffordshire Collections*, v. [1] 158).

[2] *History of London*, ii. 88. Compare Mr. Loftie's *London* ("Historic Towns"), p. 28: "The exact date of the charter is given by Rymer as 1101."

[3] Vol. iii. p. 4.

[4] *The Charters of the City of London* (1884), p. xiiii.: "To engage the citizens to support his Government he conferred upon them the advantageous privileges that are conferred in this charter."

it includes justices, points, according to my own theory, to a late period in the reign, as also does the differentiation between the justice and the sheriff. And the witnesses do the same. But there is, unfortunately, no witness of sufficient prominence to enable us to fix the date with precision. All that we can say is that such a name as that of Hugh Bigod points to the period 1123–1135, and that, of the nine witnesses named, seven or eight figure in the Pipe-Roll of 1130 (31 Hen. I.). This would suggest that these two documents must be of about the same date. Now, though we cannot trace the tenure of the shrievalty before Michaelmas, 1128, from the Roll, there is, as I have said, no sign that this charter had come into play. Nor is it easy to understand how or why it could be withdrawn within a very few years of its grant. In short, for this view there is not a scrap of evidence; against it, is all probability. If, on the contrary, we adopt the hypothesis which I am now going to advance, namely, that the charter was later than the Pipe-Roll, the difficulties all vanish. By this view, the lease for a year, to which the Pipe-Roll bears witness, would be succeeded by a permanent arrangement, that lease of the ferm in perpetuity, which we find recorded in the charter.

It is, indeed, evident that the contrary view rests solely on the guess at "1101," or on the assumption of Dr. Stubbs that the charter was earlier than the Pipe-Roll. Mr. Freeman and others have merely followed him. Dr. Stubbs writes thus:—

"Between the date of Henry's charter and that of the great Pipe-Roll, some changes in the organization of the City must have taken place. In 1130 there were four sheriffs or vicecomites, who jointly account for the ferm of London, instead of the one mentioned in the charter; and part of the account is rendered by a chamberlain of the City. The right to appoint the sheriffs has been somehow withdrawn, for the citizens pay a hundred marks of silver that they may have a sheriff of their own choice," etc., etc.[1]

But our great historian nowhere tells us what he considers "the date of Henry's charter" to have been. If that date was subsequent to the Pipe-Roll, the whole of his argument falls to the ground.

The substitution of four sheriffs for one, to which Dr. Stubbs alludes, is a matter of slight consequence, for the number of

[1] *Const. Hist.*, i. 406.

the "vicecomites" varies throughout. As a matter of fact, the abbreviated forms leave us, as in the Pipe-Roll of 1130, doubtful whether we ought to read "vicecomitem" or vicecomites," and even if the former is the one intended, we know, both in this and other cases, that there was nothing unusual in putting the office in commission between two or more. As to the chamberlain, he does not figure in connection with the *firma*, with which alone we are here concerned. But, oddly enough, Dr. Stubbs has overlooked the really important point, namely, that the *firma* is not £300, as fixed by the charter, but over £500.[1] This increases the discrepancy on which Dr. Stubbs lays stress. The most natural inference from this fact is that, as on several later occasions, the Crown had greatly raised the *firma* (which had been under the Conqueror £300), and that the citizens now, by a heavy payment, secured its reduction to the original figure. Thus, on my hypothesis that the charter was granted between 1130 and 1135, the Crown must have been tempted, by the offer of an enormous sum down, to grant (1) a lease in perpetuity, (2) a reduction of the fee-farm rent ("firma") to £300 a year. As the sum to which the *firma* had been raised by the king, together with the annual *gersoma*, amounted to some £600 a year, such a reduction can only have been purchased by a large payment in ready money.

It was, of course, by such means as these that Henry accumulated the vast "hoard" that the treasury held at his death. He may not improbably in collecting this wealth have kept in view what appears to have been the supreme aim of his closing years, namely, the securing of the succession to his heirs. This was to prove the means by which their claims should be supported. It would, perhaps, be refining too much to suggest that he hoped by this charter to attach the citizens to the interests of his line, on whom alone it could be binding. In any case his efforts were notoriously vain, for London headed throughout the opposition to the claims of his heirs. I cannot but think that his financial system had much to do with this result, and that, as with the Hebrews at the death of Solomon, the citizens of London bethought them only of his "grievous service" and his "heavy yoke," as when they met

---

[1] £327 3s. 11d. "blanch," *plus* £209 6s. 5½d. "numero."

CONCESSIONS OF HENRY I. NOT RENEWED.

the demand of his daughter for an enormous sum of money[1] by bluntly requesting a return to the system of Edward the Confessor.[2]

In any case the concessions in Henry's charter were wholly ignored both by Stephen and by the Empress, when they granted in turn to the Earl of Essex the shrievalty of London and Middlesex (1141-42).

A fresh and important point must, however, now be raised. What was the attitude of Henry II. towards his grandfather's charter? Of our two latest writers on the subject, Mr. Loftie tells us that

"Henry II. was too astute a ruler not to put himself at once on a good footing with the citizens. One of his first acts was to confirm the Great Charter of his grandfather."[3]

Miss Norgate similarly asserts that "the charter granted by Henry II. to the citizens, some time before the end of 1158, is simply a confirmation of his grandfather's."[4] Such, indeed, would seem to be the accepted belief. Yet, when we compare the two documents, we find that the special concessions with which I am here dealing, and which form the opening clauses of the charter of Henry I., are actually omitted altogether in that of Henry II.![5] This leads us to examine the rest of the

[1] "Infinitæ copiæ pecuniam . . . cum ore imperioso ab eis exegit" (*Gesta Stephani*).

[2] "Interpellata est et a civibus ut leges eis regis Edwardi observare liceret, quia optimæ erant, non patris sui Henrici quia graves erant" (*Cont. Flor. Wig.*).

[3] *London* ("Historic Towns"), p. 38. The Master of University similarly writes: "He [Henry II.] renewed the charter of the city of London" (i. 90).

[4] *England under the Angevin Kings*, ii. 471. The writer, being only acquainted with the printed copy of the charter (*Liber Custumarum*, ed. Riley, pp. 31, 32), had only the names of the two witnesses there given (the Archbishop of Canterbury and the Bishop of London) to guide her, but, fortunately, the *Liber Rubeus* version records all the witnesses (thirteen in number) together with the place of testing, thus limiting the date to 1154-56, and virtually to 1155.

[5] The omitted clauses are these: "Sciatis me concessisse civibus meis Londoniarum, tenendum Middlesex ad firmam pro ccc libris ad compotum, ipsis et heredibus suis, de me et heredibus meis, ita quod ipsi cives ponent vicecomitem qualem voluerint de se ipsis, et justitiarium qualem voluerint de se ipsis, ad custodiendum placita coronæ meæ et eadem placitanda; et nullus alius erit justitiarius super ipsos homines Londoniarum."

latter document. To facilitate this process I have here arranged the two charters side by side, and divided their contents into numbered clauses, italicizing the points of difference.

HENRY I.

(1) Cives non placitabunt extra muros civitatis pro ullo placito.

(2) Sint quieti *de schot et de loth de Danegildo et* de murdro, et nullus eorum faciat bellum.

(3) Et si quis civium de placitis coronæ implacitatus fuerit, per sacramentum quod judicatum fuerit in civitate, se disrationet homo Londoniarum.

(4) Et infra muros civitatis nullus hospitetur, neque de mea familia, neque de alia, nisi alicui hospitium liberetur.

(5) Et omnes homines Londoniarum sint quieti et liberi, et omnes res eorum, et per totam Angliam et per portus maris, de thelonio *et passagio* et lestagio *et omnibus aliis consuetudinibus.*

(6) Et ecclesiæ et barones et cives teneant et habeant bene et in pace socnas suas cum omnibus consuetudinibus, ita quod hospites qui in soccis suis hospitantur nulli dent consuetudines suas, nisi illi cujus socca fuerit, vel ministro suo quem ibi posuerit.

(7) Et homo Londoniarum non judicetur in misericordia pecuniæ nisi ad suam *were*, scilicet ad c solidos, dico de placito quod ad pecuniam pertineat.

HENRY II.

(1) Nullus eorum placitet extra muros civitatis Londoniarum[1] de ullo placito *præter placita de tenuris exterioribus, exceptis monetariis et ministris meis.*

(2) Concessi etiam eis quietanciam murdri, [*et*[2]] *infra urbem et Portsokna,*[3] et quod nullus[4] faciat bellum.[5]

(3) De placitis ad coronam [spectantibus[6]] se possunt disrationare secundum antiquam consuetudinem civitatis.

(4) Infra muros nemo capiat hospitium per vim vel per liberationem Marescalli.

(5) Omnes cives Londoniarum[7] sint quieti de theloneo et lestagio per totam Angliam et per portum[8] maris.

[This clause is wholly omitted.]

(7) Nullus de misericordia pecuniæ judicetur nisi secundum legem civitatis quam habuerunt tempore Henrici regis[9] avi mei.

---

[1] " Lond' " (*Liber Rubeus*).
[2] " Et " omitted in *L. R.*
[3] " Portsoca " (*L. R.*).
[4] " Nullus eorum " (*L. R.*).
[5] " Duellum " (*L. R.*).
[6] " Pertinentibus " (*L. R.*).
[7] " London' " (*L. R.*).
[8] " Port' " (*L. R.*).
[9] " Regis H." (*L. R.*).

(8) Et amplius non sit miskenninga in hustenge, neque in folkesmote, neque in aliis placitis infra civitatem ; Et husteng sedeat semel in hebdomada, videlicet die Lunæ.

(9) Et terras suas *et wardemotum* et debita civibus meis habere faciam *infra civitatem et extra*.

(10) Et de terris de quibus ad me clamaverint rectum eis tenebo lege civitatis.

(12) Et omnes debitores qui civibus debita debent eis reddant vel in Londoniis se disrationent quod non debent. *Quod si reddere noluerint, neque ad disrationandum venire, tunc cives quibus debita sua debent capiant intra civitatem namia sua, vel de comitatu in quo manet qui debitum debet.*

(11) Et si quis thelonium vel consuetudinem a civibus Londoniarum ceperit, *cives* Londoniarum capiant de burgo vel de villa ubi theloneum vel consuetudo capta fuit, quantum homo Londoniarum pro theloneo dedit, et proinde de damno ceperit.[4]

(13) Et cives habeant fugationes suas ad fugandum sicut melius et plenius habuerunt antecessores eorum, scilicet Chiltre et Middlesex et Sureie.

(8) In civitate in nullo placito sit miskenninga ; et quod Hustengus semel tantum in hebdomada teneatur.

(9) Terras suas *et tenuras et vadimonia* et debita omnia juste habeant, quicunque eis debeat.

(10) De terris suis et tenuris *quæ infra urbem sunt*, rectum eis teneatur secundum legem[1] civitatis ; et de omnibus debitis suis quæ accomodata fuerint apud Londonias,[2] et de vadimoniis ibidem factis, placita [? sint] apud Londoniam.[3]

(11) Et si quis *in tota Anglia* theloneum et consuetudinem ab hominibus Londoniarum[2] ceperit, *postquam ipse a recto defecerit, Vicecomes* Londoniarum[1] namium inde *apud Londonias*[2] capiat.

(12) Habeant fugationes suas, ubicumque[5] habuerunt tempore Regis Henrici avi mei.

(13) *Insuper etiam, ad emendationem civitatis, eis concessi quod*[6] *sint quieti de Brudtolle, et de Childewite, et de Yaresive,*[7] *et de Scotale ; ita quod Vicecomes meus* (sic) *London[iarum]*[8] *vel aliquis alius ballivus Scotalla non faciat.*

Before passing to a comparison of these charters, we must glance at the question of texts. The charter of Henry I. is taken from the *Select Charters* of Dr. Stubbs, who has gone to

[1] "Consuetudinem" (*L. R.*).   [2] "Lond'" (*L. R.*).
[3] "Apud Lond' teneantur" (*L. R.*).
[4] Clauses 11 and 12 in the charter of Henry I. are transposed in that of Henry II. But it is more convenient to show the transposition as I have done in the text.
[5] "Eas habuerunt" (*L. R.*).   [6] "Omnes sint" (*L. R.*).
[7] "Yeresgieve" (*L. R.*).   [8] "Londou'" (*L. R.*).

the *Fœdera* for his text (which is taken from an Inspeximus of
5 Edw. IV.). That of Henry II. is taken from the transcript
in the *Liber Custumarum* (collated with the *Liber Rubeus*).
Neither of these sources is by any means as pure as could be
wished. The names of the witnesses in both had always aroused
my suspicions,[1] but the collation of the two charters has led to
a singular discovery. It will be noticed that in the charter of
Henry I. the citizens are guaranteed " terras *et wardemotum* et
debita sua." Now, this is on the face of it an unmeaning combination. Why should the wardmoot be thus sandwiched
between the lands of the citizens and the debts due to them ?
And what can be the meaning of confirming to them their
wardmoot (? wardmoots), when the hustings is only mentioned
as an infliction and the folkmoot as a medium of extortion ?
Yet, corrupt though this passage, on the face of it, appears,
our authorities have risen at this unlucky word, if I may
venture on the expression, like pike. Dr. Stubbs, Professor
Freeman, Miss Norgate, Mr. Green, Mr. Loftie, Mr. Price, etc.,
etc., have all swallowed it without suspicion. Historians, like
doctors, may often differ, but truly " when they do agree their
unanimity is wonderful." Collation, however, fortunately
proves that " wardemotum " is nothing more than a gross misreading of " vadimonia," a word which restores to the passage
its sense by showing that what Henry confirmed to the citizens
was " the property mortgaged to them, and the debts due to
them." [2]

Having thus enforced the necessity for caution in arguing
from the text as it stands, I would urge that, with the exception
of the avowed addition at the close, the later charter has, in
sundry details, the aspect of a grudging confirmation, restricting

[1] The first two witnesses to that of Henry I. are given as " episcopo
Winton., Roberto filio Richer. (*sic*)." The bishop's initial ought to be given,
and the second witness is probably identical with Robert fitz Richard.
" Huberto (*sic*) regis camerario " has also a suspicious sound. In the second
charter the witnesses are given in the *Liber Custumarum* as " Archiepiscopo
Cantuariæ, Ricardo Episcopo Londoniarum." Here, again, the primate's
initial should be given; as, indeed, it is in the (more accurate) *Liber Rubeus*
version, where (*vide supra*, p. 367) all the witnesses are entered.

[2] This explanation is confirmed by examining other municipal charters
based on that of London. In them this clause always confirms (1) " terras
et tenuras," (2) " vadia," (3) " debita."

rather than enlarging the benefits conferred. This, however, is but a small matter in comparison with its total omission of the main concession itself. This fact, so strangely overlooked, coincides with the king's allusion to the sheriff as "vicecomes *meus*" (no longer the citizens' sheriff),[1] but explains above all the circumstance, which would be quite inexplicable without it, that the *firma* is again, under Henry II., found to be not £300, but over £500 a year.

In 1164 (10 Hen. II.) the *firma* of London, if I reckon it right, was, as in 1130 (31 Hen. I.), about £520.[2] In 1160 (6 Hen. II.) it was a few pounds less,[3] and in 1161 (7 Hen. II.) it was little, it would seem, over £500.[4] But in these calculations it is virtually impossible to attain perfect accuracy, not only from the system of keeping accounts partly in *libræ* partly in *marcæ*, and partly in money "blanched" partly in money "numero," but also from the fact that the figures on the Pipe-Rolls are by no means so infallible as might be supposed.[5]

Nor does the charter of Richard I. (April 23, 1194) make any change. It merely confirms that of his father. But John, in addition to confirming this (June 17, 1199), granted a supplementary charter (July 5, 1199)—

[1] In confirmation of this view, it may be pointed out that where this same clause occurs in charters to other towns, the words are "vicecomes *noster*" in cases, as at Winchester, where the king retains in his hand the appointment of reeve, but simply (as at Lincoln) "præpositus" or (as at Northampton) "præpositus Northamtonie," where the right to elect the reeve was also conceded.

[2] £66 17s. 1d. "blanch" *plus* £474 17s. 10½d. "numero."

[3] £445 19s. "blanch" *plus* £78 3s. 6d. "numero."

[4] £181 14s. 5d. "blanch" *plus* £335 0s. 7d. "numero."

[5] As an example of the possibility of error, in the printed Roll of 1159 (5 Hen. II.) a town is entered on the Roll as paying "quater xx. lv libras et ii marcas et dim'." The explanation of this unintelligible entry is, I may observe, as follows. The original entry evidently ran, "quater xx et ii marcas et dim'" (82½ marcs). Over this a scribe will have written the equivalent amount in pounds ("lv libræ") by interlineation. Then came the modern transcriber, who with the stupidity of a mechanical copyist brought down this interlineation into the middle of the entry, thus converting it into sheer nonsense. We have also to reckon with such clerical errors as the addition or omission of an "x" or an "i," of a "bl." or a "no." Where the total to be accounted for is stated separately, we have a means of checking the accounts. But where, as at London, this is not so, we cannot be too careful in accepting the details as given. See also Addenda.

"Sciatis nos concessisse et præsenti Charta nostra confirmasse civibus Londoniarum Vicecomitatum Londoniarum et de Middelsexia, cum omnibus rebus et consuetudinibus quæ pertinent ad prædictum Vicecomitatum . . . reddendo inde annuatim nobis et heredibus nostris ccc libras sterlingorum blancorum . . . Et præterea concessimus civibus Londoniarum, quod ipsi de se ipsis faciant Vicecomites quoscunque voluerint, et amoveant quando voluerint; . . . Hanc vero concessionem et confirmationem fecimus civibus Londoniarum propter emendationem ejusdem civitatis et quia antiquitus consuevit esse ad firmam pro ccc libris."[1]

Here at length we return to the concessions of Henry I., with which this charter of John ought to be carefully compared. With the exception of the former's provision about the "justiciar" (an exception which must not be overlooked), the concessions are the same. The subsequent raising of the *firma* to £400 (in 1270), and its eventual reduction to £300 (in 1327), have been already dealt with (pp. 358, 359).

We see then that, in absolute contradiction of the received belief on the subject, the shrievalty was not in the hands of the citizens during the twelfth century (*i.e.* from "1101"), but was held by them for a few years only, about the close of the reign of Henry I. The fact that the sheriffs of London and Middlesex were, under Henry II. and Richard I., appointed throughout by the Crown, must compel our historians to reconsider the independent position they have assigned to the City at that early period. The Crown, moreover, must have had an object in retaining this appointment in its hands. We may find it, I think, in that jealousy of exceptional privilege or exemption which characterized the *régime* of Henry II. For, as I have shown, the charters to Geoffrey remind us that the ambition of the urban communities was analogous to that of the great feudatories in so far as they both strove for exemption from official rule. It was precisely to this ambition that Henry II. was opposed; and thus, when he granted his charter to London, he wholly omitted, as we have seen, two of his grandfather's concessions, and narrowed down those that remained, that they might not be operative outside the actual walls of the city. When the shrievalty was restored by John to the citizens (1199), the concession had lost its chief importance through the triumph of the "communal" principle.

[1] *Liber Custumarum* (Rolls Series), pp. 249-251.

THE SHRIEVALTY RESTORED BY JOHN.

When that civic revolution had taken place which introduced the "communa" with its mayor—a revolution to which Henry II. would never, writes the chronicler, have submitted—when a Londoner was able to boast that he would have no king but his mayor, then had the sheriff's position become but of secondary importance, subordinate, as it has remained ever since, to that of the mayor himself.

The transient existence of the local *justitiarius* is a phenomenon of great importance, which has been wholly misunderstood. The Mandeville charters afford the clue to the nature of this office. It represents a middle term, a transitional stage, between the essentially *local* shire-reeve and the *central* "justice" of the king's court. I have already (p. 106) shown that the office sprang from "the differentiation of the sheriff and the justice," and represented, as it were, the localization of the central judicial element. That is to say, the *justitiarius* for Essex, or Herts., or London and Middlesex, was a purely local officer, and yet exercised, within the limits of his bailiwick, all the authority of the king's justice. So transient was this state of things that scarcely a trace of it remains. Yet Richard de Luci may have held the post, as we saw (p. 109), for the county of Essex, and there is evidence that Norfolk had a justice of its own in the person of Ralf Passelewe.[1] Now, in the case of London, the office was created by the charter of Henry I., granted (as I contend) towards the end of his reign, and it expired with the accession of Henry II. It is, therefore, in Stephen's reign that we should expect to find it in existence; and it is precisely in that reign that we find the office *eo nomine* twice granted to the Earl of Essex and twice mentioned as held by Gervase, otherwise Gervase of Cornhill.[2]

The office of the "Justiciar of London" should now be no longer obscure; its possible identity with those of portreeve, sheriff, or mayor cannot, surely, henceforth be maintained.

[1] "Contra Radulfum de Belphago qui tunc vicecomes erat in provincia illa et contra Radulfum Passelewe ejusdem provinciæ justiciarium" (*Ramsey Cart.*, i. 149).

[2] See Appendix K, on "Gervase of Cornhill."

APPENDIX Q.

OSBERTUS OCTODENARII.

(See p. 170.)

THE reference to this personage in the charter to the Earl of Essex is of quite exceptional interest. He was the Osbert (or Osbern) "Huit-deniers" (*alias* "Octodenarii" *alias* "Octonummi") who was a wealthy kinsman of Becket and employed him, in his house, as a clerk about this very time (*circ.* 1139-1142). We meet him as "Osbertus VIII. denarii" at London in 1130 (*Rot. Pip.*, 31 Hen. I.), and I have also found him attesting a charter of Henry I., late in the reign, as "Osberto Octodenar[ii]." Garnier[1] tells us that the future saint—

> "A soen parent vint, un riche hume Lundreis,
> Ke mult ert koneüz et de Frauns et d'Engleis,
> O Osbern witdeniers, ki l'retint demaneis.
> Puis fu ses escriveins, ne sais dous ans, u treis."

Another biographer writes:—

"Rursus vero Osbernus, Octonummi cognomine, vir insignis in civitate et multarum possessionum cui carne propinquus erat detentum circa se Thomam fere per triennium in breviandis sumptibus redditibusque suis jugiter occupabat."[2]

The influential position of this wealthy Londoner is dwelt on by yet another biographer:—

"Ad quendam Lundrensem, cognatum suum, qui non solum inter concives, verum etiam apud curiales, grandis erat nominis et honoris se contulit."[3]

In one of the appendices we shall detect him under the strange form "Ottdevers"[4] (= "Ottdeuers," a misreading for

[1] *Vie de St. Thomas* (ed. Hippeau, 1859).   [2] Grim.
[3] Auctor anonymus.
[4] Its apparent dissimilarity to the "Octod'" of Geoffrey's charter is instructive to note.

ALLUSIONS TO BECKET'S YOUTH. 375

"Ottdeners") witnessing a treaty arrangement between the Earls of Hereford and Gloucester. This he did in his capacity of feudal tenant to the latter, for in the Earl of Gloucester's *Carta* (1166) of his tenants in Kent we read: " Feodum Osberti oitdeniers i mil[item]," from which we learn that he had held one knight's fee.[1]

This singular *cognomen*, though savouring of the nickname period, may have become hereditary, for we meet with a Philip Utdeners in 1223, and with Alice and Agnes his daughters in 1233.[2]

As I have here alluded to Becket it may be permissible to mention that as the statements of his biographers in the matter of Osbert are confirmed by this extraneous evidence, so have we also evidence in charters of his residence, as "Thomas of London," in the primate's household. To two charters of Theobald to Earls Colne Priory the first witness is "Thoma Lond' Capellano nostro,"[3] while an even more interesting charter of the primate brings before us those three names, which, says William of Canterbury, were those of his three intimates, the first witness being Roger of Bishopsbridge, while the fourth and fifth are John of Canterbury and Thomas of London, "clerks."[4] Here is abundant evidence that Becket was then known as "Thomas of London," as indeed Gervase of Canterbury himself implies.[5]

[1] Hearne, who prints this entry, "Feodum Osberti oct. deniers i. mil." (*Liber Niger*, ed. 1774, i. 53), makes it the occasion of an exquisitely funny display of erudite Latinity, in which he gravely rebukes Dugdale for his ignorance on the subject ("quid sibi velit *denariata militis* ignorasse videtur Dugdalius quam tamen is facile intelliget," etc., etc.), having himself mistaken the tenant's name for a term of land measurement.

[2] *Bracton's Note-book* (ed. Maitland), ii. 616; iii. 495. A Nicholas "Treys-deners" or "Treydeners" occurs in Cornwall in the same reign (*De Banco*, 45-46 Hen. III., Mich., No. 16, m. 62). "Penny" and "Twopenny" are still familiar surnames among us, as is also "Pennyfather" (? Pennyfarthing).

[3] *Addl. MS.*, 5860, fols. 221, 223 (ink).

[4] *Cott. MSS.*, Nero, C. iii. fol. 188.

[5] " Clerico suo Thomæ Londoniensi " (i. 160).

(376)

APPENDIX R.

THE FOREST OF ESSEX.

(See pp. 92, 168, 182.)

THE references to assarts and to (forest) pleas in the first and second charters of the Empress ought to be carefully compared, as they are of importance in many ways. They run thus respectively:—

FIRST CHARTER.

Ut ipse et omnes homines sui per totam Angliam sint quieti de Wastis forestariis et assartis que facta sunt in feodo ipsius Gaufredi usque ad diem quo homo meus devenit, et ut a die illo in antea omnia illa essarta sint amodo excultibilia, et arrabilia sine forisfacto.

SECOND CHARTER.

Quod ipse et omnes homines sui habeant et lucrentur omnia essarta sua libera et quieta de omnibus placitis facta usque ad diem qua servicio domini mei Comitis Andegavie ac meo adhæsit.

A similar provision will be found in the charter to Aubrey de Vere. It is evident from these special provisions that the grantees attached a peculiar importance to this indemnity for their assarts; and it is equally noteworthy that the Empress is careful to restrict that indemnity to those assarts which had been made before a certain date ("facta usque ad diem quâ," etc.). This restriction should be compared with that which similarly limited the indemnity claimed by the barons of the Exchequer,[1] and which has been somewhat overlooked.[2]

Assarts are duly dealt with in the *Leges Henrici Primi*, and would form an important part of the "placita forestæ" in his reign. It is reasonable to presume that one of the first

[1] "Ut de hiis essartis dicantur quieti, quæ fuerant *ante diem quâ rex illustris Henricus primus rebus humanis exemptus est*" (*Dialogus*, i. 11). The reason for the restriction is added.

[2] See, for instance, *The Forest of Essex* (Fisher), p. 313.

results of the removal of his iron hand would be a violent reaction against the tyranny of "the forest." Indeed, we know that Stephen was compelled to give way upon the point. A general outburst of "assarting" would at once follow. Thus the prospect of the return, with the Empress, of her father's forest-law would greatly alarm the offenders who were guilty of "assarts."[1]

But, further, the earl's fief lay away from the forest proper. Why, then, was this concession of such importance in his eyes? We are helped towards an answer to this question by Mr. Fisher's learned and instructive work on *The Forest of Essex*. The facts there given, though needing some slight correction, show us that the Crown asserted in the reign of Henry III., that the portion of the county which had been afforested since the accession of Henry II. had (with the exception of the hundred of Tendring) been merely reafforested, having been already "forest" at the death of Henry I., though under Stephen it had ceased to be so. This claim, which was successfully asserted, affected more than half the county. Now it is singular that throughout the struggle, on this subject, with the Crown, the true forest, that of Waltham (now Epping), was always conceded to be "within forest." Mr. Fisher's valuable maps show its limits clearly. It was, accordingly, tacitly admitted by the perambulation consequent on the Charter of the Forest to have been "forest" before 1154.

The theory suggested to me by these *data* is this. Stephen, we know, by his Charter of Liberties consented that all the forests created by Henry I. should be disafforested, and retained for himself only those which had been "forest" in the days of the first and the second William. Under this arrangement he retained, I hold, the small true forest (Waltham forest), but had to resign the grasp of the Crown on the additions made to it by Henry I., which amounted to considerably more than half the county. My view that this sweeping extension of "forest" was the work of Henry I. is confirmed by the fact that his "forest" policy is admittedly the most objectionable

[1] As a matter of fact, her son's succession was marked by the exaction of heavy sums, under this head, as shown by the extracts from his first Pipe-Roll in the Red book of the Exchequer.

feature of his rule. Nor, I take it, was it inspired so much by the love of sport as by the great facilities it afforded for pecuniary exaction. In the Pipe-Roll of his thirty-first year we find (to adapt an old saying) "forest pleas as thick as fleas" in Essex, affording proof, moreover, that his "forest" had extended to the extreme north-east of the Lexden hundred. Here then again, I believe, as in so many other matters, Henry II. ignored his predecessor, and reverted to the *status quo ante*. Nor was the claim he revived finally set at rest, till Parliament disposed of it for ever in the days of Charles I.

An interesting charter bearing on this subject is preserved to us by Inspeximus.[1] It records the restoration by Stephen to the Abbess of Barking of all her estates afforested by Henry I.[2] Now, this charter, which is tested at Clarendon (perhaps the only record of Stephen being there), is witnessed by W[illiam] Martel, A[ubrey] de Ver, and E[ustace] fitz John. The name of this last witness[3] dates the charter as previous to 1138 (when he threw over Stephen), and, virtually, to the king's departure for Normandy early in 1137. Consequently (and this is an important point) we here have Stephen granting, as a favour, to Barking Abbey what he had promised in his great charter to grant universally.[4] This confirms the charge made by Henry of Huntingdon that he repudiated the concession he had made. His subsequent troubles, however, must have made it difficult for him to adhere to this policy, or check the process of assarting. His grant to the abbess was unknown to Mr. Fisher, who records an inquest of 1292, by which it was found that the woods of the abbess were " without the Regard; " and the Regarders were forbidden to exercise their authority within them.

[1] Pat. 2 Hen. VI., p. 3, m. 18.

[2] " Reddo et concedo ecclesiæ Berchingie et Abbatissæ Adel[iciæ] omnes boscos et terras suas . . . quas Henricus Rex afforestavit, ut illas excolat et hospitetur."

[3] Probably present as a brother of the abbess ("Soror Pagani filii Johannis").

[4] " Omnes forestas quas rex Henricus superaddidit ecclesiis et regno quietas reddo et concedo."

APPENDIX S.

THE TREATY OF ALLIANCE BETWEEN THE EARLS OF HEREFORD AND GLOUCESTER.

(See p. 176.)

THE document which is printed below is unknown, it would seem, to historians. It is of a very singular and, in many ways, of a most instructive character. The fact that Earl Miles is one of the contracting parties dates the document as belonging to the period between his creation (July 25, 1141) and his death (December 24, 1143). Further, the fact that the treaty provides for the surrender by him to the Earl of Gloucester of one of his sons as a hostage, taken with the fact that the Earl of Gloucester is recorded (*supra*, p. 196) to have demanded from his leading supporters their sons as hostages when he left England for Normandy, creates an extremely strong presumption that this document should be assigned to that occasion (June, 1142). It is here printed from a transcript by Dugdale, which I found among his MSS. The absence of any provision defining the services to be rendered by Earl Miles suggests that this portion of the treaty is omitted in the transcript. There is, I think, just a chance that the original may yet be discovered among the public records, for they fortunately contain a similar treaty between the sons and successors of the two contracting parties.[1] It may be, however, that the original is the document referred to by Dugdale (*Baronage*, i. 537) as " penes Joh. Philipot Somerset Heraldum anno 1640." The close resemblance between the later document [1] and that which I here print confirms the

[1] Duchy of Lancaster: Ancient Charters, Box A. No. 4 (*Thirty-Fifth Report of Deputy Keeper* [1874], p. 2).

authenticity of the latter, and is, it will be seen, illustrated by the wording of the opening clauses:—

Noscant omnes hanc esse confederationem amoris inter Robertum Comitem Gloecestrie et Milonem Comitem Herefordie.	Hæc est confederatio amoris inter Willelmum Comitem Gloec[estrie] et Rogerum comitem Herefordie.

We have also the noteworthy coincidence that Richard de St. Quintin and Hugh de Hese, who are here hostages respectively for the Earls of Gloucester and Hereford, figure again in the later document as hostages for the earls' successors.[1]

Another document with which this treaty should be carefully compared is the remarkable agreement, in the same reign, between the Earls of Chester and of Leicester,[2] though this latter suggests by its title—" Hæc est conventio . . . et finalis pax et concordia," etc.—the settlement of a strife between them rather than a friendly alliance. I see in it, indeed, the intervention, if not the arbitration, of the Church.

Both these alliances, again, should be compared, for their form, with the treaty between Henry I. and Count Robert of Flanders.[3] Although a generation earlier than the document here printed, the parallels are very striking:—

Robertus, Comes Flandriæ, fide et sacramento assecuravit Regi Henrico vitam suam et membra quæ corpori suo pertinent . . . et quod juvabit eum, etc.	Robertus, Comes Gloecestrie assecuravit Milonem Comitem Herefordie fide et sacramento, ut custodiet illi pro toto posse suo et sine ingenio suam vitam et suum membrum . . . et auxiliabitur illi, etc.
Porro Comitissa affidavit, quod, quantum poterit, Comitem in hac conventione tenebit, et in amicitia regis, et in prædicto servitio fideliter per amorem.	Et in hac ipsa confederatione amoris, affidavit Comitissa Gloecestrie quod suum dominum in hoc amore erga Milonem Comitem Hereford pro posse suo tenebit.
Hujus conventionis tenendæ ex parte Comitis obsides sunt subscripti. . . . Quod si Comes ab hac conventione exierit et . . . infra XL dies emendare noluerit, etc.	Et de hac conventione tenendâ ex parte Comitis Gloecestrie sunt hii obsides, etc. . . . Quod si Comes Gloecestrie de hac conventione exiret . . . Et si infra XL dies se nollet erga Comitem Herefordie erigere, etc.

---

[1] A somewhat similar treaty to this may be hinted at in the statement that Roger de Berkeley was connected with Walter de Gloucester "amicitia et alternæ pacis fœdere sibi astrictum" (*Gesta Stephani*).

[2] *Cott. MS.*, Nero, C. iii. fol. 178.

[3] Printed in Hearne's *Liber Niger* (i. 16-23).

The Treaty.

Noscant omnes hanc esse confederationem amoris inter Robertum Comitem Gloecestrie et Milonem Comitem Herefordie, Robertus Comes Gloecestrie assecuravit Milonem Comitem Herefordie fide et sacramento ut custodiet illi pro toto posse suo et sine ingenio suam vitam et suum membrum et terrenum suum honorem, et auxiliabitur illi ad custodiendum sua castella et sua recta et sua hereditaria et sua tenementa et sua conquisita quæ modo habet, et quæ faciet, et suas consuetudines et rectitudines et suas libertates in bosco et in plano et aquis, et quod sua hereditaria quæ modo non habet auxiliabitur ad conquirendum. Et si aliquis vellet inde Comiti Hereford malum facere, vel de aliquo decrescere, si comes Hereford vellet inde guerrare, quod Robertus comes Gloecestrie cum illo se teneret, et quod ad suum posse illi auxiliaretur per fidem et sine ingenio, nec pacem neque treuias cum illis haberet qui malum comiti Herefordiæ inferret, nisi per bonum velle et grantam (*sic*) Comitis Herefordiæ, et nominatim de hac guerra quæ modo est inter Imperatricem et Regem Stephanum se cum comite Hereford tenebit et ad unum opus erit, et de omnibus aliis guerris.

Et in hac ipsa confederatione amoris affidavit Comitissa Gloecestrie quod suum dominum in hoc amore erga Milonem Comitem Hereford pro posse suo tenebit. Et si inde exiret, ad suum posse illum ad hoc reponeret. Et si non posset, legalem recordationem, si opus esset, inde faceret ad suum scire.

Et de hac conventione firmiter tenendâ ex parte Comitis Gloecestrie sunt hii obsides per fidem et sacramentum erga Comitem Hereford: hoc modo, quod si comes Gloecestrie de hac conventione exiret, dominum suum Comitem Gloecestrie requirerent ut se erga Comitem Herefordiæ erigeret. Et si infra xl dies se nollet erga Comitem Herefordie erigere, se Comiti Herefordie liberarent, ad faciendum de illis suum velle, vel ad illos retinendum in suo servitio donec illos quietos clamaret vel ad illos ponendos ad legalem redemptionem ita ne terrâ [? terram] perderent. Et quod legalem recordationem de hac conventione facerent si opus esset, Guefridus de Waltervill, Ricardus de Greinvill,[1] Osbernus Ottdevers,[2] Reinald de Cahagnis,[3] Hubertus Dapifer, Odo Sorus,[4] Gislebertus de Umfravil,[5] Ricardus de Sancto Quintino.[6] Et ex parte Milonis Comitis Hereford ad istud confirmandum concessit Milo Comes Hereford Roberto Comiti Gloecestrie Mathielum filium suum tenendum in obsidem donec guerra inter Imperatricem et Regem Stephanum et Henricum filium Imperatricis finiatur.

Et interim si Milo Comes Hereford voluerit aliquem alium de suis filiis, qui sanus sit, in loco Mathicli filii sui ponere, recipietur.

Et postquam guerra finita fuerit et Robertus Comes Gloecestrie et Milo Comes Hereford terras suas et sua recta rehabuerint reddet Robertus Comes Gloecestrie Miloni Comiti Herefordie filium suum. Et hinc de probis hominibus utriusque comitis considerabuntur et capientur obsides et securitates de amore ipsorum comitum tenendo imperpetuum.

Et de hac conventione amoris Rogerus filius Comitis Hereford affidavit et juravit Comiti Gloecestrie quod patrem suum pro posse suo tenebit; Et si Comes Hereford inde vellet exire, Rogerus filius suus, inde illum requireret et inde illum corrigeret. Et si Comes Hereford se inde erigere nollet, servicium ipsius Rogeri filii sui prorsus perdet, donec se erga Comitem Gloecestrie erexisset.

Et de hac conventione ex parte Comitis Hereford sunt hii sui homines obsides erga Comitem Gloecestrie et per sacramenta; hoc modo, quod si Comes Hereford de hac conventione exiret, dominum suum Comitem Hereford requirerent ut se erga

---

[1] Richard de Greinvill appears in 1166 as the *late* holder of seven knights' fees from the earl (*Liber Niger*).

[2] Osbern Ottdevers (*i.e.* Ottdeners) was Osbern Octodenarii, *alias* Octonummi (see Appendix Q). He appears in 1166 as the *late* tenant of one knight's fee from the earl *in Kent* (*ibid.*).

[3] Philip "de Chahaines" appears as a tenant of the earl in 1166 (*ibid.*).

[4] An Odo Sorus is alleged to have accompanied Robert fitz Hamon into Wales. Jordan Sorus was the largest tenant of the earl in 1166, holding fifteen knights' fees from him (*Liber Niger*). His predecessor, Robert Sorus, had held of the fief under Robert fitz Hamon *circ.* 1107 (*Cart. Abingdon*, ii. 96, 106).

[5] Gilbert de Umfravill held nine knights' fees from the earl in 1166 (*Liber Niger*).

[6] Richard de St. Quintin held ten knights' fees from the earl in 1166 (*ibid.*). His family had been tenants of the fief even under Robert fitz Hamon (*Cart. Abingdon*, ii. 96, 106).

Comitem Gloecestrie erigeret. Et si infra xl dies se nollet erga Comitem Gloecestrie erigere se Comiti Gloecestrie liberarent ad faciendum de illis suum velle, vel ad illos retinendum in suo servicio donec illos quietos clamaret, vel ad illos ponendos ad legalem redemptionem, ita ne terram perdent. Et quod legalem recordationem de hac conventione in Curia facerent si opus esset, Robertus Corbet, Willelmus Mansel, Hugo de la Hese.

APPENDIX T.

"AFFIDATIO IN MANU."

(See p. 177.)

"HANC autem . . . affidavi manu mea propria in manu ipsius Comitis Gaufredi." This formula ("affidavi . . . in manu") is deserving of careful study. It ought to be compared with a passage in the *Chronicle of Abingdon* (ii. 160), describing how, some quarter of a century before, in the assembled county court (*comitatus*) of Berkshire, the delegate of the abbey, "pro ecclesiâ affidavit fidem in manu ipsius vicecomitis, vidente toto comitatu." This was a case of "affidatio" by proxy; but in the above charter we find Geoffrey stipulating for "affidatio" in person ("propria manu") by the Empress, her husband, and her son. Accordingly, when the young Henry confirms his mother's charter to Aubrey de Vere (see p. 186), he does so "manu mea propria in manu Hugonis de Inga, sicut mater mea Imperatrix affidavit in manu Comitis Gaufredi." Thus Geoffrey allowed himself the privilege, which he refused to the other contracting party, of "affidatio" by proxy, and made Hugh de Ing his delegate for the purpose.

A curious allusion to this practice is found in the words of Ranulf Flambard some half a century earlier, when he promises the captor in whose power he was to grant him all that he can ask, "et ne discredas promissis, ecce *manu affirmo* quod polliceor."—Continuatio Historiæ Turgoti (*Anglia Sacra*, i. 707). The formula was probably of great antiquity. It occurs in the lifetime of Archbishop Oswald (died 992), who obtained a lease for life on behalf of a certain Wulfric, of the provisions in which we read: "Hoc totum idem Wlfricus, sub oculis multorum qui aderant, *in manu* viri Dei qui pro eo intercessor accesserat *affidavit*" (*Chron. Ram.*, p. 81). It is found, however, as late as 1187, when at the foundation of Dodnash Priory the canons "juraverunt et fidem *in manu nostra* corporaliter . . . firmaverunt," says the bishop (*Ancient Charters*, p. 88). Another late instance is found in the *Burton Cartulary* (fol. 33), where Robert fitz Walter, that his grant "inconcussum permaneat, in toto comitatu, multis cementibus qui se ipsos testes concesserunt, in manu Vicecomitis Serlonis manu meâ hoc tenendum et servandum affidavi." So also in the Pipe-Roll of 3 John we find recorded a lease, "et quod ipse Micael et Everardus frater suus affidaverunt in manu H. Cantuarensis Arch. hanc Conventionem fideliter tenendam" (Rot. 6 *b*). An instance, in 1159, may be quoted from the *Cartulary of St. Michael on the Mount* because of its curious legal bearing. Robert de Belvoir mortgages to the abbey lands which he had settled on his wife in dower, and, in order to bar her claim, she, *by her brother*, guarantees the transaction by "affidatic in manu" to the abbot's delegate.[1] This arrangement should be compared with that which is discussed in my *Ancient Charters*, pp. 22, 23.[2] Perhaps, however, the most singular case is one which I noted in the *Cartulary* (MS.) *of Rievaulx*, and which is also of the reign of Henry II. A widow grants lands to that abbey, "et illam donationem tenendam et fideliter observandam manu propria affidavit in manu Vicecomitissæ, vid. Bert[æ] uxoris vicecomitis Ranulfi de Glanvill[a]."[3] The conjunction here of the two women, the presence of the great Glanville himself, and the part played by his wife, together with the title assigned her, all combine to render the transaction one of unusual interest.

It was by this formal and binding pledge that the leaders of the English host swore to one another to do or die on the field of the Battle of the Standard. Turning to William of Aumâle, and placing his hand in his, Walter Espec pledged his faith that he would conquer or be slain; and his fellow-

[1] "Invadiavit Rotbertus de Belueer pro sex libris Cenomannensium, terram suam quam dederat uxori sue in dotem, ipsa bene hoc concedente, Philippo fratri insuper fide sua in manu Johannis filii Bigoti illud idem sororem suam tenere assecurante" (fol. 116).

[2] Ed. Pipe-Roll Society.

[3] "Hiis testibus, Ranulfo vicecomite, Bertha vicecomitissâ, Matilda filia ejus."

commanders did the same."[1] It was, again, by this solemn pledge, towards the close of Stephen's reign, that the Bishop of Winchester, before his brother-prelates, covenanted to surrender Winchester to the duke at the king's death[2]—even as the duke himself had covenanted (April 9, 1152) with the Bishop of Salisbury concerning Devizes Castle[3]—in terms to be closely compared with those of his charter to Aubrey, and his mother's to Earl Geoffrey in 1142.

The practice is, I find, alluded to, incidentally, by Giraldus Cambrensis, who tells us that the Welsh "Adeo fidei fœdus, aliis inviolabile gentibus, parvipendere solent, ut non in seriis solum et necessariis, verum in ludicris, omnique fere verbo firmando, *dextræ manus ut mos est porrectione, signo usuali dato*, fidem gratis effundere consueverint." Here the point of the complaint is that they made light of this solemn practice, indulging in it freely on every occasion instead of reserving it for important matters. The existence of this archaic "fidei fœdus" as the *formal confirmation* of a contract is, of course, of the greatest interest. It still lingers on, not only with us, but abroad. In San Marino (Italy), for instance, "sales are conducted with much animation. Two sturdy proprietors stand back to back.... A third party stands between the two; ... he pulls one by the shoulder, the other by an elbow, and finally by an apparently acrobatic feat *he unites their hands*" ("A Political Survival," *Macmillan's*, January, 1891, p. 197). In the Lebanon, we are told by a well-informed writer: "A few months ago I had occasion to enter into a business contract with one of my Druse farmers. When we were about to draw up the agreement, the Druse suggested that, as he could neither read nor write, we should ratify the bargain in

---

[1] "Hæc dicens vertit se ad comitem Albemarlensem, dataque dextera, 'Do,' inquit, 'fidem quia hodie aut vincam Scottos aut occidar a Scottis.' Quo similiter voto cuncti se proceres constrixerunt" (Æthelred of Rievaulx).

[2] "Episcopus Wintonie in manu archiepiscopi Cantuarensis coram episcopis affidavit quod si ego decederem castra Wintonie. ... Duci redderet."

[3] "Hunc supradictam conventionem ... affidavit idem Comes (*sic*) in manu domini Cantuarensis archiepiscopi ... sine malo ingenio tenendam; et cum eo Comes Gloucestrie. ... Similiter et dominus episcopus Sarum affidavit in manu ejusdem Legati," etc. (*Sarum Charters and Documents*, pp. 22, 23).

the manner customary among his people. This consists of a solemn grasping of hands together in the presence of two or three other Druses as witnesses, whilst the agreement is recited by both parties. . . . Accordingly, the farmer brought three of his neighbours to me; and the terms of our contract having been made known to them, one of them took the right hand of each of us and joined them together, whilst he dictated to us what to say after him" ("The Druses," *Blackwood's*, January, 1891, pp. 754, 755). With us, Gerald would be grieved to hear, the ancient form survives not only for the bargain but the bet, though it only continues in full vigour as the sign of the marriage contract, where "the minister . . . shall cause the man with his right hand to take the woman by her right hand, and to say after him as followeth,"—even as the Druses, we have seen, make their contracts to-day, and as the Empress Maud sealed her own seven centuries ago.[1]

The allusion by the Empress to the "Christianitas Angliæ" refers doubtless to the fact that the breach of such "affidatio" would constitute a "læsio fidei," and would thus become a matter for the jurisdiction of the courts Christian. It was indeed on this plea that these courts claimed to attract to themselves all cases of contract, a claim against which, it is necessary to explain, an article (No. 15) of the Constitutions of Clarendon (1164) was specially directed.[2]

[1] Compare the old English term "Handfasting." The law in Austria, it is said, still recognizes the clasping of hands as a formal contract.

[2] "Placita de debitis, quæ *fide interposita* debentur, . . . sint in justitia regis."

APPENDIX U.

THE FAMILIES OF MANDEVILLE AND DE VERE.

(See p. 178.)

THE confusion on the pedigree and relationship of these two families is due, in the first place, to the fact that, for several generations, the successive heads of the family of De Vere were all named Aubrey ("Albericus"); and in the second, to a chronicle of Walden Abbey, which proves as inaccurate as to the marriage of its founder as it is on the date of his creation.[1] Dugdale, accepting all its statements without the slightest hesitation, has combined in a single passage no less than three errors, together with the means for their detection.[2] Among these is the statement that Geoffrey's wife was a daughter of Aubrey de Vere, "Earl of Oxford."[3] Accordingly, she so figures in Dugdale's tabular pedigree, and the same error has now reappeared in Mr. Doyle's *Official Baronage*.[4] Oddly enough, in his account of the De Veres, a few pages before, Dugdale makes Geoffrey's wife daughter not of the Earl of Oxford, but of his grandfather Aubrey,[5] and so enters her in the tabular pedigree.[6] And yet she was, in truth, daughter neither of the earl nor of his grandfather, but of his father, the chamberlain.[7] To establish this will now be my task.

Between the Aubrey de Vere of Domesday and the Aubrey de Vere "senior" of the *Cartulary of Abingdon Abbey*, about twenty years are interposed. Their identity, therefore, is not

[1] See p. 45.   [2] *Baronage*, i. 203 b.   [3] *Ibid.*, i. 201.
[4] "m. Rohaise, d. of Aubrey de Vere, (afterwards) Earl of Oxford" (i. 682).
[5] *Baronage*, i. 188 b.   [6] *Ibid.*, 189.
[7] Strange to say, Dugdale gives also this third (and right) version (*ibid*, i. 463 a).

actually proved, though the presumption, of course, is in its favour. But from the time of the latter Aubrey all is clear. The descent that we obtain from the Abingdon Cartulary is as follows:—

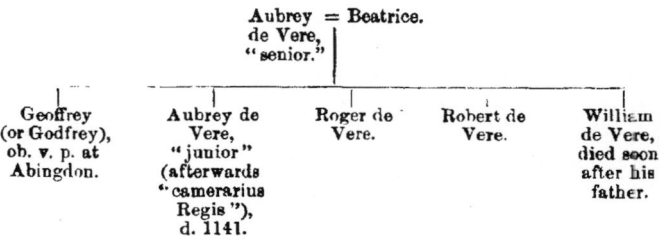

Our next source of information is the *Cartulary of Colne Priory*,[1] in combination with an invaluable tract, *De miraculis S. Osythæ*, composed by William de Vere, a brother of the first earl, and a canon of St. Osyth's Priory, Essex. Dugdale was acquainted with both documents, but lost the full force of the latter by failing to identify its author. He gives us as sons to Aubrey the chamberlain, and brothers to Aubrey the first earl, (*a*) William de Vere, (*b*) —— de Vere, canon of St. Osyth's. The identity of the two is proved, first, by a charter of Aubrey the chamberlain, in which he speaks of his "reverend" son William;[2] secondly, by a charter of Aubrey the earl, witnessed by his brother William, "presbyter;"[3] thirdly, by the charter from the Empress to the earl, in which she provides for all his brothers, the chancellorship, a clerical post, being promised to William.[4] We may further assert of this tract that it must have been written after 1163, for the canon tells us that his mother has spent her twenty-two years of widowhood at St. Osyth, and her husband had been killed in 1141.[5]

[1] In Cole's transcript (British Museum).
[2] *Ibid.*, No. 31.   [3] *Ibid.*, No. 43.   [4] See p. 182.
[5] It would seem clear that this William must have been the "Dominus Willelmus de Ver" to whom Dr. Stubbs alludes as the "early friend and fellow-student," at the University of Paris, of Arnulf, Bishop of Lisieux, and of the celebrated Ralf "de Diceto" (who may have been born, Dr. Stubbs suggests, about 1122). Bishop Arnulf, asking Ralf to come over and pay him a visit, tells him that William de Ver has promised to come too (see preface to *Radulfus de Diceto*, pp. xxxii., *note*, liv.). But some difficulty

In it he refers to his father the chamberlain,[1] as "justitiarius totius Angliæ." To this we may trace Dugdale's assertion that he held that high office, a statement which exercised the mind of Foss, who complains that "it is difficult to tell on what authority" he is introduced among its holders both by Dugdale and Spelman.[2] He further speaks of his mother as "Adeliza," daughter of Gilbert de Clare, and exults in the fact that she has spent her widowhood, not in the family priory at Colne, but in that of his own St. Osyth. He refers also to his sister "Adeliza de Essexâ filia Alberici de Vere et Adelizæ." Now, we have abundant evidence that "Adeliza de Essex" was sister to the Countess Rohese, wife of Geoffrey de Mandeville, and was aunt to their sons, Earls of Essex.[3] Accordingly, we find the Countess Rohese giving a rent-charge to Colne Priory for the souls of her father, Aubrey de Vere, and her husband, Earl Geoffrey, and we also find her son, Earl William, confirming the charter "avi mei Alberici de Vere."[4] It is quite clear

is caused by his appearing as a canon, not of St. Osyth's, but of St. Paul's, in 1162 and later (*Ninth Report Historical MSS.*, App. i. pp. 19 a, 32 a). It would seem to have been the latter William de Ver who became Bishop of Hereford in 1185, and died 1199.

[1] He had received the "Cameraria Angliæ" from Henry I., in a charter which must have passed on the occasion of the king leaving England for the last time in 1133. Madox has printed the charter (which has a valuable list of witnesses) in his *Baronia Anglica*, from Dugdale's transcript.

[2] *Judges of England*, i. 89.

[3] Thus the *Chronicle of Walden Abbey (Arundel MSS.)* relates that at the death of Geoffrey, Earl of Essex, in 1166, his mother was living at her Priory of Chicksand, with her sister "Adeliza" of Essex. On the succession of his brother William, "Alicia de Essexia" came to Walden Abbey "ordinante comite Willelmo ejus nepote," and settled and died there (*ibid.*, cap. 18). But the most important evidence is a charter of this same Earl William, abstracted in *Lansdowne MSS.*, 259, fol. 67, granting to "Adelicia of Essex," his mother's sister, the town of Aynho in free dower over and above the dower she had received from Roger fitz Richard, her lord. This charter is witnessed by his mother, "Roesia Comitissa;" Simon de Beauchamp, his uterine brother; Geoffrey de Ver and William de Ver, his uncles; Ranulf Glanville, and Geoffrey de Say, who was his cousin. He had previously granted Aynho (? in 1170) to Roger fitz Richard in exchange for Compton (co. Warwick), his charter being witnessed *inter alios* by John (de Lacy), the constable of Chester (see p. 392 n.), Ranulf de Glanville, and Geoffrey de Say (see my paper on "A Charter of William, Earl of Essex," in *Eng. Hist. Review*, April, 1891).

[4] *Colne Cartulary*, Nos. 51, 54.

PARENTAGE OF GEOFFREY'S WIFE.

that the Countess Rohese, wife of Geoffrey de Mandeville, first Earl of Essex, was sister of Alice "de Essex," and daughter of Aubrey de Vere the chamberlain, by his wife Alice, daughter of Gilbert de Clare.

But who was Alice "de Essex"? We must turn, for an answer to this question, to the *Chronicle of Walden Abbey*. There we shall find that she married twice, and left issue by both husbands. Her first husband was Robert de Essex [1]; her second was Roger fitz Richard, of Clavering, Essex, and Warkworth, Northumberland, ancestor of the Claverings. Now, "Robert de Essex" was a well-known man, being son and heir of Swegen de Essex, Sheriff of Essex under William the Conqueror, and grandson of Robert "fitz Wimarc," a favourite of the Confessor, under whom he, too, was Sheriff of Essex. The descent is proved, in a conclusive manner, by the description of the second Robert among the benefactors to Lewes Priory, in one place as Robert fitz Suein, and in another as Robert de Essex.[2] Robert had founded Prittlewell Priory as a cell to Lewes, "Alberico de Ver et Roberto fratre ejus" attesting the foundation charter.[3] Robert's son and heir was the well-known Henry de Essex.[4] So far all is clear. But, unfortunately, it is certain that Robert de Essex left a widow, Gunnor—a Bigod by birth—who was mother of his son Henry. Therefore "Alice of Essex" cannot have been his widow. Consequently she must have been the widow of another Robert de Essex, possibly a younger son of his, who held Clavering from his elder brother Henry. In any case, by her second husband, Roger fitz Richard, Alice was mother of Robert fitz Roger (of Clavering).

We are now in a position to construct an authentic tabular pedigree, showing the relationship that existed between the families of Mandeville and De Vere.

---

[1] "Domino suo primo marito Roberto scilicet de Essexiâ" (*Walden Abbey Chronicle*). Dugdale makes her, in error, the wife of Henry de Essex.

[2] This descent has not hitherto been established, and Mr. Freeman speaks of Swegen of Essex as "father or grandfather of Henry de Essex."

[3] He appears in the charters of this priory as "Robertus filius Suein" and as "Robertus de Essex filius Suein."

[4] See Appendix N. His paternity, which is well ascertained, is further proved by his confirmation, in the (MS.) *Colchester Cartulary*, of a gift by his father, Robert de Essex, to St. John's Abbey, Colchester.

392 FAMILIES OF MANDEVILLE AND DE VERE.

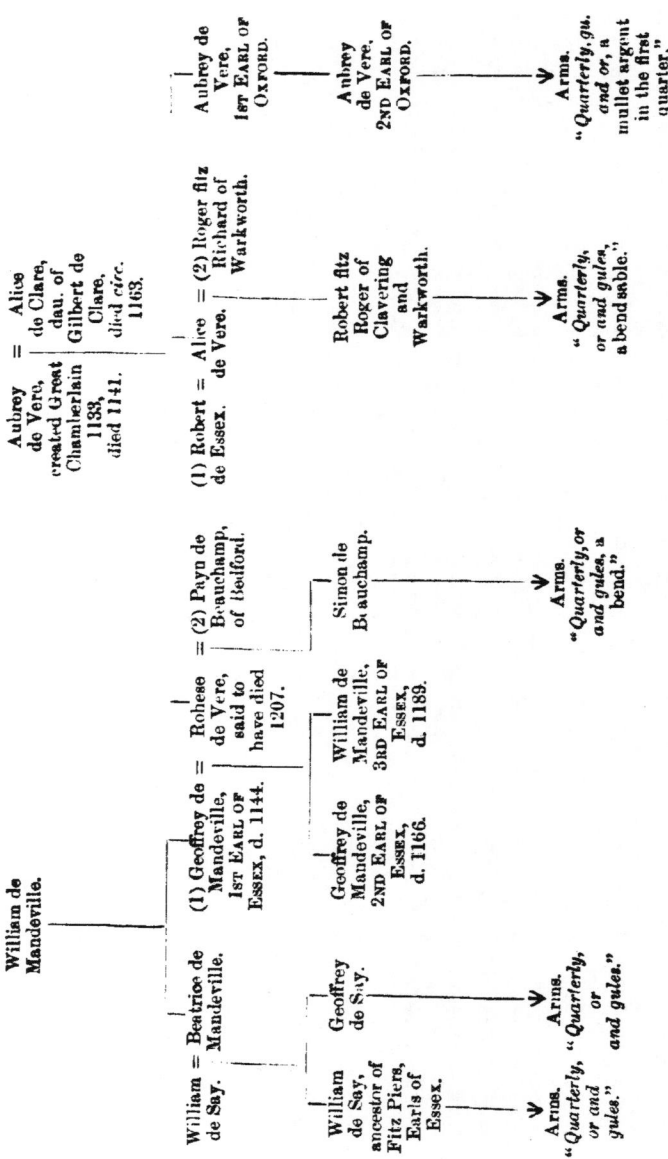

It should be observed that this pedigree is not intended to show all the children. It gives those only which are required for our special purpose. On some points there is still need of more original information. No doubt Beatrice, wife of William de Say, was sister, and not daughter, to Geoffrey de Mandeville. I know of nothing to the contrary. Still the fact would seem to rest on the authority of the *Walden Chronicle*. The re-marriage of the Countess of Essex to Payn de Beauchamp, and her parentage, by him, of Simon, are both well established, but the date of her death is taken from the *Chronicle*, and seems suspiciously late. So also does that which is assigned to her brother, the Earl of Oxford, namely, 1194, fifty-two years after the charter of the Empress. Still, the fact that his mother survived her husband for twenty-two years implies that her children may have been comparatively young at his death. Both Aubrey and Rohese may therefore have been several years junior to Geoffrey de Mandeville.

But the main point has been, in any case, established, namely, the true relationship of these baronial houses. That which is given by Dugdale contains the further error of representing Alice de Vere as wife, not of Robert de Essex, but of Henry. Mr. W. S. Ellis, in his *Antiquities of Heraldry* (p. 210), observes with truth that, as to this relationship, the existing "accounts . . . are conflicting, and that of Dugdale contradictory." But I cannot admit that his own version is "correct, or approximately so;" for while, with Dugdale, he errs in assigning to Alice de Vere Henry de Essex for husband, he transforms Roger fitz Richard, whom Dugdale had, rightly, given as her second husband, into her son-in-law.[1]

My reason for alluding to this passage is that, after I had worked out the heraldic corollaries of this descent in their

[1] I have purposely abstained from touching on the relationship of Lacy to De Vere, because there is evidently error somewhere in the account given by Dugdale, and as the descent is without my sphere, I have not investigated the question. The *Rotulus de Dominabus* should be consulted. Nor do I discuss the descent of Sackville. Mr. Ellis wrote: "The coat of Sackville, *Quarterly, a bend vairé*, is doubtless derived from De Vere, but by what match does not clearly appear." It is singular that William de Sackville, who died *circa* 1158, is said to have married Adeliza, daughter of "Aubrey the sheriff," which points to some connection between the two families.

bearing on the adoption of coat-armour, I found that I had been anticipated in this investigation by the author of that scholarly work, *The Antiquities of Heraldry*. As the conclusions, however, at which I had arrived differ slightly from those of Mr. Ellis, it may be worth while to set them forth.

Mr. Ellis writes thus of "the simple QUARTERLY shield":—

"There can be little doubt that the source of this honoured armorial ensign is to be found in the distinguished family of DE VERE, as all the families in the table who bear it are descended from the head of that house who lived at the commencement of the twelfth century." [1]

I should differ with no slight hesitation from so ably argued and erudite a work, were it not that, in this case, its conclusions are based on a false premiss. Thus we read, further on:—

"Which was the original bearer of the quarterly coat of De Vere? Was it Say, or Mandeville, or Lacy, or Beauchamp, or was it De Vere, from whom all, or their wives were descended?" [2]

Now, "the table" given by the writer himself (p. 210) disproves this statement, for it rightly shows us Say as descended from Mandeville, but *not* descended from De Vere. It is, therefore, shown by his own "table" that this *must* have been a case of the "collateral adoption" of arms, the very practice against which he here strenuously argues.[3] Thus the very case he adduces against the existence of the practice is itself proof absolute that the practice did exist. I am compelled to emphasize this point because it is the pivot on which the question turns. If "all the families in the table" who bore the quarterly coat were indeed descended from De Vere, Mr. Ellis's theory would account for the facts. But, by his own showing, they were not. Some other explanation must therefore be sought.

That which had originally occurred to myself, and to which I am still compelled to adhere, is that "the original bearer" of this quarterly coat was the central figure of this family group, Geoffrey de Mandeville himself. It being, as I have shown, absolutely clear that there must have been collateral

---

[1] *Antiquities of Heraldry*, p. 209. [2] *Ibid.*, p. 230.
[3] *Ibid.*, pp. 228–232.

adoption, the only question that remains to be decided is from which of the two family stems, Mandeville or De Vere, was the coat adopted? My first reason for selecting the former is that the first Earl of Essex was far and away, at the time, the greatest personage of the group. Aubrey de Vere figures, at Oxford, as his dependant rather than as his equal. On this ground, then, it seems to me far more probable that Aubrey should have adopted his arms from Geoffrey than that Geoffrey should have adopted his from Aubrey. The second reason is this. Science and analogy point to the fact that the simplest form of the coat is, of necessity, the most original. Now, the simplest form of this coat, its only "undifferenced" variety, is that borne by the Earls of Essex. We do not obtain recorded blazons till the reign of Henry III., but when we do, it is as "quartele de or & de goulez" that the coat of the Earl of Essex, the namesake of Geoffrey de Mandeville, first meets us.[1] But all the descendants of De Vere, it would seem, bear this coat "differenced," that of De Vere itself being charged with a mullet in the first quarter, the tinctures also (perhaps for distinction) being in this case reversed.[2] Thus heraldry, as well as genealogy, favours the claim of Mandeville as the original bearer of the coat.

It has been generally asserted in works on Heraldry that Geoffrey de Mandeville added an escarbuncle to his simple paternal coat, and that it is still to be seen on the shield of his effigy among the monuments at the Temple Church. But antiquaries have now abandoned the belief that this is indeed his effigy, and the original statement is taken only from that *Chronicle of Walden* which is in error in its statements on his foundation, on his creation, on his marriage, and on his death. Nor is there a trace of such a charge on the shields of any of his heirs.[3]

But the consequences of the theory here laid down have yet to be considered. A little thought will soon show that no

[1] Doyle's *Official Baronage*, i. 685.

[2] I must certainly decline to accept the rash conjecture of Mr. Ellis that the mullet of De Vere represents the chamberlainship, on the ground that one of his predecessors, Robert Malet, *might* have borne a mullet as an "heraldic and allusive cognizance."

[3] See p. 226 n.

hypothesis can possibly explain the adoption of the quarterly coat by these various families at any other period than this in which they all intermarried. If we wish to trace to its origin such a surname as Fitz-Walter, we must go back to some ancestor who had a Walter for his father. So with derivative coats-of-arms. By Mr. Ellis's fundamental principle we ought to find the house of De Vere imparting its coat, for successive generations, to those families who were privileged to ally themselves to it. Yet we can only trace this principle at work in this particular generation. If Mandeville, and Mandeville's kin, adopted, as he holds, the coat of De Vere, why should not De Vere, in the previous generation, have adopted that of Clare? Nothing, in short, can account for the phenomena except the hypothesis that these quarterly coats all originated in this generation and in consequence of these intermarriages. The quarterly coat of the great earl would be adopted by his sister's husband De Say, and by his wife's brother De Vere, and by those other relatives shown in the pedigree. Once adopted they remain, till they meet us in the recorded blazons of the reign of Henry III.

The natural inference from this conclusion is that the reign of Stephen was the period in which heraldic bearings were assuming a definite form. Most heralds would place it later: Mr. Ellis would have us believe that we ought to place it earlier. The question has been long and keenly discussed, and, as with surnames, we may not be able to give with certainty the date at which they became generally fixed. But, at any rate, in this typical case, the facts admit of one explanation and of one alone.

If, as I take it, heraldic coats were mainly intended (as at Evesham) to distinguish their bearers in the field, it is not improbable that these kindred coats may represent the alliance of their bearers, as typified in the Oxford charters, beneath the banner of the Earl of Essex.[1]

[1] Compare the case of Raymond (le Gros) meeting William fitz Aldelin, on his landing in Ireland (December, 1176), at the head of thirty of his kinsmen, "clipeis assumptis unius armaturæ" (*Expugnatio Hiberniæ*).

APPENDIX V.

WILLIAM OF ARQUES.

(See p. 180.)

SEPARATE treatment is demanded by that clause in the charter to Aubrey which deals with the fief of William of Arques:—

"Et do et concedo ei totam terram Willelmi de Albrincis sine placito, pro servicio suo, simul cum hæreditate et jure quod clamat ex parte uxoris suæ sicut unquam Willelmus de Archis ea melius tenuit."

The descent of this barony has formed the subject of an erudite and instructive paper by the late Mr. Stapleton.[1] The pedigree which he established may be thus expressed:—

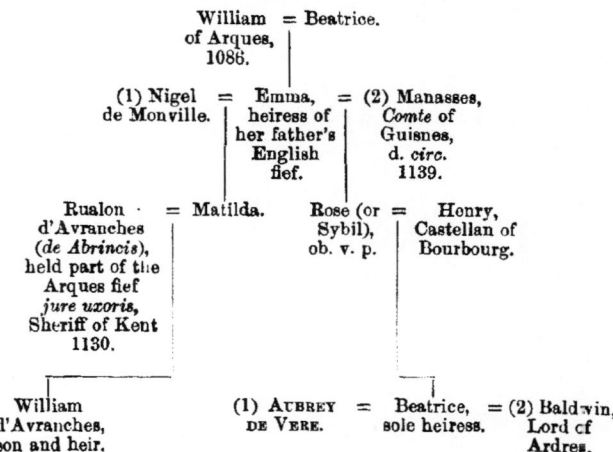

This descent renders the above clause in the charter intelli-

[1] *Archæologia*, vol. xxxi. pp. 216–237.

gible at once, for it shows that Aubrey was to reunite the whole Arques fief in his own holding *jure uxoris.*

Mr. Stapleton, who prints the clause from the translation given by Dugdale, justly pronounces it "extremely important, as establishing the fact of his marriage at its date with the heiress of the barony of Arques as well as of the *comté* of Guisnes." With Aubrey's tenure of this *comté* I have dealt at p. 188.

APPENDIX X.

ROGER "DE RAMIS."

(See p. 181.)

THE entries relating to the fief of this tenant *in capite* are probably as corrupt as any to be found in the *Liber Niger*.

The name of the family being "de Raimes"—Latinized in this charter and Domesday invariably as *de Ramis*—an inevitable confusion soon arose between it and the name of their chief seat in England, Rayne, co. Essex. Morant, in his history of Essex, identifies the two. Thus, Rayne being entered in Domesday and in the *Liber Niger* as "Raines," the name of the family appears in the latter as "de Raines," "de Reines" (i. 237), "de Ramis," "de Raimis," and "de Raimes" (i. 239, 240). The Domesday tenant was Roger "de Ramis," who was succeeded by William "de Raimes," who was dead in 1130, when his sons Roger and Robert are found indebted to the Crown for their reliefs and for their father's debts (*Rot. Pip.*, 31 Hen. I.). Further, if the *Liber Niger* (i. 237, 239) is to be trusted, there were in 1135 two Essex fiefs, held respectively by these very sons, Roger and Robert "de Ramis." So far all is clear. But when we come to the *cartæ* of 1166 all is hopeless confusion. There are, certainly, two fiefs entered in the Essex portion, but while the *carta* of that which is assigned to Robert "de Ramis" is intelligible, though very corrupt, the other is assigned by an amazing blunder to William fitz Miles, who was merely one of the under-tenants. Moreover, the entries are so similar that they might be easily taken for variants of the same *carta*.

Let us, however, now turn to the Pipe-Roll of 1159 (5 Hen. II.). We there find these entries (p. 5) under Essex:—

"Idem vicecomes reddit Compotum de xii *l.* et xiii *s.* et iiii *d.* pro Rogero de Ram'.

"Idem vicecomes reddit Compotum de xii *l.* et xiii *s.* iiii *d.* pro Ricardo de Ram'."

They require some explanation. The sums here accounted for (though it is not so stated) are payments towards "the great scutage" of the year at two marks on the knight's fee. These were in most cases paid collectively by the aggregate of knights liable. Here, luckily for us, these two tenants paid separately. Turning the payments into marcs, and then dividing by two, we find that each represents an assessment of nine and a half knights. Now, we know for certain from the *Liber Niger* (i. 240) that the assessment of one of these two fiefs was ten knights, and that its holder was entitled to deduct from that assessment an amount equivalent to half a knight. For such is the meaning in the language of the Exchequer of the phrase: "feodum dimidii militis . . . *quod mihi computatur* in x militibus quos Regi debeo." Thus we obtain the exact amount (nine and a half knights) on which he pays in the above Roll.[1]

But we can go further still. Each of the two fiefs was entitled to the same deduction (*Liber Niger*). Both, therefore, must have been alike assessed at ten knights. We are now on the right track. These two fiefs in the *Liber Niger* are not identical but distinct; they represent an original fief, assessed at twenty knights, which has been divided into two equal halves, each with an assessment of ten knights. And as with the whole fief, so with some of its component parts. Dedham, for instance, the "Delham" of Domesday (ii. 83) and the "Diham" of our charter, was held of the lord of the fief by the service of one knight. When the fief was divided in two, Dedham was divided too. Accordingly, we find it mentioned in our charter (1142) as "Diham que fuit Rogeri de Ramis, rectum . . . fili*orum* Rogeri de Ramis." It was their joint right, because it was divided between them, just as it still appears divided in the *cartæ* of 1166.[2]

But further, why is Dedham alone mentioned in this charter?

---

[1] This instance proves that payment was sometimes made on the net amount due, after making such deduction, instead of being entered as paid in full, with a subsequent entry of deduction.

[2] The forms "Diham," "De Hiham," and "Heham" are very confusing from the fact that Higham also is on the border of Essex and Suffolk.

Because it was that portion of the fief which the Crown had seized and kept, and consequently that of which the restoration was now exacted from the Empress. And why had the Crown seized it ? Possibly as security for those very debts, which were due to it from William " de Raimes " (*Rot. Pip.*, 31 Hen. I.).[1]

Dedham was not the only divided manor in the fief. "Totintuna," in Norfolk, was similarly shared, its one knight's fee being halved. This enables us to correct an error in the *Liber Niger*. We there read (i. 237)—

"Warinus de Totinton' medietatem I militis."

And again (i. 239)—

"Warinus dim' mil'.
De Todinton' feodum dimidii militis."

In the latter case the right reading is—

"Warinus de Todinton' dim' mil'.
Feodum dimidii militis[2] de Hiham, quod," etc.

Further, Robert "de Reines" is returned in both *cartæ* as holding (1166) a quarter of a knight's fee in each fief, "de novo fefamento," apparently in Higham (Suffolk), not far from Dedham (Essex). This suggests his enfeofment by the service of half a knight, and the division of his holding when the fief was divided. It is strange that on the Roll of 1159 he is entered as paying one marc, which would be the exact amount payable for half a knight.[3]

Thus the main points have been satisfactorily established. The genealogy is not so easy. Our charter tells us that, in 1142, the sons of Roger "de Ramis" were the "nepotes" of Earl Aubrey. From the earl's age at the time they could not be his grandsons: they were, therefore, his nephews, the sons of a sister. Were they the Richard and Roger who, in 1159, held respectively the two halves of the original fief (*Rot. Pip.*, 5 Hen. II.)? To answer this question, we must grasp the

---

[1] Compare the remission by Henry II., in his charter to the second Earl of Essex, of the Crown's lien upon certain of his manors, dating from the time of Henry I. (see p. 241).

[2] The words which follow are on p. 240.

[3] This has a direct bearing on the very difficult question of the assessment of the new feoffment.

data clearly. In 1130 and in 1135 the two fiefs were respectively held by Robert and Roger, the sons of *William*. In our charter (1142) we find them, it would seem, held by "the sons of *Roger*," probably of tender years. This would suggest that the Robert (son of William) of 1135 had died childless before 1142, and that his fief had been reunited to that of his brother Roger, only, however, for the joint fief to be again divided between Roger's sons. But the question is further complicated by some documents relating to the church of Ardleigh, one of which is addressed by "Robertus de Ramis filius Rogeri de Ramis" to Robert [de Sigillo], Bishop of London, while another, addressed to the same bishop, proceeds from Robert son of *William* "de Ramis," apparently his uncle. In 1159 the two fiefs reappear as held respectively by Roger and Richard "de Ramis." In 1165 (*Rot. Pip.*, 11 Hen. II.) we find them held by William and Richard de Ramis, and thenceforth they were always known as the fiefs of William and of Richard. The actual names of the holders of the fiefs in 1166 (one of which is ignored by the Black Book and the other given as Robert) are determined by the Pipe-Roll of 1168, where they are entered as William and Richard. Thus, at length, we ascertain that the *carta* assigned to William "filius Milonis" was in truth that of William "de Ramis," while that which is assigned to Robert "de Ramis" was in truth that of Richard "de Ramis." The entry on this Pipe-Roll relating to the latter fief throws so important a light on the *Carta* of 1166, that I here print the two side by side.

[1166.]

Hii sunt milites qui tenuerunt de feodo Roberti de Raimes die qua Rex Henricus fuit vivus et mortuus, viz.:—... Willelmus filius Jocelini II milites Philippus Parage feodum dim. militis. Horum servitium difforciant mihi Willelmus filius Jocelini et Philippus. Simon de Cantilupo detinet mihi Heingeham quam tenere debeo de Rege in dominio meo.

[1168.]

Ricardus de Reimis [*al.* Raimes] reddit compotum de x marcis pro x militibus. In thesauro XXXIII sol. et IIII den. Et in dominio Regis de Dedham i mar. Et debet IIII li. et VI sol. et VIII den. sed calumpniatur quod Picot de Tanie[1] habet II milites per Regem, et Simo de Cantelu IIos, et Comes Albricus dim., et Phylippus Parage dim.

---

[1] Picot de Tani (1168) stood in the shoes of William fitz Jocelin (1166), having married his daughter Alice (*Rotulus de Dominabus*).

If, as implied by our charter, the sons of Roger ("de Ramis") were minors at the time of the Anarchy, this would account for Earl Hugh seizing, as recorded in William's *carta*, five of his knights' fees in the time of King Stephen (*Liber Niger*, i. 237).

The later history of these two fiefs is one of some complexity, but the descent of Dedham, which alone concerns our own charter, is fortunately quite clear. Its two halves are well shown in the *Testa de Nevill* entry :—

"Leonia de Stutevill tenet feodum unius militis in Byh[a]m unde debet facere unam medietatem heredi Ricardi de Reymes et alteram medietatem heredi Willelmi de Reymes" (i. 276).

For this Byham, improbable as it may seem, was really the "Diham" of our charter, *i.e.* Dedham, and the two halves of the original barony are here described (as I explained above) as those of Richard and William. In a survey of Richard's portion of the fief among the inquisitions of John (*circ.* 1212),[1] we find Leonia holding half a knight's fee in "Dyham" of it, and in a later inquisition we find her heir, John de Stuteville, holding the estate as "Dyhale" (*Testa*, p. 281 *b*). As early as 1185-86 Leonia was already in possession of Dedham, as will be seen by the extract below from the *Rotulus de Dominabus*. This entry is one of a series which have formed the subject of keen, and even hot, discussion. The fact that Dedham is spoken of here as her "inheritance" has led to the hasty inference that she was heiress, or co-heiress, to the Raimes fief. This view seems to have been started by Mr. E. Chester Waters in a communication to *Notes and Queries* (1872),[2] in which, on the strength of the entries below relating to her and to Alice de Tani, he drew out a pedigree deriving them both from the "Roger de Ramis of Domesday." Writing to the *Academy* in 1885, he took great credit to himself for his performance in *Notes and Queries*, and observed, of Mr. Yeatman : " I must refer him to the *Rotulus de Dominabus* and to the Chartulary of Bocherville Abbey for the true co-heirs of the fief of Raimes."[3] But the extracts which follow clearly show (when combined with the *Testa* entry above) that neither Leonia nor

[1] Printed by Madox as from the *Liber Feudorum*.
[2] 4th series, vol. ix. p. 314.
[3] *Academy*, June 27, 1885.

Alice were the "true co-heirs of the fief of Raimes," for they were merely under-tenants of that fief, Leonia holding one knight's fee from the tenants of the whole fief, and Alice two knights' fees from the tenants of Richard's portion.

(Lexden Hundred.)

Uxor Roberti de Stuteville est de donatione Domini Regis, et de parentela Edwardi de Salesburia ex parte patris, et ex parte matris est de progenie Rogeri de Reimes. Ipsa habet j villam que vocatur Diham que est hereditas ejus, que valet annuatim xxiiij libras. Ipsa habet j filium et ij filias, et nescitur eorum etas.

(Tendring Hundred.)

Alizia de Tany est de donatione Domini Regis; terra ejus valet vij libras, et ipsa habet v filios et ij filias, et heres ejus est xx annorum, de progenie Rogeri de Reimes.

(Hinckford.)

Alicia filia Willelmi filii Godcelini quam tradidit Dominus Rex Picoto de Tani est in donatione Domini Regis, et tenet de Domino Rege, et de feodo Ricardi de Ramis; et terra sua valet vij libras; et ipsa habet v filios et primogenitus est xx annorum, et ij filias. Picot de Tani habuit dictam terram v anuis elapsis, cum autumpnus venerit.

Leonia is indeed stated to be "de progenie Rogeri de Reimes," and so is the heir of Alice (*not*, as alleged, Alice herself), but there is nothing to show that this was the Roger de Raimes "of Domesday." It may have been his namesake (and grandson ?) of 1130–35, or even (though probably not) the Roger of 1159. Whether the allusion, in our charter (1142), to Dedham being the "rectum" of the sons of Roger de Ramis, and the fact of its being in the king's hands then and in 1166–68, had to do with a claim by Leonia or her mother, or not, it is obvious that Leonia did not claim, nor did Alice de Tani, to be, in any sense, the heir of either of the above Rogers, though she may have been, as was the case so often with under-tenants, connected with them in blood.

APPENDIX Y.

THE FIRST AND SECOND VISITS OF HENRY II. TO ENGLAND.

(See p. 198.)

THE dates and circumstances of these two visits are a subject of some importance and interest. Fortunately, they can be accurately ascertained.

It is certain that, on Henry's first visit, he landed with his uncle at Wareham towards the close of 1142. Stephen had been besieging the Empress in Oxford since the 26th of September,[1] and her brother, recalled to England by her danger, must have landed, with Henry, about the beginning of December, for she had then been besieged more than two months, and Christmas was at hand.[2] This date is confirmed by another calculation. For the earl, on landing, we are told, laid siege to the castle of Wareham, and took it, after three weeks.[3] But as the flight of the Empress from Oxford coincided with, or followed immediately after, his capture of the castle,[4] and as that flight took place on the eve of Christmas,[5] after a siege of three months,[6] this would similarly throw back the landing of the earl at Wareham to the beginning of December (1142).

By a strange oversight, Dr. Stubbs, the supreme authority on his life, makes Henry arrive in 1141, "when he was eight

[1] "Tribus diebus ante festum sancti Michaelis inopinato casu Oxeneford concremavit, et castellum, in quo, cum domesticis militibus imperatrix erat obsedit" (*Will. Malms.*, 766).

[2] "Consummatis itaque in obsidione plus duobus mensibus . . . appropinquante Nativitatis Dominicæ solempnitate" (*Gervase*, i. 124).

[3] "Fuitque comes Robertus in obsidione illâ per tres septimanas" (*ibid.*).

[4] *Ibid.*, i. 125; *Will. Malms.*, 768.

[5] "Non procul a Natali" (*Hen. Hunt.*, 276).

[6] "Tribus mensibus" (*Gesta*, p. 89).

years old, to be trained in arms;"[1] whereas, as we have seen, he did not arrive till towards the end of 1142, when he was nine years and three-quarters old. Nor, it would seem, was there any intention that he should be then trained in arms. This point is here mentioned because it bears on the chronology of Gervase, as criticised by Dr. Stubbs, who, I venture to think, may have been thus led to pronounce it, as he does, "unsound."

On recovering Wareham, Henry and his uncle set out for Cirencester, where the earl appointed a rendezvous of his party, with a view to an advance on Oxford. The Empress, however, in the mean time, unable to hold out any longer, effected her well-known romantic escape and fled to Wallingford, where those of her supporters who ought to have been with her when Stephen assailed her, had gathered round the stronghold of Brian fitz Count, having decided that their forces were not equal to raising the siege of Oxford.[2] Thither, therefore, the earl now hastened with his charge, and the Empress, we are told, forgot all her troubles in the joy of the meeting with her son.[3]

Stephen had been as eager to relieve his beleaguered garrison at Wareham as the earl had been, at the same time, to raise the siege of Oxford. Neither of them, however, would attempt the task till he had finished the enterprise he had in hand.[4] But now that the fall of Oxford had set Stephen free, he determined, though Wareham had fallen, that he would at least regain possession.[5] But the earl had profited, it seems, by his experience of the preceding year, and Stephen found the fortress was now too strong for him.[6] He accordingly revenged himself for this disappointment by ravaging the

---

[1] *Const. Hist.*, i. 448; *Early Plantagenets*, p. 33. Mr. Freeman rightly assigns his arrival to 1142, as does also Mr. Hunt (*Norman Britain*).

[2] *Will. Malms.*, p. 766.

[3] *Ibid.*; *Gervase*, i. 125.

[4] *Will. Malms.*, p. 768. Compare the state of things in 1153 (*Hen. Hunt.*, 288).

[5] "Deinde [after obtaining possession of Oxford] pauco dilapso tempore, cum instructissimâ militantium manu civitatem Warham . . . advenit" (*Gesta*, p. 91).

[6] *Ibid.*

district with fire and sword.¹ Thus passed the earlier months of 1143. Eventually, with his brother, the Bishop of Winchester, he marched to Wilton, where he proceeded to convert the nunnery of St. Etheldred into a fortified post, which should act as a check on the garrison of the Empress at Salisbury.² The Earl of Gloucester, on hearing of this, burst upon his forces in the night, and scattered them in all directions. Stephen himself had a narrow escape, and the enemy made a prisoner of William Martel, his minister and faithful adherent.³ This event is dated by Gervase July 1 [1143].

I have been thus particular in dealing with this episode because, as Dr. Stubbs rightly observes, "the chronology of Gervase is here quite irreconcilable with that of Henry of Huntingdon, who places the capture of William Martel in 1142."⁴ But a careful collation of Gervase's narrative with that given in the *Gesta* removes all doubt as to the date, for it is certain, from the sequence of events in 1142, that at no period of that year can Stephen and the Earl of Gloucester have been in Wiltshire at the same time. There is, therefore, no question that the two detailed narratives I have referred to are right in assigning the event to 1143, and that Henry of Huntingdon, who only mentions it briefly, has placed it under a wrong date, having doubtless confused the two attacks (1142 and 1143) that Stephen made on Wareham.⁵

Henry, says Gervase (i. 131), now spent four years in England, during which he remained at Bristol under the wing of his mighty uncle, by whom his education was entrusted to a certain Master Mathew.⁶ A curious reference by Henry himself to this period of his life will be found in the *Monasticon*

---

¹ *Gesta; Gervase*, i. 125.   ² *Gesta*, p. 91.
³ *Gervase*, i. 126; *Gesta*, p. 92.
⁴ *Gervase*, i. 126, *note*.
⁵ This episode also gave rise to another even stranger confusion, a misreading of "Winton" for "Wilton" having led Milner and others to suppose that Stephen was the founder of the royal castle at Winchester.
⁶ "Puer autem Henricus sub tutelâ comitis Roberti apud Bristoviam degens, per quatuor annos traditus est magisterio cujusdam Mathæi litteris imbuendus et moribus honestis ut talem decebat puerum instituendus" (i. 125).

(vol. vi.), where, in a charter (? 1153) to St. Augustine's, Bristol, he refers to that abbey as one

"quam inicio juventutis meæ beneficiis et protectione cœpi juvare et fovere."

It should be noticed that Gervase twice refers to Henry's stay as one of four years (i. 125, 133), and that this statement is strictly in harmony with those by which it is succeeded. Dr. Stubbs admits that Henry's departure is placed by him "at the end of 1146,"[1] and this would be exactly four years from the date when, as we saw, he landed. Again, Gervase goes on to state that two years and four months elapsed before his return.[2] This would bring us to April, 1149; and "here," as Dr. Stubbs observes, "we get a certain date," for "Henry was certainly knighted at Carlisle at Whitsuntide [May 22], 1149."[3] It will be seen then that the chronology of Gervase is thoroughly consistent throughout.[4] When Dr. Stubbs writes: "Gervase's chronology is evidently unsound here, but the sequence of events is really obscure,"[5] he alludes to the mention of the Earl of Gloucester's death. But it will be found, on reference to the passage, that its meaning is quite clear, namely, that the earl died during Henry's absence (*interea*), and in the November after his departure. And such was, admittedly, the case.

The second visit of Henry to England has scarcely obtained the attention it deserved. It was fully intended, I believe, at the time, that his arrival should give the signal for a renewal of the civil war. This is, by Gervase (i. 140), distinctly implied. He also tells us that it was now that Henry abandoned his studies to devote himself to arms.[6] It would seem, however, to be generally supposed that the sole incident of this

[1] i. 140, *note*.
[2] "Fuitque in partibus transmarinis annis duobus et mensibus quatuor" (i. 131).
[3] i. 140, *note*.
[4] The only point, and that a small one, that could be challenged, is that Gervase makes him land "mense Maio mediante," whereas we know him to have been at Devizes by the 13th of April (*vide infra*).
[5] i. 131, *note*.
[6] "Postpositisque litterarum studiis exercitia cœpit militaria frequentare."

visit was his receiving knighthood from his great-uncle, the King of Scots, at Carlisle. But it is at Devizes that he first appears, charter evidence informing us of the fact that he was there, surrounded by some leading partisans, on April 13.[1] Again, it has, apparently, escaped notice that the author of the *Gesta*, at some length, refers to this second visit (pp. 127–129). His editor, at least, supposed him to be referring to Henry's *first* (1142) and *third* (1153) visits; these, in that gentleman's opinion, being evidently one and the same.[2] According to the *Gesta*, Henry began by attacking the royal garrisons in Cricklade and Bourton, which would harmonize, it will be seen, exactly with a northerly advance from Devizes. He was, however, unsuccessful in these attempts. Among those who joined him, says Gervase, were the Earls of Hereford and of Chester. The former duly appears with him at Devizes in the charter to which I have referred; the latter is mentioned by John of Hexham as being present with him at Carlisle.[3] This brings us to the strange story, told by the author of the *Gesta*, that Henry, before long, deserted by his friends, was forced to appeal to Stephen for supplies. There is this much to be said in favour of the story, namely, that the Earl of Chester did play him false.[4] Moreover, the Earl of Gloucester, who is said to have refused to help him,[5] certainly does not appear as taking

[1] *Sarum Charters and Documents* (Rolls Series), pp. 15, 16. The witnesses are Roger, Earl of Hereford, Patrick, Earl of Salisbury, John fitz Gilbert (the marshal), Gotso "Dinant," William de Beauchamp, Elyas Giffard, Roger de Berkeley, John de St. John, etc.

[2] See his note to p. 127. Since the above passage was written, Mr. Howlett's valuable edition of the *Gesta* for the Rolls Series has been published, in which he advances, with great confidence, the view that we are indebted to its "careful author" for the knowledge of an invasion of England by Henry fitz Empress in 1147, "unrecorded by any other chronicler" (Chronicles: *Stephen, Henry II., Richard I*, III., xvi.-xx. 130; IV., xxi., xxii.) I have discussed and rejected this theory in the *English Historical Review*, October, 1890 (v. 747–750).

[3] *Sym. Dun.*, iii. 323. Henry of Huntingdon (p. 282) states that at Carlisle he appeared "cum occidentalibus Angliæ proceribus," and that Stephen, fearing his contemplated joint attack with David, marched to York, and remained there, on the watch, during all the month of August.

[4] "Ranulfus comes promisit cum collectis agminibus suis occurrere illis. Qui, nichil eorum quæ condixerat prosecutus, avertit propositum eorum" (*Sym. Dun.*, ii. 323).

[5] The author of the *Gesta*, by a pardonable slip, speaks of the earl as

any steps on his behalf. Lastly, it is not impossible that Stephen, whose generosity, in thus acting, is so highly extolled by the writer, may have taken advantage of Henry's trouble, to send him supplies on the condition that he should abandon his enterprise and depart. It is, in any case, certain that he did depart at the commencement of the following year (1150).[1]

Henry's *uncle*. The then (1149) earl was, of course, his *cousin*. It is on this slip that Mr. Howlett's theory was based.

[1] "Henricus autem filius Gaufridi comitis Andegaviæ ducisque Normanniæ, et Matildis imperatricis, jam miles effectus, in Normanniam transfretavit in principio mensis Januarii" (*Gervase*, i. 142).

APPENDIX Z.

BISHOP NIGEL AT ROME.

(See p. 209.)

A MOST interesting and instructive series of papal letters is preserved in the valuable Cotton MS. known as Tiberius, A. vi. The earliest with which we are here concerned are those referred to in the *Historia Eliensis* as obtained by Alexander and his fellows, the "nuncii" of Nigel to the pope, in virtue of which the bishop regained his see in 1142 (*ante*, p. 162).[1] These letters are dated April 29. As the bishop was driven from the see early in 1140, the year to which they belong is not, at first sight, obvious. The *Historia* indeed appears to place them just before his return, but its narrative is not so clear as could be wished, nor would it imply that the bishop returned so late as May (1142). The sequence of events I take to have been this. Nigel, when ejected from his see (1140), fled to the Empress at Gloucester. There he remained till her triumph in the following year (1141). He would then, of course, regain his see, and this would account for his knights being found in possession of the isle when Stephen recovered his throne. The king, eager to reassert his rights and to avoid another fenland revolt, would send the two earls to Ely (1142) to regain possession of its strongholds. The bishop, now once more an exile, and despairing of Maud's fortunes, would turn for help to the pope, and obtain from him these letters commanding his restoration to his see. I should therefore assign them to April 29, 1142. This would account for the expression "per

[1] " Et negotium strennissime agentes, acceperunt ab excellentiâ Romanæ dignitatis ad Archiepiscopum et episcopos Angliæ et ad Rothomagensem Archiepiscopum literas de restituendo Nigello episcopo in sedem suam " (*Hist. Eliensis*, p. 621).

longa tempora" in the letter to Stephen. They could not belong to 1141, when the Empress was in power, and the above expression would not be applicable in the year 1140.

The following is the gist of the letter to Stephen:—

"Serenitati tue rogando mandamus quatinus dignitates et libertates.... Venerabili quoque fratri nostro Nigello eiusdem loci episcopo in recuperandis possessionibus ecclesie sue injuste distractis consilium et auxilium prebeas. Nec pro eo quod ecclesia ipsa sua bona jam per longa tempora perdidit, justitie sue eam sustinere aliquod preiuditium patiaris" (fol. 114).

To his brother, the Bishop of Winchester, Innocent writes thus:—

"Rogando mandamus et mandando precipimus quatinus sententiam quam venerabilis frater noster Nigellus Elyensis episcopus in eos qui possessiones ecclesie sue iniuste et per violentiam detinent rationabiliter promulgavit firmiter observetis et observari per vestras parrochias pariter faciatis" (fol. 113 b).

A letter (also from the Lateran) of the same date to Nigel himself excuses his presence and that of the Abbot of Thorney at a council. A subsequent letter ("data trans Tyberim") of the 5th of October, addressed to Theobald and the English bishops, deals with the expulsion and restitution of Nigel, and insists on his full restoration.

The next series of letters are from Pope Lucius, and belong to May 24, 1144, being written on the occasion of Nigel's visit (*ante*, p. 208). Of these there are five in all. To Stephen Lucius writes as follows:—

"Venerabilis frater noster Nigellus Elyensis episcopus quamvis quibusdam criminibus in presentia nostra notatus fuerit, nec tamen convictus neque confessus est. Unde nos ipsum cum gratia nostra ad sedem propriam remittentes nobilitati tue mandamus ut eum pro beati Petri et nostra reverentia honores, diligas, nec ipse sibi vel ecclesie sue iniuriam vel molestiam inferas nec ab aliis inferri permittas. Si qua etiam ... ab hominibus tuis ei ablata sunt cum integritate restitui facias" (fol. 117).

The above "crimina" are those referred to in the *Historia Eliensis* as brought forward at the Council of London in 1143:—

"Quidam magni autoritatis et prudentiæ visi adversus Dominum Nigellum Episcopum parati insurrexerunt: illum ante Domini Papæ præsentiam appellaverunt, sinistra ei objicientes plurima, maxime quod seditiones in ipso concitaverat regno, et bona Ecclesie sue in milites dissipaverat; aliaque ei convicia blasphemantes improperabant" (p. 622).

A second letter of the same date "Ad clerum elyensem de condempnatione Symonie Vitalis presbyteri" deals with the case of Vitalis, a priest in Nigel's diocese, who had been sentenced to deprivation of his living, for simony, and whose appeal to the Council of London in 1143 had been favourably received by the legate.[1] The pope had himself reheard the case, and now confirmed Nigel's decision :—

"Dilectis filiis Rodberto Abbati Thorneie et capitulo elyensi salutem etc. Notum vobis fieri quia iuditium super causa, videlicet symonia, Vitalis presbyteri in synodo elyensi habitum in nostra presentia discussum est et retractatum. Quod nos rationabile cognoscentes apostolice sedis auctoritate firmavimus," etc., etc. (fol. 117).

Then come two letters, also of the same date, one to Theobald and the English bishops, the other to the Archbishop of Rouen, both to the same effect, beginning, "Venerabilis frater noster Nigellus elyensis episcopus ad sedem apostolicam veniens, nobis conquestus est quod," etc. (fol. 116 b) :[2] the fifth document of the 24th of May (1144) is a general confirmation to Ely of all its privileges and possessions (fols. 114 b–116 b).

Last of all is the letter referring to Geoffrey de Mandeville, which must, from internal evidence, have been written in reply to a letter from Nigel after his return to England (*ante*, p. 215).

[1] "Presbyter quidam Vitalis nomine conquestus est coram omnibus quod Dominus Elyensis episcopus eum non judiciali ordine de suâ Ecclesiâ expulerit. Huic per omnia ille Legatus favebat" (*Hist. Eliensis*, p. 622).

[2] See *ante*, p. 215, for Nigel's complaint.

APPENDIX AA.

"TENSERIE."

(See p. 215.)

The mention of "tenseriæ" in the letter of Lucius is peculiarly welcome, because (in its Norman-French form) it is the very word employed by the Peterborough chronicler.[1] As I have pointed out in the *Academy*,[2] the same Latin form is found in the agenda of the judicial iter in 1194: "de prisis et *tenseriis* omnium ballivorum" (*R. Hoveden*, iii. 267), while the Anglo-Norman "tenserie" is employed by Jordan Fantosme, who, writing of the burgesses of Northampton (1174), tells us that David of Scotland "ne pot *tenserie* de eus aver." He also illustrates the use of the verb when he describes how the Earl of Leicester, landing in East Anglia, "la terre vait *tensant.* . . . E ad *tensé* la terre cum il en fût bailli." The Latin form of the verb was "tensare," as is shown by the records of the Lincolnshire eyre in 1202 (Maitland's *Select Pleas of the Crown*, p. 19), where it is used of extorting toll from vessels as they traversed the marshes. A reference to the closing portion of the Lincolnshire survey in Domesday will show the very same offence presented by the jurors of 1086.

To the same number of the *Academy*, Mr. Paget Toynbee contributed a letter quoting some examples from Ducange of the use of *tenseria*, one of them taken from the Council of London in 1151: "Sancimus igitur ut Ecclesiæ et possessiones ecclesiasticæ ab operationibus et exactionibus, quas vulgo

---

[1] "Hi læiden gæildes on the tunes . . . and clepeden it *tenserie*" (ed. Thorpe, i. 382). Mr. Thorpe, the Rolls Series editor, took upon himself to alter the word to *censerie*.

[2] No. 1001, p. 37 (July 11, 1891).

tenserias sive tallagia vocant, omnino liberæ permaneant, nec super his eas aliqui de cætero inquietare præsumant." The other is taken from the Council of Tours[1] (1163), and is specially valuable because, I think, it explains how the word acquired its meaning. The difficulty is to deduce the sense of "robbery" from a verb which originally meant "to protect" or "to defend," but this difficulty is beautifully explained by our own word "blackmail," which similarly meant money extorted under pretence of protection or defence. The "defensio" of the Tours Council supports this explanation, as does the curious story told by the monks of Abingdon,[2] that during the Anarchy under Stephen—

"Willelmus Boterel constabularius de Wallingford, pecunia accepta a Iomno Ingulfo abbate, res ecclesiæ Abbendonensis a suo exercitu se defensurum promisit. Sponsionis ergo suæ immemor, in villam Culcham, quæ huic cænobio adjacet, quicquid invenire potuit, deprædavit. Quo audito, abbas . . . admirans quomodo quod tueri deberet, fure nequior diripuisset" etc.

William died excommunicate for this, but his brother Peter made some slight compensation later.[3] It was not unusual for conscience or the Church to extort more or less restitution for lawless conduct, as, indeed, in the case of Geoffrey de Mandeville and his son. So, too, Earl Ferrers made a grant to Burton Abbey "propter dampna a me et meis Ecclesiæ predictæ illata" (cf. p. 276, *n*. 3), previous to going on pilgrimage to S. Jago de Compostella—an early instance of a pilgrimage thither.[4]

While on this subject, it may be as well to add that the grant by Robert, Earl of Leicester, to the see of Lincoln in restitution for wrongs,[5] may very possibly refer to his alleged

[1] "De Cæmeteriis et Ecclesiis, sive quibuslibet possessionibus ecclesiasticis *tenserias* dari prohibemus, ne pro Ecclesiæ vel cæmeterii defensione fidei sui Clerici sponsionem interponant." Compare the passage from the *Chronicle of Ramsey*, p. 218 *n*., *ante*.

[2] *Abingdon Cartulary*, ii. 231.

[3] William and Peter Boterel were related to Brian Fitz Count (of Wallingford) through his father. They both attest a charter of his wife, Matilda "de Wallingford," to Oakburn Priory.

[4] *Burton Cartulary*, p. 50. A pilgrimage to this shrine is alluded to in a charter (of this reign) by the Earl of Chester to his brother the Earl of Lincoln, "in eodem anno quo ipsemet . . . redivit de itinere S. Jacobi Apostoli."

[5] "Robertus Comes Leg' Radulfo vicecomiti. Sciatis me pro satisfactione,

share in the arrest of the bishops (1139), and so confirm the statement of Ordericus Vitalis.[1]

The complaint of the same English Chronicle that the lawless barons "cruelly oppressed the wretched men of the land with castle works" is curiously confirmed by a letter from Pope Eugenius to four of the prelates, July 23, 1147 :—

"Religiosorum fratrum Abbendoniæ gravem querelam accepimus quod Willelmus Martel, Hugo de Bolebec, Willelmus de Bellocampo, Johannes Marescallus, et eorum homines, et plures etiam alii parochiani vestri, possessiones eorum violenter invadunt, et bona ipsorum rapiunt et distrahunt et *indebitas castellorum operationes ab eis exigunt.*"[2]

With characteristic agreement upon this point, William Martel, who served the king, John the marshal, who followed the Empress, and William de Beauchamp, who had joined both, were at one in the evil work.

ac dampnorum per me seu per meas Ecclesiæ Lincoln' Episcopo illatorum restitutione, dedisse . . . præfatæ Ecclesiæ Lincolnensi et Alexandro Episcopo," etc. (*Remigius' Register* at Lincoln, p. 37).

[1] See his life by me in *Dictionary of National Biography*.
[2] *Cartulary of Abingdon*, ii. 200, 543.

APPENDIX BB.

THE EMPRESS'S CHARTER TO GEOFFREY RIDEL.

(See p. 234.)

THIS instrument, which is referred to in the text, belongs to the Devizes series of the charters granted by the Empress, and is enrolled among some deeds relating to the baronial family of Basset.[1] As every charter of the Empress is of interest, while this one possesses special features, it is here given *in extenso* :—

M. Imperatrix Henrici Regis filia et Anglorum Domina, et H. filius Ducis Normannorum, Archiep. Epis. Abb. Comit. Baron. Justic. Vicecom. Minist. et omnibus fidelibus suis Francis et Anglis tocius Anglie et Normannie salutem. Sciatis me reddidisse et concessisse Galfrido Ridel filio Ricardi Basset totam hereditatem suam et omnia recta sua ubicunque ea ratione poteret ostendere sive in Normannia sive in Anglia et totam terram quam pater eius Ricardus Basset habuit et tenuit jure hereditario de Rege Henrico, vel de quocunque tenuisset, in Normannia sive in Anglia, ad tenendum in feodo et hereditate. Et totam terram Galfridi Ridel avi sui quamcunque habuit et tenuit jure hereditario, In Anglia sive in Normannia de Rege Henrico, vel de quocunque tenuisset, ad tenendum in feudo et hereditate sibi et heredibus suis de ncbis et heredibus nostris. Quare volumus et firmiter precipimus quod bene et in pace et quiete et honorifice teneat in bosco et aquis et in viis et semitis in pratis et yasturis in omnibus locis cum soch et sache cum tol et them et infangefethef et cum omnibus consuetudinibus et quietudinibus et libertatibus cum quibus antecessores eius tenuerunt. T[estibus]. Cancellario et Roberto Comite Glovernie et Galfrido Comite Essex et

---

[1] *Sloane*, xxxi. 4 (No. 48).

418 EMPRESS'S CHARTER TO GEOFFREY RIDEL.

Roberto filio Reg[is] et Walchelino Maminot [et] Rogero filio (*sic*) Apud Diuis[as].

The charter with which this one ought to be closely compared is that granted, also at Devizes, to Humfrey de Bohun, early in 1144.[1] These two are the only instances I have yet met with of *joint* charters from the Empress and her son. It may not be unjustifiable to infer that Henry was henceforth included as a partner in his mother's charters. If so, it would follow that her charters in which he is not mentioned are probably of earlier date.[2] The second point suggested by a comparison of these charters is that here Henry figures as the son of the Duke of the Normans, while in the other document he is merely son of the Count of the Angevins. This is at once explained by the fact that her husband had now won his promotion (1144) from Count of the Angevins to Duke of the Normans, an explanation which confirms my remarks on the charter to Humfrey de Bohun.[3] Thus this charter to Geoffrey Ridel must be later than the spring of 1144, while anterior to Henry's departure about the end of 1146. As the (Coucher) charter to Geoffrey de Mandeville (junior) is attested by Humfrey as "Dapifer," that, also, may be placed subsequent to Humfrey's own. Again, in the charter here printed, we have proof that Richard Basset was dead at the time of its grant, if not before. There has been hitherto no clue as to the time of his decease, though Foss makes him die, by a strange confusion, in 1154. Nor is it unimportant to observe that the Bassets and Ridels were typical members of that official class which Henry I. had fostered, and which appears to have strongly favoured his daughter's cause. Lastly, in the re-grant of this charter, by Duke Henry at Wallingford (1153), we have

---

[1] See my *Ancient Charters* (Pipe-Roll Society), pp. 45-47. There are two Devizes charters of the Empress, besides this one, not included in Mr. Birch's collection, namely, her grant of Aston (by the Wrekin) to Shrewsbury Abbey, and her general confirmation to that house. They are both attested by Earl Reginald, William fitz Alan, Robert de Dunstanville, and "Goceas" de Dinan, but are later than 1141, to which date Mr. Eyton and others assign them.

[2] In the second charter of the Empress to Geoffrey de Mandeville the elder (1142) we have the first sign of a desire to secure her son's adhesion.

[3] *Ancient Charters*, p. 47.

a valuable illustration of his practice in ignoring his mother's charters, even when sanctioned by himself in his youth. For, although the terms of the instrument are reproduced with exactitude, the grant is made *de novo*, without reference to any former charter.[1]

[1] *Sloane*, xxxi. 4. The witnesses are Randulf Earl of Chester, Reginald Earl of Cornwall, William Earl of Gloucester, the Earl of Hereford, Richard de Humez ("duhumesco"), constable, Philip de Columbers, Ralph Basset, Ralph "Walensis," Hugh de "Hamslep."

EXCURSUS.

THE CREATION OF THE EARLDOM OF GLOUCESTER.

ONE of the problems in English history as yet, it would seem, unsolved, is that of the date at which Henry I. conferred on his natural son Robert the earldom of Gloucester. The great part which Robert played in the eventful struggles of his time, the fact that this was, in all probability, almost the only earldom created in the course of this reign (1100–1135), and the importance of ascertaining the date of its creation as fixing that of many an otherwise doubtful record, all combine to cause surprise that the problem remains unsolved.

Brooke wrote that the earldom of Gloucester was conferred on Robert "in the eleventh year of his father's reign," and his critic, the argus-eyed Vincent, in his *Discoverie of Errours*, did not question the statement. As to Dugdale, he evaded the problem. Ignorance on the point is frankly confessed in the *Reports on the Dignity of a Peer*; while Mr. Freeman, so far as I can find, has also deemed discretion the better part of valour.

Three dates, however, have been suggested for this creation. The first is 1109. This may be traced to Sandford (1707) and Rapin (1724), who took it from the rhyming chronicle assigned to Robert of Gloucester:—

> "And of the kynges crownement in the [ninthe][1] yere,
> The vorst Erle of Gloucestre thus was mayd there."

This date was revived by Courthope in his well-known edition (1857) of the *Historic Peerage* of Sir Harris Nicolas (by whom no date had been assigned to the creation). It may be said, by inference, to have received the sanction of the authorities at the British Museum.

[1] This, the important word, is unfortunately doubtful.]

The second is 1119. This suspiciously resembles an adaptation of the preceding date, but may have been suggested, and in the case of Mr. Clark (*vide infra*) probably was, by reading Dugdale wrong.[1] It seems to have first appeared in a footnote to William of Malmesbury (1840), as edited for the English Historical Society by the late Sir Thomas Duffus (then Mr.) Hardy. It is there stated that Robert "was created Earl of Gloucester in 1119" (vol. ii. p. 692). No authority whatever is given for this statement, but the same date is adopted by Mr. Clark (1878), who asserts that "Robert certainly bore it [the title] 1119, 20th Henry I." (*Arch. Journ.*, xxxv. 5); by Mr. Doyle (1886) in his valuable *Official Baronage* (ii. 9); and lastly (1887) by Mr. Hunt in his *Bristol* (p. 17). In none of these cases, however, is the source of the statement given.[2]

In the mean while, a third date, viz. shortly before Easter (April 2), 1116, was advanced with much assurance. In his essay on the *Survey of Lindsey* (1882), Mr. Chester Waters wrote:

"We know that the earldom was conferred on him before Easter, 1116, for he attested as earl the royal charter in favour of Tewkesbury Abbey, which was executed at Winchester on the eve of the king's embarkation for Normandy" (p. 3).

The date attributed to this charter having aroused the curiosity of antiquaries, the somewhat singular discovery was made that it could also be found in the MSS. of Mr. Eyton, then lately deceased.[3] For the time, however, Mr. Waters enjoyed the credit of having solved an ancient problem, and "the ennobling of Robert fitz Roy in 1116" was accepted by no less an authority than Mr. Elton.[4]

I propose to show that these three dates are all alike erroneous, and that the Tewkesbury charter is spurious.

[1] "He was advanced to the earldom of Gloucester by the king (his father). After which, in Anno 1119 (20 Hen. I.), he attended him in that famous battle at Brennevill," etc., etc. (*Baronage*, i. 534).

[2] A paper on the earldom was read by the late Mr. J. G. Nichols, at the Gloucester Congress of the Institute (1851), but I do not find that it was ever printed, so that I cannot give the date which he assigned.

[3] *Athenæum*, May 9 and June 27, 1885.

[4] *Academy*, September 29, 1883 (p. 207).

Let us first observe that there is no evidence for the belief that Robert received his earldom at the time of his marriage to the heiress of Robert fitz Hamon. There is, on the contrary, a probability that he did not. I do not insist on the Tewkesbury charter (*Mon. Ang.*, ii. 66), in which the king speaks of the demesne of Robert fitz Hamon as being now "Dominium Roberti filii mei," for we have more direct evidence in a charter of Robert to the church of Rochester, in which he confirmed the gifts made by his wife and father, not as Robert Earl of Gloucester, but merely as "Ego Rodbertus Henrici Regis filius."

We must further dismiss late authorities, in which, as we might expect, we find a tendency to throw back the creation of a title to an early period of the grantee's life. We cannot accept as valid evidence the rhymes of Robert of Gloucester (*circa* 1300), the confusion of later writers, or the assumptions of the fourteenth-century *Chronicque de Normandie*, in which last work Robert is represented as already "Earl of Gloucester" at the battle of Tinchebrai (1106).

The only chronicle that we can safely consult is that of the Continuator of William of Jumièges, and this, unfortunately, tells us nothing as to the date of the creation, which, however, it seems to place some time after the marriage. It is worth mentioning that the writer's words—

"Præterea, quia parum erat filium Regis ingentia prædia possidere absque nomine et honore alicujus publicæ dignitatis, dedit illi pater pius comitatum Gloecestre" (Lib. viii. cap. 29, ed. Duchesne, p. 306).

are suspiciously suggestive of Robert of Gloucester's famous story that Robert's bride refused to marry him "bote he adde an tuo name." It would be very satisfactory if we could thus trace the story to its source, the more so as the chronicle is not among those from which Robert is supposed to have drawn.

We are, therefore, left dependent on the evidence of charters alone. That is to say, we must look to the styles given to Robert the king's son, to learn when he first became Earl of Gloucester.

His earliest attestation is, to all appearance, that which occurs in a charter of 1113. This charter is printed in the appendix to the edition of Ordericus Vitalis by the Société de l'Histoire de France,[1] and as all the circumstances connected with its grant, together with the names of the chief witnesses, are given by Ordericus in the body of his work,[2] there cannot be the slightest doubt, or even hesitation, as to its date.[3] In the text he is styled "Rodbertus regis filius," and in the charter "Rodbertus filius regis," his name being given, it should be noticed, last but one. The next attestation, in order, it would seem, is found in a writ of Henry I. tested at Reading, some time before Easter, 1116, to judge from the presence of "Rannulfus Meschinus."[4] For Randulf became Earl of Chester by the death of his cousin Richard, when returning to England with the king in November, 1120.[5]

We next find Robert in Normandy with his father. He there attests a charter to Savigny, his name ("Robertus filius regis") coming immediately after those of the earls (in this case Stephen, Count of Mortain, and Richard, Earl of Chester), that being the position in which, till his creation, it henceforth always figures. This charter passed in 1118, probably in the autumn of the year.[6] Robert's next appearance is at the battle of Brémulé (or Noyon), August 20, 1119. Ordericus refers to his presence thus:—

"Ibi fuerunt duo filii ejus Rodbertus et Ricardus, milites egregii, et tres consules," etc., etc. (iv. 357).

This is certainly opposed to the view that Robert was already an earl, for he is carefully distinguished from the three earls ("tres consules") who were present, and is classed with his brother Richard, who never became an earl. We must assign to about the same date the confirmation charter of Colchester Abbey, which is known to us only from the unpublished

[1] v. 199.   [2] iv. 302.
[3] The king promised the charter on the occasion of his visit (February 3, 1113), and when it had been drawn up, it received his formal approval at Rouen, "Anno quo comes Andegavensis mecum pacem fecit et Cenomanniam de me, meus homo factus, recepit."
[4] *Abingdon Cartulary*, ii. 77.
[5] Henry remained abroad between the above dates.
[6] *Gallia Christiana*, xi. (Instrumenta), pp. 111–112. The charter is there assigned, but without any reason being given, to 1118. A collation, however, of this record with the names given by Ordericus Vitalis (iv. 329) of those present at the Council of Rouen, October 7, 1118, makes it all but certain that it passed on that occasion.

cartulary now in the possession of Lord Cowper. Robert's name here comes immediately after those of the earls, and his style is "Robertus filius henrici regis Anglorum."

This charter suggests a very important question. That its form, in the cartulary, is that in which it was originally granted we may confidently deny. At the same time, the circumstances by which its grant was accompanied are told by the monks in great detail and in the form of a separate narrative. Indeed, on that narrative is based the belief, so dear to Mr. Freeman's heart, that Henry I. was, more or less, familiar with the English tongue. Moreover, it is suggested by internal evidence that the charter, as we have it, is based on an originally genuine record. Now, the accepted practice is to class charters as genuine, doubtful, or spurious, "doubtful" meaning only that they are either genuine or spurious, but that it is not quite certain to which of these classes they belong. For my part I see no reason why there should not be an indefinite number of stages between an absolutely genuine record and one that is a sheer forgery. It was often, whether truly or falsely, alleged (we may have our own suspicions) that the charter originally granted had been lost, stolen, or burnt. In the case of this particular charter, its predecessor was said to have been lost; at Leicester, a riot was made accountable; at Carlisle a fire. In these last two cases, those who were affected were allowed to depose to the tenor of the lost charter. In the case of that which we are now considering, I have recorded in another place[1] my belief that the story was probably a plot of the monks anxious to secure an enlarged charter. Of course, where a charter was really lost, and it was thought necessary to supply its place either by a pseudo-original document, or merely in a cartulary, deliberate invention was the only resource. But, in such cases, it was almost certain that, in the days when the means of historical information were, compared with our own, non-existent, the forger would betray himself at once by the names in his list of witnesses. There was, however, as I imagine, another class of forged charters. This comprised those cases in which the original had not been lost, but in which it was desired to

[1] *Academy*, No. 645.

substitute for that original a charter with more extensive grants. Here the genuine list of witnesses might, of course, be copied, and with a little skill the interpolations or alterations might be so made as to render detection difficult, if not impossible. I speak, of course, of a cartulary transcript; in an actual charter, the document and seal would greatly assist detection. But I would suggest that there might be another class to be considered. This Colchester charter is a case in point. The impression it conveys to my mind is that of a genuine charter, adapted by a systematic process of florid and grandiloquent adornment to a depraved monkish taste. In short, I look on this charter as not, of necessity, a "forgery," that is, intended to deceive, but as possibly representing the results of a process resembling that of illumination. Such an hypothesis may appear daring, but it is based, we must remember, on a mental attitude, on, so to speak, an historic conscience, radically different from our own. After all, it is but in the present generation that the sacredness of an original record has been recognized as it should. Such a conception was wholly foreign to the men of the Middle Ages. I had occasion to allude to this essential fact in a study on "The Book of Howth," when calling attention to the strange liberties allowed themselves by the early translators of the *Expugnatio Hiberniæ*. Geoffrey of Monmouth illustrates the point. Looking not only at him but his contemporaries in the twelfth century, we cannot but compare the impertinent obtrusion of their pseudo-classical and, still more, their incorrigible Biblical erudition, with the same peculiar features in such charters as those of which I speak. Another remarkable parallel, I think, may be found in the *Dialogus de Scaccario*. Observe there the opening passage, together with the persistent obtrusion of texts, and compare them with the general type of forged, spurious, or "doctored" charters. The resemblance is very striking. It was, one might say, the systematic practice of the monkish forger or adapter to make the royal or other grantor in such charters as these indulge in a homily from the monkish standpoint on the obligation to make such grants, and to quote texts in support of that thesis. Once viewed in this light, such passages are as intelligible as they are absurd.

CREATION OF EARLDOM OF GLOUCESTER.

But, in addition to, and distinct from, these stilted moralizations, is the process which I have ventured to compare with illumination or even embroidery. This was, in most cases, so overdone, as to bury the simple phraseology of the original, if genuine, instrument beneath a pile of grandiloquence. Take for instance this clause from the Colchester charter in question:

"Data Rothomagi deo gratias solemniter et feliciter Anno ab incarn' dom' MCXIX. Quo nimirum anno prætaxatus filius regis Henrici Will's rex designatus puellam nobilissimam filiam Fulconis Andegavorum comitis Mathildam nomine Luxouii duxit uxorem."

Now, if we compare this clause with that appended to an original charter of some ten years later, we there read thus :—

"Apud Wintoniam eodem anno, inter Pascham et Pentecostem, quo Rex duxit in uxorem filiam ducis de Luvain." [1]

This peculiar method of dating charters which is found in this reign suggests that the genuine charter to Colchester would contain a similar clause (if any),[2] beginning "Apud Rothomagum eodem anno quo," etc., etc. As it stands in the cartulary, the original clause has been treated by the monkish scribe much as an original passage in a chronicle might be worked into his text, in the present day, by an historian of the "popular" school.[3] But wide and interesting though the conclusions are to which such an hypothesis might lead, I must confine myself here to pointing out that the list of witnesses,

[1] Duchy of Lancaster: Royal Charters, No. 6.

[2] Compare the Rouen charter [1113] to St. Evroul, where the clause is "Anno quo comes Andegavensis mecum pacem fecit," etc., etc. (see p. 423).

[3] This is specially applicable to the insertion of the year in numerals. Such date would be, though actually an addition, yet a legitimate inference from the event alluded to in the charter. It may be worth alluding to another case, though it stands on somewhat a different footing, to illustrate the infinite variety of treatment to which such charters were subjected, even when there were neither occasion nor intention to deceive. This is that of the final agreement between the Archbishops of Canterbury and York, of which the record is preserved at Canterbury. It has been discovered that the document from which historians have quoted (A. 1) is not really the original, but a copy "which was plainly intended for public exhibition" (*Fifth Report Hist. MSS.*, App. i. p. 452). Moreover, the real original (A. 2) was found not to contain the final clause (narrating the place and circumstances of the agreement), which is hence supposed to have been subsequently added, for the sake of convenience, by the clerk. (See my letter in *Athenæum*, December 19, 1891.)

DATE OF THE COLCHESTER CHARTER. 427

in its minutest details, is apparently beyond impeachment. Specially would I refer to four names, those of the clerks of the king's chapel. It is rare, indeed, to find so complete and careful a list. The four "capellani regis," as they are here styled, are (1) John de Bayeux;[1] (2) Nigel de Calne;[2] (3) Robert "Pechet;"[3] (4) Richard "custos sigilli regis."[4] The remarkable and, we may fairly assume, undesigned coincidence between the list of witnesses attesting this charter, and that of the king's followers at the battle of Brémulé (fought, there is reason to believe, within a few weeks of its grant), as given by Ordericus Vitalis, ought to be carefully noted, confirming, as it obviously does, the authority of both the lists, and consequently my hypothesis that the charter in the Colchester cartulary represents a genuine original record belonging to the date alleged.[5]

It is also, perhaps, worth notice that Eadmer applies to William "the Ætheling" the very same term as that which meets us in this charter, namely, "designatus."[6]

Approaching now the question of date, we note that the charter must have been subsequent to the marriage at Lisieux (June, 1119) to which it refers, and previous to the Council of Rheims (October 20, 1119), which Archbishop Thurstan attended, and from which he did not return.[7] We know that between these dates Henry was in Rouen at least once, viz. at the end of September (1119),[8] so that we can determine the date of the charter within exceedingly narrow limits.

---

[1] Natural son of Odo, Bishop of Bayeux, the Conqueror's half-brother.

[2] "Nigellus de Calna reddit compotum de j marca argenti pro Willelmo nepote suo" (*Rot. Pip.*, 31 Hen. I., p. 18).

[3] Made Bishop of Lichfield and Coventry early in 1121.

[4] *Alias* "de Sigillo." He was made Bishop of Hereford in January, 1121, as "Ricardus qui regii sigilli sub cancellario custos erat" (Eadmer).

[5] In both we have the same three earls, neither more nor less; in both we have the same two *filii regis*, Robert and Richard; in both we have Richard de Tankerville and Nigel de Albini and Roger fitz Richard.

[6] "Willelmum jam olim regni hæredem designatum" (p. 290). Compare the Continuator of Florence of Worcester, who, speaking of the very event (1119) by which this charter is dated, describes him as William "quem jam [*i.e.* 1116] hæredem totius regni sui constituerat" (ii. 72).

[7] *Florence of Worcester*, ii. 72.

[8] *Ordericus Vitalis* (ed. Société de l'Histoire de France), iv. 371.

428   CREATION OF EARLDOM OF GLOUCESTER.

The remaining charters which we have now to examine are all subsequent to the king's return and the disaster of the White Ship (November 25, 1120).

The desolate king had spent his Christmas (1120) in comparative seclusion at Brampton, attended by his nephew, Theobald of Blois.[1] In January (1121) he came south to attend a great council before his approaching marriage. By Eadmer and the Continuator of Florence of Worcester, the assembling of the council is assigned to the Epiphany (January 6, 1121). Richard "de Sigillo" was on the following day (January 7) elected to the see of Hereford, and was consecrated nine days later (January 16, 1121) at Lambeth.[2]

To this council we may safely assign a charter in the British Museum (Harley, 111, B. 46),[3] of value for its list of witnesses, twenty-six in number. It gives us the names of no fewer than thirteen bishops, by whom, in addition to the primate, this council was attended.[4] Mr. Walter de Gray Birch, by whom so much has been done to encourage the study of charters and of seals, has edited this record in one of his instructive sphragistic monographs.[5] He has, however, by an unfortunate inadvertence, omitted about half a dozen witnesses,[6] while his two limits of date are not quite correct; for Richard was consecrated Bishop of Hereford, not on "the 16th of January, 1120," but on the 16th of January, 1121 (N.S.), and Archbishop Ralph died, not "19th September," but 19th October (xiv. kal. Novembris), 1122. Thus the limit for this charter would be, not "from April, 1120, to September, 1122," but from January, 1121, to October, 1122. Mr. Birch further observes that "the

---

[1] Henry of Huntingdon.

[2] *Cont. Flor. Wig.*, ii. 75; *Eadmer*, 290.

[3] "Sciatis me dedisse et concessisse Ricardo episcopo episcopatum de Hereford," etc., etc.

[4] Five of them joined the primate in the consecration of the Bishop of Hereford (January 16). The Archbishop of York was not at the council, being still in disgrace with the king for his conduct at the Council of Rheims (October, 1119).

[5] *Journ. Brit. Arch. Ass.*, xxix. 258, 259.

[6] Reading "Willelmo, & Ricardo filiis Baldewini," where the charter has:—"(1) William de Tankerville, (2) William de Albini, (3) Walter de Gloucester, (4) Adam de Port, (5) William de Pirou, (6) Walter de Gant, (7) Richard fitz Baldwin.

date may be taken very shortly after the consecration of Richard." Here again, I must reluctantly differ, for by the practice of the time, the grant of the temporalities did not come after, but before, the consecration. The charter, in short, as I observed above, can be safely assigned to the council of January, 1121.

In it the subject of this paper attests as "Roberto filio Regis." His name occurs in its right place immediately after those of the earls, who, oddly enough, are in this charter the same two, at least in title,[1] after whom he had attested the Savigny charter in 1118.[2]

The next charters in my chain of evidence are two which passed at Windsor. We are told by Simeon of Durham that at the time of the king's marriage (January 29–30, 1121) there was gathered together at Windsor a council of the whole realm.[3] To this council I assign a charter printed by Madox from the original among the archives of Westminster Abbey.[4] I am led to do so because, firstly, the names of the witnesses are all found, with three exceptions, in charters belonging to this date; second, the said three exceptions are those of Count Theobald of Blois, who had, we know, joined the king not long before, of Earl David, from Scotland, whose visit would be due to the occasion of his brother-in-law's wedding, and of the Archbishop of Rouen, whose presence may be also thus accounted for;[5] third, the attestation of two archbishops with four bishops suggests the presence of a "concilium," as described by Simeon of Durham.

If this is the date of the charter in question, it may also be that of another charter, also to Westminster Abbey,[6] for its

---

[1] The Count of Mortain, and the Earl of Chester. The latter was, of course, now Randolf, who had succeeded his cousin Richard, drowned in the White Ship.

[2] *Vide supra*, p. 423.

[3] "Anno MCXXI Concilio totius Angliæ ante purificationem . . . apud Winderesoram adunato, Henricus rex . . . Adelinam matrimonio sibi junxit" (ii. 249).

[4] *Formularium Anglicanum*, No. lxv. (p 39).

[5] This would give us, as the principal guests assembled at the king's wedding, his brother-in-law, Earl David, his nephews Theobald, Count of Blois, and Stephen, Count of Mortain, with the primates of England and of Normandy.

[6] Madox's *Formularium Anglicanum*, No. cccсxcvi. (p. 292).

eleven witnesses are all found among those of the preceding charter. In both these cases "Robert, the king's son," attests in his regular place immediately after the earls.[1]

We now come to an original charter in every way of the highest importance.[2] I have already quoted its dating clause,[3] which proves it to have been executed at Winchester, between Easter (April 10) and Pentecost (May 29), 1121. Moreover, as the king spent his Easter at Berkeley and his Whitsuntide at Westminster,[4] the limit of date, as a matter of fact, is somewhat narrower still. Here again Robert attests ("Rob[erto] fil[io] Regis ") at the head of all the laity beneath the rank of earl.

The last charter which I propose to adduce, as attested by "Robert, the king's son," is one which, in all probability, may be assigned to this same occasion, for the whole of its thirteen witnesses had attested the previous charter, with the exception of two bishops, whose presence can be otherwise accounted for,[5] and of William de Warenne (Earl of Surrey).

The importance of this charter is not so great as that of those adduced above, for it is known to us only from the Rymer Collectanea (*Add. MSS.*, 4573), of which an abstract is appended to the *Fœdera*.[6] Moreover, in one minute detail its accuracy may be fairly impugned, for "Willielmo de Warennâ" clearly stands for "Willielmo *Comite* de Warennâ." Nor, indeed, is its evidence needed, the proof being complete without it. Yet, as the charter (*quantum valeat*) has been assigned, I think, to a wrong date, the point may be worth glancing at. In the Rymer Collectanea the date is fixed as "1115" (or "16 Henry I.") on the ground that it belongs to the same date as a charter of Henry I. to Bardney, which was granted "Apud Wynton' xvj. anno postquam rex recepit regnum Angliæ."[7] Mr. Eyton also, in a

[1] Earl David and the Count of Blois.
[2] Duchy of Lancaster : Royal Charters, No. 6.
[3] *Supra*, p. 426.   [4] *Anglo-Saxon Chronicle*.
[5] Winchester, who had attested the Windsor charters, and who here attests in his own city; and St. David's, who is constantly found at Court, and who had attested, in January, the charter at Westminster, to the Bishop of Hereford (*supra*, p. 428).
[6] "Concessio Manerii de clara Archiepiscopo Rothomagensi."
[7] *Mon. Ang.*, i. 629.

THE TEWKESBURY CHARTER CORRUPT. 431

late addition to his MS. Itinerary of Henry I.,[1] wrote that the presence of three of the bishops (Lincoln, Salisbury, and St. David's) suggested "the latter part of 1115." But we must remember that the Bardney charter is known to us only from a late Inspeximus,[2] and that the dating clause is somewhat suspicious. Yet even if the version were entirely genuine, the fact remains that the list of witnesses has only four names [3] in common with that in the charter I am discussing, which has, on the contrary, no less than ten in common with those in the original charter of 1121.[4] I cannot, therefore, but fix on 1121 as a far more probable date for its grant than 1115–1116.

This, however, as I said, is but a small matter. The really important fact is this: that we have a continuous chain of evidence, proving that "Robert, the king's son," was not yet Earl of Gloucester, at least as late as April—May, 1121.

Against this weight of accumulated evidence what is there? Absolutely nothing but that Tewkesbury charter, which is quoted from Dugdale's *Monasticon*, where it is quoted from a mere *Inspeximus* of the 10th Henry IV. (1408–9), some three centuries after its alleged date![5] I need scarcely say that this miserable evidence for the assertion that Robert was Earl of Gloucester, at Easter, 1116, is simply annihilated and crumpled up by the proof afforded by original charters that he had not yet received the earldom even five years later on (1121).

It is, however, satisfactory to be able to add that, even independent of this rebutting evidence, the charter itself, on its own face, bears witness of its spurious character. Mr. Eyton, indeed, was slightly uneasy about two of the witnesses, it being, he thought, as unusually early for an attestation of Brian fitz Count, as it was late for that of Hamo Dapifer.[6] Yet he was not, on that account, led to reject it; indeed, he not only accepted, but unfortunately built upon its evidence. He never, however, we must remember, committed his conclusions to print, so that it may be urged with perfect justice that he might have reconsidered and changed his views before he made them

---

[1] *Add. MSS.*, 31,937, fol. 130.   [2] Cart., 5 Edw. III., n. 10.
[3] The chancellor and three bishops.
[4] Duchy of Lancaster: Royal Charters, No. 6.
[5] *Monasticon Anglicanum*, ii. 66.   [6] *Addl. MSS.*, 31,943, fol. 68, b.

public. Not so with Mr. Chester Waters. Announcing the discovery which Mr. Eyton had so strangely anticipated, he wrote—

"We know that the earldom [of Gloucester] was conferred on him [Robert] before Easter, 1116, for he attested as earl the royal charter in favour of Tewkesbury Abbey which was executed at Winchester, on the eve of the king's embarkation for Normandy (*Monasticon*, vol. ii. p. 66)."[1]

When Mr. Waters thus wrote, had he observed that in this charter the king's style appears as "Henr' dei gratia Rex Angl' et dux Norm'"? And if he had done so, if he had glanced at the charter on which he based his case, is it possible that he was so unfamiliar with the charters and the writs of Henry I., as not to be aware that such a style, of itself, throws doubt upon the charter?[2] To those who remember that he confessed (in reply to certain criticisms of my own) to having "carelessly repeated a statement which comes from a discredited authority,"[3] and that he announced a discovery as to the meeting of Henry I. and Robert of Normandy, in 1101,[4] which, as I proved, was based only on his own failure to read a charter of this reign aright,[5] such a correction as this will come as no surprise.

Having now shown that Robert fitz Roy was not yet Earl of Gloucester in April—May, 1121, I proceed to show that he was earl in June, 1123.

The charter by which I prove this is granted "apud Portesmudam in transfretatione meâ."[6] It is dated in the thirty-first Report of the Deputy-keeper of the Records (in the calendar of these charters drawn up by the late Sir William Hardy) as "1115–1123." Its exact date can, however, be determined, and is 3–10 June, 1123. This I prove thus. The parties addressed are Theowulf, Bishop of Worcester (who died October 20, 1123), and Robert, Earl of Gloucester (who was not yet earl in April—May, 1121). These being the limits of date, the only occasion within these limits on which the king

[1] *Survey of Lindsey*, p. 3. See my paper on "The spurious Tewkesbury Charter" in *Genealogist*, October, 1891.

[2] "Rex Anglorum" was the normal style employed in the English charters of Henry I.: "Dux Normannorum," etc., was added by Henry II.

[3] *Academy*, June 27, 1885.   [4] *Notes and Queries*, 6th series, i. 6.

[5] *Athenæum*, Dec. 19, 1885.

[6] Duchy of Lancaster: Royal Charters, No. 5.

TRUE DATE OF THE CREATION. 433

"transfretavit" was in June, 1123. And we learn from the Anglo-Saxon Chronicle that the king, on that occasion, was at Portsmouth, waiting to cross, all Pentecost week (June 3–10). This is conclusive.

It is certain, therefore, that Robert fitz Roy received the earldom of Gloucester between April—May, 1121, and June, 1123. We may even reduce this limit if we can trust a charter in the Register of St. Osmund (i. 382) which is absurdly assigned in the Rolls edition to *circ.* 1109. The occurrence of Robert, Earl of Leicester, proves that it must be subsequent to his father's death in 1118, and consequently (as the charter is tested at Westminster) to the king's return in 1120. Again, as Bishop Robert of Lincoln witnesses the charter, it must be previous to his death, January 10, 1123. But as the king had not been at Westminster for some time before that, it cannot be placed later than 1122. Now, we have seen that in April—May, 1121, Robert was not yet Earl of Gloucester; consequently, this charter must belong to the period between that date and the close of 1122. It is, therefore, the earliest mention, as yet known to me, of Robert as Earl of Gloucester. As we increase our knowledge of the charters of this reign we shall doubtless be able to narrow further the limit I have thus ascertained.

There is, indeed, a charter which, if we could trust it, would greatly reduce the limit. This is Henry I.'s great charter to Merton,[1] which is attested by Robert, as Earl of Gloucester, and which purports to have passed August 5—December 31, 1121 (? 24th March, 1122).[2] But it is quite certain that, in the form we have it, this charter is spurious. It is true that the names given in the long list of witnesses are, apparently, consistent with the date,[3] but all else is fatally bad. Both the charter itself, and the attestations thereto, are in the worst and most turgid style; the precedence of the witnesses is distinctly wrong,[4] and the mention of the year-date would alone rouse

[1] *Cartæ Antiquæ*, R. 5.
[2] It is dated 1121, and in the twenty-second year of the reign.
[3] That is, if Archbishop Thurstan was yet restored to favour.
[4] The chancellor, for instance, instead of attesting after the bishops and before the laity, actually follows immediately after the archbishops, and precedes the whole "bench of bishops." I have been amazed to find antiquaries who thought nothing of this matter of precedence.

2 F

suspicion. Whether, and, if so, to what extent, the charter is based on a genuine document, it is not easy to decide. A reference to the new *Monasticon* will show that there is a difficulty, a conflict of testimony, about the facts of the foundation. This increases the doubt as to the authenticity of the charter, from the evidence of which, if not confirmed, we are certainly not entitled to draw any authoritative conclusion as to the date of Robert's creation.

Adhering then, for the present, to the limits I have given above (1121-1122) I may point out that Robert's promotion may possibly have been due to his increased importance, consequent on the loss in the White Ship of the king's only legitimate son, and of his natural son Richard. Of Henry's three adult sons he now alone remained.[1] It is certain that he henceforth continued to improve his position and power till, as we know, he contested with his future rival, Stephen, the honour of being first among the magnates to swear allegiance to the Empress.

Before passing to a corollary of the conclusion arrived at in this paper it may be well to glance at Robert's younger brother and namesake. This was a son of Henry by another mother, Edith, whose parentage, by the way, suggests a genealogical problem.[2] He was quite a nonentity in the history of the

[1] Robert and Richard are the two of Henry's natural sons, who are mentioned as with him in Normandy, and fighting beneath his standard at Noyon (1119).

[2] If, as suggested by the narrative in the *Monasticon* of the foundation of Osney Abbey, her father's name was "Forne," one is tempted to ask if the bearer of so uncommon a name was identical with the Forn Ligulfson ("Forne filius Ligulfi"), who is mentioned by Simeon of Durham, in 1121, as one of the magnates of Northumbria, and if so, whether the latter was son of the wealthy but ill-fated Ligulf, murdered near Durham in 1080. Should both these queries be answered in the affirmative, Edith would have been named after her grandmother "Eadgyth," the highly born wife of Ligulf. Writing at a distance from works of reference I cannot tell whether such a descent has been suggested before, but it would certainly, could it be proved, be of quite exceptional interest. Edith, as is tolerably well known, was first the mistress of Henry, and then the wife of Robert D'Oilli. Thus her son by the former, Robert fitz Edith (see p. 94, n. 4), was (half)-brother to Henry D'Oilli, and is so described by the latter in one of his grants to Osney (Dugdale's *Baronage*, i. 460). It should be added that an "Ivo fil' Forn" appears in the Pipe-Roll of 1130 (p. 25). Was he brother to Edith?

time as compared with the elder Robert; nor does his name, so far as I know, occur before 1130, when it is entered in the Pipe-Roll for that year. He is found as a witness to one of his royal father's charters, which is only known to us from the *Cartæ Antiquæ*, and which belongs to the end of the reign.[1] There is no possibility of confusion between his brother and himself, for his earliest attestations are, as we have seen, several years later than his brother's elevation to the earldom, so that they cannot both have been attesting, at any one period, as "Robert, the king's son." It is, moreover, self-evident that such a style could only be used when there was but one person whom it could be held to denote.

As illustrating the value of such researches as these, and the importance of securing a "fixed point" as a help for other inquiries, I shall now give an instance of the results consequent on ascertaining the date of this creation. Let us turn to that remarkable record among the muniments of St. Paul's, which the present Deputy-Keeper of the Records first made public,[2] and which has since been published *in extenso* and in fac-simile by the Corporation of London in their valuable *History of the Guildhall*. The importance of this record lies in its mention of the wards of the City, with their respective rulers, at an exceptionally early date. What that date was it is most desirable to learn. Mr. Loftie has rightly, in his later work,[3] made the greatest use of this list, which he describes (p. 93) as "the document I have so often quoted as containing a list of the lands of the dean and chapter before 1115." Indeed, he invariably treats this document as one "which must have been written before 1115" (p. 82). But the only reason to be found for his conclusion is that—

"Coleman Street appears in the St. Paul's list as 'Warda Reimundi,' and this is the more interesting as we know that Reimund, or Reinmund, was dead before 1115, which helps us to date the document. Azo, his son, succeeded him " (p. 89).[4]

---

[1] Charter to the church of Durham, printed in **Rymer's** *Fœdera* (Record edition), i. 13, and assigned by Sir T. D. Hardy (*Syllabus*) to "1134." It was, in any case, subsequent to Flambard's death (September 5, 1128).

[2] *Ninth Report Hist. MSS.*, App. i. p. 56.   [3] *Historic Towns: London*.

[4] Mr. Loftie elsewhere tells us (p. 27) that Reinmund "was succeeded

This is a most astounding statement, considering that all "we know," from these documents, of Reimund or Reinmund is that both he and his son Azo were living in 1132, when they attested a charter![1] Turning from this strange blunder to the fact that the Earl of Gloucester is among those mentioned in this list,[2] we learn at once that, so far from being *earlier* than 1115, it is *later* than the earl's creation in 1121–1122. And this conclusion accords well with the fact that other names which it contains, such as those of John fitz Ralf (fitz Evrard),[3] William Malet, etc., belong to the close of the reign.[4]

Before taking leave of this record, I would glance at the curious entry :—

"Terra Gialle [reddit] ii sol[idos] et est latitudinis LII pedum longitudinis CXXXII pedum."

Mr. Price, the editor of the work, renders this "The land of Gialla;" but what possible proper name can "Gialla" represent? When we find that the list is followed by a reference to the Jews being "incarcerati apud Gyhalam," *temp.* Edward I., and when Mr. Price admits that "Gyaula" is among the early forms of "Guildhall," is it too rash a conjecture that we have in the above "Gialla" a mention of the Guildhall of London earlier, by far, than he, or any one else, has ever yet discovered?

by his more eminent son Azo, the goldsmith, whom it would be interesting to identify with one of the Azors of Domesday." How does Mr. Loftie know that Azo was "more eminent" than his father, or that he was a "goldsmith"? On one point we can certainly agree with him. It *would* be most "interesting" to identify a Domesday tenant in a man whose father was living in 1132!

[1] *Ninth Report (ut supra)*, p. 67 b. For similar instances of eccentric statements on the City fathers in Mr. Loftie's book, see p. 355, and my paper on "The First Mayor of London" (*Antiquary*, March, 1887). They throw, it will be found, a strange light on Mr. Elton's unfortunate remark that "Mr. Loftie makes good use of the documents discovered at St. Paul's" (*Academy*, April 30, 1887, p. 301).

[2] "Socce Comitis Gloecestrie."

[3] Cf. pp. 305, 306.

[4] Ralf fitz "Algod," Robert fitz Gosbert, and Robert d'Ou occur in a deed of 1132 (*Ninth Report Hist. MSS.*, App. i. p. 67 b), and Osbert Masculus in one of 1142 (*ibid.*, p. 40 b).

ADDENDA.

Page 5. The assertion by the Continuator of Florence of Worcester that Stephen kept his coronation court " cum totius Angliæ primoribus " has an important bearing on the assertion by Florence that Harold was elected to the throne " a totius Angliæ primatibus." For this latter phrase is the sheet-anchor upon which Mr. Freeman relies for the fact of Harold's valid election, and which he is avowedly compelled to strain to the uttermost:—

" He was chosen, not by some small or packed assembly, but by the chief men of the land. And he was chosen, not by this or that shire or earldom, but by the chief men of the whole land. . . . All this is implied in the weighty and carefully chosen words of Florence" (*Norman Conquest* [1869], iii. 597).

So also he confidently insists that—

" There can be no doubt that the Witan of Northumberland, no less than the Witan of the rest of England, had concurred in the election of Harold. The expressions of our best authorities declare that the chief men of all England concurred in the choice " (*ibid.*, p. 57).

The only authority given for this assertion is the above statement by Florence that " Harold was 'a totius Angliæ primatibus ad regale culmen electus.' "

Now, the known authorities from which Florence worked (the Abingdon and Worcester chronicles) " are," Mr. Freeman admits, "silent about the election." The fact, therefore, rests on the *ipse dixit* of Florence (for the words of the Peterborough chronicler are quite general, and, moreover, he is admittedly a partisan), who was, strictly speaking, not a contemporary authority.

Stephen's election, as Mr. Freeman observes, " can hardly fail to call to our minds " that of Harold, and in the case of

Stephen's accession we have what he himself terms the "valuable contemporary" evidence of the Continuator of Florence." This evidence, which is better, because more contemporary, than that of Florence as to 1066, is equally precise (*vide supra*), and might, in the absence of rebutting testimony, be appealed to as confidently as Mr. Freeman appeals to that of Florence. But in this case it is proved, by rebutting evidence, to be worthless, just as it is at Maud's " reception " in 1141 (see p. 64).

Therefore, we see how dangerous it is to accept such statements, when unsupported, as exact in every detail, and are led to regard the words of Florence as a mere conventional phrase, rather than to hold, as Mr. Freeman insists, that in "no passage in any writer of any age . . . does every word deserve to be more attentively weighed."

The caution with which such evidence should be used is one of the chief lessons this work is intended to enforce (see p. 267).

Page 8. There is much confusion as to the charters of liberties issued by Stephen. The "second" charter, as explained in the text, was issued at Oxford in the spring of 1136; the other, commonly termed the "coronation" charter, is found only, it would seem, in the Cottonian MS. Claud. D. II., and has no note of date. Mr. Hubert Hall has been good enough to inform me that the authority of this MS. is first-rate; and, as to the date at which the charter was issued, that of the coronation, there is no doubt, was the most *probable*. It is important to observe that the oath stated by William of Malmesbury to have been taken by Stephen at his first arrival (and afterwards committed to writing at Oxford) was " de libertate reddenda ecclesiæ et conservanda." William's remark that this oath, " postea scripto inditum, loco suo non prætermittam," proves that he must have looked on the *Oxford* charter as the record of this oath in writing; for that is the only charter which he gives in his work. This fits in with the fact that the charter assigned to the coronation contains no mention of the Church and her liberties, while the "second" (Oxford) charter is full of them. It would appear, then, that the Oxford charter combined the original oath to the Church with the "coronation" charter to the people at large, at the same time expanding them both in fuller detail.

ADDENDA.

Page 37. (Cf. p. 354.) It would, perhaps, have been rash to introduce into the text the conjecture that in the first Geoffrey de Mandeville we have the actual " Gosfregth Portirefan " to whom the Conqueror's charter to the citizens of London was addressed, although the story in the *De Inventione*, the known connection of the Mandevilles with the shrievalty, and the striking resemblance of the two names (even closer than in " Esegar " and " Ansgar "), all point to the same conclusion.

The association of the custody of the Tower with the shrievalty of London and Middlesex is a point of considerable interest, because in other cases—such as those of Worcestershire, Gloucestershire, Wilts, and Devon—we find the custody of the fortress in the county town and the shrievalty of the shire hereditarily vested in the same hands.

Page 74. The phrase " in regni dominam electa " must, as explained in the text, not be pressed too far, as it may be loosely used. But the parallel is too curious to be passed over.

Page 92. The grant of " excidamenta " confers on Geoffrey the escheatorship of Essex to the exclusion of any Crown officer.

Page 93. The closing clauses of this charter suggest that Geoffrey was even then guarding himself against the consequences of future treason.

Page 103. The grants of knight-service to Geoffrey should be carefully compared with those, by Henry I., to William de Albini " Pincerna," as recorded in the *carta* of his fief (*Liber Rubeus*, ed. Hall, p. 397), and are also illustrated by the charter to Aubrey, p. 189.

Page 112. "Archiepiscopo Cant." is, of course, a transcriber's wrong extension for " Arch[idiacono] Cant."

Page 116. The phrase " senatoribus inclitis, civibus honoratis, et omnibus commune London " may be compared with the " cent partz et a laut poble et comunautat de Baione " on p. 248.

Page 182. The expression " una baronia " should be noted as a very early instance of its use.

Page 189. The name of Abbot Ording dates this charter as between 1148 and 1156 (*Memorials of St. Edmundsbury*, I. xxxiv.).

Page 190. " Mauricius dapifer " was Maurice de Windsor,

steward of the Abbey. For him and for the Cockfield family, see the Camden Society's edition of Jocelyn de Brakelonde.

"Alanus filius Frodonis" was probably the heir of Frodo, brother to Abbot Baldwin of St. Edmund's (see Domesday).

Page 205. Compare William of Malmesbury's criticism on Stephen's conduct in attacking Lincoln (1140) without due notice: "Iniquum id visum multis," etc.

Page 235. The transcriber is responsible, of course, for the extension of the king's style.

Page 242. It is only fair to add that the peculiar strength of the words of inheritance might be held to support the view that hereditary earldoms were a novelty.

Page 267. The charters of Henry II. to certain earls in no way affect my real contention, namely, that no "fiscal" earls were, as is alleged, deprived by him of their earldoms.

Page 275. On the gradual resumption of crown-lands, see my *Ancient Charters*, page 47.

Page 286. "Navium applicationibus" (cf. *Domesday*, 32: "De exitu aquæ ubi naves applicabant") is a phrase occurring elsewhere as "appulatione navium." It there equates "theloneum," and was doubtless a payment for landing-dues. So, "de teloneo dando ad Bilingesgate" is found in the Instituta Londoniæ of Æthelred.

Page 312, note 1. Compare the charge against Harold (in the French life of the Confessor) that he "deners cum usurer amasse."

Page 314. The occurrence of "salinis" among the general words in this charter is clearly due to the rights of the Beauchamps in Droitwich and its salt-pans.

Page 371. The amount of the *firma* seems to be determined by an entry in the Pipe-Roll of 15 Hen. II. (page 169), which makes it £500 "blanch," *plus* a varying sum of about £20 "numero."

Page 372. Henry's jealousy of the Londoners might also be due, in part, to their steadfast support of Stephen and opposition to his mother. His restriction of clauses (1) and (10) to lands within the walls is illustrated by a citizen having to pay, in 1169 (*Rot. Pip.* 15 Hen. II., p. 173), "ut placitet contra W. de R. *in civitate Lund'* de terra de Eggeswera" (Edgware), as a special favour.

INDEX.

A

Abetot, Geoffrey d', 314
———, Urse d', 314, 315
Abingdon Abbey, its treasury robbed, 213; its troubles, 415, 416; its delegate, 384
——— ———, Ingulf, abbot of, 265, 415
Adeliza, Queen (wife of Henry I.), her "election," 74, 439; marries Henry I., 429; William de Albini, 319, 322, 323; dowered by Henry I., 322, 324; her grant to Reading, 325
Ælfgar ("Colessune"), 310
———, Nicholas, son of, 309, 310
Affidatio, 170, 176, 182, 384-387
Aino, William de, 230
Albamarle. *See* AUMÂLE.
Albini, Nigel de, 427
———, William de ("Pincerna"), 262, 263, 324, 428, 439. *See also* ARUNDEL.
Aldreth (Camb.), 161, 162, 209
Alexander, Pope, absolves Earl Geoffrey, 224
Algasil, Gingan, 60
Alvia, Andrew de, 172, 183
Anarchy, incidents of the, 127-132, 134, 206, 209-220, 323, 403, 414-416
Andover, Stephen at, 47; burnt by his queen, 128
Angers, Ulger, bishop of, pleads for Maud at Rome, 8, 254-257
Anjou. *See* GEOFFREY
Ansgar. *See* ESEGAR
Anstey (Herts.), 141
Appleby Castle, 331
Arch', Gilbert, 314
Ardleigh (Essex), 402

Ardres, Baldwin d', 188, 397
Arms, collateral adoption of, 394; date of their origin, 396
Arques, Château d', 340-346; its keep built by Henry I., 333
———, Count William of, 341-343, 345, 346
———, William of, 180, 188, 397
Arras, Baldwin of, 310
Arsic, Geoffrey, 190, 230
Arundel, Robert, 93, 263, 264, 266
———, Empress lands at, 55, 273, 280
———, William (de Albini), earl of, 143, 145, 146; "pincerna," 324; created earl, 322; styled Earl of Chichester, 318, 320; Earl of Sussex, 146, 319, 320; Earl of Lincoln, 324, 325; his charter from Henry II., 240; his "third penny," 293; holds Waltham, 324; at St. Albans, 204-206; dies, 317; his character, 323
———, earldom of, 316-325; its earliest mention, 146, 271, 322; not an earldom by tenure, 316, 324; its various names, 320, 321; similar to other earldoms, 322, 325
Assarts (forest), 92, 168, 182, 376-378
Aston (Salop), 418
Auco. *See* Ou
Aumâle, William of (Earl of York), 143, 145, 146, 157, 262-264, 276, 385
Avranches, Rhiwallon d', 397
———, Turgis d', 46, 52, 144, 149, 158, 207
———, William d', 154, 180, 397
———, bishop of, Richard, 262, 263
Aynho (Northants), 390
Azo. *See* REINMUND

B

Baentona. *See* BAMPTON
Bailiffs, represent, in towns, the sheriff, 110
Balliol, Joscelin de, 236
Bampton, Robert de, 140
Bareville, Walter de, 231
Barking, Stephen at, 320; his charters to, 320, 378; Alice, abbess of, 378
"Baronia," grant of a, 182, 439
Barstable, hundred of, grant of the, 320
Basset, Ralf, 419
———, Richard, 265, 297, 298, 417, 418
Bath, Stephen grants his bishopric of, 18, 21
———, Robert, bishop of, 18, 64, 263
Battle, Warner, abbot of, 265
Bayeux, John de, 427
———, Odo, bishop of, 427
Bayonne, customs of, 247
Bazas (Aquitaine), customs of, 247
Beauchamp, Maud de, 313
———, Stephen de, 314, 315
———, Walter de, 313-315
———, William de, 154, 409, 416; constable, 285, 313; his charter from the Empress, 313-315
——— (of Bedford), Miles de, 171, 183, 314, 315
———, Payne de, 171, 392, 393
———, Robert de, 171
———, Simon de, 171, 231, 262, 263, 390, 392, 393
Beaudesert Castle, 65
Beaufoe, Henry, 230; Ralf de, 373
Beaumont, Hugh de. *See* "PAUPER"
Becket, Thomas, his youth, 374, 375; as chancellor, 228, 236. *See also* CANTERBURY
Bedford, earldom of, 270, 271, 276
"Begeford," 286
Belmeis, Richard de (archdeacon), 123
Belun, Adam de, 144, 158, 201, 320
Belvoir, Robert de, 385
Benwick, 211
Berkeley, Henry I. at, 430
———, Roger de, 380, 409
Berkshire, earldom of, 181

Berners, Ralf de, 229-231
Bigod, Gunnor, 391
———, Hugh (Earl of Norfolk), 403; with Henry I., 265, 365; asserts the Empress was disinherited, 6; with Stephen at Reading, 11, 13; at Oxford, 263; rebels, 23; attacked by Stephen, 49; created earl, 50, 188, 191, 238, 270; with the Empress, 83, 172, 178, 183; opposed to Stephen, 195; rebels, 209; his earldom East Anglian, 273; created anew by Henry II., 277
———, Roger, 329
Bigorre, customs of, quoted, 58
Birch, Mr. W. de Gray, on a charter of Henry I., 428; on the charters to Geoffrey, 44, 87; on the seals of Stephen, 50, 139; on the election of the Empress, 59-61, 63; on the charters of the Empress, 66, 76; on the styles of the Empress, 75-78, 83; on the seal of the Empress, 299; his remarkable discovery, 71-73
Bishopsbridge, Roger of, 375
Bishop's Stortford, 167; its castle, 174
Bisset, Manasser, 236
Blois, Count Theobald of, 91, 428-430; forfeited by the Empress, 102, 140
Blundus, Gilbert, 190
———, Robert, 229
Bocland, Hugh de, 309, 328, 355
———, Walter de, 201
Boeville, William de, 142, 231
———, Otwel de, 229
Bohun, Humfrey de, 125, 234, 263, 265, 281, 286, 314, 315, 418
Bolbec, Hugh de, 201, 416
———, Walter de, 264
Bonhunt. *See* WICKHAM BONHUNT
Boreham (Essex), 214
"Bosco, de," Ernald, 228
Boseville, William de, 142
Bosham, Herbert of, on the Emperor, 301
Boterel, Geoffrey, 125
———, Peter, 415
———, William, 415
Boulogne, Count Eustace of, 1, 2, 143, 168

Boulogne, Geoffrey de, 147
——, Pharamus de, 120, 144, 147
——, Richard de, 120
——, honour of, 121, 141, 147, 168, 182
Bourton, young Henry attacks, 409
Boxgrove Priory, 320
Brampton, Henry I. at, 428
Braughing (Herts.), 141
Breteuil, William de, 327
Bristol, Empress arrives at, 55, 278; Stephen imprisoned at, 56, 65; Empress and her followers at, 135, 163; young Henry at, 407
——, St. Augustine's Abbey, 408
Brito, Mainfeninus, 52, 201, 360
——, Ranulf (? Ralf), 143
Brittany, Alan of. *See* RICHMOND
Buccuinte, Andrew, 305, 309
Buckenham Abbey, foundation of, 318
Buckingham, earldom of, 272
Bumsted Helion (Essex), 181
Bungay (Suffolk), the foundation at, 318
Burwell, besieged by Geoffrey, 220; who falls there, 221
Bury, Richard de, his "Liber Epistolaris," 261
Bushey (Herts.), 92, 156

C

Caen, castle of, 331, 333
Calne, Nigel de, 427
Cambridge, sacked by Geoffrey, 212
Cambridgeshire, "tertius denarius" of, 181, 193, 194
——, earldom of, 181, 191-193, 271, 273
"Camera abbatis," annuity from the, 190
Camerarius, Eustace, 231
——, Fulcred, 355
——, Richard, 355
——, William, 355
Camville, Richard de, 159
Cantelupe, Simon de, 402
Canterbury, Gervase of, his accuracy confirmed, 137, 375; his chronology discussed, 284, 406-408

Canterbury, John of (clerk), 375
——, archbishops of, Lanfranc, 326, 337;—Anselm, sanctions marriage of Henry I., 257;—Ralf, 307, 428;—William, 265, 306; extorts oath from Stephen, 3; crowns him, 4-8, 253; with him at Reading, 11; at Westminster and Oxford, 262; his clerk "Lovel," 253; builds keep of Rochester, 337, 338;—Theobald, 311, 370, 386; meets the Empress, 65; hesitates to receive her, 260; attends her election, 69; at her court, 125; supports her cause, 208; forfeited by Stephen, 251; with Henry II., 236; patron of Becket, 375; papal letters to, 214, 215, 412, 413;—Thomas (Becket), confirms compensation to Ramsey, 225; claims Saltwood, 327. *See also* BECKET
——, archdeacon of, Geoffrey, 112, 439
——, Stephen at, 1; granted to Earl of Gloucester, 2; Stephen re-crowned at, 137-139; Henry II. at, 236, 237
—— and York, charter of settlement between, 426
Capella, Aubrey de, 190
Capellanus, Hasculf, 231
—— regis, 427. *See also* FECAMP
Capra. *See* CHIÉVRE
Carbonel, Hugh (fitz Ralf) de, 190
——, Ralf de, 190
Carlisle, Athelwulf, bishop of, 262, 263
——, "firma" of, 363
——, young Henry at, 408, 409
—— Castle, 331
Cartæ of 1166, erroneous headings of, 399, 402; carelessly transcribed, 401; illustrated by Pipe-Rolls, 402
"Castellum," special meaning of, 331-334, 337, 338, 340, 343
Castles, erection of, and license for, 142, 154, 156, 160, 168, 174, 175; misery caused by, 217, 416; surrender of, extorted, 202, 207; their character, 331, 334, 343, 346; in hands of sheriffs, 439
"Castrum." *See* "CASTELLUM"

INDEX.

Catlidge (Essex), 90, 140
Celestine, Pope, favours the Empress, 252, 258, 259
Cerney, 281
Chahaines, Philip de, 382
——, Reginald de, 382
Chalk (Kent), 306, 308
Chamberlainship of England, the, 180, 187, 390
Chancellors (Stephen's), Philip (de Harcourt), 46-48;—Roger (le Poor), 262, 263
—— (the Empress's), William (fitz Gilbert), 93, 123, 171, 182, 195;—William de Vere, 182, 195
—— (of Henry I.), Geoffrey, 265
Charters of Henry I., 19, 25, 422-434; to London, 109, 347, 356, 359, 364, 367, 370; to Aubrey de Vere, 187, 390; to church of Salisbury, 265; to Gervase of Cornhill, 305; to Bishop of Hereford, 428; to Colchester Abbey, 423-427; to Westminster, 429; to Tewkesbury, 431; to Bardney, 430; Eudo Dapifer, 328
—— of Stephen, 18, 19, 23, 25, 27, 438; to Miles of Gloucester, 11-14, 176; to church of Salisbury, 46; to Geoffrey de Mandeville, 41-53, 138, 156; to Monks Horton, 158; to Earl of Lincoln, 159; to Abingdon, 201; to St. Frideswide's, 201; to Barking, 320, 378
—— of the Empress Maud, 82, 83, 194; to Geoffrey de Mandeville, 41, 42, 86-113, 139, 163-177, 294; to Miles of Gloucester, 56, 60, 123, 165, 288; to St. Bene't of Hulme, 67; to Thurstan de Montfort, 65, 66; to Glastonbury, 83; to Haughmond, 123; to Aubrey de Vere, 178-195; to Geoffrey de Mandeville, jun., 233; to Roger de Valoines, 286; to William de Beauchamp, 313-315, 440; to Geoffrey Ridel, 417; to Humfrey de Bohun, 418; to Shrewsbury Abbey, 418
—— of Queen Matilda, to Geoffrey, 118-121, 139, 156; to Gervase, 120

Charters of Henry II., 112; to Wallingford, 200; to Feversham Abbey, 147; to Aubrey de Vere, 184-186, 237, 239; to Geoffrey the younger, 234-241; to Earl of Arundel, 240, 277; to Hugh Bigod, 239, 277, 288; to London, 367-371, 440; to Geoffrey Ridel, 418
—— of Richard I., to Colchester, 110
—— of John, to London, 372
—— of Henry III., to London, 358
——, dating clauses in, 426, 431, 433: archaic *formulæ* in, 241; forged, altered, and enlarged, 424, 425, 431; garbled, 426, 433; granted at Easter court (1136), 18, 19, 262-265; of Henry I. and Henry II. to London, compared, 368-371; of Mandeville family, 228-233, 390; of Basset family, 417
Chester, Randulf, earl of, 146, 160, 262, 263, 265, 380, 423, 429; at Easter court (1136), 265; at siege of Winchester, 128; reconciled to Stephen, 159; his wrong doings, 268; arrested by Stephen, 203; joins Henry, 409, 419; dies, 276; his charter of restitution, 415
——, Richard, earl of, 423, 429
——, Roger, bishop of, 83, 253, 265; died, 251
——, John (de Lacy), constable of, 390
Chiche, Maurice de, 142
Chichester, Seffrid, bishop of, 83, 262, 263, 265
——, earl of. *See* ARUNDEL
Chicksand Priory, 231, 390
Chiévre, Geoffrey, 169
——, Michael, 169
——, William, 169
Chreshall (Essex), 168
"Christianitas Angliæ," 172, 177, 183, 387
Cirencester, Empress at, 57; captured by Stephen, 197; Earl of Gloucester reaches, 199, 406
Clairvaux, Payne de, 172, 183
——, Robert de, 172, 183
Clare, Richard "fitz Gilbert" de (I.), 321

Clare, Gilbert "fitz Richard" (I.) de, 329
——, ——, Baldwin "fitz Gilbert" de, 13, 144, 145, 148, 159
——, ——, Richard "fitz Gilbert" de (II.), 40, 148, 270, 271
——, ——, Walter "fitz Gilbert" de, 159
——, Robert "fitz Richard" (I.) de, 11, 13, 14, 262, 263, 370
——, Roger "fitz Richard" (I.) de, 265, 427
——, Walter "fitz Richard" (I.) de, 13, 14, 264, 265
——, Alice de (wife of Aubrey de Vere), 390
——, earldom of. *See* HERTFORD
—— *See also* PEMBROKE, earl of; EXETER, Baldwin of
Clarendon, Stephen at, 378
——, Assize of, 111-113
Clark, Mr. G. T., on Gloucester Castle, 330; on the Tower of London, 334; on Rochester Castle, 338; on the keep of Newcastle, 339, 346; on the Château d'Arques, 340-346; his authority, 346
Clavering (Essex), 391
Clericus, Hugh, 231
——, Lovel, 253
——, Roger, 231
——, Simon, 231
Clinton, Geoffrey de, 265, 297
Cluny, Peter, abbot of, 253, 254
——, abbey of, favours the Empress, 254
Cnihtengild, the London, 307-309
Cookfield, Adam de, 190, 440
——, Robert de, 190
Coffin, story of the Empress escaping in a, 134
"Cokeford," 314
Colchester, charter of Richard I. to, 110
—— Castle, granted to Eudo Dapifer, 328; to Aubrey de Vere, 180, 185, 328
—— Abbey (St. John's), 391; charter of Henry I. to, 423-427
—— ——, Hugh, abbot of, 194
Coleville, Robert de, 314

Coleville, W. de, 159
Colne Priory, 390
Columbers, Philip de, 419
"Communa." *See* LONDONERS
"Communio." *See* LONDONERS
Compostella, St. Jago de, pilgrimages to, 415
Compton (Warwick), 390
Constableship, hereditary, 285, 314, 315, 326
"Constabularia" (of knights), the, 155
"Constabularie, Honor," 326, 327
Corbet, Robert, 383
Cornhill, Edward de, 306, 307
——, ——, his wife "Godeleve," 306-308
——, Gervase de, 304-312; his loan to the Queen, 120, 305; justiciar of London, 121, 305; sheriff of London, 304; of Kent, 311; a money-lender, 311; his descendants, 312
——, ——, his wife Agnes, 306, 308; his brother Alan, 310, 311
——, Henry de (son of Gervase), 305, 310
——, Ralph de, 310
——, Reginald de, 310
——. *See also* "NEPOS HUBERTI," Roger
Cornwall, Reginald ("filius regis"), earl of, 68, 82, 123, 125, 172, 183, 234, 236, 263, 264, 271, 418, 419
——, earldom of, 68, 271
Coronation, its relation to election, 5; its importance, 6; in the power of the Church, 7; performed at Westminster, 78, 80; repeated by Stephen and by Richard I., 137
Coroners represent, in towns, the "justiciar," 110
Councils, 17-24, 48, 69, 136, 165, 202, 264, 265, 278, 412, 413, 415, 423, 427-429
Courci, Robert de (Dapifer), 170, 183
——, Alice de, 310
Courtenay, Hugh de, 296
Coutances, "Algarus," bishop of, 262, 263
——, Geoffrey, bishop of, 290
Crevecœur, Robert de, 158

INDEX.

Cricklade, young Henry attacks, 409
——, " third penny " of, 289
Crown, hereditary right to the, 25, 26, 29, 30, 32, 33, 55, 186, 200, 253-256; elective, 26, 29, 34; kept at Winchester, 62
Crown lands, grants of, 99, 101, 140, 142, 149, 154, 167, 269, 275, 440; their rents, 100, 268, 293
Culham, 415
Cumin, William, 85
Curci. *See* COURCI
" Custodes " distinct from sheriffs, 297

D

Dammartin, William de, 53
Danfront, Picard de, 141
Danish district, peculiar payments in the, 289
Danvers, Henry, 232
Dapifer, Eudo, 154, 328; his fief and office, 167, 173
——, Hamo, 431
——, Hubert, 382
David, King of Scots, with Henry I. (as earl), 429, 430; invades England, 16; joins the Empress, 80, 84; at her court, 123, 124; knights Henry, 409; his earldom, 181, 192
Dean, Forest of, 56
Dedham (Essex), 181, 400-404
Deforcement, 351
Depden (Essex), 90, 140, 141
Derby, earldom of, 193, 270, 271
——, earl of. *See* FERRERS
Devizes, castle of, 46; Empress flees to, 133; its story, 134, 386; councils of the Empress at, 165; young Henry at, 408, 409; charter granted at, 417, 418
Devon, earldom of, 271, 272, 296
——, " tertius denarius " of, 296
——, Baldwin (de Redvers), earl of, 93, 125, 172, 183
" Dialogus de Scaccario," the, 154, 293, 304, 312, 322, 376, 425
" Diffidatio," the, 28, 284, 285

Diham. *See* DEDHAM
Dinan, Gotso (or Goceas) de, 409, 418
Dispenser, Robert le, 154, 314, 315; his inheritance, 313
Dodnash Priory, foundation of, 385
D'Oilli. *See* OILLI
Domesday values, 101, 102, 140, 241, 361; the " tertius denarius " in, 287-291
Domfront. *See* DANFRONT
" Domina,", the Empress as, 14, 56, 57, 63, 67, 70, 73-75, 80, 83
" Dominus," the king as, 14, 70, 73, 74
Dorset, earldom of, 95, 181, 193, 194, 271, 272, 277. *See* MOHUN
——, " tertius denarius " of, 291
Douai, Walter de, his fief, 141
Dover, Stephen at, 1; granted to Earl of Gloucester, 2; held against Stephen, 2, 94; Henry II. at, 237; a " castellum," 332
—— Castle, 340, 345
Dower, 385
Droitwich, 440
Dublin Castle, 331
Dugdale, his errors, 37, 38, 44, 87, 166, 327, 388, 391
Dunstanville, Alan de, 123, 325
——, Robert de, 236, 418
Durham, Stephen at, 16
——, see of, contest for, 85; privileges of, 112
——, bishops of, Ranulf (Flambard), 384;—Geoffrey, 265

E

" Eadintune," 306, 307
Earldoms, always of a county, 273, 320; or joint counties, 191-193, 273; hereditary, 53, 242, 440; formula of creation, 97, 187, 191, 238; of confirmation, 89, 97, 188, 190, 238; dealings of Henry II. with, 234, 239, 274-277
Earls, their privileges, 52, 93, 98, 143, 160, 169, 181, 182, 235, 292; at siege of Winchester, 128; at Stephen's court, 139, 144, 159; origin of their

titles, 144, 181, 191, 272, 273, 320, 321; their "third penny," 239, 240, 269, 287-296
Earls, Stephen's, 266, 270; dates of their creation, 270, 271; choice of their titles, 272; their alleged poverty, 267, 269; not "fiscal," 267-277, 440; their alleged deposition, 274-277
Easton (Essex), 141
Edgware, 440
Edward I., his dealings with London, 358; with Nottingham, 359
Eglinus (? de Furnis), 53
Ellis, Mr. W. S., on the arms of Mandeville, 394; of Sackville, 393; of De Vere, 395
Elmdon (Essex), 143
Elton, Mr., on Mr. Chester Waters, 421; on Mr. Loftie, 436
Ely, Stephen marches on, 48; Geoffrey despatched against, 161, 411; Geoffrey occupies, 209, 215; Geoffrey's doings at, 213, 215, 218; Stephen's vengeance on, 214; famine and misery at, 219
——, Nigel, bishop of, 45; at Stephen's court, 262, 263; rebels, 48; joins the Empress, 64, 161, 411; attends her court, 82, 83, 93, 314; appeals to Rome against Stephen, 161, 411; restored to his see, 162, 412; visits the Empress, 208; goes to Rome, 208, 209; returns, 215; with Henry II., 236
——, William, prior of, 83
Emperor, style of the, 300, 301
Epping Forest. *See* WALTHAM
Esegar (the staller), succeeded by the Mandevilles, 37; sheriff and portreeve, 353, 354
"Esendona," 286
Espec, Walter, 263, 385
Essex, hereditary shrievalty of, 92, 109, 142, 150, 166
——, —— justiciarship of, 92, 105, 109, 142, 150, 167
——, "firma" of, 92, 142, 150, 166, 298, 360
——, "third penny" of, 89, 92, 235, 237, 239

Essex, earldom of, created by Stephen, 51-53, 97, 270, 271; confirmed by the Empress, 89; assigned to Geoffrey the younger, 234, 417; re-created by Henry II., 234-239; extinct, 243
——, escheatorship of, 92, 439
——, forest of, 376-378
——, earls of. *See* MANDEVILLE and FITZ PIERS
——, Henry of, 52, 172, 183 (?), 195, 236, 268, 326, 327, 391, 393
——, Robert of, 52, 391
——, Swegen of, 52, 391
——, Alice of, 169, 390
Eu, the count of, 158
Eugene III., Pope, 224, 251, 258, 416
Eustace, son and heir of Stephen, his betrothal, 47; his intended coronation, 7, 250, 259
Evreux, Audoen, bishop of, 262, 263
"Excambion," formula of, 102, 167, 180-182, 230
Exchequer system, 108, 293, 352, 355, 360, 400; not destroyed by the Anarchy, 99, 142, 154
——, pensions on the, 267-269, 274
Exeter, held against Stephen, 24
——, William, bishop of, 265
——, earldom of, 272. *See* DEVON
——, "third penny" of, 289
—— Baldwin, (sheriff) of, 289, 329
——, ——, his wife Emma, 329
——, ——, Robert, son of, 329
——, ——, Richard, son of, 329, 428
—— Castle, 343
Eynsford, William de, 158, 298, 360
Eyton, Mr., on the charters to Geoffrey, 41-44, 86, 97; to Aubrey de Vere, 179; on the charters of the Empress, 67; on Richard de Luci, 146; on Robert de Vere, 147; his MSS., 44, 421; on the Tewkesbury charter, 431

F

Fecamp, Roger de, 46, 263
Fenland campaign, 209-212
Ferrers, Robert de (Earl of Derby), 13, 94, 143, 146, 159, 263, 266, 415

INDEX.

Feudalism, its aims, 105, 108, 109, 111, 176, 372. *See also* "DOMINUS," "DIFFIDATIO"
Feversham Abbey, 147
Fiennes, Sybil de, 147
"Firma burgi," 361-363
—— comitatus," 99, 102, 142, 150, 154, 156, 298, 313, 360, 362; its constituents, 100, 287, 293, 361
"Fiscus," meaning of, 268
Fitz (*Filius*) Adam, Ralf, 190
—— ——, Warine, 190
—— Ailb', William, 190
—— "Ailric," Robert, 190
—— Alan, Roger, 310, 311
—— ——, John, 316
—— ——, Walter, 123
—— ——, William, 123, 125, 418
—— Algod, Ralf, 436
—— Alvred, William, 53, 229, 230
—— Baldwin. *See* EXETER
—— Bigot, John, 385
—— Brian, Ralf, 142
—— Count, Brian, with Henry I., 265, 431; meets Earl of Gloucester, 281; is besieged and relieved, *ib.*; at Stephen's court, 19, 262, 263; escorts the Empress, 58, 82, 83, 93, 125, 130, 135, 170, 182, 286, 314; his letter, 251, 261
—— ——, Otwel, 307
—— ——, Reginald, 320
—— Ebrard, Ralf, 305
—— Edith, Robert (son of Henry I.), 66, 82, 94, 125, 129, 170, 183, 234, 418, 434, 435
—— Ernald, William, 53, 229
—— ——, Ranulf, 229
—— Frodo, Alan, 189, 440
—— Gerold, Henry, 229, 230
—— ——, Robert, 142
—— ——, Ralf, 142
—— ——, Warine, 190, 228, 229, 236, 241
—— Gilbert. *See* CLARE
—— ——, John (the marshal), 82, 125, 129-132, 171, 182, 183, 234, 314, 409, 416. *See also* "HISTOIRE"
—— ——, William. *See* CHANCELLORS
—— Gosbert, Robert, 436

Fitz Hamon, Robert, 382, 422
—— Heldebrand, Robert, 95, 171, 183
—— ——, Richard, 95
—— Herlwin, Ralf, 309, 310
—— ——, his sons, 310
—— ——, Herlwin, 310
—— ——, William, 310
—— Hervey, William, 142
—— Hubert, Robert, 134, 281
—— Humfrey, Geoffrey, 190
—— ——, Robert, 190
—— Jocelin, William, 402, 404
—— John, Payne, 11, 12, 263, 265, 378
—— ——, Eustace, 159, 264, 378
—— Liulf, Forn, 434
—— Martin, Robert, 94, 135
—— Miles, William, 399
—— Muriel, Abraham, 229
—— Osbern, William (Earl of Hereford), 154
—— Osbert, Richard, 53, 229, 231
—— Other, Walter, 169
—— Oto, William, 86
—— Otwel, William, 169, 229, 231
—— Piers, Geoffrey, Earl of Essex, 39
—— Ralf, Brian, 142
—— —— (fitz Ebrard), John, 305, 306, 436
—— —— ——, Robert, 305, 306
—— Richard. *See* CLARE
—— ——, Osbert, 53, 231
—— ——, Roger, 169, 390-392
—— Robert, Walter (of Dunmow), 169
—— ——, William, 142
—— —— (fitz Walter), John, 52
—— Roger, Robert, 391
—— Roy. *See* CORNWALL, FITZ EDITH, GLOUCESTER
—— ——, Richard (son of Henry I.), 423, 427, 434
—— Urse, Richard, 53, 159
—— ——, Reginald, 53
—— Walter, Fulcred, 360, 363
—— ——, Geoffrey, 229
—— ——, Ranulf, 229
—— ——, Robert, 385
—— ——, William, constable of Windsor, 169

Fitz Wimarc, Robert, 391
Flanders, Count Robert of, 176, 177, 380
Flemings, expulsion of the, 275
Florence of Worcester, his continuater's chronology, 278, 279, 284, 285; accuracy, 437, 438
Foliot, Gilbert, attends council at Rome, 251, 253; his letter to Brian Fitz Count, 251, 252, 254-257, 261; becomes Abbot of Gloucester (1139), 285; Bishop of Hereford (1148), 251, 260
Fordham (Camb.), 209, 211, 220, 222
Fordwich, "third penny" of, 290
Forests. See ASSARTS
France, King of, 171, 177, 183
Fraxineto. See FRESNE
Freeman, Professor, his errors, 16, 62, 63, 68, 224, 250, 261, 290, 291, 294, 325, 333, 335, 338, 346, 349; Mr. J. Parker on, 280
Fresne, Roger du, 320
Fulcinus, Albot, 231
Fulham, 117

G

Gainsborough Castle, 159
Gamlingay (Camb.), 120, 305
Gant, Walter de, 264, 266, 128
——, Gilbert de, 327
Geoffrey of Anjou, 167, 168, 171, 183, 184; was to succeed Henry I., 33; summons Stephen before the Pope, 10, 259; invited to England, 165, 177, 195; sends his son to England in his stead, 33, 185, 198; detains the Earl of Gloucester, 198; conquers Normandy, 418; cedes Normandy to Henry, 251, 259; admits no legate, 260
Gerardmota, Simon de, 120
Gerpenville. See JARPENVILLE
"Gersoma," 298, 360, 363, 366
"Gesta Stephani," its accuracy impugned, 12, 409; confirmed, 32, 63, 115, 130, 132
"Gialla." See LONDON
Gifard, John, 364
Giffard, Elyas, 409
"Ging'." See ING
Glanville, Ranulf de, 385, 390
——, ——, his wife Bertha, 385; his daughter Maud, 385
Gloucester, Empress reaches, 55, 278; leaves it, 57; returns to it, 115; leaves it again, 123; flees to it, 134
—— Castle, 13, 329, 330
——, earldom of, its creation, 420-422, 431-434
——, honour of, 11
——, Robert (son of Henry I.), earl of, 181; marries heiress of Robert fitz Hamon, 422; his earliest attestation (Rouen, 1113), 423; attends his father at Reading, ib.; at the battle of Brémulé, ib.; at Rouen, 424, 426; in England, 429, 430; created Earl of Gloucester, 432; attends his father at Westminster, 433; at Portsmouth, 432; his increasing greatness, 434; attests charters at Westminster, 306; at Northampton, 265; receives lands in Kent, 2; does homage to Stephen at Oxford, 22, 23, 263; "defies" Stephen, 28, 284; lands at Arundel with the Empress, 55, 279; reaches Bristol, 55, 281; escorts the Empress to Winchester, 58; to Oxford, 68; said to have created earldom of Cornwall, ib.; at Reading, 82; in London, 87, 93, 286; advises moderation in vain, 114; withdraws from London, 115; goes to Oxford with Maud, 124, 314; visits Winchester, 124; joins in its siege, 126, 127; captured at Stockbridge, 133; released and goes to Bristol, 135; removes with Maud to Oxford, 163, 170, 182; his treaty with Earl Miles, 379; goes to Normandy, 163, 165, 184, 196, 379; returns and captures Wareham, 185, 198, 405; joins Maud at Wallingford, 199, 406; is

with her at Devizes, 234, 417; routs Stephen at Wilton, 407; dies, 408; his *Carta*, 375, 382; his *tertius denarius*, 292-294; his London soke, 436; his wife, 381

Gloucester, William, earl of, 380, 409, 419; confused with his father, 410

——, Walter, abbot of, 265

——, Gilbert, abbot of. *See* FOLIOT

——, Miles de (Earl of Hereford), employed by Henry I. (1130), 297; with him at Northampton (1131), 265; meets Stephen at Reading (1136), 12; obtains charters from him, 11, 13, 14, 28; attends his Easter court as constable, 19, 263; and witnesses his Oxford charter, 263; is with him at siege of Shrewsbury (1138), 285; abandons Stephen (1139), 128, 284; receives the Empress, 55, 60; obtains charter from her, 56; loses constableship, 285; relieves Brian fitz Count, 281; sacks Worcester and captures Hereford, 282; escorts the Empress to Winchester (1141), 58, 65; to Reading (as constable), 82; to London, 83, 93, 286; to Gloucester, 123; is created by her Earl of Hereford, 97, 123, 271, 273, 288, 315, 328; is with her at Oxford, 123, 314; and at siege of Winchester, 125; escapes to Gloucester and Bristol, 135; with the Empress at Oxford, 170, 182; his treaty with the Earl of Gloucester, 379; his grant to Llanthony, 329; his death, 276; his son Roger, *see* HEREFORD, Earls of; his son Mahel, 382

——, Walter de (father of Miles), 13, 428

Grantmesnil, Hugh de, 289

Greenfield (Linc.), 169

Greinville, Richard de, 382

Greys Thurrock (Essex), 181

Guisnes, *Comté* of, 188, 398. *See* VERE, Aubrey de

——, Manasses, Count of, 189, 397

——, Ralf de, 190

H

Hairon, Albany de, 286

Ham (Essex), 141

"Hamslep," Hugh de, 419

Handfasting. *See* AFFIDATIO

Harold, his accession compared with Stephen's, 8, 253, 437

Hartshorne, Mr., on Rochester Castle, 337

Hastings, William de, 171

Hatfield Broad Oak (Essex), 100, 140, 141, 149

"Hattele," church of, 233

Haughley (Suffolk), 326

Haye, Ralf de, 159

Hearne as a critic, 375

Hedenham (Bucks.), 337

Hedingham (Essex), 402

Helion, barony of, 229

——, Robert de, 143

——, William de, 181, 194

Henry I., secures Winchester, 63; his style, 25, 432; at St. Evroul and Rouen, 423, 426; at Brampton and Westminster, 428; marries Adeliza, 74, 426, 429; visits Winchester, 426, 430, 421, 432; Portsmouth, 432; Westminster, 433; secures succession to his children, 2, 30-32, 34; dies, 322; his widow's dower, 324; his gifts to Cluny, 254; his reforms, 104, 298; his ministers, 111, 418; his exactions, 101, 105, 150, 360, 361, 366; his forest policy, 377; his dealings with London, 347, 358, 359, 365-367; his chaplains, 427; his military architecture, 333, 334, 341-343, 345, 346; his charter to Eudo Dapifer, 328; his treaty with the Count of Flanders, 176, 380; his knowledge of English, 424

——, his son William, heir to the crown, 30, 427; married, 426; drowned, 434

——, his children. *See* MAUD, GLOUCESTER, FITZ EDITH, FITZ ROY

——, his widow. *See* ADELIZA

Henry II., mentioned in charters of

the Empress, 171, 183, 417, 418; confirms his mother's charter, 184-186, 384, 418; his hereditary right, 186, 200; lands with his uncle (1142), 198, 405; joins the Empress, 199, 406; resides at Bristol, 407; his gifts to St. Augustine's, 408; lands afresh (1149), 279, 408; visits Devizes, 409; knighted at Carlisle, 408; unsupported, 409; leaves England, 410; his third visit and negotiations, 176, 386, 418; strength of his position, 35; his policy, 112, 372, 378; his alienations of demesne, 269; his charters to Aubrey de Vere, 237, 239; to Hugh Bigod, 239; to Earl of Arundel, 240; to Wallingford, 200; his dealings with London, 358, 367, 370, 372, 440

Henry III., his charter to London, 358
Henry VIII., confirms charter of the Empress, 179, 328
Henry (V.), the Emperor, 300, 301
Henry of Scotland. *See* HUNTINGDON
Heraclius, the Patriarch, consecrates the Temple church, 225
Heraldry. *See* ARMS, QUARTERLY
Hereditary right. *See* CROWN
Hereford, Stephen at, 48; seized by Miles, 282
——, its "tertius denarius," 288
—— Castle, 328, 329
——, earldom of, created by the Empress, 97, 123, 187, 271, 273
——, earl of, William Fitzosbern, 154, 276
——, earls of. *See* GLOUCESTER
——, Roger, earl of, 234, 329, 380, 382, 409, 419
——, Richard ("de Sigillo"), bishop of, 427, 428
——, Robert, bishop of, 46, 64, 82, 83, 93, 262, 263, 265
Hertford (or "Clare"), earldom of, 39, 40, 146, 270-272
——, Gilbert, earl of, 143, 145, 159, 271, 276
——, Roger, earl of, 236
——, mills of, 286

Hertfordshire, shrievalty of, 39, 142, 150, 166; justiciarship of, 142, 150, 167; "firma" of, 142, 150, 166
Hexham, John of, his accuracy confirmed, 19
Hinckford hundred (Essex), 404
"Histoire de Guillaume le Maréchal," extracts from, 130-133; its authority, 130, 194
Historia Pontificalis, editorial errors in, 253
Holland, Great (Essex), 141
Howard, Thomas, 316
Howlett, Mr., on the landing of the Empress, 278-280; on an unknown landing by Henry II., 409, 410
"Hugate," 232
Huitdeniers, Osbert, 170, 374, 375, 382
——, Philip, 375
Humez, Richard de, 236, 419
Huntingdon, its "tertius denarius," 288
——, Henry of, his chronology discussed, 407
——, Henry (of Scotland), earl of, 19, 192, 262, 263, 265
——, earldom of, 191-193, 265, 272
Hyde Abbey burnt, 127

I

Ickleton (Camb.), 141
"Inga" (Essex), 140, 186
Ing, Goisbert de, 142
——, Hugh de, 185, 186, 190, 384
Innocent, Pope, hears Maud's appeal against Stephen (1136), 250, 252; dismisses it, 9, 257; "confirms" Stephen, 9, 257, 258, 260; writes to Stephen, 412; to Henry of Winchester, *ib.*
Ipra. *See* YPRES
Ipswich, "third penny" of, 290
Irvine, Mr., on Rochester Castle, 338
Issigeac (Perigord), 247

J

Jarpenville, David de, 231
——, ——, Symon, his brother, 231

Jarpenville, Geoffrey de, 229, 230
Jerusalem, pilgrimage to, 306, 308
Jingles in charters, 241
John, his charters to London, 358, 371
Juga. *See* INGA *and* ING
Jurisdiction, the struggle for, 105, 108, 111
Justicia, the, localized, 105, 373; termed "capitalis," 106; differentiated from the sheriff, 107, 109, 153; feudalized, 109; represented by "coroners," 110; has precedence of the sheriff, 110

K

Kent, faithful to Stephen, 2, 138
Kingham (Oxon), 230-233
Kirton-in-Lindsey (Linc.), 159
Knightsbridge, the Londoners meet kings at, 84
Knights' service, grants of, 91, 103, 142, 155, 167, 189, 439

L

Laci, Hugh de, 331
——, Ilbert de, 263
Læsio fidei, 9, 387
Lea, the river, 168, 175, 337
Ledet, Wiscard, 231
Legate, the papal. *See* WINCHESTER, Henry, bishop of; CANTERBURY, Theobald, archbishop of
Leicester, "third penny" of, 289
——, Robert, earl of, 146, 154, 236, 265, 380, 415, 433
Leicestershire, "tertius denarius" of, 295
Le Mans, tower of, 336
Leofstan (of London), 309
Leominster, Stephen at, 282
Lewes Priory, 391
Lexden hundred (Essex), 378, 404
Librata terræ, the, 99, 104, 140, 141, 241, 305, 314
Liege homage, 315
Lincoln, excludes the sheriff, 362; its "firma burgi," 362, 363; Stephen besieges, 46, 159, 440; battle of, 54, 56, 140, 148, 149
Lincoln Castle, constableship of, 160
——, earldom of, 271, 325
——, Robert (I.), bishop of, 329, 433
——, Alexander, bishop of, 51, 64, 82, 83, 93, 123, 262, 265, 416
——, Robert (II.), bishop of, 236
——, William, earl of, 146, 159, 271, 415
Lisieux, Arnulf, bishop of, Stephen's envoy (1136), 252, 253, 260, 389
Lisures, Warner de, 120, 320
——, William de, 231
Little Hereford, Stephen at, 282
Lodnes, Ralf de, 190
Loftie, Mr. W. J., his strange errors, 152, 349-351, 354-356, 364, 436
London, its name latinized, 347; inseparable from Middlesex, 347, 352, 353, 357, 359; not a corporate unit, 356; its organization territorial, 357; earliest list of its wards, 351, 435, 436; its *auxilium*, 352
——, portreeve of, 439; ignored by Henry I., 350, 351; difficulty concerning, 354, 356; replaced by Norman *vicecomes*, 353, 354
——, mayor of, 356, 357, 373, 436
——, chamberlain of, 355, 366
——, Tower of, its custody, 439; held by the Mandevilles, 38, 89, 117, 141, 143, 149, 156, 166; its importance, 98, 113, 119, 139, 164; Stephen at, 48; surrendered by Geoffrey, 207; explanation of its name, 336; its inner ward, 334
——, Guildhall (?) of, earliest mention of, 436
——, St. Michael's, Cheap, 309, 310
——, bishops of, Maurice, 68, 328;— Gilbert, 265;—Robert ("de Sigillo"), 45, 67, 117, 118, 123, 167, 194, 402; —Richard, 236, 370
——. *See also* TEMPLE; CNIHTENGILD
London and Middlesex, spoken of as London, 348, 351, 372; as Middlesex, 347; sheriff of, replaces portreeve, 353, 354, 356; *firma*, of, 142,

INDEX.

150, 151, 166, 347-349, 352, 355, 357-359, 362, 366, 371, 372, 440; shrievalty of, 110, 141, 150, 166, 347-349, 358, 359, 363, 364, 367, 372, 439; justiciarship of, 110, 141, 150, 167, 347, 373

London and Middlesex, sheriffs of, Esegar, 353; — Ulf, 353, 354; — Geoffrey de Mandeville (I.), 354, 439;—William de Eynsford, 360. *See* also MANDEVILLE

———, justiciars of, Gervase (de Cornhill), 120, 121, 373;—Geoffrey de Mandeville, 141, 150, 167, 373

Londoners, the, obtain from Henry I. shrievalty of Middlesex, 347, 349, 359, 363, 364, 366; dislike his system, 366; elect Stephen, 2; their compact with him, 3, 27, 247-249; faithful to him, 49, 116, 354; at the election of the Empress, 69; slow to receive her, 81; admit her conditionally, 84, 248; harassed by the Queen, 114; expel the Empress, 115, 117; join the Queen, 119, 128; record Stephen's release, 136; abandoned by him to Geoffrey, 153; whose mortal foes they are, 168, 174; treatment of, by Henry II., 370-372, 440; join Simon de Montfort, 358; their charters from the Conqueror, 354, 439; from Henry I., 109, 347, 356, 359, 364; from Henry II., 367-370, 440; from Richard I., 371; from John, 358, 371; from Henry III., 348; their *communa*, 116, 247, 357, 373, 439; their alleged early liberties, 152, 372, 440; their "wardmoot," 370

Lords' Reports, error in, 39

Lovel, Ralf, 94

Luci, Richard de, 101, 109, 112, 137, 146, 373; with Stephen at Norwich, 49; at Canterbury, 144; at Ipswich, 158; at Oxford, 201; with Henry II., 236

Lucius, Pope, 208, 215, 258, 412

Ludgershall, the Empress flees to, 133

"Luffenham," 314

M

Magn', Ralf, 230

Maldon (Essex), 90, 92, 99, 100, 102, 140

Malet, Robert (I.), great chamberlain, 180, 395

———, Robert (II.), 93, 262

———, William, 93, 436

Malmesbury, Stephen at, 47, 281

———, William of, his accuracy confirmed, 11, 61; impugned, 63, 115, 132; discussed, 283, 344, 438

Maminot, Walchelin, 2, 94, 264, 286, 314, 418

Mandeville family, origin of, 37; heirs of, 232, 233, 243, 244; charters of, 228-233, 390; pedigree of, 392

Mandeville, Geoffrey de (I.), 89, 235, 236, 358; receives fief from the Conqueror, 37; founds Hurley Priory, 38; sheriff of three counties, 142, 166; said to be "portreeve," 152; and may have been, 439

———, Geoffrey de (II.), Earl of Essex, 181-184; his parentage, 37; succeeds his father, 40; at Stephen's court (1136), 19, 263, 264; detains Constance in the Tower, 47; his first charter from the king, 41-53, 292; created Earl of Essex, 52, 270, 272; with Stephen at Norwich, 49; strengthens the Tower, 81; his first charter from the Empress, 87-113, 292; made justice, sheriff, and escheator of Essex, 92; deserts the Empress, 119; seizes Bishop of London, 117; obtains a charter from the Queen, 118; his second charter from the king, 138-156; made justice and sheriff of Herts. and of London and Middlesex, 141, 142; with Stephen at Ipswich, 158; sent against Ely, 161; aspires to be king-maker, 164; his second charter from the Empress, 165-178, 183; obtains charter for Aubrey de Vere, 183, 184; his plot against Stephen, 195; is with him at Oxford, 201; arrested by

INDEX.

Stephen, 202-206; surrenders his castles, 207; breaks into revolt, *ib.*; secures Ely, 209; seizes Ramsey Abbey, 210; holds the fenland, 211; sacks Cambridge, 212; evades Stephen, 213; his atrocities, 214, 218; wounded at Burwell, 221; dies at Mildenhall, 222, 276; fate of his corpse, 224-226; his alleged effigy, 226, 395; his heirs, 232, 244; he founds Walden Abbey, 45; burns Waltham, 323; his policy, 98, 153, 164, 173, 439; his greatness, 164, 203, 223, 323; his arms, 392-396

Mandeville, Geoffrey de (II.), his sister Beatrice (de Say), 169, 392, 393

——, ——, his wife Rohese (de Vere), 171, 229, 232, 388, 390-393

——, ——, his father-in-law, Aubrey de Vere, 81

——, his brother-in-law, Earl Aubrey, 178. *See also* VERE

——, Geoffrey de (III.), Earl of Essex, 112, 169, 238; succeeds his father, 233; styled earl, 238, 417; his charter from Henry II., 235; procures his father's absolution, 225; his charter to Ernulf, 230, 231; his grant of Sawbridgeworth, 241; his death, 242; struggle for his corpse, 226

——, ——, his wife Eustachia, 229

——, Geoffrey de (IV.), Earl of Essex, 229; confused with Geoffrey de Mandeville (II.), 39

——, William de (I.), constable of the Tower, 38, 166, 169, 392

——, William de (II.), Earl of Essex, 169, 390; his charter to Ernulf, 231; succeeds his brother as earl, 242; devoted to Henry II., 243; becomes Great Justiciar, *ib.*; dies, *ib.*

——, Ernulf (or Arnulf, or Ernald, or Hernald) de, grants to him, 141, 142, 149, 155, 167, 168, 174; fortifies Wood Walton, 211; holds Ramsey Abbey, 223; surrenders it, 227; exiled, *ib.*; reappears, 228, 238; occurs in family charters, 229-233; disinherited, 233

——, ——, his wife Aaliz, 232, 233

Mandeville, Ernulf de, his son Geoffrey, 232

——, ——, his son Ralf, 231

——, ——, his grandson Geoffrey, 232

——, ——, his heir Geoffrey, 229

——, Geoffrey de, 233

——, Hugh de, 232

——, Robert de, 232

——, ——, Ralf, his brother, 232

——, Walter de, 229, 230

——, William de, 233

Mansel, William, 383

Marmion, Robert, 313

Marshal, Gilbert the, 171

——, John the. *See* FITZ-GILBERT

Martel, Eudo (?), 263

——, Geoffrey, 147

——, William, 46, 144, 146, 158, 159, 206, 262, 263, 320, 378, 407, 416

Masculus, Osbert, 436

Mathew, Master, 407

Matilda (of Boulogne), Stephen's queen, 262; advances on London, 114; her charter to Geoffrey, 118-121, 139; rallies her party, 119; her charter to Gervase, 120; gains the legate, 122; wears crown at Canterbury, 138, 143; visits York, 157; her charters and seal, 302; at Barking, 320

Matom, Alan de, 233

——, Serlo de, 89

Maud, the Empress, her legitimacy, 256; marries the Emperor, 300; oath sworn to her (1127), 6, 10, 31, 255; appeals to Rome (1136), 8, 32, 253-257; her claim to the throne, 29-34; lands in England (1139), 55, 278-280, 283; reaches Bristol, 55; resides at Gloucester, 56; joined by Miles, 56, 285; joined by Bishop Nigel, 161; received at Winchester (1141), 57, 64, 79; her style, 63-67, 70-77, 300-302; visits Wilton and Oxford, 65-67; elected "Domina," 58-61, 69; forfeits Count Theobald, 102, 140; visits Reading, 66, 82; advances to St. Albans, 83; reaches London, 84; her intended coronation, 78, 80, 84, 302; her Valoines charter, 286; her first charter to Geoffrey, 86-113, 149-155, 238; deals with see of Durham, 85; expelled from London, 85, 115, 117; flees to Gloucester, 115; returns to Oxford, 123; her Beauchamp charter, 313-315; marches on Winchester, 124; besieges the legate, 126-128; flees from Winchester, 130, 132, 133; reaches Gloucester, 134; visits Bristol, 135; again returns to Oxford, 163; holds councils at Devizes, 165; sends for her husband, 165, 177; her second charter to Geoffrey, 165-177; her charter to Aubrey de Vere, 179-184, 187, 190-195; is besieged in Oxford, 198; escapes to Wallingford, 199; visited by Bishop Nigel, 208; quarters her followers on Wilts, 230; her charter to Geoffrey de Mandeville the younger, 233; to Geoffrey Ridel, 234, 417; her court, 64, 82, 95, 124, 178, 286; her earls, 271-273; her seal, 299-303; her arrogance, 96, 114, 367; her gifts to Cluny, 254

Mauduit, Ralf, 142

Mayenne, Juhel de, 172, 183

Meduana. See MAYENNE

Melford, Geoffrey de, 190

——, Helias de, 190

Mercata terræ, 232

Merton, charter to, 433

Meulan, Robert, count of, 329

——, Waleran, count of, 46, 145, 262, 263, 271, 313, 314; escorts the Empress, 55; faithful to Stephen, 120; his brother Hugh, 171

Middlesex, comprised London, 347; archdeaconry of, 348. See LONDON AND MIDDLESEX

Mildenhall (Suffolk), Geoffrey dies at, 222, 223

Moch' (? Woch[endona]), William de, 229

Mohun (Moion), William de (Earl of Somerset or Dorset), 93, 125, 266, 272, 277

Money-lending denounced, 311, 312, 440

Monks Horton Priory, 148, 158, 326

Montfort, Hugh de, 148, 326

——, Robert de, 148, 327

——, Thurstan de, 65, 327

Montgomery, Arnulf de, 331

——, Roger de, 322

Montreuil, 331, 338

Mortgage. See VADIMONIUM

'Mottes,' shell-keeps termed, 328, 330, 333, 336, 337

Mountnessing (Essex), 169

N

Napier, origin of the name, 324

"Navium applicationes," 286, 440

"Nepos Huberti," Roger, 305, 306, 308-310

——, ——, Ingenolda, his wife, 305, 308, 310

Neufbourg, Robert de, 52

Neufmarché, Henry de, 320

Nevill, Hugh de, 310

Newburgh, William of, his chronicle, 47, 203, 205

Newcastle, keep of, 339, 346

Newport (Essex), 89, 90, 92, 99, 100, 140, 156

Newtimber (Sussex), 325

Norfolk, earldom of, 191, 270, 271, 273, 277. See BIGOD

Norhale, William de, 231

Northampton, Stephen ill at, 160, 164; its burgesses, 414

——, Simon (de St. Liz or Silvanecta), earl of, 120, 143, 145, 159, 192, 262-264, 276

Northamptonshire, earldom of, 192, 264, 272

Norwich, Stephen at, 49

——, Ebrard, bishop of, 83, 262, 263, 265

——, William, bishop of, 45

——, John, bishop of, 318

Novo burgo. See NEUFBOURG

—— mercato. See NEUFMARCHÉ

Noyon, battle of, 423, 427

Nuers, Ralf de, 230

Nunant, Roger de, 125

INDEX.

O

Octodenarii. *See* HUITDENIERS
Oilli, Fulk d', 46
——, Henry d', 94, 434
——, Robert d', 46, 65, 66, 94, 171, 183, 263, 434
——, Roger d', 125
Ordgar (of London), 309
Osney Priory, 171; charters to, 232
Osonville, Sewal de, 231
Ottdevers. *See* HUITDENIERS
Ou, Hugh d', 229, 230
——, Robert d', 436
——, William d', 53, 142, 170
Oxeaie, Richard de, 205
——, Walkelin de, 205, 206
Oxford, Stephen at (1136), 15, 16, 23, 201, 282; the Empress at, 65, 66, 123, 163, 314; arrest of the bishops at, 202, 203, 416; conspiracy against Stephen at (1142), 162, 195, 203, 207; fortified by the Earl of Gloucester, 197; stormed by Stephen, 197; who besieges its castle, 198, 405; from which the Empress escapes, 199, 405, 406; leaving it to Stephen, 406
——, St. Frideswide's, charter to, 201
——, house at, 232
——, earl of. *See* VERE, Aubrey de
Oxfordshire, earldom of, 181, 194, 239, 240, 270, 271, 295
——, "tertius denarius" of, 295

P

Parage, Philip, 402
Paris, Mathew, his accuracy confirmed, 205
Park', Isnardus, 314, 315
——, ——, his son Nicholas, 314
Parker, Mr., on Professor Freeman, 280; on Rochester Castle, 337
Pascal, Pope, anoints the Empress, 257
Passelewe, Ralf, 373
"Pauper," Hugh (? Earl of Bedford), 171, 270, 276

Paynell, Ralf, 94, 171, 183, 286
Pechet, Robert, 427
Pedigrees, of Gervase de Cornhill, 308, 310; of Aubrey de Vere, 389; of the Mandevilles and De Veres, 392; of William d'Arques, 397; of Ernulf de Mandeville, 232
Pembroke, Gilbert, earl of, 143, 145, 158, 159, 161, 162, 172, 178, 181-183, 188, 194, 276
——, earldom of, 270, 271
Percy, William de, 264
Peterborough chronicle, the, on the Anarchy, 214, 220, 416
Petrivilla. *See* PIERREVILLE
Peverel (of London), William, his fief, 90, 91, 140-142
—— (of Nottingham), William, 263, 266; forfeited, 195; his fief, 181
——, Mathew, 143
Pharamus. *See* BOULOGNE
"Phingria" (Essex), 140
Pierreville, Geoffrey de, 320
Pincerna, Audoen, 230
——, ——, Ralf, brother of, 230
——, Geoffrey, 229
Pirou, William de, 428
Pleas, dread of, 93, 105, 167, 169, 170, 180; farming of, 108, 287, 293, 295, 361
—— of the Crown, 105, 110; of the forest, 376-378
Pleshy (Essex), 207
Plessis, Walter de, 229
——, William de, 230
Ploughteam, importance of the, 218
Poitiers, Richard, archdeacon of, 112
Pont de l'Arche, William de, 4, 11, 12, 46, 62, 234, 263, 265, 297
Popes. *See* ALEXANDER, CELESTINE, EUGENE, INNOCENT, LUCIUS, PASCAL
Port, Adam de, (I.) 233, (II.) 428
——, ——, Matildis, his wife, 233
——, ——, Henry, his brother, 233
——, Henry de, 264
Portsmouth, alleged landing at, 278-280; Henry I. at, 432
Predevilain, Alfred, 230
Presbyter, Vitalis, 413

INDEX. 457

Prittlewell Priory, 391
Protection, money exacted for, 415
Prudfot, Gilbert, 350, 351

Q

Quadripartitus, quotation from, 312
Quarterly coat of Mandeville, the, 392-396
"Queen," the Empress styles herself, 63, 64, 66, 83, 302

R

Radwinter (Essex), 168
Raimes, family of de, 399-404; Roger (I.), 399, 403, 404; William (I.), 399, 401; Roger (II.), 181, 399-404; Robert (I.), 399, 402; William (II.), 402, 403; Richard, 400-404; Robert (II.), 401
Rainham (Essex), 141
Ramis de. *See* RAIMES
Ramsey Abbey, grant of a hundred to, 101; occupied by Geoffrey, 209; fortified by him, 210, 211, 213, 216; claimed by Abbot Walter, 216, 218; sweats blood, 217; avenged, 221; surrendered to the abbot, 223, 227; compensated for its losses, 225
——, Walter, abbot of, 83, 210; goes to Rome, 215; returns to Ramsey, 216; his misery, 217; at Geoffrey's death-bed, 223
——, Daniel, abbot of, 210, 215, 218; goes to Rome, 216
——, William, abbot of, 225
Ravengerus, 89
Rayne (Essex), 399
Reading, Stephen at, 10, 46, 48, 283; the Empress at, 66, 82
——, Anscher, abbot of (1131), 265
——, Edward, abbot of (1141), 117
Redvers, Baldwin de, 266, 272, 278
——, Richard de, 272
Reinmund (of London), 435, 436; his son Azo, *ib.*
Richard I., his second coronation, 137

Richmond, earldom of, 157
——, Alan, earl of, 143, 145, 157, 276
——, Conan, earl of, 290
Ridel, Geoffrey (II.), 417-419; his grandfather, 417
Rochelle, Richard de, 231
——, John de, 231
Rochester, its early name, 332, 339; charter to church of, 422
—— Castle, 337-339, 345, 346
——, Gundulf, bishop of, 334, 337-339
——, John, bishop of, 262, 263, 265
Rome, appeal of the Empress to, 8, 250-261; appeals of Bishop Nigel to, 161, 208, 209, 411-413; Abbot of Ramsey appeals to, 215
Romeli. *See* RUMILLI
Rouen, Hugh, archbishop of, 113, 262, 263, 412, 413
——, the Tower of, 334-336
Rumard, Absalom, 172, 183
Rumilli, Alan de, 170
——, Mathew de, 170
——, Robert de, 170

S

Sablé, Guy de, 172, 183
——, Robert de, 172, 183
Sackville, William de, 393; arms of, *ib.*
Saffron Walden (Essex), 89, 90, 149, 156, 174, 207, 236
Sai, Ingelram de, 11-13, 46
——, Geoffrey de, 231, 243, 390, 392
——, William de, 169, 209, 227, 392, 396
St. Albans, the Empress at, 83; Stephen arrests Geoffrey at, 202-207; consequent struggle at, 204-206; abbot of, Geoffrey, 206, 265
St. Augustine's, Hugh, abbot of, 265
St. Briavel's, castle of, 56
St. Clare, Hamo de, 263, 264
——, Osbert de, 231
——, William de, 52
St. David's, Bernard, bishop of, 58, 82, 83, 93, 262, 263, 314, 430
St. Edmundsbury, Anselm, abbot of, 174; Ording, abbot of, 189, 439;

INDEX.

William, prior of, 190; Ralf, sacristan of, 190; Maurice, dapifer of, 190; Goscelin and Eudo, monks of, 190

St. Evroul, charter to, 423, 426
St. Ives, 212, 213
St. John, John de, 409
St. Liz. *See* NORTHAMPTON
St. Osyth's Priory, 389, 390
St. Quintin, Richard de, 382
Salamon Presbyter, 181
Salisbury, Stephen at, 46, 283; held for the Empress, 407
——, earldom of. *See* WILTSHIRE
——, bishop of, Roger, builds Devizes Castle, 134; receives Stephen as king, 4; attends his coronation, 5; with him at Reading, 11; at Westminster, 262, 263; at Oxford, 262; repudiates his oath to the Empress, 32, 256; his death, 46, 48, 282; his nephew Nigel,] 265 (*see* ELY, bishops of)
——, Edward de, 404
——, Walter de, 46, 264, 266, 276
——, ——, Sibyl, his wife, 276
——, William de, 125, 276
——, Patrick de (Earl of Salisbury or Wilts), 194, 271, 276, 409
Saltpans, 440
Saltwood (Kent), 326
Savigny, charter to, 423
Sawbridgeworth (Herts.), 228, 236, 241
Scotale, 361, 369
Scutage of 1159, the, 400
Seals, great, of Stephen, 50; of Maud, 299, 303
——, keepers of the. *See* SIGILLO, de
Seez, Arnulf, archdeacon of. *See* LISIEUX
——, John, bishop of, 262, 263
Sherborne Castle, 146
Sheriff, the, as "justicia," 107, 109; as an officer of the "curia," 108; as "firmarius," 360-363; feudalized, 109; his "third penny," 289; distinct from the "custos," 297
——. *See also* BAILIFFS
Ships, toll from, 414, 440

Shrewsbury, Stephen besieges, 285
Shropshire settled on Queen Adeliza, 322
Sigillo, Robert de, 265. *See* LONDON, bishops of.
——, Richard de, 427. *See* HEREFORD, bishops of
Silvanecta. *See* NORTHAMPTON
Soilli, Henry de ("nepos regis"), 262-264
Someri, Adam de, 143
——, Roger de, 143, 168
Somerset, earldom of, 95. *See* MOHUN
Sorus, Jordan, 382
——, Odo, 382
——, Robert, 382
Southwark, Edward of, 307, 308
——, his son William, 307, 308
Stafford, "third penny" of, 289
——, Robert de, 289
Stamford, 159
Stapleton, Mr., on William of Arques, 188, 397
Stephen, King, attends Henry I. (as Count of Mortain), 423, 429; lands in England, 1; his treaty with the Londoners, 247-249; his election and coronation, 2-8, 437, 438; his embassy to Rome, 9, 253-257; his charters to Miles of Gloucester, 11-14; visits Oxford, 15; Durham, 16; keeps Easter at Westminster, 16-21, 262-265; his Oxford charter of liberties, 22, 258, 438; his title to the throne, 25, 29, 258-260; besieges Shrewsbury, 285; his movements in 1139, 281-283; besieges the Empress at Arundel, 55; his movements in 1140, 46-49; his first charter to Geoffrey, 49-53, 98, 238; captured at Lincoln, 54; imprisoned at Bristol, 56; receives the primate, 65, 260; released, 135; holds council at Westminster, 136; crowned at Canterbury, 138; his second charter to Geoffrey, 99, 103, 119, 138-156, 175; betrays the Londoners, 153; goes north, 157; visits Ipswich, 158; Stamford, 159; recovers Ely, 411;

ill at Northampton, 160, 164; restores Nigel to Ely, 161, 412; captures Wareham, 196; storms Oxford, 197; besieges the Empress, 198, 405; his charters to Abingdon and St. Frideswide's, 201; recovers Oxford Castle, 406; besieges Wareham, *ib.*; attends council at London, 202; routed at Wilton, 407; arrests Geoffrey at St. Albans, 202-207; visits Ramsey Abbey, 210; attacks Geoffrey, 213; forfeits monks of Ely, 214; arrests Earl of Chester, 203; forfeits the primate, 251; marches to York, 409; stated to have assisted Henry, 410; seeks coronation of Eustace, 250, 259; his seal, 50; his "fiscal" earls, 276, 277, 295, 440; his faults, 24, 35, 174, 267, 269; grant to his brother Theobald, 102, 140; his forest policy, 377, 378; papal letters to him, 257, 412

Stephen, King, his wife. *See* MATILDA
——, his son. *See* EUSTACE
——, his nephew, Henry (de Soilli), 262-264

Stockbridge (Hants.), 133
Stortford. *See* BISHOP'S STORTFORD
Stuteville, John de, 403
——, Leonia de, 403, 404
——, Robert de, 404
Sumeri. *See* SOMERI
Sussex, question as to "firma" of, 322
——, earl of. *See* ARUNDEL

T

Taid', Jurdan de, 230
Talbot, Geoffrey, 182, 263
Tamworth, 313, 314
Tani, Picot de, 402, 404
——, Alice de, 402-404
——. *See also* TANY
Tankerville, Richard de, 427
——, William de, 428
Tany, Graeland de, 91, 104, 142
——, Hasculf de, 91
——, Gilbert de, 91
——. *See also* TANI
Templars, at Geoffrey's deathbed, 224; their red cross, *ib.*; retain Geoffrey's corpse, 226

Temple (London), the old, 224
—— ——, the new, 225, 226, 395
Tendring hundred (Essex), 377, 404
"Tenserie," 215, 218, 414-416
Terræ datæ. *See* CROWN LANDS
"Tertius denarius," the, 287-296; grants of the, by the Empress, 292, 293; by Henry II., 239, 240, 293; only given to some earls, 269, 293-295; its two kinds, 287-290; attached to manors, 291; amount of, 294. *See also* EARLS

Tewkesbury, spurious charter to, 421, 431, 432
Theobald. *See* BLOIS
"Third penny," the. *See* "TERTIUS DENARIUS"
Thoby Priory, 169
Thorney, Robert, abbot of, 413
Tilbury by Clare (Essex), 181
Tiretei, Maurice de, 228, 229
Titles, peerage, origin of, 145. *See also* EARLS
Tolleshunt Tregoz (Essex), 142
Torigny, castle of, 334
Totintone, Warine de, 401
"Towers," rectangular keeps termed, 328-331, 333, 336, 338, 341, 343
Treason, appeal of, 93, 156, 204, 327
Treaties between sovereign and subject, 176
Tresgoz, William de, 142
Treys-deners, Nicholas, 375
Trowbridge (Wilts), 281, 282
Tureville, Geoffrey de, 170
Turonis (?), Pepin de, 172, 183
Turroc'. *See* GREYS THURROCK

U

Ulf the portreeve, 353, 354
Umfraville, Gilbert de, 382
Usury. *See* MONEY-LENDING

V

"Vadimonium" (or "Vadium"), 214, 236, 305, 369, 370

INDEX.

Valderi, Richard de, 320
Valoines, Peter de (I.), 39
——, Peter de (II.), 172, 183
——, Robert de, 172
——, Roger de, 172, 264; Maud's charter to, 286
Venoiz, Robert de, 171
Vercorol, Richard de, 231
Vere, Aubrey de (I.), great chamberlain, his pedigree, 389, 392; father-in-law of Geoffrey de Mandeville, 388; "justiciar of England," 390; slain (1141), 81, 147, 188, 389; mentioned, 180, 187, 262, 263, 265, 297, 298, 309, 378, 388-391
——, ——, his wife, Alice de Clare, 390
——, ——, his brothers, Roger de (brother of Aubrey (I.)), 189, 389;— Robert de, 389, 391 ;—William, 389
——, Geoffrey (fitz Aubrey) de, 182, 190, 390
——, Robert (fitz Aubrey) de, 147, 182
——, William (fitz Aubrey) de, 182, 195, 231, 389, 390. *See* CHANCELLORS
——, Alice de, 169, 390
——, Aubrey de (II.), Earl of Oxford, 154, 172, 195, 230, 231, 270, 271, 402; brother-in-law to Earl Geoffrey de Mandeville, 178; his charter from the Empress, 179-195; to be Earl of Cambridgeshire, 181, 191-193; his charter from Henry of Anjou, 186; was Count of Guisnes, 188, 189, 240; became Earl of Oxford, 194, 239; his charter from St. Edmund's, 189, 439; from Henry II., 237, 239; his wife Beatrice, 188, 189, 397; his arms, 394-396; his connection with De Rames, 401
Ver, Robert (fitz Bernard) de, 46, 144, 147, 148, 158, 201, 262, 263, 326
——, ——, his wife, Adeline de Montford, 326

W

Wac (Wake), Hugh, 159, 160
Wace, authority of, 344
Walden. *See* SAFFRON WALDEN

Walden Abbey, chronicle of, 38, 45, 203, 205, 210, 388, 390, 393, 395
—— ——, William, prior of, 224, 226
Walensis, Ralf, 419
Wallingford, Stephen besieges, 188, 281; Empress escapes to, 198, 199, 406; young Henry at, 419; charter of Henry II. to, 200
Walterville, Geoffrey de, 314, 381
Waltham (Essex), 236, 323, 324; forest, 377
Waltham Abbey, Geoffrey's doings at, 323; avenged, 222
—— ——, Chronicle of, 322-324, 439
Waltheof, Earl, 192, 276
Wareham, 165; captured by Stephen, 196, 407; besieged by Earl of Gloucester, 198; captured by him, 199, 405; Baldwin lands at, 279; its defences, 332; besieged by Stephen, 406, 407
Warenne, William, Earl, 120, 143, 145, 158, 206, 262, 263, 265, 430
Warranty, 182, 230
Warwick, Henry, earl of, 329
——, Roger, earl of, 65, 125, 159, 262, 263, 265
Warwickshire, "tertius denarius" of, 291
Waters, Mr. Chester, on the family of De Raimes, 403; on the earldom of Gloucester, 421, 432; his authority, 432
Way, Mr. Albert, on the styles of the Empress, 70, 73
Welsh, levity of the, 386
Westminster, charters tested at, 18, 53, 86, 95, 262-264, 286, 302, 306, 329, 428, 433
——, Herbert, abbot of, 265
Weston, 314
Wherwell, Empress at, 57; burning of, 127, 129-131
White Ship, loss of the, 423, 428, 429, 434
Wickham Bonhunt (Essex), 90, 140
Wilton, the Empress at, 65; affair of, 146, 276, 407
Wiltshire, earldom of, 181, 194, 271

INDEX. 461

Winchester, Stephen received at, 4, 47; Henry I. at, 421, 430, 432; Empress received at, 57-64; importance of its possession, 60; its castle and treasury, 62, 63, 125, 128, 386, 407; election of the Empress at, 69; its siege by the Empress, 124-132; its royal palace, 126, 127
——, William (Giffard), bishop of, 329
——, Henry, bishop of (and papal legate), 265; receives Stephen as king, 3, 4; attends his coronation, 5; with him at Reading, 11; at Westminster, 262; at Oxford, 263; at Arundel, 55; receives the Empress, 57; his mandate to Theobald, 260; conducts Maud's election, 69; escorts her, 82, 83, 93; opposes her as to William Cumin, 85; deserts her and joins the Queen, 121, 122; besieged by the Empress, 125; his palace, 126; burns Winchester, 127; restores Stephen, 136; at his court, 143; with him at Wilton, 407; opposed to Nigel of Ely, 413; goes to Rome, 208; his letter to Brian Fitz Count, 261; his covenant with Henry, 386; papal letters to, 412
Windsor, Maurice de (dapifer of St. Edmund's), 190, 439
—— Castle, 169; Henry I. at, 429
Wiret, Ralf de, 53

Wood Walton, 211
Woodham Mortimer (Essex), 141
Worcester, Stephen at, 48, 282; sacked by Miles, 282; its "third penny," 290
—— Castle, 313, 328
——, Simon, bishop of, 262, 263, 265
——, Theowulf, bishop of, 432
Worcestershire, earldom (?) of, 271
——, shrievalty of, 313
Worth (Wilts), 229, 233
Writtle (Essex), 140, 149, 214
——, Godebold of, 214
Wymondham, the foundation at, 318

Y

York, Stephen visits, 157, 409
——, Roger, archbishop of, 236
——, Thurstan, archbishop of, 262, 263, 265, 427, 428, 433
——, earldom of, 270, 271, 276
——, earl of. *See* AUMÂLE
Ypres, William of, in England, 45, 52, 144, 158, 201; not an earl, 146, 270, 275; in charge of Kent, 147, 275; burns Wherwell, 129, 131, 132; tries to burn St. Albans, 206; robs Abingdon, 213; persecutes the Church, 271; grants to him, 269, 275

Printed in Great Britain by
Amazon.co.uk, Ltd.,
Marston Gate.